Museum
Registration
Methods
5th Edition

MRM5

Museum Registration Methods
5th Edition

EDITED BY REBECCA A. BUCK AND JEAN ALLMAN GILMORE

©2010 The AAM Press
American Association of Museums
1575 Eye St. NW, Suite 400
Washington, DC 20005
www.aam-us.org

TO DOROTHY H. DUDLEY AND IRMA BEZOLD WILKINSON

Those of us who follow walk a straighter path because of them.

MUSEUM REGISTRATION METHODS 5TH EDITION
EDITED BY REBECCA A. BUCK AND JEAN ALLMAN GILMORE

©2010 The AAM Press, American Association of Museums, 1575 Eye St. NW, Suite 400, Washington, DC 20005.

The opinions expressed by the authors in this book are their own and are not to be taken as representing the views of any institution or organization, including the American Association of Museums.

Cover: Luce Foundation Center, courtesy of the Smithsonian American Art Museum. Photo: Timothy Hursley.
The Smithsonian American Art Museum's Luce Foundation Center, which opened in 2006, is an innovative public space that serves as a study center and visible art storage facility. More than 3,300 artworks from the museum's permanent collection are on display in a three-story, sky-lit space, providing new ways to experience and interpret American art.

Library of Congress Cataloging-in-Publication Data
Museum registration methods / edited by Rebecca A. Buck and Jean Allman
Gilmore. -- 5th ed.
    p. cm.
 Previous ed.: Washington, DC : American Association of Museums, c1998,
under title The new museum registration methods.
 Includes bibliographical references and index.
 ISBN 978-1-933253-15-2 (paper)
 1. Museum registration methods. I. Buck, Rebecca A., 1946- II. Gilmore,
Jean Allman, 1946- III. American Association of Museums. IV. New museum
registration methods.
 AM139.M78 2010
 069'.52--dc22
                    2010014963

2nd printing October 2011

Contents

Acknowledgements

T HE PEOPLE involved in the production of this book are legion. The authors and those contributing their knowledge are foremost, but the thousands of collections staff who have made presentations, written articles, discussed issues on Internet listservs, responded to phone calls, and offered help and support to each other over the decades have developed some basic agreement on standards in the field. We have tried to gather the best of these standards as the profession continues to build on common discoveries and good communication.

The 5th edition is organized differently from the last, and there are over 30 new essays. Many topics are here for the first time: dealing with contemporary art, history of the profession, the Green Museum, and Data Asset Management Systems, among others. The marking section has undergone major revision, and we anticipate that it will form the basis of a profession-wide standard. Preventive care also shows a very new point-of-view. Many subjects were extensively reworked, and all were edited to show changes and updates from the 4th edition. Some were diminished even as the size of the book continued to grow. The bibliography is small, as is the glossary, but the American Association of Museums plans a "back-of-book" web page where long versions of these former appendices will be compiled and updated. It may contain a forms library, links to relevant laws as they change, and the latest and greatest resource lists for the field. The possibilities are very exciting, and we look forward to the publication of the web page.

We decided that a reference book that had become a textbook as well could use discussion points and hypotheticals, and you will find them throughout the book. They provide something new for the classroom or for Friday afternoon tea. Many thanks to Antonia Moser of the Newark Museum and Seton Hall University for writing and discussing so many good ideas and situations. Batja Bell, also of the Newark Museum collections staff, tossed in a few as well. The museums represented in the hypotheticals can be found somewhere in the hundred or so years of experience the perpetrators have lived or read about. The only quiz we offer: which photograph has stayed the same yet changed over the 3rd, 4th, and 5th editions?

We asked for input from the registrars on the RC-AAM listserv: Which books form the basis of your library? Will you share your forms? Please let us know what your organizational chart tells and what your job descriptions demand. To everyone who responded, you enriched this book. We appreciate that, and give special thanks to Ramona Banayon, Janice Klein, and Martha Mayberry. Betsey Bruemmer and Jacqueline M. Cabrera provided us with important leads.

We are especially pleased to be able to reprint the collections sections of several ethics policies, with appreciation to John Strand of the American Association of Museums, Andy Finch of the Association of Art Museum Directors, Cherie Cook of the American Association for State and Local History, and Nadine Amorim and Bernice Murphy of the International Council of Museums. Masterpiece International was generous in updating the Transportation Security Agency guidelines for the publication. And as always, Kittu Longstreth-Brown's humor was lurking there in the background.

The Newark Museum and the Brandywine River Museum have again offered generous and continued support for this project. Our heartfelt thanks go to our directors, Mary Sue Sweeney Price and James H. Duff, and to Meme Omogbai, Chief Operating Officer at Newark. The entire collections division, especially Jeffrey Moy, Olivia Arnone, and William Peniston, responded quickly and positively to all crazy requests. Richard Stomber, Newark's Director of Facility Operations, double-checked the things that engineers know well. By their daily concern with the welfare of objects and close observation of safeguards and standards, the staff of Brandywine's curatorial division provide ongoing support and inspiration. Special thanks to Bethany Engel for her help.

Finally, we are certain that John Strand, publisher of The AAM Press, is pleased to see this very large book finished, and we thank him for his patience and good advice. Jane Lusaka and Susannah C. O'Donnell worked again with us as editors, and Polly Franchini is responsible for the clear design. As for our husbands, Jim Reuter and G. L. Gilmore, we appreciate every minute of their encouragement and endurance.

REBECCA BUCK AND JEAN ALLMAN GILMORE
APRIL 2010

Letter from the RC-AAM chair

Tremendous changes have taken place in the world since the first edition of *Museum Registration Methods* was published in 1958. Changes in the world of the registrar have paralleled them: new methods of shipping and packing have emerged, new technologies for documentation started with computerization in the 1980s, and new laws and legal situations have increased the complexity of the registrar's tasks. Most important, a profession that was scarcely recognized in 1958 has become a major player in the museum world. The world of museum registration continues to evolve and encompass more responsibilities, but the word "registrar" rings historically true. We do not need to change what we are or to change the name of our committee to something that reflects a new paradigm. If the basics are not done, the museum cannot succeed. Registrars are there to make certain that the basics are done properly.

When Dorothy Dudley and Irma Bezold Wilkinson wrote the first registration book, it was to get information out to the country's museums. When the Registrars Committee of the American Association of Museums was formed many years later, it led the struggle to professionalize the registration field and ensure recognition of the value of the work being done. Things have changed again, and we are now involved in maintaining an established professional committee and providing educational opportunities that allow our members to stay at the edge of change.

MRM5 incorporates new material that reflects some of the changes of the last decade. New chapters treat the green museum, data asset management, and documenting and caring for contemporary art. It reflects increased attention to standards in the field, as well. Although the book was trimmed in some areas, the subject matter has again broadened and this book is larger than the last. But the real value remains with information on all of the basic areas that museum registration has come to encompass: acquisitions, loans, deaccessions, exhibitions, storage, preventive care, intellectual property, and the many details that make up collections management and risk management.

We thank the co-editors of *MRM5*, Rebecca Buck and Jean Allman Gilmore, for reshaping and refreshing this basic text. Over 30 new authors contributed to this edition. As a result, if we look back through the decades, we find the minds of well over 100 registrars at work to bring this book to publication. Each of them and each of you who have presented at AAM annual meeting sessions, worked on publications, produced and revised forms and web sites, participated in the legislative process to make laws we can use, taught registration or acted as a mentor, or participated in discussions on the RC-AAM listserv have added to the body of knowledge that makes the profession work.

JEANNE BENAS
CHAIR, REGISTRARS COMMITTEE OF THE AMERICAN ASSOCIATION OF MUSEUMS

PREFACE | THE EVOLVING ROLE OF THE REGISTRAR

THE TERM "risk management" can be defined as the application of analysis and common sense to perceived risks. It is an aggressive approach to problem-solving where one seeks in advance to identify potential problems and determine how they can be avoided or mitigated. The goal is to learn how to "do it right" the first time so that there are few, if any, unfortunate consequences. Early in my museum-related career I witnessed a small group of registrars apply the risk management approach to their duties and the results were a dramatic change in the way museums operated and a dramatic change in the professional status of registrars. Here is what happened.

Back in the mid-1970s I was a young attorney at the Smithsonian just beginning to learn how to spell "museum." Before long I found myself getting a number of questions from some Smithsonian registrars. They explained that they were concerned about certain aspects of their work and thought a lawyer might offer some help. Their questions included such issues as how to handle "old loans," "objects without documentation," and "deaccessioning." As I looked into these questions I learned that there was no widely promulgated guidance in the profession on such issues. In other words, we were on our own.

This group of registrars agreed to meet with me on a regular basis so they could explain in more detail how they were currently operating, and I could then come up with legal advice about how to handle their existing problems. In addition we could explore how to avoid such problems in the future. This went on for many months. We ended up realizing that many of the existing problems had no easy legal solutions, so it was imperative to focus on how to put into place procedures that would help a museum avoid making these mistakes in the future. And, as the saying goes, "The rest is history."

With the help of the registrars, an informal "collection management initiative" was started within the Smithsonian. The result was the development of a set of guidelines on how to write a collection management policy, a policy that set forth the appropriate procedures to follow when acquiring and managing museum objects. Using these guidelines, each one of the collecting organizations within the Smithsonian was then required to produce its own collection management policy. Before long the museum profession was beginning to pay attention to the importance of having collection management policies, and within museums it was invariably the registrars who were promoting the development of such documents and keeping them up-to-date.

It is conceded today that a good collection management policy is the most important "risk-management" tool available to a museum. It is also recognized that registrars, as experts in creating and maintaining such policies, have clearly entered the ranks of museum professionals. Many years ago museum registrars played a passive role, dutifully following long established patterns. Today they have a pro-active role that grows more challenging each year.

This latest edition, *MRM5 or Museum Registration Methods 5th Edition,* covers what registrars need to know now, and hints at new challenges that may lie just over the horizon.

MARIE C. MALARO

SECTION 1 | THE PROFESSION

REBECCA BUCK

INTRODUCTION

In 1881, when the new U. S. National Museum building, now the Arts and Industries Building, opened in Washington, D.C., Stephen C. Brown was named to head the Office of the Registrar.[1] Brown had been the Assistant Keeper of Reptiles, and had proven his talents in dealing with systems for collections during the 1876 Centennial Exposition in Philadelphia. He was appointed because G. Brown Goode, then Assistant Director of the museum and a serious student of museum administration, felt strongly that good records formed the foundation for collection access. Goode was heavily influenced by London's South Kensington Museum (known now as the Victoria and Albert) and by 1895 he had developed the comprehensive document, *Principles of Museum Administration*. His philosophy about objects,[2] which became the rationale for museum registration, follows:

Museum Records

1. The value of a collection depends in the highest degree upon the accuracy and fullness of the records of the history of the objects which it contains.
2. A museum specimen without a history is practically without value, and had much better be destroyed than preserved.[3]

The Oxford English Dictionary traces 'register' to 1390, "to set down (facts, names, etc.) formally in writing." In 1515, a "regester-booke" was used in Galway. The "registrar" showed up in Bathurst in 1675, as "one whose business it is to keep a register; an official recorder." It is logical that the one who formally records objects in a museum, using a bound ledger to record gifts, bequests, loans and purchases, is called registrar. The profession is old, the iteration in museums is fairly new.

SMITHSONIAN INSTITUTION ARCHIVES, STEVEN C. BROWN, REGISTRAR, UNITED STATES NATIONAL MUSEUM, 1881-1919. PHOTOGRAPH 1892 RECORD UNIT 95, BOX 4 FOLDER 42. IMAGE NUMBER 2002.32230.TIF

The profession of museum registration has roots in the 18th century, but it was not until the last half of the 19th century that the title, as noted above, was used. Museums, as the International Council of Museums once noted, "provide a location where objects of various kinds are assembled with the intention of collecting, preserving, and making them accessible to the public at large. A catalogue of a museum offers a printed list of the objects in any systematic order, preferably with a description that at least enables the reader to identify the object."[4]

Many private collections from the 1700s, particularly those of royal origin, had personnel who maintained descriptive lists.[5] After museums formed and began to gather collections for the use of the public, museum personnel began to systematically describe and order their collections to make them accessible. The prefiguration of the catalog in private collections became the museum catalog and the staffing and expertise necessary to access and preserve collections began to emerge.

Many of the first museums of the United States started with collections of scientific and natural history specimens, a direct outgrowth of museums of curios and natural history specimens in Europe.

Some of these early museums—such as the Charleston Museum in South Carolina—flourished from the late 1700s. Scientists, with their penchant for systems and orderly thinking, established many of the early museum systems.

Museums evolved slowly through the late 1800s, and the turn of the century brought a strong concentration of interest in collections and systematic business methods that coincided with the founding of the American Association of Museums in the first decade of the 20th century. The registration of art, artifacts, and specimens had become a focal point of the museum's basic work by the early 1900s. In concert with the development of systematic communication in the industrial world that began in the 1850s with railroads and culminated in the 1920s, museums began to recognize that new business methods were necessary.

Librarians worked on systematic approaches to book access as well during this period. Melvil Dewey developed the Dewey Decimal System while working as a librarian at Amherst, Mass., from 1874–1877. The timing was right. Steeped in the evolving philosophies of librarianship, Henry Watson Kent of the Metropolitan Museum, New York, and John Cotton Dana of the Newark Museum led the librarian-turned-museologist school of thought. Kent was a member of Melvil Dewey's first class in 1887 at Columbia University's then-new library school. In 1901 he had devised, with Richard Hoe Lawrence, a system of classification for the library of the Grolier Club.[6] Dana studied at Dartmouth College and then went west. He opened library stacks to the public for the first time while librarian in Denver, Colorado, then returned east and directed the Newark Public Library; by 1909 he had become the founding director of the Newark Museum and was a friend and rival to Kent.

A reference in Henry Watson Kent's memoir *What I Prefer to Call My Education* indicates that the title registrar was in use at the Metropolitan by 1905. In that year he says of the Metropolitan Museum of Art, "The Registrar . . . carried a Latin Bible in his pocket, from which he would ask you to read passages, to test your scholarship." It all became official in the Metropolitan's February 1906 *Bulletin*: "By vote of the Trustees, the office of Assistant Curator of Art Objects and Textile Fabrics has been abolished, and Mr. P. H. Reynolds, who held that position, has been appointed Registrar of the Museum." A 1907 Bulletin fleshes out the position.

Bulletin of the Metropolitan Museum of Art, Volume 2, April 1907. No. 4

"The duties of this officer have been systematized and co-ordinated to those of the Director and other members of the Museum staff. All objects of art offered either by way of gift or purchase, are received by him and duly receipted for. If not accepted, they are returned to the owner by him. After the Trustees have accepted an object, it is immediately numbered, accessioned, sent to the photographer's studio to be photographed, returned to the Registrar's Office, and there awaits placement in the room for recent accessions. A list for the monthly Bulletin, classifying and describing the different objects, is then prepared and temporary labels are attached to those so accepted.

The business of the Museum in receiving and dealing with all objects of art received by it has been thoroughly systematized."

The Museum of Fine Arts, Boston, also established the position of registrar in 1906:[7]

It shall be the duty of the Registrar of the Museum to receive and deliver objects of art at the Museum, to attend to Custom House business and to loans and deposits with or by the Museum; to attend to the immediate accessioning of objects, and to render assistance to those in charge of departments in their further registry; also to verify the registers of the Museum under the Director and when desired by him; to record any restrictions attached to objects and to aid the Director in maintaining these restrictions; to attend to the photographing of the objects; to aid the Director and those in charge of departments in arranging for the storage, installation, cleaning and repair of objects, and to direct any persons assigned to this work not already responsible to others; and to render such other assistance in the work of the Museum as the Director may determine.

The job description is remarkably current, with only repairing and cleaning removed from the tasks.

A title like Secretary or Secretary-Registrar meant an administrative position, not simply a clerical one. Henry Watson Kent, Assistant Secretary at the Metropolitan, used the term "business methods" to describe accessioning procedures and described taking over the records of the museum from General Cesnola's secretary, saying that they were "docketed in the old-fashioned way and bound up with red tape," noting that his job was to "catalogue and file them in new-fashioned cases of Dewey's devising." His position was thoroughly professional and built on a career as librarian and museum director.

The first surge of standardization was underway, and with the founding of the American Association of Museums in 1906 and its first full presentations of papers in 1907, professionalism for museum workers was formally launched in the United States.

Frederick A. Lucas, Curator-in-Chief, Museum of the Brooklyn Institute of Arts and Sciences, presented the paper "Evolution of Museums" in 1907 at the first annual meeting of the American Association of Museums in Pittsburgh, Pa. Lucas stated that collections should not be made haphazardly, that they should have definite purposes, and that collections should be a consistent whole. He discussed the changes that took place from the earliest museums through the end of the 19th century, and states:

"Thus museums have passed through several distinct states; at first they were indiscriminate gatherings of 'curios,' objects of art, and specimens of natural history. Then, by the inevitable process of segregation, natural history came to have a place by itself, the collections of scientific societies developed as storehouses of material, mainly for the use of the specialist and the public

museums derived from these were largely dryly scientific in their character."

In terms of use and content, museums moved from cabinets of curiosities held by individuals to collections that represented specific disciplines. Lucas lamented the number of curiosities that remained in museums of the United States at the turn of the century:

"... a vast number of objects were of that class rightly called curiosities, a comprehensive term that embraces a vast and miscellaneous category of objects, including the familiar and ever-present petrified potato and four-legged chicken. If there is anything that a museum has no use and no place for, it is the mere curiosity, but, as John Minto says in a recent article, 'It will take years to do away with the idea of museums still entertained by many that they are storehouses of curiosities.'" [8]

The Charleston Museum, formed in 1793, collected natural history and ethnology, and in the 1900s it began collecting material culture. The age and nature of the collections make it impossible truly to count the objects, which are said to be in the millions. A justified inventory was even more difficult, since the first accession ledger was put in place around 1902. That first systematic ledger, and the extended system it represented, was also discussed at the 1907 AAM meeting. Paul M. Rea, then director of the Charleston Museum, said it was devised to meet the conditions of "extensive collections . . . the accumulations of more than a century . . . data, scattered on loose labels and in old memorandum books, [which] had to be associated with their specimens . . ." The museum put in place a four-part record system to control its collections: accession ledger, with sequential numbers from 1 to infinity, representing lots; specimen records with unique numbers for each specimen that were then placed on the specimen; a finding list with numbers, specimen name, and location; and a list of sources.

During the ensuing years many museums were founded, and sometimes museums were developed with careful choices and carefully crafted systems for collecting, collections care, and collections documentation. Often, though, wheels were reinvented and curios or uncontrolled collections were the order of the day.

Early collection control systems evolved from prototypes found in the world of libraries, and no major breakthroughs in museum documentation and object tracking methods occurred from the early 1900s until computers became commonplace in the late 1990s. There were, however, some developments toward the systems that are currently most popular. Museums first used the simple sequential system employed by libraries in their accession ledgers—1, 2, 3, 4, 5—to number lots of objects. By 1909, two-part systems came into use. Some museums bypassed the idea of the accession as a group and applied sequential object numbers in each year, e.g., 9.1, 9.2, 9.3 for the first three objects in 1909, whether or not from the same source. By 1927 there is evidence of the three-part system in some museums: 27.1.1 marks the first object of the first accession of 1927. Such registration evolution has created many of the collection control problems museums now face. It resulted in inconsistent systems within institutions. Museums might have two or three, or in some cases even 15 different systems in place. They might have used the three-part system and gone back and forth between that and other systems. Confusion still abounds.

By 1925 programs to train general museum personnel were in force, and registration was a definite part of the program. The Newark Museum offered that year a 12-month apprentice program, which produced one of the most important registrars in the history of the profession, Dorothy H. Dudley.

In that year 1925, there was a registrar's job description at the Newark Museum. While registrars no longer color band files of trade and exhibit catalogs, much of the position remains unchanged.

During its first 50 years, the American Association of Museums worked to establish standards for the care and use of museum permanent collections and to apply those standards, as needed, to museum activities other than accessions. AAM's first code of ethics, called *Code of Ethics for Museum*

THE NEWARK MUSEUM
J.C.D. (JOHN COTTON DANA) APRIL, 1925

Here is a list of the workers in this museum, with a statement of the duties of each one.

III. Registrar.

Registry and care of collection: combination of schedules of registrar and assistant.

A. Receive, record, accession, label, store and follow up all gifts, purchases, and loans: prepare and list objects for storage warehouse: care for all storage and working equipment within the building.

B. File and care for all labels and posters, replace soiled ones.

C. Care of photos and negatives: accessioning, mounting, labeling, filing.

D. Books, etc. in Museum library: periodicals, record and binding: catalog, shelve, inventory.

E. Color band files of trade and exhibit catalogs

F. Exhibitions, particularly physical care of objects on exhibition.

Workers, dates to 1925, the year Dorothy H. Dudley graduated.

Loans became a popular way to generate broader exhibitions than a single museum could produce alone. When it became obvious that loans had to be monitored, museums came together and devised procedures to do that. Museums slowly established standards, with bursts of activity in the 1880s, 1900s, 1920s, and 1950s.

The period of the 1950s was a vital period in the development of standards for collections care, and it culminated in the publication of Museum Registration Methods in 1958. Dorothy Dudley and Irma Wilkinson were joined by a diverse group of registrars, administrators and conservators, including Geraldine Bruckner, registrar at the University Museum, University of Pennsylvania; Richard D. Buck, Conservator at the Intermuseum Laboratory in Oberlin, Ohio; and David B. Little, Secretary-Registrar of the Museum of Fine Arts, Boston. The

American Association of Museums proclaimed its stance on collection care in the foreword, written by William M. Milliken, President of the AAM:

> "The American Association of Museum is deeply concerned with the question of standards in the museums it serves. One of its main purposes is to place the career of the museum employee upon the highest possible professional level, and to do this it has from time to time issued publications which bear upon one or another of the many problems which concerns museums, large or small. One of the most fundamental of them is the basic function of the Registrar.
>
> "The vitality of the Association depends increasingly upon its usefulness and the cooperation of its members. The Registrars as a group have recognized this and by united action they have prepared the essential information which is contained in this important volume."

In the 1950s and 1960s registrars and their standards became more focused, and their community continued to develop. An AAM task on loans presented a report that is still vital in its directives regarding safe lending policies. *Museum Registration Methods* was revised and published again in 1968. The scene was set for the major jump in training and professionalization that occurred in the late 1960s and early 1970s. Accreditation, the hallmark of a professional institution and of a profession, was in the making.

That jump was precipitated by the popularity of museums (by 1967 there were 5,000 museums in the United States) and the finances needed to make them run well. Museums sought federal support from newly created federal endowments for the arts and humanities. In order to be trusted with public monies, the profession needed an accreditation system to assure federal grant-givers of the standard of stewardship in individual museums. President Lyndon B. Johnson formed

Dorothy H. Dudley studied at Wheaton College in Massachusetts and upon graduation left knowing only that she did not want to teach. A New York *World Telegram* article from 1961 states that she "jumped at the chance to join an apprentice program at the Newark Museum at a salary of $50 monthly and stayed for ten years." A note from the Newark Museum says she "left Museum Oct. 1, 1936 for Museum of Modern Art." There, as registrar, she worked on standardization of many aspects of registration. She met Irma Bezold Wilkinson of the Metropolitan Museum of Art and they decided to write it all down to lessen the constant inquiries they received from other museums. Together they developed the first edition of *Museum Registration Methods,* published in 1958.

a commission to study museums, and in 1968 he received the Belmont Report: "The Condition and Needs of American Museums," which led directly to the AAM's accreditation program. In 1971, 16 museums received accreditation.

The process of accreditation accelerated everything professional in museums, including creation

DOROTHY H. DUDLEY, 4TH FROM LEFT, GRADUATING FROM THE NEWARK PROGRAM IN 1925. PHOTO COURTESY OF NEWARK MUSEUM.

of more positions for collection managers, collection technicians, exhibition managers, registrars, and curators. There was a growing demand for museum training programs, which had begun early in the century with courses at Harvard and later an apprentice program at The Newark Museum. The Cooperstown Graduate Program, started in 1964 by Dr. Louis C. Jones, then Director of the New York State Historical Association, was positioned to train professional staff for the growing number of history museums. The Winterthur Program in Early American Culture, established in 1952 to foster connoisseurship, was joined in 1972 by the University of Delaware's Museum Studies Program to train professionals in other areas of museum and collections management. The JFK University program in San Francisco began in 1974, and the George Washington University museum program started in 1976. Since the early 1980s a growing number of professional training programs have sprung up around the country, affiliated with art, history, anthropology, or science programs in universities.

In the 1970s The American Association of Museums was growing, and it offered a new possibility for professional recognition and involvement. Specific groups within the museum profession — educators, registrars, curators, exhibition personnel — had the opportunity to form professional groups within the parent organization. The benefits were large: recognition of the professions, official program planning for continuing education, a potential board member or at least an inside view of the current affairs of the organization. The educators were the first to take advantage, and they became the first Standing Professional Committee of the American Association of Museums.

There were sessions in the AAM meetings for conservators and registrars, at least from the 1950s, but there was that urgent sense that registrars needed more recognition and that the profession needed to move forward. Registrars were not part of the program planning group, and only those who came from large and rich organizations could usually attend. Kittu (Gates) Longstreth-Brown notes that in 1974 there were conversations in Boston, at a workshop on standards and professionalism, about organization.

The conversation continued in Los Angeles in September: registrars, Kittu says, found out there were others "facing the same tasks and responsibilities, and that solutions and help could be shared."

Pat Nauert, who had worked with Dorothy Dudley before moving to the Los Angeles County Museum of Art, was instrumental, in the mid-1970s, in the formation of the committee. She worked on mailing lists and started the journal *Registrars' Report,* a staple of basic information during the early days of the committee which was separate from, but sanctioned by, the Registrars Committee when it was formed. By 1976 the registrars were organized enough to send out a list of sessions for the Washington, D.C., AAM meeting, noting the sessions that were of interest to registrars, and asking the question, "to organize, or not, and how to make it work." In the west, Kittu Longstreth-Brown says, people on Pat Nauert's mailing list received copies of the sessions and questions.

Diane Green wrote:

At the Registration Seminar that Pat Nauert held at LACMA, the first place that I remember hearing the idea of forming a Registrars Committee, all of us there were struck with how many concerns we shared as a group and how far we had to go to become accepted as professionals in the museum world. I can remember resolutions that registrars should be paid at least a $10,000 per annum salary, something hardly any of us could claim (I myself was making $4,800 at a small outdoor museum). I remember the flurry of correspondence about standards and procedures in that pre-computer world. Almost all of us on the committee were women, and I can recall that our work was suffused with the energy and excitement of '70s feminism. I can recall at one point grabbing the hand of a totally uncomprehending Gloria Steinham at a speech of hers in San Antonio and explaining that there were people in the museum field who were at work on feminist issues, too.

Ellen Myette wrote in the article "How This Book Came To Be" in *Registrars on Record*:

Washington, D. C., in June is a very appealing town, especially to the visitor. The temperature does not yet rival that of New Delhi, the Mall is green and inviting, and the city's many garden plots are still in flower. Furthermore, from the Sheraton Park Hotel, site of the 1976 annual meeting of the American Association of Museums (AAM), it is an easy walk to wonderful museums, historic mansions, and the federal monuments. Why then, after a full day's workshops and meetings, would forty-three registrars choose to remain indoors?

In a crowded hotel room, these registrars were in fact taking the first step of a professional journey. The immediate goal of this late afternoon conclave was to establish a registrars' steering committee, choose its officers, and determine its structure. Its most pressing long-term goal was to become a standing professional committee of the AAM. Both of these goals were a means to an end; the underlying and most critical objective of the assembled registrars was to advance their profession.

In 1976, registrars' concerns were scarcely reflected in the annual meeting program, nor were registrars represented on the AAM council. The registrars were convinced that something had to be done to inform their museum colleagues of the changing role of the registrar and to promote communication among themselves.

Kay Paris was appointed Chair of the Steering Committee. Her Dudley Wilkinson Award of Distinction speech details the work that was done during the year of the committee's formation.

She writes, as part of an award acceptance speech:

After everyone had left, working through the night, we prepared for another special session, which I had called for the following morning. There were a number of objectives, imperatives, if you will, which I hoped could eventually be reached:

1. Development of a museum-wide understanding of, and appreciation for, registrarial responsibilities.

2. Recognition of the importance of the Registrar as a member of each museum's professional staff.

3. The active organization of informative sessions, specific to registrars, at state, regional and national meetings, in order that registrars could share information, improve their skills, supplement their knowledge, have greater opportunity for networking, on all those levels, and have funds budgeted by their institutions for attendance at such meetings.

4. The appointment of task forces, each of which would give in-depth study to a topic of specific importance to registrars.

5. A concerted effort to see that, through established standards of required educational background, job skills, and management abilities, the museum registrar would attain the professional stature of the chief curator and receive a commensurate salary.

To move us toward the perceived objectives, twelve long-range goals were envisioned:

1. Develop the structure for a national organization, which reaches out to the regions and the states.

2. Propose by-laws for a Standing Professional Committee to AAM.

3. Prepare a Statement of Professional Practices.

4. Registrars programs and

5. Ad hoc sessions at regional conferences.

6. Registrars programs and

7. Ad hoc sessions at the annual meeting.

8. Petition AAM Council for recognition as a Standing Professional Committee.

9. Petition nationally for nomination to an at-large position on the AAM Council.

10. Publish a Registrars newsletter.

11. Develop a national mailing list.

12. Undertake a national position and salary survey.

Item 8, petition AAM Council for recognition as a Standing Professional Committee was undertaken with vigor. A first mailing reached nearly 100, and was sent off to AAM. On 28 April 1977 Joseph Veach Noble, President of the American Association of Museums, wrote to Katherine Paris in acceptance.

Registrars were the second professional group to become organized, after the educators; they took only the year, from Washington, D.C., until the Seattle, Washington, meeting. They sailed by the curators, who were also working to form a committee, and entered into a new phase of professionalism.

Some things should be noted about the importance of the early transactions of the Registrar's Committee. It is apparent that the Registrars Committee was first concerned with inclusion, that everyone who might benefit was kept informed (this has continued to the present day with free listserv subscription outside of any committee affiliation). There was concern from the beginning that involvement reach all the regional organizations.

By 1980 two registrars were nominated for AAM Council: Ellen Myette, by the nominating committee, and Mary Edgar Patton, by petition. The election of these two to AAM Council was a high point for the committee's involvement with the larger board and was the time of largest possible impact on the greater museum community. By 1990 the situation was more difficult. A report in the Summer 1990 RC Newsletter indicates that the names of two registrars were submitted to the AAM Nominations for consideration and that neither was approved. RC-AAM then circulated petitions to acquire at least 100 signatures for both candidates. In the end, one, Cordelia Rose, was elected as AAM Councilor-at-large. In more recent years the AAM board has been reduced in size and it has become nearly impossible for any museum personnel below the level of deputy director to serve on the AAM Board. In 2001 the slate for election to the American Association of Museums Board was limited to one candidate for each vacancy, and the work of the AAM Nominations Committee grew in importance.

The AAM continually refines the accreditation process. Museum Assessment Programs and peer review of museums provide important means to assure standards. On a parallel track, professional committees formed to further the process of ongoing education for AAM members. Among other museum disciplines, these committees include Small Museum Administrators, Curators, and Registrars.

The Registrars Committee of the American Association of Museums has produced a myriad of workshops and publications to further best practices and standards for collections stewardship. These include (but are certainly not limited to) work on condition reports, insurance, loan practices and agreements, ethics, couriering, deaccessioning, emergency planning, and the standardization of facility reports. In 1998 more than 70 RC-AAM members wrote the fourth edition of the book on museum registration, *The New Museum Registration Methods,* edited by Rebecca Buck and Jean A. Gilmore. This volume, 2010, updates and expands *NMRM.* The latest iteration of programming, started in the 2000s, is the establishment of the International Registrars Symposium, which alternates with its counterpart, the European international conference. There is also an active Australasian Registrars Committee that provides active programming for Australia, New Zealand, and Asia.

Mechanisms are in place to create and perfect the standards needed to care for museum collections. Standards to deal with problems left from the past are now being examined, and strong support for wise and careful collecting as well as judicious deaccessioning in museums is needed. In 2004 the American Association of Museums published *Collecting Guidelines for Museums,* which may serve as a template for developing collections and provide the basis for limiting collection problems in the future. The combination of best practices in collections stewardship with an institutional ability to make responsible collection choices can be the foundation for solutions to current problems and prevention of future conundrums.

The 2005 AAM Accreditation Handbook offers the following explanation:

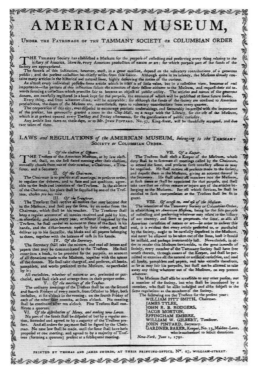

COPY PHOTOGRAPH COURTESY THE
METROPOLITAN MUSEUM OF ART

PHOTO COURTESY NEWARK MUSEUM

DEALING WITH EARLY COLLECTIONS: *Early Collecting Policies*

Museums proliferated in the 20th century, and in their early days operated with very broad missions and collection policies. There are major collections of objects of national historical importance in some museums, but many general and history museums collect and display humble objects used by the local people. Museums often opened themselves up as the community attic, the repository for objects that people did not want but could not throw away. The early collections were less likely to be well catalogued and tracked, and many of the registration issues faced today spring from the early days of museums.

On June 1, 1791, the Tammany Society of New York City issued a Broadside publicizing its American Museum, which had opened to the public on May 21st. The founders had a collecting plan: "Everything, from whatever clime, will be acceptable."

The National Museum also had a broad scope of collections:

". . . [I]t is not unreasonable to hope that examples of every kind of object known to man may be acquired, and that this museum may be able, by means of a thorough classification . . . to illustrate the history of human culture better than has ever been done before."

—*George Brown Goode, Assistant Director, National Museum of the United States, 1881*

THE NEWARK MUSEUM also had a broad, albeit specialized collection that promoted the intense focus of the museum on education. This poster (above) dates from 1914.

Plans for museum accreditation began in earnest in 1967 when President Lyndon B. Johnson asked the U. S. Federal Council on the Arts and Humanities to conduct a study of the status of American museums and recommend ways to support and strengthen them. The council enlisted AAM's assistance and in 1968 the association established a committee to study the idea of an accreditation program for museums. Based on AAM's input, on November 25, 1968, the council issued *America's Museums: The Belmont Report,* which stated: "It is urgent that the American Association of Museums and its member institutions develop and agree upon acceptable criteria and methods of accrediting museums." •

NOTES

1. This is the earliest date found for the title, though not for the duties. Should anyone have evidence of an earlier use of registrar in a museum, please contact the author.

2. Goode, G. Brown, *Principle of Museum Administration,* Annual Report of the Board of Regents of the Smithsonian Institution for the year ending June 30, 1897

3. Goode did admit "there will be many legitimate exceptions to this rule, but it can do no harm to state it forcibly, since the museum curator is more likely to err on the side of saving too much."

4. Keers, p. 26

5. See Frits Keers, "Preliminaries for a Bibliography of Museum Collection Catalogues," *Art Libraries Journal,* 22/2, 1997.

6. The Grolier Club was founded in 1884 and is the oldest club for bibliophiles and friends of book arts. Kent and John Cotton Dana, librarian at Newark's Free Public Library and founding director of the Newark Museum, had a close relationship fraught with arguments and comparisons about systems for museums and libraries.

7. From MFA Boston documents, thanks to Jill Kennedy-Kernohan

8. Lucas, F. A. Evolution of Museums, AAM proceedings, 1907, pp. 82-91

REBECCA BUCK

Museum Registration Methods 5 was written for and by museum collections personnel. John Cotton Dana often used the term "museum worker" to describe his staff, and it might have been easier to continue that practice than to try to account for the breakdown and specialization of collections roles as museums become more and more complex. Registrars became Head or Senior or Chief, with divisions of associate and assistant and assistant to, and then some became Directors of Registration, and then there were divisions in exhibition and permanent collection work. Some have gone on to become Deputy or Assistant Directors. An emerging group of administrative exhibition officials with a rainbow of titles has added extra depth. This proliferation of titles, in addition to the age-old discussion of where registrars and curators and collection managers and conservators stand in the museum hierarchy and vis-à-vis each other, make the topic of the registrar's role perhaps more interesting than it need be.

There are, or can be, some distinctions among the group. Some are important, some are not. It is important to check the history and tradition of the museum one is reviewing, or working in, to determine how titles and organizational charts came into their current form, and more importantly, why the museum took its present form. The determinants can be size, discipline, or age; in other than small museums and museums with only volunteers, it is likely that the real determinants were personality and circumstance.

Throughout this book we refer to the registrar as the staff member who undertakes the task at hand. That person may, in reality, be a registrar (chief, head, associate, assistant, assistant to), collections manager, curator (associate, assistant), director (executive, deputy, assistant), project director, keeper, conservator, collections technician, computer specialist, exhibition technician, mount maker, archivist, consultant,

board member, or volunteer. There are, within some organizations, even greater proliferations of titles.

The most important point about collection roles is not the title itself, nor the description of job responsibilities. Collection personnel should be placed at the right level in the organizational chart. Heads of the registration, curatorial, and conservation departments should be peers on the organizational chart. If they are not responsible to the same authority, be it director or deputy director for collections, there are potential problems. They must be equal so that a serious dialogue can exist among departments. If a registrar reports to a curator or conservator, a curator reports to a registrar or conservator, or a conservator reports to a registrar or curator, there is no healthy balance of roles within the museum. At some point, it is almost assured that the ego of a past or present staff member will overtake efficiency and teamwork in favor of individual gain. Collections managers and registrars have also played this particular game. Neither title is superior. A museum can set up its system to have collections managers overseeing registrars or registrars overseeing collections managers. Historically, "registrar" wins hands down as the title of choice.

In order to understand a position and be effective in it, a prospective staff member should become familiar with the organizational structure, history, and culture of the specific museum. Titles may be similar, but working within the framework of a large science museum is far different from working in a small history museum.

Small museums may have only one paid staff member. That person is charged with everything from development to housekeeping and may call on volunteers to perform registration and collections management tasks. Small to mid-size museums often rely on a curator, sometimes called a curator of collections, for the performance of collection work.

Basic collection roles

Registrar

Registrars are responsible for risk management and documentation of the collection. They develop and maintain record systems and are often responsible for storage systems. Registrars are academic generalists.

Collection Managers

Collection managers form the hands-on problem-solving component of the museum staff. They move objects, carry out re-housing and relocation projects, and may oversee basic housekeeping, IPM, packing, and preparatory staffs. They often have graduate degrees in museology.

Curator

Curators are responsible for the intellectual and, in art museums, aesthetic control of the collection. They collect, develop exhibitions, catalog, and write. Curators are usually the creative stars of the museum; they are specialists in their academic areas.

Conservator

Trained conservators do all invasive work on museum collection objects. When on staff, they oversee the physical care of collections. They are highly trained in chemistry and practical techniques for repair and restoration.

In addition: Exhibition coordinators, preparators, art handlers, cataloguers, installers, technicians, projects directors, keepers, computer specialists, and intellectual property officers may find a place in the museum collections officescape.

As the museum grows, an employee with the title registrar may be hired to take over many of the collections functions. Some museums include a collections manager who focuses on the physical aspects of handling and storage, while the registrar concentrates on records, logistics, and legal matters.

Registrars in art museums, where the department is central to collections management and documentation, are often charged with a full scope of collections tasks. The registrar, among other things, organizes storage; oversees computer projects; processes accessions, loans, and exhibitions; and drafts collections policy and procedures.

In very large art museums, collection departments that are defined by institutional collecting focus and history (European Art, Prints & Drawings) care for and document specific parts of the overall collection. In these cases, the registrar serves a more specialized and centralized function; the registrar's office generally deals with accessions, deaccessions, loans, exhibitions, and many administrative tasks related to collections. Large history museums may be similarly organized.

Science museums rely on collecting departments, often staffed with collections managers in addition to curators, to care for collections. The registrar's function in the science museum may also be centralized and is often removed from collection activities, except for accessioning, deaccessioning, and loans. If departments are responsible for inventory and care, the registrar may be the auditor who assures accountability.

The following description of a registrar's job encompasses a wide range of work related to collections. It is culled from job descriptions requested for the RC-AAM journal REGISTRAR in 1993, from the job descriptions on file with the RC-AAM, from updates and queries that have appeared on the RC listserv and the observations and personal correspondence in response to them, and from a model drawn up for a management seminar. Depending on the type and size of museum, the Registrar's Office may do many, most, or all of the tasks that are listed, alone or in concert with other departments in the museum. •

1c | The Administrative Placement of Registration and Collections Care in Museums

MARK JANZEN

The overall purpose of most museums is to collect, preserve, research, and exhibit materials of artistic, historical, archaeological, and natural significance for the benefit of the public. Constantly improving procedural, material, and ethical practice has led to the development of several professional fields of endeavor within the larger museum community. The development of new positions in response to both a need to serve the public and to protect our irreplaceable collections has shaped the nature and direction of museum practice.

One of those fundamentally altered fields is collections care, which includes all of the specialists dealing with the handling and documentation of artifacts. Registration and collection management are often merged as the twin endeavors of professional collections care. As the museum field has grown and professionalized, increasingly complex training and skills have become necessary to accomplish the wide array of required collection tasks. Collection care is now not only one of the critical elements of museum function but is also recognized by the American Association of Museums as one of the most important factors to be considered in evaluating an institution seeking professional accreditation.

An often overlooked factor in the professionalization of collections care has been its administrative placement within the broader museum structure. Early incarnations of registrars and collection care professionals were often marginalized as secretaries and janitors by institutions and professionals who did not understand their growing value and expertise. Continuing reports of instances in which collections care best practice are set aside and in which collections care specialists and modern professional standards are ignored in deference to curatorial expediency and the need to raise money make it clear that problems still exist.

Registrars and collections managers should be the administrative equivalent of their curatorial peers in order to prevent conflict and help shield the collections against ill-informed or unethical behavior regarding care and documentation. A significant percentage of museums have already moved to this administrative standard, and it should be encouraged for all institutions. All professional groups should be encouraged to recognize and support the proper administrative placement of registrars and collection care professionals. •

1D | A COMPOSITE JOB DESCRIPTION FOR THE REGISTRAR

REBECCA BUCK

PROFILE

Academic background

B.A., M.A., or Ph.D. in museum's specialty field and/or museum studies; information sciences and business/legal studies a plus

Reports to

Director or head of collections division

Supervises

Assistants for loans, collections, and information management; preparators, packers, handlers, and photographers; interns, work-study students, and volunteers; rights and reproduction, and, in some cases, library and archives. Coordinates conservation as necessary

AREAS OF RESPONSIBILITY

Information management: manual and computerized

Creates/compiles and maintains legal documents, histories of use, and physical histories of permanent collections objects and/or specimens

Legal forms and acknowledgments

Permanent collections catalog and files

Loan, conservation, condition, publication records

Exhibition, insurance, and location records

Organizes and implements inventory projects

Coordinates/assists with computer projects

Systems specs and software choices

Data standards committees

Data input management

Disseminates information as needed to other departments, researchers, and students

Coordinates object identification services

Coordinates or is involved with DAMS projects

Collections management

Monitors legal and ethical implications and care standards of transactions

Facilitates care and control of collections on site

Initiates, drafts, and, upon adoption, implements collection policies

Oversees object movement, internal and external

Oversees packing and shipping

Acts as courier or designates courier

Implements security procedures / works closely with security forces

Designs and controls storage areas

Works with contractors

Determines storage methods

Oversees integrated pest management programs
Contracts for outside services as needed
Conservation, rigging, packing, crating, shipping, photography, insurance
Exhibitions
Borrowed exhibitions
Negotiates loan contracts
Schedules and supervises packing, shipping, condition reporting, and object movement
Prepares grant reports as necessary
Produces indemnity applications as necessary
In-house exhibitions
Provides information to other departments as needed
Coordinates object movement and record keeping
Prepares or helps in preparation of label copy
Traveling exhibitions
Drafts/reviews contracts
Prepares and coordinates documentation, packing, shipping
Provides courier service
Other services and responsibilities
Maintains archives
Manages photographic services
Supervises collections photography
Stores photographic collections
Provides rights and reproduction services

ADMINISTRATIVE RESPONSIBILITIES

Administers department
Hires, trains, and evaluates staff
Develops and runs internship program
Prepares and implements budgets, in whole or part
Departmental
Exhibitions
Storage and other special projects
Contracts for services
Purchases office and collections management equipment and supplies
Prepares rate structures
Loans, traveling exhibitions
Photographic services

1E | THE ROLE OF THE REGISTRAR IN THE MUSEUM'S WEB

CHARLES HUMMEL

Where in the museum's organizational structure is the registrar best able to carry out his or her responsibilities and act as counselor to the director? That question, of course, raises issues related to a registrar's authority and status as well as to the budget level and management style of the institution served by a registrar.

Museums do function as stewards, responsible for collecting, preserving, interpreting, and displaying collections for the public in exchange for tax exemption in the United States. Trustees assign responsibility to a director and staff for carrying out policies and activities that are responsible and accountable both to trustees and to the public.

The public of a museum consists of many constituents: trustees, curators, educators, registrars, physical plant personnel, conservators, librarians, archivists, photographers, marketing and business personnel, development staff, volunteers, scholars, students, politicians, collectors, dealers, and the general museum-going public. Who is going to help a director decide on policy recommendations and activities that serve all of these constituencies while still maintaining accountability and responsibility for the collections? Who helps the director "bell the cat"?

Based on my experiences in the museum profession, the answer should be those division or section managers just below the director or deputy-director levels in an organization's management chart. The registrar should have the same standing and level of authority as a senior curator, head of physical plant, head of public safety, head of an education division or section, and so on. In most small or medium-size museums, the registrar should report independently to the director. In large museums the registrar should report, as appropriate, either to the Director, Deputy Director for Collections or Deputy Director for Exhibitions. If the organization is so large that it has three or more deputy directors, there should be a position at that level to whom the registrar reports.

So much responsibility and authority should be vested in the registrar, first of all, because of that position's audit of collections function. Museums are unique educational institutions because of their use of collections to educate and inspire their constituents. In Steve Weil's collection of essays about museums entitled *Beauty and the Beasts*, he devotes some attention to "The Museum as Bureaucracy." Weil states,

> Museums, like any other organization, cannot devote their full energies to carrying out programs. Some substantial part must be reserved for . . . ensurance of their continuity. Continuity is far more critical to an art museum than it is to, say, a ballet company or a publishing house. . . . No one is going to entrust valuable works of art to a museum without some reasonable certainty that the museum will continue year after year to look after them.

The audit function includes inventory of collections, which, if truth be told, is more often honored in the breach than in practice. Registrars are not usually given sufficient human and financial resources to carry out complete inventories of collections on a regular schedule. The integrity of records, accession books, accession number assignment to objects and corresponding catalogue cards, computerized information systems, object folders, conservation records, scientific examination records, photography, CD-ROM discs, and control of the level of access to records — all are part of the registrar's audit function. If carried out properly, this responsibility results in "one-stop shopping" by staff and the public for information about an institution's collections.

Permanent, current, and temporary location of collections is also an important part of this audit function. The movement and handling of collection objects due to special exhibitions, event-driven

•Why I Love Museum Registrars!

One Curator's Personal Perspective | JANET BURNETT GROSSMAN

As a recent retiree, I finally have the time and the inclination to reflect upon my experience as Associate Curator of Antiquities at the J. Paul Getty Museum, and upon my relationships with various staff members. As an intern, my first exposure to registrars was through a rather dry, academic presentation of a profession that to my mind did not sound particularly interesting or intellectually demanding, because it seemed like a type of statistical accounting. I clearly had a lot to learn.

In due course, after I had completed my PhD, I was fortunate to be hired as a curator at the Getty. Gradually, over the course of several years, I began to appreciate the many talents of our registrars. For example, in the days before there was a separate collections management staff, and as collections records began to be entered into a computerized system, they helped me learn to maximize all the information stored therein and to conduct increasingly sophisticated searches. And when I was called upon to courier objects to foreign places, they made my responsibilities much easier by providing me with step-by-step instructions and support. But my greatest admiration for registrars developed when I began to organize and mount loan exhibitions, especially those containing art from institutions outside the United States. I now believe that the realm of loan exhibitions calls upon all the skills of registrars, especially their diplomatic ones. In fact, I credit one registrar in particular for the success of two exhibitions that I organized that were particularly challenging: "Stories in Stone: Conserving Mosaics of Roman Africa: Masterpieces from the National Museums of Tunisia," and "Greeks on the Black Sea: Ancient Art from the Hermitage." (http://www.getty.edu/visit/exhibitions/past.html) It was this registrar's skill in developing a personal connection to her Tunisian and Russian counterparts that ensured the objects' safe arrival to this country in a timely fashion. She wholeheartedly committed herself to these projects and went the extra mile to make them happen. She and I worked in tandem with our respective registrarial and curatorial colleagues in both Tunisia and Russia, and it took both our efforts to ensure the realization of these exhibitions.

I know for a fact that some of my curatorial colleagues think that registrars are an irritating fact of museum life. They complain about a registrar's obsession with numbers, audits, and statistics, considering it a hindrance to the creative process that most curators imagine themselves engaged in. What these misguided curators do not seem to realize is that it is absolutely wonderful to have registrars take care of the more statistical aspects of collection management.

In conclusion, I shall report on what Wikipedia had to say about museum registrars. Under the general heading of registrars (http://en.wikipedia.org/wiki/Registrar there is this one line statement: "a museum professional who keeps permanent and loan collection records and oversees risk management for all museum collections." This is certainly a terse description that, in my opinion, does not begin to convey the complexity and importance of the job that registrars perform day in and day out behind the scenes of our nation's museums, both great and small.

attendance, and rental of museum gallery space to affiliated or outside organizations has become especially critical in house, history, and decorative arts museums. In art museums, where often up to 95 percent of collection holdings are somewhere in storage, audit, movement, and handling are equally critical.

When an institution becomes involved with major or minor renovations to its physical plant, carries out routine maintenance in its building or buildings, or undertakes new construction, it is the registrar who is the logistics general, planning the movement and storage of objects in temporary location and the return of the same objects when work is completed.

Registrars are often in a key position to remind a director or deputy director of limitations in facility space, staff resources, financial costs of materials, temporary storage, and overtime required when planning new programs or expansion of existing activities.

No one needs a reminder of the registrar's knowledge, patience, and skills in implementing temporary exhibitions.Examination of objects for condition, crating, packing, shipping, movement, and handling are all overseen by the registrar. The reverse side of this coin, obviously, is the loan of objects, on a temporary or long-term basis, to other institutions. The registrar monitors these loans as well.

Copyright and control of matters related to commercial activity programs, publication activity, fees for photography and the use of color negatives, slides, or photographic prints have also become a major activity for many registrars.

As a retired museum professional who has now switched to the trustees side of museum activity, it seems clear to me that in this period of history, the post-heroic mode of management style posited by the Museum Management Institute calls for institutions to provide registrars with the authority and status that their responsibilities have earned. Directors and deputy-directors are made "stars" by the efforts of highly competent staff. Key positions in an organization deserve highly visible recognition and those positions should include that of the registrar. •

•Insurance and the Importance of the Registrar

BILL ALLEN, RETIRED COLLECTIONS INSURANCE BROKER

To a collections insurance broker, the most important person in the museum community is the registrar. The coverage provided by insurance policies for museum collections is so broad that it cannot even be offered to the general public. The underwriters who provide collections insurance for museum professionals count on registrars more than any other museum staff member because it is the job of the registrar to know, at any given moment, the whereabouts of every collections object and the security surrounding that object. Registrars are the risk managers for underwriters. Without registrars, it is extremely doubtful that anyone would want to take on the risk of providing any kind of insurance for collections objects.

What makes good registrars?
•They need to be very compulsive. There is no room for people who are hysterics. When a van pulls up to the loading dock to take away a collections piece, it takes a compulsive personality to think of checking the tire treads on the truck to be certain that it will make it to its destination!

•They need to be "clear thinkers," able to immediately intuit the problems associated with any particular course of action. Do you allow that courier to take that Van Gogh in a gondola if it is the only way to deliver it in Venice?

•They need to be assertive. They need to be able to say no to even the most self-important staff members.

•They need to be diplomats in order to get the agreement of others on the staff and make their "no" stick.

•And of course, to their loved ones at home, they occasionally have to play the role of sweetheart.

The Registrar's Bookshelf
Compiled by Rebecca Buck

Basics

Buck, Rebecca A. and Jean Allman Gilmore, ed. *Museum Registration Methods 5,* The AAM Press, American Association of Museums, Washington, D.C., 2010.

Gardner, James and Elizabeth Merrit, *AAM Guide to Collections Planning,* American Association of Museums, Washington, D.C., 2004.

Malaro, Marie. *A Legal Primer on Managing Museum Collections, 2nd Edition.* Smithsonian Institution Press, Washington, D.C., 1998.

Merritt, Elizabeth E., ed. *National Standards and Best Practices for U.S. Museums.* The AAM Press, American Association of Museums, Washington, DC, 2008.

National Committee to Save America's Cultural Collections. *Caring for Your Collections,* Henry N. Abrams, New York, 1992.

Simmons, John E. *Things Great and Small: Collection Management Policies* American Association of Museums, Washington, D.C., 2005.

Registration and Collections Management

Benedetti, Joan M. *Art Museum Libraries and Librarianship.* Scarecrow Press/Art Libraries Society of North America, 2007.

Bourcier, Paul and Ruby Rogers, The AASLH Nomenclature Committee, *Nomenclature 3.0 for Museum Cataloging,* AASLH/AltaMire Press, 2009.

Buck, Rebecca A. and Jean Allman Gilmore. *On the Road Again: Developing and Managing Traveling Exhibitions.* American Association of Museums, Washington, DC, 2003.

Heritage Preservation, The National Institute for Conservation, *Emergency Response and the Salvage Wheel.* Washington, DC, Heritage Preservation Inc., 2005.

National Parks Service, *Museum Handbook, Part I, Museum Collections.* National Park Service, Washington, DC, 200.7

The National Trust Manual of Housekeeping: *The Care of Collections in Historic Houses Open to the Public.* Butterworth-Heinemann, Oxford and Burlington, MA, 2006.

Ogden, Sherelyn, ed. *Caring for American Indian Objects: A Practical and Cultural Guide,* Minnesota Historical Society Press, 2004.

Texas Association of Museums, *Museum Forms Book.* Texas Association of Museums, Austin, Texas, 1999.

Rose, Carolyn L., Catharine A. Hawks, and Hugh H. Genoways. *Storage of Natural History Collections: A Preventive Conservation Approach,* 1995.

Rose, Cordelia. *Courierspeak.* Smithsonian Institution Press, Washington D.C., 1993.

Wythe, Debora, ed. *Museum Archives: An Introduction,* American Society of Archivists, 2004.

Visual Resource Association, *Cataloging Cultural Objects: A Guide to Describing Cultural Works and Their Images.* ALA Editions, Atlanta, Ga., 2006.

Conservation

AIC Directory, American Institute of Conservation, released yearly.

Bachmann, Konstanze, ed. *Conservation Concerns: A Guide for Collectors and Curators.* Smithsonian Institution Press, Washington, D.C., 1992.
Ellis, Margaret Holben. *The Care of Prints and Drawings.* New York, AltaMira Press, 1995.

Frey, Franziska, Dawn Heller, Dan Kushel, Timothy Vitale, Jeffrey Warda, and Gawain

Weaver. *The AIC Guide to Digital Photograph and Conservation Documentation.* AIC, Washington, DC, 2008.

Gorman, G. E. and Sydney J. Shep, ed. *Preservation Management of Libraries, Archives and Museums.* Facet Publishing, London, 2006.

Long, Jane S. and Richard W. Long. *Caring for Your Family Treasures.* Harry N. Abrams, Inc. Publishers, New York, 2000.

National Trust. *The National Trust Manual for Housekeeping: The Care of Collection in Historic Houses Open to the Public.* Elsevier, Amsterdam, 2006.

Thomson, Garry. *Museum Environment.* Butterwork-Heinemann, Oxford and Woburn, Ma., 1999.

History and Philosophy

Alexander, Edward P. and Mary Alexander. *Museums in Motion: An Introduction to the History and Functions of Museums*, AASLH/AltaMira Press, 2007.

Case, Mary, ed. *Registrars on Record: Essays on Museum Collections Management*, American Association of Museums, Washington, DC, 1988.

Schwarzer, Marjorie. *Riches, Rivals and Radicals: 100 Years of Museums in America.* American Association of Museums, Washington, DC, 2006.

Weil, Stephen E. *Making Museums Matter.* Smithsonian Institution, Washington, DC, 2002.

Legal and Ethical

ALI-ABA (American Legal Institute, American Bar Association), *Course of Studies Materials: Legal Problems of Museum Administration.* Published annually since 1973.

Malaro, Marie C. *Museum Governance: Mission, Ethics, Policy.* Smithsonian Institution Press, Washington, DC, 1994.

Steiner, Christine, ed. *A Museum Guide to Copyright and Trademark* Michael Shapiro & Brett I. Miller, Morgan, Lewis & Bockius, American Association of Museums, Washington, DC, 1999.

Sullivan, Lawrence E. and Alison Edwards. *Stewards of the Sacred.* American Association of Museums, Washington, DC, 2004.

Various. Code of Ethics and Practice of Interest to Museums, American Association of Museums 2000.

Weil, Stephen E. *A Deaccession Reader.* American Association of Museums, Washington, DC, 1997.

Yeide, Nancy, and Akinsha Konstantin and Amy Walsh. *The AAM Guide to Provenance Research*, American Association of Museums, Washington, DC, 2001.

Websites

American Association of Museums
www.aam-us.org

Association of Art Museum Directors
www.aamd.org

Canadian Heritage Information Network
www.chin.gc.ca

Getty research institute vocabularies
www.getty.edu/research/conducting_research/vocabularies

International Council of Museums
icom.museum

Registrar's Committee AAM
www.rcaam.org

Thanks to: Jean Gilmore, Ramona Bronkar Bannayan, Lynn A. Bethke, Karen Christenson, Susan Colletta, Janice Klein, Martha Mayberry, Chris McNamara, L. J. Richards, Stephen B. Ringle, John Simmons.

The Profession | HYPOTHETICALS

1

The registrar examines the legality of the object's presence in the United States, finds it questionable, and determines that this information must be made transparent to those who make decisions about acquisitions. The curator acquiring the piece, however, is the registrar's direct supervisor.

How does she proceed?

2

A major permanent gallery in the museum is being refurbished and reinstalled. Two large sculptures in the gallery have been carefully wrapped and sealed for protection. The education department is pushing for an early opening to allow class use that corresponds to curriculum in the state, while the operations department forecasts delays because of staff shortages, and special events has already scheduled a wedding that uses this supposedly painted but uninstalled space as a reception area.

Where does the registrar fall in the negotiations for use of this gallery and how does it get sorted out?

3

Questions/Discussion:

Sum up a registrar's job in 20 words or less.

What kind of organizational model best balances the collections staff with other divisions in the museum?

Through what activities does a registrar most effectively carry out the museum's mission?

What are the differences and similarities among registrar, collection manager, and preparator positions?

SECTION 2 | **POLICIES**

2A | COLLECTIONS MANAGEMENT POLICIES

JOHN E. SIMMONS

Collections management includes everything that is done to document, care for, and develop museum collections and make them available for use. There are fundamental commonalities among all collections summarized in the principles that form the basis for collections management policies:

1. Each object or specimen entering the museum must be documented.

2. Collections should be stabilized for long-term preservation and housed in a proper storage environment.

3. The collections must be regularly inventoried and monitored.

4. The collections storage environment must be regularly monitored.

5. All collection activities and monitoring must be documented.

The purpose of the collections management policy is to minimize risk to the collections. The policy identifies the staff responsible for the collections and provides a framework for management. In practice, the collections management policy is actually a set of related policies. The core policies of acquisition, loan, deaccession, access, and collections care are augmented by ethics policies, emergency preparedness policies, and collecting plans and framed by the mission and scope of collections. (Table 1) Enacting and enforcing good collections management policies helps the museum achieve its mission, demonstrates commitment to professional standards and practices, and enables the governing authority to meet its legal and ethical obligations to protect and make accessible the collections in the public trust.

Three fundamental concepts underlying collections management policies reflect the past history of the collections while anticipating future policy evolution (Pearce 1993):

1. The collections management policy describes a relationship among the museum and its collections, its authorities and staff, and the outside world.

2. The trajectory of this relationship is set by the sum of the previous relationships among these three parties, all of which have to be taken into account whenever decisions are made.

3. These relationships are in a constant state of interaction. The policy regulates activities in the present and the future, but it takes its character from what has happened in the past.

The museum's organization and legal status affect some collections management policies and determine the nature of the responsibility of the governing board and the administration. In general, because a museum holds its collections in the public trust, the governing authority is responsible for:

1. maintaining the highest legal, ethical, and professional standards,

2. establishing policies that guide the institution's operation, and

3. delegating specific responsibilities to the staff, volunteers, and consultants (via the collections management policies).

Collections management policies explain why a museum is in operation and how it goes about its business, and define the professional standards for managing the objects in its care. These policies are accompanied by collections management procedures, which are the detailed instructions that specify how the staff should apply the policies in their day-to-day activities. Although policies and procedures often are discussed together, it is important to understand the differences between the two. *Policies* establish the standards that regulate the museum's activities by identifying what needs to be done and providing a framework to help the staff make

Table 1 Issues Addressed by the Collections Management Policy

Introduction		
Mission Statement		
Administrative and Personnel Functions	Statement of authority	
	Scope of collections	
	Categories of collections	
	Ethics	•Institutional code of ethics
		•Discipline-specific codes of ethics
		•Private collections
	Documentation	•Standards
		•Requirements
	Risk management	•Disaster plan
		•Insurance
	Intellectual property	•Rights and reproduction
		•Copyright
		•Commercial use of intellectual property
	Health and safety	
Collections Acquisition and Deaccession	Collections plan	
	Acquisition of collections	
	Documentation	
	Repository agreements	
	Registration and cataloging	
	Deaccession and disposal	
	Appraisals and identifications	
Collections Care	Conservation	•Standards for storage environment and housing
		•Environmental monitoring
		•Standards for object/specimen supports and containers
		•Standards for storage furniture
	Security	
	Inventory	
	Integrated Pest Management	
	Access and use of collections and collections information	•Public access
		•Professional use
		•Non-professional use
		•Commercial use
		•Destructive sampling
	Loans	•Incoming loans
		•Outgoing loans
		•Courier policy
		•Loan insurance
	Objects in custody	
Policy review	Compliance review	
	Policy revision	

decisions. Policy statements are approved by the governing authority. *Procedures* tell the staff how to do things and provide the mechanism for implementing the policies in a series of succinct and unambiguous action steps. Procedures are developed at the staff level and do not have to be approved by the governing authority. There should be separate documents to make clear what is policy and what is procedure. Because revisions of procedures do not have to be approved by the governing authority, maintaining separate documents makes it easier for the staff to adjust or revise the procedures as necessary to carry out the policy.

A policy is created to accomplish a specific goal or address a particular issue. Collections management policies should address any issues that might have a significant impact on the collections, museum operations, staff, or collections users. Because the issues that affect collections vary from one museum to another, the set of policies included in the collections management policy will vary somewhat from one museum to another. The policies should reflect current professional standards, be sensible and logical, and be stated clearly. The individual policies that are part of the collections management policies are interrelated and may address other museum functions as well (e.g., security, pest management, or exhibitions).

Collections management policies should be written to meet the needs of a specific museum, its collections, and the use of those collections. Reference to policies from similar institutions can help prepare a policy, but wholesale adoption of documents from other institutions will prove inadequate. The policies must be institution specific, simple, and up-to-date. Complex, confounded, or out-dated policies will simply be ignored.

The policies should define areas of responsibility (taking into account staff size, expertise, museum mission, type and size of collections, and collections use) and delegate decision-making authority to the appropriate individuals or committees. It is also important to identify who has the authority to make exemptions to the policies when necessary. The policies should direct the staff to maintain complete written records regarding all collections-related decisions and activities.

DEVELOPING AND WRITING COLLECTION MANAGEMENT POLICIES

The most successful method of preparing collections management policies involves a team with wide constituent input and a careful process:

- The director appoints a team leader and assembles a team that can provide input from all sectors of the institution.

- The team makes a careful review of current legal, ethical, and professional standards.

- A draft of the policy circulates to staff for comment.

- Drafts are redone, reviewed, and revised until complete.

- Polices are submitted to the institution's governing authority for endorsement.

A small museum with few staff members can solicit help from colleagues in other institutions. The staff should understand how the policies are developed and should have the opportunity to participate during each stage of the process it is recommended that several drafts of the policy documents be circulated to the staff for comment. Input from a variety of viewpoints will ensure that the policies support the institutional mission and have support of the staff members who must implement them.

Museum staff should develop procedures for implementing the policies and review them periodically for effectiveness.

COLLECTIONS MANAGEMENT POLICIES

Detailed information about writing collections management policies can be found in the references listed in the bibliography, including John E. Simmons, Things Great and Small: Collection Management Policies and Marie C. Malaro, A Legal Primer on Managing Museum Collections.

Introductory Sections
The collections management policy document should begin with the museum's mission statement, followed by an introduction summarizing the museum governance structure and history. The

introduction addresses how the collections management policies were developed in the context of the museum's history, mission, and collections plan and delineates other considerations that guide the process of determining the museum's collections-related activities. The collections plan establishes a vision for the collections that will best serve the museum's mission, compares the existing collections to this vision, and maps out how the museum will achieve these ideal collections (Gardner and Merritt, 2004).

The scope of collections reviews the history of the collection; considers its strengths, weaknesses, and current uses; and states what the museum does and does not collect. The collections management policy should define categories of collections (e.g., research, exhibit, public education), if any. The policy should include or refer to the museum's institutional code of ethics and any discipline-specific codes of ethics the professional staff may follow. The ethics section should address personal collecting and any restrictions the institution wishes to place on staff and board members in this regard.

The documentation policy sets standards for recording collections activities, including environmental monitoring results and regular collections inventories. The policy should require documentation to be written in simple, plain prose (using appropriate technical terms as needed), in a permanent format (using archival materials), and be legible and comprehensive.

Acquisitions

An acquisition policy is developed based on the collections plan and directs how objects and specimens are acquired or brought into the museum under the terms of a repository agreement. The policy should state clearly which staff and board members are authorized to make decisions regarding the various collections held by a museum: permanent, loan or use, research, hands-on, or other types of collections.

Acquisitions of all types of collections should be relevant to the purposes and priorities of the museum. The criteria for decision, in addition to those laid out in the collecting plan, may include intended and potential use, basic integrity, and cost and space for care and storage. The policy should require a receipt to be issued for any object or specimen left at the museum (e.g., for identification) and to all donors and sellers of collections, and that the receipts include the owner's contact information and signature over a clear statement of intent.

To protect the museum from liability issues, the policy should state that title (ownership) must be obtained free and clear for any accessioned material. The policy should require the staff to make appropriate efforts to ensure that accessioned collections have been obtained legally (e.g., documentation that includes permissions to possess, transport, export, and import the objects or specimens). The accession policy also can be written to protect the museum from donor demands for restricted gifts or partial gifts.

Repository agreements are increasingly common in museums, particularly for archaeological and natural science collections. Under the terms of a repository agreement, one institution takes on the responsibility for the care and management of a collection owned by another institution. In most cases, this means that the managing institution catalogs, cares for, and manages those collections as it does for its own. It is recommended that the repository agreement policy parallel the accession policy as closely as possible, and that the required repository documentation parallel accession policy documentation as closely as possible. The repository agreement policy should require the agreement to be detailed in a written contract between the museum and the outside agency or institution with a definite beginning date, ending date, and description of what objects or specimens will be covered. The policy should specify standards for the collections storage environment, containers, and storage furniture; standards for collections care and management (which should be the same as those for the museum's own collection); required staffing; responsibility for paying to pack up and return the collections when the repository agreement terminates; and compensation (if any) due to the curating museum for the services it provides. The policy also may address restrictions on a repository agreement, such as the collections are to be studied on site but not loaned to another institution; loans must be approved by the agency that owns the collections; and either party may terminate the agreement at any time.

Appraisals and Authentications

The appraisals policy must reflect the legal restrictions on donor tax deductions and ethical considerations for making appraisals. In general, this means that the policy should require appraisals to be done by outside professionals to avoid conflicts of interest and prohibit museum staff members from doing appraisals for collections or donations involving their current institution or one where they have recently worked. It is critically important to be scrupulous in avoiding both conflicts of interest and the appearance of conflicts of interest. The policy should reference internal appraisals of owned collections, which often are used for insurance purposes.

The museum may or may not allow authentications. If it does, the policy may state that when professional staff members authenticate objects or specimens, the museum is not responsible for the accuracy of their determinations.

Deaccessions

The deaccessioning policy covers objects or specimens that are to be removed from a collection in order to strengthen it. Deaccessioning is a way for a museum to refine and focus its collections to serve its missions better. Deaccessions may be done when objects no longer fit the museum's mission, for legal reasons (NAGPRA, illegal export, theft), for various reasons dealing with the physical integrity of the object (poor condition, part/whole relationships), or because of poor quality or redundancy.

The policy should ensure that the responsibility for deaccessioning rests with more than one person and that the board of trustees gives the final approval. The means of disposal of deaccessioned objects should be in the best interests of the museum, the public, and the professional community. Some deaccession policies require that historical, cultural, and scientific material of a state or country remain in a certain geographic area. The deaccession policy also may promote the use of exchanges with other public trust institutions as the preferred means of disposal. The policy should mandate that deaccessioned objects and specimens will not be given or sold to museum staff, volunteers, board members, or their representatives and that any proceeds

gained should be, depending on the museum's discipline, used only for the acquisition or direct care of collections. (Direct care may include conservation studies and treatments, monitoring technology, and improvements to collection storage.) The Association of Art Museum Directors, for instance, mandates that its members can use funds raised from deaccessions only for the purchase of other collection objects.

Collections Care

This policy should make it clear that all museum staff members share the responsibility for collections care, and it should identify the lead players in all areas. The policy includes risk management, conservation, storage, and environmental concerns. Documentation of the objects and their inventories also should be covered.

The collections care policy mandates the level of training for staff members who handle museum objects and requires other users to confirm via signature that they have read the instructions for handling collections. The policy should set standards for each area: registration and cataloging, maintenance and regular monitoring of appropriate storage environment, and inventory. It addresses collection security (in conjunction with the general institutional security policy) and mandates periodic collections inventories. The policy should establish a program of integrated pest management. Some museums also require specific policies to cover off-site storage of collections.

Access

The access and use policy must balance the requirements for collections care and security with the museum's public trust responsibilities. This policy designates the staff members who may approve access to and use of collections and related information. Such access will be different for museum professionals than it is for the public, scholars, and commercial users. The policy also imposes reasonable restrictions on access and use if such limitations are in the best interests of the collections' long-term care and preservation.

Loans

The loan policy should define appropriate reasons for loans and specify that they be made to other peer institutions rather than to individuals or commercial corporations. It should require the use of borrowed objects or specimens be in keeping with standards in the field and with the museum's own goals.

The policy should be clear on the process and authority to approve a loan to another institution and borrowing objects from another institution. The loan policy also addresses insurance and documentation of loans, the length of the loan period (no loan should be open-ended), and the use of photographs and other images of the objects or specimens. It should specify that physical requirements and security protocol be maintained for loans and indicate a decision-making process for sending couriers or installers to accompany a loan object. It also should provide a mechanism for recalling loans.

Many museums draw up separate policies for outgoing and incoming loans. They also may create a policy that clarifies all work related to exhibitions produced for loan to other institutions.

Review and Revision

Each collections management policy must be reviewed and revised on a regular basis. Collections management policies, like any other policy, are useless if they are outdated, ignored, too complex to be followed, too simplistic to be useful, or not congruent with the museum's mission. A simple statement—either in conjunction with each policy or with the group of policies as a whole—should outline time periods for review. Staff also should keep abreast of changes in museum standards and the law so that they can update policies when necessary. •

2B | AD HOC POLICIES FOR COLLECTIONS MANAGERS

ROBIN MEADOR-WOODRUFF

Ad hoc: for the particular end or case at hand without consideration of wider application. (Merriam-Webster Online Dictionary, 2009)

All collections managers will accommodate requests to use their museums' collections. Such requests may involve a visitor who wants to snap a photo of an object or event staff who inquire about the possibility of serving a bit of wine and cheese in the galleries.

Collections form the core of a museum, and their display and use are central to the fulfillment of the institution's mission. Museums balance their desire to use objects against their overarching responsibility to safeguard the collections in their care. The competing needs of collections use and collections safety mean that the collections management department must have good ad hoc policies that relate to specific instances of collections use by both museum staff and visitors. It is important that the museum's collections staff participate in policy-making discussions in other departments that might affect collections, particularly the security, visitor services, education, and facilities departments. These divisions interact with the public in the museum's physical space in a variety of ways, and principles of responsible collections management must take into account in situations that involve the collections or the space in which they reside.

Ad hoc policies sometimes are found within a museum's collections management policy (CMP), but usually they are ancillary to the CMP and do not need the approval of the board of trustees. They often are developed to interpret the broad access and use and collections care sections of a CMP for specific areas in the museum (e.g., those related to education activities or special events) or to accommodate rapidly changing laws and technologies (e.g., regarding photography). Ad hoc policies are a flexible response to ongoing and often quickly developing requests by

a museum's staff and audience; these policies give staff consistent ways of dealing with these situations.

Some ad hoc policies, such as those concerning photography in the galleries, will be relevant to most types of museums; others, such as those establishing terms and requirements for scientific sampling, will be relevant to a much smaller subset. But all such policies aim to preserve the museum's collections and minimize risk while accommodating judicious collections use.

Ad hoc policies may be very directly related to the collections or, from a collections manager's perspective, they may be tangentially related. The following examples are presented as subsets and represent situations in which an ad hoc policy might be needed. They are meant to serve as a tool to assist collections managers as they consider the often-evolving ways to accommodate collections use. These examples are intended to be representative and are by no means exhaustive, since all institutions have unique needs.

IMAGES: CAPTURE AND USE

A typical collections manager, if there is such a thing, might find that the most frequently asked questions concern images of the materials in the collection. While a museum's general rights and reproduction policy within the CMP sets the tone for image duplication and use, ad hoc policies address the physical act of image capture. Photography of collections stored in secure, non-public areas of the museum usually is accomplished by and under the direction of collections management staff in controlled circumstances. However, it is critical to have a short and clear policy governing photography of the collections on display in the galleries. Will it be allowed at all and, if so, under what circumstances? Questions answered by the ad hoc policy might include: Should people register their cameras with security or visitor services staff as soon as they enter the building? Are tripods or video-filming dollies allowed? Are additional lights or flash permitted? Given the ubiquity and the increasing popularity of cell phone cameras, how will these be managed, particularly if the museum has a policy against cell phones in the galleries? It can be argued that most images of museum collections are now captured digitally. If image capture is permitted in the galleries, how will the museum let visitors know about its image-use constraints?

Although photography is the most prevalent, many institutions also accommodate other types of image capture, such as the time-honored practice of copying works in the museum's collections. Although some museums do not allow this type of activity, others encourage it as an extension of their mission. The conditions under which an individual will be allowed to sketch, draw, or paint in the galleries should be addressed by collections managers, particularly in instances where the materials used have the potential to affect the collections adversely. A related but less frequent example is the physical reproduction of three-dimensional objects, such as models. Although a museum's CMP usually governs the reproduction of images for commercial ventures, ad hoc policies often address the activities of individual visitors making non-commercial reproductions.

PHYSICAL USE OF THE COLLECTIONS

The use of collections objects for non-display purposes is one of the more problematic situations that can arise for collections managers. The mandate to protect the collection from harm would seem to take precedence against a request to perform an action that could result in varying degrees of physical change, including destruction. However, such requests may be legitimate uses of the collection and may serve to further the museum's mission.

Collections of ethnographic and natural history materials are subject to requests for scientific sampling, which usually is accomplished by using invasive techniques to harvest the sample. It is critical to have good policies that govern the vetting process for the approval of the sampling request as well as

policies that dictate the ultimate disposition of any samples taken. Will the samples be destroyed during the examination process, or will they be returned to the museum? Where will irradiated samples be stored upon their return to the museum? How will the information about the results of the sampling be disseminated to the museum, and will there be any restrictions on staff who want to use this information?

Artifacts in museum collections that have been produced by indigenous peoples are another type of ethnographic material that poses unique challenges. The evolving relationship and dialogue between museums and indigenous peoples, particularly Native Americans, has yielded rich rewards in the form of increased sensitivity toward and greater understanding of the material culture. Many museums now perceive more fully their custodial capacity regarding these collections and, acting in cooperation with the indigenous groups from which the artifacts derive, permit ceremonial use of the materials under controlled circumstances. Collections managers whose institutions accommodate this type of use must ensure that collections safety is balanced with the needs of the users. Ceremonies may incorporate the use of consumable organic materials, such as tobacco or grain, or utilize an open flame. Ad hoc policies can stipulate the conditions that must be met in order to accommodate ceremonial use, such as employing tobacco that has been processed through a thermal treatment. It is also important to consider issues such as whether residues or byproducts will be generated and whether the objects can be cleaned.

The physical use of artifacts of a mechanical nature or artworks with moving parts also may call for ad hoc policies. Under what, if any, conditions will such use be permitted and by whom? A museum with a collection of antique musical instruments may have a policy in place that dictates they are never to be played, whereas a historic house might have a functional piano that benefits from being tuned and played periodically. If that is the case, who may tune or play the piano, and with what frequency should such uses occur? Machines that are still functional and are housed in a collection pose a similar problem. Again, conditions for maintenance and use must be stipulated. Does the nature of the machine dictate that a conservator must perform maintenance, or is it appropriate for a technician or mechanic to provide those services? Under what condition is the machine to be operated: as a scheduled demonstration for the public or as part of a routinely occurring maintenance protocol?

Ad hoc policies can apply to the use of demonstration or instructional collections. Museums that have an active education departments often use their collections to facilitate directed learning activities in a classroom, laboratory, or gallery. It is important to clarify which portions of the collections may be used for this purpose—the museum's accessioned permanent collections or only those artifacts that have been designated for demonstration.

Libraries and archives may fall within the administrative oversight of the collections management division, or they may be more autonomous divisions within the museum. In instances where the museum has no formal library or archive, collections managers often are called upon to administer these materials, in addition to the artwork and artifacts that comprise the accessioned collections. Library and archive materials have the potential to be among a museum's most heavily used resources, and it is important that they are administered in a responsible manner. Many of the constraints governing the handling and use of artifact collections are not applicable to materials that, by their nature, serve as either primary or secondary source references. Ad hoc library and archive policies can set parameters for the use of such materials.

THE MUSEUM'S PUBLIC SPACE

The collections manager will help generate a variety of policies that affect the museum's public space. Often these policies are drafted in collaboration with other divisions of the museum that will be affected by any constraints the policies set. While collections managers usually are not responsible for initiating policies addressing gallery conduct, facility use, and housekeeping in public spaces, they or their representatives should be included in the development of those policies. The collections manager must

advocate for participation in the policy-making process of other divisions in all cases where the policies generated might have an impact on the collections.

An overarching question for collections managers should be, "What is in the museum building other than the collections themselves, and what risks do those things pose to the collections?" The answers can be myriad, and although such threats will be found throughout the building, they are particularly critical when they occur in close proximity to collections on display. Food and drink, living plants and cut flowers, chemicals in the form of cleaning solvents and inks—and visitors—can be seen as risky introductions into the museum's environment. Policies that regulate the museum's physical space are intended to minimize risk to both the collections and the people who use the facility.

Many museums have learned the hard way that organic materials must be monitored closely. Spilled food and drink can stain artwork. The spills, when inadequately cleaned, have the potential to draw insects that will damage the collections and furnishings of the museum. Collections managers may advocate for policies that limit the type of food and drink that may be served and the areas within the museum where food and drink service may occur. Similarly, they should work with events staff to ensure the existence and enforcement of adequate policies stipulating that live plants and cut flowers must be treated for insects before they can be introduced into the museum environment. Policies about food, drink, plants, and flowers should be part of any facility use agreement that the museum enters into with third parties.

Collections managers should work to ensure that acceptable standards for visitor conduct are articulated in their institutional ad hoc policies. They should be concerned about unruly visitors because they may damage the collections, either intentionally or accidentally. In addition, many museums have institutional policies restricting the use of strollers and requiring visitors to check umbrellas, coats, bags, and oversized packages. Collections managers should recognize the potential these items have to inflict damage on exhibitions and urge the museum to adopt policies if they do not currently exist.

Education departments often orchestrate demonstrations, tours, festivals and concerts that, depending on the nature of the event, may use some gallery space. Policies may limit the size of the tour, the materials that a class may use in a gallery, and spaces that can be used if an outside event is rained out. ●

AD HOC POLICIES

The policies noted here are ad hoc because they differ from museum to museum. A historic house museum may need a strict policy regarding use of rooms but an art museum with large, spacious reception areas may not. A museum may or may not receive requests for scientific testing on its collections. If the museum ends up with a fire muster or a circus on the premises, there may be many more areas to address. The list provided is not exhaustive; each policy, however, should be approached with the whole museum in mind. Financial concerns are important, care of the collections is vital, and policies that will be taken seriously and implemented must be creative and take all aspects of the mission into consideration.

LIST OF AD HOC POLICIES

Public
Photography in the galleries
   General public
   Public relations
   Movie shoots
Special events
   Access
   Plants allowed
   Food and beverage allowed
Photography in storage areas
Sketching in the galleries
Educational programs in galleries
   Size
   Materials for workshops
   Physical activities (dancing, drumming, singing, etc.)
Family festival guidelines
Animals in the galleries/gardens

Staff
Scientific testing

Treatment and display of sacred objects

Sacred ceremonies

Allowable living exhibitions (insects, plants)

Using historic objects
   (musical instruments, music boxes, etc.)

Documentation and care of contemporary art

Maintenance of galleries/vitrines/objects

Staff access to storage

Access to exhibition areas in preparation

Art in offices (personal, museum-owned)

Art on campus

Policies | HYPOTHETICALS

1

After careful consideration and staff discussion, the museum's administration has decided not to allow public photography in the galleries. This measure has been taken for reasons of safety, copyright, and security. In one day you receive the following five queries.

How do you reply?

•A local high-school student wants to photograph an artwork on view to illustrate a paper he is writing.

•An artist whose work is on display wants to take photos of the installation.

•The artist-in-residence wants to make a documentary of the galleries, filmed from a model airplane.

•A television news program wants to shoot opening and closing scenes for its own documentary, unrelated to the museum, in the American galleries.

•A fashion magazine wants to use the galleries as a background for an upcoming photo shoot.

2

An important trustee, a doctor, asks to borrow a gift he made to the museum several years ago; it will be displayed in his office.

How do you respond?

3

Imagine that you have deaccessioned and sold more than 100 low-value objects that have clogged your storage for decades.

How do you account for the income, and how do you assign credit lines?

4

The curator who is very sensitive to the ethics of collecting has found an artwork at auction that may have been purchased and imported after 1970. She comes to you, the registrar, for advice about the ethics of purchasing the work and to determine your requirements for complete provenance.

How do you respond?

5

The special events coordinator has scheduled a vital (her description) wedding in the museum between two important exhibitions. As the date approaches, it becomes evident that the weather will be terrible and that all the bars will have to be moved inside. She wants to put them in a multi-purpose area where only a few pieces of art are installed.

What is your response?

6

A loan request comes from a small historic house museum without environmental controls.

How do you address it?

7

A local conservator asks the museum if she could have some deaccessioned, low-value objects for her students to use as practice pieces.

How do you respond?

8

The public relations director and special events manager in a historic house museum have planned an exciting, crowd-pleasing activity for Halloween: "Let's exaggerate the long-standing rumors that the historic house is haunted by its previous inhabitants, open the museum late one night, and invite a local ghost-hunter with all of his 'scientific' equipment designed to detect paranormal activity. Meanwhile, the docents can tell people about the history of the house and the family."

How do you respond?

9

The curator of contemporary art wants to acquire a sculpture made of plastic that will surely degrade. The conservator advises against it: not only will it be a daunting, if not impossible, task to preserve the artwork, the off-gassing of the deteriorating plastic may harm other objects. The curator, however, insists that this artwork will be an important addition to the collection.

How do you respond?

10

A couple from the community approaches the museum and asks if they can be married at an altarpiece in the collection. They promise to invite no more than 10 guests to the ceremony.

How do you respond?

SECTION 3 | THE BASICS

3A | INITIAL CUSTODY AND DOCUMENTATION

REBECCA BUCK

An object comes to the museum for the first time. It may be on approval for gift or purchase; it may be a loan for exhibition or study. If preparations have been made and all goes according to plan, the object can be tracked forever if it enters the permanent collection, or it can be used in the short-term without error or loss while on loan. The museum can exercise physical and intellectual control over the object, and an accurate history of status and condition that assures accountability will accrue. In order to make that initial moment successful, a well-defined process has to be in place, and curatorial and registration personnel have to communicate and follow the process every time, for every object, with almost no exceptions.

Keeping object entry under control relates directly to museum mission and collection management policies. The process that emerges from those documents can strengthen a museum's ability to decrease risks associated with abandoned property, old loans, partially processed objects, and the objects that eventually become found-in-collection objects. Guidelines about object entry should be established. If the museum can control entry and allow only those objects that are destined for the permanent collection or for loan exhibitions, very few problems arise. The more defined the guidelines are, the greater the success. Sample guidelines:

- A temporary custody or incoming loan agreement must be in place before an object arrives at the museum.

- All collection objects coming in to the museum must be approved in advance by the museum's curatorial staff and/or director.

- First curatorial review should take place by photograph or visit, then arrangements for a temporary custody agreement should be made as necessary.

- No object may be accepted for gift or for review by front-desk personnel, guards, or other staff, including registrars, collection managers, and exhibition staff.

- If the museum does object identification for the public, it must be done only by photograph.

- The museum should have a statement about the fate of objects left on the property without process and receipt. This statement should apply to cases where the source is known as well as to property with no identification attached. The museum should follow state law regarding such property.

The initial process happens in two major ways, one for objects coming in for loan and another for those coming into permanent collection.

For loans, a very well defined process *(See chapter on Loans)* must be in place. Most museums do not let a loaned object onto their premises without a signed loan agreement, and the reasons are valid and clear: responsibilities and actions are well defined. It is less often that museums require signed agreements in advance of objects entering their permanent collections, but it is highly advised that such requirements be put in place. The questions and problems involving misunderstandings or lack of proof of intent that can often lead to a museum's inability to complete an acquisition process disappear when the intent and actions are clearly defined at the beginning of the process.

For permanent collection entries, the museum enters into a temporary custody agreement for an object that is being reviewed for purchase or gift. The custody agreement should be put in place as soon as the decision is made to consider the object for the collection. If there is any question about who is responsible for loss or damage, whether that happens in the vendor's showroom or donor's apartment, during shipment or arrival at the museum, the custody agreement will define that responsibility and allow claims that might arise to be answered cleanly. If the vendor closes shop or claims damage, the responsibilities are clear. If a donor does not return a deed of gift or disappears into the ether, there is a signature saying that the intent is to give, and the museum can then act on that information.

The temporary custody agreement requires significant information, some of which is difficult to track down in advance. Contact information should include the source's name—both owner and agent, if appropriate—address, phone, and email information, with alternates where necessary. Object identification should include complete essential information: object name, object date, artist/maker/manufacturer, title when applicable, location of origin when known, materials/medium, and measurements. The purchase price is necessary for objects under purchase consideration, and it is always useful to get an approximate value for potential gifts. There should be some negotiation regarding shipping and packing costs and insurance coverage. Much variation is possible in these areas: Is the object local or long-distance? Are packers on site or must they be hired? Is international movement involved? Are there applicable laws (Endangered Species, CITES, UNESCO agreements) that must be observed? Each transaction should be entered with an open mind, with common sense, and with the grace to keep all parties in harmony.

The difficulties of these procedures are obvious. The relationships and respect between museum departments must be such that they communicate with each other and work in tandem. There must be adequate personnel to track down information and produce documentation. The administration and board of trustees must be educated and must know the importance of these activities so that they are supported. If a museum does not develop a "pre-admission" custody agreement, however, it must rely for direction on a shipping receipt with basic

---

Object Meets Museum Meets Object: Best Case/Worst Case

Best:
Registrar receives complete information about object and source of each incoming gift, bequest, purchase, or loan.
Custody agreement, with signatures from both parties, is drawn up to include:
  Names and all contact information from source and museum.
  Intention for the outcome: gift, purchase, bequest, loan.
  Responsibilities for insurance, packing, shipping.
  Description of the object
All attendant information regarding special considerations, restrictions, etc.
Registrar arranges shipping.
Registrar receives object.
Tracking number is assigned and informational receipt is issued.
Object begins its journey through museum activities.

Worst:
The director or curator calls to tell the registrar that s/he has:
  An object brought into the museum for perhaps a gift or perhaps a purchase on approval.
  An object that has been dropped off that may be used in an exhibition but may be a gift
  An object left by a trustee for storage.
The registrar receives a call from the front desk saying a visitor has left an object as a gift.
A non-collection officer agrees to have someone drop off an unsolicited gift.

information or an informational temporary receipt issued after an object has arrived. If no agreement is in place, the museum can initiate tracking and documentation but cannot assure intent unless that intent occurs in supplemental documentation.

NEXT STEPS:

The temporary custody form is in place, signed, and delivered. The object arrives at the museum with a shipping receipt, usually a simple receipt that notes shipment date and type and can be issued at the moment of receipt or delivery. This receipt may be the incoming or outgoing receipt in use, or it may be a slightly different form. It may say "three crates" or "ten dresses" without identifying objects in enough detail to identify each one. The names of the receipts, sometimes obvious, sometimes not, should be consistent within an institution; it is the use of receipts and the procedures that surround them that are most important.

Once the object(s) has arrived at the museum, the informational receipt, sometimes called a temporary receipt (TR), temporary deposit (TD), or simply an incoming receipt, should be issued. Issuing this receipt confirms the temporary custody agreement and/or the shipping receipt and its content guides the first phase of the registration process.

The receipt includes all contact information, object descriptions including measurements and, where possible, a small photo of the object. This receipt should confirm the date, conditions and terms under which a museum has received the object. If this receipt serves as an after-the-fact temporary custody or temporary deposit agreement, it is vital that it include intent as well as insurance, shipping, and packing information and it is best if it can be countersigned.

The registrar should process the object(s) as follows:

1. Assign a temporary number to the transaction and to each object within the transaction.

2. Unpack and condition report the object(s).

3. Tag the object(s) with the temporary number(s).

4. Create database and/or hardcopy files about each object:
   a. All known contact information, relationship of contact to objects
   b. Reason/intent for entry into the museum
   Gift on approval
   Purchase on approval
   Bequest
   Exhibition loan
   Long term loan
   *Any other reasons a particular museum may allow (photography conservation, etc.)
   c. Description of each object (essential/label information)

5. Take digital photograph of each object, transfer to database if possible.

6. Start tracking by noting the first location in storage of the object.

Three bits of information were included on the initial receipt in the first *Museum Registration Methods* description in the 1950s that are no longer included: value or price, location in museum, and record of condition. These three elements are important parts of the TR or TD file but should not be integral to the actual receipt. Value is best kept as privately as possible, thus should only be noted as necessary in the letter or computer file for the transaction. Complete condition reports should replace a brief record of condition whenever possible. Record of location should be kept within the system the museum uses to keep all locations: if a card system, a card for each TR or TD object should be added and locations updated on the card. If a computerized database is used, the tracking system in place should be utilized to update locations in the database as necessary. Tracking is vital and must be included in the process, but it should not be disclosed to anyone without a direct need to know.

The TD or TR receipt, if object information is entered in a database, can be produced through a report. If done as a word processing form, the completed form should be kept in a computer file designated for acquisitions. If truly manual, copies should

---

TEMPORARY NUMBERS are never written or painted directly on the incoming object. The object housing may be numbered, and tags may be attached to objects with temporary numbers on them.

Museums' names for their temporary systems are not standard; internal consistency is what is important. Don't ever be surprised by the twists and turns that numbering patterns have taken within an individual institution; do introduce or maintain consistency where possible.

TR for temporary receipt
    TR2009.1 or TR1.2009—followed by expansions for specific objects
TD for temporary deposit
    TD2009.1 or TD1.2009—followed by expansions for specific objects
L for loan
    L1.2009 or L2009.1—followed by expansions for specific objects
No designation, simply a reverse numbering system
    1.2009—followed by expansions for specific objects

See the chapter on numbering systems for a full explanation.

---

be made and filed with other acquisition material. The registrar who processed the information should sign the form.

The curator may keep a file on active gifts and purchases in the designated department, so s/he needs a hard copy of the receipt information. One copy is always sent to the source to confirm conditions of transfer and safe arrival. The registrar keeps a hard copy in an active acquisitions file, and it is good practice to keep a year binder with copies or a bound register for notation. This allows multiple staff members to assign temporary numbers without redundancy and allows one-stop end-of-year reconciliation. It is also useful to note those objects that have stayed and those that have been returned to their owners or gone on to other exhibitions to be certain that all object tasks have been completed. The entry in the bound register or on cover pages in a binder should include number assigned, curatorial sponsorship, status, reason for entry, and date of entry.

Once the TR or TD is in place and the initial registration has been carried out completely, the future tracking and documentation of the object(s) becomes simple. Status changes can be made,

updates in location and condition can be tracked, and, in the case of permanent collection additions, complete cataloging can take place. TR files in a database can be switched to permanent collection files, when appropriate.

This process is, without doubt, one of the best ways to avoid problems with objects left in the care of the museum. It is time-consuming at point of entry but saves untold time in future months and years. It allows museums to avoid serious problems with insurance claims, with unclear intent of donors and claims of vendors, and with problems in identifying objects and determining reasons why they are in the museum's custody. If instituted thoroughly, it will prompt the museum to develop policies that do not allow objects to enter informally and will encourage sound and professional practices. ●

MRM5 Museum
123 Any Street, Any Town, Any State 00000
tel. 000-000-0000, fax 000-000-0000

INCOMING AGREEMENT for TEMPORARY CUSTODY

For objects placed on deposit for less than six months

AGREEMENT

The undersigned ("Lender") hereby places the object(s) described herein in custody of the MRM5 Museum for the purposes, and subject to the terms and conditions, set forth.

PURPOSE: _____ Examination for possible acquisition
_____Examination for possible exhibition loan
_____Research
_____Other_____

PROJECT OR EVENT:

DATES OF CUSTODY PERIOD:

MRM5 MUSEUM REGISTRAR:

LENDER:

Address:

Telephone: FAX: E-mail:

Contact Person:

OBJECTS Object/Title/Description/Artist/Medium:

INSURANCE   Total value (estimated fair market value in US $):

MRM5 Museum will insure unless otherwise advised. Please see reverse for conditions.

SHIPPING METHOD: Incoming:
Return (if applicable):

Date required for receiving item(s):

Date required for return of item(s) (if applicable):

Special instructions for handling, packing, shipping or installation:

SIGNATURE   The Lender acknowledges that he/she has read the conditions above and on the back of this form and that he/she agrees to be bound by them.

Signature:

Date:
Lender or authorized agent

Signature:

Date:
For MRM5 Museum

Please complete, sign and return both copies to the MRM5 Museum Registrar. A countersigned copy will be returned to Lender.

Version 11/1/05

CONDITIONS GOVERNING INCOMING TEMPORARY CUSTODY

Care and Handling

1. MRM5 (the "Museum") will exercise the same care with respect to the object(s) on deposit as it does with comparable property of its own.

2. The Museum will not alter, clean or repair objects on deposit without transfer of the object to formal incoming loan status and written approval of lender.

Packing and Transportation

1. The Lender certifies that the objects are in good condition and will withstand ordinary strains of packing and transportation. Evidence of damage to objects on deposit at the time of receipt or while in the Museum's custody will be reported immediately to the Lender.

2. If applicable, objects will be returned packed in the same or similar materials as received unless authorized by the Lender.

3. Costs of transportation and packing will be borne by the Museum unless the loan is at the Lender's request, unless agreed otherwise in advance, or unless lender requests delivery to another location than the original pickup site.

4. International shipments may not be placed on Incoming Temporary Custody, but should be covered by formal incoming loan agreement. Customs regulations will be adhered to in international shipments in this case.

Insurance

1. Unless the Lender expressly elects to maintain his/her own insurance coverage, the Museum's general insurance policy will cover the objects against risks of physical loss or damage from time of release to Museum staff authorized to receive on premises, in the case of delivery by Lender or Lender's agent. If transport is arranged by the Museum, coverage will begin at time of objects' physical release to Museum staff or to professional contract art handling services designated to act as shippers/agents for museum.

2. Insurance will be placed in the amount specified by the Lender which must reflect fair market value. In case of damage or loss, the insurance company may ask the Lender to substantiate the insurance value. If the Lender fails to indicate an amount, the Museum will set a value for purposes of insurance only for the period of the loan. The Lender agrees that in the event of loss or damage, recovery shall be limited to such amount, if any, as may be paid by the insurer, hereby releasing the Museum and the Trustees, officers, agents and employees of the Museum from liability for any and all claims arising out of such loss or damage.

Reproduction and Credit

1. The Museum assumes the right, unless specifically denied by the Lender, to photograph the objects placed on deposit for documentation purposes only. Photography, videotaping, and reproduction for publicity, publication and educational purposes connected with an exhibition or research project must be covered by a formal loan agreement.

Ownership and Change in Ownership

1. The Lender hereby warrants that he/she has full legal title and copyrights to objects placed on temporary custody, or that he/she is the duly authorized agent of the Owner or Owners of them.

2. The Lender will notify the Museum promptly in writing of any change of ownership of the items in custody whether by reason of death, sale, insolvency, gift or otherwise. If ownership shall change during the period of custody, the Museum reserves the right to require the new owner, prior to the return of the work, to establish his or her right to possession by proof satisfactory to the Museum. The new owner shall succeed to Lender's rights and obligations under this agreement, including, but not limited to, the custody period and any insurance obligations.

Custody Period, Extension, Return

1. The objects in temporary custody may remain in the possession of the Museum for the time specified on the reverse, but may be returned to Lender at any time earlier by the Museum. If a time extension is requested by curatorial or administrative staff for long-term research or further examination prior to acquisition, the transaction will be transferred to a formal incoming loan agreement.

2. Unless the Lender requests otherwise in writing, the Museum will return the items only to the Lender and only at the address specified in this agreement. The Lender shall promptly notify the Museum in writing of any change of address. The Museum assumes no responsibility to search for a Lender who cannot be reached at the address specified in this agreement. The Lender will may be required to pay additional costs, if any, if the Lender requests the return of the work to another address.

3. The Museum's right to return the objects from custody shall accrue absolutely at the termination of the loan. If, after two weeks beyond termination of loan date noted above, pursuing all possible means of contact, and in accordance with any legal requirements, the Lender cannot be found or the Lender refuses to accept the return of the items on temporary custody, it shall be deemed abandoned property, and become the property of the Museum.

Interpretation

1. This agreement constitutes the entire agreement between the Lender and the Museum and may be amended or modified only in writing signed by both parties. Any changes herein of printed text or written additions must bear the initial of both parties. This agreement shall be governed and interpreted according to the laws of_____.

2. If the terms of this agreement conflict with the forms, agreements or correspondence of the Lender, the terms of this agreement will be controlling.

CLARISSE CARNELL AND REBECCA BUCK

INTRODUCTION

The acquisitions section of a collection management policy carefully defines the types of collections that a museum holds: art, history, archival, science, anthropology, archaeology, etc. It should mention all permanent collections and should acknowledge special collections, such as those for educational use or special loan. The policy should also stipulate the means by which decisions are made for accepting objects to the permanent collections, who is responsible for the decisions, and the legal and ethical framework that is followed by the museum. The acquisitions policy should be augmented by a set of procedures that allow objects destined for the permanent collection to be accessioned and objects for secondary collections, research, or sale to be accounted for.

All accessioned objects are acquired, but not all acquisitions are meant to be accessioned. An acquisition is made by a museum when title of an object is transferred and the museum becomes the owner. Accessioning is the two-part process of acquiring an object (acquisition) and documenting an object (registration) into the permanent collection. The two parts of the process hinge on transfer of title to the museum.

The word accession may be used to denote (1) an object acquired by a museum for its permanent collection or (2) the act of recording/processing an addition to the permanent collection. It is the act of recording an addition to the permanent collection by means of assigning a unique number that allows the museum to connect an object to its documentation. *(See chapter on Numbering Objects.)*

It is not necessary for a museum to accession every object that it acquires. However, the process of deciding what to accession must be very clear. If the object is a gift, the donor should be informed of the museum's intended purpose for the gift before it comes to the museum. How the museum intends to use the object affects the tax consequences of the gift for the donor. *(See chapter on Tax Issues.)* Objects acquired by the museum may go, as noted above, to the permanent collection, to an educational project or hands-on loan collection, or to the library or archives. They may be accepted for research (which may mean the eventual destruction of the object) or to be sold at a later date.

ACQUISITIONS

Acquisitions may be made by:
- Gift (title passes during the life of the donor)
- Bequest (title passes under a will)
- Purchase
    Direct, Auction, Bargain Sale, Exchange, Commission
- Field Collection
- Conversion (the unauthorized assumption of ownership of property belonging to another. *(See chapter on Old Loans.)*

GIFTS

Gifts may be
- Outright
- Fractional
- Promised

Gifts may be
- Unrestricted
- Made with some restrictions

Outright Gifts

Outright gifts are very straightforward. The donor offers the museum a gift by showing his/her intent. The museum accepts the gift. The gift is delivered to the museum. Intent, acceptance, are delivery are the three necessary legal actions that transfer title.

Intent may be oral, written informally, or

expressed in a deed of gift. Acceptance may be oral, but is usually written in a formal letter and often expressed in countersignature on a deed of gift. Delivery is vital; the museum must take possession of the object for the transaction to be complete.

Fractional Gifts

Fractional gifts are generally made for tax reasons, because a taxpayer's deduction in any one year is limited. *(See chapter on Tax Issues.)* Upon advice from his or her tax advisor, the donor offers the museum a percentage interest in an object amounting to the allowable deduction. If the museum accepts the offer, a deed of gift detailing the arrangement is produced by the museum in consultation with its legal counsel or by the donor's lawyer. The deed may convey one portion only, or it may transfer title automatically to further portions of the work through several years. *(See chapter on Creating Documentation.)* Fractional gift law has been changing rapidly in the United States since the Pension Act of 2006. It is important that the registrar and curators remain aware of changes in the laws affecting fractional gifts. The American Association of Museums and the Association of Art Museum Directors can be contacted for updated information; the Internal Revenue Service web site (www.irs.gov) can also be searched.

A fractional gift should go through the same acquisition process as an outright gift. As a rule, a fractional gift must be in the museum's possession for a part of each year equal to the percentage owned by the museum. A fractional promised gift in the custody of the museum is treated as an accessioned object, as long as the pledge of the donor to the museum is binding.

Promised Gifts

Promised gifts may be made by a donor in the form of a letter expressing the donor's intent to give a specific object to the museum at some future time. Although many museums have a draft format for promised gifts to act as a guide for donors, it is preferable to have the donor initiate the promised gift letter on the donor's letterhead before signing a binding pledge agreement.

The museum may wish to encourage the donor to include the gift to the museum in his or her will

ALLOCATION was a term often used by the Works Progress Administration of the Federal Government to indicate transfer of title for works created during that project. The Operating Procedures in the Public Works of Art Program Bulletin, March 26, 1934, indicates in Section 32, Part A, 1st paragraph: "For the purposes of this section 'allocated' shall mean transfer of title." However, a later part of the procedure notes a restriction regarding release from the responsibility of custody. The General Services Administration (GSA), in 2000, interpreted the manual to mean that allocated works included transfers of restricted title, and that the "receiving agency or institution received legal title to the works of art limited by the purpose stated in the allocation forms and by the regulations." Works of art produced by the Works Progress Administration programs are often allocated but may also be lent to an institution.

Allocations are most often, in museums, indications of use of funds. If a museum does hold federal project works that it received from the federal government, however, it is important to become familiar with GSA terms and uses. All WPA objects should be carefully checked for transfer of title, and communication with the GSA, which currently oversees WPA works, should be initiated if there is any question of status.

to ensure that the donor's promise is carried our if the donor is unable to make the gift during his or her lifetime.

A promised gift be in the custody of the museum should be treated as a loan. *(See chapter on Incoming Loans)*. A promise does not confer transfer of title. Museums may make very specific rules about public announcements of promised gifts, as such announcements convey some benefit to the donor and put the museum at some risk if the gift is not fulfilled.

Unrestricted Gifts and Gifts with Restrictions

An outright and unrestricted gift is always preferred, although there will be some circumstances in which the object is so important an addition to a collection that some restrictions are acceptable. Depending on the donor and the nature of the restrictions requested, it is often possible for appropriate museum personnel to discuss the potential restrictions with the donor, discover the reasoning behind the restrictions, and negotiate a more acceptable gift agreement.

Requests to exhibit permanently or to keep a collection together are the most common restrictions requested by donors. Neither is practical, and this type of request should be discouraged. A reasonable restriction might be one to keep an important album of photographs together in its original binding rather than unbind and mat each one separately; the museum must weigh its current desire to have the album with the possibility that future generations will be hampered by the restriction. All restrictions must be carefully considered and, if accepted, carefully documented in the object records.

BEQUESTS

A bequest is a gift from a deceased person that passes to the museum under the terms of that person's will. It is important to have on record, as evidence of the transfer of title, a copy of the provision of the will that concerns the gift to the museum. If objects come to the museum not under the terms of a will but as gifts by heirs of objects included in the estate, that is, if title passes first to the heirs and they, in turn, make a gift to the museum, the appropriate evidence of transfer is a deed of gift and the appropriate credit line, rather than "Bequest of" is generally "Gift of the estate of."

A museum may or may not know of a bequest in advance. Museums are usually notified of an active bequest by the executor (legal representative) of the estate or the law firm representing the executor. It is important to deal with the official representative of an estate. The museum should ask for a copy of the will that concerns the bequest to the museum. The museum should then decide whether it wishes to accept the bequest, accept only part of the bequest, or refuse the bequest. It should communicate its wishes to the legal representative of the estate. It is not mandatory that the museum accept bequests. If a museum does accept and receive the object(s), it will usually be asked to sign a receipt and release—a receipt for the objects and a release for the estate that indicates nothing more is expected from the estate. The museum should be aware of the fact that the transfer to the museum is not final until the probate of the estate is finally approved by the court. The receipt and release agreements, however, are not usually made until an executor is certain that the estate can pay its bills and give legatees their designated bequests.

PURCHASES

Purchases for museum collections can be made in a variety of ways: at auction, from or through dealers, or directly from individuals. Objects can be commissioned, and they may also be exchanged through orchestrated deaccession of objects of like value.

Purchase from a Dealer or Gallery

If an object is purchased from a dealer or gallery, it is important that the museum have a bill of sale and proof of payment in addition to any internal curatorial documentation required, and such documentation should be part of the acquisition file. Curators should always research provenance and should add all provenance information to the file. They are also responsible for working out discounts with vendors and they are in good position to initiate discussions regarding copyright releases for contemporary works.

As issues of provenance and legal export and import become more important, most museums require at least a warranty of title and indemnification for purchase of an important object. If the object purchased is of sensitive nature or of very high value, it may have a contract of sale to clarify all points of purchase. As Ildiko deAngelis states in the chapter on Ethics of Collecting, it is best to go beyond warranties and to confirm legality by review of customs papers and searches of provenance indices and art loss registers.

Bargain Sale

A hybrid form of purchase is a "bargain sale." In this instance the vendor offers an object to a museum at substantially lower than fair market value with the intention of benefitting the museum by virtue of the reduced price. The vendor, therefore, is also a donor. Properly done, there may be tax benefits for the vendor/donor. The method of transfer of title is a bill of sale, but the museum acknowledges in correspondence to the vendor/donor the fact that the price of the object has been reduced to favor the museum. It is up to the donor to establish his/her tax benefits with the IRS. The museum, for its part, wants to be secure in its opinion that the sale price is substantially reduced. An independent appraisal is advisable to document the discount. The bill of sale and all related correspondence should be part of the acquisition file.

Exchange

Exchanges are in fact a form of purchase. In this case the payment is in kind, not in currency. The museum trades objects of equal value to the objects it receives from another museum. This must involve deaccession of the objects it trades, and deaccession requires full documentation as well. The terms of an exchange should be set forth in writing and a museum, for its records, should establish the fairness of the exchange by means of appraisals and other expert opinions. The written agreement concerning the exchange and all relevant documents concerning the justifications for the exchange and the execution of the exchange should be part of the acquisition file. This is a rare form of purchase and is done primarily between museums. *(See chapters on Appraisals and File Management.)*

FIELD COLLECTIONS

Field collections are made more frequently by science, anthropology, history, and archaeology museums than by art museums. They may be a series of purchases acquired during an expedition, or they may be collections of scientific or archaeological specimens that are collected in a field research project or archaeological excavation. Purchases are

generally made from persons who made or used the objects, and the recording of provenience, materials, techniques and use are vital to the purchase record. Archaeological material should also be accompanied by complete field notes.

Field collections are increasingly subjected to legal restrictions, particularly regulations on export from the country of origin and laws dealing with repatriation to Native American or Native Hawaiian groups and endangered species. *(See chapter on NAGPRA.)* The museum must be aware of all potential restrictions and obtain applicable permits and customs releases before bringing material from the field to the museum. The registrar should, with help of legal counsel, research the legal title to the collections returned to the museum before they go through the acquisitions process and are accessioned into the permanent collection.

CONVERSION

Most museums have objects on loan that remain unclaimed by the owners. Several states have adopted legislation to enable a museum to acquire title to these objects if the owners cannot be located and if specified procedures are followed and waiting periods met. *(See chapter on Old Loans.)* Conversion may also be necessary for Found-in-Collection objects; if the museum's state has a statue regarding FIC objects, it is important for that museum to follow state guidelines.

THE ACQUISITION PROCESS FOR PERMANENT COLLECTION OBJECTS

A cogent collecting policy that takes into account current collection strengths and weaknesses must be in place for each collecting area if the museum is to acquire collection objects intelligently. A typical museum policy sets forth the practical and legal considerations that precede an acquisition.

Practical considerations:
- Is the object consistent with the collection goals of the museum and the specific goals of the curatorial department?

•Will the object be useful for exhibition and educational purposes and for research and scholarship?

•Is the object in a reasonably good state of preservation?

•Can the museum properly exhibit and/or store the object?

•Is the price asked for purchased objects reasonable?

•Will the acquisition of the object result in major expenses for the museum for conservation or maintenance or because it opens a new area of collecting?

•Can the acquisition of the object be construed as a commercial endorsement?

Legal and ethical considerations:

•Can valid title to the object be passed to the museum? Is the possessor of the object the sole owner or the legal agent of the owner?

•Is the object authentic?

•Can all rights in the object be conveyed to the museum?

•Does the acquisition of the object violate applicable state, national, or international laws or conventions that protect the rights of artists or the rights of countries to their cultural history or that preserve endangered species?

•Is the object subject to repatriation to a Native American or Native Hawaiian group?

•Is the object free of donor restrictions or qualifications that inhibit prudent use of the object by the museum?

Acquiring objects for the permanent collection is a complicated process for most museums. It must be thoughtful and undertaken with care. It usually begins with curators who seek gifts by cultivating donor relationships and seek objects for purchase by becoming familiar with the market and galleries in their area of specialization. Gift offers and purchase opportunities also come unsolicited to most museums. In science, anthropology, history, and archaeology museums, field collecting has been important

in the past and is still a possibility in some collecting areas.

Between the time an object becomes available to the museum and the time it is actually acquired, a number of things take place (the order differs among museums):

•Director and curator agree on importance of object's acquisition.

•The object is transported to the museum.

•Curatorial research on provenance and cost is conducted.

•Curatorial proposal for acquisitions and/or worksheet is completed.

•Consultation between curator, director, outside specialists, or board members takes place.

•Conservators are consulted regarding costs for preservation and conservation.

•Registrars/collections managers are consulted regarding storage needs and costs.

•Legal concerns (permits for endangered species, copyright licenses, title issues) are reviewed.

•If the object is a gift, intent to give is established, usually by the issue of a deed of gift, which is sent to the donor for signature.

•If the object is a purchase, warranty of title and indemnification agreement is executed.

•The object is placed on the agenda for the acquisitions committee.

The curator usually consults with the director after an initial gift offer is received or a purchase opportunity arises. Museums have many variations of the acquisition process that follows after the director and curator decide to pursue an acquisition, but the registrar is always central to that process.

The registrar is generally charged with coordinating objects and their documentation, bringing objects to the museum, and making recommendations, in conjunction with a conservator when possible, about the feasibility of caring for and properly storing new objects. It is also the responsibility of the registrar to make certain that title to the object is transferred and needed licenses and permits are acquired.

If the object offered for gift or purchase is not already in the museum's custody for loan or examination, the registrar must arrange to bring it to the museum. The curator writes a proposal for acquisition, which should explain in detail the reasons the object is desirable for the collection. The registrar begins an acquisition file and makes certain that a temporary number is assigned to the object and that proper receipts have been issued, condition reports completed, and the location of the object noted. It is also wise to have a digital photograph made at this point. *(See chapters on File Management, Numbering and Condition Reporting.)*

The deed of gift, a document that is drawn up with help of legal counsel, is generated by the registrar. It can serve as evidence of both an intent to donate and an acceptance by the proper museum authority.

Three elements are normally needed to complete a gift.

- •Intent to donate, preferably in writing. A Deed of Gift is the preferred instrument to demonstrate this intent.
- •Proof of physical receipt of the object by the museum.
- •Written acceptance of the gift by the proper museum authority.

At least two original copies of the Deed of Gift are sent to the donor with a letter requesting that the donor sign and return both copies to the museum. The signed copies are held until the acquisitions committee meets and approves the gift. After the committee meets, the designated officer for the museum, usually the director, countersigns the Deed of Gift and sends one copy to the donor with a letter of appreciation. The other signed copy goes to the registrar for inclusion in the acquisition file. In some museums, three originals are made and the third is sent off-site for security purposes. *(See chapter on Creating Documentation.)*

Many museums do not include copyright releases in the Deed of Gift. Often the donor is not the holder of copyright. If copyright in the object is an issue and it is not covered in a Deed of Gift, a separate non-exclusive use agreement should be sent to the copyright holder. The donor of an object, unless that donor is the artist, is usually unaware of whether he or she holds copyright to a work. *(See chapter on Copyright.)*

Depending on the acquisition policy of the museum, gifts, purchases, bequests, or exchanges proposed for accession will be reviewed and/or approved by a collections or acquisitions committee. That committee may meet monthly, quarterly, semiannually, or as needed and may consist of board members, staff members, collectors, specialists in the field, friends of the museum, and, in a university museum, faculty members. This committee may have the authority to approve or reject acquisitions, or the authority to recommend objects to the board of trustees for final approval. In any case, acquisitions are formally recorded in the minutes of the board meeting.

The agenda for the acquisitions committee is usually prepared by the registrar. It should be a clear listing of all objects to be considered for acquisition. The listing should include complete descriptions of the objects, donor and vendor names and addresses, credit lines for gifts where possible, and, as appropriate, the price and funds to be used for purchases. The recording secretary for these meetings may be the registrar, deputy director, chief curator, or other member of the staff appointed by the director. Regardless of recorder, the registrar should be officially notified as soon as possible after the meeting of works accepted or rejected for acquisition. Rejected objects should be returned to the donor or vendor. Accepted gifts should be acknowledged with a letter of appreciation from the director (and in some cases the curators) and a countersigned deed of gift or other official form that describes the gift(s).

ACCESSIONING

Once the object(s) has been approved for acquisition into the permanent collection and the deed of gift signed or the sale completed, title passes to the museum and the registrar completes the process of accessioning. The second part of accessioning is the act of recording or processing an addition to the permanent collection. An accession number is assigned, and the file that has been made to track the potential acquisition becomes the accession file. *(See chapters on Numbering and Creating Documentation.)* The file is checked for supporting documentation and completion of accessioning begins. The process includes:

• Gathering all gift or purchase documents and noting the accession number(s) on each.

• Creating a curatorial worksheet. If one has not been done, the registrar completes the basic worksheet and sends it to the curator for approval and additions, if any.

• Numbering the object. *(See chapter on Marking.)*

• Photographing the object in high resolution.

• Entering information into the manual system. This may include:

  • Source card (vendor or donor)

  • Fund card (for purchase)

  • Cross-reference cards, as used by the museum

  • Biography card or artist card, as used by the museum

  • Location card (or new card changed from the temporary to the permanent number)

  • Accession or catalog card, as used by the museum.

• Entering information into the computerized system and printing out the cards outlined above. Some museums decide to keep none, all, or some manual files, generated by computer.

• Creating accession and/or object and/or source vertical files as necessary.

The accession number associates the object with its file and all its documentation. It is vital to have unique accession numbers that will take the staff member, curator, or researcher directly to the documentation. *(See chapter on Object Numbering.)* An accession folder may be produced and stored by consecutive number; if a volume of documentation exists for a single object within the accession, an object file may be broken out from the accession file to hold that information. Some museums have files for every object; others have accession files; still others keep both accession and source files so that all information about an accession can be retrieved or all transactions with a single donor or vendor can be traced. *(See chapter on File Management.)*

After the accessioning is complete, the registrar must review the file for compliance with the Collection Management policy. The accession file becomes the repository of all information that comes to the museum regarding the group of objects in it, and object files fill with research, photography, condition reports, loans, conservation work, and publications.

Policies and procedures should be developed to govern access to permanent collection records. Confidential information such as shipping and insurance histories, appraisals, tax documents, purchase orders, donor addresses, and telephone numbers may be available only to certain members of the professional staff. Condition notes, conservation treatment reports, and some provenance information may also have limited access. The general public should have access (usually in the form of the accession card) to descriptive information about the object, the accession number, credit line, reference notations, and the exhibition and publication histories of an object. In developing policy about access to records, legal advice should be sought concerning the existence of any applicable freedom of information or privacy laws. •

Thanks to Jeanne M. Benas, Jan W. M. Thompson, and Ted Greenberg. Many thanks to Marie Malaro.

•Accession, Accessioned, Accessioning

Accessioning is the two-part process of acquiring (acquisition) and documenting (registration) an object. The two parts of the process hinge on transfer of title to the museum.

The word most often tossed about without thought of its clear definition is accession; that word and its variations are at the core of collection status. Accession is a noun, a verb, and an adjective. The word is not an alternate of acquisition but is used in conjunction with that word to describe some of the processes and committees museums use when adding objects to their permanent collections.

First, there are published sources that define the terms[1]:

Museum Registration Methods, 3rd Edition, Dorothy Dudley and Irma Wilkinson, American Association of Museums, 1979:

> Accession: (1) an object acquired by a museum as part of its permanent collection; (2) the act of recording/processing an addition to the permanent collection.

Introduction to Museum Work, 3rd Edition, G. Ellis Burcaw, Altamira Press, 1997:

> Accession: One or more objects acquired at one time from one source constituting a single transaction between the museum and the source, or the transaction itself.

Burcaw goes on to clarify accession by adding a definition for registration: "Assigning a permanent number for identification purposes to an accession and recording this number according to a system." Thus he identifies accessioning, though obliquely, as a process.

Marie Malaro, in *A Legal Primer on Managing Museum Collections,* devotes four pages to the meaning of the word "accession." She notes that accessioning is "the formal process used to accept and record an item as a collection object." Everyone dealing with collection status problems should review Malaro's seminal work, *A Legal Primer on Managing Museum Collections,* whenever title questions are addressed.

The important point is that the word "accessioning" currently includes the process of acquiring, that is, the acquisition of the object as well as its recording. The 1979 edition of *Museum Registration Methods* notes the process only in conjunction with recording, and Burcaw's work does not clarify the process.

Dorothy Dudley was a product of the Apprenticeship Program at The Newark Museum, Class of 1925-26, and the meaning of accessioning at Newark was very clear at the time. Margaret White, registrar there from 1925 through 1940, wrote for *The Museum*, journal of The Newark Museum, an article called "How a Museum Accessions Objects" in 1925. It indicates that the process started when an object already slated for the permanent collection arrived at the museum.

John Cotton Dana found a bottle in a Vermont shop in September 1925 that he wanted for the museum's permanent collection. White says:

> "One morning, soon after, the Museum received the bill and later a box marked "Fragile–Glass." The bottle was unpacked and sent to the Museum registrar. She connected it with the bill, checked the bill and pasted a bit of adhesive tape on the base of the bottle. On the tape she wrote the source, price and date.
> "Already the gentle art of accessioning . . . has begun."

Dana was a friend of Henry Watson Kent, who developed early "business methods" for the Metropolitan Museum of Art. Dana was certainly aware of Kent's methods. Kent discussed his procedures for acquiring and recording collection objects at the 6th Annual American Association of Museums meeting in Boston in 1911. The process of accessioning is clearly the recording part of the process:

> "At the time of the receipt of the object, the registrar sends to the secretary a card, called from its color

"the blue card," upon which he notes as much information concerning the thing itself as has come under his observation. The return of this card, filled in with additional data furnished by the curator, serves as his notification of the trustees' action. The registrar then accessions the object in a volume which follows in its general arrangement the accession book perfected by libraries."

The current process for accessioning most often includes choice of object, research by curators on origin and provenance, a review of practical considerations, a run through the personnel and/or committees that a museum has deemed necessary, the legal title transfers and warranties, the delivery of an object to the museum, assigning and numbering the object(s), producing a base catalog card and/or computer record, placing the object physically in storage or on exhibition, and recording the assigned location. If we use the verb accession to include the entire process of bringing an object into a collection, we are better served when we discuss accessioning in relation to partially accessioned, found-in-collection (FIC), or supplementary collections.

The noun accession is best used to describe the transaction, while the objects involved in the transaction are best represented by the adjective, i.e. accessioned objects. If, as Dudley/Wilkinson used the word, accession denotes an object rather than the transaction, the clearest and simplest way to track legal status becomes more complicated. If each object is separate, grouping objects with a single source that came in at one time is difficult. The first *Museum Registration Methods* follows through with the "accession as object" definition by assigning either two-part accession numbers or, possibly, three-part numbers if the museum receives groups of objects at one time.

The definitions we use for accession, then, follow:

•Accession, verb: to acquire or accept and register or record an object for the permanent collection of a museum. Acquisition and registration are generally linked by transfer of title.

•Accession, noun: as in Burcaw, one or more objects acquired at one time from one source constituting a single transaction between the museum and the source, or the transaction itself.

•Accessioned or accession, adjective: describes an object that has been accessioned or something related to the process of accessioning. EXAMPLES:

> Accession file
>
> Accession number
>
> Accession card
>
> Accessioned object

NOTE

1. *The New Museum Registration Methods*, Buck/Gilmore, 1998, presents both the Dudley/Wilkinson and Burcaw definitions in its glossary.

DEALER PROVENANCE QUESTIONNAIRE

OBJECT: Artist _____

           Title/Date _____

           Medium/Dimensions _____

PROVENANCE: _____

At what date did you acquire the object? _____

Please provide the name of the source from which the artwork was acquired, or, if acquired at auction, the name and location of the auction house and date of sale:

_____

_____

Please list all known former owners and dates of ownership, if known:

_____

_____

_____

For antiquities and archaeological materials:

When did the object leave its country of modern discovery? _____

Do you have export documents from the source country? _____ (Please attach copies)

Do you have import documents? _____ (Please attach copies)

EXHIBITION HISTORY: _____

_____

_____

_____

PUBLICATION HISTORY: _____

_____

_____

_____

DOCUMENTS (attach copies):

[   ] Art Loss Register Report, if any _____

[   ] Import/Export Documents _____

Signature: _____

(Vendor)

Date: _____

DONOR QUESTIONNAIRE

[For works of art that could have been in Nazi-era Europe (1933–1945) and antiquities and archaeological materials]

Please complete the following questionnaire to the best of your ability. For many reasons it is important that the Museum have a complete history of the ownership of works of art offered as gifts. To that end, it would also be helpful if you will forward any additional information or documentation which you may have with respect to your ownership, the exhibition or publication history of the object, and any known prior ownership information.

Donor(s) name(s): _____

Object (or group of objects, if acquired at the same time and from the same source):

_____

How long have you owned this object? _____

How did you acquire it?

Purchase	date
Inheritance	date
Gift	date
Found	date
Other	date

If this object was purchased, do you have a bill of sale, certificate, or any items relating to the transaction or authenticity?_____ If yes, please attach a copy to this questionnaire.

Were there any previous owners? _____

Please list all known previous owners and their relationship to the donor(s): _____

_____

Do you have any published information or press clippings about the object? _____

If yes, please attach a copy to this questionnaire.

Do you know the exhibition history of the object? _____ If yes, please list: _____

_____

Have you performed any repairs, made changes to the object or contracted a conservator to perform cleaning or repairs while this object was in your care? If yes, please list names, dates, cleanings, changes, etc., and attach copies of any pertinent paperwork and photographs.

Do you know if this work was conserved/restored prior to your ownership? If yes, please list all known treatments, dates, and conservators used.

_____

Donor(s) Signature(s) _____   Date _____

WARRANTY AND INDEMNIFICATION

This Warranty and Indemnification (the "Warranty") is made and delivered to _____ (the "Museum") as of the _____ day of _____ 20__ from the undersigned (the "Seller/Agent"), who is (a) the seller of, or (b), the authorized agent of the owner of, the work (the "Work") described below and in the attached Bill of Sale dated _____ and the Invoice previously provided to the Museum:

The Seller/Agent represents, warrants, covenants, certifies, and agrees that:

a. Seller/Agent has lawful authority to sell and transfer the Work and upon the consummation of the sale, the Museum will have good and marketable title to the Work, including, without limitation, any proprietary or copyright rights in the Work, free and clear of all liens, mortgages, pledges, security interests, encumbrances, claims, charges or liabilities whatsoever.

If Seller/Agent is not the owner, Seller/agent is fully authorized by the owner of the Work to, and, on behalf of the owner does, enter into this Warranty and the Bill of Sale and accepts all terms and makes all representations, warranties, covenants, certifications, and agreements set forth herein.

b. The Work is authentic, conforms in all respects to the description set forth above and in the said Invoice (collectively, the "Documentation") and is of the period indicated.

c. Any exportation of the Work from any foreign country has been in full compliance with the laws, rules, and regulations of such country.

d. The country of origin of the Work as set forth in the customs declaration for the importation of the Work into the United States is true, accurate, and complete.

e. The country of modern discovery is

_____

f. Any importation of the Work into any foreign country has been in full compliance with the laws, rules, and regulations of such country.

g. Any importation of the Work into the United States of America ("USA") has been in full compliance with the laws, rules, and regulations of the USA.

h. No customs, tax, patrimony or other laws, rules or regulations applicable to the Work, its sale, export or import have been violated.

i. Seller/Agent has provided to the Museum all information known to Seller/Agent (including after due inquiry information known to the principals and agents of Seller/Agent) regarding the Work and the provenance of the Work, and all information and documentation provided by Seller/Agent to the Museum with respect to the Work is true, accurate, and complete in all material respects.

j. No license or other right has been granted to any person by Seller/Agent or, to Seller/Agent's knowledge after due inquiry, by any other person that would in any manner limit or restrict the Museum's rights in and to the Work, including, but not limited to, any rights derived from ownership of the copyright included in the Work or in any derivative of the Work.

Seller/Agent agrees to indemnify, defend, and hold harmless the Museum and its trustees, directors, officers, employees, and agents from and against any and all claims, allegations (pending or threatened), costs, and fees, including without limitation attorneys' fees and costs, losses, damages, judgments or liabilities arising from, connected to or as a result of any breach or alleged breach of this Warranty or a good faith challenge of the Museum's title to all or any part of the Work or the Museum's right to the free use and enjoyment of Work.

In addition to, and not in limitation of, the foregoing, in the event of any breach of this Warranty and, in connection therewith, the Museum loses or otherwise fails to have or retain the lawful right to own, possess, display, sell, enjoy, mortgage, pledge, grant a security interest in or encumber the Work, the Museum shall be entitled, at its election and without regard to any otherwise applicable statue of limitation or repose, to receive a full refund of the purchase price of the Work. The foregoing shall be in addition to, and not in limitation of, any other remedies to which the Museum may be entitled and shall not be construed to limit the Museum's right to elect any of such other remedies.

This Warranty and the Documentation taken together constitute the entire agreement between the parties. In the event of any conflict between the Warranty and the Documentation, the Warranty shall control. The Warranty and the Documentation and the transactions contemplated hereby shall be construed in accordance with the laws of Any State and the Warranty shall be binding upon and inure to the benefit of the Seller/Agent and the Museum and their respective successors, assigns, heirs, executors, administrators and legal representatives.

Agreed to by:

_____
Seller/Agent
_____
Name
_____
Address
_____
Telephone
_____
Date:

Courtesy of the Art Institute of Chicago, Association of Art Museum Directors, Cleveland Museum of Art, Getty Museum, and the Metropolitan Museum of Art. With thanks to Rebecca Noonan Murray.

MRM5 Museum
CONFIRMATION OF GIFT

MRM5 Museum
123 Any Street
Any Town, USA 00000

Gentlemen:

I hereby confirm my agreement to give to the MRM5 Museum ("Museum"), at or before my death, the work or works of art listed below or on the attachment hereto:

You have informed me that other collectors, Trustees and friends of the Museum have indicated their intention of giving to the Museum works of art which they own in order to enhance the Museum's collection. As I believe that definite commitments to make such gifts or bequests will be of great value to the Museum, I have agreed to give the above described work of art to the Museum on the understanding (I) that you will do your best to obtain similar commitments from others and may refer to this agreement in inducing others to make such commitments; (ii) that this agreement shall be governed by the laws of Any State.

I may, according to my own convenience, give this work of art to you during my lifetime. Should this gift not be completed during my lifetime, it is understood that this agreement shall be binding on my heirs, executors, and administrators, and that omission from my Will of a specific bequest of this work of art to the Museum shall not release them from delivering the aforementioned work of art to the Museum in accordance herewith, or otherwise impair the force and effect of this agreement.

Neither the Museum nor I shall be under any obligation to insure this work of art during my lifetime. In the event I do not own this work of art at my death because of loss by casualty, the Museum shall have no claim against my heirs, executors or administrators with respect to this undertaking on my part.

I have entered into this agreement on the date indicated below with the full intention that I will be legally bound hereby pursuant to the applicable provisions of the law relating to written obligations and that this agreement shall be binding as well on my heirs, executors, administrators and assigns.

Very truly yours,   Notarized

(signed)   (signed)

(dated)   (dated)

                                           (seal)

We confirm that the above correctly states the agreement between us.

For the MRM5 Museum

(signed)   (dated)

MRM5 MUSEUM
123 Any Street, Any Town, USA 00000
Telephone 000-000-0000 FAX 000-000-0001

DEED OF GIFT

Date   Page   of

Donor:
Name
Address
Telephone

Description of object(s)

Donor hereby transfers and assigns without condition or restriction all right, title and interest free of restrictions or encumbrances in the tangible personal property listed above (the "Object"), and all rights (including trade marks and copyrights) associated with it (the "Rights") to the MRM5 Museum Association, a corporation existing under the laws of the State of AnyState for use and disposition by the MRM5 Museum.

Donor warrants and represents that Donor has the full power and authority to transfer the Object to the MRM5 Museum Association.

Donor certifies that to the best of the Donor's knowledge, the Object has not been exported from its country of origin in violation of the Laws of that country in effect at the time of the export, nor imported into the United States in violation of United States laws and treaties.

Donor   Date

Donor   Date

Accepted for the MRM5 Museum

by   Date

          Director
                    (See reverse for additional terms)

[On back of form] This deed of gift represents an agreement between the MRM5 Museum and the donor(s) named on the face hereof. Any variation in the terms noted must be in writing on the face of this form and approved in writing by both parties.

Gifts to the MRM5 Museum are deductible from taxable income in accordance with the provisions of Federal income tax law. However, Museum employees cannot, in their official capacity, give appraisals for the purpose of establishing the tax deductible value of donated items. Evaluations must be secured by the donor at his/her/their expense.

The donor received no goods or services in consideration of this gift.

Limited gallery space and the policy of changing exhibitions do not allow the Museum to promise the permanent exhibition of any object.

3c | REPOSITORIES

KARA J. HURST

Museums, particularly those with archaeological and natural science collections, often serve as repositories for collections that are federally or state-owned, or owned by another institution. The repository takes on the care and management of a collection and, in most cases, catalogs, cares for, and manages the collections as it does its own collections. (revised from Simmons chapter)

The Antiquities Act of 1906 (16 U.S.C. 431-433) was the first United States federal law to provide general protection for cultural and natural resources. It gave the President authority to declare "historic landmarks, historic and prehistoric structures, and other objects of historic or scientific interest...to be national monuments." Permitting of archaeological undertakings by scientific or educational institutions was implemented with the caveat that all artifacts and data were to be permanently preserved in a public museum. The accompanying Code of Federal Regulations (CFR) for the Antiquities Act, 43 CFR 3, asserted federal jurisdiction over "ruins, archeological sites, historic and prehistoric monuments and structures, objects of antiquity, historic landmarks, and other objects of historic and scientific interest," while 43 CFR 3.17 discusses preservation of collections and the requirement of collections to be held in public museums and be accessible to the public.

Twenty-nine years later the Historic Sites Act was passed to "provide for the preservation of historic American sites, buildings, objects, and antiquities of national significance, and for other purposes." An additional 25 years later the initial Reservoir Salvage Act was passed, with amendments over the next 14 years that resulted in the Archeological and Historic Preservation Act (AHPA) of 1974 (16 U.S.C. 469). AHPA built on the Historic Sites Act of 1935 to protect historic and archeological data that may be lost to such activities as flooding, road and dam construction or an "alternation of terrain due to Federal or licensed construction, activity or program." During this period, the National Historic Preservation Act (NHPA) of 1966 (16 U.S.C. 470) was enacted to provide a basis for federal protection of cultural resources and generally encourage preservation of culturally significant resources through public and private efforts. NHPA's mandatory federal review is triggered by listing on, or eligibility for, the National Register, a current listing of districts, sites, buildings, structures and objects deemed significant in American history, architecture, archaeology and culture. With regard to archaeological collections, Sec. 106 of NHPA helped spawn the Cultural Resource Management industry and is the driving force behind most federal collections placed in museums and/or repositories.

In 1974 a significant court ruling was appealed by defendant Ben Diaz. In U.S. v. Diaz (499 F.2d 113), the defendant was charged with violating the Antiquities Act but won on appeal, with the circuit judge ruling the "use of undefined terms of uncommon usage, is fatally vague in violation of the due process clause of the Constitution." Clearly a better law protecting cultural resources was necessary. Five years later, the Archaeological Resources Protection Act (ARPA) of 1979 (16 U.S.C. 470) became law. ARPA provided more detailed descriptions of prohibited acts, provided larger financial and incarceration penalties for convicted violators and, with the 1988 amendments, increased archaeological resource management oversight. The Federal government reasserted ownership of archaeological resources from public lands, stating that "archaeological records and data will be preserved by a suitable university, museum, or other scientific or educational institution." The accompanying regulations (43 CFR 7) provide details on implementing ARPA. At this time, federal cultural resource laws and regulations remain unfunded, with the burden of caring for

LAWS AND REGULATIONS CITED

1906   Antiquities Act of 1906; 16 U.S.C. 431-433
http://www.nps.gov/history/local-law/FHPL_AntiAct.pdf

1935   Historic Sites Act of 1935
http://www.nps.gov/history/local-law/FHPL_HistSites.pdf

1954   43 CFR 3: Preservation of American Antiquities
http://archnet.asu.edu/Topical/CRM/usdocs/43cfr3.html

1960   Archeological and Historic Preservation Act, as amended; 16 U.S.C. 469
http://www.nps.gov/history/local-law/FHPL_ArchHistPres.pdf

1966   National Historic Preservation Act of 1966; 16 U.S.C. 470
http://www.nps.gov/history/local-law/FHPL_HistPrsrvt.pdf

1974   U.S. v. Ben Diaz (499 F.2d 113). U.S. Court of Appeals for the Ninth Circuit.

1979   Archaeological Resources Protection Act of 1979; 16 U.S.C. 470
http://www.nps.gov/history/local-law/FHPL_ArchRsrcsProt.pdf

1984   43 CFR 7: Protection of Archaeological Resources
http://www.nps.gov/history/local-law/43cfr7.htm

1990   36 CFR 79: Curation of Federally-Owned and Administered Archaeological Collections,
U. S. Dept. of the Interior
http://www.nps.gov/history/archeology/tools/36cfr79.htm

1990   Native American Graves Protection and Repatriation Act, as amended; 25 U.S.C. 3001
http://www.nps.gov/history/nagpra/MANDATES/25USC3001etseq.htm

1995   43 CFR 10: Native American Graves Protection and Repatriation Regulations
http://www.nps.gov/history/nagpra/MANDATES/43CFR10_12-4-95.htm

1997   Department Manual 411, U.S. Dept. of the Interior
http://www.doi.gov/museum/policy.htm

2009   Paleontological Resources Preservation Act; P.L. 111-011, Sec. 6301
http://frwebgate.access.gpo.gov/cgi-bin/getdoc.cgi?dbname=111_cong_public_
laws&docid=f:publ011.111.pdf

collections left to the often-meager resources available to the public museums accepting collections from federal lands.

In 1990, the Native American Graves Protection and Repatriation Act (NAGPRA) (25 U.S.C. 3001) was enacted, requiring that federal agencies and museums receiving federal funds inventory their Native American human remains and funerary objects and provide written summaries of other cultural objects. Regulations on how NAGPRA would be implemented were provided by 43 CFR 10. Although positive in spirit, NAGPRA was yet one more unfunded federal regulation for museums, although some funds are made available through granting programs for museums and tribes. However, 1990 also saw the implementation of 36 CFR 79: Curation of Federally-Owned and Administered Archeological Collections. Again, the federal government asserts ownership of collections recovered from public lands under Antiquities Act, AHPA, NHPA and ARPA, but for the first time regulations are made applicable to preexisting as well as new collections. It is significant that federal agencies are now held responsible and accountable for collections obtained from their respective lands.

With roles more clearly defined in 36 CFR 79, museums and federal agencies can come to agreement regarding management of federal collections. Museums must meet guidelines as outlined in the U.S. Department of the Interior, Department Manual 411 (DM411), which are similar in many aspects to accreditation standards of the American Association of Museums. Museums desiring to be a repository for a federal collection should enter into a written agreement with the respective agency (or agencies) to clarify the roles of each party regarding "curatorial services" as outlined in 36 CFR 79.4(b) (1–6). This agreement would take the form of a Memorandum of Understanding (MOU) or Memorandum of Agreement (MOA). Generally, agencies prefer to work with museums to be repositories for local or regional collections, as they provide the most research potential when paired with other collections held by the museum or other landowners (i.e., state lands). When a museum undertakes the responsibility of being a repository for federal collections, the

museum will still accession the collection(s) into its accession records, but with the understanding that the museum is the steward of the collection(s), while the respective agency is the responsible party and the U.S. Government retains title. There may be certain cataloging requirements regarding federal collections that are important to know prior to accepting any collections.

Until 2009, federal laws and regulations pertained only to cultural collections, but with the Omnibus Public Land Management Act (Public Law 111–011) signed by President Obama in March 2009, the Paleontological Resources Preservation Act (PRPA) became law. PRPA applies only to federal lands and provides the legal authority for protection of paleontological resources with criminal and civil penalties for fossil theft and vandalism. PRPA requires federal land agencies to manage and protect paleontological resources on Federal lands using scientific principles and expertise. Similar to ARPA, PRPA requires paleontological resources and associated data and records to be deposited in an approved repository.

It is important that museums set bounds on acceptable reposited materials so collections fall under the mission and collecting scope of the museum. Likewise, it is important for the museum to set policies on how reposited collections come into the museum and how much cataloging and processing is done by the repositing contractor (such as in the case of NHPA Sec. 106 mitigation projects) or the repositing federal agency. Many states have adopted laws and regulations similar to federal with regard to collections acquired from State lands. However, states vary considerably and it is important to ascertain the legal and regulatory duties to be undertaken by the museum accepting collections from state lands. •

REPOSITORIES AT A GLANCE

Repository Agreement:
Points to consider before a museum becomes a repository for field-generated collections:

•Is the contractor a member of his or her professional organization and does he or she uphold those professional ethics (i.e., Register of Professional Archaeologists [RPA])?

•Does the museum have a MOU or MOA with the land agency with which the contractor will be working (i.e. Bureau of Land Management [BLM])?

•Is the project a NHPA Sec. 106 mitigation project?

•Is the undertaking a Phase I, II or III archaeological project? If Phase III, does the museum have adequate collections storage space?

•Does the project fit within the museum's mission and scope of collections?

Accessioning:
Points to consider when a museum accessions field-generated collections:

•Does the contractor hold a current Repository Agreement with the museum?

•Was the entire project undertaken on land owned by a single land agency or are there multiple agencies (state and/or federal) and private landowners involved?

•Can the contractor provide the museum with copies of written permits and agreements from all land agencies and owners involved?

•Was the work undertaken in a professional, legal and ethical manner?

•Did the contractor abide by all museum policies and procedures for processing the collection?

•Did the contractor pay the museum-levied reposited box fees (if applicable) for the collection when it was brought to the museum?

•Did to the museum alert the land agency (if different from the contractor) that the collection has formally entered the museum?

Cataloging:
Points to consider when a museum generates cataloging procedures for field-generated collections:

•Consider culling the collection (i.e., does the museum need 200 historic aluminum cans when three representative samples are enough?).

•Does the museum prefer to assign cataloging numbers to the contractor processing the collection or does it use the site number: field specimen numbering system?

•Does the museum have a written cataloging manual to provide contractors so the cataloging process is clearly defined?

Packaging:
Points to consider when a museum accepts field-generated collections:

•Will the contractor supply acid-free boxes or will the museum provide specific acid-free boxes for a cost?

•Are requirements clearly stated so only appropriate materials such as acid-free paper and board, polypropylene or polyethylene materials, and pigment ink pens are used for packaging and labeling artifacts?

•Do the museum's policy and procedures state whether or not multiple sites can be packaged in one box or whether each site must have its own box?

3D | PROVENANCE RESEARCH IN MUSEUM COLLECTIONS

A Collections Management Perspective

KAREN D. DALY

INTRODUCTION

The word "provenance" literally means "origin"; yet, it also refers to the history of ownership, particularly of an artwork or artifact.[1] The objective of provenance research is to trace the ownership history and location of an object, ideally from its creation to the present. Documentation of the provenance of a work of art has long been a valuable component of art historical research. In addition to providing insight into the history of art collecting, it can serve as a way to authenticate an object. Increasingly, provenance information is necessary to determine the legal status of an object.

Museums have traditionally conducted provenance research as part of the overall curatorial research on a collection. However, within the last few decades, there has been an increased focus on the provenance of museum objects.[2] As such, provenance has evolved into an individual category of importance for museums. In effect, information that was once seen as beneficial is now further understood as crucial.

Provenance research supports a museum's mandate to ensure that all collections in its custody are lawfully held and rightfully owned; in turn, this kind of responsible stewardship helps to maintain a high level of public trust. Whether an object has been in a museum's permanent collection for many years or is being considered for acquisition, incoming loan, or outgoing loan, its documented history of ownership can be a fundamental factor in making ethical decisions that abide by museum standards. From primarily a collections management perspective, this chapter offers practical suggestions and approaches to the important and complex work of Nazi-era provenance research and documentation.[3] It also considers how a museum can prepare for, and effectively respond to, possible claims of ownership of an object(s) within its collection, while fulfilling its fiduciary obligations.

In the United States, the standards and practices for the museum field are ultimately determined by the museum community itself, and are expressly developed through its professional associations, the American Association of Museums (AAM) and the Association of Art Museum Directors (AAMD).[4] With respect to Nazi-era provenance issues, the standards and guidelines developed by the AAM *(Guidelines Concerning the Unlawful Appropriation of Objects During the Nazi Era)* and AAMD *(Report of the AAMD Task Force on the Spoliation of Art during the Nazi/World War II Era)* give museums a strong basis for identifying and applying consistent methods most appropriate for their respective staff and collections.[5] In addressing provenance issues, each museum is entrusted to incorporate these standards and guidelines into their own policies and procedures, determine the appropriate staffing and funding, organize existing provenance information, establish their own priorities for further research, and make provenance information publicly available.

Although the focus of this chapter is primarily on provenance issues related to the World War II era, it is hoped that this information might help address other provenance issues and cultural property concerns throughout a museum's collection.[6]

HISTORICAL BACKGROUND

From 1933 until the end of World War II in 1945, the Nazi regime conducted one of the largest confiscations of art and cultural property known in history. The Third Reich enacted an elaborate and premeditated system of theft, confiscation, coercion, and destruction, with millions of objects being unlawfully and forcibly taken from rightful owners.

After World War II, great efforts were made by the Allied forces and other governments to return objects to their countries of origin and to original owners. Many members of the American museum community played leading roles in the success of the post-war restitution effort.[7] Although large amounts of artwork were restituted, some works entered the art market and eventually found their way into various collections in Europe, the U.S. and elsewhere, often with lost, obscured, or false provenance information.

Within the last two decades, museums have become increasingly aware of issues of looted art and restitution, particularly of objects possibly misappropriated during the Nazi era. In 1998, the Presidential Advisory Commission on Holocaust Assets in the United States (PCHA) was created to study and report to the President on issues relating to Holocaust victims' assets in the United States. The Department of State and the United States Holocaust Memorial Museum then co-hosted the Washington Conference on Holocaust-Era Assets. This conference resulted in the release of a document of 11 principles created to help resolve issues related to Nazi-looted art and assets.[8]

From 1998 to 2000, important guidelines issued by AAM and AAMD began to reshape museum policies across the U.S. In a joint agreement reached with the PCHA in 2000, AAM and AAMD further recommended that museums should strive to: (1) identify all objects in their collection that were created before 1946 and acquired by the museum after 1932, that underwent a change of ownership between 1932 and 1946, and that were or might reasonably be thought to have been in continental Europe between those dates, hence identified as "covered objects"; (2) make currently available object and provenance information on those objects accessible; and, (3) give priority to continuing provenance research as resources allow. AAM, AAMD, and PCHA further agreed that the initial focus of museum research should be European paintings and Judaica.[9]

In 2003, AAM launched the Nazi-Era Provenance Internet Portal (NEPIP), which provides a searchable registry of objects in U.S. museum collections that possibly changed hands in Continental Europe during the Nazi era, from 1933 to 1945.[10] Through the Portal, museums are able to submit and manage their own data on covered objects from their collections. The participating museum provides descriptive and provenance information for each object, sometimes accompanied by links to additional information on a museum website. The Portal continues to be a tremendous help for many museums, especially for those who may have limited resources to make collections information available through their own websites. NEPIP has been a crucial development in providing American museums a direct way to fulfill their responsibility of making provenance information publicly accessible. Moreover, in addition to the guidelines, AAM has led the way in assisting American museums in this area, providing online resources, specialized seminars, and crucial publications.[11]

PROVENANCE RESEARCH

"Provenance research is a study of absence. As we try to determine the history of a painting, a drawing, a piece of furniture or porcelain, or an East Asian work of art, we follow the traces of collections that were dispersed years, decades, even centuries ago. In the case of Holocaust-looted art from European Jewish collections, there is a double absence."[12] —Stephanie Tasch

As these words poignantly express, provenance research is challenging and complex work, particularly for objects possibly misappropriated during the Nazi era. Ownership records of art objects are often incomplete, as many factors over time have made it difficult to locate information. Among numerous factors, the upheavals of World War II, the inaccessibility of many archives during the Cold War, destruction from natural disasters, and changing standards of record keeping over time, have all added to the difficulty of determining a complete provenance for an object. Sometimes provenance records simply reflect a past owner's wish for anonymity. Other times, the attribution of an artwork may change over time, creating confusion in tracking the documentation. Furthermore, many dealers and auction houses are no longer in business and their records may have been lost or destroyed.

Provenance research is inter-disciplinary by its

nature, requiring the ability to consult many types of sources from different fields of study. It also requires an extensive knowledge of art history, the expertise to physically examine works of art, and the patience to thoroughly examine numerous sources for possible information. Particularly, World II-era provenance research requires a methodical investigation of the object itself, museum object records, museum archives, auction and exhibition catalogues, catalogues of collections, catalogues raisonnés, dealer records, photographic archives, and publications of the wartime activities of dealers and collectors. This kind of specialized research also requires proficiency in foreign languages, with at least a reading knowledge of German and French.

At times, provenance research requires examination of archives in other countries and access to documents that may not be publicly accessible. In many cases, museums find it necessary to employ a provenance researcher with a more specific expertise and background.

To date, one of the most important provenance research resources for museums is *The AAM Guide to Provenance Research* by Nancy H. Yeide, Konstantin Akinsha, and Amy L. Walsh, published by AAM in 2001. Full of historical information, recent methodologies, essential indices, valuable resources and case studies, this guide remains an essential reference for any museum addressing Nazi era provenance and related issues. *Museum Policy and Procedures for Nazi-Era Issues,* also published by AAM in 2001 and compiled by Helen J. Wechsler, Teri Coate-Saal, and John Lukavic, is an indispensable resource for collection managers, registrars, and curators, especially valuable through the numerous examples of policies and documentation.

At any stage of provenance research, the work can take considerable time, diligence, and expense. However, for most museums, the most substantial amount of time is required to establish and document what is already known about its collection. Subsequently, these provenance data need to be organized and formatted in a systematic and consistent manner. For example, in *The AAM Guide to Provenance Research,* there is a suggested standard format for recording provenance.[13] Yet, as the

AAM guide states, "an institution can develop its own format as long as it is explained in publications and/or other media. . . ."[14] Essentially, a provenance record, whether published or included in a museum's internal database, should clearly establish a sequence of ownership and document the sources of information.

STAFF ROLES

The work of provenance research and its documentation requires the support of an entire institution. Often, various museum departments intersect and overlap in the overall goal of making provenance information accurate, consistent, and available to researchers and the general public. However, each museum should decide on key staff members who will undertake the necessary duties in achieving this goal.

As part of their general responsibilities, curators are the staff members who most often conduct and review provenance research of their respective collections. Many museums, however, need to appoint at least one additional staff member as a primary contact for provenance information and as a coordinator of the museum's provenance research. It is ideal if one person, or a small group, can oversee and organize the museum's provenance information, as well as prioritize museum objects for further research. Likewise, it can be particularly helpful to have one person as a point of contact for outside inquiries on provenance, and for possible claims of ownership. Whether or not an inquiry evolves into a claim of ownership, having it proceed through an initial contact can help maintain a consistency of records.[15]

As provenance research staff and their specific roles are designated, their contact information should be included in a museum directory and on the museum's website, if applicable. Many museums also include a section on their museum website dedicated to the topic of provenance research, outlining the museum's efforts in this area, as well as a statement of the museum's position on Nazi-era provenance and other related cultural property concerns.

At this time, the museum professionals who primarily work in the area of provenance research

TWENTY CATEGORIES OF OBJECT AND PROVENANCE INFORMATION
Template Recommended by AAM for Submission to NEPIP

Category	Comments
Artist/Maker	To include artists' names, alternate names, and previous attributions.
Nationality of Artist/Maker	—
Life Dates of Artist/Maker —	
Place or Culture of Object Only if artist unknown.	
Object Title or Name	To include alternate titles.
Date of Work	To include approximate date, if specific date is unknown.
Medium/Materials	—
Measurements	—
Date of Acquisition	—
Accession Number	—
Object Type	Painting, sculpture, decorative arts, etc.
Subject Type	Landscape, portrait, mythological subject, historical, religious, genre, Judaica, etc.
Signature and Marks (obverse)	To include signatures, inscriptions, and marks; for paintings, what appears on the front
Labels and Marks (reverse, frame, mount, etc.)	To describe marks and labels (prior to 1960) on the reverse of an object (including frame, mount, etc.). Indicate if images are available.
Description	To contain description of object (its content, subject, etc.). Museums should make this a priority.
Provenance	To contain, at the minimum, known owners, dates of ownership, places of ownership, method of transfer (sale, gift, descent, etc.). To include, if known, lot numbers, sale prices, buyers, etc. To include information on unlawful appropriation during the Nazi era and subsequent restitution. Museums should ensure that provenance information is understandable and organized chronologically.
Exhibition History	—
Bibliographic History	—
Other Relevant Information	To contain anything about the object that would be useful in identifying it for this purpose. If the object fits the definition of Judaica contained in this document, so state.
Image	An image is key to identifying an object. Museums should make every effort to include an image with their records.

and related issues are curators, collection managers, registrars, and archivists. It is ideal that the staff member(s) who primarily work in this area have an extensive knowledge of the museum's collection, a familiarity with the various types of museum records, and experience working with the objects. Additionally, museum directors, senior level administrators, and their staff are often closely involved in the supervision and management of these important and ever evolving issues. Furthermore, a museum's legal counsel plays a crucial role, particularly with cultural property concerns and possible claims of ownership.

Regardless of which staff members are primarily responsible for provenance research, it is clear that registrars and collection managers play a significant role in the success of any provenance research effort. As museum professionals trained to think in terms of the integrity of records and documentation, registrars and collections managers are often well suited to work in this area. Also, collections management staff typically have a comprehensive knowledge and understanding of the institution's records, related legal issues, its collection management policy, and the collection itself.

There is an increasing call for museum professionals with expertise in provenance research who are knowledgeable about current cultural property laws and concerns. As such, it is certain that those who work in the field of museum collections management will continue to encounter these issues and make significant contributions to this area.

EXISTING COLLECTION

One of the primary objectives of provenance research of a museum's permanent collection is to ascertain what is currently known about the ownership history of the collection. In this process, it is important to establish goals and working methodologies to achieve those goals. Any methodology used should be clearly documented so the process and results can be understood and expanded upon by future researchers.

A. Covered Objects

The initial goal, per the AAM Recommended Procedures, is to determine how many "covered objects" are in a collection: "objects created before 1946 and acquired by the museum after 1932, that underwent a change of ownership between 1932 and 1946, and that were or might reasonably be thought to have been in continental Europe between those dates. In the event that a museum is unable to determine whether an object created before 1946 and acquired after 1932 (a) might have been in continental Europe between 1932 and 1946 and/or (b) underwent a change of ownership during that period, it should still be treated as a covered object."[16]

It is easy to become paralyzed when considering how to calculate the number of covered objects in a collection. Without a doubt, this task can turn into a challenging and complex process. Yet it is important to first evaluate, at least in a general sense, how many objects within a collection will require further provenance research. As such, this step can help a museum estimate the necessary staffing, funding and an overall timeline for a Nazi-era provenance research project.

The speed of calculating a museum's total number of potentially covered objects depends greatly on the type of museum collection. For example, if it is a small, focused collection, established mostly before the 1930s, this might be a quick and straightforward process. However, many American museum collections grew significantly after 1932 and include numerous works created before 1946. Also, numerous collections are encyclopedic and diverse in nature, with a number of different categories for consideration. From the outset, researchers are greatly aided if there is an ability to systematically search museum records, especially through an effective collections management database system.

At the beginning of such a project, it can be difficult to assess the amount of time needed to achieve a completely accurate calculation of the number of covered objects in a collection. While it is not complex to determine how many objects were created before 1946 and acquired after 1932, it is more complicated and time consuming to find out whether an object may have been in Continental Europe between

1933 and 1945, as this requires object records to be researched, at least to some degree.

After establishing the overall number of objects which were created before 1946 and acquired by the museum after 1932, one might further refine the figure by eliminating certain categories of objects, or individual objects known to have not been in Continental Europe during the Nazi era. For example, it might be known that a group of artworks given by a certain patron were in the United States throughout the Nazi era, and thus can be subtracted from the overall count. Also, as AAM, AAMD and the PCHA have recommended, the focus should first be on any Judaica and European paintings.[17] Museums should try to determine an overall timeline for those areas that will need further research beyond holdings of European paintings and Judaica, such as European sculpture, decorative arts, drawings, and prints. After those categories are completed, and if applicable, museums could estimate the time to examine any remaining potential covered objects in their respective collections.[18]

To make the research of covered objects a more manageable project, it helps to break a collection into smaller groups to research, such as paintings associated with a certain dealer, or a patron, or from a particular time period.

With each covered object, all related museum records should be thoroughly examined: accession records, database entries, object files, wills, bequests, correspondence, and exhibition and publication histories. Furthermore, it is necessary to physically examine the work in its entirety, documenting the backs of paintings and all sides of objects, looking for any kind of collectors' stamps, labels, numbers, marks, auction house codes or lot numbers. If there is no existing photography, have the object fully photographed, preferably in a digital format so the images can be easily uploaded to different online formats.

When conducting this internal research, it is time-efficient to fill out a template or format, through which the data can eventually be made public on the museum's website and on NEPIP. It is recommended that museums follow AAM's "Twenty Categories of Object and Provenance Information" as a format.[19] Using such a template not only helps to create consistent provenance records internally, but it also serves to systematize information for outside researchers and possible claimants.

B. Prioritizing Research

During the internal research process, some covered objects may appear more problematic than others. Therefore, the prioritization of provenance research is a necessary phase of the overall research. It is important to critically evaluate the provenance gaps of covered objects through consideration of a few general factors.

First, there is the potential location of an object during the Nazi era. Although any gap in provenance could be problematic, it helps to look at any known locations and associations of the object. For example, a gap in the provenance history for a painting known to have been in the United States or United Kingdom prior to and following World War II would not be a likely candidate for misappropriation by the Nazis. Yet, an object associated with a German collection and with a provenance gap between 1933 and 1938 would warrant further research and higher prioritization.[20]

Another factor to take into account during the research process is the identification of "red-flag" names. One of the most often cited lists of "red-flag" names is found in records of the Office of Strategic Services (OSS) Art Looting Investigation Unit's (ALIU) "Biographical Index of Individuals Involved in Art Looting."[21] Additionally, researchers should become familiar with "red-flag" names of collections that are known to have been looted within this time period. Although there is no single list of names of all the victims of looting, there are various resources and archives to aid in such research.[22] It is important to keep in mind that the discovery of any type of "red-flag" names only indicates a need of further research. Many objects associated with these names were sold by dealers or in collections before or after the war. Moreover, thousands of these objects were returned to rightful owners following the war, thanks to the Allied restitution effort.

Another aspect to keep in mind during research is a general recognition of the types of objects highly desired and sought by the Nazis throughout this time period. Although their confiscations were certainly wide-ranging, there are certain art historical categories that were valued higher and pursued by the Third Reich officers more intensely than others, such as German art of the Renaissance period.[23]

The provenance researcher should assemble all in-house information first, seeking to close any provenance gaps before going offsite to other sources. Once the internal records are thoroughly examined and the information is critically evaluated, staff should contact relevant archives, existent databases, and any art dealers, auction houses, or donors, as may be necessary. Additionally, there are scholars and other researchers who may be able to provide information. As part of a recently emergent field, those who work in the area of provenance research benefit from sharing information with each other, as much as may be possible, given occasional circumstances of required confidentiality.[24]

C. Making it Public: Museum Website and NEPIP

Following recommendations by the AAM, AAMD and PCHA, museums should make current information on their covered objects as available and accessible as possible. Making this information available to the public helps museums fulfill their mandate of responsible stewardship of their collections. Fortunately, the Internet provides a direct way for museums to share information on covered objects with the public, researchers, and potential claimants. It also provides an opportunity for others outside the museum to share further information that may clarify the provenance of objects.

In addition to posting information on a museum website, there is the Nazi-Era Provenance Internet Portal (NEPIP), designed and managed by AAM on behalf of the U.S. museum community. If a museum does not have provenance information on its covered objects ready and formatted for inclusion in NEPIP, the museum should still register on the portal as a participating museum. Initially, a museum must provide a contact name, contact information, links to their museum website, and information on whether the museum has any Judaica holdings in its collection.

As research develops and the information is organized, museums can continue to submit and manage their own data on their covered objects. Due to the challenging nature of provenance research, the posting and updating of information on a museum website and NEPIP should be understood as an ongoing endeavor.[25]

D. Discovering Evidence of Misappropriated Objects

Per AAM, if in the process of researching a museum's existing collection, researchers find credible evidence of unlawful appropriation without subsequent restitution, there should be a procedure in place to inform key museum staff. In consultation with qualified legal counsel, the museum should make every effort to resolve the status of the object. This may include making such information public and possibly notifying potential claimants. In such a situation, museums should strive to be as open and transparent as possible, seeking ways to address the situation responsibly and appropriately.[26]

ACQUISITIONS

Among the many criteria used for determining whether an object should be added to a collection, the provenance of the object is a factor of increasing consequence. Although museums have historically sought to obtain provenance information on objects intended for acquisition, in recent decades has it has become imperative to obtain and document such information. Currently, museums are proceeding with great caution in acquisitions, not only with respect to Nazi-era provenance, but with acquisitions of various archaeological materials and ancient art objects originating outside the United States.[27]

AAM has clearly stated that museums should take all "reasonable steps to resolve the Nazi-era provenance status of objects before acquiring them for their collections whether by purchase, gift, bequest, or exchange."[28] Since the late 1990s, museums have incorporated more rigorous guidelines and procedures into their collection management policies with respect to acquisitions and Holocaust-era provenance.[29]

For example, many museums send a provenance questionnaire to all potential donors or dealers of art being considered for acquisition, including a specific request for any provenance information from 1932 to 1945. Often, the registrar or collections manager is directly involved in this documentation and should work in tandem with the curator in obtaining, analyzing, and documenting all provenance information.

In certain cases, it is prudent for museums to require a warranty as part of a purchase agreement to ensure the museum obtains good title to an object, which may offer protection from potential future claims.[30] Notably, in the 1998 "Report of the Association of Art Museum Directors (AAMD) Task Force on the Spoliation of Art during the Nazi/World War II Era," the AAMD advises that museums, when purchasing works of art, "seek representations and warranties from the seller that the seller has valid title and that the work of art is free from any claims."[31]

Another step of due diligence in the acquisition process is to check an object's descriptive information and known ownership history against various databases of stolen art, most of which are accessible online.[32] At present, it appears that most museums employ the Art Loss Register (ALR), which is one of the largest private databases of lost and stolen art, antiques. and collectibles.[33] The ALR has a great deal of experience with museums in providing their search services, research capabilities, and expertise in a number of areas. While their services are not free, it is a worthwhile investment and necessary expense for many museums to include in planning budgets, whether related to the care and research of the collection, exhibitions, or other related museum projects. With respect to the ALR and to other established databases, there is an important caveat to keep in mind. Submitting a search through the ALR is just one step of due diligence, checking objects that have been registered with the ALR as lost or stolen. It does not replace further research that might be warranted, nor does it guarantee any protection against possible provenance issues in the future.

Per AAM, when the provenance is incomplete or uncertain for a proposed acquisition, the museum should consider what "additional research would be necessary to resolve the Nazi-era provenance status of the object before acquiring it."[34] This section of the guidelines can become a murky area in both interpretation and application. Therefore, it falls to individual museums to determine how these decisions will be made within their institution. It is best to incorporate very clear responsibilities and procedures into an "Acquisitions" section of a museum's collection management policy, and update as necessary over time.

During the research phase of an acquisition, if credible evidence of unlawful appropriation without subsequent restitution is found, it is recommended that the museum notify the donor, seller, or estate executor of the evidence, and not proceed with acquiring the object until there is an acceptable resolution and planned course of action. As circumstances and complexities can vary greatly depending on the situation, any decisions should be made in consultation with qualified legal counsel.[35]

Once an object has been accessioned into a collection, the object and provenance information about the acquisition should be made public as soon as possible, especially if it qualifies as a covered object, per AAM guidelines. Press releases on new acquisitions, published in local newspapers or on a museum's website, help to convey an overall transparency to the general public. Furthermore, it is recommended that new and recent acquisitions be put on display, as is possible and appropriate.

In the museum's acquisition process, the goal is to be as open and transparent as possible, making the objects available for further research, public review, and accountability.

LOANS

In recent years, issues of provenance have filtered into almost every collections-related practice within a museum. As no exception, an institution's approach to loans, both to and from its collection, includes a thorough consideration of provenance information.

A. Incoming Loans

Per AAM, museums should be aware of their ethical

responsibility to consider the status of material they borrow as well as the possibility of claims being brought against a loaned object in their custody.[36] Also, AAMD urges museums to review provenance information regarding incoming loans.[37]

With incoming loans, museums should request that lenders provide as much Nazi-era provenance information as possible. Museums may also want to consult published sources on their own to see if there are potential provenance concerns. As applicable with the provenance research of an existing collection or of proposed acquisitions, the borrowing museum must have and maintain clear documentation of this provenance information.

Per AAM, when the provenance is incomplete or uncertain for a proposed loan, the museum should consider what "additional research would be prudent or necessary to resolve the Nazi-era provenance status of the object before borrowing it."[38] This section entrusts individual museums to formulate their own policies on how such decisions will be made within their institutions. As with other collections-related practices, it is recommended that museums incorporate and update as necessary very clear responsibilities and procedures into a "Loans" section of their respective collection management policies.

During the research and planning phase of an incoming loan, if credible evidence of unlawful appropriation without subsequent restitution is found, the borrower should notify the lender of the nature of the evidence and should not proceed with the loan until taking further action to clarify these issues. To reiterate, circumstances and complexities can vary greatly in these situations; therefore, any decisions should be made carefully and in consultation with qualified legal counsel.[39]

In recent years, museums have increasingly included conditions in loan agreements and exhibition contracts that stipulate terms regarding the lender's legal status as sole owner of the loaned object(s). Some agreements stipulate that the borrower will only release or take instructions concerning the loan from the lender or the lender's authorized agent.[40] Furthermore, to limit liability during an exhibition, a borrowing museum may apply, as appropriate and necessary, for Immunity from Judicial Seizure

of Cultural Objects, administered through the U.S. Department of State.[41]

B. Outgoing Loans

As indicated by professional standards, potential lenders should submit to borrowers, as requested, all known provenance information on objects proposed for loan. For loans from the collection, designated staff should conduct and document, as appropriate, a provenance review of the proposed loan. In addition to an institution's established criteria for considering loans, there are a few factors to consider with respect to Nazi-era provenance.

If the proposed loan qualifies as a covered object, and it has not yet been fully researched as part of an overall provenance research assessment of the collection, all efforts should be made to check internal records and publications, determining if there are potential concerns or if further research is necessary. As standard practice, the museum should clearly document all the related provenance research of potential outgoing loans.

If any provenance concerns develop in the review process, designated staff should critically evaluate all known ownership, exhibition, and publication history of the object(s), weighing potential risks against the potential benefits of increased public knowledge and possible further scholarship that might result from the exhibition of the object(s). In such a situation, an appropriate step of due diligence would be to submit the known information about the proposed loan to the Art Loss Register (ALR) for a search against their database. Furthermore, depending on where the loan is traveling for exhibition, it is prudent to be aware of current and applicable immunity from seizure laws that may be in place. Depending on the circumstances, an exhibition's organizer(s) may have secured immunity from seizure for all lenders, but it is certainly best to confirm these details from the borrower in documented form.

The provenance review, research information, and summary of the museum's decision regarding provenance issues of an outgoing loan should be completely documented as part of the process.

With incoming and outgoing loans, museums should incorporate practices that carefully consider issues of Nazi-era provenance, not only to protect the interests of the museum, but also to responsibly participate in the shared goals of education and scholarship within the field.

CLAIMS OF OWNERSHIP

AAM states that museums should address claims of ownership of objects in their custody "openly, seriously, responsively, and with respect for the dignity of all parties involved" and that each claim "should be considered on its own merits."[42] Furthermore, both AAM and AAMD affirm that museums should review Nazi-era related claims "promptly and thoroughly."[43]

While these statements represent the important and ethical commitments of the field, professional guidelines regarding ownership claims of objects possibly misappropriated during the Nazi era are somewhat general in nature. Realistically, when faced with such a claim, museums can find themselves in the challenging situation of attempting to respond promptly while simultaneously ensuring their responsibility of due diligence in the matter. More often than not, such claims are complicated, each one with its own unique set of challenges. The process of thoroughly reviewing a claim, while meeting a museum's fiduciary responsibility to its public, can require a significant amount of time, dedicated staff, and resources. Therefore, it is essential for museums to be as prepared as possible to respond to all inquiries and restitution claims.

Overall, the museum's goal should be to build a framework that will help support and facilitate a potential claim process. Although claims can vary greatly through unique circumstances and requirements, there are basic factors for consideration.

Whether incorporating relevant language into an existing collection management policy, or creating a separate policy, museums should first consider what their response procedure would be throughout a claim process, together with the designation of an internal chain of communication.[44] Part of this chain of communication should be a core group of staff members including, but not limited to: the director; senior, deputy or associate-level directors,

as appropriate; the chief curator; the curator associated with the claimed object; the head of the museum's public relations department; collections manager and/or registrar; legal counsel; and provenance research staff, if applicable.[45]

The museum should determine a primary museum contact(s), who could best correspond with the claimant or the claimant's representative. Also, it is recommended that one staff member create and maintain a documented chronology of the claim, recording the claim's history, including such information as: the date and content of an initial contact or correspondence; any requests for information; submission or receipt of evidence; summaries of phone calls, other contacts and correspondences; and summaries of evolving internal questions and opinions.[46] This kind of documentation can be an efficient way to keep key staff and trustee members clearly and consistently informed on the evolving status of a claim. The primary contact(s) may also be the ideal staff person(s) to maintain the claim chronology, if appropriate.[47]

Per AAM, museums ought to conduct their own research during a claim process and should also "request evidence of ownership from the claimant in order to assist in determining the provenance of the object."[48] Depending on what is currently known and documented about the claimed object, all efforts should be made by the museum to pursue further information on the history and provenance of the object.

Although museums must individually determine what level of documentary evidence is necessary to consider deaccession and restitution of an object, or possible compensation for an object, it is recommended that museums ask for receipt of any and all related information from the claimant, with specific requests for evidence that satisfactorily addresses the following: (1) that the object was confiscated by the Nazis or was subject to a forced sale, with no subsequent restitution or compensation; (2) the claimant or claimants are the sole legal heir(s) to the object, representing the entirety of those who could possibly make a claim on the object; [49] and, (3) documentary evidence, photographic or of an adequate visual description and documentation, that clearly matches and identifies the claimed object with an actual object held in the museum's custody.

If these important questions are not fully answered or adequately addressed, the resulting unresolved status of the object(s) can present a difficult situation for all parties. Although museums are completely committed to thoroughly responding to all claims, they also hold their collections in trust for the public and have a legal and fiduciary duty not to deaccession and restitute objects from their collections without sufficient evidence. For example, museums are not free to restitute a work to a claimant on the basis of ambiguous evidence of ownership, when a subsequent claimant might appear with evidence of ownership, thus making the museum liable to an additional claimant. Furthermore, if a museum decides to transfer a work held in public trust, this decision may have to be approved by an appropriate government regulator, such as an Attorney General.

It should be further noted that the due diligence that a museum must undertake before considering restitution of an object should not be dependent on a question of monetary market value. As museums hold all of their works in trust for the public, that standard should not be based on any monetary value of an object.

If, however, a museum does discover or receive evidence that supports the claim and addresses the major areas of concern, the museum then must determine what kind of official internal documentation is needed to proceed with a recommendation and resolution. Also, as part of the necessary documentation of the claim process, the museum should ensure that it receives a formal request for restitution or compensation from the claimant or claimant's representative.

Both AAM and AAMD state that if a museum determines that an object in its collection was unlawfully appropriated during the Nazi era without subsequent restitution, the museum should seek to resolve the matter with the claimant "in an equitable, appropriate, and mutually agreeable manner."[50] Furthermore, both organizations strongly suggest that museums seek "methods other than litigation" to resolve such claims.[51]

In such cases, it is ideal to negotiate any and all terms of restitution outside of litigation.[52] Any claim

and art restitution process is certainly difficult and complex enough for all involved without the added expense and potential stress of litigation. If possible, when both museums and claimants are able to cooperate and coordinate all the necessary documentation and terms of an agreement, the entire process can sometimes provide a positive and educational opportunity for a museum and its public community.

Once a museum has come to a decision to resolve the claim, there remain considerations and steps of museum procedure and documentation.

If a museum negotiates to keep the object in the collection via some form of compensation to the claimant, there may be mutually agreeable conditions that guarantee the museum will educate the public about the object's provenance and Holocaust-era history through future gallery texts and publications. Any legal agreements should be coordinated and executed through a museum's legal counsel.

If a museum and claimant agree that the work should be removed from the collection and restituted, there are actions that must be considered and taken by a museum's governing body, such as its board of trustees.

DEACCESSION AND RESTITUTION

As part of its collection management policy, a museum should have clear deaccessioning procedures in place. Many of these policies typically include a museum's specified criteria for considering the removal of an object. In preparation for a possible restitution, museums may choose to update their policies by adding a potential criterion that conveys the need to remove works of art that "are subject to restitution or repatriation on the basis of clear evidence proving past illegal appropriations."[53]

In the case of proposed restitution, a deaccessioning recommendation could be submitted to a museum's board of trustees to take such an action. Ideally, such a recommendation would include a summary of the claim and clearly convey the intent of restitution.

If a museum does not have a clear deaccessioning policy, museum staff may want to consider creating a special recommendation or resolution in consultation with the museum's legal counsel. This special recommendation, to be submitted to the museums' board of trustees for an action, should summarize the claim and clearly outline the reasons for deaccession and restitution.

If a museum's board of trustees votes to deaccession and restitute an object, then plans must be made for the transfer of ownership of the object. As part of this phase, the museum should work with its legal counsel and the claimant or claimant's representative to prepare a satisfactory legal transfer agreement. If there are potential issues or expenses involved regarding the physical return of the object, such as packing, shipping, and insurance, those terms should be negotiated and clearly documented either prior to the transfer as part of the transfer of ownership agreement.

Although ownership claims of objects possibly misappropriated during the Nazi era can vary greatly in their historical context, evidence, and outcome, it is certain that throughout any claim process, a museum must follow a clear, consistent, and thorough documentation process in order to ensure due diligence and to meet its fiduciary responsibility.

CONCLUSION

Early 21st century is a transitional time with respect to the collecting practices of American museums. In recent years, it is apparent that the greater museum field has experienced a paradigm shift, with the increased focus on the provenance of objects acquired by museums, as well as an ever expanding scrutiny of objects held in museum collections. As such, there is an increased need for staff with expertise in provenance research and with extensive knowledge of current cultural property issues and laws.

Museums continue to hold these collections in the public trust and remain committed to their responsible stewardship. Also, museums stand committed to following the highest ethical standards and professional guidelines set by the greater museum community. Moreover, it is clear that museums will continue to review and adapt their policies and procedures as warranted over time.

In the area of World War II provenance research, the museum community remains dedicated to helping Holocaust survivors and heirs by the research of existing collections, proposed acquisitions, and loans and by working to make all provenance research on potential Holocaust-era looted objects available and accessible.

Although U.S. museums have set an impressive record of resolving Nazi-era claims of ownership, they must remain vigilant in the provenance research of their collections and be prepared for potential claims in the future. •

NOTES

1. The term "provenience" also denotes "origin" and is most often referred to within an archaeological context. According to the 2009 Archaeological Institute of America glossary: "Provenience (provenance): The three-dimensional context (including geographical location) of an archaeological find, giving information about its function and date." Please see http://www.archaeological.org

2. After the fall of the Berlin wall in 1989 and the dissolution of the Soviet Union in 1991, historians began to obtain access to formerly closed archives in Eastern Europe and in the former Soviet Union. This access allowed for a new awareness of the extent of looting in the World War II era, thereby raising the issue of art and assets misappropriated by the Nazis. The declassification of archival documents in the United States further contributed to the increased scholarship on this topic. In recent years, media attention paid to various high profile cases has added to the increased scrutiny of holdings in museum collections. In addition to concerns regarding possible Nazi loot, there is an increased interest in art and archeological objects that might have been looted and illegally removed from countries of origin since the 1970 United Nations Educational, Scientific and Cultural Organization (UNESCO) Convention on the Means of Prohibiting and Preventing the Illicit Import, Export and Transfer of Ownership of Cultural Property. See http://portal.unesco.org/en/ev.php-URL_ID=13039&URL_DO=DO_TOPIC&URL_SECTION=201.html

3. The National Socialist German Worker's (Nazi) Party was founded in 1919 and was headed by Adolf Hitler from 1921. The "Nazi era" refers to the time period of 1933–1945 when the Nazi party was in power in Germany. This time period is also sometimes referred to as the "World War II era" or the "Holocaust era."

4. Although U.S. museums are not overseen by a governmental regulatory agency, they must comply with all applicable laws. See Helen J. Wechsler. "U.S. Museums and the Nazi-Era Assets Issue." In *Vitalizing Memory: International Perspectives on Provenance Research* (pp.12–15). Washington, DC: American Association of Museums, 2005.

5. For official guidelines and procedures regarding museums

and Nazi era provenance issues, please see the American Association of Museum's website: http://www.aam-us.org/museumresources/ethics/index.cfm and the Association of Art Museum Directors website: www.aamd.org.

6. For guidelines and standards regarding museums and the provenance of archaeological materials and ancient art, please see the American Association of Museums' website: http://www.aam-us.org/museumresources/ethics/index.cfm and the Association of Art Museum Directors' website: www.aamd.org.

7. See Appendix A: Suggested Resources for Provenance Research in Museum Collections for publications and websites related to this topic and time period.

8. See Helen J. Wechsler, Teri Coate-Saal, and John Lukavic, compilers. *Museum Policy and Procedures for Nazi-Era Issues,* American Association of Museums, 2001, p. 93, Appendix C. The principles can also be found online: http://www.state.gov/www/regions/eur/981203_heac_art_princ.html

9. See the AAM Recommended Procedures for Providing Information to the Public about Objects Transferred in Europe during the Nazi Era http://www.aam-us.org/museumresources/prov/procedures.cfm. Please also see Helen J. Wechsler, Teri Coate-Saal, and John Lukavic, compilers. *Museum Policy and Procedures for Nazi-Era Issues,* American Association of Museums, 2001.

10. See www.nepip.org for more details on how AAM manages this portal on behalf of the U.S. museum community.

11. AAM offered some scholarship assistance to help applicants attend training seminars in 2002 and 2003 in Washington, D.C. AAM also coordinated an international conference in Washington, D.C., in 2004, offering some scholarship assistance. See Nancy H. Yeide, Intro. *Vitalizing Memory: International Perspectives on Provenance Research.* Washington, DC: American Association of Museums, 2005.

12. See Stephanie Tasch (2005). "Women Collectors of the Weimar Republic." In *Vitalizing Memory: International Perspectives on Provenance Research* (pp.76-79). Washington, DC: American Association of Museums, 2005.

13. See Nancy H. Yeide, Konstantin Akinsha, and Amy L. Walsh. *The AAM Guide to Provenance Research.* American Association of Museums, Washington, DC, 2001, pp. 33–34.

14. Ibid., p. 33.

15. Please note these observations are based on the author's experiences and research of six years, and also on an informal survey of twenty museums of various sizes taken in 2006 through a professional provenance listserv, which requested information on provenance issues and staffing. (Listserv: PROVENANCE-LIST@HOME.EASE.LSOFT.COM)

16. See the AAM Recommended Procedures for Providing Information to the Public about Objects Transferred in Europe during the Nazi Era http://www.aam-us.org/museumresources/prov/procedures.cfm

17. Per AAM, Judaica is broadly defined as the material culture of the Jewish people. This includes ceremonial objects for communal or domestic use. Judaica also comprises historical artifacts relating to important Jewish personalities, momentous events, and significant communal activities, as well as literature relating to Jews and Judaism. See the AAM Recommended Procedures for Providing Information to the Public about Objects Transferred in Europe during the Nazi Era http://www.aam-us.org/museumresources/prov/procedures.cfm

18. Per AAM, museums should incorporate Nazi-era provenance research into their standard research on collections and into funding proposals for museum projects, if applicable. Depending on their particular circumstances, museums are also encouraged to pursue special funding to undertake Nazi-era provenance research.

19. See Appendix B: AAM's Twenty Categories of Object and Provenance Information.

20. See Nancy H. Yeide, Konstantin Akinsha, and Amy L. Walsh. *The AAM Guide to Provenance Research.* American Association of Museums, Washington, DC, 2001, pp. 49–51.

21. Ibid., pp. 55–56; pp. 259–296 (ALIU lists included in indices).

22. Ibid., p. 51; pp. 55–68.

23. Ibid., pp. 41–44.

24. For example, if a museum is in the middle of a lawsuit regarding a claim of ownership, staff involved may be asked to keep all information confidential.

25. See www.nepip.org for contact information.

26. See AAM Guidelines Concerning the Unlawful Appropriation of Objects During the Nazi Era: http://www.aam-us.org/museumresources/ethics/nazi_guidelines.cfm

27. See AAM Standards Regarding Archaeological Material and Ancient Art: http://www.aam-us.org/museumresources/ethics/index.cfm. See also Appendix A: Suggested Resources for Provenance Research in Museum Collections, which lists helpful websites related to these issues.

28. See AAM Guidelines Concerning the Unlawful Appropriation of Objects During the Nazi Era: http://www.aam-us.org/museumresources/ethics/nazi_guidelines.cfm

29. See Helen J. Wechsler, Teri Coate-Saal, and John Lukavic, compilers. *Museum Policy and Procedures for Nazi-Era Issues,* American Association of Museums, 2001, pp. 1–27. The chapter on Acquisitions includes many helpful examples of how the AAM guidelines have been incorporated into working documents in museums.

30. Ibid., pp. 1–11. (See examples of warranties).

31. See Report of the Association of Art Museum Directors (AAMD) Task Force on the Spoliation of Art during the Nazi/World War II Era (1933-1945), Washington, DC, June 1998: www.aamd.org

32. See Appendix A: Suggested Resources for Provenance Research in Museum Collections, which lists some of the online databases related to the Holocaust era.

33. The ALR includes item registration, search and recovery services to collectors, museums conducting due diligence in provenance research, the art trade, insurers, worldwide law enforcement agencies, and private individuals. See http://www.artloss.com/ for more information.

34. See AAM Guidelines Concerning the Unlawful Appropriation of Objects During the Nazi Era: http://www.aam-us.org/museumresources/ethics/nazi_guidelines.cfm.

35. Ibid.

36. Ibid.

37. See Report of the Association of Art Museum Directors (AAMD) Task Force on the Spoliation of Art during the Nazi/World War II Era (1933-1945), Washington, DC, June 1998: www.aamd.org.

38. See AAM Guidelines Concerning the Unlawful Appropriation of Objects During the Nazi Era: http://www.aam-us.org/museumresources/ethics/nazi_guidelines.cfm.

39. Ibid.

40. See Helen J. Wechsler, Teri Coate-Saal, and John Lukavic, compilers. *Museum Policy and Procedures for Nazi-Era Issues,* American Association of Museums, 2001, pp. 29–40. In the chapter on Loans, see examples of agreements with specific language included as to the lender's ownership status.

41. See U.S. Department of State: Immunity from Judicial Seizure–Cultural Objects: http://www.state.gov/s/l/c3432.htm. In recent years, there have been a number of cases relating to immunity from seizure, both in the United States and abroad. In general, this is an ever-evolving area of concern for museums and it is wise to stay as informed as possible. Information on some of the more prominent cases can be found online. For example, see the International Foundation for Art Research's section on Art Law and Cultural Property: http://www.ifar.org/art_law.php.

42. See AAM Guidelines Concerning the Unlawful Appropriation of Objects During the Nazi Era: http://www.aam-us.org/museumresources/ethics/nazi_guidelines.cfm.

43. See AAM Guidelines Concerning the Unlawful Appropriation of Objects During the Nazi Era: http://www.aam-us.org/museumresources/ethics/nazi_guidelines.cfm, and the Report of the Association of Art Museum Directors (AAMD) Task Force on the Spoliation of Art during the Nazi/World War II Era (1933-1945), Washington, DC, June 1998: www.aamd.org.

44. See Helen J. Wechsler, Teri Coate-Saal, and John Lukavic, compilers. *Museum Policy and Procedures for Nazi-Era Issues,* American Association of Museums, 2001, pp. 65–85. See examples from museums of related procedures.

45. Museums may also include a trustee member in this group, or designate someone to keep their trustees informed through the claim process.

46. This suggestion is based on shared accounts from some American museums that have experienced Nazi era restitution claims within the last twelve years. It is informally suggested as a tool that could be adapted, updated and changed as to the needs of a particular institution.

47. Depending on the situation, some museums may designate only legal counsel be in contact with a claimant or a claimant's representative.

48. See AAM Guidelines Concerning the Unlawful Appropriation of Objects During the Nazi Era: http://www.aam-us.org/museumresources/ethics/nazi_guidelines.cfm.

49. This kind of request, for example, can require significant research into inheritance records, such as wills, which, in some countries are not accessible to researchers without the consent of the family. It would be helpful for claimants and museums if there were a mutually agreed upon mechanism in place to authenticate such records for all parties. As an example, the Holocaust Claims Processing Office (HCPO) of the State of New York is an organization that facilitates many of these crucial documentation requirements for all parties involved in such claims. See the New York State Holocaust Claims Office: http://www.claims.state.ny.us/art.htm.

50. See AAM Guidelines Concerning the Unlawful Appropriation of Objects During the Nazi Era: http://www.aam-us.org/museumresources/ethics/nazi_guidelines.cfm, and the Report of the Association of Art Museum Directors (AAMD) Task Force on the Spoliation of Art during the Nazi/World War II Era (1933-1945), Washington, DC, June 1998: www.aamd.org.

51. Ibid.

52. See Monica Dugot, "An Introduction to the Holocaust Claims Processing Office." Helen J. Wechsler, Teri Coate-Saal, and John Lukavic, compilers. *Museum Policy and Procedures for Nazi-Era Issues,* American Association of Museums, 2001, pp. 66–68. Dugot provides an interesting point of view as someone who has facilitated dialogue and coordinated efforts with both claimants and museums in successful Holocaust era restitutions.

53. This language is taken from the Virginia Museum of Fine Arts (VMFA) Deaccessioning Policy, which is part of the VMFA Collections Management Policy, updated and approved by the VMFA Board of Trustees in 2007.

TERMS RELATING TO PROVENANCE, CULTURAL PROPERTY

Covered object: Any object created before 1946 and acquired by a museum after 1932 that underwent a change of ownership between 1932 and 1946, and that was or might reasonably be thought to have been in continental Europe between those dates ("AAM Guidelines Concerning the Unlawful Appropriation of Objects During the Nazi Era").

Fiduciary obligation: The responsibility of a museum to the collections it holds in trust, for the public.

Nazi era: The period 1933-1945 when the Nazi Party was in power in Germany. In related resources, this is sometimes also referred to as the Holocaust era.

Ownership: the legal right of possession; lawful title (to something); proprietorship.

Patrimony laws: laws enacted by a county claiming ownership by the country of all art that it defines as part of the patrimony of that country. These types of laws can range from less-intrusive screening mechanisms to total embargoes on the export of cultural property, such that it becomes theft of public property to remove patrimony objects without permission.

Provenance: the documented history of ownership and location of an object.

Provenience: an archaeological term meaning the three-dimensional context (including geographical location) of an archaeological find, giving information about its function and date.

Restitution: the return of an object(s) or payment of compensation to an object's original owner or legal successor, or the return of a work of art to the ownership of a source country, or country that claims to be the source country.

Title: regarding personal property, the possession of rights of ownership in that property. Separate rights of possession may include copyright interests, trademark rights, and any specific interest that previous owner may have reserved (adapted from *A Legal Primer on Managing Museum Collections,* 2nd ed.).

Unlawful appropriation: objects that were acquired through theft, confiscation, coercive transfer, or other methods of wrongful expropriation, or may be considered to have been unlawfully appropriated, depending on the specific circumstances ("AAM Guidelines Concerning the Unlawful Appropriation of Objects during the Nazi Era").

GLOSSARY RELATING TO PROVENANCE, CULTURAL PROPERTY

ALR (The Art Loss Register): the world's largest private database of lost and stolen art, antiques and collectables. It includes item registration, search and recovery services to collectors, museums conducting due diligence in provenance research, the art trade, insurers, worldwide law enforcement agencies, and private individuals. It uses state of the art technology and a team of specially trained professional art historians. The worldwide team has been deliberately constructed so as to offer a range of language capabilities as well as specialties.

ARPA (Archeological Resources Protection Act of 1979): United States statute establishing requirements to protect archaeological resources and sites on public lands and Indian lands and to foster increased cooperation and exchange of information between governmental authorities, the professional archaeological community, and private individuals. The Act established civil and criminal penalties for the destruction or alteration of cultural resources. The U.S. Department of the Interior regulates under the ARPA and the National Park Service regulates under the ARPA for the care of federally owned and administered collections.

CPIA (Convention on Cultural Property Implementation Act): the United States' legislation, passed in 1983, implementing the 1970 UNESCO Convention.

Interpol List (Interpol Cultural Property Database): a database of stolen objects maintained by Interpol

Headquarters, Lyon, France, with access through Interpol Washington, D.C. Requests for stolen objects to be added to the database or searches to be performed must be made through a law enforcement agency.

NAGPRA (Native American Graves Protection and Repatriation Act, 1990): United States statute providing for the return of certain Native American cultural items—human remains, funerary objects, sacred objects, or objects of cultural patrimony—to lineal descendants, and culturally affiliated Indian tribes and Native Hawaiian organizations. NAGPRA includes provisions for unclaimed and culturally unidentifiable Native American cultural items, intentional and inadvertent discovery of Native American cultural items on Federal and tribal lands, and penalties for noncompliance and illegal trafficking.

NSAF (National Stolen Art File): an FBI computerized index of stolen art and cultural property as reported to the FBI by law enforcement agencies throughout the US and internationally. The NSAF consists of images and physical descriptions of stolen and recovered objects, in addition to investigative case information.

NSPA (National Stolen Property Act, 1934): United States statute that extended the National Motor Vehicle Theft Act to other property. Originally intended to coordinate state and federal prosecution of the illegal interstate movement of fraudulent securities, counterfeit money, and stolen goods. Recently, federal attorneys have used the NSPA to prosecute the illegal importation of cultural property into the U.S.

Nazi Era Provenance Internet Portal (NEPIP): co-created and hosted by AAM, a searchable online registry of objects in U.S. museum collections that changed hands in Continental Europe during the Nazi era (1933-1945).

UNESCO Convention (1970 Convention) (The Convention on the Means of Prohibiting and Preventing the Illicit Import, Export and Transfer of Ownership of Cultural Property): the 1970 UNESCO Convention declares as illegal the import, export or transfer of ownership of cultural property. By ratifying this Convention, each signing country agrees to adopt the necessary measures:

(a) to prevent museums within their territories from acquiring cultural property which has been illegally exported;

(b) to prohibit the import of cultural property stolen from a museum or a public institution after the entry into force of the Convention;

(c) at the request of the country of origin, to recover and return any such cultural property stolen and imported. The UNESCO Convention of 1970 has no retroactive effect; it only enters into effect on the day of its official ratification. [US signed the 1970 Convention and implemented it through the CPIA (Convention on Cultural Property Implementation Act) in 1983.]

3E | DOCUMENTING CONTEMPORARY ART

MARK B. SCHLEMMER

INTRODUCTION

Conserving, documenting and defining the parameters of contemporary art are major issues for registrars. It is a reality that has emerged from necessity. The issues are not new, but the volume of material that needs a non-traditional approach has increased greatly in the last decade. The materials artists choose in creating work obviously have no limits. In addition to traditional media like wood, paint, stone, paper, and canvas, artists increasingly use ephemeral materials, detritus, and digital content to meet their creative needs. A painting or drawing may be partially defined by its two-dimensionality, but with much of contemporary art, installation art in particular, nailing down such defining parameters has become all but impossible. That is not to say that attempts to identify or give meaning to such issues were ignored or not important in the past, but rather that situations were dealt with ad hoc as they emerged. Frequently, museum professionals are forced to install, and perhaps more significantly re-install, contemporary work without sufficient guidelines. *The key to dealing with newly created art is in its documentation.*

Traditionally, the documentation of artwork has focused on materiality and issues of authenticity. Materials are undeniably important to the way we understand art. A working knowledge of and familiarity with various media will allow a registrar to forecast storage needs, foster collections care, and recommend exhibition guidelines. In other words, the materials indeed may be important, but the conceptual core remains the essence of the work. The new challenge is how to effectively document a conceptual idea.

In order to document contemporary art, strategies that incorporate broader definitions of *how* to document, in addition to a new perspective on recording the perception of the work itself, will aid in creating the object files at the core of all museum collections.

ARTIST QUESTIONNAIRES AND INTERVIEWS

Often, the best source of information regarding how artwork is defined comes directly from the artists. It is vital for any museum that is acquiring, or thinking of acquiring, art by a living artist to devise a documentation strategy to record the artist's intent. Not only is this an ethical mandate in relation to the museum's mission to safeguard acquired artwork for perpetuity, but it is increasingly a response to protect the museum from potential litigious situations involving copyright and other artists' rights. Questionnaires and interviews are a good starting point to reach this end.

The main purpose behind documenting the artist's intent via interviews and questionnaires is to record his or her views regarding potential changes to the parameters of subsequent installation. The interview will provide more complete results, but the questionnaire seems to be more widely utilized. Written questionnaires, which tend to focus mostly on very factual information like the brand of playback equipment (for work that incorporates video), dates of production, materials used, etc., are indeed very useful to the museum. However, even art museums that advocate for the persistent use of questionnaires admit that they are not enough. Not every hypothetical situation requiring a resolution can be imagined at the time of acquisition.

Fortunately, these questionnaires need not be created from scratch. "Media Matters," a research project from England's Tate on the care of time-based media works of art, has created resources and templates that anyone can freely adapt and use. The sample questions are straightforward and of vital importance: "What are the essential vs. desirable exhibition conditions, including space requirements?" and "What can and cannot be changed in the display?"[1] These are just a sample of the questions directed at the artist to help the museum in assessing the impact the work will have if it becomes a part of the permanent collection. A deeper investigation into the artist's thoughts regarding his/her work is often best elaborated via direct interviews.

As a response to museum professionals who were seeking guidance on formulating questionnaires, The International Network for the Conservation of Contemporary Art (INCCA) established an effective general resource guide to conducting artists' interviews for the purpose of garnering insight into their oeuvre. With a view to collecting and effectively exhibiting art in keeping with the artists' intent, the guide proposes seven approaches or methodologies to conducting artist interviews: communication via letter, questionnaire, phone call, face-to-face conversation, brief or limited interview, extended interview, and working together with the artist.[2]

The most basic communication with the artist begins with a letter or email, composed with very explicit and concise questions in mind. The goal is not only to acquire insight, but also to create a document for the object file. Unfortunately, the museum cannot always rely on receiving a timely or appropriate response to a letter or email. The same holds true for a more elaborate questionnaire. Letters and questionnaires demand a lot of the artist's time, and motivation to complete them may not be a top priority for the artist. Similar to a letter, a questionnaire cannot, however, be depended upon to elicit the breadth and complexity needed to document an artwork. Certain queries would be too unwieldy to answer succinctly in a written format.

To address the relationship among the various components that comprise a total work usually requires being physically in the space with the installed work. This is especially true of work that has a highly interactive quality, is composed of complicated arrangements, or employs the accumulation of many parts of seemingly random detritus. To address such issues, oral communication is usually a better alternative.

Phone calls are often effective in clarifying very precise details or in obtaining answers to specific concerns. They also permit a more fluid conversation which may lead to direct questions not previously anticipated. As with any type of communication, the person initiating the call will be at the mercy of the artist, and certain questions may be construed as an interruption to his or her work or an invasion of privacy. Additionally, not everyone communicates effectively via telephone. Face-to-face conversations may be the better all-around strategy.

The best face-to-face conversations take place in the physical presence of the artwork itself. As in all cases, extensive preparation on the part of the interviewer will provide the best results. Careful consideration should be made regarding the duration of the conversation and to judiciously controlling the direction of the dialogue. These interviews can be either brief undertakings or extended investigations.

In either case, it is often beneficial to prepare the artist with the content of the interview ahead of time. For brief or limited interviews, documentation techniques should be determined in advance and confirmed with the artist. Audio, video, and notes are all viable recording options, but video provides more content upon which to base future conclusions.

An extended interview allows one not only to probe more deeply into particular works, techniques, or intents, but also permits far-reaching exploration of larger themes and connections in the artist's oeuvre. The questions for an extended interview are usually more open-ended and can provide deeper layers of content. Obviously, the extended interview shows a commitment on the part of the artist to documenting effectively as much about his or her thoughts and expectations as possible, providing a very useful level of information.

Finally, observing an artist's working session, or, better yet, an installation of his or her work in which he or she is participating, may provide information that goes far beyond responses to questions. A certain level of trust and comfort must exist for an artist to agree to such a session. The interviewer must be able to read the situation well and know how far to take the conversation. As with all interviews, the key is in the preparation.

It is recommended that notes and annotations

of the interviews always be presented to the artist afterwards for approval. The end result of all interviews and questionnaires is a record that provides the museum with vital information to turn to in the future.

The timing of these interviews and of the documentation in general is important. The more time that has passed from the creation of the work to the documentation of it, the more removed the artist will be from it. Additionally, after the work is created, it takes its place in art history while the artist continues to develop and advance his or her personal progression. Delayed documentation of a work can leave the artist too far removed from what was important and influential at the time of creation.

INCCA encourages multiple interview sessions and even multiple voices in conducting the interview (curator, conservator, technician, art historian, arthandler, registrar, etc.) Of course, there will be limits on the extent of these interviews depending on budget, time, and available personnel, all factors that have in the past been used as arguments or justification for not conducting interviews in the first place. It is also worth emphasizing that the artist's opinion is only one to be taken into consideration. The museum has a voice, and a very strong one, in making decisions as to the future of its collections. Conservators have another voice, sometimes in concert with the artist, sometimes with the museum. In the end, a collaborative agreement between all parties is the ultimate goal.

DOCUMENTING INSTALLATION ART

In recent years, more installation art has found its place among the permanent collections of art museums. The complex environments of installation art prove to be popular with artists who seek to branch out into a fourth dimension (interactivity) with their artistic creation. However, the inherently complex nature of installation art, in particular those works which comprise elements of new or time-based media, require a new approach to museum procedures, especially the need to draw upon a wide body of experts from both within and outside the museum community. Conservators, curators, registrars,

technicians, artists' assistants, architects, and the artists themselves may be called upon to help create a precisely documented account of the installation for the museum's object file. Once again, budget, time, and personnel will have an impact on the extent of the documentation, but almost any institution can undertake video documentation of the installation.

The benefits of video documentation of installation art include capturing the "overall impression, visual aspects of components, relation of components, relation to space/architecture, sound, movement, choreography, time-specific aspects, interactivity and presence (and experience) of the audience."[3] All of these aspects would be extremely unruly, or even impossible, to document in written form. Just as proponents of artist questionnaires concede the benefit of video recording, the same is seen in reverse. Video does not render written documentation obsolete, but rather augments it in ways that make a more nearly complete package. Video documentation fills in the gaps of information essential to understanding what cannot be written down.

The key to video documentation for the purpose of facilitating the re-installation of the work is exactitude. Describing the relationship and position of individual components to each other and to the complete installation is the core of why video documentation should be utilized. In order for this information to be useful for re-installations, this visual record must be paired with an explanation from the artist as to the importance of these relationships and the extent of their variability. Without this key idea, re-installations could exaggerate details and relationships which are not so tightly defined in the mind of the artist.

In addition to documenting relationships, it is essential to record processes. One video documentation strategy that can capture the installation process is the use of static surveillance cameras. Long-exposure recordings, not helpful in their original form, are viewed in a sped-up or fast-forward manner to provide a record of the specific installation process that will benefit those undertaking the same in the future. However, this type of documentation lacks an essential level of detail and should only be used in a very general way to steer future installations.

A complete video documentation package for the purpose of guiding re-installation (as opposed to a publicity video, etc.) should include a general installation (static) overview, zoom views of details, recordings of sounds, and voice-overs indicating elements that may not be clear from a merely visual standpoint.[4]

Even though it seems that video documentation is the best way to guarantee a successful and true iteration of future installations, the issues of cost and time loom above every project. The budget will dictate to what degree video documentation takes place, and the cost to do so should be included in the pre-acquisition considerations by museum acquisition committees. Videos can be prepared by staff members, contracted out to semi-professionals, or in the best-of-all-worlds completed by video specialists. The latter will be able to provide the best post-production options.

Augmented with research, the results of artist questionnaires, and other written documentation, the complexities of documenting installation art are more effectively tackled by utilizing video for registrarial ends.

FURTHER STRATEGIES FOR DOCUMENTING NEW MEDIA ART

One of the key concepts to adopt in documenting new art is the need to approach it in ways that embrace what is at the core of the work independently from how we document the media. Minimal, conceptual, and much of new media art are often not reliant on any physical object. Still, the work must be documented in a way that renders such complex realities in a usable registrarial format. "Preserving the Immaterial," a conference at the Solomon R. Guggenheim Museum in New York from March 30–31, 2001, addressed these issues head on. One of the results was the creation of "The Variable Media Approach," a strategy that remains relevant for capturing essential and core concepts in our documentation of art. At the center of this approach is a way of identifying the essence of the conceptual base of the work.

As proposed by almost everyone involved in any aspect of documenting contemporary art, the approach to variable media is based upon formulating a questionnaire and dialogue with the artist to serve as a springboard in identifying non-media specific concepts. The Variable Media Questionnaire is broken down into eight sub-topics, each addressing a particular behavior. These ideal states are:

•installed: implying that the work has more complex exhibition requirements than mounting on a wall or placing on a pedestal; issues of site-specific placement, scale, access, and lighting are addressed.

•performed: emphasizing that the process is integral to the end product/object created; the artist therefore provides instructions for performers, installers, etc., in addition to specifications of sets, props, etc.

•interactive: referencing not only computer-based work, but also any installation in which the visitor is essential to the work through active participation with it; this method documents how and to what extent external participation is carried out, and whether this interaction is recorded.

•reproduced: documenting any medium, such as film, audio, or video, in which the result of producing a copy from an original master results in a loss of quality.

•duplicated: explaining that a work does not lose any quality when copied from the original; most works of digital media and ready-made, mass-produced objects typically are considered as duplicated.

•encoded: implying that the essence of the work is created with a computer code or special language; depending on the nature of the code, it may be possible to archive the transcript or notation separately and independently from the work.

•networked: designating that the work is experienced via the Internet or some other electronic system; websites, email, surveillance, etc., are all networked behaviors.[5]

Identifying work in terms of behaviors references

it in its ideal state. However, any changes or alterations over time, whether happening naturally or as a result of conservation interventions, produce a shift away from this ideal. The documentation of the artist's philosophy over these questions will aid the museum in making decisions about dealing with these eventual changes.

CONCLUSION

Proper documentation does indeed take many hours of staff time to produce correctly. Museum environments are undeniably hectic and there is always high demand on making the best use of limited staffs. However, when it comes to documenting much of contemporary art, making the effort will save both time and money for the museum in the long term. Re-installations have the potential to create an overwhelming array of problems. If registrars can anticipate, even to the slightest extent, future installation requirements, they will alleviate the burden of tedious and time-consuming tasks required to answer questions of appropriate, ethical, and realistic re-installations. This positive outcome will become widespread only when museum administrators make proper documentation a routine undertaking.

In conclusion, the multivalent and complicated challenge of properly documenting the conceptual and technical variance for the reinstallation of contemporary art can be summed up by five key ideas:

1. There is no need to reinvent the wheel! Various resources already exist online that any museum can exploit to assist in preparing condition reports, installation guides, facilities reports, etc., with an emphasis on the specific needs and idiosyncrasies of contemporary art.

2. It is important to document the artist's intent. Again, by turning to existing guides for advice, registrars can effectively formulate questions that elicit the most beneficial information for the future installations of the work.

3. Proper documentation necessitates calling upon the expertise of others. Curators, registrars, and conservators are logical allies within the museum community, but architects, technicians, and artist assistants may all help provide essential details.

4. New media are at the same time new and familiar. To document time-based media one must look at it in terms beyond aesthetics or materiality. By learning to reference the behaviors of a work, one can reach the essence of the digital content.

5. Documentation involves more than creating a written record. Photography and, more importantly, video will serve the documentation process well and permit a visual and aural record of the complicated relationships of installation components and of abstract concepts like interactivity. Again, online sources can teach museum professionals the ins and outs of effectively documenting an installation with video.

Every new work of art is its own unique world. Because of that, it may be impossible to approach any kind of preferred practice for its documentation. Still, guidelines and suggestions from those who have studied and researched new media, conceptual, minimal, and installation art can provide insight and encouragement to aid in formulating effective strategies to assess the documentary requirements for each individual work. In the end, not only will the museum professionals charged with the stewardship of collections be permitted to address the specific requirements of contemporary art ethically and responsibly, but they will also be providing their future colleagues with the tools they will need, and will appreciate, when called upon to oversee subsequent installations. •

NOTES

1. "Acquisitions: Pre-Acquisitions." *Media Matters.* Tate. 7 Feb. 2007 http://www.tate.org.uk/research/

tateresearch/majorprojects/mediamatters/acquisitions/preacquisition.html/>.

2. "Guide to Good Practice: Artists' Interviews." *International Network for the Conservation of Contemporary Art.* 7 Oct. 2007 <http://www.incca.org>.

3. Wijers, Gaby. "Video Documentation of Installations." Inside Installations. 10 Mar. 2008 <http://insideinstallations.org>.

4. Ibid.

5. Depocas, Alain, Jon Ippolito, and Caitlin Jones, eds. *The Variable Media Approach.* New York: Guggenheim Museum Publications. 2003. 46.

The Basics I | HYPOTHETICALS

1

You have arrived at a new job in an anthropology museum. One of your first finds is a metal cabinet in the "holding area" for collections. It contains various objects, some with handwritten notes under them, some with no notes at all. The first you look at says "Possibly a gift, 1982" and the second says "M. Campbell identification request, 12/91." The list goes on.

What are the issues with these objects and how do you resolve them? What do you recommend for a system that will keep this from happening in the future?

2

Everything is in place for an important exhibition. The couriers for several loans have come and gone and are in agreement with placement, security, and installation. You then receive three unanticipated requests: special events needs a bar in the entrance gallery for a major donor reception, education has come up with an innovative activity and requests that it be conducted (with blunt scissors and color pencils) in the exhibition space, and adult programs calls to say that they are getting so many group requests for tours that they need to raise the number of people allowed in the gallery at one time

Your response?

3

How do you determine whether a donor has full authority to give an object to the museum?

What do you do when you believe a gift has been finalized and another party arrives with a claim to the object?

4

If you could develop the most efficient and thorough procedure possible for accepting and processing gifts into your museum's collection, what would it be?

5

You have received a major contemporary work that has a life-span of perhaps 30 years because of the off-gassing material from which it is made.

Discuss documentation, storage, care.

6

What are the various ways that you can prove that a gift for the museum collection has been finalized?

What constitutes intent, acceptance, and physical receipt?

7

A major donor calls on Dec. 24, offering a substantial year-end gift. However, your curator is out of the country until the new year.

The director worries about offending the donor, but can you accept the donation without the curator's approval?

8

What procedures can you initiate to help the year-end gift-processing run more smoothly?

9

Your museum has acquired a piece by a living artist. The artist has supplied specific installation instructions; however, these instructions will not provide adequate support and protection for the piece in the gallery.

What steps can you take to find a solution?

Would there be any difference if the piece were on loan, not acquired?

10

Your museum is hosting an exhibition of digital and media art. You receive on loan many DVDs with digital artwork. The insurance values differ widely: some lenders place a value on the intellectual artwork, while others require insurance only for the physical disk.

How do you bring some equality to this situation?

Do you need to?

11

A trustee has for many years kept objects on deposit at your museum; he simply does not have room to store them at home. The problem is, your storage space is limited as well. This trustee has been very generous to the museum and the administration is concerned about offending him.

What can you do?

12

How and when does your museum offer insurance coverage to objects on temporary deposit?

When do you require lenders to maintain their own insurance?

3F | OLD LOANS

ILDIKO POGANY DeANGELIS

Very few museum registrars are spared the vexing problem of "old loans." The term refers to expired loans or loans of unlimited duration left unclaimed by lenders who cannot be readily located by the museum.[1] These objects may have come in to the museum under formal loans for exhibition purposes or under temporary custody arrangements for examination or study by museum staff.[2] The lenders have long since died, moved, or in any case, have failed to maintain contact with the museum. As registrars are routinely assigned responsibility to monitor loans and to account for objects and their documentation in the custody of the museum, it is to this office that the task of resolving the old loan conundrum is usually assigned.

Because daily tasks quickly consume a registrar's time, often little or none remains to spare on old loans.[3] Nevertheless, museums and registrars are well advised to make time for old loans because the mere passage of time will not cure the problem. Often the older the loan gets, the harder it may be to resolve. Lacking legal title to the unclaimed objects, the museum can only make limited use of them, all the while bearing the costs and burdens of storage space, record maintenance, climate control, security, periodic inspection, insurance, and general overhead.[4]

To understand what must be done, it is important to appreciate the legal constraints involved. The basic legal relationship between the lender and the museum is a bailment, under which the museum as bailee (borrower) generally has the obligation to care for the object until the bailor (lender) comes to claim it.[5] This obligation can go on indefinitely because the passage of time will not alter this legal relationship. For example, if a lender dies, his or her ownership interest in the object will pass to heirs. Often, determining the identity and location of heirs entitles to the object may be a difficult and time consuming, if not impossible, task. To make things worse, returning the object to the wrong party may open the museum to liability for a claim brought by the rightful owner.

The key to resolving the old loan dilemma is for the museum to break the bailment relationship as soon as possible. Unfortunately, this is not easily done under general legal principles.

In recognition of these difficulties, 40 states, as of 2009, have passed old loan statutes that specifically make this task easier for museums.[6] These old loan laws spell out the mechanisms by which the lender's ownership of the object can be cut off, making it possible for the museum to move with some assurance toward gaining title to the object. With the title secure, the museum then may use or dispose of an object as it sees fit. More will be said about these state statutes and the general approaches they take, but first a discussion of common law principles (principles that govern in absence of a statute) is in order. These principles usually prevail in states without specific old loan statutes, and a knowledge of these principles also assists in appreciating and/or interpreting specific old loan statutes.

THE COMMON LAW SOLUTION

In states without old loan statutes, museums are left with general principles of common law to guide them. Common law refers to principles that do not rest for their authority on any express statute, but upon statements of principles found in court decisions. The application of these principles to old loans has not been fully tested in court. As a result, museums are left with some legal uncertainties.[7] Nevertheless, under these principles, to break the bailment relationship, the museum must take actions inconsistent with the terms of the bailment and call the lender's attention to the fact that title to the object is being challenged and could be lost if the lender remains silent. For example, the museum should send a letter to the lender stating that the museum is terminating the loan, and unless the lender comes forward to claim the objects or make arrangements for their successful return by a certain date, the museum will take title to the objects as of that date. If the lender is aware of the museum's conversion (a legal term meaning unauthorized assumption of ownership of property belonging to another), the lender, under general principles of law, must come forward to protect his or her ownership interests. If the lender fails to claim the object or to bring his or her claim or suit to court within a specific time after the museum's conversion of the object, the lender's ownership rights may be lost.

The specific time periods to bring claims to court are provided in state laws, and are called statutes of limitations. Lawsuits are barred that are not brought within prescribed limitation periods. The purpose of statutes of limitations is to encourage claimants to take timely action before evidence fades and witnesses die. Statutes of limitations vary from state to state and with the nature of the claim. For example, a claim for breach of contract will have a different limitation period from a claim based on negligence causing personal injury. Although it is relatively simple to determine the length of the limitation period in any state for a claim of conversion, the more difficult issue is to determine when the limitation period begins to run against an owner to extinguish his claim. The general rule is that the owner of property converted by another must bring his or her claim to court within the limitation period that begins after his or her "cause of action" arises. A cause of action is a set of facts that give a person the right to file a suit in court.

Under the law of bailment, the cause of action usually arises when the lender demands return of the object and the borrower refuses. The lender's cause of action may also arise when he or she is put on notice that the borrower is claiming title to the object, in effect, refusing to return the object. Thus, to utilize the statute of limitations to extinguish a lender's right to an unclaimed object, the goal for the museum is to make sure the lender has notice that

the museum intends to terminate the loan and to claim the loaned object as its own if the lender fails to come and get it or arrange for its return.[8]

To ensure that the limitations period is triggered, the museum should notify the lender by certified mail, return receipt requested, to prove that the lender received actual notice of the museum's actions. Upon receipt of the notice, the limitations period should begin to run and after its expiration, the lender who has failed to take action should be barred from any further claim to the object. Title to the object, in effect, then belongs to the museum. At this time, the museum is free to do whatever it wishes with the object, to keep it, to lend it, or to dispose of it.

Anyone who has ever worked with old loans inevitably would ask the next question: What if the lender is unknown or the lender or heirs cannot be located? Are there any alternatives to actual notice? One court decision from the District of Columbia, in the McCagg case, involved an old loan, and the court suggested that constructive notice to the lender might be legally sufficient where actual notice is not possible. The term "constructive notice" refers to notice to unknown or missing individuals by publication in a newspaper. If done properly, the law will presume that the notice reached the individual whether or not he actually saw the notice in the newspaper. All the old loan statutes discussed below have implemented the constructive notice approach to notify missing lenders. The question remains whether constructive notice will be legally sufficient without an applicable state statute in place that provides how and when this may be done. Until this has been tested in court, museums must face an element of uncertainty in this area. This uncertainty should not prevent museums from proceeding, because doing nothing affords no chance of yielding any positive results. Each museum is urged, however, to consult with its legal counsel before initiating notice to lenders by publication.

In any event, the court in the McCagg case cautioned that constructive notice may be available only if actual notice is not possible. Thus, a museum must be in a position to show that the lender or heirs could not be located after reasonable efforts by the museum to do so. As to what constitutes reasonable efforts, once again there is little guidance in existing legal precedents. One commentator suggests that the following sources in addition to the museum's own records should be consulted in the course of a reasonable search for the lender: probate records, telephone directories, real estate records, and vital (death) records.[9] Depending on the circumstances, other avenues such as social registers or cemetery records may be available. It is absolutely essential that the museum document every effort taken to locate lenders because the museum's records may become evidence should a lender or heir suddenly surface years later and demand return of the object. The value of the objects in question may have an impact on the extent of the efforts to locate the lenders. If after reasonable efforts, the whereabouts of the lender or heirs are still unknown, the museum may try constructive notice by publication in a newspaper.

The notice in the newspapers should include as much of the following information as possible:

•Date of the notice

•Name of the lender

•Description of the item loaned

•Date of the original loan

•Name and address of the museum staff to contact

•Statement that the museum is terminating the loan and will take title to the object if it is not claimed by a specified date

It is suggested that this notice should be published once a week for three consecutive weeks in a newspaper of general circulation in the county of the lender's last known address and the county or municipality where the museum is located.[10] The statute of limitations should begin to run after the date set in the notice as a deadline for contacting the museum—whether or not the lender or heirs have actually seen the published notice.

If the lender fails to come forward before the date given by actual or constructive notice, the museum should amend its records immediately to reflect the ownership change for the object as of that date. In addition, the museum should note in the records the date of expiration of claims under that state's statute of limitations. Although the museum asserts ownership from the date the object is accessioned, its title to the object would be subject to challenge in a claim brought to court by the lender or heirs up to the time the applicable limitations period for filing suit had expired. Therefore, the file should note that prior to the expiration of the statute of limitations, the object should not be disposed of by the museum. For example, in the museum's published notice, the date in which title is claimed is June 1, 1995. Having failed to hear from the lender or heirs, on June 1, 1995, the museum accessions the object. Having been advised by counsel that the limitations period for conversion is three years, the museum will note in the records that the object should not be disposed of prior to June 2, 1998.

In planning a systematic approach to resolve old loans in states where no statute exists, museums are well advised to seek the advice of counsel in establishing procedures and forms for this purpose. One publication highly recommended to aid museums and their counsel in this effort is entitled *Practical Guidelines in Resolving Old Loans: Guidelines for Museums* by Agnes Tabah (see bibliography). This paper has step-by-step instructions and sample forms that may be very helpful. It can be found in Marie Malaro's 1998 *Legal Primer on Managing Museum Collections*, pp. 304–311.

However, because of a lack of clear precedents, even if all recommended steps are taken, there are no guarantees that claims will not be brought against the museum for conversion of the loaned object. In the worst case, a lender or heirs may surface years later and institute a lawsuit. At this point, if a court should determine that the steps taken by the museum to gain title were legally insufficient, the museum may need to return the object. If the object was disposed of in the interim, the museum may be ordered to compensate the lender for the value of the object, possibly as of the date of the lender's return. Although the risk of a legal suit with the attendant adverse publicity should not be underestimated, this risk needs to be balanced against the substantial benefits gained by freeing the museum's collections from unwanted objects that are costly to maintain, and by having reliable, up-to-date records of objects in its collections. If the objects are of little value, it is unlikely that anyone is ever going to sue. If someone does threaten a lawsuit, it is a relatively simple matter to offer to pay him or her the value of the object to make the claim go away. If the museum has disposed of the object after acquiring title, it should have an excellent record of the object's value at the time of disposal. In any event, the museum's counsel may be able to negotiate a settlement without the need to resort to a formal legal proceeding.

LEGISLATIVE SOLUTION: STATE OLD LOAN STATUTES

A list of states that have passed old loan statutes appears in a table format. For a museum located in one of these states, resolving old loans will require following the dictates of the applicable statute in Chapter 3G. While state old loan statutes vary in approach, they all establish specific mechanisms by which the museum may terminate the loan and take title to objects left unclaimed by lenders. In operation, the legislative solution mimics the common law approach but adds clarity and some degree of certainty about the adequacy of the procedures. In some cases, old loan statutes eliminate some cumbersome steps required under the common law approach. The usual scheme is for the law to prescribe a notice procedure by which lenders are notified by the museum that the loan is terminated. The notice procedures may apply to expired loans as well as to indefinite loans that have been at the museum for an extended period.

The notice may take two general forms. The first is by mail to the lender of record at his last known address and the second is notice by publication in newspapers. Some statutes only require notice by mail to the name and address of the lender as it appears in the museum's records. If that information is not accurate or if it is incomplete, no further search for the lender is required. Other statutes require a "reasonable search" for the lender, often not giving much guidance as to what the term means. If the lender cannot be reached by mail, the museum may proceed with notification by publication in a

newspaper. If, after notice, no one comes forward to make a claim within the prescribed time period (ranging from 30 days to seven years), title to the object passes to the museum. Several states allow museums to take title to an object without giving notice if there was no contact between the museum and the lender for a long time. For example, California allows the museum to take title if there has been not contact with the lender for at least 25 years as evidenced in the museum's records.[11]

In addition, old loan statutes may impose obligations on lenders to notify museums of change of address and changes in ownership of the property.[12] Some statutes address the issue of undertaking conservation work on unclaimed loans.[13]

An important question not yet answered is whether these statutes will pass constitutional challenges that may be brought to court by disgruntled lenders. Such challenges to state laws may be brought under the 14th Amendment of the U.S. Constitution, alleging that the old loan statute deprives the lender of his or her property without the due process of law. The question presented in such cases is whether the law affords owners adequate notice and opportunity to protect their ownership rights before such rights are cut off. As of 2010, there have been no published court decisions testing the constitutionality of any state old loan statute, and we have yet to see how a court may view these statutes with regard to due process questions.

One unpublished study indicates that many museums may not have begun to implement applicable old loan statutes. This conclusion is based on the sparse replies to a questionnaire on implementation of old loan legislation.[14] The study posits the following reasons for this sluggishness. To use the statutes systematically, museums need to inventory their collections to determine which objects are in fact old loans. Inventories require time and effort and are too easily relegated to the back burner. Also, some museums may be reluctant to implement the statutes, fearing that important objects will be lost if lenders actually come forward and reclaim loaned objects. Finally, some may fear the administrative burdens that may be presented by spurious claims. The experience reported by the few museums that have implemented their legislation shows the opposite.

Contrary to fears, large numbers of people did not come forward to claim objects. Moreover, implementation of the old loan statutes gave registrars a useful instrument to provide vacillating lenders incentive to make decisions on disposition of their loaned property.[15]

HOW TO AVOID THE PROBLEM OF OLD LOANS IN THE FUTURE

Given the time, effort, and costs involved in resolving old loans, museums should institute safeguards to avoid this problem in the future. Museums should borrow objects for a limited duration only (usually one year) with the expiration date specifically stated in the loan agreement. If the object is needed longer, it is better to renew the loan than to agree to a longer initial term. More frequent contacts with lenders will avoid the missing lender situation. Loan agreements should specify that it is the lender's obligation to notify the museum of a change in the lender's address or a change in the ownership of the loaned object. Moreover, loan agreements should state that if, at the expiration of the loan, the museum is unable to contact the lender to make arrangements for the return of the object, the museum will store the object for a set period of years at the lender's expense. If, after this period, the lender still fails to come forward after notice by mail is sent by the museum to the lender's address of record, the museum will deem that an unrestricted gift of the object is made by the lender to the museum. In effect, the loan agreement will put the lender on notice of the museum's claim to the object after a set period of time if the lender fails to maintain contact or refuses to pick up the object.

Objects left at the museum for identification, authentication, or examination are more likely to be left unclaimed than objects borrowed by the museum for exhibition purposes. The negligible value of some of these objects may remove an incentive for their owners to return to claim them. To avoid this risk, these objects should be processed immediately by the museum. Each should be documented with a temporary custody receipt, signed by the owner. If an object

was mailed unsolicited to the museum, the package should be returned within days to the sender. If more time is needed, the temporary custody receipt should be mailed to the sender for signature. The length of the museum's custody specified in the receipt should be limited to a period significantly shorter than the duration of a standard incoming loan. For example, a museum may decide that the maximum time for temporary custody is three months, subject to extension by special permission only. The temporary custody receipt should specify the exact method to be used for return of the object and include a provision, similar to one used in a formal loan agreement, that infers a gift to the museum if the object is not claimed after a limited storage period subsequent to the expiration date on the receipt.

CONCLUSION

As a public trust, a museum has a legal responsibility to make the best use of its assets. Prudent collections management dictates that museums should pursue systematic efforts to clean up old loans that eat up valuable storage space and consume scarce staff and financial resources. But procedures should also be in place to avoid these situations. It is the registrar's office that usually plays a critical role in developing and implementing ways to banish the old loan problem in a museum. ●

NOTES

1. The term "permanent loan" was used in the profession some years ago. Loans by definition are temporary and therefore it is unclear what the parties had in mind when the arrangements for "permanent loans" were made. Often a review of the museum's records may indicate that a gift was actually intended or completed. However, if title to the object still rests with the lender, then permanent loaned objects should be treated as loans of unlimited duration.

2. It is important to note that "old loans" does not include undocumented objects found in the museum's collections. These "found-in-collection (FIC)" objects lack any documentation as to how they were acquired by the museum. This chapter deals with objects that are accompanied by documentation that a loan to the museum was intended by the owner. With FIC objects, there is no evidence held by the museum that someone else owns these objects. Rather, the museum's undisturbed possession for an extended period supports a presumption that ownership was transferred to

the museum at the time the objects were acquired. Unless and until someone shows up at the museum and can overcome this presumption with evidence that he or she has clearer title to a FIC object, the museum generally may treat a FIC object as its own. However, disposal of objects of unconfirmed ownership should involve further considerations and assistance from the museum's legal counsel. (See deaccession risk chart)

3. This situation may be getting worse as many museums are forced to down-size due to budgetary constraints.

4. Wise, L.K. Old Loans: A Collections Management Problem, *Legal Problems of Museum Administration,* ALI-ABA (1990), at 44; Tabah, A. The Practicalities of Resolving Old Loans: Guidelines for Museums, in Malaro, M. A Legal Primer on managing Museum Collections, pp. 304–311.

5. For a full discussion of the legal problems of unclaimed loans and possible solutions, see Malaro, M. Unclaimed Loans, *A Legal Primer in Managing Museum Collections,* Chapter VII, Smithsonian Institution Press, (1985), pp. 183–203.

6. In addition to these 40 states, the Mid-Atlantic Association of Museums Registrars Committee established an Old Loan Task Force in the late 1990s to draft model legislation for that region that includes Pennsylvania, Maryland, Virginia, Washington, D.C., Delaware, New York, and New Jersey. That model has been included in Chapter 3H.

7. In the one reported court decision from the District of Columbia involving an old loan, the court held that the paintings on loan to the museum for decades had to be returned to the lender's heirs. In re Therese McCagg, 450 A.2d 414 (D.C. 1982). The court noted that the museum had failed in that case to make a reasonable effort to notify the lender's heirs and refused to find that the loan had expired at the lender's death. However, the court noted in a footnote that if the lenders cannot be located by the museum after reasonable efforts, notice to the lenders or heirs by publication in a newspaper may be legally sufficient. Notice by publication was not directly at issue in the case. Id. at 418.

8. In addition to the statute of limitations approach, the legal doctrines of adverse possession and laches may help a museum successfully defend a case brought by a long overdue lender for return of an old loan. The usefulness of these doctrines is discussed in Malaro, M. *Legal Primer* at 189–94 and DeAngelis, I. AOld Loans—Laches to the Rescue? *Legal Problems of Museum Administration,* ALI-ABA (1992) at 202. Actions taken by the museum under the statute of limitations approach discussed in this chapter will also support these alternate defenses and are not separately addressed here.

9. Tabah, A. The Practicalities of Resolving Old Loans: Guidelines for Museums, *Legal Problems of Museum Administration,* ALI-ABA (1992), at 330–31.

10. Id.

11. Cal. Civil Code Sec. 1899.10(b)

12. For example, see the old loan statutes of California, Wyoming, Missouri, and Kansas.

13. For example, see the old loan statutes of Indiana, Missouri, and South Carolina.

14. Tabah, A. Old Loans: State Legislative Solutions, unpublished research paper dated December 4, 1991, prepared for the George Washington University Museum Studies Program course on Collections Management: Legal and Ethical Issues.

15. Id.

3G | OLD LOANS: STATE LEGISLATION THROUGH 2009

UPDATED AND EDITED BY KATHRYN SPECKART

SUMMARY			
States with Old Loans laws only	15		
States with Old Loans and FIC laws	25		
States with no Old Loan or FIC laws	11 (with DC)		

State	Citation	Comments	FIC provision
Alabama	§ 41-6-70 to 41-6-75	Applies only to collections held by the Department of Archives and History	"Undocumented property" must be held for 5 years or longer and remain unclaimed. The Museum must publish a notice at least once each week for two consecutive weeks with specified information. If after 90 days from the second notice, no one claims title, it become property of the Department.
Alaska	§ 14.57.200 to 14.57.290	Article 1 (starting with 14.57.010) applies to the State Museum only. Article 3 (starting with 14.57.200) applies to property held by museums; notifications of all Native American FIC property must be sent to all Native Corporations	"Undocumented Property" must be held for 7 years or longer, verified by museum records, with no contact or claim by any person. The museum must publish a notice once a week for four weeks including specified information. If the property is not Native American, the museum can claim title on the 46th day after the last notice.*
Arizona	§ 44-351 to 44-356	—	"Undocumented Property" must be held for 7 years or longer, verified by museum records, with no contact or claim by any person. The museum must: publish a notice for two consecutive weeks including specified information, wait 65 days, then publish a second notice including specified information. If no claims are made, title passes to the museum.
Arkansas	13-5-1001 to 13-5-1013	—	"Undocumented Property" that is documented by the museum for 7 years, to which no person has made a claim, becomes the property of the museum. However, ownership is not vested if the undocumented property is determined later to be stolen property or property whose ownership is subject to federal law.
California	§1899 to 1899.11	—	No
Colorado	§ 38-14-101 to 38-14-112	—	No

State	Citation	Comments	FIC provision
Connecticut	—	No museum-specific legislation 2009	—
Delaware	—	No museum-specific legislation 2009	—
District of Columbia	—	No museum-specific legislation 2009	—
Florida	§ 265.565.1-12	—	No
Georgia	§ 10-1-529.1-7	Georgia Museum Property Act excludes American Indian human remains and burial objects	Undocumented property that is held by the museum for 7 years and remains unclaimed can become property of the museum after publishing a notice once a week for two consecutive weeks with specified information.
Hawaii	—	No museum-specific legislation 2009	—
Idaho	—	No museum-specific legislation 2009	—
Illinois	chap. 765 § 1033/1 to 1033/50	For FIC, no notice is necessary. The only requirement is for the seven year waiting period to end.	"Undocumented Property" that is held by the museum for 7 years, to which no person has made a claim, becomes the property of the museum. However, ownership is not vested if the undocumented property is determined later to be stolen property or property whose ownership is subject to federal law.
Indiana	§ 32-34-5-1 to 16	—	"Undocumented Property" must be held for 7 years or longer. The museum must publish a notice including specified information. If no claims are made within three (3) years of the publication of the notice, title passes to the museum.
Iowa	§ 305B.1 to 305B.13	—	"Undocumented Property" must be held for 7 years or longer, with no contact or claim by any person. The museum must publish a notice including specified information. If no claims are made within three (3) years of the publication of the notice, title passes to the museum.
Kansas	§ 58-4001 to 58-4013	—	"Undocumented Property" must be held for 7 years or longer, with no contact or claim by any person. The museum must publish a notice including specified information. If no claims are made within one year of the publication of the notice, title passes to the museum.
Kentucky	§ 171.830 to 171.849	—	A museum may initiate action to gain title to property (pursuant to KRS 171.840) after it has held property for seven (7) years, other than by the terms of a loan agreement

State	Citation	Comments	FIC provision
Louisiana	§ 25.345	Applies only to Louisiana State museums	Any property that is held at a museum for 10 years or more, to which no person has made a claim, becomes the property of the museum if: the museum publishes a notice once a week for two weeks containing specified information. If no claims are made within 65 days, title passes to the museum.
Maine	tit. 27, § 601	—	Any property that is held at a museum for 25 years or more, to which no person has made a claim, becomes the property of the museum if: the museum publishes a notice once a week for two weeks containing specified information. If no claims are made within 65 days, title passes to the museum.
Maryland	—	No museum-specific legislation 2009	—
Massachusetts	—	No museum-specific legislation 2009	—
Michigan	§ 399.601 to 399.613		Beginning January 1, 1993, a museum may give notice on "Undocumented Property". The museum must publish a notice for two consecutive weeks including specified information, wait at least 60 days, then publish a second notice including specified information.
Minnesota	345.70 to 345.74	—	Effective August 1, 2004, property that: (1) is found in or on property controlled by the museum; (2) is from an unknown source; and (3) might reasonably be assumed to have been intended as a gift to the museum, is conclusively presumed to be a gift to the museum if ownership of the property is not claimed by a person within 90 days of its discovery.
Mississippi	§ 39-19-1 to 39-19-21	—	No
Missouri	§ 184.101 to 184.122	—	"Undocumented Property" must be held for 7 years or longer, with no contact or claim by any person. The museum must publish a notice including specified information. If no claims are made within ninety days of the publication of the notice, title passes to the museum.
Montana	§ 22-3-501 to 22-3-523	22-3-523. Applicability. This part applies only to property loaned to a museum on or after October 1, 1985, or to existing loaned property with a market value of $1,000 or less at the time of disposal.	No

State	Citation	Comments	FIC provision
Nebraska	§ 51-701 to 51-712*	—	"Undocumented Property" must be held for 7 years or longer, with no contact or claim by any person. The museum must publish a notice including specified information. If no claims are made within three years of the publication of the notice, title passes to the museum.
Nevada	§ 381.009	Applies only to certain Nevada State museums and historical societies	Any property that is held at a museum for 3 years or more, to which no person has made a claim, becomes the property of the museum if: the museum publishes a notice once a week for two weeks containing specified information. If no claims are made within 60 days, title passes to the museum.
New Hampshire	§ 201-E:1 to 201-E:7	—	Any property held by a museum within the state, other than by terms of a loan agreement, must be held for 5 years or longer, with no contact or claim by any person. The museum must publish a notice including specified information. If no claims are made within 90 days of the publication of the notice, title passes to the museum.
New Jersey	—	No museum-specific legislation; as of 2009, the legislation is written and the legislative process is beginning.	—
New Mexico	§ 18-10-1 to 18-10-5	—	No
New York	§ 233-a; § 233-aa	§ 233-a applies only to the New York State museum. § 233-aa, signed in 2008, amends that law to include other museums in the state.	"Unclaimed or undocumented property" requires three newspaper publications, 180 waiting period, then publication on the Unclaimed Funds Registry of the Comptroller's website. 30 days after that posting, the museum acquires the property. For "Unsolicited" property, the museum acquires rights 90 days after delivery if no one comes forward to establish ownership.
North Carolina	§ 121-7(c) and 121-7(d)	Applies only to North Carolina State museums (Department of Cultural Resources)	"Undocumented Property" must be held for 5 years or longer, with no contact or claim by any person. The museum must publish a notice including specified information. If no claims are made within 30 days of the publication of the notice, title passes to the museum.
North Dakota	§ 47-07-14	Applies only to museums about to close.	No
Ohio	tit. 33 § 3385.01 -.10	—	No

State	Citation	Comments	FIC provision
Oklahoma	60.683.2	Pursuant to section 60.683.2(c) of the Oklahoma statutes, a museum is exempted from the provisions of the state's Uniform Unclaimed Property Act, but may avail itself of the act by complying with its provisions	
Oregon	§ 358.415 to 358.440	—	No
Pennsylvania	—	No museum-specific legislation 2009	—
Rhode Island	—	No museum-specific legislation 2009	—
South Carolina	§ 27-45-10 to 27-45-100	—	No
South Dakota	§ 43-41C-1 to 43-41C-4	—	Abandoned Property: Any property that has been held by the museum for ten years or more, other than by terms of a loan agreement, shall be deemed abandoned. The museum must publish a notice with specific information. If no claims are made within sixty five days, title passes to the museum.
Tennessee	§ 66-29-201 to 66-29-204	—	Abandoned Property: Any property that has been held by the museum for twenty years or more, other than by terms of a loan agreement, shall be deemed abandoned. The museum must publish a notice with specific information. If no claims are made within sixty five days, title passes to the museum.
Texas	§ 80.001 to 80.008	—	No
Utah	§ 9-8-801 to 9-8-806	—	Any materials that are not accompanied by a transfer of title are considered a gift when more than 25 years have passed from the date of the last written contact between depositor or his successors and the collecting institution.
Vermont	§ 27-12-1151 to 1158	—	Any property held by a museum that is not subject to a loan agreement and has been held for 10 or more years and has remained unclaimed shall be deemed to be abandoned. The museum must publish a notice once each month for three consecutive months. After 180 days from the date of the third published notice, if no claim has been made, title passes to the museum.
Virginia	§ 55-210.31- § 55-210.38	—	No

State	Citation	Comments	FIC provision
Washington	§ 63.26.010 to 63.26.050	—	Abandoned Property: Any property that has been held by the museum for five years or more, other than by terms of a loan agreement, shall be deemed abandoned. The museum must: publish a notice with specific information at least once a week for two weeks. If no claims are made within ninety days, title passes to the museum.
West Virginia	—	No museum-specific legislation 2009	
Wisconsin	§ 171.30 to 171.33	—	No
Wyoming	§ 34-23-101 to 34-23-108	—	No

Thanks to students in the George Washington University Museum Studies Program.

3H | MODEL–MUSEUM UNCLAIMED PROPERTY LAW

MID-ATLANTIC ASSOCIATION OF MUSEUMS REGISTRARS COMMITTEE

SECTION I: PURPOSE

The people of this state have an interest in the growth and maintenance of museum collections and in the preservation and protection of unclaimed tangible property of artistic, historic, cultural and/or scientific value left in the custody of museums within this state. Loans of such property are made to these museums in furtherance of their educational purposes. When lenders fail to stay in contact, museums routinely store and care for loaned property long after the loan periods have expired or should reasonably be deemed expired. But, museums have limited rights to the use and treatment of such unclaimed loaned property, all the while bearing substantial costs related to storage, record keeping, climate control, security, periodic inspection, insurance, general overhead, and conservation. It is in the public interest to:

(a) encourage both museums and their lenders to use due diligence in monitoring loans;

(b) allocate fairly responsibilities between lenders and borrowers; and

(c) resolve expeditiously the issue of title of unclaimed loans left in the custody of museums.

The purpose of this chapter is to establish uniform rules to govern the disposition of unclaimed property on loan to museums and this act should be interpreted with these goals in mind.

SECTION II: CITATION OF LAW

This law shall be known and may be cited as the Museum Unclaimed Property Act.

SECTION III: EFFECTIVE DATE

The effective date of this act is [date].

SECTION IV: DEFINITIONS

(a) "Lender",—an individual, corporation, partnership, trust estate, or similar organization, whose name appears on the records of the museum as the entity legally entitled to control property on loan to the museum;

(b) "Loan",—"On loan", or "Loaned",—property in the possession of the museum, accompanied by evidence that the lender intended to retain title to the property and to return to take physical possession of the property in the future;

(c) "Museum",—a public or private non-profit agency or institution located in this state and organized on a permanent basis for essentially educational or aesthetic purposes, which unitizes a professional staff, owns or utilizes tangible objects, cares for them, and exhibits them to the public on a regular basis;

(d) "Museum records",—documents created and/or held by the museum in its regular course of business;

(e) "Property",—a tangible object, in the custody of a museum, that has intrinsic historical, artistic, scientific, or cultural value;

(f) "Restricted certified mail"—certified mail that carries on its face, in a conspicuous place where it will not be obliterated, the endorsement "deliver to addressee only" and for which the post office provides the mailer with a return receipt showing the date of delivery, the place of delivery and the person to whom delivered;

(g) "Unclaimed property",—property meeting the following two conditions: (1) property is on loan to the museum; (2) the original lender, or anyone acting legitimately on the lender's behalf, has not contacted the museum for at least 25 years from the date of the beginning of the loan, if the loan was for an indefinite or undetermined period, or for at least 5 years after the date upon which the loan for a definite period expired.

SECTION V: MUSEUMS' OBLIGATIONS TO LENDERS

1. Record Keeping for New Loans: For property loaned to a museum on or after the effective date of this act, the museum shall do all of the following at the time of the loan:

(a) Make and retain a written record containing at least all of the following:

(i) The lender's name, address, and telephone number

(ii) A description of the property loaned in sufficient detail for ready identification;

(iii) The beginning date of the loan; (iv) The expiration date of the loan.

(b) Provide the lender with a signed receipt or loan agreement containing at least the record set forth in subsection (a) above.

(c) Inform the lender of the existence of this act and provide the lender with a copy of this act upon the lender's request.

2. Record Keeping for Existing Loans: Regardless of the date of a loan of property, the museum shall do the following:

(a) Update its records if a lender informs the museum of a change of address or change in ownership of property loaned, or if the lender and museum negotiate a change in the duration of the loan.

(b) Inform the lender of the existence of this act when renewing or updating the records of an existing loan and provide the lender with a copy of this act upon the lender's request.

SECTION VI: LENDERS' OBLIGATIONS TO MUSEUMS

1. Notices Required of Lenders: As of the date of this act, the lender, or any successor of such lender, shall, regardless of the date of a loan of property in the custody of a museum, promptly notify the museum in writing:

(a) of a change in lender's address; and/or

(b) of a change in ownership in the property on loan to the museum.

2. Documentation establishing ownership: It is the responsibility of a successor of a lender to document passage of rights of control to the property in the custody of the museum.

(a) Unless there is evidence of bad faith or gross negligence, no museum shall be prejudiced by reason of any failure to deal with the true owner of any loaned property.

(b) In cases of disputed ownership of loaned property, a museum shall not be held liable for its refusal to surrender loaned property in its possession except in reliance upon a court order or judgement.

SECTION VII: NOTICE BY MUSEUMS TO LENDERS TO TERMINATE LOANS FOR UNCLAIMED PROPERTY

A museum may terminate a loan for unclaimed property in its possession as follows:

1. Good Faith Search: The museum shall make a good faith and reasonable search for the identity and last known address of the lender from the museum records and other records reasonably available to museum staff. If the museum identifies the lender and the lender's last known address, the museum shall give actual notice to the lender that the loan is terminated pursuant to subsection 2(a) below. If the identity or the last know address of the lender remains unknown after the above described search, the museum shall give notice by publication pursuant to subsection 2(b) below.

2. Notice: (a) Actual Notice: Actual notice of termination of a loan of unclaimed property shall take substantially the following form. The museum shall send a letter by restricted certified mail to the lender at the lender's last known address giving a notice of termination of the loan, which shall include the following information:

(i) Date of notice of termination; (ii) Name of the lender;

(iii) Description of property in sufficient detail for ready identification;

(iv) Approximate initiating date of the loan (and termination date, if applicable), if known;

(v) The name and address of the appropriate museum official to be contacted regarding the loan;

(vi) Statement that within 90 days of the date of the notice of termination, the lender is required to remove the property from the museum or contact the designated official in the museum to preserve the lender's interests in the property and that failure to do so will result in the loss of all rights in the property pursuant to Section VIII of this act.

(b) Notice by Publication: If the museum is unable to identify sufficient information to send actual notice pursuant to section (a) above, or if a signed return receipt of a notice sent by restricted certified mail under subsection (a) above is not received by the museum within 30 days after the notice is mailed, the museum shall publish the notice of termination of loan containing all the information available to the museum provided in subsection (a) (i–v) above at least twice, 60 or more days apart, in a publication of general circulation in the county in which the museum is located, and the county of the lender's last known address, if known.

SECTION VIII: MUSEUM GAINING TITLE TO PROPERTY; CONDITIONS

As of the effective date of this act, a museum acquires title to unclaimed property, under any of the following circumstances:

(a) For property for which a museum provides actual notice to a lender in accordance to Section VII 3(a) above and a signed receipt is received, if a lender of that property does not contact the museum, within 90 days after the date notice was received.

(b) For property for which notice by publication is made pursuant to Section VII 3(b) above, if a lender or anyone claiming a legal interest in that property does not contact the museum within 90 days after the date of the second publication.

SECTION IX: CONTRACTUAL OBLIGATIONS

Despite this act, a lender and museum can bind themselves to different loan provisions by written contract.

SECTION X: EFFECT ON OTHER RIGHTS

(a) Property on loan to a museum shall not escheat to the state under any state escheat law but shall pass to the museum under the provision of Section VIII above.

(b) Property interests other than those specifically addressed in this act are not altered by this act.

SECTION XI: TITLE OF PROPERTY ACQUIRED FROM A MUSEUM

A museum which acquires title to property under this act passes good title to another when transferring such property with the intent to pass title.

SECTION XII: MUSEUM LIEN FOR EXPENSES OF EXPIRED LOANS

As of the effective date of this act, a museum shall have a lien for expenses for reasonable care of loaned property unclaimed after the expiration date of the loan. •

Thanks to Marie Malaro and Ildiko Pogany DeAngelis.

31 | DEACCESSIONING

MARTHA MORRIS, UPDATED BY ANTONIA MOSER

INTRODUCTION

Museums have engaged in the practice of deaccessioning for decades. In fact, disposing of collections that have been acquired and cared for by museums has been a common practice. The concept of deaccessioning in the last 35 years has frequently been controversial as the profession has been ever more alert to issues of legal responsibilities, the public's expectations of museums, and ethics codes for institutions and individuals. Museums became painfully aware of the need for strong deaccession policies and practices in the early 1970s when several institutions, including New York's Metropolitan Museum of Art and the Museum of the American Indian, were scrutinized for certain collections disposal practices. The Brooklyn Museum, the Henry Ford Museum in Dearborn, Michigan, the Barnes Collection in Merion, Pennsylvania, and the New-York Historical Society are just a few of the institutions whose actual or proposed deaccession activity created public or professional controversy throughout the 1980s and 1990s. Twenty-first century examples include the Museum of Northern Arizona in Flagstaff, the Albright-Knox Art Gallery in Buffalo, and the National Academy Museum in New York; moreover, libraries and universities—Fisk University in Nashville, Jefferson Medical College in Philadelphia, and The New York Public Library—have brought more public attention to the issue of deaccessioning by selling or seeking to sell important artworks in their possession. In some cases the criticism emanated from offended donors disappointed that their gifts were no longer worthy of museum status. Frequently, certain objects were considered treasured cultural assets of the community. In other cases legal and ethical codes were violated when museum staff or trustees personally benefited from collection sales or when proceeds of deaccession sales were used to support operations or reduce financial obligations of the institution. Internally, controversy swirled as museum staff were reluctant to dispose of objects that might be significant treasures in the future.[1]

These experiences have caused museums to perform much more conscientious reviews of their decisions to dispose of collections and this is reflected in the types of policies, procedures, and ethical statements that have been adopted in more recent years by their governing bodies. A museum's fundamental mission to preserve and build collections for the benefit of present and future generations can be challenged when it seeks to remove objects from the collections. Such activity, if not carried out in a thoughtful and careful manner, can be a serious liability for the museum. There is probably no more sensitive current issue for museums, unless it be the repatriation of cultural property or the blurring of lines between the non-profit, public, and for-profit sectors.

However, there is a compelling case for the practice of deaccessioning, despite its controversy. Many museums have collected material that is clearly outside the scope of their mission, that may be deteriorated beyond a useful life, or that could be better used by other educational institutions. Managing collections is a rigorous and costly task, and some museums simply do not have the resources to care for properly or make accessible all of their collections. Informed and responsible choices and decisions have to be made. To assure the highest level of public accountability museums must codify policy and procedure for deaccessions, and these policies must be endorsed and fully embraced by the museum's governing body and staff.

The following outlines practices which all museums should employ in the process of developing deaccession policies and procedures, including collecting plans, deaccession criteria, decision processes, disposal options, record keeping, alternatives to deaccessioning, and special problems. The registrar's role in deaccessioning is to be vigilant about the creation of and adherence to the museum's policy and procedures, to track the transaction and maintain records of it, and to remain knowledgeable about preferred practices of the profession.

THE FIRST STEPS: DEFINING COLLECTIONS RATIONALE

In order for a museum to make intelligent decisions regarding deaccessions, it must first have clearly articulated collecting goals. A museum defines its collections by reference to its operating charter and mission statement. From its mission the museum must define its scope of collections in a written document approved by its governing body. Once the museum defines a broad scope of collections, which at a minimum should cover object type and origin, intellectual themes and subjects, there is a need to form a Collecting Plan. This plan, usually crafted by the curatorial staff, evolves from the scope statement to a formal assessment of the strengths and weaknesses of existing collections. This assessment looks at collections in specific collecting areas, comparing them to other objects in the museum and to similar collections in other museums. The assessment process can be a time-consuming effort and in some cases may require hiring outside specialists to supplement the expertise of existing staff. The registrar, collections manager, curator, and conservator will be active partners in this effort as they provide information about the legal and physical status of objects as well as critical information about their provenance. Once the assessment is completed, the priority of collecting objectives must be established in order to target new acquisitions. Certain items in the collection can be earmarked for deaccession and disposal, if not within the parameters of the plan. The museum can benefit from an analysis of the ongoing costs associated with collecting and maintaining collections, including not only the cost to acquire—e.g., purchase cost, transportation and insurance, initial conservation—but also long term costs such as cataloging, storage, conservation,

photography, and inventory control. This analysis is particularly important as a tool to project the costs of ongoing maintenance and the future growth of collections. It will assist museum management in strategic planning for new resources and inform the governing body as it makes decisions. This type of analysis is complementary to the planning that should be ongoing for developing inventory control systems, full documentation of collections, and surveys for preservation. Once these analyses are completed they will be helpful to the museum as it participates in the AAM Museum Assessment Program, undergoes Accreditation review, applies for funding for programs, or mounts a capital campaign.

DEACCESSION POLICY AND PROCEDURE

The museum's collections management policy must clearly explain criteria for making decisions about deaccessions. Deaccession and disposal are two different things.

Deaccession is the formal change in recorded status of the object. Disposal is the resulting action taken after a deaccession decision. No matter what the object's accession status, it should go through a thoughtful disposal process. Indeed the museum's collections management policies should define the various categories of objects and the steps needed to acquire, deaccession, and dispose of them. For example, a collection that is composed of materials used for school programs, study, or exhibition props probably would require less rigorous levels of review before disposal. In fact, such items might be disposed of at the discretion of the curator or educator. Other objects, such as those in the permanent collection, usually may only be disposed of after review by the museum's management and the Board's unanimous written approval. Of course, the type of objects and their monetary or intrinsic value determine the best approach. All decisions must take into consideration the processes associated with proper records review and disposal options. In all cases, the Collections Management Policy should clearly address the criteria and process associated with decisions and actions to deaccession and dispose of collections.

Decision criteria are needed in order for the

museum's Collections Committee (usually a trustee group working closely with staff) to make thoughtful and justifiable decisions. With reference to the museum's mission and its Collecting Plan, deaccessions should be considered only when the objects in question are

•Not within the scope or mission

•Beyond the capability of the museum to maintain

•Not useful for research, exhibition, or educational programs in the foreseeable future

•Duplicates of other collections

•Poor, less important, incomplete, or unauthentic examples

•Physically deteriorated/hazardous materials.

•In the case of living collections, the death of a specimen

•Originally acquired illegally or unethically

•Subject to a legislative mandate, e.g., repatriation

•Subject to contractual donor restrictions the museum is no longer able to meet

•Found to be part of a set that belongs to another institution, or more appropriate to the collection of another institution

Decision Process

Deaccessioning is the result of a thoughtful and well-documented process.

The following are critical steps in the process and should be documented. The Registrar plays a key role in coordinating the steps in this process and providing key information from the museum's records.

•Written curatorial justification linked to the collecting plan, outlining the decision criteria that apply.

•Verification of official legal title, checking records to ascertain if any restrictions exist from the original gift, bequest, or purchase. In particular, any copyright or trademark restrictions might be reviewed by legal counsel, since those rights will not automatically transfer to a new owner.

•Physical examination by conservator to help establish appropriate means of disposal, including possible sale or destruction.

•One or more outside appraisals, especially for objects of value and those which might be sold or traded.

•Outside opinions for items of value, especially if there is any uncertainty about provenance or authenticity.

•Internal review by all curatorial staff to assure full awareness of the plan to dispose of a collection item.

•CEO/Director and governing board approval. This is where the final decision is made. In most cases, deaccessions must be approved by the Board, often by unanimous vote. Some decisions may be delegated to the CEO/Director, depending on the value of the objects. Beyond the governing body, each museum should check its own charter and relevant state laws to see if there are any external limitations on disposal.

•Working with external stakeholders. There is no obligation to notify the donor if the gift was unrestricted and the museum owns the material free and clear. However, many museums do contact donors or relatives as a courtesy. Conferring with members of local community advisory groups is important to assure concurrence and avoid possible public outcry when the deaccession is officially announced. Special interest groups may include collectors, other museums, volunteers, and museum membership groups.

Disposal Options

The following are common options for disposal of deaccessioned material. The best course may vary from case to case based on the type of material and the needs of the museum. Of course, no items should be acquired by museum staff, board or their relatives. Of concern to most museums is the need to assure that items are seriously considered for placement in other educational institutions. There may also be some need to retain an object in the community, region, or country, if it has any relevance as an item of cultural patrimony.

•Donation of the objects to another museum, library, or archive for educational purposes. A museum can determine if there is a way to retain the objects in the community or develop an ongoing collecting agreement with another museum. For example, the National Park Service maintains a Clearinghouse for material that can be placed in other museums. Other regional or national networks could be a valuable outlet for disposal.

•Exchange with another museum or non-profit institution. This option is also a customary method of assuring that objects stay accessible to the public. Exchanges should be made in such a way that there is relatively equal value of the items involved. Trading objects with private dealers or collectors can be perilous, and it is most important to be sure that the monetary and historical value of the exchanged materials is equal. Furthermore, the museum should be able to justify the trade, including any exceptional circumstances that would favor a particular dealer or collector. As earlier noted, obtaining good independent appraisals of the items being acquired is mandatory.

•Educational and Research programs. Often, items can be used for scientific study, school programs, hands-on demonstrations, exhibition props, or testing in conservation research. In these cases it is expected that the objects will be subject to physical deterioration or destruction over time.

•Physical destruction. Objects may have deteriorated due to inherent vice, natural disaster, vandalism, accident, or other causes. In other cases, items may be considered hazardous, such as those objects containing drugs, chemicals, explosives, or asbestos, and should be disposed of. There are strict standards for disposal of these types of material which can be determined by consulting appropriate regulatory agencies or experts in the field. Another possible justification for physical destruction might be to eliminate from circulation unauthorized or counterfeit materials. The method of destruction will vary depending on the type of material, but generally it should be done so as to be irreversible. Records of the method of disposal should be retained. Archival collections are frequently destroyed as a method of disposal. There is also the possible use of collections in research, often the case with natural history museums, where collections go through destructive analysis. In this regard the importance of the test results should be weighed against the loss of the object and its value as a specimen.

•Repatriation and/or cultural sensitivity. Repatriation is a legal issue which can have an impact on the method of disposal of objects. Human remains or certain items of religious or cultural sensitivity might need to be handled in a prescribed way in order to meet legal requirements or cultural standards. (See chapters in this volume on NAGPRA and the handling of sacred objects.)

•Private sale. This method is not a standard alternative but may be justified in some circumstances. If it is pursued, the museum must keep good records and be ready to respond honestly to outside inquiries. In some cases where public auction is not possible or practical, material can be consigned to a dealer for sale.

•Return to donor. This alternative is not usually the best option for the museum. Museums hold collections in trust for the public, and putting objects into the hands of private citizens does not meet this objective. The danger of returning objects to donors also lies in setting a precedent and raising expectations of such actions in the future. There might also be tax complications. The most legitimate reason for returning material would likely be that the museum has failed to meet the requirements or conditions of the original gift or bequest. In any event, this option should be used rarely and only after careful consultation with legal counsel.

•Public Auction. One frequently selected option for disposal of deaccessioned collections is a public sale. This method is especially important when there is a need to generate funds to improve the prospects for future collecting. In considering this option the museum should, among other things, weigh the staff time and other costs associated with an appropriately administered sale in comparison to the anticipated proceeds. Since this option is one which is subject to close public scrutiny, it is important to review the procedures in some detail.

Selection of Auction House

It is important to interview several potential auction houses and check their references carefully with other museum clients. Issues that should be considered are the costs that will be covered by the firm, its marketing strategy, its reputation for reliability and timeliness, and the location of the sale if that has an impact on potential market or publicity.

Request for Proposal

Customary procurement and contracting practices of the organization will determine the method used, but in general the request for proposal should include a scope of work, describing the collection and requirements for the sale. Several firms should be asked to bid on the sale to allow for a fair competition among possible auction houses and give the museum an opportunity to select the best possible firm for the material to be sold. The scope should include expectations for the sale, a description of the material, the time frame, and criteria by which the bidder will be judged. These criteria might include the production of fully illustrated sales catalogues, previous sales records, or specialized staff expertise.

Museum Records and Provenance

Before entering into a consignment agreement be sure to make every effort to catalog the objects fully, checking provenance and reviewing the museum's official registration records. Any problems of provenance or attribution should to be discussed with the auction house. If objects are on loan to another museum, be sure to alert the museum so the objects can be recalled with plenty of lead time. This step will be a primary job for the registrar.

Contracting with the Auction House

A detailed sales/consignment contract must be prepared. Most auction houses have a standard contract.

The museum should carefully review this document, sharing it with legal counsel. In some cases a customized contract may be needed to cover all contingencies. For example, one may want to specify how publicity will be handled, how commission and fees will be arranged, how a reserve will be placed, how unsold materials are to be handled, the date for the sale, physical care and insurance for the objects, responsibilities for photography, and potential for withdrawal of items.

Be sure that auction house staff are fully conversant with the terms of the contract. Invite them to meet with museum staff to discuss concerns and expectations. It is important to determine roles and responsibilities of various players and to clarify who speaks for the firm and who speaks for the museum. Likewise, the museum should assign a principal spokesperson. If any questions arise during the course of the sales period, be sure that they are clarified in writing and that all parties know who is authorized to make commitments or amend the agreement.

Care and Handling

The Registrar will negotiate with the auction house regarding costs and methods of packing, shipping, insurance, staff travel, interim storage, and availability of objects for previews. Insisting that a museum staff member be present as an escort or handler is a legitimate request. The museum should invest in sending a staff member to inspect the firm's facilities, security, and handling to underscore that the sale is of paramount importance and concern.

Marketing

Be sure to agree on how advertising is to be done and on who approves the final ad copy, issues and approves press releases, and conducts press interviews. In addition, previews and receptions may also be used to promote the sale, and the museum should consider how it will be portrayed in those settings. Care should be taken to assure the museum's collections are not mixed in with materials from other sales if there is any concern about the sensitivity of the sale.

Post-sale Activities

A press release may be issued to announce the

result of the sale and to explain once again how the museum intends to use the proceeds. Unsold materials may remain the property of the museum or the auction house, depending on contract terms. Be sure to negotiate how to handle these remaining objects, either through inclusion in future auctions or in private sales.

Public Relations and Deaccessioning

Whether it is a sale, a donation to another museum, or destruction, the museum usually must face the issue of public relations. Concerns can be raised inside the museum, among staff and volunteers, or with any number of public stakeholders. Generally the museum can and should provide at the earliest possible time as much information as possible. Keeping staff informed throughout the process of a deaccession is critical. The public can be informed through issuing a press release targeted to museum members, donors, funders, and the general public. For major deaccessions, it might be advisable to host a formal press conference where general and trade (specialty) press could actually see the objects being deaccessioned. Providing a statement from the Director or Board Chair, possibly also a supporting statement from the donor or other significant stakeholder in the community, along with photographs and descriptions of the items and a full disclosure of the proposed use of proceeds is recommended for a major deaccession. Assure that an official statement from the Director or Board Chair is printed in the sales catalog. Statements from the museum should address the rationale for deaccession, the decision-making and approval process, and the proposed use of proceeds. Notifying the donors of the deaccession and then acknowledging them in any publicity is critical. Remember to communicate with colleagues at other museums, as your plans might raise interest or questions in their museums. Appointing a spokesperson for the museum is helpful in keeping various parties fully and accurately informed.

Ethical Considerations and Use of Proceeds

Several professional codes of ethics exist that address deaccessioning. All museums should consider ethics codes as they develop their own policies. Common in these codes is the prohibition on sale or transfer of collections items to museum trustees or staff or their relatives, and the need to restrict the use of proceeds of sales. In looking at the latter restriction, the following represent recommended practices in 2009:

• Association of Art Museum Directors: Proceeds should be restricted to acquisitions of new works of art, with the added caveat of a potential penalty for violating this code.[2]

• American Association of Museums: Requires disposal solely for advancement of the museum's mission. Proceeds from the sale of nonliving collections are to be used consistent with the established standards of the museum's discipline, but in no event shall they be used for anything other than acquisition or direct care of collections.[3]

• American Association of State and Local History: Collections shall not be deaccessioned or disposed of in order to provide financial support for institutional operations, facilities maintenance, or any reason other than the preservation or acquisition of collections.[4]

• International Council of Museums: Proceeds should be applied solely to the purchase of additions to the museum collections.[5]

• Society of American Archivists: Each museum must determine the best approach for its own mission and circumstances. However, the use of proceeds should be restricted to maintenance of collections.[6]

Record Keeping

The registrar is responsible for record keeping during the deaccessioning process. Since official documentation is critical to the fair and thorough approach needed to remain accountable, the registrar plays a very important role. The following steps are needed in reviewing and maintaining records of the deaccession.

• Fully document justification and review process as well as disposal and include transfer of title and negotiated transfer of copyright, if owned.

• Before deaccession approval, clearly research title and note any restrictions on disposal, particularly if specific expectations were written into the deed of gift or the purchase or bequest instruments.

•Notify the donor in advance of actual disposal.

•The Internal Revenue Service may require notification when a donated object is deaccessioned. Current regulations should be reviewed and the museum must comply with them. *(See chapter on Tax Issues.)*

•For FASB requirements, assure appropriate records are made in the museum's annual audit process.

•Photograph the objects for the record.

•Retain all records permanently.

•Produce an annual report on deaccession activity.

•Give credit to the original donor via a fund name which is applied to any purchases made with the proceeds of sales.

ALTERNATIVES TO DEACCESSION

Long-term loan

Many museums lend collections for an extended period, usually three or more years, for public display or study by other qualified museums or educational organizations. Clearly, there is value in considering this practice in order to meet a number of concerns:

•Relieve overcrowded storage areas

•Provide the public access to collections that might otherwise remain in storage

•Assure that the objects remain the property of the museum, thus meeting expectations of donors and assuring curators that future generations may benefit from access to the collections

Drawbacks to this approach include:

•The costs associated with monitoring the use of the objects by borrowing organizations

•Possible loss of interest in the material (out of sight, out of mind)

•Reassignment of storage space to new collections

•Lack of access to objects for study and research

•Possibility of borrower's inability to return objects, due to financial problems

Shared Ownership

Some museums have elected to enter into agreements with other museums for shared ownership of specific objects. This allows the museum to retain and display the object for a certain time in consideration of community interests, while sharing the costs of its care with the co-owner.

Collaborations

Another option is a special affiliation between or among museums and other organizations to share collections and exhibitions that is like a long-term loan arrangement. Collaborations among museums, such as the Smithsonian and the University of Alaska museum, or the Whitney Museum and San Jose Museum of Art, illustrate long-term affiliations that involve a transfer of collections for exhibition or research over a long period of time, such as 10 years. This collaboration often includes an exchange of staff or collaboration between staff working on exhibitions, publications, conservation, or research projects.

SPECIAL PROBLEMS WITH DEACCESSIONING

The Shared Collection

In some instances the museum may not be the sole owner of an object. The object may have been jointly purchased with another museum or not-for-profit agency or the museum may have acquired only a partial gift. In such cases it is important to seek legal advice before deaccession action is taken.

What if there is no record of ownership?

The only risk-free deaccession is one in which the museum's title is clear. However, a museum may wish—or need—to balance the risk of deaccessioning objects that lack perfect documentation with the benefits gained from removing material that clearly does not belong in the museum's collection. The "Deaccession Risk Chart" was designed to help museums measure the various levels of risk associated with deaccessioning objects with incomplete documentation. If the item is clearly not an unclaimed loan, and it has been in the museum's possession for some time, and it is no longer relevant to the museum's mission, deaccessioning may be considered, despite no record of ownership. Move carefully toward disposal of this type of material. After checking all records, including loan files, for evidence of title, create a file and assign an accession number if this has not already been done. The next steps regarding disposal should consider the consequences of any future claim of ownership to the objects. A sale may not be a prudent alternative if the museum cannot provide an absolute warranty to the buyer. Again, such situations should be fully reviewed with a legal advisor.

What if the museum owns it, but it is not accessioned?
In this case, the process of disposal should follow similar steps to assure that a careful decision is made. Even if items have not been accessioned because they are unrelated to the mission of the museum, they are museum assets and thus require care in the decision to dispose. Therefore, going through the process of reviewing the stated decision criteria for deaccessions is a prudent approach.

What if the object was brought in for the permanent collection but not processed?
If there is strong evidence that the object was originally meant to be part of the permanent collection, but the process of assigning numbers and numbering the objects was never completed, it is logical to assign the accession number and use it to create deaccessioning documentation and to track the object during the process. Accessioning includes both acquisition and processing; the lack of processing does not define the object as unaccessioned. Information about objects processed outside the museum's comprehensive collection systems (manual and computerized) can easily become impossible to access after deaccession and disposition.

What code of ethics should one follow?
In light of the varied ethics codes promulgated about the deaccession of collections, the museum's board of trustees must consider what constitutes an appropriate deaccession policy, given its charter and mission. Being aware of the various ethics codes is critical to the decision process. Once selected, the code should be formally adopted as a part of the deaccession policy and fully understood by all board and staff members.

In conclusion, it is important to weigh all the factors associated with deaccessioning, including museum mission and collecting objectives, ethical codes, policy and procedure for justifying the action, as well as the most appropriate disposal options before embarking on deaccession activity. Thoughtful review of legal, ethical, and practical implications of deaccessioning and clearly articulated policy and procedure should allow the museum to move with confidence in this area. •

NOTES

1. There are many references that detail specific cases listed in the bibliography. A consistent source of information on this topic is the published proceedings of the ALI-ABA Course Study: *Legal Problems of Museum Administration,* 1973-present.

2. Association of Art Museum Directors *Professional Practices in Art Museums,* New York, 1992.

3. *Code of Ethics for Museums,* AAM, Washington DC, 1994, p. 9.

4. A Statement of Professional Ethics, American Association for State and Local History, Nashville, Tennessee, 1992.

5. Malaro, Marie. *Museum Governance,* Smithsonian Institution Press, 1994, p. 155.

6. Ham, F. Gerald. *Selecting and Appraising Archives and Manuscripts,* Society of American Archivists, 1993, p. 92.

3J | DEACCESSIONING RISK CHART

REBECCA BUCK

	Value	Disposition method	Clarity of Title	Object type
MOST RISK	**$1 million +**			
		Destroy	Undocumented/FIC	Unique
		Return to source	Accession number only	Small series
		Sell privately	Unsigned deed of gift (no value)	
		Sell at auction	Unclear documentation	Limited edition, artist
		Exchange	Object and/or source card file	
		Repatriate	Annual reports	Limited edition, manufacture
		Give to non-profit	Report to trustees	
LEAST RISK	**$0**	Internal Transfer	Countersigned deed of gift/intent and acknowledgement/clear bill of sale	Mass produced (man-made) Abundant (natural)

3K | FOUND-IN-COLLECTION

REBECCA BUCK

OVERVIEW

Almost all museum collections contain some objects that have no number to connect them with documentation. They have no tag, no number written on them, no indication of source in their packaging, and they have no characteristic that connects them to records of gifts, purchases, or loans. They are found during inventories, they are discovered during work on an exhibition or a re-housing project, or they pop up when someone leaves the institution and desks and shelves are cleaned out.

These objects may have entered the collection at any time in the museum's history. They may have been gifts, purchases, bequests, or objects left in spaces taken over by the museum; they may have been loans or objects left from special events or educational programs. They may have been objects belonging to former staff, brought in for decoration; they may even have been former utilitarian objects that, by their age and manufacture, have attained some historical or aesthetic value. Though their status may be uncertain, it is more likely than not that they belong to the museum.

What are the sources of undocumented objects?

- Gift
- Gift on approval/deposit
- Bequest
- Bequest on approval/deposit
- Purchase
- Purchase on approval/deposit
- Commission
- Unclaimed or "Old" loan
- Abandoned property
- Exhibition prop
- Special events prop
- Made on site
  Educational programs
  Arts workshop
  Exhibition workshop
- Acquired with real property
- Decoration
- Former office/storage equipment
- Staff personal property
- Awards and trophies (museum or staff)

Undocumented objects are mysteries that can many times be solved. If the mystery is solved, the undocumented object returns to its true status as a loan, gift, or purchase. If it cannot be solved, then the object may properly be considered a found-in-collection (FIC) object. In order to protect the museum's interests should claims regarding these objects arise, it is necessary to differentiate between the two status types.

The museum profession has not unanimously decided on terminology for this collection problem, and discussion about these objects is often confusing. It is important that the museum community come to a more uniform understanding of the definitions used to discuss the problem. The two important terms, with proposed definitions, are "undocumented object" and "found-in-collection (FIC)."

Undocumented Objects:

Undocumented objects are those objects similar to collections and found in collections areas with no numbers, no information in their housing, nor any characteristics that might connect them to documentation.

Found-in-Collection:

Found-in-collection objects are undocumented objects that remain without status after all attempts to reconcile them to existing records of permanent collection and loan objects are completed.

The difference between the two is research and the museum's ability to assume ownership of the object. It is vital to track undocumented objects from the moment they are found, but it is not possible to know definitively if they can be connected to existing documentation until a complete inventory and reconciliation process is done. When it is, the remaining objects are and may be considered museum property.

Many factors influence the type and quantity of objects that are undocumented. If a museum collects objects or works of art with a fairly narrow focus, if almost all objects are high value, if the museum is fairly young and/or if the collection has historically been tightly controlled, then the chances of having FIC material is slight. New museums, and many established art museums, either do not have FIC or have a very minor occurrence of this type of object. Unfortunately, these museums are few and FIC objects are common across the museum field. The problem is widespread, not attributable to one cause, and certainly not anything that should incur blame on current staff. Most FIC are the product of the vagaries of past collecting practices and the lack of caretakers for the collections.

What types of practices lead to undocumented objects?

•Documentation systems were not regularized for museums until the early 1900s. The dissemination of those systems was slow, and staff to implement them scarce.

•Different systems were embraced—and reinvented—by different museums. Several systems for accessioning and documenting objects often exist within one museum.

•Natural history, history, anthropology, and archaeology museums work with such large volumes of material that adequate staffing is rarely an option. Some objects just never got processed.

•Volunteers have been used extensively for collections work, and they are neither always well trained nor clearly committed to finishing tasks at hand. Supervision and checking of work are not always possible because of the volume of work and the lack of professional staff.

•The entire tenor of society in the first part of the 20th century, when museums were forming, was very informal with regard to property transfer. The litigious nature of the early 21st century was virtually unknown.

•Tax laws have, especially since the middle of the 20th century, pushed recording of gifts in a timely fashion to the forefront of collection activities. Before there were IRS incentives or IRS reporting, timelines for gifts were much more casual.

•Human nature is probably the largest cause. Directors and curators took in unimportant objects from important donors. Board members felt that the museums were an extension of their own collections and deposited, donated, and purchased accordingly.

POLICY

There are divergent opinions about undocumented and FIC objects and how they should be treated by a museum. The first and perhaps most difficult task is to find all undocumented objects and to reconcile as many of them as possible to existing documentation. *(See chapter on Inventory.)* At the end of the inventory process a museum is usually left with a number of objects that are lost in inventory and a number of objects that are undocumented. The reconciliation process has, in the past, been hit-or-miss, long, protracted, and difficult. Searching through a card catalog system or inventory books, however well developed, was like searching for a needle in a haystack. The advent of computerized collection databases has improved this process tremendously. While card systems were arranged, at best, by three or four identifiers (e.g., accession number, artist, culture, object name), computer systems can enable searches on most words entered. If all object names, cultural affiliations, materials, artists, publishers, manufacturers, and geographic origins can be easily searched, it is infinitely easier to match undocumented objects to their records than it was before computers.

A case in point comes from the Northwest Museum of Arts and Culture (MAC), in Spokane,

Washington. In 1978 the museum, then the Cheney Cowles Memorial Museum, completed its first comprehensive inventory, checking each object in the collection against a set of notebooks containing accession lists for the entire collection. At the end of the process there were over 2000 undocumented objects and over 2000 lost-in-inventory pieces. The reconciliation process included laying out all objects of one type (guns, Plateau material, textiles, domestic objects) and going through all lost-in-inventory descriptions, trying to match materials with records. Perhaps a quarter of the objects were reunited with their documentation after a process that lasted more than six months.

In 1994, when the last of NAGPRA inventories was being processed, staff at the MAC came across a box of five Native American artifacts with a note from 1978 that they had not been reconciled. The database was checked for objects without location with characteristics that matched the found objects. Within an hour all were reunited with their original documentation.

Most museums assign tracking numbers to objects when they are discovered without documentation. These numbers, starting with (among many variations) N or NN (no number), X, or 00 for the year, allow the museum to begin documentation without the long process of accessioning approvals and decisions. If the museum uses a tracking number, however, rather than an accession number for an undocumented object, it may not be making as strong a case for ownership as it might.

On the other hand, if a museum applies an accession number to an undocumented object, and thus makes a stronger ownership case, it implies that some thoughtful and careful process has been completed. The practical problems that arise from this conundrum are numerous. It is extremely difficult for museums with large, unwieldy collections to complete and reconcile inventories. It is even difficult for medium size collections, perhaps 30,000 to 50,000 pieces, to finish and reconcile an inventory. If records are complicated, and were not clearly kept, it could take years for a reconciliation process to take place.

In order to deal effectively with the problem of undocumented objects and FIC, museums should first discuss and devise policy, and provide guidance on how to proceed with undocumented vs. FIC objects. If policy is not written and approved, museum staff will deal ad hoc with the problem, and the results will be uneven and confusing as changes in staff occur over the years. The policy on undocumented and FIC objects should be a subsection of the institution's acquisitions policy, approved by the institution's governing board.

The time gap between inventory and complete reconciliation must be taken into account when policy is established. It is even possible that a museum will not be able to complete an inventory, and that undocumented objects will be found from time to time during projects. There are differences of opinion on this complex and problematic subject and laws that leave little room for opinion. Policy choices for dealing with each problem follow, along with a recommended policy in each instance.

Museum staff should first research, with legal counsel, the laws that deal with property that might be similar to undocumented or FIC objects in their state. (See chart on property laws.) These laws may be called lost property, unclaimed property, or abandoned property laws; they also may be found as sections in many of the museum-specific laws that deal primarily with old loans. If state law makes specific demands and/or denies the museum title without a claim process, the first decision is made; if it does not, the museum must devise its own procedures for assimilating FIC objects.

1. Definition

a. Undocumented objects are those objects similar to collections and found in collections areas with no numbers, no information in their housing, nor any characteristics that might connect them to documentation. Found-in-collection objects are undocumented objects that remain after all attempts to reconcile them to existing records of permanent collection and loan objects fail.

•A list of undocumented objects should not include objects with partial documentation, objects that have numbers consistent with the museum's accession numbers (even without backup documents), or objects that have not been completely processed. A systematic process will consider how to deal with the partials, temporaries, and incompletes, but documentation should exist for most of those objects. True FIC objects are those that remain after a reconciliation process without extant clues to their origin or status.

2. Museum's considered perception of undocumented objects:

a. Museum A considers undocumented objects to be the property of the Museum.

b. Museum B considers undocumented objects to be of uncertain status.

c. Museum C considers undocumented objects to be accessioned objects owned by the museum which have lost the numbers that connect them to documentation.

d. Museum D holds undocumented objects that must be processed under state museum property law.

•Preference goes in order from 2a through 2d. Unless the museum has specific state law to follow, 2b is closest to the reality of most situations. 2a, however, is the preferred stance, and is most often used by museums; except in unusual situations, the majority of undocumented objects are owned by the museum that holds them. They may be of uncertain status, but there is nothing to indicate that an undocumented object may belong to someone else; only a claim will bring that possibility forward.

There are times when the museum does know where the property came from. Consider the use of "found in collection" by the National Postal Museum: "In an attempt to fill gaps in the older issues, we have resurrected material set aside as 'duplicate' in the 1980s. We have finished the review of selection of good mint examples from this source and have inventoried them. Their reintroduction to the collection will be complete when they are given FIC numbers and cataloged."[1] Records for the duplicate collection were obviously not as complete as those for the permanent collection, but there is reason to consider them owned by the museum.

A museum may originate from the gift of an entire estate that may include a house and its contents. Such a gift may also occur at any time; for example, the Brandywine River Museum's acquisition of the N. C. Wyeth house and studio in the 1990s. If the first sweep in the process of accessioning was not complete, and if all objects were not identified and numbered, undocumented objects and FIC objects may well be unprocessed parts of the original accession.

A second and very common scenario is the lost accession number. For example, in the 1920s some collections of Native American baskets were numbered by stapling small, thick paper tags to their rims. The paper was acidic and over the years it cracked and crumbled. In some instances, the staples rusted out as well, and the baskets were left with partial tags or no tags at all. Even partial tags are a useful clue, however, since a museum worker may know the types of tags and inks used in the collection during specific time periods. The tag may even point toward a single gift. In many cases there is no way to reconcile the basket to a record, because records noting baskets in the collection may just say "coiled basket," or "woven basket," or even just "basket."

The baskets with no identifications left must be treated as undocumented objects and FIC. It is possible that they might have been loans, but a museum worker will have a sense of the proportion of loans to permanent collection objects in an individual museum, and of the type and quality of object that existed in the major collections gathered in the early days of the museum. That worker should be able to place the preponderance of the evidence with either gift/purchase or loan.

Museum workers are also aware of the collecting policies that were in place in the early days of their institutions. Some museums took everything that came their way and put aside material that they felt was secondary. These secondary objects, left for future generations to deal with, are now found-in-collection. Sometimes they can be reconciled with some vague list; usually they can't.

Museums in small towns have often found

themselves the recipient of objects they really do not want, from "donors" who refused to make a clear declaration of gift but wanted the museum to keep the property. Their collections may also be filled by donors who insisted on giving the museum all of the bric-a-brac they own. All of the standards and policies and procedures and professional associations in the world have failed to convince directors and curators that they can risk offending the town's richest or most powerful citizen, and collections fill up with unwanted and often undocumented objects.

3. The museum's preliminary action

a. Undocumented objects will receive tracking numbers and be used in accordance with approved uses of museum collections.

b. The museum will make every attempt to reconcile undocumented objects with existing documentation, considering objects that are not reconciled to be FIC.

•Most museums assign tracking numbers to objects when they are discovered without documentation. This is necessary for several reasons, but is primarily done to avoid the long process of accessioning approvals and decisions and allow immediate tracking.

Many museums, however, stop at this point. They assign tracking numbers but make no affirmative decision that the object should be in the collection; some museum policies, however, note that any object found in collection is to be considered an accessioned object.

4. Decisions about FIC

a. FIC objects may be accessioned into the collection or disposed of according to approved deaccession policy.

b. Any FIC objects that might be a loan, i.e., of the object type listed in an unresolved old loan, will be converted to museum property using applicable state law.

c. All FIC objects may be converted to museum property and then accessioned into the collection.

d. All FIC objects will be converted to museum property according to applicable state law.

During inventory reconciliation, it is common to find several objects that are probably a part of an accession or an old loan, but it is not possible to determine for certain which of the objects were included in a given transaction. For example, after the inventory there are five dolls without numbers and four dolls lost in inventory.

Three dolls in an accession list have not been found:

Small cloth doll, bad condition.
Ceramic doll with blue eyes
Doll

One doll has a loan status, and its documentation reads:

Cloth doll, 6 inches

After reviewing all the records and inspecting the dolls, it may be impossible to determine whether any of them are actually the dolls noted on the loan receipt and in the accession list. In this case, it is prudent to go through an old loan process for all the dolls, listing them as unknown source when publishing constructive notice *(see chapter on Old Loans)*, and accessioning them (or deaccessioning them) when that process is complete.

FIC objects are often inferior to already accessioned objects. Constraints on staff time generally translate into taking more care to document and track objects that are considered very valuable. Lesser objects receive less time and less documentation. While some FIC material may be considered relevant to the mission of the museum, not affirming it by accessioning when it originally arrived is a major indicator that it never fit, and should be processed out of the museum. The process of dealing with FIC objects presents the ideal time to review each object, affirm or reject it, and if affirmed, to process it into the collection.

Accessioning the object implies that it may be used in the same way other museum objects are used: that it may be exhibited, loaned, photographed, published, conserved, or deaccessioned. If FIC objects receive a tracking number rather than accession number, the museum's policy should state that tracked FIC objects may also be used in accordance with policies and procedures covering accessioned objects.

5. Accessioning FIC material

a. The process of accessioning FIC objects will begin with

a decision of the director and curator

a decision of the curator

and/or

The process for accessioning will not include review by the acquisitions committee of the museum.

and/or

FIC acquisitions will (or will not) be reported in the annual report.

b. FIC objects will be accessioned into the permanent collection following all steps in the museum's acquisitions (or accessions) policy.

c. The assignment of a number to the object when it is found will indicate that it is accessioned.

•If a museum takes the approach that FIC objects are already theirs and that there is institutional evidence to believe that most FIC objects were simply missed or have lost their documents, the process of accessioning may be the more internal affirmation (curator or curator/director). Reporting accessions with an FIC source, however, is important so that collection size and sources are updated and transparent. It may be, as well, another source of notice that would make the museum's case more strongly if a claim is made. The museum might also require that an affidavit be signed and dated by either the person assigning the original tracking number or by a curator or other staff member with knowledge of possible ownership, e.g., recollection of a group of objects coming in together or knowledge of the type of material that appeared in an early collection.

6. Deaccession

a. FIC objects slated for disposition will follow the deaccession process as if they are owned objects.

b. Ad hoc decisions regarding claims for title under applicable state law relating to deaccession of FIC objects will be made by a committee of professional staff.

c. FIC objects slated for deaccession will be claimed under applicable state law.

d. FIC objects will be claimed under applicable state law before they are either accessioned or deaccessioned.

There is no evidence, with FIC objects, that the museum does not own the object. Ildiko DeAngelis, in a 2005 AAM Annual Meeting discussion, states the following:

"Legally, actually, you're in a much better position with FICs than you are with old loans, because the undisturbed possession by the museum of this object, often for decades, is in itself evidence that supports a presumption that the title is owned by the museum. In other words, because you own it and you possess it, and you lack evidence that it's not yours, the law gives you a break. It actually is on your side.

"The burden of proof would be on anyone who wants to claim that object as theirs. In other words, the museum can sit there on its laurels and say, this is ours, prove to us otherwise. So the claimant has the burden of proof, and honestly, that burden is often heavy."[2]

DeAngelis holds that the accession number is far better than a tracking number in the event that a claim for title is made. She notes that getting rid of FIC is in harmony with the responsibilities of a museum that holds objects in the public trust.

If a museum adds a FIC object to its permanent collection, the worst that can happen is a future claim, the success of which will diminish as time passes. If a successful claim is made, the worst that can happen is the return of an object to its rightful owner. The museum might even negotiate a gift, if the situation warrants it.

If a museum disposes of an object by sale, it does open itself up to penalty should a successful claim ever be made. Each state's version of the Uniform Commercial Code applies, and if a successful claim is made, the museum may have to pay the current value of the object, rather than the value for which the object was sold. If instead the museum donates the object, or sells it with notice of a flawed title (in all likelihood reducing the price), there is less recourse for the owner whose claim has succeeded. Review Malaro's text on claims, pp. 356–359 , applicable state law, and the risk chart in this section.

7. Possible actions if original documentation is found or a claim is made.

a. If original documentation is found for an object that has been tracked or accessioned into the collection using a FIC number, it will be returned to its original number and the FIC number will be retired.

b. If a claim is made on a FIC object, either accessioned into the collection or disposed of, the museum will make ad hoc decisions on accepting or fighting the claim.

If a claim is made, the museum must request proof that the object claimed from the collection is the object described in the claimant's documents, and that the claimant is either the sole owner or that he or she has complete authority from all of the owners to make the claim. The first part may require very precise documentation, e.g., a "flowered vase" will hardly describe one of five vases of different periods made of different materials that exist in the collection with FIC documentation only. It may also be difficult for a person to claim he or she is the only heir. As time goes on, it often happens that more than one person inherits from an estate. If this is compounded, the more time a museum has held an object, the less the chance of a successful claim.

The museum must respond to a claim as soon as is feasible. If the proof is strong, the museum should return the object quickly. If the proof is weak, the museum should reject the claim in writing. This starts a statute of limitations (usually three to six years) to bring a suit against the museum. If a suit is filed, the museum may decide whether to fight the claim or return the object. This, too, is often dependent on the value and uniqueness of the object.

The preferred policy options suggest the following model:

Policy on Undocumented and Found in Collection Objects

Undocumented objects are those objects similar to collections and found-in-collections areas with no numbers, no information in their housing, nor any characteristics that might connect them to documentation. Found-in-collection (FIC) objects are undocumented objects that remain after all attempts to reconcile them to existing records of permanent collection and loan objects fail.

The museum will make every attempt to reconcile undocumented objects to existing documentation. Objects that are not reconciled will be considered FIC.

The museum considers undocumented and FIC objects to be the property of the museum. Undocumented objects will be tracked and documented from the time they are found, and may be used as any permanent collection object is used. FIC objects may be accessioned into the collection or disposed of according to approved deaccession policy. The decision to accession may be made by the curator with the approval of the director, as documented on an acquisition proposal form. FIC objects accessioned into the permanent collection will be given numbers in the year of accession and included in the annual report of objects.

If original documentation is found for an object that has been tracked or accessioned into the collection using a FIC number, the object will be returned to its original status and number and the FIC number will be retired.

If a claim is made on an undocumented or FIC object, either accessioned into the collection or disposed of, the museum will make ad hoc decisions on accepting or fighting the claim.

Unclaimed objects and FIC objects slated for disposition will follow the approved deaccession process as if they are owned objects.

PROCEDURES

1. Assign and apply a tracking number.

Objects without documentation should be assigned a number immediately.

If the number is to serve as both a tracking

number and an accession number (that is, museum policy considers all undocumented objects to be FIC property of the museum from the time they are found), it is good to put it at the beginning of the year's accessions. If an accession number, it should follow the same pattern used for all of the museum's accessions. Example:

2005.00.1

00 is given the accession group with the source "Unknown." It could as easily be 0 or 000, depending on the numbering system used by the museum. Again, one number can be used for all of the FIC objects accessioned in the calendar year.

If the number is simply for tracking, and decisions about accessioning are to be made after some review, the number might be a reverse of the usual accession number. With a standard tripartite system, for example, the first undocumented object of the year might be:

00.2005.1

The sequence can continue throughout the year, with museum staff adding as many objects as found, i.e., 00.2005.2, 00.2005.3, etc. In 2006, 00.2006 is reserved for FIC accessions.

Museums have used a variety of tracking systems to indicate undocumented objects: numbers prefixed by X or N, 00 numbers followed only by sequential numbers, and prefixes used on a yearly basis, for example.

It is not advisable, especially with a numbering system that will probably see many retired numbers, to change what exists in records already created. It is advisable, however, to alter the system slightly for the present and future if a year is not indicated in the existing number system. Because of various state laws it is important to be able to prove how long an object has been in the museum if a claim is made. It is also important because of the constraints on staff time in most museums; the process may not get past the numbering stage for years or even decades.

Current system: 00.1, 00.2, 00.3, etc.

Change to: 00.2005.1, 00.2005.2, etc., then 00.2006.1, etc., for the next year.

Current system: N1, N2, N3, etc.

Change to N2005.1, N2005.2, etc., then N2006.1, etc., for the next year.

The number assigned may be applied immediately, using the same methods used to number a permanent collection object. Whereas loans are not usually permanently marked, both undocumented and FIC objects may be. Or the object may be tagged during inventory reconciliation and a permanent physical number applied only after it is reconciled and accessioned as a FIC object.

2. Gather basic registration information.

Describe all undocumented objects in the system used for recording permanent collections. For most museums, this has become a computerized collections database from which a catalog card can be printed. Using the database or a regular worksheet, measure the object. Do a condition report. Collect and record as much information as can be taken from the object itself, particularly information about any marks, collector's numbers, or other characteristics that can differentiate it from other objects. Photograph the object, and if possible, put a photo in the computer, on the printout of the catalog card or on the manually produced catalog card, and/or in the object folder.

- Describe
- Measure
- Report Condition
- Photograph

3. Do an institutional search for information.

Record for the FIC object file comments from staff members who might remember details about the object. For example, the director might have seen the object at a particular time or remembers using it in an exhibition a decade before it is "found." Perhaps a curator or a registrar remembers bringing in a group of similar materials and believes that the object in question is a part of that group. A nondescript mark or number on the object may "ring a bell" with someone aware of the habits of a certain collector who marked his objects in a particular way.

Write down any information that is found, and sign and date the document. An affidavit form can help formalize the information gathered. Such a document adds to the strength of the museum's claim of ownership.

4. Reconcile undocumented objects with lost-in-inventory objects.

Inventory reconciliation is the process of matching objects to documentation; for undocumented objects, it is the more complicated process of trying to match objects without numbers to documentation without objects. It is generally and most easily accomplished with the aid of a complete inventory. Trying to find a single object without a good catalog, preferably entered into a computerized database, can be one of the most frustrating collection tasks possible. The process of reconciliation of FIC objects is best done as the final part of a reconciled inventory. Records of objects that have not been found in that inventory are prime candidates for matches with objects with no numbers.

If a collections database is available, first make certain that there is at least a "place-holder" file for each object noted in either catalogue cards or accession ledger, and keep track of all moves in the database. Over time, even without a complete inventory, locations are noted and a history of where objects have been and are currently located emerges. Databases allow easy searches for objects named but with no location. For example, a rifle is found in the collection and a computerized search for rifles that have no known locations yields a list of perhaps five examples with which to begin comparisons.

This process is long and arduous. It can sometimes be done in pieces, i.e., locate and inventory every doll in the collection. Find all of the doll records. Compare them all. It is even better if this step can be done before any numbers are assigned, in order to avoid the necessity of retiring tracking or mistaken accession numbers. Such an ideal sequence, however, generally cannot and does not happen unless there is ample and dedicated staff to work on the specific project.

When is lost in inventory truly lost in inventory?
Never. Although one can never be certain an object is truly lost, a museum may decide to claim the loss on their insurance policy after a careful check of all areas where the object might reasonably be (storage, conservation, exhibition, loan) and after checking with all staff who might have had reason to interact with the object. A new inventory of suspect areas and records should find the object or leave staff relatively certain that it has been inadvertently disposed of or stolen. Records for lost property should never be removed from files or databases.

5. For reconciled objects, affirm and apply original number. Retire tracking number.

Keep a record on the object's card, in its file, and/or in its computer record, of the tracking number that was assigned to it. It is not always possible to eliminate or change all of the records where a number was used. That tracking number will pop up somewhere and will need to be linked to the current object number.

6. For remaining objects, decide whether to accession or dispose.

The museum's policy will outline the process for making this decision. The registrar or collections manager who is working on the FIC objects should alert the curator responsible for a particular collection when it is determined that an object is truly without documentation. Decision to accession or dispose can be made in accordance with the guidelines for accession or deaccession outlined in the museum's collection management policy and in accordance with the process outlined in the policy for FIC objects.

Review the FIC object to determine if any federal or state laws regarding materials or origin affect the status of the object. If this has not already been done when the FIC object was found, check whether the object is covered under the Native American Graves Protection and Repatriation Act, the Endangered Species Act, or other laws that control the use and movement of species or specific types of material taken from them. If a curator knows of possible stolen or looted objects, or objects removed from their countries in violation of laws in place, the museum may move to restore or repatriate, as well.

7. Accession the FIC object.

Add the object to the permanent system as if it were an object on approval from any other source. Change the number (see 1 above) and record the object in the current year. Should this object be deaccessioned in the future, it should be deaccessioned in accordance with the deaccession policy in place, and its former

FIC status should be noted and used to make decisions regarding the risk the museum is taking. If the museum pursues title to FIC objects before deaccessioning, that policy would apply.

8. Dispose of an undocumented or FIC object.

Undocumented and FIC objects are in their most sensitive moment when they are deaccessioned. Regardless of whether the object was accessioned or just tracked, it is imperative that the complete deaccessioning process in accordance with the museum's policy be used to dispose of it. Trustees must know if there is a risk of future claims against the museum. As noted on the risk chart, it is likely that objects that are multiples, of small or no monetary value, or given to other not-for-profit institutions, pose little or no risk. The museum may not have the time, staff, or resources to use legal processes to convert small or minor objects. Consider, for example, how many Sears and Roebuck cast-iron irons will be claimed and whether they are worth a lawsuit. Even differentiating among five irons cataloged briefly as "clothes irons" may not be possible. Use common sense, and document everything very carefully.

The risk for unique objects, especially those of high value, is a different matter. Legal counsel should be sought, and using available laws to take title to the property may prove a positive factor in fighting future claims. •

NOTES

1. Lawson, Mary H. How One Collection is getting its Groove Back: Revitalizing the National Postal Museum's Exhibit and Master and Reference Collection of U. S. Stamps, EnRoute, 1998.

2. DeAngelis, Ildiko. Old Loans and Found in Collection, presentation at the American Association of Museums Annual Meeting, Indianapolis, Indiana. May, 2005.

3. Malaro, Marie C. *A Legal Primer on Managing Museum Collections.* Smithsonian Institution Press, Washington, D.C. 1998

The Basics II | HYPOTHETICALS

1

During a recent inventory, you found nearly one hundred objects whose cards have been marked "deaccessioned," but the objects are clearly still present in the museum. There are no records of deaccession in the object files, and you have no idea when the deaccessioning might have been done.

How do you proceed?

2

Amanda Smith arrives at the museum and requests that the piano her great-grandmother loaned to the museum in 1917 be given to her on the spot. She hands you a loan form that indicates the spinet was left with the museum on September 17, 1917.

Do you have the piano?

Will you hand it over?

What are the processes, proofs, prerequisites for returning a loan from the past to a person in the present?

3

Define "found in collections" for your museum and write a clear policy to place FIC in context.

Develop as well a process to incorporate FIC intelligently into the permanent collections.

4

Who in the museum is responsible for research on provenance for existing collections?

For new collections?

How is the research used and how is the information integrated into records?

3L | LOANS

SALLY FREITAG AND CHERIE SUMMERS, UPDATED BY SALLY FREITAG AND JUDY CLINE

Loans are made between museums or between museums and private individuals or commercial entities for a number of reasons. The term "loan" covers a broad spectrum of categories for all works of art—owned or borrowed—under the museum's care.

•Loans for exhibition are the most common type. Objects are borrowed for specific periods of time for a specific purpose.

•Loans for traveling exhibitions are similar to single venue loans, but the issues are multiplied by the number of venues.

•Exchange loans are made for two reasons. They may be for the mutual benefit of the museums, or an institution may request a loan to fill a gap in its permanent exhibition that occurs when another museum borrows an important work.

•Study loans are made between museums or between museums and individuals. The latter type of study loan is more common in science and archaeology museums than in art or history museums.

•Promised gifts in the museum's custody are loans until title has passed to the museum.

•The donor's remaining interest in a partial gift (also called a fractional-interest gift) should be treated as a loan whenever the object is in the museum's custody. New tax laws require careful monitoring of the time the partial gift remains in the donor's custody prior to final transfer of title.

•Long-term loans from individuals to a museum or from one museum to another are common. The former was standard fare for many museums in the early and middle decades of the 20th century but is less common today, and these loans should always be reviewed annually.

•Objects coming in for purchase or acquisition

consideration also can be treated as loans until title has passed to the museum.

•Unsolicited objects often are received for loan or acquisition. The sender should be notified immediately that the unsolicited parcel will be returned at his/her expense and in the same manner that it was packed and shipped. The sender also should be notified that he/she will be required to carry and pay for any insurance he/she desires.

•Property with unidentified sources in the museum's custody should be treated as a loan until it has been identified. *(See chapter on Old Loans.)*

Loans should be requested and made with great care. A written loan policy should include sections on both incoming and outgoing loans. It should be supplemented by written procedures that are implemented as thoroughly as possible.

APPROVAL PROCESS: INCOMING LOANS

Museum administrative policies differ regarding the internal approvals needed to request a loan. If the borrowed object is to be exhibited, the director, curator, and/or project manager usually must approve. Long-term loans or loans of promised gifts may require the approval of a committee within the museum or may follow the museum's established acquisitions procedure. The department that controls the budget for the loan arrangements must be consulted.

Customary protocol for requesting loans calls for the director, curator, or project manager of the borrowing institution to send the prospective lender a detailed letter describing the purpose of the exhibition or loan activity and the objects desired. This "loan request" should contain the following key information:

•Title of the exhibition and/or purpose of the loan

•Length of the loan period

•Location(s) of the exhibition with dates

The borrower's responsibility to pay for all expenses incurred in preparing a loan (e.g., packing, shipping, insurance, immunity from seizure) should be acknowledged at this time. The deadline for the lender's response should be noted to allow sufficient time for the loan approval. A copy of the lender's letter, which typically is addressed to the director or curator if the borrower is an institution, must be forwarded to the registrar as soon as possible, so he/she can begin processing the loan and respond to the lender's queries. Often a loan agreement form accompanies the official loan request letter. Other documentation, such as contracts that cover unusal circumstances, also may be appropriate. *(See chapter on Documentation.)*

APPROVAL PROCESS: OUTGOING LOANS

When a request for a loan is received, the lending institution's approval procedure for outgoing loans should involve the following "key players":

•The curator evaluates the project in general and indicates the availability of the loan based on any unannounced projects he/she may know about. Provenance issues also should be considered in case there are gaps in ownership history and obtaining immunity from seizure becomes necessary.

•The conservator or registrar examines the condition of the object(s) to be loaned. Size, weight, and shipping logistics to the borrower's location are major factors.

•The registrar also checks for other commitments during the period in question and for any other legal restrictions, such as the donor's requirements or U.S. Customs or Fish and Wildlife regulations.

•Final approval by the director and/or the board of trustees is required in many institutions after the various departments have submitted their input.

In general, there should be good communication within the lending institution from the time a loan is requested until it is returned. It is critical that the curator, registrar, conservator, and director keep one another apprised of any pertinent information. It is up to the registrar to coordinate the process and make certain that the object and the borrowing institution are evaluated.

In evaluating the object's condition, the following questions should be considered:

•Is the object able to withstand the rigors of travel and additional handling?

•Is the object too fragile to be displayed safely?

•Should special restrictions be placed on light levels or general environmental exposure?

•Has the object recently traveled extensively or been subjected to long periods of light exposure?

•Will it fit through the borrower's doors crated or uncrated?

Many objects, such as works on paper, photographs, or latex materials, can be exposed to light and adverse climate conditions only for a limited length of time during packing, display, and shipping. If your museum does not have an in-house conservator, it is advisable to seek professional advice from a freelance conservator before deciding whether the object can travel safely. This cost may be passed on to the borrower.

The borrower's current facility report must be considered when evaluating a loan request. The General Facility Report form developed by the Registrars Committee of the American Association of Museums (RC-AAM) often is used by American museums; some institutions, especially foreign museums, may submit their own forms. The RC-AAM form is extremely thorough in the questions it contains and is highly recommended. Accuracy and honesty are essential when filling out the facility report, and information on the form should be updated on a regular basis or as changes occur. The borrower must be prepared to meet certain minimum

MRM5 MUSEUM
123 Any Street, Any Town, USA 00000
Telephone 000-000-0000 FAX 000-000-0001

OUTGOING LOAN AGREEMENT

AGREEMENT   The MRM5 Museum hereby lends to the borrower identified below the object(s) described herein for the purposes and subject to the terms and conditions set forth.

BORROWER
Borrower:
Address:
Telephone: FAX:
Contact: Title:

OBJECT
Accession Number:
Artist/Maker:
Object/Title:
Medium:
Date of Work:
Dimensions of actual object: with frame or mount:
        Weight (if applicable):
Credit Line (for use in exhibit label and catalog):

EXHIBITION   Period of Loan:
Exhibition Title:
Venue(s) and Date(s):

INSURANCE
Insurance value (in U.S. dollars):
❏ To be carried by borrower
❏ To be carried by the MRM5 Museum, premium billed to borrower

---

SHIPPING/
PACKING
Unless otherwise specified, all objects will be released from and returned to:
The MRM5 Museum, Receiving Entrance, 123 Any Street, Any Town, USA

DISPLAY
Temperature range: Humidity range: Light levels:
Special display requirements:

SIGNATURE
The borrower acknowledges that he/she has full authority and power to enter into this agreement, that he/she has read the conditions above and on the back of this form and that he/she agrees to be bound by them.

Signature: Date:

The MRM5 Museum

Signature: Date:

Borrower

Please sign white original and return to the MRM5 Museum Registrar. The copy is for your files.

OUTGOING LOAN CONDITIONS

Care and Preservation
Objects borrowed shall be given proper care to insure against loss, damage or deterioration. The borrower agrees to meet any special requirements for installation and handling. The MRM5 Museum (the "Museum") certifies that the objects lent are in condition to withstand ordinary strains of packing, transportation and handling. The Museum is to be notified immediately, followed by a full written and photographic report, if damage or loss is discovered. If damage occurred in transit, the borrower will also notify the carrier and will save all packing materials for inspection. No object may be altered, cleaned, repaired or fumigated without the written permission of the Museum, nor may framing, matting, mounting or glazing be changed without written permission; not may objects be examined by scientific methods without written permission. Objects must be maintained in a fireproof building under 24-hour physical and/or electronic security and protected from unusual temperatures and humidity; excessive light and from insects, vermin, dirt or other environmental hazards. Objects will be handled only by experienced personnel.

Packing and Transportation
Packing and transportation arrangements for the loan must be approved by the Museum. The borrower agrees to meet any special requirements for packing and shipping. Shipping requirements include: dual drivers, air-ride and climate control truck, last on/first off, direct non-stop delivery, or exclusive use shipping. At no time should the truck be left unattended. Unpacking and repacking must be performed by experienced personnel. Repacking must be done with either original or similar materials and boxes and by the same methods as the object was received.

Insurance
Objects shall be insured at the borrower's expense for the value stated on the face of this agreement under an all-risk wall-to-wall policy subject to the following standard exclusions: wear and tear, insects, vermin, gradual deterioration or inherent vice; repairing, restoration or retouching processes; hostile or warlike action, insurrection, or rebellion; nuclear reaction, nuclear radiation or radioactive contamination. The Museum shall determine whether the borrower insures the objects or whether the Museum insures them and bills the borrower for the premium. If the borrower is insuring the objects, the Museum must be furnished with a certificate of insurance or a copy of the policy made out in favor of the Museum prior to shipment of the loan. The Museum must be notified in writing at least 30 days prior to any cancellation or meaningful change in the borrower's policy. Any lapses in coverage, any failure to secure insurance and/or inaction by the Museum will not release the borrower from liability for loss or damage.

Reproduction and Credit
The Museum will make available, through an outside service, photographs of objects lent, which may used for catalog, routine non-commercial educational uses, publicity and registrarial purposes. No further use of such photographs can be made and no other reproduction of objects lent can be made without the written permission from the Museum. Each object will be labeled and credited to the Museum in the exact format provided on the face of this contract, both for display labels and publication credits.

Costs
The borrower will assume responsibility for all expenses incurred by the Museum in work by conservators to prepare the object for loan, in packing, crating, transportation, couriers, insurance, photography and any and all other related costs. The Museum will make every effort to provide the borrower with estimates in advance of all applicable costs.

Cancellation/Return/Extension
The loan is made with the understanding that the object will be on view during the entire exhibition period for which it has been requested. Any intention by the borrower to withdraw the loan from the exhibition at any time must be communicated to the Museum immediately. The Museum reserves the right to recall the loan or cancel the loan for good cause at any time, and will make effort to give reasonable notice thereof. Objects lent must be returned to the Museum by the stated return date. Any extension of the loan period must be approved in writing by the Museum Director or his designate and covered by written parallel extension of the insurance coverage.

Interpretation
In the event of any conflict between this agreement and any forms of the borrower, the terms of this agreement shall be controlling. For loans to borrowers with in the United States, this agreement shall be construed in accordance with the laws of the State of New Jersey.

Additional Conditions for International Loans
Government regulations will be adhered to in international shipments. Unless otherwise stated in writing, the borrower is responsible for adhering to its country's import/export requirements. The borrower will protect objects from possible damage during its customs inspections and will make every effort to ensure that customs examinations are made only the borrower's premises. If the nature of the material to be exported falls within the types addressed by the UNESCO Convention, its status in the importing country should be verified before this loan agreement is signed by the borrower. The Museum requires a declaration of immunity from seizure if available. The provisions of this loan agreement are subject to the doctrine of force majeure. If U.S. Government Indemnity is secured, the amount payable by indemnity is the sole recovery available to the Museum in event of loss or damage, and objects will be insured in U.S. dollars at their value as of the application date. Current fluctuations affecting value of claims at a later date are not recognized under indemnity.

museum standards to secure loans, such as proper climate controls, fire suppression, and security. The lender wants assurance that the borrower has a history of professional and responsible care of museum artifacts. Because information can be checked by the lender, false answers may jeopardize the loan or future exchanges. When reviewing the borrower's facility report, the lender should question any unclear answers and work with the borrower to improve unacceptable conditions, if at all possible. Although not applicable to foreign institutions, AAM accreditation can indicate that a borrowing institution has met certain minimum standards.

Shortly after the loan request has been received, the borrower should be given preliminary notification of all standard loan terms and fees required by the lending museum. Standard protocol between museums and collectors calls for the borrower to pay all expenses relating to temporary and long-term loans, incoming gifts, study or research loans, or any other loans of primary benefit to the museum. The lender may be asked to pay costs associated with loans of benefit to the lender, such as objects deposited for private conservation, photography, consideration for purchase, or exchange. Responsibility for costs should be discussed prior to the loan or prior to any charges being incurred. Museum collections management policies or manuals should designate clearly which museum personnel have authority to approve these costs.

Loan costs include the expense (materials, labor, delivery, storage, and rental fees) of all crating, preparation, display case, base or mount, matting and framing, glazing, conservation, deinstallation and reinstallation, shipping, courier, insurance, and loan fee. Prior to the actual loan contract or loan agreement, the lender may ask the borrower to sign a preliminary form acknowledging unusual loan conditions such as special environmental or shipping requirements. After reviewing the costs and special conditions, the borrower can decide if it is in a position to proceed with the loan request. Some museums have preprinted forms stating their general loan conditions, regarding care of the object(s), insurance, courier costs, publication, publicity, conservation, and rights and reproduction of the items being requested. The borrower is usually responsible for all the costs incurred in the loan arrangement unless otherwise discussed with and agreed to by the lender. Some institutions have reciprocal agreements with other museums to waive certain costs, such as loan fees. In cases where the fee makes the loan impossible for the borrower, the lender may be willing to negotiate a fee reduction.

The delicate condition or high value of some objects may dictate special loan conditions. It is important that these conditions be justified and essential for protecting the object. All costs or requirements must be clearly stated with as much notice given as possible so that the borrower can budget adequately. These costs can include a special frame, base, mount or environment, alarms or barriers, a courier or supervisor, or an insurance premium.

The lender may stipulate that a courier must accompany his/her loan whenever the object is in transit. The lender may allow another museum professional to act on his/her behalf as a courier in consolidated shipments or may agree to let his/her own courier take the object to the first venue and bring it back from the final venue in the case of exhibition tours. It is typically the borrower's responsibility to arrange and pay for costs related to the courier, including transportation, lodging, and per diem. The loan agreement may stipulate the per diem amount to be allotted. If not, the amount should be negotiated in advance. The courier may receive the per diem in cash upon arrival, or the lender may bill the borrower later for reimbursement of expenses. Arrangements should be clear and in writing. *(See chapters on Couriers and the Courier Code of Ethics.)*

Final approval or denial of a loan should be communicated in writing in a timely fashion once all in-house and board of trustee approvals have been received. Should a loan be denied, the reason(s) should be clearly stated so the borrower can improve any aspects of his/her facility or methods that need it. If the loan is approved, the approval letters and completed loan-agreement forms then are signed and returned to the borrower. Any special conditions should be restated on the loan form. In-house records should be "flagged" or "coded" to indicate that the object is reserved for a loan.

LOAN DOCUMENTATION

Either the borrower or lender can issue the final loan agreement; it is usually done by the borrower but the lender's form takes precedence if they insist on having their loan agreement signed. All special requirements or charges must be approved by the borrower before the lender begins to prepare the loan. The borrower must decide if the lender's special requirements can be met, both physically and financially. Further negotiations between museums may be necessary.

The loan contract or loan agreement is a binding legal document between the lending and borrowing institutions. This document protects both parties by specifying all agreed-upon conditions. The signed loan agreement overrides all other documents and understandings, whether written or verbal. It is completed by the registrar and signed before any preparation of the objects begins or costs are incurred. Institutions differ on who signs this form, director, curator, loan officer, exhibition officer, project manager, or registrar. If someone other than the registrar signs the contract, the registrar should review it first. Most museums have a general loan contract containing certain standard clauses including but not limited to care and handling of object, insurance coverage, and environmental conditions. To this, an addendum can be made to address any special clauses needed for individual objects.

Many museums have a standard contract for outgoing loans and a separate one for incoming loans. Occasionally, museums will tailor a unique loan contract for a particular exhibition. Standard or special loan contracts should be reviewed by legal counsel as well as by the museum's insurance broker.

The borrower should never commit itself to conditions that it cannot uphold or that cannot be supported under the terms of its insurance policy. Approving special requirements placed by the lender may require various internal approvals. Unanticipated loan fees and unexpected requests may have such an impact on the borrower's budget that the loan request must be withdrawn.

The lender signs and returns the loan contract with an accompanying letter calling special attention

---

Traveling Exhibition Organizer to Host INFORMATION TIMETABLE

One year to six months prior to exhibition opening at each venue
Send publicity packets containing:
  a. Checklist
  b. Press release
  c. Selected black-and-white photos and color transparencies for news articles
  d. Slides and/or digital photos with slide/photo list
  e. Clippings from prior venues (if available)
  f. Request that attendance figures and clippings be sent to organizer

Six to four months prior to exhibition opening
Send registration packet containing:
  a. Checklist
  b. Slides and/or digital images
  c. Special handling requirements
  d. Special equipment needs
  e. Pedestal and vitrine requirements
  f. Photography permissions and/or restrictions
Discuss and agree on shipping arrangements

Two months to one month prior to exhibition opening
  a. Send crate dimensions
  b. Send crate contents list (identify which crate has the condition report notebook)
  c. Confirm special handling requirements
  d. Confirm courier costs and arrangements
  e. Confirm shipping schedule

With thanks to Dixie Nielson

to any changes; the contract then should be counter-signed by the borrower.

INSURANCE

It is standard loan protocol for the borrower to accept responsibility for insuring loans. A few museums have administrative policies stipulating that they, as lenders, must keep their own coverage in effect when making outgoing loans. The borrower then is billed for the cost of the insurance premium; this should be agreed upon in the early stages of the loan negotiation.

In accepting the borrower's coverage, lenders are advised to review a copy of the borrower's current insurance policy to ensure the coverage is indeed adequate. Key areas to look for are:

- Limits of coverage
- Terrorism
- Deductibles
- Exclusions
- Property insured
- Policy terms
- Terms of cancellation

Coverage should be "all risk," not based on "named perils," which are less inclusive. Coverage also should be "wall to wall" or "nail to nail," meaning that the loan object is insured from the moment it is picked up to the moment it is examined upon its return to the lender. Various government indemnities are now available. The indemnification coverage should be the same as or better than commercial policies and should be considered by the lender to save costs.

A certificate of insurance or indemnity from another institution acts only as evidence of coverage. Even with this certificate in hand, the borrower has no real assurances that the policy has not been amended or canceled. The certificate should name the lender as "additional insured" and must be issued to the lender before the object is released for shipment. If the lender prefers to maintain his/her own coverage, the borrower should request an insurance certificate or waiver of subrogation from the lender. *(See chapter on Insurance.)*

Insurance values for each object are determined by the lender. The assigned values should reflect the "fair-market value," the price at which the property would change hands between a willing buyer and a willing seller, neither being under any compulsion to buy or sell and both having reasonable knowledge of the relevant facts. Auction values often are used as the basis for insurance values. The borrower should question an exceptionally high value or one that seems out of line with similar objects. A third-party appraisal may be required in some instances, such as for indemnity applications. All values should be confirmed internally by the curator. It is the lender's responsibility to keep the value of the loan up to date.

If a lender insists on a specific situation the borrowing institution believes may be hazardous to the loan object—e.g., installing the object without a barrier, using push pins to mount the work, displaying the art work in harsh light, or allowing the general public to touch the object—the lender should be asked to sign a "hold harmless" agreement.

PACKING AND SHIPPING ARRANGEMENTS

Packing and shipping arrangements must be mutually agreed upon by the lending and borrowing registrars. The borrowing registrar normally contacts the lender to discuss considerations for packing, shipping methods, elevator or loading dock limitations, door heights and egress issues, scheduling, and courier needs. The borrowing registrar may wish to consolidate the loan with others. The lending registrar must state specific requirements clearly in the loan agreement if there are special needs, courier schedules, and preferred modes of transportation. Frequently, the borrowing registrar will contact the lending registrar many months in advance to obtain estimates for packing and preparation, insurance, and courier costs in order to prepare a budget for the loan.

In August 2007, the U. S. Congress approved the Recommendations of the 9/11 Commission Act of 2007. This legislation is being implemented in three stages and will directly affect air-cargo shipments. The goal of the Transportation Safety Administration (TSA) is to screen by electronic, manual, or canine means 100 percent of the cargo transported on passenger aircrafts by August 2010. As this book was prepared for publication, it was unknown how this would affect the policies or procedures for shipping works of art via passenger aircrafts. Updates on regulations should be checked often while this process evolves.

The packing method to be utilized is determined by many factors, including travel distance, route, type of conveyance and object size, media, fragility, and value. Whether soft packing for short trips or crating for longer trips or extra safeguards, the same packing principles apply; that is, the need to protect the object from shock, vibration, and rapid changes in temperature or humidity is of primary importance. The packing technique should be simple enough for the average person to understand easily.

In the post-9/11-heightened security environment, hand-carried objects on commercial aircraft are strongly discouraged. While an object may be small enough to carry by hand, it will be subject to inspections that may include opening the package; the crew may even bar it from entering the airplane. An extra seat for the object in first or business class often is required, which drives up costs. Hand-carried objects also have additional security risks when the courier is unescorted by TSA authorized agents, when problems arise in securing odd-shaped packages to the airplane seats (extra straps may be required), and when sizes or weights are unwieldy. *(See chapters on Packing and Crating, and Shipping.)* Packing the object in a case suitable for cargo gives the work stable temperature, provides adequate shock and vibration protection, and allows it to be closely monitored by agents.

Instructions for unpacking and repacking should accompany the shipment in the form of written instructions, diagrams, photographs, or video. Appropriate packing materials should be used. Wood must be in compliance with the International Standard for Phytosanitary Measures requirement for wood packaging (ISPM15), which was implemented in October 2001. *(See chapter on Packing.)*

If the lender has the facility, staff, and time to do its own packing, it will do so and bill the borrower for expenses. Packing charges can be based either on an exact record of the hours worked and the actual cost of materials used or on a system of flat rates that cover different sizes of boxes or special packing jobs. If a crate or packing material already exists for the loan object, the lender may pro-rate the cost of this existing material or may not charge the borrower at all. If the lender does not have a suitable crate or the capability to produce one, a commercial packer must be engaged, either by the lender or the borrower; it should be approved by both registrars. The lender must communicate its special packing, handling, or shipping instructions to the commercial packer. The commercial packer may bill the borrower directly, or occasionally the lender will pay the bill and be reimbursed by the borrower.

The borrowing museum generally makes arrangements for transporting the loans, again, subject to the lender's approval; it also is responsible for all shipping costs. The registrar discusses such factors as preferred routing, mode of transportation, agents, special rigging needs, consolidations, and any additional security requirements. The shipping schedules will determine the deadline for packing and must be negotiated with the lender to make sure both dates can be met as planned. In general, depending on the nature of the object and the cost to the borrower, the lender should request the most direct route and the shortest travel time. Consolidated shipments can be the most cost-efficient option for the borrower if the safety of the object is not jeopardized in the process. *(See chapter on Shipping.)*

Couriers to accompany shipments may be required for a variety of reasons, such as to oversee the transit or to hand carry or install the object. RC-AAM has established guidelines that define and discuss acceptable reasons for requiring a courier. Per diem payments should cover the courier's travel and living costs for the period he/she is attending to the loan. *(See chapter on Couriers.)*

International loans generally are handled through shipping or forwarding agents in the countries where the borrower is located. The borrower's registrar or agent contacts the foreign shipping agent for a bid on packing, shipping, and export/import documentation. An agent is selected and approved by the lender; in many museums the selection is determined through a public tender or bidding process.

The agent prepares all the necessary documentation for the export/import; he/she also can arrange packing, delivery to the airport, and airport supervision. Qualified agents can be recommended by the lending institution, by forwarding agents in the United States, or by other U.S. museums that have negotiated loans in foreign countries. Some export documentation and licenses take several weeks to prepare; international loans should be arranged far in advance. *(See chapter on Export/Import.)*

Confirm all packing and shipping arrangements, as well as cost estimates, in writing. Specific deadlines, special requirements, and the names and phone numbers of contact persons should be communicated to vendors and agents.

PROCESSING THE OUTGOING LOAN

The outgoing object must be prepared adequately for travel. A conservator may need to make minor repairs, reattach loose fragments, or touch up small losses. Major conservation treatments required prior to the loan should be negotiated with the borrower first, if the borrower will be expected to take responsibility for any of the cost. Generally the borrower is expected to pay for all preparation expenses, but conservation treatment needed despite the loan is open for negotiation.

The registrar or preparator should check the framing, glazing, mounts, hardware, and accompanying vitrines or bases to ensure they are fit to travel. The object must be secured in the frame with mending plates and spacers. Glass should be substituted with UV-filtered Plexiglas for works on paper (excluding pastels), textiles, or other light-sensitive media. If glass is not removed, it must be taped with low-tack tape to prevent damage if it breaks in transit. Any loose elements must be removed and wrapped separately. Two-dimensional framed objects must be protected with backing boards. Finally, all mounting hardware should be checked to ensure it is adequate for display and has not become "fatigued" from wear. *(See chapter on Preparation.)*

If a documenting photograph does not already exist in the object file, one should be taken for identification, condition, and insurance purposes.

An outgoing condition report is prepared to document any obvious blemishes, instabilities, old repairs, or preexisting conditions. A condition report is made for the frames, bases, or other accompanying elements as well. Annotating a photograph, in addition to written notes, is an effective way of describing the object's condition. A space should be provided on the form so the borrower can add comments or note any changes. All condition reports should be dated and signed by the person who wrote them. *(See chapter on Condition Reporting.)*

The lending museum sends a receipt to the borrower, along with a copy of the outgoing condition reports. The receipt, signed by the registrar of the borrowing institution, serves as formal notification of the loan's arrival and provides the lender with the borrower's official acknowledgment of the loan. It is standard for two copies of an outgoing loan receipt to be sent on the same date that the loan is shipped. One copy is returned with the borrower's signature and the date on which the loan arrived. The other copy is retained by the borrower. The borrower often sends its own receipt as well to document the transaction. The outgoing loan receipt should reiterate the conditions under which the loan has been granted. These conditions should be identical to those detailed in the loan-agreement form.

Once the loan has been shipped to the borrower, the lending registrar updates internal files and computer systems to indicate the new location of the object. Pertinent departments, e.g., curator, education, information office, are notified of the absence of the object and the estimated date for its return.

TRACKING OBJECTS ON LOAN

The registrar must establish a system for tracking the object while it is out of the museum. It should include the object's estimated return date or the date it is anticipated to move to the next venue. Loans occasionally are made for extended periods (e.g., more than a year). It is important that the registrar have an effective system for remembering or "calling up" all loans that are out. Tracking systems can be manual (e.g., a tickler file) or on a computer database. Some museum auditors require annual confirmation of loans that are out and will send letters to borrowing museums to verify the location of objects.

WHEN THE LOAN OBJECT ARRIVES

Upon receipt of the loan object, the registrar of the borrowing institution should carefully check the exterior of the packing case or soft-pack material for signs of damage. The registrar also should document any damage in case the contents are affected. A photograph should be taken of any exterior damage to the crate.

When unpacking the loan, the registrar should carefully note how the object was packed so that it can be returned to the lender in the same manner. Museums generally agree that objects should be repacked in the same manner in which they arrived. A photograph of how the object is situated within the case may help document the packing method. The borrowing museum should save the packing materials for reuse; if that is not possible, the replacement material should duplicate the original. If problems are experienced or if packing materials are inadequate, packing may be changed with lender approval.

The original case or packaging material should be stored in a clean, dry area, preferably in a climate-controlled environment. If an offsite storage facility or non-climate-controlled space is used, the case should be brought back into the museum environment in adequate time to acclimatize it prior to repacking.

As soon as the objects are unpacked, they must be inventoried; condition reports should be done promptly. It is important that the contents of a crate or other packing container be assessed to verify that all the objects have been received. Written notes and/or a photograph should be taken of all removable parts, elements, or accessories. Each element should be tagged or labeled until the object is installed or returned to the lender.

The condition report prepared by the lender becomes the basis for comparison upon receipt of an incoming object. Condition reports often become key documentation in the event of an insurance claim, and it is important that they be thorough and understandable. The condition report also is referred to at the end of the loan period to check for any changes to the object. Condition report formats vary from museum to museum and according to the type of material. They should be brief but accurate and should clearly describe the nature, location, and extent of irregularities in the object's condition. A photograph of the object documenting its condition upon arrival is a highly recommended addition to the written report. Condition reports should be produced for deposits, study loans, and other miscellaneous loans to protect the museum in case of future claims. (*See chapter on Condition Reporting.*)

The lender should be notified immediately if objects or parts of objects have not been received or if the registrar believes an object has been damaged or has experienced a change in condition. If the registrar thinks the damage may warrant an insurance claim or if the lender requests a claim, the museum's insurance agent should be notified immediately. (*See chapters on Condition Reporting, Forms, and Insurance.*)

Each loan and each object within that loan must be assigned a unique number and be promptly tagged or labeled. The number may be a "temporary deposit" number or a catalog number in the case of a special exhibition. A temporary label can be used until the object's final disposition is determined. All labeling or marking methods that are utilized for loan objects must be reversible. (*See chapters on Numbering Systems and Marking Objects.*)

Handling and installing the loan must be done in a fashion consistent with the lender's requirements and be based on high standards of museum care. Care should be taken to pad and protect each object during movement until it is installed or stored. The borrower also must seek the lender's approval before modifying the loan object in any fashion or employing the object for a purpose other than that originally agreed. Adding hanging devices or a mount, displaying the object in an outdoor atmosphere, etc., must be discussed in advance. Hardware that is removed should be saved and returned to the lender with the loan object. Any issues that might arise concerning the safety of the object also should be discussed with the lender. All modifications to the loan, its accessories, or packing should be documented for the file to facilitate their replacement at the end of the loan. *(See chapter on Handling.)*

Entry records and receipts must be prepared to document the loan transaction properly. If the lending institution sends a receipt, it should be completed and returned by the borrower. If the lender does not do so, the borrower should produce a receipt and send it to the lender. Receipts may be done by both institutions. Information should include:

- Name and full address of lender, preferably with telephone and fax numbers and e-mail address

- Purpose of loan, e.g., long-term loan, special exhibition

- Exhibition title

- Curatorial department responsible for loan

- Arrival date and method of shipment

- Loan numbers assigned to objects

- Name of artist/maker

- Exact title of work or name of object

- Medium or materials

- Dimensions

- Insurance value or name of insurer, if lender is to insure

- Condition

An entry record includes location of the work, crate/packing information, and hardware or special devices accompanying the work. Receipts must be issued promptly and accurately. The wording of terms and conditions on the loan receipt should agree with the conditions stated on the loan-agreement form regarding purpose, duration, insurance coverage, and value. Only the registrar should issue receipts and record loan information; this guarantees consistency and proper loan management. *(See chapter on Creating Documentation.)*

Ongoing Loan Management

Loans must be tracked and updated by the borrowing museum on a regular basis; an annual inventory can identify expired loans and help the museum avoid any potential problems. Loan expiration dates should be carefully monitored so that loans are returned to the lender on time. If the object is to remain on loan, the loan contract must be updated annually and the insurance coverage extended. Insurance values should be reviewed periodically by the lender. If contact has been lost and the lender cannot be found, the loan is regarded as an "old loan." Many states in the United States have established laws regarding the disposition of old loans. The registrar should seek legal advice for disposition of unclaimed or old loans within his/her jurisdiction. *(See chapter on Old Loans.)*

When the Loan Is Returned

Requests for the return of a loan must agree with the terms of the original loan agreement. All objects should be returned to the lender at the same place from which they were collected unless otherwise stipulated in writing by the lender and agreed to by the borrowing museum. In the event of a possible dispute between lenders, such as a divorce or dissolved partnership, the registrar should seek legal advice. A loan should not be returned to one partner without the written consent of the other. If the loan is to be returned to a different location or address, the change should be documented in writing. If the loan is to be returned to a location farther away than the original point of collection, any additional cost associated with the new location can be negotiated, unless this change was a condition of the loan. If someone else imported the object, the registrar should seek proper import documentation. *(See chapter on Export/Import.)*

When the loan period has expired, the registrar at the borrowing institution contacts the lender to arrange the return. The return-shipment date and method of transit should have been discussed with the lender in advance. The registrar prepares the object for the return by inventorying all elements and accessories. If the object was framed or reframed, or if the original hardware was removed, these elements returned to their original status unless otherwise agreed to by the lender. The registrar must make an outgoing condition report that refs to the incoming report or any interim reports and ensure that the object returns in the same condition it was received. The object should be repacked in the same fashion as received unless packing modifications have been approved. Finally, an outgoing receipt should be issued; the lender is asked to sign and return a copy after verifying that all objects have been returned in satisfactory condition.

The loan file should closed by noting the destination, date, and method of return. Internal departments should be apprised of the loan return as necessary. All bills for packing, shipping, agents, insurance premiums, and courier costs should be processed for payment upon receipt. In the event that some costs are to be shared by the lender, or other museums in the case of a touring exhibition, invoices must be prepared for such costs as shipping, couriers, photography, and insurance premiums. If the loan object happens to be acquired by the museum, the registrar will accession and catalog the object, changing the incoming loan numbers to permanent accessions numbers. *(See chapter on Accessions.)*

PROCESSING LOANS BEING RETURNED

Upon return of the object, the lending registrar unpacks the object as promptly as possible after acclimatization (about 24 hours[1]) and compares it against the outgoing condition report for any significant changes. If new conditions or damage are apparent or suspected, the borrowing registrar should be contacted immediately. The registrars should decide whether to file an insurance claim. Photographs should be taken if any changes have occurred. If the damage could have occurred during transit, all packing material must be saved and photographed, too. The lending registrar should check to see that all loan objects as well as all parts or accessories and installation hardware have returned.

An "incoming receipt" is signed by the lender, evidencing the receipt of the loan in satisfactory condition. Either the borrower or lender can issue this receipt. Files and/or computer records are updated as to location of the object. A loan history for the object is maintained to document its exposure. *(See chapter on Managing Files and Records.)*

A history file on different borrowers should be kept to document problems or concerns for future reference. This file can include notes on agents or shippers used by the borrower that proved problematic, fees charged, extreme courier costs, or facility problems. Loan histories also can be useful in negotiating later loans should the lender wish to borrow objects from the borrower in the future.

• Shortly after the conclusion of the loan, either the registrar or the museum's business office prepares a final invoice, billing the borrower for all agreed costs related to the loan, e.g., crating, conservation, courier costs not paid directly by the borrower, and insurance premiums. Timely accounting of these costs is appreciated by both the borrowing and lending institution. Agent's bills should be directed to the borrower, or the lender should be reimbursed for agent's costs, as appropriate. Loans can be shipped to borrowers "prepaid" with the borrower invoiced later or can be shipped "collect" to avoid billing.

LOAN ISSUES

•**Damage.** If the object is damaged at any time, the lender must be contacted immediately. Any damage, however slight, must be documented. A conservator should be consulted regarding possible remedies that can be carried through if the lender approves. If damage is serious, an insurance claim should be made.

•**Change of ownership.** If the object's ownership or status changes—e.g., if it is donated, promised, or placed on extended loan—the change must be documented in writing. A new loan agreement must be signed by lender and borrower.

•**Change of information.** If loan information simply needs to be updated, a new agreement is not required. However, the change in information should be confirmed in writing by the lender or his/her representative.

•**Loans to third parties.** In the case of loans to third parties (i.e., an object currently borrowed by your museum and loaned to another museum), the owner must provide written permission for the object to be released. The borrower usually is responsible for paying all charges in connection with a third-party loan. There should be a clear understanding of exactly when the borrower's insurance takes effect. If the loan is to return to the museum, its file and loan number can be continued. When the loan finally returns, it is prudent to ask the lender if any information needs to be changed.

•**Requests for loan extensions.** Requests for loan extensions or date or venue changes are subject to the same review and approval process as the original loan request. Minor changes in dates can be handled by a simple letter from the borrower, countersigned by the lender.

•**Loans to traveling exhibitions.** Several concerns may be raised by loans to traveling exhibitions. Facilities reports for each venue should be reviewed by the lending institution. Large gaps in time may exist between venues, and it is the borrower's responsibility to inform lenders of the arrangements that will be made to accommodate such lapses: shipments to the next venue may be postponed, or the loans may be stored. No loans should ever be stored at sites other than the exhibition venues without the lender's advance permission. The organizing institution is usually responsible for insuring the tour, processing invoices, and relaying lender requirements to venues unless other separate arrangements have been made with each venue. Should an early release from the traveling exhibition occur, all parties concerned should be informed in advance. *(See chapter on Organizing Traveling Exhibitions.)*

•**Exchange loans.** Exchange loans may be reciprocal loans for long or short periods, or they may happen when an object requested for loan must be replaced at the lender's site for the duration of the loan. They are handled in the same fashion as other outgoing loans, with outgoing and incoming loan contracts to document the transaction. Shipments to and from the same lender often can be consolidated for a savings. Since both institutions benefit, it is important that there is a clear understanding regarding which museum is responsible for which costs.

In recent years, the cost of organizing exhibitions has mushroomed. It is incumbent upon museums to work cooperatively to find ways to control loan costs. Without risking the safety and long-term preservation of the object, costs often can be reduced by waiving or consolidating couriers, waiving loan fees, invoicing expenses "at cost" only, or reusing recycled crates. Since the 9/11 terrorist attacks, the requests for terrorism-insurance coverage have escalated. Many major museums have agreed to waive this requirement to save costs. Loans will remain a mainstay of museum exhibitions for the foreseeable future, and it is vital that the process be as efficient as possible. •

NOTE

1. *Acclimatization* refers to the amount of time a work of art needs to return to a temperature level above the dew point. A delay in unpacking reduces the risk of condensation on the surface of objects. In a room at 72°F and 50-percent RH, condensation would occur on any object colder than the dew point (52°F). Since the interior temperature of a crate is usually unknown, it is prudent to wait 24 hours. However, a shorter period is acceptable when packing cases are well insulated and transported in climate-controlled vehicles.

3M | ORGANIZING LOAN AND TRAVELING EXHIBITIONS

JULIA BAKKE

The registrar's role in organizing a traveling exhibition begins during the planning stage. In cooperation with the exhibition team, the registrar contributes to the development of the exhibition budget. Early in the organization process, the curator of the exhibition provides the registrar with a preliminary checklist of objects and perhaps an exhibition schedule, including the proposed number and location of venues. The registrar usually is asked to provide estimates for crating, shipping, insurance, and any other projected expenses related to the loans to the exhibition, such as loan fees, courier expenses, and costs of preparing objects for loan, such as framing or special mounts. These will be passed on to the organizing institution by individual or institutional lenders. Based on the material to be exhibited, its relative fragility and value, and the level of complexity of the installation, the registrar, in consultation with a conservator when possible, determines whether couriers will be needed. A courier may accompany the shipment of the objects between venues and/or may travel to each venue to supervise the unpacking and installation of the exhibition and later the deinstallation and repacking. The registrar budgets for these costs accordingly.

When the exhibition venues have been confirmed, the organizing registrar obtains facilities reports from each participating institution, so that, upon request, lenders can be sent copies of those reports for their own review. The registrar is often responsible for drafting an exhibition contract that will be sent to and signed by each participating host institution. This contract should clearly and specifically delineate responsibilities—both financial and logistical—between the organizing institution and each host institution. *(See chapter on Contracts.)*

At this point, the organizing institution sends loan-request letters, accompanied by loan forms. While the letters usually are generated by the director or curator, the loan forms most often are generated by the registrar. *(See chapter on Loans.)* As loans are approved and loan agreements returned, the registrar reviews the forms and notes any special lender requirements and restrictions, such as specific light levels, climate control, security hangars, locked cases, floor barriers, shipping specifications, and photography and rights and reproduction limitations. In larger institutions, this information often is distributed by the registrar to the various departments (e.g., Rights and Reproductions, Curatorial, Exhibitions). When the exhibition travels, the registrar must provide each venue with a list of installation requirements and photography restrictions well in advance of the objects' arrival at each venue. This information, in fact, might be included in a preliminary packet of exhibition information, consisting of a final checklist of the exhibition, a press kit, and installation photographs.

INSURANCE

It is the organizing institution's responsibility to make all the insurance arrangements for the exhibition, and it is usually at this point in the exhibition-planning phase that the method of insurance and the insurance carrier are determined. Three types of insurance applications may pertain to any one exhibition. Objects may be insured:

- By the organizing institution
- By the lender, which then may bill the organizing institution for the premium
- By government indemnity

An exhibition may incorporate any and all of these insurance arrangements. It is up to the organizing registrar to ensure that adequate and accurate coverage is provided for all objects from the time they leave the lenders' premises to the time they are returned.

INSURANCE BY THE ORGANIZING INSTITUTION

All works may be covered for the entire exhibition tour under the organizing institution's own insurance policy or under a special policy negotiated with the organizing institution's usual insurance carrier. For budgetary purposes, the organizing institution may elect to cover the entire tour of the exhibition under its own fine arts insurance policy if one of the following conditions applies:

- The total value of the exhibition falls under the appropriate limits of maximum probable loss.

- Extra layers of insurance can be purchased to raise the limits of liability to cover the total value of the exhibition.

While this method is the least costly way of insuring an exhibition, it is also the riskiest for the organizing institution because it essentially puts the institution's permanent collection at greater risk by "borrowing" a portion of its coverage. Thus, it is more usual for the organizing institution to negotiate a special insurance policy for a particular exhibition. In either case, however, the organizing institution bears the burden of ultimate responsibility and accountability for any damages that might occur over the course of the exhibition tour. For this reason, it is essential that the organizing registrar be completely familiar and comfortable with each venue's facilities and staff. In addition, regarding exhibitions with particularly fragile and/or high-value works, it is the usual practice for the organizing institution's registrar to travel to each venue prior to the exhibition opening and when it closes, to monitor the condition of objects and supervise object handling.

INSURANCE BY LENDERS

Often individual lenders prefer to maintain their own insurance coverage. The organizing institution is then responsible for the cost of the insurance premiums for these loans. This extra cost must be anticipated when establishing the initial exhibition budget. The organizing registrar should review all outside insurance policies and their provisions, passing on any unusual stipulations to the other host institutions. The registrar should obtain a waiver of subrogation from the lender's insurance company to ensure that it will not sue any of the participants in the exhibition. *(See chapter on Insurance.)* The organizing registrar is responsible for obtaining certificates of insurance for these loans, often directly from the individual insurance companies.

GOVERNMENTAL INDEMNITIES

Application for U.S. indemnity must be made well in advance of the exhibition opening, and the registrar must be prepared to provide detailed checklists and support documentation. The registrar should be aware of the various requirements of U.S. indemnity and budget for the probable expenses that will be incurred as a result of these requirements, e.g., arranging for condition reports for all objects before they leave the lender's premises and after they are returned at the close of the exhibition. The organizing registrar is responsible for providing each venue with copies of the indemnity provisions and for informing the indemnity office of any changes to the conditions outlined in the original indemnity application that may occur during the course of the exhibition, such as a change in exhibition site, exhibition dates, security, or shipping arrangements. U.S. indemnity is available for both international and domestic exhibitions. There is a deductible layer, the amount of which is based on the total value of the exhibition, which applies to the exhibition as a whole (not per object) and must be covered by other insurance. Objects made of certain fragile materials may be excluded from coverage.

GATHERING THE LOANS

Shipping Arrangements

Once the majority of the loans have been confirmed, the registrar establishes an overall shipping schedule, based on the projected installation schedule, and considers the methods of transportation available: air, overland, or, in some cases, a combination of the two. *(See chapter on Shipping.)* The registrar then reviews the lenders' loan agreements, noting any special shipping requirements, such as couriers or preference for a particular carrier or shipping agent. It is often helpful at this point to generate a shipping worksheet (see sample) to organize and keep track of the information pertaining to each loan. The worksheet can be organized geographically, grouping the loans by location to produce a working list of possible ways to consolidate some of the shipments. At this stage, the registrar can solicit bids from different commercial carriers. For domestic loans, this usually means contacting one or more fine arts trucking firms and providing them with a list of loans to be collected and any other pertinent requirements, such as exclusive use, climate control, two drivers, nonstop, overnight security, courier on the truck, etc. For international loans, shipping estimates can be obtained in one of two ways: by contacting the foreign agent or by providing the museum's own shipping agent with a list of foreign loans to be collected and asking that agent to obtain the bids. *(See chapter on Import/Export.)*

Crating

It usually can be assumed that private lenders do not have crates for their works and that the organizing registrar will need to make crating arrangements. Most lending institutions prefer to make their own crating arrangements, either in-house or with their own preferred commercial packer. For those loans that do need to have crating arrangements made, it is helpful, again, to group the lenders by general region. The registrar then obtains bids from one or more commercial fine arts packing firms in each region by providing each packer with a list of works to be crated and any specific crate design requirements, such as thermal insulation, waterproofing, reusable closure system, or travel frames. For loans coming from smaller towns where no commercial packing firms are known to the organizing registrar, it is helpful to contact a colleague in a museum or gallery in close proximity to the lender in order to obtain names of one or more small packing companies or even an individual whose work is reputable and known locally. For foreign loans, most international shipping companies provide crating services as well, and it is usual practice to use the same company for both shipping and packing. *(See chapter on Packing and Crating.)*

Contacting the Lenders

Once the various carriers, packers, and agents have been selected, the registrar contacts the lenders. While most fine arts firms will handle this entire process, if necessary, it is good professional practice for the registrar to make initial contact with each lender to discuss proposed packing arrangements, shipping method, and dates and then have each commercial firm follow up directly with the lenders to confirm precise pickup dates and times. At the same time, the registrar can find out other specific information about the works to be borrowed. It is important to know if a two-dimensional work is framed or unframed, if there are any known condition problems, and if there are any logistical problems in getting the object out of the lender's residence. (Ideally, in lieu of this step, a condition report will be made at the lender's premises, prior to making final packing and shipping arrangements.) Most commercial crating companies are able to provide secure, climate-controlled storage and therefore can consolidate the objects at their warehouse, doing the actual crating there. Not only is this more cost-effective for the borrower, but in many cases private lenders prefer this method to on-site crating. If the registrar believes this arrangement to be appropriate, it should be discussed with the lender to ensure that he/she has no objections or concerns about the object being transported locally with minimal packing.

After all of the lenders have been contacted, the registrar refines the list of works that must be crated and gives it to the various packing firms, discussing in more detail the exact packing method and crate design desired. For large exhibitions, where there are many loans from one location, it is often desirable for several works to be packed in one crate, particularly if there are many small objects. The registrar needs to take into consideration whether there are objects in the exhibition that will not travel to all of the venues; if so, those items should not be included in a crate with multiple objects.

Receiving the Works at the First Venue

Most often, the first venue of the exhibition is the organizing museum. However, there are occasions when the first venue is a museum other than the organizer. If that is the case, it should be decided, and clearly stated in the exhibition contract, what the first venue's responsibilities will be, e.g., whether the loans will be delivered directly to the museum or consolidated in a nearby warehouse and then delivered en masse to the museum. This will have an effect on the overall exhibition budget and should be planned for accordingly.

Once the works are received at the initial host institution, the registrar carries out the usual procedures for receiving and documenting incoming works of art:

- Confirms crate dimensions, noting how each work is packed, including whether any packing revisions should be considered

- Labels or tags each object

- Makes incoming condition reports

- Sends out receipts to the lenders, confirming safe arrival of their loans

THE EXHIBITION TOUR

Documentation

Once all of the information is gathered, the registrar can begin to organize the pertinent documentation that will be passed on to the various exhibition venues. The documentation should include the following:

- A checklist of the exhibition, including complete object data and credit line for each work

- A crate list, including crate sizes and, when possible, crate weights, and a list of the crate contents (it is common practice to establish a crate-numbering system, specific to the particular exhibition, and to mark the crates accordingly when they arrive at the first venue)

- A list of equipment necessary to receive the exhibition and/or install objects (e.g., forklift, dollies, gantry, crane, etc.)

- A list of display furniture, mounts, and graphics that will travel with the exhibition

- A packing list with explicit packing instructions for each object

- A list of lenders' special requirements, such as light levels, relative humidity and temperature levels, barriers, photography/filming restrictions, etc.

- A certificate of insurance naming each museum as additionally insured

- Indemnity documents, when appropriate

THE CONDITION REPORT NOTEBOOK

The format for the traveling condition report should be clear, concise, and easy to use. In many institutions a photograph forms the basis for the condition report, thereby minimizing the need for a detailed written description. Black-and-white, 8" x 10" photographs or printouts of digital images work best, as they provide the clearest images for reference. Photos can be requested from lenders for this purpose; the extra cost will be included in the exhibition budget. The photo can be inserted into a plastic sleeve, on which notations can be made with colored markers. When photographs are not available, color proofs from the exhibition catalog or photocopied images can be used. However, these images are often not accurate in color or sharpness, so they are used more as a way to indicate the location of a particular condition note than as photographic documentation of a preexisting condition. *(See chapter on Condition Reporting.)*

The condition report sheet itself should include the following information:

- Checklist or catalog number for the object

- Complete object data

- Incoming condition report, including condition notes on frame, glazing, and mounts

A space, adequate in size, should be provided where each venue can make incoming and outgoing notes and comments. Each space should include a line for the signatures of the people doing the incoming and outgoing condition checks and the dates. (See sample form.)

If a lender's condition report is sent with the object, it should be incorporated into the master condition report notebook, and subsequent condition notes and comments should be made directly on the lender's condition report. At the close of the exhibition tour, the organizing registrar is responsible for returning these condition reports to the lenders.

If damage to an object occurs while the exhibition is on tour, it is the organizing institution's responsibility to report the damage to the lender and to determine, with the lender, the appropriate course of action: conservation treatment, insurance claim, and/or withdrawal of the work from the exhibition. Whether the damage is significant or insignificant, the organizing institution's registrar must be contacted immediately. The organizing institution's registrar handles all aspects of any insurance claim. If conservation treatment is required, the organizing institution, in consultation with the lender, chooses a conservator and arranges for the treatment to be done, coordinating the logistics and scheduling with the host institution's registrar.

Shipping Arrangements between Venues

Several months before the exhibition is due to open at the next venue, the organizing registrar contacts the registrar at the next host institution to discuss a proposed shipping schedule. The organizing registrar then determines the shipping method and carrier and later informs both institutions of the proposed shipment delivery date or dates. The organizing registrar is responsible for making arrangements, if required, for a courier on the truck or in a follow car. The organizing registrar is also usually responsible, unless otherwise agreed by the host institution, for making per diem and hotel arrangements for lenders' couriers at each venue, as required.

Dispersal of the Exhibition

Dispersal of the exhibition usually is done directly from the last exhibition venue. The organizing registrar must be in especially close contact with the last venue's registrar well before the exhibition closing date in order to set a concise and workable shipping schedule. Again, the organizing registrar makes all shipping arrangements, including accommodation for the couriers. Before the exhibition closes, the registrar should review the exhibition loan list and/or loan forms, noting any frame, mount, or hanging device changes that were made during the course of the exhibition, so that the works can be returned to the lenders in their original state (unless the lender has specially requested otherwise). The registrar also reviews special instructions for the return of each work, such as returning it to a location other than the lender's premises. If a lender's condition report accompanied the loan, the registrar removes it from the condition report notebook after the final condition check is done and returns it with the loan to the lender.

After all of the works are dispersed from the last exhibition venue, the organizing registrar generates receipts and sends them to all lenders for their signatures to confirm the safe return of the objects. •

Thanks to Alice Whelihan

3N | IN-HOUSE EXHIBITIONS

GWEN BITZ

In-house exhibitions are important to museums and must be planned and executed as carefully as loan and traveling exhibitions. They may be long-term or temporary exhibitions that afford the museum an opportunity to display objects from its own permanent collection. The focus on permanent collections does not preclude the inclusion of loan objects from important local collections, so loan procedures may be involved. On the whole, however, in-house exhibitions are less complex than major loan or traveling exhibitions and consequently are easier for the registrar to coordinate. There are usually few packing, shipping, and insurance problems to solve; the budgets are typically small and easy to manage. As a result, the main challenge of the in-house exhibition is to frame an efficient preparation and installation schedule that is sensitive to the needs and safety of the objects and the workloads of the personnel involved.

EXHIBITION PLANNING

Museums may have prescribed exhibition production schedules. Some have committees in place to plan exhibitions, while others make planning a primary responsibility of a curator or an exhibition coordinator. Timelines for exhibition development also vary from museum to museum; it is ideal to have a year to plan an in-house exhibition, a preproduction meeting approximately eight weeks before opening, and all pre-installation work completed three weeks before the opening date.

Exhibition preparation, however, begins with two documents: the preliminary checklist and the budget. These two documents will become the basis for the exhibition. The checklist, drafted by the curator, includes the following:

- Accession number (or loan number if loans are involved)
- Artist or maker
- Title or object name
- Object date
- Medium or materials
- Dimensions
- Credit line (always used in art museums, sometimes used in history museums, seldom used in science museums)

The budget is based on the preliminary checklist. The curator, registrar, and exhibition personnel should have input into the budget, and categories for all exhibition costs should be included. The registrar's section should cover all packing, shipping, and insurance costs if loans are included and, when an in-house conservator is not available, consultation and conservation costs. If there will be a need to hire preparators or art handlers to work on the exhibition or truck objects from offsite storage areas, those costs should be included as well.

EXHIBITION DEVELOPMENT

In all stages of planning and development, the tracking of objects is the responsibility of the registrar. Accession numbers and, if loans are included, loan numbers, are vital for tracking. *(See chapter on Numbering.)*

As the curator works on the exhibition concept and develops a floor plan, the checklist will undergo many transformations. The entries on the checklist should not be numbered (i.e., from 1 consecutively to the last number on the list) until it is certain that the checklist is final. The list might not become final until the exhibition is completely installed, at which time a final accurate checklist with numbers can be completed. The final checklist is valuable for security and registrarial checks and serves as archival information about the museum collection.

Upon receipt of each draft of the checklist, the registrar will consider the availability of each work from the permanent collection and pass on the necessary information about the objects to the curator. This is most important in early stages of planning. The following questions should be asked about each work:

•Is it in good condition? If not, will it require conservation treatment?

•Is it out on loan or promised for loan during the exhibition period?

•Is it stored at an offsite facility?

•Are special mounts, cases, or security devices necessary for installation?

•What are the lighting restrictions for the object?

•Does the object include new technology? If yes, is the equipment available and in good running condition?

•Are there existing preservation and running copies of the originals of any new technology works (videotapes, audio tapes, videodiscs, CD-ROMs, etc.)?

•Are there good instructions in the files for complicated installations?

•Will special signage be needed, e.g., "Do Not Touch" or "Touch the Screen to Start the Program"?

The answers to these questions will help the curator make the final selections for the checklist.

To determine if the permanent collection objects on the first draft of the checklist are in good condition, the registrar should inspect each work physically and research the object file for condition history. *(See chapter on Condition Reporting.)* If the registrar learns during this inspection and research that the condition is questionable, a conservator should inspect the work and prepare a treatment proposal with cost estimates. The curator and registrar then can determine if the exhibition budget can bear the total cost of all estimated treatments.

When the conservation proposal is approved, the registrar immediately schedules the treatment to ensure that it can be completed several weeks prior to the opening date.

In its working stages, the checklist may be entered into an exhibition database which will then serve as the digital file from which all other documents needed to track the objects during the exhibition process can be generated. Traditional manual files may also be established to record the history of the planning and production of the exhibition. *(See chapter on Files.)* All information pertaining to an exhibition should be available and accessible not only to the registrar in charge of the project but also to anyone in the registration, exhibition, and curatorial departments who needs it. A typical in-house exhibition file eventually will include:

•Budget

•Checklist

•Conservation information

•Installation notes

•Label copy

•Alphabetized list of lenders, if any

•Loan agreements and receipts, if needed

•Packing, shipping, and consolidation information

•Photographic materials

•Security notes

A preproduction meeting should be held several weeks before the opening; at this meeting, the curator, registrar, and exhibition staff, along with other staff members who are involved, study the floor plan and develop strategies for installation. A schedule can then be developed to make each department accountable for a timely completion of its responsibilities. The number of extra art handlers or technicians required to accomplish the installation safely also can be decided.

The registrar oversees the completion of conservation work and, depending on the organization of the museum, sometimes has responsibility for cleaning and basic preparation of the objects in the exhibition. The registrar also may be responsible for preparing label copy for the objects; if not, it will be his/her responsibility to review and check the label copy for accuracy. Each museum has a specific in-house procedure and style for producing label copy, and those museum must be carefully followed.

INSTALLATION

Approximately three weeks prior to the opening of the exhibition, all of the objects that will be included should be on-site. Conservation should be complete, and all of the tasks that the many museum departments did for the preparation of the gallery space and objects should be finished. The objects are then moved into the galleries.

The gallery floor plan serves as a map for the placement of the works, and installation begins. For large exhibition installations, many museums hire art handlers to supplement their staff. The registrar should conduct an object handling briefing for this temporary staff and ask permanent employees to attend as well. It is important that all crew are as alert as possible to the basic rules of object handling. *(See chapter on Handling.)*

There probably will be some changes in the final placement of the works as the curator oversees the installation. When it is certain the placements are final, the appropriate security devices can be installed, labels can be distributed and placed, and lighting can be adjusted.

The day before the exhibition opens, the registrar and curator should walk through the exhibition with security staff to explain potential guarding problems. During this tour, identify specific safety needs for each work, point out audible alarms, and review the instructions for responding to the alarms when they are activated by patrons. Explain vulnerable surfaces and complicated installations, and determine the best vantage point from which to observe the works easily. The security staff can express concerns they have about protecting the objects as they are installed. If there are interactive works or objects with many parts, instructions and inventory lists should be distributed for easy reference.

It is important that the objects on exhibit be monitored carefully. Security, registration, and exhibition staff all share this task. In-house rules for department and staff responsibilities should be followed.

DEINSTALLATION

Prior to the last week of the exhibition period, the registrar and the exhibition staff should plan the deinstallation of the objects; arrange the return of any exhibition loans to local collectors; and prepare the final paperwork, including receipts for signature upon delivery. Permanent collection objects slated for offsite storage must be packed, and local drayage arranged. Other permanent collection works will be returned to their appropriate locations in the storage vaults.

The registrar continues tracking of the objects after deinstallation and records the location information in databases, manual files, or both places. An exhibition history is prepared for each object and filed in the appropriate place. The exhibition file is closed, and the in-house exhibition is officially concluded. •

30 | HOSTING TRAVELING EXHIBITIONS

DEBORAH SLANEY

As an integral part of the exhibition team, the registrar plays a major role when a museum hosts a traveling exhibition. The registrar must understand the ramifications of contracts negotiated with the organizing institution, insurance providers, and shippers in the course of hosting an exhibition in order to ensure that the terms of these contracts are carried out. In essence, the registrar's role is to facilitate the safe shipping, handling, movement, tracking, storage, and display of the objects for the duration of the exhibition at the hosting museum. This role also may extend to the care and tracking of non-collection items, such as props, exhibition furniture, mounts, educational materials, and packing and crating materials. Through the reduction of risk, the registrar helps the museum meet its contractual obligations and ensures that the exhibition arrives at the next venue having received the best care possible.

The responsibilities assigned to the hosting registrar of a traveling exhibition vary greatly from museum to museum. In smaller museums, the registrar often assists with many of the functions of the exhibition team, including exhibition selection and scheduling, gallery design, collections care and preventive conservation, risk management, and gallery security. In larger museums, the role of a registrar within the exhibition team is usually more specialized. To work well with the team, it is essential that the registrar understand the team's professional makeup and how internal responsibility for various aspects of each exhibition is delegated. In addition, every traveling exhibition is different, each shipment presents new challenges, and every traveling exhibition project is a learning experience. Ultimately, the registrars who are able to tackle these responsibilities the most effectively are the ones who are organized, flexible, and unflappable!

PLANNING

Advance planning is critical to the success of a traveling exhibition. Exhibition meetings, attended by the registrar, are the best places to plan, discuss progress, present issues, and make group decisions. The kinds of questions raised during initial exhibition meetings, which the registrar must be prepared to discuss, usually relate to the logistics of getting exhibition materials to the facility by a specified time. Early on, the registrar may be asked to provide a facility report to the organizing institution and should be prepared to discuss its contents with the organizer, if questions arise.

As soon as they are available, the registrar should review the marketing materials and legal documents provided to the exhibition team by the organizer. Marketing materials may provide basic but useful information, such as the number and types of objects, gallery environment and security requirements, and current venues. Catalogs with object illustrations may be available as part of the marketing package.

As one who is knowledgeable about the museum facility from a collections-care point of view, the registrar often assists with the review and negotiation of the exhibition contract. The registrar reads the contract carefully and should be prepared to call attention to any requirements that cannot be fulfilled by the hosting institution. Particular attention is paid to clauses describing requirements for environment, security, and insurance and borrower responsibilities for packing, shipping, couriering, conservation, and storage of ancillary materials. Because many parts of an exhibition contract often overlap with loan agreements, the registrar checks with the organizer to determine if the contract will serve as the loan agreement, or if a separate loan agreement will be negotiated. If there will be two separate documents, both should be reviewed and discussed internally with the team, then negotiated with the organizer.

As soon as they are available, the registrar reviews inventories of objects and other exhibition materials; the crate list and individual crate inventories; a condition report notebook with photographs, condition reports, and conservation information; instructions for unpacking, handling, and installation; a full list of venues; shipping documents and copies of export and customs documents; and indemnity instructions, if applicable. These documents, which often arrive in the form of an exhibition manual, can help determine how the exhibition materials will be managed once they arrive at the museum. Crate statistics, for example, allow the registrar to determine points of entry into the museum, the number of staff required to unload and unpack the exhibition, the type of moving equipment needed, and the space required for staging and crate storage.

The registrar also contributes information that helps the exhibition team formulate a project budget. Crate statistics, combined with the list of venues, may be used to obtain quotes from shippers for transporting the exhibition to or from the museum; or the organizing institution may be able to provide rough estimates. If the contract stipulates that new packing materials are to be provided, crate and object inventories, packing instructions, and condition reports may be used to create materials lists; supply catalogs then can be used to compile the estimates. Offsite storage space, couriering and customs costs, environmental monitoring devices, installation, and insurance costs may be required to fill out the budget.

Exhibition Documentation

Since planning for a traveling exhibition requires that information be provided in advance of the exhibition itself, records received by the registrar usually are compiled into a working exhibition file. Appropriate documents then are converted to an incoming loan file when the exhibition is received. Ideally, these records are assigned a loan number and stored in acid-free folders in a locking, fire-resistant file cabinet. The loan and exhibition files might include

•The exhibition contract

•Loan agreement

•Relevant checklists and instructions from the organizing institution

•Gallery layouts and lists of object locations

•Conservation records

•Computer reports

•Installation photographs

•Gallery climate and pest-monitoring records

•Purchase requisitions

•Shipping records

•Correspondence relating to the exhibition

In addition, the file may include information about where related materials, such as condition report notebooks and crates, can be found. If incoming or outgoing changes to condition reports are noted, copies of the reports should be included in the loan file as permanent documentation. If loan records are maintained in computer files, backup disks are created and hard copies generated for the loan file (or the document names are listed in the loan file). The loan file should be set up so that other curatorial staff can coordinate the tracking and return of the exhibition in the registrar's absence. *(See chapter on Files.)*

Prior to the actual release of the shipment by the organizer, additional documents are requested from the hosting museum. Copies of hygrothermograph records may be requested as proof that the museum can maintain a stable climate for the exhibition. If insurance is to be provided by the borrower, the lender may request that a certificate of insurance be issued by the insurer as proof of coverage for the duration of the exhibition. If the organizer provides insurance coverage, the registrar requests a certificate of insurance naming the hosting museum as an additional insured or a waiver of subrogation from the organizer.

Receiving the Exhibition

It is important to become as familiar as possible with the lender's intentions for shipping and installing the exhibition. The exhibition contract may stipulate which institution is financially responsible for inbound or outbound shipping, but it might not state who will be responsible for making shipping arrangements. Although the organizer usually takes on this responsibility, the registrar of the hosting institution should be prepared, if questions or problems arise, to communicate with the packer, shipper, customs broker, freight forwarder, or courier. The registrar informs both lender and shipper about any unusual characteristics pertaining to arrival at the loading dock. Specifically, the shipper should be made aware of the museum's loading dock hours and any special equipment needs. The museum must be prepared to borrow, buy, or rent the equipment and operators needed if they are not or cannot be provided by the shipper.

If the exhibition is to be accompanied by a courier or the organizer provides an installation team, the registrar must learn how responsibilities will be shared once the exhibition arrives. Some organizers prefer to unpack, condition report, and install the exhibitions with minimal assistance; others expect the hosting institution to supply the human resources needed. Finding out in advance if the courier will assist with unpacking and condition reporting, if the conservator will help with installation, and if the drivers will move crates into the facility (i.e., beyond the loading dock) allows the registrar to coordinate in-house resources more effectively.

As the hosting institution prepares to receive the exhibition, the registrar should maintain communication with the organizer's registration staff. Both institutions should agree on a receiving date that takes into account the shipper's schedule, the hosting museum's loading-dock hours and workload, and personnel resources. The registrar works with the shipper to determine the approximate arrival time and often must be prepared to mobilize earlier or later than expected. Security personnel should be alerted to the impending arrival. If security monitors progress at the loading dock, it can be helpful to provide them with a copy of the crate list.

In further preparation for arrival, in-house travel routes are checked and cleared in advance. The loading dock is cleared of unnecessary materials and equipment, vehicles, and unauthorized persons. Any required equipment must be on hand. The route should be free of onlookers to reduce distractions and minimize the risk of damage. If entryway dimensions are restrictive, the registrar should determine alternate routes in advance and test them with prototypes, if necessary. If special environmental requirements have been requested, condition the display cases should before the objects arrive.

When the exhibition arrives, the registrar meets the shipper and communicates the route to the receiving/holding area. As crates and other exhibition materials are brought into the building, the registrar uses the crate list to account for all materials. Although the shipper may conduct an inventory, it is important that the museum keep its own institutional records and confirm that the complete exhibition has arrived. The waybill should not be signed until all materials have been accounted for and a visual inspection has verified that the containers have not been damaged in shipment.

Any missing or damaged containers are noted on the waybill, and photographs are taken to document any suspected damage. At this point, the registrar determines whether it is necessary to unpack damaged containers in order to document the extent of damage prior to signing the waybill. After the shipment has been secured, the registrar advises the organizing institution that the shipment has been received; and together they determine if materials are missing. Alternative arrangements then can be made to locate the original or obtain replacement materials.

Incoming exhibition containers should be provided a "rest period" prior to unpacking. A rest period allows the containers and their contents to reach an equilibrium with their new environment; 24 hours is a standard acclimatization period. In some cases, the temperature and relative humidity of the receiving/ holding area must be adjusted to meet the requirements in the organizer's exhibition contract or loan agreement. Incoming materials should be stored in an area that meets the environmental requirements of the objects in the exhibition. If an exhibition manual, condition reports, or receipts were sent with the exhibition, the registrar determines the location of these items and retrieves them first. The receipt then is signed, dated, and mailed back to the organizer to document receipt of the exhibition.

UNPACKING AND STAGING

A secure staging area is furnished with clean, padded storage equipment (tables, pedestals, shelving, and cabinetry are ideal) in preparation for unpacking. The order of unpacking may be governed by a variety of conditions, including size or fragility of objects, space, organization of the condition reports, and installation needs. In general, it is best to work with one crate at a time, so that crate inventories can be used as a checklist to confirm receipt of each item on the object list. This way, if the registrar must break away from the unpacking, the integrity of the inventory can be maintained. In addition, packing materials (if they are to be reserved) can be replaced in the crate and the crate re-secured for storage.

Before individual objects are unpacked, the registrar reviews their condition reports and handling instructions to get a sense of how best to handle and examine each one. As the objects are unpacked, the registrar puts notations on the crate regarding repacking, checks that no parts of objects have been left in the packing materials, and notes whether any packing materials need to be replaced or if existing silica gel needs to be reconditioned. Using his/her knowledge of how handling, shipping, and environmental conditions affect different types of materials, the registrar looks for evidence of changes as well as condition information that may not have been recorded prior to shipping. By recording this information, the registrar protects the museum from claims for damage that actually occurred prior to receipt.

Condition reports should be completed as soon as possible after receipt of the exhibition. If objects are placed into temporary storage for an extended period of time, the organizer may require a second review prior to installation. If the organizer does not require condition reports, it is best to produce in-house condition reports or a summary condition report and send a copy to the organizer as a safeguard against a potential future claim.

Other exhibition materials such as props, furniture, mounts, graphics, and educational materials are not usually treated as collections objects and may be subject to different levels of storage, handling, and security. However, these materials are part of the loan and often are included in the total value of the exhibition for insurance purposes. Therefore, the registrar tracks the condition and location of these materials in a general way until the exhibition moves to the next venue.

The location of each collection object should be tracked individually until the exhibition is installed. Since the objects should be handled as little as possible, it is best if staging can occur in the gallery itself, provided that storage-level security is provided. If not, objects may need to be relocated to a temporary holding or staging area or to the museum's collections storage area until installation. If the storage area must be utilized for traveling exhibition storage, the registrar should be aware of several concerns. Intellectual control must be maintained; exhibition objects are tagged with loan numbers and segregated from the museum collection to avoid confusion with the permanent collection or possible misplacement of objects. In addition, there is the potential of introducing undesirable activities and materials (such as wooden containers, organic packing materials, debris, and pests) into the storage area. To reduce these risks, the registrar checks each object thoroughly for pest activity, bags any suspect items, isolates the objects from the permanent collection, stores the material near the storage entrance if possible to avoid as much activity as possible in the storage area, and stores as much packing material as possible in an alternative location approved by the organizer.

If pest activity or active deterioration of an object is noted during unpacking and condition reporting, the registrar should contact the organizer as soon as possible. Permission may be granted to freeze infested objects or to use an in-house or contract conservator to stabilize them. If a conservator or registrar travels with the exhibition, this person usually will coordinate arrangements for treatment. However the process takes place, the registrar will receive copies of any treatment proposals, reports, and photo documentation and ensure that the organizer also receives this documentation. In cases where an object cannot be stabilized for further exhibition and travel, the registrar may be asked to return it to the organizer. Keep in mind that removal or replacement of objects from a traveling exhibition affects many of the exhibition documents, including the loan agreement, certificate of insurance, object list, crate list, crate inventory, condition report notebook, and shipping waybill, which are then modified.

INSTALLATION

During installation, the registrar provides assistance to the exhibition team using his/her knowledge of object handling, movement, tracking, monitoring, and security procedures. Objects are protected during movement by pads, weighted bags, and wedges until they are installed. If professional handlers or installers are part of the team, the registrar provides them with handling instructions. If customized interior boxes are provided by the organizers, objects are stored and moved in them until they are installed. During installation, objects are checked off the inventory again, and their new locations are noted.

Before exhibition cases and vitrines are secured, the registrar checks again to be certain gallery climate and light levels meet the specifications provided in the contract. Hygrothermographs, data loggers, and thermohygrometers can provide information on temperature and humidity levels in the gallery, as well as inside the cases and pedestals themselves. This information can determine how adjustments may be made to the gallery's HVAC system or if buffering materials will be needed to meet the organizer's climate requirements. Lux meters and ultraviolet meters establish current light levels; this information will determine how to adjust the gallery lighting or relocate light-sensitive objects. As final adjustments to casework are made, the registrar also may provide temporary security or assistance to the installers. In some cases, the registrar provides inert materials for padding folds, creating protective surfaces, and otherwise cushioning objects on display to protect them from structural stress.

Prior to opening the gallery, the registrar takes a moment to review the exhibition from a security perspective. Small, valuable, and "fenceable" or "approachable" objects are particularly vulnerable to theft or vandalism. Any concerns the registrar may have are communicated to the team member coordinating gallery security, so that they may be addressed before the public opening.

MAINTENANCE

Once the exhibition has opened to the public, periodic inspections of the gallery are desirable and often are required by the exhibition contract. The registrar, who may be one of a number of staff keeping watch over gallery conditions, communicates with the design team and the organizer to provide solutions to any breakdown of educational materials or audiovisual equipment discovered during gallery inspections. If the registrar is responsible for the museum's integrated pest-management program, the gallery is monitored in selected locations so that potential infestation can be discovered before damage occurs.

If an object is damaged during the course of the exhibition, the registrar completes a condition report, photographs the damage, and works with the exhibition team to determine if the object should be removed from the gallery. A note indicating that the object has been removed from exhibition, by whom, and the removal date is left in its place, and the organizer is contacted for instructions on how to proceed. In the event an object is noticed to be missing from the gallery, the registrar notifies security to set internal risk-management procedures into motion. If the object then is determined to have been removed without authorization and is actually missing, the organizer is notified immediately so that its procedures also may be set into motion. The registrar works with administrative staff and the organizer to provide information on the object's value and determine whether an insurance claim will be filed.

Before the exhibition closes to the public, the registrar begins planning the outbound shipment. Together with the organizer, the shipper, and the contact at the next venue, a shipping date is identified, and the waybill and any necessary permits or documents are completed and forwarded. If the next shipment requires exportation, the organizer's preferred customs broker assists the registrar with preparation of export declarations and customs documents. *(See chapter on Import/Export.)* If the organizer arranges the outbound shipping, a completed waybill is mailed to the registrar, or blank waybills may be obtained in advance from the shipper.

DEINSTALLATION

While most exhibitions are disassembled and repacked in the reverse of the order in which they were installed, some details may have changed during the course of the exhibition, especially if objects or other exhibition materials have been replaced. The registrar checks to make sure that all crating materials are sound, or have been repaired, prior to repacking. Silica gel or other buffering materials requiring conditioning are readied for packing. The organizer may request modifications to the crates, based on the information provided on the incoming condition reports. New packing materials may be required by the exhibition contract, so the registrar will obtain the materials and have them ready to use by closing time. After the gallery has been secured, the exhibition objects are inventoried, condition reported, and repacked as they were received. Props, furnishings, mounts, graphics, and educational materials also must be accounted for and repacked prior to shipment.

DISPERSAL

Occasionally, a museum that hosts the last venue of an exhibition will be asked to take on the responsibility of dispersing the exhibition for the organizer. As dispersal can add complexity to the project, it is important for the exhibition team to consider the impact of the request upon time, space, budget, and personnel. The exhibition contract, or a separate contract, should define which institution will pay for shipping objects back to original lenders, as well as crate construction and renovation costs. The contract also should stipulate which organization will take possession of non-collection materials. The registrar should make sure that the organizer provides the information required to determine which objects are returned to which lenders.

SHIPPING

When the entire exhibition has been accounted for, the crate lids are secured and, where security procedures require, the crates are inspected and sealed by security staff prior to loading. The registrar uses the venue list to determine the street address, phone number, and contact for the next venue. This information is added to the waybill, and new individual address labels are affixed to the containers in place of the former label. Each container must be accounted for by the registrar as the exhibition is being loaded by the shipper. The registrar also must be attentive to the manner in which the exhibition is loaded and discuss any unusual circumstances with the shipper and the organizer before the shipment leaves the loading dock.

After the exhibition has left for its next destination, the registrar informs the organizer and the contact at the next venue that the shipment is on its way. Copies of condition reports that reflect changes during the course of the exhibition are forwarded to the organizer, along with a release that is signed, dated, and returned to the hosting institution as documentation that the museum has released custody of the materials. In addition, the next venue contacts the registrar to advise that the exhibition has been received. The loan files are closed, and all loan and exhibition records are maintained as part of the permanent exhibition history of the hosting museum. •

The Basics III | HYPOTHETICALS

1

You carefully discuss all of the requirements for a large African mask that you're lending to another institution: its crate is oversized and will need a very large door and elevator; it needs to be mounted on a pedestal with a Plexiglas vitrine; the shipping estimate does not include offsite stops or offsite storage of the crate. Agreements are made. The week before you ship, you receive a note from the borrower asking that you eliminate the vitrine requirement.

How do you react?

Then, when the courier arrives with the work, it will not fit through the door, and there is no elevator.

What can the courier do?

Is there a positive way to resolve all issues?

2

Discuss the various ways in which museums can partner with each other in developing and showing exhibitions.

What are the positive and strong reasons for partnering?

What types of problems does partnering bring?

How does the museum track such exhibitions, and who should be responsible?

3

You book a traveling exhibition for your main temporary exhibition gallery and build a strong program around it. At the last minute, your designer tells everyone that part of the exhibition cannot fit into the space. The organizing institution is unhappy about changing the number of objects, so the designer works to fit them all. It then is discovered that there are several conflicts with other exhibitions. The checklist for a permanent gallery change is affected, as is another temporary exhibition.

How do you resolve the problems?

4

How do you track in-house exhibitions? Discuss the importance of the checklist, the conservator's review, the creation of mounts and labels, and strategies for recording location changes.

How do you review exhibitions after they are mounted, security checks, and condition of objects?

SECTION 4 | RECORDS MANAGEMENT

4A | TYPES OF FILES

KITTU LONGSTRETH-BROWN, UPDATED BY REBECCA BUCK

Creation and maintenance of transaction and object documentation are the essential tasks of a museum registrar. Information about objects and transactions involving objects—once it is organized or compiled into records and documents—has traditionally has been stored in various physical files. The filing system in a museum may reflect the kind of information stored or the activity to which the information relates. Typical files in the registrar's office, before computerization of information came into existence, included:

- Card catalog
- Category/subject/classification
- Accession (also referred to as object or document)
- Source or donor
- Maker/artist/manufacturer
- Location
- Object photo
- Insurance
- Incoming loan
- Outgoing loan
- Exhibition

It is important that the registrar understand how the files and the business methods of the past govern the information that is available today.

Records about objects in the collection are maintained on an ongoing basis for permanent reference. Activity files are compiled, maintained, and searched while the activity itself is current. Once an exhibition is concluded, or loans have been returned to owners, some of the information may be added to a history sheet for the object file, while the actual documents may be moved to less accessible archival storage. Other activity files—temporary custody, loan, acquisition—may be restarted each year.

Since the value of storing information about objects and activities lies in retrieval, the registrar should organize data and documents in the way in that most users will logically look for them. The arrangement of files should be alphabetical, numerical, or chronological, depending on the type of information and how it will be used. Retrieval from any system is easier if the information has been entered in a uniform format, with consistent spellings and modes of display. Filing systems should be simple, clear, and consistent. Strive for systems that can be understood even if the registrar is not there to explain them. Simple systems that are kept up to date are better than models of sophistication too cumbersome to be completed by the current staff.

CARD CATALOG

The registrar compiles and maintains a central file that lists all of the objects in the permanent collection. This file contains a record for each object, retrievable in accession-number order, incorporating some or all of the information that was gathered on the worksheet. It sometimes includes a small identification photograph. It also may encompass cross-reference files that provide a way to identify specific objects or groups of objects by means other than the accession number, such as maker or artist, donor, subject matter, classification system, or geographic origin.

This list of the entire collection in numerical order is essential to the accountability of the museum registrar. The form of the central record and the complexity of data in the file depend on the resources allotted to the registrar's functions over the history of the museum. Enough information should appear to distinguish one object from all others and to identify what it is, where it came from, and where it is currently located. The central file may be a stepping stone to the greater information that the registrar collects on an object, may display all of that information, or may provide something between the two. In some museums, the card catalog has been discontinued in favor of computer files. If that is the case, care must be taken to back up and protect all information.

CATEGORY/SUBJECT/CLASSIFICATION FILE

A category reference file should be based on an appropriate classification system, materials, or subject matter. Each discipline has its own intellectual or hierarchical categories; some are more complete or systematic than others. A museum should clearly define the standard classification systems it uses.

Category files may present difficulties in a manual system, and are made less often as computerization progresses. Often the categories are not really parallel to each other, although they may reflect the way a particular museum has divided up responsibility for its varied collections: portraits, Chinese, farm tools, wood carvings, for example. These divisions are useful to those who started them and to those who get used to them but do not always aid the researcher or new staff. Form, content, and intellectual analysis can become intertwined and confused. Accurate assignment of a particular object to one of these categories may become a matter of chance.

ACCESSION/OBJECT/DOCUMENT FILES

Documents created by others are also appropriate to the registrar's object files, although copies may be filed in a curatorial department as well. It is important that the museum have a central document file, similar to its central card catalog, a place where records for the entire collection will be reliably found. Accession/object/document files usually are kept in accession-number order, although some museums may divide them by curatorial department. In an acid-free folder are kept documents and correspondence relating to the object and its acquisition:

- Legal documents associated with the accession, such as the bill of sale or deed of gift, although some museums file these by donor
- Correspondence about the delivery and acquisition of the object
- Shipping information, documents, or invoices
- Copy of a bequestor's will
- Photograph
- Worksheets
- Condition and treatment reports from conservator
- Valuation or appraisal information
- Copies of research reports or correspondence, especially those documenting changes in attribution
- Bibliographic references
- Exhibition and loan history
- Deaccession information

These files are archival in themselves, as the documents are primary sources of information about the object. The object file is a continuing and growing history of the object as well, incorporating bibliographic history, appraisals and valuation, exhibition history, and research notes. Information should be date-stamped when it is added to the folder. Object files are most useful when the contents are organized and duplicate pages removed.

MAKER/ARTIST/MANUFACTURER FILES

A frequently used reference is the maker or artist file; like some other types of files, it is becoming more common to keep these only in a computer database. The format of names, regardless of how the files are kept, should be consistent and clear. There are often standard references for names, and the curator is the institution's arbiter. Collection or long-term loan objects may be listed for ready capsule view. The maker—whether individual, manufacturer, or cultural group—may be described by life dates, active dates, places worked, manufacturing sites, biographical notes, nationality, or a designation for group, tribe, or culture. A file folder with detailed information about the maker may be maintained, although this type of information usually resides in a curatorial file.

SOURCE OR DONOR FILES

The source or donor file, identifies the donors of objects, vendors, purchase funds, archeological sites, expeditions, lenders, or trading institutions. It should have a consistent and clear format for names.

LOCATION FILES

Each museum must devise a workable way to report and record object movement. Location files are key to the accountability of registration. Inventory and tracking of the objects is as important as descriptive information. Location files are searched or modified as often as staff need to look at or take inventory of objects or move them. This frequency of use means that location files must be easy to read and easy to modify.

In large museums, a written work request often is used to initiate object movement and record new locations, with a copy to the registrar for marking cards or changing a computer entry. At another museum, a location log may be kept in the storage room, the new locations or object movements written in as they occur and the central location file on cards or computer updated periodically.

In another system, duplicates of accession cards may be filed by location (another cross-reference file). When an object is moved, its card is refiled by the new location; this cumbersome method does not always record the date of the move. Still another museum may use a rotating file of small cards by accession number. Locations are crossed out when they are changed, and dates are added. New cards also are added as needed.

Frequent moves are difficult to record in a timely manner. Backlogs of object-movement work orders or logs in storage soon lead to poor inventory control. Periodic physical inventories must be done to confirm the accuracy of location information. Constant vigilance by the registrar is required to enforce reports of object movement from curators and object handlers; self-discipline is required to stay up to date with location records. A location file that is simple and straightforward will be maintained better than an elegant and elaborate tracking system that has too many steps or maneuvers.

OBJECT PHOTO FILES

Photographs document the collections and aid identification, condition recording, insurance claims, study, research, education, exhibition planning, publication, and publicity. The registrar's older photo files may consist simply of a negative number with the photo date or may encompass storage of the photographic materials themselves.

Photographs come in several formats: negatives (individual or rolls), contact sheets, black-and-white or color prints, color transparencies, color slides, snapshots and Polaroids, and digitized images on CD-ROM or computer hard drives. Types of access needed and the materials being stored determine the organization of photo files. If the files are used mostly by the registrar's staff, they can be arranged by accession number. If others need regular access, it may be more useful to organize them alphabetically by artist, classification, place of origin, or medium or materials. The registrar should choose a method that works best for the collection and for the institution's users and avoid complicated or idiosyncratic systems of organization.

If the negatives are kept by the archivist or, perhaps, a photography or rights department, it is helpful to have the negative number in the object records. Photographs should be kept in acid-free folders. Negatives, slides, and transparencies should be kept separated from prints, in acid-free or metal boxes or in acid-free envelopes, Mylar D, or polypropylene or polyethylene sleeves. Prints and negatives should not be stored with rubber bands or paper clips.

INSURANCE FILES

Insurance values for individual objects are part of the continuing document file. Some insurance policies require a periodic schedule of new or revised values, or, as part of its own risk-management program, the museum may track values by gallery. The organization of the information and the files depends on how the information is used by the registrar, the insurer, and the museum: chronological by date of the report, location of the objects, or collection group. As with all files, simplicity of the system and clearly marked labels make the information easier to find and use.

Incoming Loan Files

Incoming loans may be received for exhibition, research and study, long-term custody, or consideration for acquisition. The files document ownership, object condition, object use, and agreed-upon conditions of the loan, such as location, length of loan, or any special needs. Paperwork about loans for temporary exhibitions should be kept with the rest of the exhibition file. (See below.)

Long-term loans to the museum's collection are recorded, stored, exhibited, or studied the same as collection objects, except that the registration numbers assigned should immediately distinguish loans from accessions. A prefix L and a separate compound numbering sequence for transactions is a common and simple method. *(See chapter on Assigning Numbers.)* Central loan records, maintained in L-number order in a separate file, further aid distinction. Loan object folders should contain the loan agreements, incoming receipts, condition reports, photographs, correspondence, and other documents. An alphabetical lender file is useful in museums that deal with many object and exhibition loans to the collection, while a separate tickler file may alert the registrar to the return or renewal date.

Short-term loans will not be in the museum''s custody long enough to require extensive files. Six months is a useful dividing point. These loans will be given a tracking number, perhaps with the prefix T for temporary or SL for short loan. A log is needed to record these numbers. Each separate numbering system used by a museum (the fewer the better) must have its own integral sequence and a clear prefix or other identifier to avoid confusion between owned and borrowed materials.

The various documents pertaining to the transaction should be annotated with the tracking number and filed by the activity for which the objects were borrowed. Once incoming loan transactions have been concluded and works returned to their owners, the records should be annotated and folders or paperwork placed in a Closed File. Information about long-term loans may be kept for future research in the same way that information about deaccessioned objects is kept. For all loans, the registrar may establish both an owners' alphabetical reference file and a loan-number reference in case of future questions. Documents kept should include the loan agreement, official correspondence, and copies of incoming and outgoing receipts, especially those signed by the owner on return.

Outgoing Loan Files

Files for outgoing loans should contain the following:

- Correspondence with the borrower prior to and during the loan
- Loan agreement spelling out terms of the loan
- Shipping papers
- Borrower's receipt
- Condition reports
- Insurance certificates

Exhibition Files

From initial planning through actual installation and opening of a particular exhibition, the registrar accumulates documents and notes that are used to get the work done. The registrar's working exhibition files may include the following:

- Original loan forms
- Receipts
- Correspondence with lenders, shippers, insurers
- An inventory of the show by case, catalog, hanging order, and/or accession number

•List of lenders, if any

•Contact names, telephone numbers, e-mail addresses

•Condition reports

•Photographs

•Treatment reports

•Related in-house notes and memos

•Shipping bids and bills of lading

•Budget notes and estimates

•Purchase orders

•Related conservation or exhibit maintenance schedules

•Insurance lists

•Copies of information from other departments

This kind of working file has the order, or disorder, that meets the particular registrar's needs or time available. It is prudent to keep everything, even notes on scraps of paper during this time. An exhibition file may grow to become an exhibition "box" or a series of folders sorted by activity.

At the conclusion of a temporary exhibition, after all loaned works have been returned and collection objects put away, or once a "permanent" exhibit is in place, it is time to organize the contents of the file. Keep those papers with information that someone may need to find in later years in a way that will aid finding, and dispose of any redundant pages and now-irrelevant scraps and notes. A closed exhibition file should be as useful as any research document with papers in logical order and an index or table of contents.

Exhibition files should be kept chronologically by exhibition date. All or part of the registration materials may become part of the institution's master archive file for that exhibition. Information about the logistics, lenders, shipping arrangements, insurance, and costs may be useful in future exhibition planning; the registrar may keep the information, if not the actual documents, in an Exhibition Planning file for reference. •

Thanks to: Anne Fuhrman Douglas, Connie Estep, Paulette Dunn Hennum, Monique Maas, and Dominique Schultes.

4B | MANUAL SYSTEMS

KITTU LONGSTRETH-BROWN, UPDATED BY REBECCA BUCK

CREATING DOCUMENTATION

The registrar manages information about the museum's collection and about transactions and activities involving works in the collection or in temporary custody. Several documents, or variants of them, are common to most museums and form the basic records about collection objects. These documents describe the object, record transactions involving the object, and define the legal status of ownership or custody. The format of any of these documents will be specific to the systems in place in a given museum, but the functions are the same for all. Essential documents include:

- Receipts
- Master log
- Worksheets
- Condition reports
- Gift agreements
- IRS Forms
- Proofs of purchase
- Copyright licenses

LOAN AGREEMENTS

Information in these documents may originate with the registrar, curator, donor, maker, vendor or others, but the registrar gathers originals of the documents for the files and tracks the steps between receipt and consideration of objects through accessioning into the collection or return to the owner.

- Receipts
- Receipts should be issued for all objects coming into the museum's custody for any reason. Elements of a receipt include:
- Name and address of the owner of the object
- Daytime phone and fax numbers
- E-mail address
- Date the object was received by the museum
- Why the object is at the museum
- How the object came to the museum
- Description of the object
- Temporary or catalog numbers
- Insurance value (if appropriate) and insurer of record
- Expiration date or duration of deposit

The terms and conditions under which the museum receives objects usually appear on the back of the form. The registrar and the depositor sign and date the receipt. The owner of the object receives a copy, and the registrar keeps one or more copies for the museum files.

If many objects are received in a single deposit, it may take time to complete an accurate count and descriptive list. A temporary receipt may be issued, indicating that details will be added later; an addendum or a superseding receipt should follow. Such a list, complete and accurate, will form the basis of all future documentation of the transaction and should be completed as soon as possible.

GIFT AGREEMENTS

The gift agreement—also known as deed of gift, deed of reconveyance, statement of gift, or certificate of gift—substantiates the transfer of title of an object from the donor to the museum. The agreement is generated by the recipient museum and forwarded to the donor for signature. A gift agreement is issued on museum letterhead or on a special form bearing the museum's logo. The paper should be acid free. Two or three originals are generated, and all are forwarded to the donor for signature; the donor is asked to return all to the museum. The museum director or other authorized official countersigns them and returns one to the donor for his/her records. The signed and dated gift agreement is kept in the object document file or, in some museums, in an alphabetical file organized by donor's last name. If there is a third copy, it can be kept in a safe place offsite.

The gift agreement should contain the following information:

- Museum's name, address, and phone and fax numbers

- Registrar's e-mail address

- Donor's name, address, e-mail, and phone numbers

- A description of the object(s) to be accepted, including the type of object, artist or maker, country of origin, date of object, materials or medium, and dimensions

- Accession number assigned to the item (optional)

- A credit line, standard to the museum, which presents an option for change by the donor

- Expression of intention to donate

- Language waiving all right of ownership

- Language indicating that the person giving the object has the legal authority to give it

- Language that the gift is unrestricted (any restrictions that are accepted by the museum should be written into the deed of gift; those restrictions then supplant this statement)

- Language confirming the donor's belief that the object neither was exported from its country of origin in violation of the laws of that country in effect at the time of the export nor imported into the United States in violation of U.S. laws and treaties

- A statement that the gift was not acquired illegally

- Language indicating that the donor received no goods or services in consideration of the gift

- If dealing with the artist or copyright owner, a statement passing ownership or granting non-exclusive use to the museum

- If not dealing with artist or copyright owner, a statement giving up all rights to the gift

- Language acknowledging the museum's acceptance of the gift

- A line for signature and date of signing of the donor(s)

- A line for signature and date of signing of the museum authority

While possession of a completed gift agreement may be the optimum manner of substantiating title to an object, alternate documentation—such as correspondence from the donor expressing an intent to make a gift and a gift-acknowledgment letter from the museum—may serve the same purpose. If, however, it is determined that the documentation on hand does not support title, the museum may wish to have the donor sign a confirmation of gift statement, indicating that the item was donated and the date on which donation took place. If the donor is unwilling to provide such a statement, the registrar should send a letter to the donor by certified mail, indicating that unless advised otherwise by a given date, the museum will consider the item a donation to the collection as of that date. *(See chapter on Old Loans.)*

Fractional gifts (or gifts of fractional interest) are those in which title to a portion of a work is given to a museum; the museum often stipulates that full title must be received at a later time. It is important to note that in the case of a fractional gift, a separate gift-agreement document must be issued as title for each portion of the gift is transferred to the museum, unless the initial gift contract stipulates the progressive transfer on a predetermined schedule. Legal counsel must be consulted to ensure transfer of title for fractional gifts.

A letter of acknowledgment usually is issued with the gift agreement. Sent as a cover letter to the agreement, this document serves to thank the donor for the gift and to provide instructions about completion of the gift agreement. The acknowledgment letter typically is signed by the director or the curator of the department and includes a description of the donated items. A copy of this letter is kept on file with the gift agreement.

IRS FORMS

The U.S. tax code changes as new legislation is passed and new regulations are accepted. It is imperative for registrars, development officers, curators, and directors to keep abreast of new tax developments. Information in this text reflects laws in place at the time of publication.

The museum may be asked by a donor to complete Internal Revenue Service (IRS) Form 8283 (Noncash Charitable Contributions) after an item has been accepted for the collection. It is the donor's responsibility to obtain, circulate for completion, and file Form 8283, but as a service to donors, the museum may wish to keep on hand blank copies of IRS forms relating to such donations. The museum is required to complete only those sections of any IRS form that apply to its action and should avoid giving tax advice, inappropriate assistance, or the appearance of inappropriate assistance to a donor completing a tax return. The museum's signature confirms only the receipt of the gift as described on the form. It does not imply agreement with values assigned by the donor. *(See chapter on Appraisals and Tax Issues Related to Gifts.)* A copy of Form 8283 signed by a museum official should be placed in the object file with the gift agreement and the original returned to the donor.

If the museum sells, exchanges, or otherwise disposes of property described in Form 8283 (or any portion thereof) within 3 years (or the period prescribed by current law) after the date of receipt, the museum must file Form 8282 (Donee Information Return) with the IRS.

PROOFS OF PURCHASE

Copies of paperwork approving the purchase, invoice or bill of sale, purchase order, and receipt for payment related to objects purchased for the collection are appropriate to include in the registrar's document files, along with any warranties the museum may require from the vendor. Recent trends have made it imperative for the museum to have a warranty of title and indemnification for the purchase of most objects.

MASTER LOG

Identification numbers form the link between each object and the information about that object and should be assigned as soon as the item enters the museum's charge. Sometimes the only way to distinguish objects from one another is by number. The number for each piece must be unique, and it must appear on the object as well as on the records. The numbering system selected must be adaptable, simple, and capable of expanding as the collections grow. Since descriptive information about the object will be found in the records, it need not be coded into an identification or accession number. *(See chapter on Assigning Numbers.)*

A master log, maintained by one person, prevents numbering inconsistencies and ensures that a number is not skipped or duplicated. This log provides a readily available running list of the year's accessions, in order, which serves as a reference to the card catalog and other files in which object information is kept. It need not be elaborate, but should be clear, orderly, easy to read, and difficult to alter. A typical log consists of a bound ledger with information entered in ink. Numbers should be listed in order with enough information to identify the object and source. With the influx of computers, it is often a computer "read only" list that is kept; at the end of a year the full list of this log, and the year's accessions can be printed and bound. More detailed information or tracking of actions is better kept in other files. On a periodic basis the pages should be microfilmed or photocopied for offsite storage. Computerized files should be backed up systematically.

WORKSHEETS

Once an object has been purchased or formally accepted for the permanent collection, an information form called a worksheet, accession sheet, or catalog sheet should be completed. The registrar uses this form to compile, either from the curator or directly from the object, as much information as is available about the item and its acquisition. Although accession information and catalog information often are used interchangeably, there is a distinction. Accession information includes a physical and material description of the object, acquisition information, current condition, and accession number. Depending on the type of museum, monetary value and status of copyright may be included as well. Catalog information includes provenance and history, bibliographic references, an assignment into intellectual categories as followed by the museum or its discipline, and in some museums a catalog number that differs from the accession number. This record-keeping, too, is migrating to a computerized form that can be accessed and added to by curators, researchers, and registrars alike.

CONDITION REPORTS

A condition report should be completed when an object enters the museum's custody to provide a baseline against which future examinations can be compared. *(See chapter on Condition Reporting.)* Condition reports are also appropriate when placing an object on exhibit or taking it down, lending an object or receiving it back, or monitoring a particularly vulnerable or deteriorating object. A condition review also may be part of a collection inventory. Condition reports on objects owned by others are particularly important and should be completed or annotated any time a change is detected. The condition report form may be a checklist or free text but should include the following elements:

- Owner of the object
- Object number
- Maker or artist
- Object name or title
- Object description or type (optional)
- Classification
- Date
- Measurements

- Materials
- Condition: general and specific, using standard terminology
- Description and condition of any accessories: base, frame, cover
- Date, and name of person completing report
- A dated photograph

COPYRIGHT LICENSES

In some museums, documents about copyright in the object form another part of the record. Documentation relating to the copyright status of the item ideally should be generated at the time of acquisition. The museum may desire an exclusive or non-exclusive copyright license for an object it acquires. If the item is acquired from the artist, maker, or copyright holder, language addressing copyright status can be incorporated into the gift or sale agreement. If the donor is not the copyright holder, a separate document may be sent to the owner of copyright with a request for signature. *(See chapter on Copyright.)* These documents become part of the object file.

LOAN AGREEMENTS

A loan agreement for works coming into the museum's custody either for exhibition or on a long-term arrangement is completed before the museum accepts delivery. *(See chapter on Loans.)* The loan agreement describes the object or objects to be lent, the lender, the borrower, terms and conditions of the loan (including who will pay what expenses), and importantly the term of the loan. Like the gift agreement, this form will have a museum logo and the museum's address and phone numbers clearly indicated. Other elements of the loan agreement include:

- Name, address, phone, and fax numbers of the owner of the object(s); for institutional lenders, the name of the contact person
- Purpose of the loan: research, exhibition, loan to collection, etc.
- Beginning and ending dates of the loan arrangement

•Credit line listing how donor wishes to be acknowledged for catalog, label, and/or publicity purposes

•Description of the object, including maker or origin, materials, dimensions, and accessories such as containers or bases

•An insurance value and indication of who is insuring

•Provisions for shipping

•Permissions for photography

•Dated signatures of borrow and lender

Often the reverse side of this agreement lists conditions that pertain to all loans the museum accepts, with language about responsibility, notification to lender of any damage, reference to any state laws about unclaimed property, and limits or exclusions to insurance coverage.

A similar agreement is used when the museum lends objects from the collection to other museums. Usually the agreement generated by the borrowing museum is used for the transaction, although the lending museum may negotiate changes and make modifications as its own policies dictate, or even substitute its own agreement form. The information about an outgoing loan becomes part of the object's history, so the loan agreement or reference to it is added to the object's document file or record.

MANAGING FILES AND RECORDS

RECORD MAINTENANCE

Data about objects are put in the registration files when the objects are incorporated into the collection. Over the years, information reflecting research results, exhibition and publication history, and changes in object status will be added to the files. The addition to, modification of, or deletion of information must be monitored by the registrar. In a manual system, it is often obvious that information has been changed; erasures, crossing out, different typeface or handwriting, and different card stocks tell the tale. Nevertheless, a record of who made

changes on what date will provide a means of verifying the information and its reliability. Typically, only designated staff are permitted to amend information. Subjective information, such as attributions or interpretations of subject matter, and time-sensitive information, such as condition assessments or insurance values, should be initialed and dated by the person amending the file.

Within the time constraints of the museum's activities, the registrar should assign a high priority to the timely updating of information and filing of new materials. In addition to maintaining and updating information, the registrar takes physical care of the files. Acid-free papers should be used for folders, cards, and documents. To preserve contents and information, folders and cards should be replaced when worn or degraded. Documents in folders must be protected from creasing, paper clips, and staples. If prongs are used to hold papers, care must be taken that they do not damage the documents or neighboring files. File labels must be firmly attached, neatly typed or printed, and replaced as required.

Documents that simply carry information that can be transferred to another card or paper do not need to be acid free. Acid-free materials should be used for documents and records that in themselves are archival, for instance, signature copies of gift agreements. A long-term view of preservation is essential in organizing and maintaining these files.

DUPLICATION / PROTECTION

Responsibility for the safety and security of objects extends to the safety of the documentation connected with them. Disasters do happen. Off-premises storage of duplicate records will safeguard essential collection information in the event of loss. Various methods of duplication have been successfully employed. If object cards are typed, carbon copies can be made at the time of production. Cards and documents can be photocopied, full-size or reduced. Copies can be made on microfilm or microfiche, or documents can be scanned into computers. Duplicate records should be stored in a secure offsite area with controlled access, such as a bank vault. More than one person should know where records are stored and how to retrieve them.

Duplicate object records with basic descriptive information and, if possible, a small photo should be made. A record of current loans with insurance values should be made and secured regularly. If the budget allows, store copies of acquisition records (deeds of gift or bequest, receipts of sale, etc.). Establish a schedule for routinely producing and storing duplicate collection records to stay up to date with new acquisitions and new versions of records. If there is an index or "table of contents" for stored records, be sure it is dated, and keep a copy at the museum as well. The frequency of updating duplicate records will depend on the quantity of new records, the value of the objects, and an evaluation of the risks to registration records.

SECURITY OF RECORDS

Registration files with information about the collection are valuable assets to the museum. The information is essential to exhibiting and interpreting as well as responsibly accounting for the collection; insurance values and object condition make a difference in situations of loss or damage. These files must be secured and the integrity of the information safeguarded. The registrar should list risks against which to secure files, periodically evaluating these risks and taking steps to protect against them.

Fast-acting hazards that can destroy or damage records include fire, water, and theft. Slower acting events can deteriorate or destroy as well: dirt, exposure to light, pests, handling, acidic papers, malicious alteration of data, or well-meaning but misguided and unsupervised alteration of data.

In each museum, safeguards and solutions must be devised within the context of the building itself, the budget, support from museum administration, and the registrar's ability, resources, and creative problem solving. Safeguards for records in the registration area include:

- good housekeeping practices
- a smoking ban
- restricting food and drink
- a good automatic fire-suppression system
- fire extinguishers and training in how to use them
- storing files off the floor and protecting them with water barriers
- locking files and maintaining good key control
- monitoring access and enforcing sign out and sign in procedures whenever files are removed
- protection from ultraviolet light exposure
- clean hands and respect for materials
- acid-free papers and folders
- metal file containers
- a procedure for affecting modifications to files, including a written record of changes and clear lines of authority to make them

Records can be considered secure if there are good, up-to-date duplicate records offsite, a staff that understands and respects the importance of records, enough staff to monitor access to files, more than one reference to objects to check information against, the registrar looks at the files often and is very familiar with the contents, the museum's general security practices and procedures are good and the building is protected against fire and intrusion, and access to the registration files is well controlled.

As computers become an integral part of the museum workplace, much of the duplication for security is assigned to computer files, either collections management systems or word-processing documents that hold all basic information. In order for this hybrid system to work, back-up tapes must be made daily, and tapes, at intervals, must be stored offsite in secure and climate-controlled spaces. Electronic files must migrate to new platforms as technology changes, and the rotating back-ups must follow that migration. It is important to produce and maintain hard copies to make certain that the records are secure. *(See chapter on Computerized Records.)* •

Thanks to: Anne Fuhrman Douglas, Connie Estep, Paulette Dunn Hennum, Monique Maas, Dominique Schultes.

4c | COMPUTERIZED SYSTEMS

SUZANNE QUIGLEY, UPDATED AND EXPANDED BY PERIAN SULLY

Collections management activities are greatly enhanced by computer technology. The registrar's use of computers is now widely accepted for the storage and retrieval of catalog information, but computer systems can go much farther. Many registrars track object locations, prepare exhibition lists, generate a myriad of forms (receipts, insurance forms, deeds of gift, etc.), manage images (photo records, rights and reproduction, and images themselves), and organize conservation, publication, exhibition histories, provenance, and curatorial information on the computer.

Implementation of a collections management system (CMS) also benefits other functions within a museum. Education, membership, accounting, and administration use information internally, while the public searches the system in a gallery or on the internet. To aid the registrar, who is often the system manager or program administrator, in planning for and getting the most out of the museum's CMS, this section provides a comprehensive account of CMS requirements, the system selection process, the structured nature of data management, online access, and a brief introduction to imaging.

COLLECTIONS MANAGEMENT SYSTEMS

System Requirements

A system consists of hardware, software, and the network on which they are used within the museum. It is run by human beings and must be managed. Each museum must determine who will choose, manage, and maintain a CMS before it begins the process of implementation.

Choosing a system requires a thorough analysis of:

- The information that is to be stored
- Who will enter data

- How, why, and by whom the data will be used
- Present computer capabilities
- Existing data structures
- Anticipated future growth of institutional needs

Based on this analysis, the choice is among proprietary museum data-management systems, professionally designed custom systems, or in-house designed systems.

Hardware should be selected only after the foregoing analysis and selection of software have been made to ensure its adequacy for the type of data being stored, the database size, the operating system, and network capabilities. Conversely, existing hardware may limit the type of data-management software that can be used.

Database Structure

A database is a collection of information about something. Manual collections records are a database. The advantage of computerizing collections data is that the computer can sort data more quickly and in many more ways than a person using a manual system can. A CMS refers to the database and the application software interface with which the user interacts.

The key to a useful computerized database is the method of data organization, that is, the database structure. There are a number of different types of database systems, but only three are commonly referred to when discussing collections management systems: flat file, relational, and object-oriented relational. Flat file databases keep information in a single large table, while relational databases keep data in separate tables, each "related" to the other by means of a common field, such as accession number or donor number. The object-oriented relational database is a relational system that utilizes the same type of fields within the database and the application, removing the need for software to translate between the database fields and the output programming; it permits the system to run more smoothly as a whole. Flat file databases are rarely used for today's complex information management needs, though they are frequently utilized for simpler tasks.

Relational and object-oriented relational databases have many advantages over flat files. A collection might contain a number of objects given by a single donor. While there will be a separate record for each object in the collections table, there need be only one record for the donor in the donor table, linked to every record of an object in the collection table that was given by that donor. If information about the donor should change, this information needs to be altered in only one location in the database, thus saving work and ensuring accuracy.

A cardinal rule of good database structure is that no piece of information should ever be entered more than once. The exceptions to this are the common fields that link related tables together, such as the donor number, which must be present in both tables to enable the link.

Although the terminology and precise way they work vary among different software products, most computerized database systems have four components: tables, queries, forms, and reports.

Tables hold stored data. Each table is comprised of records, which consist of sets of data about a particular type of item, such as objects or donors. Individual pieces of information that make up a record are placed in fields, the equivalent of the blanks that must be filled in on a paper form.

Some fields can hold only text data, some only numerical data, and others only dates. Other fields can display various calculations from other fields. The collections management software may "require" that certain fields be entered (such as the accession numbers), while it may leave other fields to the discretion of the data-entry operator.

Queries, also known as searches, extract information from a database. They may be simple, such as one that calls up a record pertaining to an object with a specific accession number. Queries can also be complex, for instance, a request for a list of all objects given by a particular donor in a given year whose value was greater than a certain amount.

Forms generally are used for one of two purposes. Designed to represent paper records, they visually organize and simplify the data-entry process and speed data entry. They can use lookup tables in the database to ensure that information placed in certain fields is valid and that it is correctly spelled or formatted. Forms also frequently are used to specify search or sort criteria to be used by predefined queries. The query is selected from a menu presented by the software, and the criteria the query uses then are entered on an associated form.

Reports are the means by which the results of a query are displayed or printed. They may be part of the software itself, may be designed by the user, or both, depending upon the capabilities of the particular software. Queries, if properly structured, can use predetermined reports to display or print their results. If a report is not used, a query usually results in a simple list that may be displayed, printed, or imported into a word-processing program for editing and formatting.

Functionality

It is important for a CMS to be flexible. The system should allow a museum to begin with the data it already has and to expand as need and opportunities arise. The sum of the information about any object comes from a variety of sources, such as registrars, curators, and risk managers. Each should be responsible for the timeliness and accuracy of his/her piece of information and should be able to enter it without transmitting it to a third party. The system should incorporate methods to ensure that only authorized persons are able to enter, edit, or view various pieces of information about an object. In all but the smallest museums, this generally means a networked system of computers, the software and data residing on a central computer called a server.

Hardware Comparability

At the end of the first decade of the 2000s, the majority of both proprietary collections management systems and commercial database systems run on Microsoft Windows operating systems, although there are some systems that run on Apple Macintosh or Linux-based operating systems. Many Apple and Linux systems today have the ability to run Windows on the same computer, on a "virtual hard drive." This means that computers running non-Windows operating systems also can access Windows-only software.

Ideally, the computer or computers should be chosen only after the collections management software has been selected. If this is not possible, the software must be selected so that it does not exceed the limitations of the hardware. In such instances, it is important to select software that can be expanded in its capabilities as future hardware upgrades occur. Consulting a technology professional to ensure compatibility of the hardware and software is desirable, regardless of whether the selected software is a stand-alone system or a networked system.

This compatibility is especially critical if the software selected runs on a network with multiple desktop computers accessing it. In that case it is important to hire a technology professional who has experience not only with the type of server and operating system selected but also with the networking requirements of the system. He or she will be able to advise on infrastructure upgrades needed to implement the system and will be the person responsible for setting up the server running the software. In many cases, however, the vendor of a proprietary CMS will install the software on the server and networked computers. Prior to selecting the software, it is necessary that the system administrator, the technology professional, and the vendor(s) discuss the requirements of the system and the infrastructure of the institution. They must determine if the software is compatible with the existing framework, such as network wiring, electrical outlets, Internet speeds, and physical space requirements. If not, the institution must determine if it is possible to upgrade its infrastructure; if an upgrade is not feasible, a different system must be selected.

The computer and server hardware must be evaluated on the basis of several criteria. The hardware should be produced by a reputable manufacturer who stands behind its warranty and should be purchased from an established vendor. A number of manufacturers claim that their product is equal to those of major manufacturers, and this is often true. However, unless the museum is a large organization

(or part of one, such as a governmental agency) with an information management department that can handle alternate arrangements should the producer suddenly go out of business, a computer produced by an established manufacturer and serviced by an established vendor is worth the difference in cost.

In general, the rule is to buy the fastest, most powerful computer(s) affordable. Speed and power are especially important if electronic documents, images, videos, audio files, or other multimedia will be used as part of the CMS. The computer must have an adequate amount of "Random Access Memory" (RAM), a more than adequate amount of hard disk or other storage space, and hardware for internal and external backups. The computer upon which the data are stored, whether a server or a stand-alone desktop computer, should have a redundancy feature called a RAID (Redundant Array of Inexpensive Disks). A RAID consists of multiple hard drives, mirroring the data. In the event one hard drive fails, the computer can retrieve data from one of the other disks on the RAID. This is not a substitute for external backups, however, and should be used in conjunction with backup hardware. There are a number of different RAID configurations, and the technology professional can advise on which configuration is appropriate.

If the system is a stand-alone installation, the computer must have adequate expansion slots to accommodate equipment additions. Connecting the computer to a network, a scanner or other electronic image-capturing device, or a soundboard requires the installation of a card to handle the external connections. Some external storage method is also necessary, such as CD-ROM, DVD-RW, tape drives, and external hard drives, which may be swapped out as backup storage.

SOFTWARE SELECTION AND DEVELOPMENT
Software Selection
Before selecting software for a database system, the institution must decide whether it will purchase commercial, non-museum-specific database software and contract with a computer programmer or computer company, or use a staff member to create

custom software, or buy a CMS from a commercial vendor. Current staffing, immediate and future budgets, long-term needs, and the stability of the museum must be considered when determining if a commercial CMS or a customized in-house database product is the right solution. Each solution has certain advantages and disadvantages, but many, if not most, museums today purchase their CMS from a vendor and work with the vendor to tailor the product to the institution's specific needs.

Commercial Databases

Commercial database software, such as SQL, Access, and FileMaker Pro, are economical, powerful, and flexible database systems capable of being configured for collections management purposes. Although this software is designed to be customized by the user for particular applications, a reasonable knowledge of the software is required to do so. Use of commercial databases can be an economical way to begin a CMS. However, if it is not carefully thought through and managed, this option also can be the most expensive of all the routes and the most difficult to scale up for future needs, ensuring ongoing development throughout the lifetime of the system.

One of the primary advantages of using in-house designed systems is the relatively small initial investment in equipment and software. If building a new system from scratch, the computerization project can start out small, using the information already contained in paper records, and then expand as the need and opportunity arise. This approach is also very flexible, allowing the system to be designed to fit a particular museum's needs.

There are major disadvantages to this approach as well. If done by someone whose primary task is not collections management, that person's time will be diverted from other duties. During the early stages of development, the amount of time required can be significant. A poorly designed system can waste time and money and in the end be worse than no computerized system at all. If the person who designed it leaves the museum, it may be impossible to maintain, especially if the software in question is modified to such a degree that advice and information become difficult to obtain from outside sources.

An institution with a truly customized database system also may be at a major disadvantage if it decides to share its information on the Internet or directly with other museums or consortiums. Creating a system using commercial database software requires recognition of and adherence to established standards and practices, as well as a broad understanding of information management practices at other institutions.

A museum no longer needs a computer guru on its staff to produce an in-house system, but if there are no dedicated staff on-hand, it is recommended that the museum contract and work with a software developer to design the software. If not contracting with a developer, it is necessary to provide the person who will establish the system with training in database design, testing, and documentation. Initially, the system should be kept simple. Only when one aspect is working well should another be added; it is not wise to try to incorporate every desirable feature or function all at once. The new system should be integrated into office routines slowly, preferably by starting with the processing of new transactions. If properly designed and used, the computerized system should save time and effort. Only after the new system is functioning satisfactorily and the staff are comfortable in its use is it appropriate to computerize the entire collection.

Commercial Collections Management Systems

A commercial CMS, fully adapted for cataloging and collections management use, offers a museum many advantages. The system often comes to the museum as a complete package and use can begin soon after system installation and initial training are finished. Technical support is often available by telephone, via e-mail, or on a website; training is usually available from the vendor; and upgrades come without museum staff spending time on software development. Established vendors use client feedback to focus development and make certain that needs are met. The museum can form user groups with other clients and share information, problems, and solutions.

A major drawback of the commercial CMS can be the amount of money that must be spent for initial implementation. The commitment to a yearly maintenance agreement—which usually is based on the number of user licenses (i.e., the number of users who can use the system over the network at one time) a museum has purchased—is also serious. There may be concerns about the stability of the company that sells the program and questions about the continuance of software maintenance should the company cease to exist. There are now free, open-source options available that have the potential to significantly reduce startup and maintenance costs, but the drawback is that open-source CMS cannot be tailored to the institution's needs by a vendor; the institution must staff or hire a programmer to make modifications.

A museum must plan the configuration and implementation of a commercial system very carefully. Since development is not done in-house, it is possible to overlook the careful review of data as they are collected and used by various departments.

A single staff member should serve as liaison between the software company and other museum users. A second staff member should learn the program administration thoroughly and be ready to step in if needed. The program administrator is often the registrar or a member of the registrar's department; whoever takes the position should know collections management processes and collection information needs. Ideally, the program administrator should be a staff member dedicated solely to information and system management, help-desk functions, report writing, and communication with vendors and IT professionals.

Most commercial CMSs offer room for growth. Additional users can be enabled and new features may be added at the request of the museum or included free of charge as part of an upgrade. As these changes may be expensive to implement, it is important to anticipate future needs and select a system that already has most features present at time of installation.

The popularity of commercial systems proves that they meet an extremely important need in the museum community. With the fast pace of developing technologies, it is logical that museums rely on specialists who can use new developments to improve functionality quickly. Commercial programs have become the collection management programs of choice in most museums.

Determining What Type of System to Select

Before software or hardware selections can be made, a comprehensive list of system requirements must be prepared. The Canadian Heritage Information Network (CHIN) has produced a number of guides to help institutions in planning their digitization projects. CHIN's *Criteria Checklist*[1] outlines a number of features commonly included in a commercial CMS, which can assist a museum in determining which features have priority. It is also helpful to interview similar institutions about their systems and determine which features they find especially useful.

Request for Proposal

Whether a museum has decided to purchase a commercial CMS or to hire a programmer to develop an in-house system, a request for proposal (RFP) is the appropriate document to send to a small group of selected vendors. Look for vendors who have experience working within the institution's discipline. Educating the vendor about work flow will be much easier if the vendor has worked with similar institutions.

The RFP must provide the vendor with an exact, comprehensive, and clearly written outline of the product the museum needs. It must include a cover letter describing the museum and the project, a description of the existing computer environment, a functional requirement section, and instructions for returning a proposal to the museum.

The bulk of the RFP will be the functional requirements section, which states the desired characteristics of the CMS as determined above. It is advisable to divide this section into parts. For example, the section on system requirements will contain information about the network in place and whether the museum intends to continue to use it. If it does, the vendor's system must be compatible with the network. The museum may request that the system have a web-based output, be compatible with different operating systems, or accommodate different user groups with various levels of security. All questions throughout the RFP should be phrased so that they can be answered by the vendor with "yes," "no," or "modify."

Further subdivisions of the functional requirements section address specific issues for each of the modules the museum expects to use (e.g., object tracking, exhibition registration, accessioning, multimedia, etc.).

The other significant section of the RFP contains directions for the vendors' responses:

•The deadline by which the museum must receive the proposal (usually four weeks from the date of the museum's cover letter)

•The format in which the proposal is to be sent to the museum, often via certified mail (it is important for the museum staff to be able to compare each of the proposals directly to each other, and to do this consistency of format is necessary)

•Clear instructions as to what must be included, including license fees, annual maintenance costs for a specified number of users, training costs, accessibility of support staff, extra costs for data transfer, and anticipated project timeline

It is crucial that all vendors be treated equally. Due dates must be met and the proposal must be complete for the vendor to be eligible for consideration.

Note: A vendor is legally liable for answering the RFP truthfully, as it serves as the basis for a future contract.

Evaluation

Evaluation of proposals and selection of a vendor is a surprisingly labor-intensive task, and it is important to let the vendors know of your selection as quickly as possible.

Upon receipt of each proposal, check to see that all the items requested in the RFP are present. As soon as the deadline has passed, organize the proposals so that they may be easily compared. Establish a rating system that everyone agrees upon; give each person on the selection committee a set amount of time to scrutinize, compare, and rate the responses.

Narrow the selection to no more than three vendors and observe the selected systems in use. If possible, ask the vendor to preload some of the museum's existing data for the demonstration.

•At large museums, ask the vendors to demonstrate the system on-site.

•At medium-sized museums, ask the vendors to come and demonstrate to your staff and those from other museums in the area as well.

•At smaller museums, have staff attend a national or regional professional meeting where vendors regularly demonstrate their products.

Alternately, one may request to view the product online, using a remote desktop connection or a live webcast. Depending on the institution's network infrastructure and internet speed, online demonstrations can be effective.

After the demonstrations, contact colleagues at similar institutions who have already installed each of the systems under consideration. Ask them for a frank and honest evaluation of what they like and don't like about the systems; ask about the vendors' responsiveness and any unanticipated costs they encountered during or after installation. If at all possible, the internal selection committee should visit other museum sites where the systems under consideration are installed and running.

The committee should then be able to reach consensus on the product.

Contract Negotiation

Once the vendor is selected it is time to buy. Even if the system is for a single user, it is advisable to have a contract with the vendor outlining exactly what is included. The proposal provided by the vendor in response to the RFP is the cornerstone of the agreement and should be referenced in the contract. The contract need not be elaborate. Many vendors will provide a sample contract which both parties are free to amend, as long as they both agree on the amendments. The contract should set dates for acceptance of the system, a schedule of payment to the vendor, return policies, training and support agreements, data conversion, and requested modifications to the system. *(See chapter on Contracts.)* It may also state that the source code will be placed in escrow in case the company should dissolve at a later date, but there is usually an extra cost associated with this.

IMPLEMENTING A COLLECTIONS MANAGEMENT SYSTEM
Implementation
The who, what, where, when, and how of a com-

puterized data-management system come together in a concrete fashion during the implementation process, when the system manager, using the chosen hardware and software, strives to achieve a working system. The adequacies of the chosen system, hardware, software, and site must be tested during the initial implementation process. The objective of this phase is to identify and correct defects so that the ultimate goals of efficiency and productivity can be achieved.

Site Preparation

Site preparation takes into account the safety and efficiency of all aspects of the system: hardware, software, and the people using the equipment. Sites can take many forms, each of which requires a different type of preparation. Sites can be centralized or dispersed, independent or connected, and permanent or mobile.

Centralized versus dispersed

Centralized sites avoid the need for extensive networking and may allow for the design of a specialized computer room. Such a room should have requirements for temperature, relative humidity, and dust filtration similar to collections storage areas and should provide maximum efficiency of computer use: technical support easily available, comfortable and safe working conditions, strong security, etc.

Dispersed sites enable customized or specialized workstations that fit the needs of particular museum users. For example, registrars can enter acquisition information, loan inventories, etc., from their workspace without having to take materials into a central area with a higher level of traffic flow. Likewise, conservators can set up a work station to use when doing condition and treatment reports, or secure work stations can be set up for visiting researchers in areas that will not be in the way of other museum functions.

Independent versus connected

Whether sites are centralized or dispersed, connectivity may or may not be desirable. Connected sites permit easy communication, standardization, and control, but these networked sites almost always require a system administrator, increased security, higher costs, and modifications to architectural infrastructure. Wiring a museum for networking can be a problem; the construction of many of the old buildings that house museums is so solid that passing cables through walls, ceilings, or floors may not be possible. In these cases, wireless networks may be the solution. Thinking ahead and wiring during times of remodeling or new construction will save money and headaches in the future.

Permanent versus mobile

The mobility of a computer site also is important to consider. Permanent workstations usually provide greater computing power, full-sized keyboards, and larger monitors. When computing sites are permanent, ergonomic furniture, lighting, and security issues also are easier to resolve. The ability to move computers, however, is advantageous in many situations. Computers can be taken into collection areas for direct data entry during inventory, condition checks, or environmental monitoring. Having the means to take computerized records or images to meetings, libraries, and offsite locations is convenient and can solve potential access and security problems. Mobile computing, however, has its drawbacks. Theft becomes a greater issue when using small, portable computing equipment and, if networking is required, using a wireless system becomes the only practical solution.

Whatever the configuration of computing sites, the computers and network equipment should be assembled and tested prior to installation. If possible, the data servers should be kept in a secure area where they are accessible to authorized personnel but protected from vandalism and theft. CDs, DVDs, backup tapes or hard drives, and other portable data storage units also should be put in a safe and secure place.

Like other machinery, computer hardware should not be exposed to extreme changes in temperature and humidity and should be protected from particulates (dust, crumbs, etc.), liquids (leaky pipes, spilled coffee, etc.), and other debris. Adequate and stable energy sources and sufficient access to them should be provided to avoid data loss and undue stress on the computer hardware. Like other electrical equipment, computer hardware should be placed in a low-static area away from magnetic fields.

Wires and cables should be isolated in such a way that people do not walk or trip on them, equipment does not roll over them, and animals do not chew them. Cables and the backs of computers should still be easily accessible. System disks, warranty, and other legal documentation should be safely stored in a place where they will be safe but accessible when needed.

Many work-related injuries are caused by inadequate equipment and poorly designed work areas. Chairs and desktops should be ergonomically designed and organized to avoid injuries from typing at a keyboard, sitting, and viewing a monitor. Light sources should be as low as possible; focusing them away from computer monitors will help eliminate eyestrain.

The goal of an efficient workspace is data integrity. Ideally, the workspace will have a large enough space to organize necessary paperwork and support documentation without jeopardizing the quality of data entry or the safety of equipment and objects. If accessioned objects are to be worked with at the computer for cataloging, condition and treatment reports, etc., the work space must be arranged so that the risks of knocking pieces over, placing documents or other objects on top of them, or losing pieces altogether are eliminated.

Schedule

The schedule for implementing a CMS can be divided into two stages: installation and execution. The actual time needed to achieve a functioning system will depend on the hardware and software planning and testing that was completed prior to implementation. The implementation process actually begins when a museum undertakes a needs assessment and concludes that change is needed and can be achieved. Whether a museum chooses an in-house solution or purchases a commercial CMS, a similar implementation process follows: analysis of the institution's needs; assessment of available resources; evaluation and selection of a system; and purchase, installation, and testing of the system.

Loss of a certain amount of time is expected when switching between old and new systems. At a minimum, conversion to the new system will involve training existing employees to use it. If importing files or data from another system is needed and possible, converting the data and then getting it ready for use in the new system may be quite time consuming. It is helpful to take the time to examine the information structure of the new system and clean up or reorganize existing data to correspond to the new system, especially if data entry in the past has been inconsistent or incomplete. Find out how this conversion will work prior to starting the implementation process. At the other extreme, interruption in use of the file-management system may involve hiring and training new employees to transfer data manually (initial entry from manual card files, clean up and "tweaking" of existing data, etc.) and training existing employees on future applications.

Good system design results from reverse engineering. Starting with the needed results will naturally lead to appropriate software and, in turn, hardware. Some museums start a new system without knowing what they will or will not be able to do with it. This usually results in further "downtime" of the system, general frustration, and low morale. How these factors affect individual institutions depends on such factors as size, type of system, and type and frequency of use of that system. Ideally, scheduling will be structured enough to be completed at a time that is appropriate for the museum (based on impending deadlines for system-generated data or reports, etc.) yet flexible enough to allow for unpreventable or unexpected set-backs (sudden limitations in staffing or staff time, faulty hardware or software, etc.).

Testing

Testing should be done in stages. A museum should know the quality and requirements of the hardware, software, and technical support available for a product prior to purchase and certainly prior to the testing process. During the testing process, the museum should derive the actual long-term cost of the system in staff time. This includes the length of time it takes staff members to be trained on the system, to enter data, to conduct queries, to generate reports, and to make changes in the format of the system. Initial testing is best done by those designing or installing the system. Secondary testing is essential and should be conducted by those who are the day-to-day users of the system; small, workable amounts of actual data should be used for tests. All operations of the system that are desired should be tested, as should vendor's claims about capacity and performance. Although this may not prevent software errors that result from using larger amounts of data, more files, or different configurations of data, it is an initial, short-term way of testing a system prior to becoming fully engulfed in it.

DATA MANAGEMENT

Data are both resources and assets. The data preserved about an object gives that object its depth of meaning and value. A computerized system opens up new avenues of access to the information recorded about an object, and the most important elements of any information management system are the data entered into it. Poorly managed information in a manual system will continue to be poorly managed information when moved into a computer database. All of the expected benefits of digital record keeping—especially the sophisticated searching, comparison possibilities, instant retrieval of related information, and statistical reporting—will not be met if the data are inconsistently entered and controlled.

In the process of choosing a computerized system, a museum will review its requirements and the intended uses of the system. The institution will examine how information is currently maintained in paper files or in an existing database. It will determine how it anticipates a new database system to streamline existing processes and increase its current capabilities. It will produce a data model that outlines how information will relate to other data in the new system. The institution must understand what it expects of a new system before it is installed.

The collections database manager should undertake an inventory of existing documentation systems and standards, both manual and automated, to determine which departments or individuals collect and record data and how they do so. This not only will identify data sources within the museum, it also will help determine what data should be used in a

new software system and who will provide or enter it.

When information is added by a variety of sources, each source must be responsible for the accuracy and consistency of the information that it enters. Each department must understand its responsibilities toward the object and the object's documentation; all users need a clear idea of precisely where in the system they enter their data and how they relate to other information and other users. If there are a large number of sources for the data, it is a good idea to route entered records to one person, often a registrar, a collections information manager, or the database administrator, who can review it for accuracy and consistency.

Data entry and upkeep are expensive processes, and the data entered should be considered just as valuable and priceless as the object(s) they represent. Much like caring for objects, the process of caring for data can be complex. Data must be managed with optimal conditions, primarily consistency and a standardized level of completeness, and multiple backup copies must be made to ensure longevity. Unlike many physical objects, electronic data often can be recreated and rebuilt, but the resulting cost in staff time can have an impact on other activities within the museum.

While it is useful and often desirable to access all the available information about an object in a CMS, there may be data-entry constraints. Not all data must be entered online; it is perfectly acceptable to decide that certain kinds of information will remain in a manual system with pointers from the automated system. For instance, complicated dimensions, confidential donor information, bibliographic references, detailed provenance information all may remain in a manual file, each having some indication in the automated file that directs the user to the manual file, e.g., "See curatorial file for provenance."

Define what the institution considers to be the minimum content of a record to identify, locate, and otherwise control the object that the record represents. All information that goes into a CMS should be dictated by the museum's needs and not by the computer system. It is not necessary to enter data just because there is a field in an automated system that will accommodate it. If possible, the system administrator may wish to hide certain unused fields to prevent users from entering information into them. Doing so will help ensure consistent locations of specific information.

Create documentation standards that will guide users to enter correct and complete information concerning an object. It is often possible to set required fields to prevent users from adding new records unless they enter certain fields, such as an accession number, title, or a location. For guidance in developing documentation standards for an institution, it may be useful to review the *Categories for the Description of Works of Art* (CDWA) developed by the Art Information Task Force or *Cataloging Cultural Objects: A Guide to Describing Cultural Works and Their Images* (CCO) from the Visual Resources Association (VRA). These projects provide guidelines to encourage the creation of documentation standards that will help the museum community preserve information that is required to identify, locate, and control objects. Other documentation standards include SPECTRUM from the Museum Documentation Association in the United Kingdom. Each of these standards has a slightly different focus on the type of material it is designed to describe, so it is important to select the one that is most useful for those materials and then adhere closely to the standard. In certain institutions, it will not be possible to find a perfect match, so selecting one and modifying the standard slightly to fit the museum's needs may be necessary. The important thing is to adhere to a standard.

Types of material each standard describes:
•CDWA: art museums

•CCO: museums that collect art, architecture, and material culture and their associated visual resources

•SPECTRUM: designed for museums in the United Kingdom, but useful elsewhere; no specific materials described

Data Dictionary

When a museum establishes data content standards, a data dictionary can provide a useful tool for documenting and preserving information about those standards. A data dictionary furnishes a definition of each of the fields or data elements that combine to create a documentary record of an object. It allows a museum to examine the nature of the object information it preserves by breaking it up into and documenting data elements.

Data dictionaries are particularly valuable in a museum in which more than one department enters information about an object. They provide a reference to guide users throughout an institution in entering data consistently. When provided with a data dictionary, each department has documentation that details the scope of its own and other departments' responsibilities for entering data concerning an object. It is helpful to establish a cataloging manual in conjunction with the data dictionary. Outline the steps required to catalog an object within the institution and the steps a cataloger must take, in combination with the data dictionary, to enter data into the CMS.

While a data dictionary usually will be developed in-house, one also may be provided by the vendor of an automated CMS. Users should review a vendor-provided data dictionary carefully, determine if they agree with the definitions for the data elements that the vendor proposes, and revise them, if necessary, to suit their own particular needs.

When developing a data dictionary, concentrate on those things that assist in effective use of the documentation. A selection from the following information is useful when creating a data dictionary entry, although not all of the following information is required:

•Module name. In a relational database there may be more than one area into which information is entered. Identify the module (objects, locations, exhibitions, etc.) where the user will find this particular data element.

•Field name. The name of the category, field, or data element.

•Field code. The code the system uses internally.

•Standards. The various data standards to which the field corresponds. Such standards may include terminology dictionaries, such as the *Art and Architecture Thesaurus* or *Nomenclature* (discussed below) and metadata protocols.

•Attributes. Identify the attributes of the field; note whether it is a fixed or variable length, alpha or numeric, repeatable, etc. Note if there is a controlled vocabulary that will verify this field or special keystroke commands or controls that are required to use this field.

•Access. Identify which departments or users may access and enter or change data within this field.

•Description. Define the field, stating its purpose and the character of the information that will be entered into the field.

•Data-entry rules. Provide a list of conventions for data entry in this field. Note any exceptions to the rules; for instance, is a different standard applied to backlog records? Note, among other things, if names are inverted or if dates are entered month or day first, etc. If an authority or controlled terminology is in use for this field, provide directions for using the authority, provide definitions of controlled terms, or direct the user to the appropriate information.

•Examples. Provide examples of data entered in the field.

•Indexed. Note whether the field is indexed.

•Remarks. It may be helpful to users to note whether the field is related to other fields in the database or in another database.

A sample data dictionary entry for an accession value field might include:

Field name: Accession number (required)

Field code: ACCNUM

Standards.

CDWA: Current location (repository numbers)

ISAD code: 3.1.1

EAD tag: <unitid>

Attributes: Alphanumeric (unique value)

Access: Write access for registration and administration groups. Input for curatorial group for new records only. Read access for all.

Description: The accession number is the unique

identifier assigned to objects as they are received into the museum. For detailed accessioning and numbering procedures, refer to the Acquisition Procedures manual, located in the Registrar's office.

Create individual records for each object. An "object" refers to an item that is cataloged and displayed individually. For example, a portfolio containing seven prints would have seven or more objects, including the cover, colophon, and any additional materials. A cup and saucer is considered one object in two parts, and denoted with parts letters (a–b). In this example, each piece of the portfolio is cataloged individually, while the cup and saucer have only one record entered into the CMS.

Examples:
2007.5
2007.1 a-c
2007.2.1
2007.7.1.3
2007.7.1.1 a-b
87.2.2 LIB
2006.011.6.1 a-b ARC

Data-entry rules:
•Always use periods between the numeric values of the number.

•Use hyphens between parts letters (e.g., a–c).

•For objects with parts letters or special collection distinctions (LIB, ARC), insert a space between the numeric values and the letters.

Useful data dictionaries are never created in a void, and no matter how thorough the documentation is, there is always a unique problem or detail that will be exceptional. Meetings with users provide the opportunity to discover elements of information that each field entry in a data dictionary can and cannot accommodate. Meetings should include information supervisors such as curators and registrars, should be regularly scheduled, and should be goal oriented.

•Hold meetings with users while the data dictionary entry is being generated.

•Listen to suggestions and implement them.

•Use meetings as an opportunity to build

consensus because data dictionary conventions that are imposed on users will be ignored.

•Always provide a reason for a convention; users are more likely to use a data dictionary that makes sense.

Finally, data dictionary entries constantly evolve and adapt to new uses and unique situations. It is essential that they be kept up to date; otherwise, users will not be able to depend upon them as reliable and definitive sources of information.

Data Standards and Validation

In a museum, there are many different applications of standards and many contexts in which they are used. Data standards focus on how information is structured and entered into a collections management/cataloging system (manual or automated) and how that system maintains the information and provides a framework through which the information may be retrieved and manipulated. Data standards are concerned with three elements: structure, content, and value.

Data structure standards provide guidelines for the structure of a documentation system: what constitutes a record, what fields or categories of information are considered essential information, what fields are optional, and how those fields relate to one another. Data structure standards determine how much and what kind of documentation will meet the organization's criteria for security, accountability, and access to the object. These standards are established both by the strictures of the database system and by the demands of the museum. Using national or international documentation standards as a guide, it is the museum that should choose all the categories of information that are required for its needs. A CMS may determine the structure of the files and how information is recorded, but it should never determine what information is recorded.

Data content standards provide guidelines for defining each individual data element or field and what information should be entered into it. Data content standards clearly describe the content of a defined field or data element and provide guidelines for controlling the syntax, style, grammar, and abbreviations used within each field. These standards are usually internally developed cataloging rules with

institutional data dictionaries and procedural manuals that outline the rules and applications.

Data value standards determine the vocabulary to be used for individual fields or data elements and the authorities that will build consistency into a database or documentation system. Terminology standards that are used consistently enable a computerized system to provide indexes that find like objects quickly and connect them to other objects in interesting and sometimes unexpected ways. A consistent use of data value standards protects the museum's investment in its data and provides many more points of access to an object than can be provided in a manual system. These standards may be externally or internally developed authority files, lexica, thesauri, and controlled vocabularies.

The benefits of the consistent application of data standards in a CMS include:

•Maximized investment in the data in a system

•Enhanced accountability for a collection

•Enhanced access to records and, thereby, to objects

•Consistency in retrieval of related information

•Enhanced quality and accuracy of the individual record

•Data that adapt more easily to new technological and documentation developments

•Data that can be exported more efficiently into a new system

•Simplified exchange of information with other programs within an institution or with other institutions

Even when data standards have been established and are in use, it is necessary to review and revise them. Examine where they do and do not work. When the information that will go into an automated system is first organized, strict controls can be instituted for fields that are never used for searching or indexing. Review usage patterns and consider whether it is useful to control information that is not being utilized. There invariably will be object information that cannot easily fit into any organized system. Remember that while the aim of using standards is to be consistent, it is also necessary to be flexible enough to accommodate unique situations.

It is useful to become familiar with current efforts in the museum community to create data standards. Much work already has been done to define the categories of information that combine to form a record and the terminology standards to use in those categories. Use these efforts to guide the development of standards in the museum and to avoid repeating work that others have already done.

The following list, by no means comprehensive, provides some information about organizations that are currently or have been involved in the development of standards in the museum community:

•The Getty Research Institute promotes the development of art information standards, sponsoring the development of the *Art and Architecture Thesaurus,* the *Union List of Artist Names,* and the *Thesaurus of Geographic Names* to encourage institutions to use common terminology and reference resources. The Getty Art Information Task Force (AITF) is one of several of the Getty's Art History Information Program (AHIP) projects involved in the development and dissemination of standards. AITF developed the *Categories for the Description of Works of Art,* a comprehensive set of categories for describing works of art and related images and a format for electronic exchange of information. Contributors include art historians, curators, and registrars.

•The Museum Computer Network (MCN) is an organization that seeks to promote the development and use of computer technology in the museum community. MCN sponsors an annual conference with workshops to promote the growth of knowledge and understanding of computer applications for museums. The conference also provides an opportunity for developers to demonstrate products.

•The Canadian Heritage Information Network (CHIN) offers a variety of services to Canadian museums, including an automated collections management system, advice on documentation standards and new technology, and data dictionary standards for data entry. The organization maintains three national databases of Canadian collections that cover humanities and natural sciences objects and archaeological sites. CHIN is primarily concerned with promoting and supporting the development of documentation standards and computerization in the Canadian museum community.

•The Collections Trust (previously the Museum Documentation Association) promotes the development of documentation standards in the United Kingdom. The Collection Trust publishes *SPECTRUM,* which outlines the procedures required to provide documentation for museum objects and for collections management activities and describes the information needed to support those procedures.

Terminology Control: Resources

A CMS expands the points of access through which an object or group of objects may be located. Many manual systems use catalog cards that provide only a limited number of access points for information retrieval, for instance, by accession number, classification, or medium. A CMS can provide many additional points of access, and many more in combination with each other. A computerized system, however, demands a much greater degree of precision in the use of language for cataloging and data retrieval than does a manual system.

Terminology control is necessary because natural language has a number of different words that mean the same thing (synonyms) and identical words that mean different things (homonyms). If synonym terms have been entered in a field, it will be impossible to retrieve all the similar objects without knowing and searching for each synonym term individually. To control synonyms in a CMS, it is necessary to choose a single "preferred" term and use it in place of all "non-preferred" terms. Some advanced systems have internal synonym dictionaries that can retrieve all items, regardless of the term entered in the query, but this requires all synonyms to be manually entered into the dictionary. If homonym terms have been entered in a field, a search on that field will retrieve unrelated terms. To control homonyms, it is necessary to distinguish one homonym term from another, for instance "barrel (container)" and "barrel (firearm component)"; otherwise, the system may not be able to differentiate one from the other in a search.

To develop a consistent vocabulary, it is necessary to use some form of terminology control, for instance, an authority list or a thesaurus for each data element or field in a CMS for which it is determined that there are terminology control requirements. An authority list is a controlled list of terms considered to be acceptable for entry in a field. A list of acceptable vocabulary terms can be assembled for each controlled field and, often, the system can verify that only one of the terms from that list has been entered into the field.

Authority lists vary in sophistication. A simple authority list may provide only a set of preferred terms, while a more complex authority list may provide non-preferred terms with cross-references to the preferred terms. It also may provide terms that relate to the preferred term in a broader or narrower sense, and it may provide some levels of hierarchical structure.

A thesaurus is a highly structured authority that defines the terminology and vocabulary that most accurately describe an object or concept for indexing and retrieval purposes. Terms in a thesaurus may be restricted to a selected meaning, because a single meaning serves indexing purposes best. If the same concept can be expressed by two or more terms, one term is chosen to be the preferred term for indexing purposes. A thesaurus is structured to distinguish one term from other similar terms and to note if these terms are non-preferred terms, synonyms, homonyms, variant spellings, narrower and broader terms, or related terms.

Thesauri and authority lists may or may not be controlled within the system. At their simplest, they are developed as a simple document or spreadsheet and shared between departments. More complex thesauri, such as the *Getty's Art and Architecture Thesaurus,* can be purchased and "plugged" into the system directly, without manual entry of the terms.

It is not necessary to control the vocabulary for every data element in a CMS record. Focus on those fields that will be essential for indexing and retrieval purposes. Fields in a cataloguing and collections management system for which a museum may

decide to develop terminology controls include:

- Classification
- Object name
- Subject heading
- Location name
- Medium
- Technique
- Condition
- Geography place names
- Period/Style
- Acquisition terms
- Deaccession terms
- Department names
- Artist/Maker names
- Artist/Maker roles

When considering what terminology controls to use in a database, it is paramount that a museum first consider the use of established resources that are available for the entire field before developing in-house resources. While in-house terminology controls do provide a level of consistency for the individual institution, they do not conform to a standard that will unify the whole community of museum users. On a more practical level, developing internal authorities can be a time-consuming and labor-intensive process. An externally developed authority may help a museum to avoid repeating authority work that already has been done and accepted as a standard by the museum community. Internally developed terminology controls will reflect only the content of the local collection and, often, will lack a hierarchical structure or links to related terms, unless the users have spent time building an authority in accordance with standards developed by the International Organization for Standardization (ISO).

When an institution chooses external standards, it joins a larger group that uses those standards and contributes to the development of consistent terminology controls throughout the museum community. An externally developed authority will provide a carefully developed and structured framework for its users in accordance with international standards. There are some disadvantages: it takes time to familiarize users with an externally developed authority, terms that are irrelevant to an individual museum's collection will be included, and updates may take some time to reach users. The benefits of an externally developed authority are that a community of users have agreed on the use of the terms and have contributed their expertise to develop the terminology. If the developers of the terminology are committed to long-term maintenance and updating of the terminology and structure of the authority, the benefits far outweigh the disadvantages.

Authorities and Lexicons

Many projects have developed terminology and terminology standards. A sampling includes:

•*The Art and Architecture Thesaurus* (AAT) is a thesaurus of art historical and architectural terminology developed as a controlled indexing language for the use of libraries, archives, and museums in cataloging book and periodical collections, image collections, and museum objects, particularly art-related objects. AAT terminology has been validated by users in the scholarly community and includes index terms that may be used to control a variety of fields in a cataloging/collections management system, including object names, object genres, attributes, style and period terms, people roles, materials, and techniques. The AAT provides a list of single concepts arranged both alphabetically and hierarchically. It is designed for use in indexing and retrieval. The AAT is an ongoing project that continually develops terminology and is especially responsive to user feedback. It is available in both an electronic and a print edition and is sponsored by the Getty Research Institute of the J. Paul Getty Trust.

•*The Revised Nomenclature for Museum Cataloguing (Nomenclature)* is an authority list of object names for manmade artifacts designed as a tool for cataloging museum collections; it is particularly useful for collections of historical objects. Nomenclature is indexed alphabetically and hierarchically. Object terms in the

Nomenclature system are based on the original function of the object, with hierarchical divisions that include structures, building furnishings, personal artifacts, tools and equipment for materials, etc. Under the category "building furnishings" additional subdivisions include bedding, floor covering, furniture, etc. Object terms are inverted with the noun first, followed by a comma and the modifier: chair, dining; chair, easy; chair, folding. In an alphabetical listing of object names, all the chairs or other like objects will display in the same place in the list. Preferred terms are displayed in capital letters and non-preferred terms direct the user to the preferred terms. *Nomenclature* is available in a print edition and is sponsored by the American Association of State and Local History (AASLH).

•*The Thesaurus of Geographic Names* (TGN) is a thesaurus of hierarchically arranged geography terms to aid libraries, museums, and archives that enter and index geography terms for object and people records. Place names are arranged in a structure that illustrates their context in terms of broader and narrower localities, and the thesaurus features preferred and non-preferred terms. Available in electronic form, TGN was developed by the Vocabulary Coordination Group, a project of the Getty Research Institute of the J. Paul Getty Trust. *The Union List of Artist Names* (ULAN) is neither an authority list nor a thesaurus. Instead, it was developed to serve as a terminology resource for museums, libraries, and archives that research and use artist names. It is a database that lists approximately 200,000 names that are linked to 100,000 individual artists. ULAN features a "cluster" format that displays and links all the variant spellings and versions of an artist's name, as well as basic biographic data that includes life dates, roles, and nationality information. It is up to the user to choose the name that is preferred for cataloging and indexing, although ULAN provides some helpful information concerning the sources of the names and the use preferences of the sources from which the names have been drawn. It is available in both electronic and print editions and was developed by the Vocabulary Coordination Group, a project of the Getty Research Institute of the J. Paul Getty Trust.

•Iconclass is a system of iconographic classification designed to provide subject and content terminology for art and historical visual images. It features a series of decimal codes with a hierarchic structure. It has nine main divisions that feature the primary subject headings of religion and magic; nature; human beings, man in general; society, civilization, culture; abstract ideas and concepts; history; the Bible; literature; and classical mythology and ancient history. Within these numbered divisions are additional numbers and letters that, when combined in a string, represent important elements in an image using a descending hierarchy of concepts, beginning with a major concept, such as "history," and ending with a specific concept, such as a precise event in history.

Ionclass is not the only system that concentrates on subject content; other projects include the Garnier System (Thesaurus Iconographique, Systeme Descriptif de Representations) used widely in France; the Yale Center for British Art Project; and the Glass System (Subject Index for the Visual Arts) developed for the Victoria and Albert Museum. Iconclass is available as a printed edition or on CD-ROM (in various languages), or online via the Iconclass Libertas Browser.

The above-mentioned projects do not form a comprehensive list of available resources. As terminologies shift and consortiums are formed to develop new dictionaries, it is useful to talk to other professionals in similar institutions to determine which thesauri they are using. If there are no existing thesauri, it can be helpful to request the lexicons of similar museums, in order to build on their existing work.

DATA ENTRY

Training

Museums frequently hire museum information specialists, often people with museum registration or curatorial backgrounds who can manage the information needs of the institution. They also have a background in database management and understand the importance of data consistency and adherence to standards. Such personnel must bridge the protocols developed internally with the standards created by the broader museum community. Because of this, it is important to include information management staff in any discussion about data standards, registration methods, and information access. They should share their expertise while adapting practices to existing needs. Information specialists are also often responsible for training new and existing staff how to enter data into the system.

Training responsibilities can be divided into two categories: initial and ongoing. Initial training is generally for those who are new to a specific software program and must be shown the basics. Such training must be repeated whenever a major change in hardware or software takes place, such as the installation of a network or a new CMS, or when new staff are hired. Ongoing training includes keeping the museum staff informed of software upgrades and new software and often can be as simple as reminding staff of the importance of good housekeeping for computer files or the importance of backups.

Staff training can be accomplished through different methods, including outside training or contracting with private companies, CMS vendors, or individuals for in-house training. To receive outside training, staff must travel to another location to learn a specific program or programs. Museums located on university campuses or those with access to such facilities can explore options offered through staff-enrichment programs focusing on computer use.

Vocational or technical colleges provide similar programs. A determination has to be made whether it would be a good investment for the entire staff to go for outside training or if sending one member who can come back and conduct training for the rest would be more efficient. Museums purchasing proprietary museum software can explore offers by the vendors for training sessions to teach their particular programs.

With in-house training, companies or consultants come to the museum to conduct training for staff. This allows more flexibility for the museum, which may find it difficult to operate with staff members away. If it is decided to keep all training in-house, the museum might establish a user group that meets periodically to exchange issues and ideas. Many museums have internal e-mail newsletters that offer tips. Collegial sharing of information through e-mail, users groups, and conferences greatly enhances the staff's ability to remain aware of new technology advances.

Training staff to perform data entry is the most exacting computer task within a museum because of the need to establish an accurate database. Training data-entry personnel for this task has been effectively accomplished by many museums through the use of data standards and carefully designed manuals to explain the process (see section on Data Dictionaries). The fewer decisions the data-entry person has to make, the cleaner the database. It can be beneficial to hold regularly scheduled training sessions for those working in the different areas of the museum. These classes can be presented by staff members whose job it is to oversee the production and maintenance of the data being collected and entered.

Data Entry

Data entry into a new system can be one of the most expensive and time-consuming aspects in implementing a CMS. It must be planned as carefully as the other CMS aspects. Furthermore, data entry is never completely done unless the collection is static. Not only does retroactive data entry often have to be done, but responsibility for ongoing data entry must be delineated. If there are data in "machine-readable form," such as an electronic spreadsheet, then there is a good chance they can be "mapped" by the vendor into a new data structure. It is a good idea to plan this conversion into a computer project rather than to reenter all the data from another system manually.

When there are no data in machine-readable form, manual entry into a system is necessary. The museum may have personnel enter data from cards or catalog sheets, a time-consuming task because source material is often inconsistent and because there is a tendency to attempt to record all information possible for each object into the database.

Depending on the size of the collection, it is generally better to identify ten or twelve key fields of data to enter for each object so that there is a minimal identifying record for each object. Initial records can be elaborated on later, as time permits. Data entry by hand can be exceedingly slow. Six to ten records per hour may be entered, if a data entry person is really fast. Even at ten records per hour, that is only 60 to 75 records per day, 300 to 450 records per week, or (assuming a 48-week year) about 14,400 to 21,600 records in a year. Even a collection of modest size would require hiring a full time person to do nothing but data entry.

Planning Data Entry

A commitment to record all current collections management activities on the computer as soon as the database structure is up and running is important, and a plan must be made for the systematic data entry of backlog records. Priorities for data entry may be determined by the museum's mission. For example, an art museum might plan to enter the most valuable items in the collection first to accommodate insurance tracking and reporting. A history museum might choose the items currently on exhibit.

It is logical to enter backlog records chronologically, working from the most recent to the oldest. Other approaches may be based on object type, donor or source, least problematic, or objects currently loaned out. Whatever the priority, a goal-oriented plan should be drawn up to complete data entry systematically and make the database useful immediately.

Establish a system for keeping track of progress; count or estimate the number of paper records and measure daily progress against this total. Objects with no accompanying records should be given current numbers, assigned the source as "found in the collection," and have minimal working fields entered for each object.

Ideally, a staff member will be responsible for evaluating records as they are completed. This person is often the information manager, a curator, or the registrar. In some cases, it is a multi-person effort, with a select few staff members entering data into a few fields for which they are responsible. One person, such as the collections information manager, will have final authority to approve a record as correct and complete. For example, the registrar will enter information about an object's accession number, its location, and its provenance. The curator will write a detailed description, assign a date, and identify the maker. The information manager will then check these fields for proper data-entry conventions and correctness of completion.

Data Cleanup

Raw data can be entered as it exists and cleaned up later, or it can be corrected before or during data entry. Clean up during entry will necessitate using highly skilled data-entry people who have subject-specific knowledge and understand the need for consistency. Clean up during data entry rarely works, so a plan must be developed to clean up data either before or after entry.

Cleaning up data before entry will almost double the time required to get a database up and running. If all of the existing data is entirely in paper form, you must first transcribe the existing data to another paper form with a standardized format and correct for content, spelling, and punctuation. This procedure yields good results and allows the use of minimally skilled people for data entry, but it is very time consuming. Alternately, while transferring data from one system to another, exporting the data from the old system into an electronic spreadsheet can greatly assist in data cleanup. The spreadsheet's "find and replace," sorting, and filtering capabilities allow the data cleanup person to see inconsistencies and informational blank spots at a glance. The spreadsheet can be mapped to the new data structure, greatly facilitating the import of information into the new system. Depending on the quality of information contained in the old system, this may take a few weeks to several months. It may be of use to clean up the data in batches, by object type or department, and import it as each batch is completed. Keeping a duplicate master copy available will allow other staff to access the information during the data cleanup process, even if they cannot make changes.

Most museums cannot afford the time required to correct data before data entry and therefore must rely on cleaning it up after it is entered. Reports can be generated for registrarial or curatorial editing, with subsequent corrections made individually or globally, depending on the type and amount of information being corrected.

Proofreading

Human beings make mistakes, and any computer database will reflect the mistakes made by the person who entered the data. If minimally skilled people enter data, the chances are great that many mistakes in spelling, punctuation, capitalization, etc., will occur. These mistakes may be derived from the original paper records. It is important for the person overseeing the project to identify the source of the errors and take corrective action. A representative sample of entered records, selected either randomly or in conjunction with another project, should be proofread on a regular basis. Proofreading and corrections should be the responsibility of only one person, the person in charge of the project. Error-prone data-entry personnel should be replaced if they cannot improve.

SYSTEM MANAGEMENT AND INTEGRATION

System Management

Management is the backbone of a computerized file system. Systems management, supervised by the system administrator, involves the maintenance and protection of the system hardware, software, and data and their integration into museum operations. While the system administrator is the designated leader, all individuals using the system should take part in systems management. Researchers and other individuals who may have access to the system should be trained in how to report problems and inconsistencies in the directions for using the system or malfunctions in the computer; and staff members should have an efficient means for communicating their needs to the system administrator.

Systems management in museum settings may include scheduling with an in-house system manager, online technical support from an outside vendor, data-logging notebooks or "bug sheets" that are periodically reviewed, and e-mails and phone calls to non-institutionally affiliated technical support advisors. Effective systems management relies on honest and thorough communication among all individuals working with or supporting the system. An institution with many computer applications may designate a systems manager and a program administrator. The registrar is often one or both.

Maintenance

Maintenance relies on thorough and efficient communication between system users and system managers. While scheduled maintenance tasks—such as backing up, spot-check testing of data, and monitoring for dust and debris in keyboards and on monitors—should be conducted regularly, meetings with systems users to determine the continued usefulness of the system as a whole are also a part of general maintenance. If the system no longer functions at its maximum level of usefulness, changes or upgrades to the system should be considered and, if possible, implemented. Many institutions face the simple problem of staff members acquiring certain types of data and saving it on their desktop computers. Maintenance of the system involves centralizing information so that all users can report what they have completed, what they are working on, and what projects using the system may be ready to start. The systems or program administrator should maintain a master schedule of projects and progress.

Security

A computer system, and the information it contains, represents a major institutional investment. Just as employees are informed of the general museum security plan, users of the computer system must be educated regarding electronic security. There are three main aspects to computer security, which are very similar to the security requirements for a museum collection:

- It must be protected from physical loss or damage by human actions or environmental causes.

- Information must be protected from unauthorized changes or deletion, either by accident or design.

- Information that must remain confidential for legal, ethical, or security reasons must be safeguarded. Confidential information includes records regarding donors, valuations, and storage locations; museum security systems and procedures; and employee records and personnel files.

An institution with more than two employees, or one that is part of a wider electronic network, needs password protection for its computer system. For relatively simple systems, single password entry may be sufficient. Do not rely on screen-saver password programs; they are easy to defeat. If a system has multiple users, is on a network, or relies heavily on computerized collections management data, a hierarchical system of passwords should be in place. Password protection can cover an individual's files or the official museum records. Levels of access and authority can range from "read only" access to the capability to add information to the capacity to change or delete information. Confidential fields in a database may be restricted to holders of certain passwords.

A password is most secure if it is a random string of uppercase and lowercase letters, numbers, and if permitted, special characters. However, it is also the most difficult for the user to remember, at least initially. Random passwords are worth using for the highest levels of access and security. Lower-level users may have passwords that they find more memorable. Care should be taken to choose passwords that are not easy to guess. For continued effectiveness, passwords need to be changed periodically.

To protect the museum's records against an external threat, it is necessary to construct an electronic firewall to prevent unauthorized access. Security systems, however, are not foolproof. Much like professional burglars, hackers have the knowledge and "tools" to defeat security systems.

Computer viruses, programs that interfere with the normal healthy operation of the computer system, are another external threat. Viruses are carried by vectors such as downloaded programs and utilities. The harmful program deploys when the program file that contains it is opened or executed or when the computer's internal clock initiates a program command upon reaching a particular time and date. Vaccines exist in the form of virus detection and eradication programs, but they must be used conscientiously and updated frequently to be effective. To prevent contracting viruses, users should not be permitted to install personal software or software downloaded from external sources.

Physical security includes not only restricted access but also favorable environmental conditions. Computers should be cleaned and maintained on a regular basis. Much like collections objects, computers and computer media require a relatively high level of environmental control. They are especially sensitive to heat. Keep computers and media at an even temperature and away from windows and internal heat sources. Avoid power surges by using a good suppressor and an outlet dedicated to computer equipment. Ideally, the data servers at the very least should be connected to an uninterruptible power supply (UPS). Other electric appliances and equipment, especially heavy power users, should be plugged into a different circuit. In any event, keep hard copies of computer files and backup media in a separate, protected location, preferably offsite. Computer media must be protected from magnetic fields, such as those in telephones, office magnets, and electronic equipment, including computers themselves!

Backups

Unlike museum collections items, information can be duplicated. A regular backup schedule is the key to a computer disaster recovery plan. "Backup" can be used as a verb (back up) or a noun, referring to creating a copy of computer files or to the copy itself. As a precaution against information loss, this activity is so important that it must be considered when choosing computer software and hardware. When determining a backup schedule, the key question is: how much work can the museum afford to lose? The frequency will depend upon how often computer files are updated or how fast information is added. Full backups, a copy of everything on the computer system, can be made periodically, for example, weekly. Incremental backups, copies of all files that have been added or amended, can be scheduled more frequently.

Very active or very cautious computer users may wish to maintain backups of their own files, but generally, a system manager is responsible for the backup program. The process of backing up computer files on a networked system is best done during slack times, at night or on weekends, as the activity degrades computer performance and currently open files are not included in the backup. However, the backup system can be fully automated, so a system manager need not be physically present during the process. Computer backup media (magnetic tape, optical disks, external hard drives, etc.) exist in a number of different formats. CD-ROM and DVDs are not a reliable backup mechanism, but frequently are used for short-term backup or for transferring large quantities of data into another medium, such as an external server. Each type of backup medium has advantages and disadvantages based on the medium's reliability and cost per byte of data stored. For the short-term purpose of backing up files, longevity of the medium is not a critical factor, but the ability to reuse it reliably may be very important and should be researched as part of the cost analysis conducted when selecting a system.

For long-term backup, "live storage" is the most reliable method. The data are continuously rewritten in multiple electronic or physical locations, ensuring that information is not degrading from the effects of time or the failure of one single piece of hardware. Live storage methods include "cloud computing," in which the data are distributed across a network of servers in geographically diverse locations, or in RAIDs, where the data are duplicated across multiple hard drives within a single server.

System Administrator

Information systems managers or system administrators may interact with the museum in a variety of ways. They may or may not also be the collections information manager. Whether an outside contractor or an in-house staff member, whether working on a full-time or part-time basis, his/her abilities to train staff, handle unforeseen problems, and manage the overall system play a pivotal role in the success of the system as a whole. If the system administrator is a full-time museum staff member, he/she will be the person most likely responsible for troubleshooting, adding and deleting users on the network, and coordinating with other museum personnel for disaster preparedness and emergency backups needed during evenings, weekends, and holidays.

When deciding on a systems manager, museum administrators need to consider both short-term and long-term costs. If staff members are adding systems administration to their already overtaxed schedules, the short-term costs may be low because no new employees will be added. The long-term costs, however, can be quite high as these employees attempt to find time in their schedules to get the systems in running order and enable other employees to work. Contract system administrators may be cost effective, as they can be used on an as-needed basis, but scheduling these individuals may be difficult or inconvenient.

Ideally, a systems administrator keeps a database of all of the hardware and software for each workstation within the museum as well as the types of files and data in use. This ensures protection against problems with software licensing, crashes, theft, configuration problems, and unrelated software that tends to fill up hard drives. The system administrator also may be the person responsible for determining whether or not an upgrade to the computer or network systems is needed and then coordinating the upgrade within the museum.

Managing a computer system involves not only administering hardware and software but also checking and ensuring data integrity. A systems manager should coordinate with the collections information manager to determine the percent of a museum's records that are within the CMS, the accuracy percentage of the information, and how up-to-date the digital records are. These accuracy data are important for insurance purposes, management and planning, and research. Many times, the systems administrator will have museum staff members spot-check the data relevant to their particular area of expertise. Systems administrators also should work with museum staff to build redundancy checks into databases. Most important of all, a comprehensive data backup plan should be maintained and duplicate data sets kept offsite. (See section on Backups.)

System Manual
A system manual can take many forms: a web page, an electronic document within the museum's intranet, a bound paper manual, or a loose-leaf binder that allows for changes to the system or improvements in documentation. A system manual may include the following:

•Information on the specific hardware and software being used (including identification or serial numbers that may be needed for access to the technical assistance departments of specific vendors)

•The name(s) and ways to contact the systems manager or other technical assistance people

•Policies on systems use

•Instructions on how to use the systems

For a system manual to be effective, it needs to provide employees with step-by-step guidance on exactly how to use the system, how to enter the information for which it is being set up, and exactly how to get out what is needed. A system manual should not be seen as a static document. As technology and an institution's computer needs change, the systems manual should reflect those changes and continue to provide the service that is expected from it. Currently, many museums do not use systems manuals or even have them in place because they are seen as bothersome to produce, and many museums that do have systems manuals do not keep them updated because they hope to avoid the cost in staff time that it takes to do so. Actually, systems manuals can save staff time by answering questions people may have about the system and by serving as a tutorial on systems use. Writing out instructions for what one already knows how to do may seem like an exercise in redundancy, but documenting procedures so that they can be followed by any anticipated user will save an institution time and money in the long run. System manuals also can help ensure that any additions or changes to the system, such as new software, are compatible with existing hardware and software.

Integration into Museum Operations
The ideal computerized CMS involves the entire realm of museum records relating to collections. Links should eliminate the need for entering information more than one time. Museum objects, whether accessions or loans, should be constantly tracked once they enter an institution. Once basic information is entered, the system should be able to

produce necessary receipts, loan forms, gift agreements, etc. Bar coding of objects may simplify object tracking while eliminating typographical errors *(see chapter on Object Marking)*, and the inclusion of digital images greatly enhances a CMS.

In addition to tracking an object and being a repository for the object's data, the CMS should make data available to various departments. Networked computers should be available in storage areas, collections management areas, curators' offices, exhibit design areas, and/or central locations where staff can efficiently utilize the information. Crosslinks may be made with photo files, exhibition files, and membership and development files to simplify access. Within the institution, public access to object-level data can be made with computers in areas set aside for researchers as well as terminals in exhibit galleries. Public access outside the institution may be made available through the Internet.

ONLINE ACCESS

Since the 1970s, museums have been sharing their collections information online. Initially, they shared information with other museums and research institutions, but with the increase in public interest in collections holdings and the relative ease with which such information could be shared on the Internet, museums began to feel substantial pressure to release certain types of information freely to the public.[2] Often, it is the dual responsibility of the registrar and curator to ensure that the information is accurate, complete, and easily discoverable.

Providing public access to collections information serves multiple purposes. It helps fulfill a museum's mission to educate the public and prove that the objects held in public trust are used to public benefit. Sharing information with a diverse group of people and scholarly bodies can encourage the institution to be careful with its data entry. As a result, many museums have become more aware of the importance of consistency and the use of standards in their descriptive practices.

In addition, preparing object information for public viewing online has the effect of supporting basic collection stewardship. The process of documenting an object for online publication follows the same basic registration procedures outlined in this book. The only difference is that information must be input into the system with the understanding that the museum's holdings are known by more than a select few staff members and scholars.

Virtually *anyone* can view items of interest in digital form online, so the registrar may see an increase in requests for loans or in-person viewings of those objects available. Curators may see an increase in requests for additional information about a number of collection items. Management may become convinced that additional support for collections documentation is needed and development may look for additional funding sources for inventory and documentation. In fact, many funding bodies, including the Institute of Museum and Library Services, as well as many private donors will fund "accessibility" projects, which require photographing and documenting objects before their information can be placed online. Other grant opportunities for collections care will have an online-access requirement for the award.

Types of Online Access

Museums employ a variety of methods for sharing collection information online. Today "online access" is synonymous with displaying collection items on the World Wide Web, either on the museum's website, on a consortium website, or through some other third-party application or web page.

Curated online exhibitions

Some institutions have very few collection items available for viewing on their websites. They offer a curated selection of important objects with lengthy descriptions and histories, almost always including ages of the objects. These "highlights from the collection" function much as in-gallery exhibitions do, either informed by a specific story being told or self-guided by the online visitor. Sometimes other supporting materials, such as video, audio, or links to related texts, will be displayed within the exhibition.

The curated method of sharing collections online has the advantage of providing educational interpretive materials to the public. It also can serve as a way for curators to extend their physical exhibitions to visitors who cannot visit the museum in person, or to ensure that the efforts they expend to create physical exhibitions live on far past the usual lifespan of the traditional museum presentation. The downside to the curated online displays is that they require additional effort by staff to make the materials available. Curators must write the didactic texts necessary to support the objects. Registrars must check credit lines and are often responsible for creating a digital photograph for use on the website. The webmaster must collect all information and images and create a number of pages to display the materials.

Database-driven collections online

Some museums will display information from the CMS directly on a specific "online collections" area of the museum's website. These database-driven pages are extensive, displaying information about every object that has been approved for public viewing, often thousands or tens of thousands of records. The information displayed varies among institutions. Most museums display the accession number, title, creation date, maker, maker birth and death dates, material or medium, credit line, and an image, if available. Other museums publish links to related materials, detailed provenance information, descriptive texts, subjects and categories, artist biographies, videos, and high-resolution images for download or viewing within the web browser.

Since the web pages are database-driven, any changes made within the CMS will appear automatically on the website. This may be immediate if the networking structure between the system and the web display allows it, or if administrative permissions allow immediate changes. More frequently, any changes made to the records will be uploaded to the server managing the web module of the system on a nightly, weekly, or quarterly basis. Any changes to the information should be reviewed by the collections information manager, who has final authority to approve the information for dissemination on the website.

Database-driven online collections often require a CMS that offers a module for web-based display. Some museums without such systems have chosen to hire programmers who build complex scripts to bridge their collections database to a website. In either case, a web designer will be needed to design the graphical layout of the web pages in which the information will be displayed.

If database-driven online collection access is important to the institution, as it is to an increasing percentage of museums, the web-output capabilities of the system should be evaluated along with all other functionalities under consideration at the time of selection. It can be helpful to view the online collections of museums using the system for that purpose, bearing in mind that the graphical interface is often separate from the functionality of the system itself. Speaking with the staff responsible for bridging the internal system with the web-based display can help clarify any issues with the software.

Another consideration about this approach is that materials are presented without many explicitly defined contextual relationships, unlike curated exhibitions. Many scholars and members of the public are self-driven to explore the material and make their own connections, but this inclination is not true for everyone. Utilizing both mediated and unmediated displays for online collections information can be mutually supporting and enhance public education, sometimes in unexpected ways. •

NOTES

1. *Collection Management Software Review—Criteria Checklist, Canadian Heritage Information Network. http://www.chin. gc.ca/English/Collections_Management/Criteria_Checklist/ index.html* (accessed August 2008).

2. Robert G. Chenhall, *Museum Cataloging in the Computer Age (*Nashville: American Association for State and Local History, 1975), pp. 86–87.

Thanks to: Lynn Adkins, Olivia Arnone, Rebecca Buck, Connie Estep, Leslie Freund, Roberta Frey Gilboe, Suzanne Quigley, David Ryan, Holly Young. For institutional support: Roger Lidman, Director, Pueblo Grande Museum; for expertise: Dr. Robert W. Layhe, Research Computing Facility Manager, Mayo Clinic, Scottsdale, Ariz.

4D | DIGITAL ASSET MANAGEMENT

OLIVIA ARNONE

INTRODUCTION TO DIGITAL ASSET MANAGEMENT SYSTEMS

Overview

A museum holds many shared images and documents on its institutional network. A search or a random access may reveal the existence among these shared files of extraneous duplicates, multiple versions, and various edits and updates of any given image or document file. It may not be apparent who created them, whether they are still viable, or if they are authentic. Knowledge of the existence of some of them might have saved time on a previous project; eliminating redundancy among them definitely would ease the demand for network capacity. Such problems are common in the museum community, and information managers are increasingly aware of the need to control electronic files through a system that can aid in their organization, identification, searching, and retrieval in an easy, efficient, automated, and reliable manner.

Many museums are turning to digital asset management systems, otherwise known as DAMS. These systems historically have been used by advertising and marketing professionals, but cultural institutions now investigate and implement them to provide efficient access to files and to centralize operations. While an asset management system can be, at its most basic level, an organized folder structure on a server, more sophisticated enterprise level or proprietary systems are designed to manage, track, display, and authenticate various types of files, their versions, and related information (or metadata) that exist within an institution's spectrum of media and document resources.

Much like any physical object cared for by a museum, digital files increasingly are recognized as valuable assets that require preservation and management. The lifecycle of a digital file—the time and money invested in its creation or capture; the frequency with which its content is used, extracted, or repurposed; the amount in which this file is shared cross-departmentally, and the need to archive its content as institutional history—demonstrates its value. Asset management systems can be programmed to facilitate the oversight of file relevance, quality, and longevity, ultimately making extremely efficient use of extant human and electronic resources. The following sections will explain the functionality of a DAMS, its various components, as well as the investments that an institution must consider before developing, implementing, and maintaining the system.

1. Function

What exactly does a DAMS do? What goes into the system and how does it work? How does an institution choose a system? According to the National Initiative for a Networked Cultural Heritage's *NINCH Guide to Good Practice in the Digital Representation and Management of Cultural Heritage Materials,* implementing a DAMS involves:

> creating an efficient archive that can hold digital resources (images, audio and text) as well as the metadata used to describe them, implementing an infrastructure to ensure that these electronic data are managed and preserved in such a way that they will not become obsolete, enacting search facilities that enable users to identify, locate and retrieve a digital object.

Before implementing a DAMS, a museum must first know what it wants from a system. In order for a DAMS to function properly, one must also identify and organize available resources in a manner that will produce positive results for these specific needs. The maintenance of files needs to be addressed for their ultimate usability and preservation. This preparation involves establishing and implementing policies that address the standardization of file types, formats, sizing, and, in some cases, naming.

a. Images

Image collections are commonly a shared resource for curators, registrars, exhibition designers, marketing teams, public relations managers, education professionals, membership departments, and web and IT staff. While many individual departments within an institution may manage their own image collections, DAMS introduces the ability to share images of objects, archival and historical images, and activity, program, and exhibition-related images. With new forms of publication and dissemination such as blogs and podcasts comes increased activity for new and existing images by various departments. As a result, the types of digital files and frequency at which they are used and repurposed is increasing, virtually flooding shared drives with images. Before implementing a DAMS, it is important to distinguish the types of images that exist, what they can be used for, and which can be eliminated.

b. Master and Derivative Images

The results of a search within a DAMS interface often will display its results by listing, either by file name or thumbnail view, the various versions of an image that exist in an institution's repository or server. It is important to know the intended output format, such as a printed publication or screen use for web or presentations, and to determine whether the available images are sufficient. Included in the available resources are often a *master* file, an original, archival, un-manipulated version, as well as a variety of *derivatives,* files derived from the original master file, resized for website or printed materials.

Master files should remain the preferred and preserved archival copy of a file, stored in an uncompressed, unaltered format, such as RAW or TIFF (see section on file formats below). This version of an image best represents the visual information of the object, person, or event displayed. Considering that many images are used and repurposed by many departments, it is important to preserve a master version of a file.

Depending on storage parameters designated by your institution, master images may be stored as RAW, which take up less space, or uncompressed TIFF files, which take up significantly more space depending on the pixel dimensions. It is important to keep in mind that each camera model has its own RAW image setting that is not universally readable. For this reason, many institutions may prefer to convert RAW master images to DNG (digital negative), which is managed by the Adobe Corporation and thus is a more universally used file format. The master image should remain unaltered over time. The California Digital Library recommends that this file should have a lifespan of approximately 50 years.

Derivative files are commonly suitable for reuse and should consist of a version that is sufficient for print (a 300 ppi JPEG or JPEG 2000; see section on "file formats"), as well as a version created for database use or web output (72–96 ppi JPEG; see chapter on Photography for more information about image sizing). It is imperative that a policy be developed to standardize the quality of master images, as well as their derivatives. The master file should be reliable enough to reproduce a variety of derivatives for many intended uses without having to rescan or recapture the original.

Careful consideration should be given to the long-term preservation of born digital images—images that were not created using a physical medium—as they remain the primary source file with no analog format to rely upon as a backup. A strategy should be employed to oversee the long-term preservation of these assets so that they can be retrieved for future generations. Procedures that will maintain accessibility, quality, and integrity of the digital master should be maintained throughout the entire lifecycle of a digital object. (See section on Digital Preservation.) This is not the case for analog media, which are now commonly digitally reformatted to serve as the primary archival records and sources for derivative files. Digital media also serve to protect the information contained on the original analog from loss if it is misplaced when sent out for publication, borrowed by other departments and not returned, or physically degraded over time through use or inherent vice.

c. Image File Formats

Long-term preservation of digital files begins with understanding the purpose and use of various file formats. "Lossless" file formats are the preferred archival formats, as the data stored within the file are not compressed in such a way as to discard information. These file formats are TIFF, RAW, and DNG. "Lossy" file formats, such as JPEG, are preferred for applications such as web pages or embedding images into collections management systems, as they are smaller in file size. Lossy formats cannot, however, be used for archival purposes, as the method in which their file sizes are made smaller requires that some data be discarded upon saving.

1. Lossless
RAW. The preferred capture mode that produces a superior quality image. Contains unprocessed data from a digital camera and is sometimes considered a digital negative (DNG). Camera make and model determine the size of the RAW file.

DNG (digital negative). Adobe's archival RAW format, the preferred archival or lossless file format to convert RAW files after image capture.

TIFF (Tagged Image File Format). The most widely used archival format to save processed images. Flexible and universally supported across operating system platforms, TIFF files maintain all of the original color information and support embedded color profiles needed for printing, as well as metadata in the file.

2. Lossy
JPEG (Joint Photographic Experts Group). The most widely used format for distribution but not for archival purposes. Each time an image is opened, saved, and closed the image is compressed further. If it is opened and closed without saving, it is not altered.

3. Both
JPEG2000. Published in 2002 to be superior to the original JPEG. This format provides both lossless and lossy compression. It is not currently widely supported in consumer photography equipment or in Internet web browsers but is becoming a more widely accepted format for distribution.

PDF (Portable Document Format). The preferred long-term storage and distribution method for text and image-based content. Universally supported across platforms, PDF files store text, images, and graphics embedded in a single file. It can be opened at any time in the future without changes. Although this format is technically proprietary because it was developed by Adobe Systems, Inc., it has been adopted by public as well as private institutions for its reliability. Some organizations use this format for long term storage of document files.

d. Unique Numbering and Persistent Identifiers
As physical objects in a collection have accession numbers, so also a unique identifier (i.e., an alphanumeric naming scheme) may be assigned to each digital asset to help locate and identify the resource. In addition, all physical media and hard copy documentation should be marked with this unique number allocated to the resource, along with any additional information required by the institution to identify its content and formats.

With different versions of digital assets located in different areas of an institution's collections management system (CMS) and DAMS, a distinctive naming scheme will help identify the differences between the various purposes of extant versions of any given file. One option is to use qualifiers to keep all versions of a file consistently named (such as adding 001, 002, etc.). However, this number should not interfere with any existing system of naming conventions, such as for the page numbers of an album or catalog. Qualifiers should differentiate between the various types of derivatives, such as versions that are purposed for screen use, such as the Internet or Power Point presentations, versus those used for print publications. These can consist of numbers or letters that prefix or append an image identifier, such as "p" for published version and "w" for web version. Numbers also can be used, such as 300 for images that are printable, and 72 for images that are for screen use.

Files should be numbered without the use of special characters (&, @, #, <, >, ", ?, spaces, periods, etc.); file names should be lowercase and be no more than 120 characters. Although most computers today can read spaces and long filenames, they cannot understand special characters, and it is good practice to ensure the files are readable across a wide range of applications. What is important to keep in mind is that the convention must be consistent.

For example: 1992.55_72.jpg represents a compressed derivative file that is suitable for screen use, while 1992.55_300.jpg represents a compressed derivative file that is suitable for printing.

Consideration should be given to the way in which various perspectives or versions of the same subject are named, such as aspects of three-dimensional objects, different views inside the same gallery or event, and so on.

It may also be helpful to store the various types of image files in separate directories according to type of file, output format, or intended use. For example, images can be divided among a master image directory with access restricted to those administering image collections; a low-resolution directory for web images; and a print-resolution directory, etc., with related legal documents in a legal document directory.

e. More Examples of Persistent Identifiers

1. Master Images
Accession #.TIF or Accession #.RAW or .DNG

If there are two standards in place for TIFF images, the filename can include the size of the file such as Accession #_300.TIF, or Accession #_600.TIF

2. Derivative Images
Images that are derivatives from master images for linking to a CMS or for screen use, often with various perspectives of one object. These images will be the primary images, or default images, that will be seen as representative of a given object and are derived from professional photographs.

Accession #.jpg (primary or main image)
Accession #_view1.jpg
Accession #_view2.jpg
Accession # view3.jpg and so on depending on how many perspectives there are for any given image

3. Identification Images
Images in which no professional image has been obtained; snapshots. These images may also link to the CMS and are used as a record image or to document condition.

Accession #-1.jpg
Accession #-2.jpg
Accession #-3.jpg

4. Non-object related images
Gallery views, archive images, events, and other related images often end up as reusable assets. It is important to retain any information in the filename that will enable retrieval later. There are numerous possibilities, but it may be favorable to use prefixes that include dates, content, or even departments to which the images relate.

For example, an event such as an exhibition opening that took place on February 1, 2009, could be named as follows:

Ex 2-1-09_72.jpg for screen use or Ex 2-1-09_300.jpg for print use

OR

Exhibition name 2009_72.jpg or Exhibition name 2009_300.jpg for print use.

5. Documents
At this time, there has not been enough research or historical models to determine the best practices for storing and retrieving text documents for long-term access. Currently, most institutions that are implementing DAMS are doing so to manage their image and media collections. The primary concern with documents is that some formats may not remain supported in the future due to regular updates and changes in proprietary software. On the other hand, the problem with choosing a non-proprietary file format (or standard) for long-term access is that formatting preferences and design elements, such as fonts, are sometimes lost because the file is reduced to its textual elements.

Currently, three standard file formats are considered preservation formats because they rely on web-based technologies:

1. HTML—Hypertext Markup Language
Used on the World Wide Web to display pages. Very widely used and supported and can be viewed

in any browser. Commonly used for output from other systems, such as databases.

2. XML—Extensible Markup Language

Widely used for structured files such as spreadsheets. This file format does not require licensing, is well supported, and is not specific to any platform or system type, such as "MAC" or "PC." XML is considered by some experts to be the current and future file format because it is able to store document content along with descriptive information (metadata).

3. PDF—Portable Document Format

The preferred long-term storage and distribution method for text and image-based content. Universally supported across platforms, PDF files store text, images, and graphics embedded in a single file which can be opened at any time in the future without changes. Although this format is technically proprietary because it was developed by Adobe Systems Inc., it has been adopted by public as well as private institutions for its reliability. Some organizations use this format for long term storage of document files. (source: Hunter, Gregory S., *Preserving Digital Information,* 2000 (New York, London: Neal Schuman Publishers), pp 60–62).

f. Metadata

While DAMS are designed to display the related information of an image, its metadata, the metadata also are used to search for files on a server. Metadata are the information attached to digital objects. In addition to a small thumbnail image and the various versions of a file that may exist within an institution's image resources, the title, size, and other related information will be displayed as search results within a DAMS. There are numerous types of metadata that can be related to a given file, such as:

- Descriptive metadata: the content of the image, such as title, artist, date of work, subject

- Administrative metadata: the creator/author, input device settings, and rights information

- Preservation metadata: information relating to the condition of the object, data migration and refreshing schedule, and technical information, such as authentication and security data

The types of and amount of metadata that appear in a DAMS are entirely at the discretion of the institution and are in compliance with policies and procedures that are either in place or are adopted with the implementation of a DAMS. It is good practice to confer with other institutions to determine what types of metadata they regularly embed in their assets. Some metadata are necessary to ensure the longevity and vitality of the digital file, but that which is needed will differ depending upon the type of file and its intended use.

g. CMS and DAMS: Harvesting Content and Metadata Management

One of the ways in which one can link information about images of collection objects (metadata) and other related images, such as exhibition and installation/gallery images, to their sources is through an institution's CMS. DAMS allow a user interface to mimic the information found in cataloging information, such as "tombstone" or label information, creator/author identification, administrative information about the file (a creation date or input device, such as a scanner, for example), the intellectual property, or copyright status of an art object, and just about any other information the institution deems pertinent.

As information in a CMS is cataloged and updated, it can be synchronized with a DAMS as required. Through the process of performing scheduled checksums (programmed operations that check for errors and redundancies in files), which will decipher changes that have been made, and a deployment agent that systematically delivers all new information to the DAMS, the system can also be set up to feed information from the DAMS back to the CMS. In order to maximize access potential for future content, placeholder records can be created for catalog records that do not have matching images, indicating that there are existing media available, but that it is has not been digitized and linked to the system. The DAMS also can automatically recognize any changes that have been made to an image, such as color-correction or cropping.

h. Security

It is also possible to program the system to be selective in its choice of information and the types of images it chooses to deploy. A security matrix can be designed to block private information or information that should not be available to end users from object records, including information about loaned objects or donor information. Default ranking, a system designed to indicate, in a specific order, the preferred file to be used for an intended output format, can be set up to maintain selectivity so as not to overload the system with substandard images.

Programming permissions for any file or folder in the repository gives an end user the limited capability of viewing, reading, or seeing a list but not to make changes to the information in the document or its metadata. Some institutions choose to limit the information in their DAMS to tombstone data, which includes any intellectual property information for the artwork or image, and any potentially restricted uses.

i. Choosing a System

Many factors contribute to the decision about the type of system an institution chooses to implement. Most often, budgetary and staff commitment are the main determining factors for the architecture and design of a DAMS. Enterprise level systems are time consuming and very costly to implement, support, and license. Some organizations may choose an open source system or a trusted repository, models that archives and libraries have historically used. Like an enterprise level system, they are somewhat usable "off the shelf," but in order to customize these systems, institutions tend to rely mostly on technical support from on-site staff.

2. Digital Preservation

It is recommended that a strategy be enforced to actively manage the information in electronic records, along with the media on which they are stored. These procedures should ensure that the media remain reliable and authentic without losing the integrity of the original. Preservation metadata, unlike descriptive and administrative metadata, are the information infrastructure that support the processes associated with digital preservation. Preservation metadata are defined by PREMIS (PREservation Metadata: Implementation Strategies) as "the information a repository uses to support the digital preservation process." For more information on the structure and contents of preservation metadata, see the *PREMIS Data Dictionary for Preservation Metadata* published in March 2008 (available online as a PDF download).

More specifically, preservation metadata are necessary in order to:

- maintain viability of the readable bit stream (the contiguous or non-contiguous series of bytes that make up a file, i.e., 11000011001)

- ensure renderability, or the ability of humans and computers to translate the bit stream

- secure understandability, or the capacity of users to interpret the bit stream

a. Media Migration

Data format and software obsolescence pose a large threat to the long-term accessibility of digital objects. As file formats continue to evolve with new versions and updates to software, files can potentially become indecipherable. Media also may become unreadable over time due to physical damage to the storage device or technological developments in hardware devices that render preexisting formats obsolete. Two strategies have been formulated to deal with these problems:

1. Media migration. Moving files from an obscure or outdated medium to a prevailing, current media format. This process applies to both file formats and storage media and ensures "bit level" preservation, or preservation of the data sequence of bytes that make up a file (the 1's and 0's of a file).

2. Emulation. Allows a modern system to mimic the interface of an obsolete system in order for a digital object to be viewed and understood. Use of emulation software can help recover old files and migrate them to a new format.

The use of file-converter software will allow easy migration from one file format to another. Outsourcing format migration is an option, as is investing in new software technologies that can automatically scan and report the compatibility of files, which then can be selected and converted to new version formats.

The Council on Library and Information Resources recommends that file-conversion software:

- Read the source file and analyze the difference

Stages identified in the lifecycle of physical collections
  selection
  acquisition processing
  cataloging and press-marking or numbering objects
  preservation, conservation, storage, retrieval
    deaccession

Stages identified in the lifecycle of digitized material
  selection
  checking intellectual property rights
  conservation check and remedial conservation costs
  retrieval and reshelving costs of physical media
  capture of digitized master
  quality assurance of digital master and production of
    service copies
  metadata creation cost
  access cost over time
  storage costs over time

---

between it and the target format

•Identify and report the degree of risk if a mismatch occurs

•Accurately convert the source file(s) to target specifications

•Work on single files as well as large collections

•Provide a record of its conversions for inclusion in the migration project documentation

In addition to migration and emulation, the *NINCH Guide to Good Practice* also recommends:

•Enduring Care. Takes into consideration the safe storage and handling of digital objects and storage media.

•Refreshing. Moving data from one medium to another, such as from a CD to a DVD. (Not to be confused with migration, this process moves just the content and does not change the format of the file.)

•Digital Archaeology. Rescuing content from damaged or obsolete media or hardware/software.

b. Lifecycle Management and Associated Costs
According to the Digital Preservation Coalition, tracking the lifecycle of a digital file can be used to allocate costs. The Digital Preservation Coalition based its calculation models on various studies completed by researchers interested in determining the economic impact of managing these files on cultural institutions. The following table outlines a

structured approach to reinforce the cyclical costs associated with the various stages in the life of a digital file.

Because of innumerable variables, it is extremely difficult to gauge the costs associated with these stages. Open Archival Information Systems (OAIS) has developed its own reference models that describe each stage of the lifecycle as a cost event. Then each stage is evaluated for likely cost sources. Depending on the purpose of the study, a total cost may then be calculated per item, per time period for preservation of all collection material, or per process. (See tables 1 and 2 below.) Even if these models are not utilized for estimating associated costs, they provide a good foundation for thinking about the cyclical nature and the accumulated activity surrounding digital files.

Conclusion

Unfortunately, by the time this book reaches its readers, some of the information in this section may already be outdated. It is a disadvantage of technology that many new developments in software or hardware are replaced by something newer and greater at very brief intervals. Museums are now faced with the gargantuan task of managing *digital files* in a way that is conducive to access and preservation. Methods of managing information before the digital age no longer apply. We are in an era of transition, as new means of providing access to collections replace the old in exciting ways. In the meantime, as

Table 1 TYPICAL COST EVENTS

Activities	Cost Events
System creation and management activities	Creating organizational infrastructure Creating repository architecture Archive administration, repository operation, and maintenance upgrades
Digital material workflow/ life cycle activities	Selection, acquisition, validation, creation of digital collections, conversion of deposited material, rights negotiation and management, resource description (e.g., cataloging metadata and preservation metadata creation), storage, evaluation and revision, disposal/deaccession
Specific preservation activities	Technology planning activities, such as technology watch, long term strategies, e.g., migration and emulation
Specific access activities	Access to objects, access to catalogs, user support

Table 2 TYPICAL COST SOURCES

Cost Type	Cost Sources
Digital object / data acquisition	Purchase price/licensing cost
Labor	Personnel include dedicated staff as well as varying proportions of senior management, supervisor, IT staff, curatorial staff, etc.
Technology	Hardware, software, level of requirements (e.g., speed, availability, and performance)
Non-labor operational costs	Facilities and space (e.g., rent and electricity), materials and equipment, communications, insurance, legal costs

we continue to learn how to utilize available technologies, we must maintain and strengthen the integrity of our existing resources. •

NOTES

1. *NINCH Guide to Good Practice in the Digital Representation and Management of Cultural Heritage Materials,* p. 195.

2. The California Digital Library, www.cdlib.org/inside/diglib/guidelines/bpgimages/introduction.html.

3. California Digital Library, www.cdlib.org/inside/diglib3.uidelines/bpgimages/introduction.html.

4. California Digital Library, www.cdlib.org/inside/diglib/guidelines/bpgimages/introduction.html.

5. Archives of New Zealand, http://continuum.archives.govt.nz/files/file/standards/s6/s6-app6.html.

6. Digital Preservation Coalition, www.dpconline.org/graphics/handbook/.

7. PREMIS Data Dictionary, www.loc.gov/standards/premis/v2/premis-2-0.pdf.

8. www.oclc.org/research/projects/pmwg/pm_framework.pdf.

9. Council on Library and Information Resources, www.clir.org/pubs/reports/pub93/risk.html.

10. Digital Preservation Coalition, www.dpconline.org/graphics/digpres/stratoverview.html.

11. Ibid.

12. Ibid.

4E | BASIC COMPONENTS OF AN INSTITUTIONAL ARCHIVE

K. SHARON BENNETT

Archives are created and maintained to preserve records of lasting value and to make them accessible for use. In addition to providing physical control of the materials, a museum must consider the intended use and intellectual control of these materials. The maintenance and retention of important records can be relatively simple once proper policies and procedures are established by the board, administration, and archivist or person serving in an archival capacity. Since there are similarities between the registrar's record-keeping activities and the archivist's responsibilities, the registrar may be charged with administering the institutional archives in small and medium-sized museums. There are several excellent publications on starting and maintaining an archive that will aid the successful archival administrator. Some of these resources are noted in the bibliography.

Among the initial difficulties faced in establishing an archive are determining what to consider archival and understanding the terms applied to various types of materials. As stated by Julie Bressor in *Caring For Historical Records*, the term "archive" can have several meanings, depending on its use. It can be the physical area housing the records; the agency responsible for selecting, preserving, and making the materials available; or a non-current record of an institution preserved because of its continuing value.

In many institutions, for convenience of storage and handling, library and archival materials are housed in the same areas. There are, however, some important distinctions that must be made between library and archival holdings, which differ in both form and function. Library materials generally are published resources concerning a single topic or series of related topics, whereas archival materials are generally the non-published and non-current records of an institution. These materials are usually compilations of records important to the operation or history of the institution but no longer active or needed for their original purpose. Some, such as annual reports, may be published. Other materials include manuscripts and printed items and might include departmental records, correspondence, financial and personnel information, minutes, publicity, membership records, etc. These records come in a variety of formats, including ledgers, scrapbooks, photographs, audio or video tapes, and others. Computer-generated and digital records are also created using a variety of formats and operating systems.

ESTABLISHMENT OF POLICIES AND PROCEDURES

For the most part, the archival records retained will be the products of institutional activities. A vital step in beginning an archive is to establish the policies and procedures that will govern the acquisition, arrangement, and use of both analog and digital material. The policies should be approved by and have the full support of the administration and governing body. They provide the framework for procedures and decisions. The following statements should be created.

Mission Statement

Essentially a statement of purpose and goals, the mission statement should indicate the authority under which the archive is established and define its place in the overall organization of the institution. This statement also may define which records will constitute the archive and who has the responsibility for carrying out the necessary task. Statements regarding collecting focus should be included. The mission statement should clearly indicate which materials created or compiled in the course of business are the property of the organization.

Statement of Authority/Organizational Placement

A clear and concise statement of authority is necessary to establish internal support and should indicate where in the organization of the institution the archive is positioned. The higher the archival program is placed in the overall organizational structure, the greater the chance of achieving the goals set forth. This statement can be, but does not necessarily have to be, a part of the mission statement, according to Elizabeth Yakel in *Starting An Archives.*

It should make clear the authority, schedule, and frequency by which materials will be collected or transferred to the archive, the availability of the information, and conditions or restrictions governing the retention of materials. The policy also may indicate the types of materials that will not be included because of overlap with another department. In any organization, certain materials and records have a defined period of use, beyond which the frequency of use declines. It is at that point that the materials should be transferred to the archive, provided that the information is considered to have lasting value. Establishing a schedule for transfer to the archive can facilitate the separation of vital from valueless and prevent the archive from becoming a storage area for unwanted records. Transfer schedules also help discourage an accumulation of inactive records that can lead to the loss of vital records through improper "house-cleaning." These schedules, as well as access policies, should be reviewed by counsel.

Access and Use Policies

Every archive should have a policy defining its intended use. This should include statements regarding general access, restrictions, and use limitations. Procedures for requesting and copying records are based on this policy. In some cases, it may be necessary for several staff members to have daily access to the archival materials. In such cases, the development and implementation of standardized procedures regarding access is critical to maintaining good control over the records. It is important to have general statements about which records are considered open and which are subject to restrictions, about the conditions of restriction, and about the procedures required for use.

Collections Development/Management Policy

The needs of the institution, its staffing, and its financial ability to maintain the records it creates are important considerations in establishing an archival collection policy. Collecting priorities should be based on input from the staff and administration. The collections policy should state what materials are acceptable and set priorities and limitations for collecting.

SCOPE OF THE COLLECTION

Acquisition

Once physical control over the collection has been established, it is necessary to consider intellectual control and to make a determination regarding the permanent value of records. This will determine what will be kept.

Various types of media, including paper, audio or video tapes, computer-generated or digital records, photographs, film, other works on paper, and objects often are included in the archival record. Arguments can be made against the archive assuming responsibility for artifacts and some types of media. However, if no one else in the organization is able to care for these materials, the archivist may choose to assume the responsibility.

Appraisal is the process by which archivists evaluate the enduring value of records. The archival value can be assessed by projecting possible uses of the records for reference and research determined by the information they contain on personnel, places, events, and activities. In some cases, individual items have an intrinsic value, that is, they are deemed worthy because of the creator, use, physical form, or content. Items or documents with intrinsic value are always kept in their original form.

In *Selecting and Appraising Archives and Manuscripts,* F. Gerald Ham notes five considerations that form the basic tools necessary to appraise records and identify and select those of enduring value. There should be:

• A record's functional characteristics—who

created the record and for what purpose

•The vital information contained in the record and how this information relates to other documentary sources

•The potential uses for the record

•The physical, legal, and intellectual limitations on access

•The cost of preserving the record weighed against the benefit of retaining the information

Records should be evaluated on the basis of their administrative, fiscal, legal, historical, and informational value. Typically, institutional archival records should include architectural and building plans, financial records, personnel records, board minutes, annual reports, publications, photographic records, audio and video tapes, correspondence, departmental records, ephemera, and memorabilia.

Arrangement and Description of the Collection

Archival arrangement is based on two important principles: provenance and original order. Most records of institutions will come to the archive with a preexisting order indicating the particular way they were handled by the person or department creating them. The most important factor in the organization of archival records is their provenance, maintaining the context in which the records were created. As stated by Ann Pederson in *Keeping Archives*, the term provenance refers to the place of origin of the records, i.e., the organization or person that created, received or accumulated, and used the records in the conduct of business or life. Since archival records are the byproduct of an institution, activity, or person, maintaining the context in which the record was created is essential to the future historical understanding of the organization, individual, or activity. Materials from one records creator or compiler, as Yakel notes, should not be intermingled with those of another, despite similarities in subject matter.

The second principle of arrangement is original order. In other words, groups of records should be kept in their original order and not rearranged by the archivist. Any order originally imposed by the creator of the records should be observed and followed. For example, it is not necessary to organize materials in a chronological manner if the creator

did not. This again provides information about the context of the records. Rearrangement can be very time consuming and subjective. As a result, archivists tend to keep almost all existing coherent filing systems, even if they are not ideal. As Frederic M. Miller, author of *Arranging and Describing Archives and Manuscripts* points out, the original order is preserved unless it is clearly detrimental to the use of the records being retained. If records do need to be rearranged, a careful plan should be prepared and outlined before any materials are actually moved. It may be necessary to remove special forms of materials from a collection, formats such as photographs or architectural drawings, to provide them with proper safe storage. If this is done, a note should be inserted identifying the item removed and its new location. This will preserve the context while allowing for safe storage. *Guidelines For Arrangement And Description Of Archives And Manuscripts,* a manual for historical records programs in New York state, provides these and other useful recommendations on arrangement.

Archival description is the process of gathering information about the origin, context, provenance, and original order of a group of records, as well as describing their physical and intellectual arrangement and recording that information in a standardized form. In order to describe a collection adequately, information should be included on the filing structure, format, scope and content, relationships with other records, and the ways in which information can be located.

For the most part, institutional records are in the form of a series, defined as a body of documents, maintained as a unit, and arranged according to a filing system. As stated by Pederson, "a series consists of records which have been brought together in the course of their active life to form a discrete sequence. This sequence may be a discernible filing system, or it may simply be a grouping of records on the basis of similar function, content, or format." Typical series include minutes, correspondence, reports, newsletters, ledgers, etc. See Frederic Miller's list of "Common Types of Functional Records Series."

The primary goal of description is to provide access to the information easily. The level of description chosen for each record should correspond to the research value and anticipated need for the information contained in the record.

When materials are transferred to the archive, the archivist must determine whether value of the individual record is sufficient to warrant description by the item, or by the file, or whether an overall description will be adequate to retrieve the necessary information.

Two excellent resources on what to consider and how to begin describing institutional records can be found in the publications *Guidelines for Arrangement and Description of Archives and Manuscripts,* published by the University of the State of New York, and *Starting an Archives* by Elizabeth Yakel.

Finding Aids

Archives exist to house non-current records in a useful manner. In institutional archives, use will be primarily by staff of the institution for internal research and documentation. On occasion, the records will be used by historians and other researchers. To provide ready access to the information, finding aids are necessary.

The finding aid, whether in the form of an index or narrative, should include the following:

- Information on the creator
- The volume of materials—a file folder or several boxes?
- Type of record—paper-based materials, photographs, maps, or magnetic media?
- Intellectual contents and arrangement—organized by topic or medium, chronologically or alphabetically?

A condition statement is important, particularly if the materials are in poor physical condition. Any use restrictions or limitations due to condition or content should be noted.

It may be necessary to take the processing of some collections to a more detailed level than others. As varying levels of arrangement and description can be used in the processing of collections, flexibility is needed in the types of finding aids or user guides that are provided. For example, use by institutional staff may require the best stated, most current, or succinct records available; a historian or external researcher may require all available sources on a particular topic for a historical approach to the subject.

When examining a set of records and during the arrangement and description inventory, all possible uses of the collection should be noted; this can save time when writing the finding aid for the records.

Depending on the overall size of the collection, it may be necessary to provide physical finding aids for locating particular items within the collection. This is best handled by creating a container list indicating which box contains which information. Sometimes a folder list for each box is helpful or necessary.

Records Transfer/Retention Schedules

The administration should establish a schedule of periodic transfer from the creator of the records to the archive. Prior to the transfer, it may be helpful to establish procedures that outline the steps to be followed when preparing the material for transfer. It may be necessary to provide a receipt for the items. Due to the nature of institutional records and record keeping, the archive will receive transfers from the same provenance over time. The establishment of transfer guidelines will help ensure that the records are received in the same format and can be more easily integrated into the established series. Some records, such as personnel and financial materials, may be considered sensitive, and any restrictions on their use and access should be noted at the time of transfer.

Storage and Handling

As with all museum collections, the storage and handling of archival materials play a critical role in their longevity and thus comprise an important factor in the determination of the formats used to retain the information. Good storage equipment and cabinetry must be accompanied by proper handling by staff. In some cases, it will be necessary to limit use of certain records groups; any digitization, photocopying, and handling of such records should be conducted by trained personnel.

Most, if not all, of the records retained by the archive, no matter what the medium—paper, disc, tape, photographs—will deteriorate over time due to their inherent vice. In paper collections, this can be the amount of acid incorporated in the paper during production. For discs and magnetic media, it could be the result of binder failure or deterioration of the binder layers. Digital formats are dependent upon storage and retrieval equipment and changes in technology over time. These problems often are exacerbated by poor environmental conditions, including exposure to light, humidity, high temperature, air pollution, pests, and mold. *(See chapters on Preventive Care and Storage).*

Most archival records are housed within a micro-environment provided by folders and boxes. Any materials that come into contact with records should be conservationally sound. Housekeeping is often a problem in records storage areas, and particular attention should be given to keeping these areas neat and dust free. There should be no eating, drinking, or smoking in the storage area or in any areas where the collections might be used. For a comprehensive discussion on the storage and housing of archival materials, before any new housing materials are acquired, see *Preserving Archives and Manuscripts* by Mary Lynn Ritzenthaler.

Shelving and Cabinetry

All shelving and cabinetry used in the storage of archival records should be heavy-duty, non-damaging metal, strong enough to provide good physical support for the collection. Shelving with any physical problems such as sharp or damaged edges or rust should be avoided. To prevent falling, all shelving should be secured and bolted to the floor, to the wall, or to each other across the top. The location of the storage units is important. If possible, shelving should not face a window, since natural light can cause fading and produce heat. If this is not avoidable, shades or curtains can provide some protection from light damage. It is also important to avoid housing cabinetry units on exterior walls, since the danger of moisture problems and leaks in those areas is greater. Bottom shelves should be at least 6 inches from the floor to guard against problems from water damage due to flood. If the institution has a sprinkler system or other water pipes near the ceiling, it is advisable to have canopies over shelving to prevent water problems from above.

Materials and finishes to be avoided include wood and wood products containing formaldehyde and materials that produce harmful gas as they age or deteriorate. These include press-board, chip board, plastic laminates, polyurethane paints and varnishes, and pressure-sensitive materials. Wooden shelves, drawers, and filing cabinets are not suitable storage and should be avoided since they typically off-gas, and the acids that occur in wood naturally can leach into the items stored. As a general rule, if the storage container or cabinet has or is producing an odor, it is not suitable storage for archival records.

Storage of Paper Records

In most cases, paper boxes, folders, envelopes, and sleeves provide the best storage for archival records. Any materials that come into contact with the records should be non-acidic and buffered. While many companies advertise "archival" materials, it is important to make sure that the advertising is truthful and that proper supplies are purchased.

The terms "acid free," "lignin free," and "100-percent rag" are all designations for conservationally sound materials. A variety of enclosures meet these criteria, each with a different feature, such as reinforced hinges or a wider margin at the top; if possible, examine several different styles to determine those best suited to the collection. Paper enclosures have a number of advantages for storage: they provide support for the item enclosed, the alkaline reserve can help slow or prevent acid migration, and they are easily labeled.

One recognized disadvantage of paper enclosures is the inability to view the contents without pulling the object out. This can result in mechanical damage of some items, particularly brittle paper. When ordering supplies, it may be best to purchase those enclosures that do not have a thumb cutout so that the contents are not always grasped in the same spot. All marking and labeling should be done in pencil, not ink, since many inks are water soluble or can flake off when dry. Pressure-sensitive adhesive labels are not suitable as they have a tendency to peel off over time, leaving a sticky residue.

Plastic enclosures are also available for archival material but should be used with caution; moisture problems can develop inside the sleeves if there are any problems with temperature and humidity fluctuations. The plastic should not exude harmful material or gas. Plastic should be internally plasticized so that the plasticizer does not migrate into the stored materials. Good choices include polyethylene and polyester. These sleeves have a number of advantages, particularly for housing photographic collections; they are clear and allow immediate identification of the materials inside without the problem of fingerprints being transferred to the object inside. There are several disadvantages to the use of plastics; in addition to possible moisture problems, they can be difficult to label; they do not provide any support due to their inherent flexibility; and they are less permeable than paper and can trap decomposition products rather than allow them to dissipate. Plastic enclosures are not suitable for some media, such as pastels, or for any items with loosely adhered media since plastic can generate static electricity.

Both paper and plastic folders are suited for housing in archival boxes or in hanging-file systems. For most purposes, acid-free boxes on proper shelving are considered optimum storage. Storage in boxes creates a micro-environment that protects against light damage, dust, and fluctuations in temperature and relative humidity. Folders and boxes come in a variety of sizes. Housing for a collection should be determined by the physical size of the documents to be stored. Due to the depth of standard shelving units, it will be advantageous to use letter or legal-sized supplies where possible. The size of container used for a group of records should be determined by the dimensions of the majority of items in the set. Mixing folders of different sizes within the same box is not good practice.

Boxes should be relatively full to prevent the folders from sagging or curling and to keep the records from shifting unnecessarily as they are being transported. The use of additional support inside a partially full box, such as acid-free mat board interspersed with the folders, can help alleviate this problem. In some cases it may be necessary to use a filler, such as an envelope or folder rolled into a tube or a commercially available box spacer to keep the records upright. Most plastic sleeves are very flexible and will require additional support. Care should also be taken not to overfill a box, as this can result in mechanical damage to the records as they are removed and replaced.

Before archival objects are placed in permanent housing, non-paper materials and metal fasteners, such as rubber bands and paper clips, should be removed, since they will deteriorate over time and damage the items. The use of post-it notes on anything considered archival is not acceptable, since they are known to leave a slight residue that over time will attract fingerprints and dust. All items should be unfolded and should fit inside the folder with no edges exposed in order to prevent damage.

Oversize items, such as mechanical drawings, blueprints, and maps, should be housed in cabinetry or boxes designed to accommodate them. Many vendors provide a custom box service and can make enclosures to the exact dimensions needed. Storage of oversize boxes can be a problem, since they need to be stored flat on a secure table. It is tempting to stack numerous boxes on top of one another, but this practice should be avoided or limited to stacks of no more than three boxes depending on the weight of the records inside. The optimum storage for oversize materials is to group them roughly by size for storage in a map or architectural file. The same rules for folders and labeling will apply. Many large items require additional support for storage and transport. Ideally, they should be placed in heavyweight folders within the drawer and supported by pieces of mat board, cut to the size of the drawer and interspersed between every few folders. This will aid in the retrieval of items in the bottom of the drawer. It is important to have adequate work space in areas where large records will be stored. This will minimize the distance for transport and encourage the user to take greater care in their use. While several items may be placed in the same folder, common sense should dictate the number, based on the weight and fragility of the records.

Items such as blueprints should be stored separately since they emit gas and are considered chemically unstable. Likewise, newsprint, which is highly acidic, should not be intermingled with other records in storage. A suitable photocopy on acid-free paper should be made to replace the newsprint in the record group and the actual newsprint itself stored separately.

Storage of Photographic Material

Special care should be taken with photographic materials, as they are highly susceptible to changes in temperature and relative humidity, light levels, and air purity. Easily damaged through environmental factors and improper handling, photographic prints and negatives require good storage and use practices to ensure their longevity. Under improper storage conditions, particularly high temperature or relative humidity, both positive and negative images will stick to an enclosure.

As with works on paper, there are several types of storage enclosures available, each with distinct advantages and disadvantages. It is important to take note of several factors in determining the proper care of photographs. Due to the diversity of photographic processes, and the inherent problems of each due to the chemical processes used, photographs are best stored individually. When organizing photographic collections care should be given to note any materials, such as nitrate negatives, that are unstable and highly combustible. These materials should be isolated and stored apart from the rest of the collection. Ideally, a copy negative of the image should be made on safety film and the unstable materials removed to a safe storage area. Some instuitutions make the decision to save only the safety copies. For guidelines about preservation of film, see http://www.loc.gov/avconservation/.

Black-and-white photographs are much more stable than color. When generating photographs as a means of documentation, good quality black-and-white film is a better choice than color. The film should be processed by a professional photographic lab which adheres to ANSI (American National Standards Institute) standards. In some institutional archives, there is a photographic file which documents the activities of the organization. In other cases, the photographs may be supplementary information in an existing records file. In cases where a photograph will remain in another file, it is important that it be housed in a stable enclosure that separates it physically from the rest of the file.

Prints should be stored separately from negatives, due to differences in the chemical stability and to guard against a complete loss in the event of disaster. Photographs taken in digital formats should follow the recommendations for organization and storage of electronic records.

Storage of Electronic Records/Magnetic Media

Increasingly, electronic records are being created and stored on discs, microfilm, microfiche, audiotape, videotape, CD-ROM, and a variety of other media that require special storage considerations. Since technology is rapidly changing and many types of media have not been in existence long enough to establish set guidelines for their care and use, the term archival is not considered applicable. Many paper-based records will deteriorate over time due to inherent instabilities, overuse and handling, and possible environmental problems. Reformatting heavily used paper items as digital or magnetic media can be essential to their preservation. The disadvantage of some of these media is that they will constantly require upgrading as technology changes; it will be necessary to maintain the equipment on which the media was generated in order to use it unless it is transferred to another medium each time the technology changes.

The newer the technology, the less known about its stability and longevity. The following section discusses some considerations necessary for the proper storage and handling of these items, based on current practices and information available on their longevity.

Storage of Magnetic Tape

Magnetic tape is essentially comprised of a magnetic recording layer on a flexible support. Manufacturers consider the physical makeup and particular characteristics of their tapes a trade secret. This makes it difficult to obtain reliable information on the physical components of various brands. The quality of both audiotape and videotape varies greatly between manufacturers and types of tape. The formats currently used are housed within either a cartridge, which has one spool, or a cassette, which has two spools. Magnetic tapes housed on open or "reel to reel" spools are considered obsolete and should be reformatted. When purchasing tape for archival use, buy the highest grade possible. Shorter reels, while more expensive, are preferred as the tape is thicker and thought to have greater durability.

Most magnetic media have a static charge and can easily attract a variety of debris. If possible, storage of magnetic media should be in uncarpeted, unwaxed areas that are damp-mopped. Storage should be on fixed metal shelving away from sources of heat, light, airborne contaminants, and mechanical equipment that might create magnetic fields. Tapes should be stored vertically in enclosures that protect them from dust and debris. The housing that tapes are purchased in is rarely suitable. Good quality, inert plastic enclosures provide the best support and should include an interior hub to support the weight of the tape during storage. For long-term storage, tapes should be played through at normal speed in the environment in which they are to be stored. On occasion, rewinding the tape can result in the breaking of the leader at the beginning of the tape; stopping in the middle of the tape can result in cinching or fold-over of the tape in the pack and can irreparably damage it. Tapes should be rewound and played through at least every three years to help prevent any sticking or transfer of information. The tape itself should never be marked, as this can introduce contamination.

Storage of Optical Disks

Digital technology allows the storage of large quantities of information and will probably provide the basis for records storage in the future. There are two types of optical discs: compact discs (CD) and digital versatile discs (DVD). Both are available in read-only, recordable, and rewriteable formats. No standards have been developed, and there is insufficient information to judge the physical stability of the discs themselves since this technology is still in flux. According to the Digital Preservation Department of the National Archives, research suggests that recordable CDs (CD-Rs), which use a gold reflective layer and phthalocyanine-based dyes, are the most suitable for archival purposes. These often are referred to as "gold/gold" discs. While differing claims as to the stability of various brands and types of discs have been made, it is believed that they will last longer than the associated technology and are suitable for archival preservation. Rewritable discs should not be used as a long-term storage option. The DVD is

considered a recent development and the archival qualities of are not yet well understood. If used, the same recommendations for the selection of compact discs apply.

The general storage requirements governing magnetic media also apply to discs. Discs should be handled by the edges or center hole; the recording area should not be touched. While both surfaces of the discs should be handled with caution, the upper surface is the data-carrying layer. Adhesive labels should never be used as they can damage the data layer; discs can be marked on the upper surface using water-soluble ink. Archival quality plastic cases made from inert polyester are recommended. Rigid cases should be used, as they provide greater protection than paper enclosures. It is important never to leave any type of magnetic media lying in the open where it is susceptible to dust, damage, or scratching. This is especially true of the common practice of placing the discs on top of the computer, a source of heat, between use. Use lint-free cotton gloves when handling archival storage discs to safeguard against the transfer of fingerprints and debris. Electronic records should be stored vertically with support; leaning or slanting can cause a distortion of the disc.

Solid State Media

Solid state storage devices include compact flash, SmartMedia, and other formats used in digital cameras, laptops, and similar devices. Referred to as memory cards or sticks, these are developing technologies and, as such, are not considered suitable for archival storage. These often are used for the transfer of information and require the same care in handling as other media. The contacts should not be touched, and any labeling should be applied within the approved label area.

Digital Archival Collections

Today much of the ongoing business of institutions—large and small—is created digitally. Physical copies of information resources are often no longer produced. This includes event and collection photographs, cataloging records, correspondence, loan requests, minutes, etc. Many museums have begun to build and maintain digital archives related to the business they conduct using digital technology as well as for their records. These collections should be retained and managed in the same manner that paper-based records are kept. Digitization also allows access and use of friable paper-based collection items, while creating a preservation copy of the original.

Digital Repositories

Many institutions utilize digital formats on a daily basis; records that once were created and stored in analog/paper formats are now created—and must be stored—digitally. Use of digital formats requires a plan for the long-term availability and access to the information. A digital repository consists of records in digital format; some have been created digitally, and others have been reformatted from analog or paper records. Creating a digital archive or repository that continues the organization and retrieval historically used for institutional records produced on paper and other mediums will ensure access to information.

Digital Collections Management

Like the analog collections they are replacing, digital collections require a collection management strategy, an ongoing commitment to staff training, and dedicated financial resources. Unlike paper records, which can be utilized long after creation even if poorly housed, electronic records require constant attention. Integrating a digitization policy into the normal staff workflow along with providing written guidelines and ongoing staff training is an important component of any digital collection policy.

The choice of hardware and software systems should be based on the type of information, intended users, identified search parameters, and type of display or retrieval necessary. For example, a storage and retrieval system suitable for photographs may not be as suitable for other types of records. The hardware and software systems must be maintained, upgraded, and converted to new formats as technologies change; current methods for backup systems, such as external memory sticks and compact discs, will be obsolete in the future, requiring continual reformatting to new technology. Otherwise, valuable information will be lost due to the inability to retrieve it.

Standards

Digital technology is still considered very new, and countless types of formats, hardware, and software are available. Some choices will result in a long-term commitment to a specific technology, and it may not be possible to archive formats that are dependent on specific programs or equipment as the field is rapidly developing and changing. Before undertaking a digitization effort, each institution needs to examine the purpose of the project; its ability to sustain it financially; the ability, dedication, and interest of the staff; the growth of the information over time; and the intended use of the information.

The Association of Research Libraries has accepted digitization as a preservation formatting method and has published accepted standards and best practices for maintaining digital collections long-term. The life span of any electronic storage medium is reliant both on the physical longevity of the equipment needed to retrieve it and on the current technology.

Strategies

There are numerous reformatting methods and strategies, each has strengths and weaknesses. Most institutions employ a combination of methods that suit their needs and are in keeping with their staffing and financial resources. For example, many institutions use digital cameras to record events, document incoming loans, and record individual collection items as part of their basic condition reporting, while still creating paper documents for correspondence, minutes, etc. Most institutions use both paper records and e-mail records to carry out business. Each institution needs to determine a strategy for reconciling information in different formats by either printing out important e-mails or digitizing the paper copies in order to have a complete record.

Libraries have taken a leading role in identifying system design and business models to sustain collections of digital objects. In addition to the standards set by the Association of Research Libraries, work is being done at the national level by the Library of Congress, which has been charged to develop a National Digital Information Infrastructure for Preservation, and the National Archives and Records Administration, which has established an Electronic

Records Archive. These organizations can provide ongoing guidance regarding research, digital preservation, models, and strategies.

As with all museum collections, archival records should be examined periodically as a preventive measure. Since many records will be housed in folders and boxes, and in a variety of formats, it may be difficult to discover a developing problem unless a collections survey, if only a random sampling, is done on a periodic basis. •

Documentation Systems | HYPOTHETICALS

1

We rely increasingly on computers to store and manage information for us.

Do you consider all types of paper records—such as bound accession ledgers and card catalogs—to be archaic, or do they still have their uses?

Will the significance of paper records continue to diminish?

2

A curator at your museum asks why she must prepare a detailed, written acquisition proposal when most of the information it contains—description, provenance, condition, appraisal, and so forth—will exist in electronic form in your collections management database.

How do you respond?

3

Past inconsistencies in your museum's filing procedures have left you with some documents filed by object number and some by the donor's or vendor's name. Some documents are duplicated and filed in both source and object files. Some donor files contain documentation relating to multiple gifts and are consequently very thick and disorganized. Some object files, on the other hand, are practically empty.

Devise a plan to sort out your filing system and to bring some order to this chaos.

What challenges do you anticipate, and how might you solve them?

4

You have accumulated a large number of digital photographs taken as records of conservation work.

What is the best way to manage these images?

Should they all be linked to object records in your collections database, or stored separately?

Do you need to print hard copies for the paper files?

5

Your museum began collecting in the late 1800s, and the science collection was based on field collection records of the time. You have cards organized only by species and vague collecting notes. Your history collection, however, was numbered consecutively from 1 to the current record, accession files are in place, and the catalog has followed the Chenhall system since the early 1970s. It's now 2011, and you're faced with integrating the system for computerization.

Where do you begin?

6

The museum's most famous painting has constantly been in the spotlight. It has been loaned many times, exhibited on-site, and featured in publications, videos, banners, and posters; it has been X-rayed and tested scientifically. It was once stolen and returned. It has even been the center of a major lawsuit.

Discuss efficient ways of keeping manual records for the object's history.

Calvin and Hobbes

by Bill Watterson

SECTION 5 | COLLECTIONS MANAGEMENT

5A | NUMBERING

UPDATED AND EXPANDED FROM THE 4TH EDITION BY REBECCA BUCK

In order to track museum collection objects, to differentiate between permanent, loan and subsidiary collections, and most importantly to provide access to the documentation of objects in a collection, it is vital that a systematic numbering scheme be used. The number assigned to an object is marked on most permanent collection objects, tagged onto objects in temporary custody, and prominently noted on all documentation associated with the objects.

PREFERRED NUMBERING SYSTEMS

Permanent collection, legally owned objects; compound numbers:

2010.1	Transaction, first of year 2010
2010.1.1	First object is a single unit
2010.1.1.1-10	First object is a set of ten pieces
2010.1.1a,b	First object is a pair, two parts

Suggestions for temporary records, short and long-term loans:

TR1.2010	Transaction, first of year 2010
TR1.2010.1	First object in the transaction
L.2010.1 or	
L1.2010	First loan of the year 2010
L2010.1.1 or	
L1.2010.1	First object of first loan of the year 2010

Museums may also develop numbers for long-term loans to differentiate them from exhibition loans, and for long-term incoming loans. Supplemental collections may have yet another number. It is always best to keep numbering systems to a minimum and to keep them as simple as possible.

Museums have tried many numbering systems over the years. The most important thing about a number, either permanent or temporary, is that it be unique. It must be the key between the object and its documentation. Without a unique number that relates to specific files, an object is at risk of losing its context and information relating to its legal status.

Sequential numbering (1, 2, 3, 4) is based on early library accessioning systems. It is simple and has been used by many museums. Typically, the first object gets number 1, the second object is number 2, and on into infinity. But this system will not adapt and expand with a collection. The same limitation exists with a two-part system (year and object, 76.21-27, 76.28, etc.). An object found after the original count is made cannot be numbered with its original group, making it much more difficult to keep information that should stay with a group of objects – receipts, deeds of gift, warranties of title – accessible for all objects in the group.

Computerization can overcome the difficulties caused by varied early systems, if every number used by the museum is unique. It is possible, for instance, to impose a transaction number on sequential or separated items and pull them together in a database. For instance, in the two-part system, 21.3-10 and 21.15 are found to be from the same transaction. The registrar can review the year and systematically assign a transaction number to which all pertinent object records can be attached. Perhaps the transaction number for this example will be 1921.3.

Systems with alphabetical prefixes become cumbersome if the prefix refers to a collection category, a geographical location or a department. All of those categories may become obsolete or inaccurate with the renaming or reorganization of the referenced categories. A prefix may be useful for loan collections, temporary custody or for subsidiary collections used for teaching purposes but is not recommended for permanent collections.

Prefixes gone wrong:
P for Persia
Y for Yugoslavia
C for crosses and coins, Cambodia or Ceylon
S for science or sculpture

Museums with several numbering systems may find their record filing complicated and the systems confusing. Some museums have found it helpful to retire old complicated systems and implement a single standard system; however, there can be no attempt to re-number a large permanent collection. A single system applied from a certain date forward will simplify record keeping for current and future activity. Attempts to renumber usually end in chaos.

It is important for a museum to be consistent in its numbering once it has decided on a preferred system. Systems must be used for both temporary and permanent holdings, and each system must have its own sequence. If several departments use different systems they must communicate and make certain that their systems do not overlap and create duplicate numbers. Collections management databases often use the assigned number to identify a record about an object, and duplicate numbers lead to confusion.

TEMPORARY HOLDING NUMBERS

A temporary number system helps track objects until they are accessioned and given a permanent number or are returned to the owner. The temporary number may be structured the same as an accession number, as described below, but with a T (Temporary) or TR (Temporary Record) or other prefix (L for loan, E for exhibition, etc.) to distinguish it; or it may be structured as an accession number in reverse, that is, "16.1996" instead of "1996.16."

PERMANENT ACCESSION NUMBERS

The most common accession numbering system now used is a compound number separated by a point or hyphen. The first number indicates the year the object is accessioned and may be the whole year: 1995; or a part: 995, 895, 001 or 95, 34, 76. The whole year is recommended; if it was not used in the past, it should have been started with the year 2000.

The second number indicates the sequence of the transaction by which the object/s were formally taken into the collection; 1995.1, 1995.2, 1995.3 indicates the object or group of objects that comprise each gift, bequest, exchange, expedition or purchase.

If there is only one object in the transaction, the two-part number typically suffices. If title to more than one object passes to the museum in a given transaction, a third number is assigned to each item in the group: 1995.4.1, 1995.4.2, 1995.4.3. If an object is a set or portfolio of objects, the accession number for each individual part within the whole can reach four parts: 1995.4.3.1, 1995.4.3.2. An object may also be one item with component parts, such as a box with a lid, a chest with removable drawers, or a sculpture that can be disassembled. The whole object is assigned an accession number, such as 1995.5.2, and each part of the whole is given a letter suffix: 1995.5.2a, 1995.5.2b, 1995.5.2c. If there is any question about whether the objects have part/whole or set relationships, the curator in charge of the collection should be consulted. It is generally not within the registrar's realm to know these details in every instance. Registrars deal broadly with objects across a wide range of disciplines; asking the curator helps build relationships and increase accuracy.

Examples of the Standard Numbering System:

10 objects from one donor:
Portfolio of 8 photographs: 1997.1.1.1-8
Six separate photographs: 1997.1.2-7
Coffee pot with tray: 1997.1.8a-c (pot, cover, tray)
Painting: 1997.1.9
Pair of shoes: 1997.1.10a,b

Single object purchased: 1997.2

In this compound numbering system, each separate item has its own distinct identification through the accession number. The accession transactions for each year can be accounted for and the years noted separately from each other. The system allows for growth but does not demand it; each year starts with transaction 1 and ends with the last transaction. Parts can be identified with wholes. Future research that changes the intellectual classification of objects will not interfere with an identification system based on when and in what order the museum acquired them. If an object was overlooked, it still has a place at the end of the sequence for an individual transaction.

Subsidiary or departmental number systems that refer to a systematic classification of the objects, the archaeological site of origin, or some other information useful in research may also be used within a museum. Cross-reference lists to and from the accession numbers are useful for identification of the correct object, for rapid retrieval of stored information or object location. These different numbers should be maintained separately, using the cross-reference lists to move back and forth.

Numbering systems are fascinating, but in the end it is most important that a number used to connect an object to its documentation be unique. That said, there are some very good reasons to used standardized systems.

In the 1st edition of *Museum Registration Methods* (American Association of Museums, 1958), Dudley and Bezold describe the identification numbers in the broad context of their use for accessions, extended loan, or loan for exhibition. There was a reference to a type of catalogue number, called "curatorial" number. By the third edition (1979), the glossary compiled by Patricia Nauert was specific in differentiating between the two:

> Accession Number: a control number, unique to an object, whose purpose is identification, not description.

> Catalogue Number: a term used in a variety of ways in museums: (1) in some museums, a catalogue number is assigned to a an object or specimen based on its class; its purpose is description; (2) in some museums, the number described in this book as an accession number is called a catalogue number, in which case its purpose is identification; (3) the number assigned to an object in a printed publication or catalogue of a special exhibition or collection.

Some museums also refer to object number and differentiate that from the accession number. The accession number in this case, for the tripartite system, includes the first two parts and object number includes all three.

2010.1.1	2010.1 is the accession numbe
2010.1.1	2010.1.1 is the object number

NUMBERING UNPROCESSED COLLECTIONS

Registrars are often faced with an array of unprocessed material from the near and distant past *(see Found in Collection chapter)*. Some objects have only temporary numbers assigned while others have permanent numbers that never made it onto the object itself. The range of documentation for objects goes from none whatsoever to a full file complete with deed of gift or bill of sale and acquisition committee reports.

Title must be transferred to a museum before an object can be considered part of the permanent collection and accessioned as a permanent collection object. Thus loans, old or new, never become permanent collection objects. Purchases need proof of purchase—a document that shows the museum paid for the object. Gifts need three distinct parts: donor intent, institutional acceptance, and institutional possession of the object. In the early to mid-19th century everything—loans, gifts, purchases, bequests—was "accessioned." Accession was more about tracking than it was about permanent collection. In current museum practice only objects that are owned by the museum are accessioned into the permanent collection.

Against this background the registrar can begin to work through the material in a museum that was not previously completely processed. If an object arrived in 1972 and in 1972 there was a letter from the donor saying she wanted the museum to have it; and if the curator or director wrote a note back thanking the donor; and if the museum has possession of the object, then the number entered in finishing the process is the next available number in the year 1972. If there was a deed of gift at the time, then 1972 is the year.

If the same object had everything except donor intent, the choice is two-fold: send the donor a letter of confirmation acknowledging that the gift was made in 1972 and assign 1972 as the accession number; or send a new Deed of Gift and record it in the current year (if the DOG is returned to the museum by the donor). The letter of confirmation is preferred because it places the gift firmly within the museum's collection for the complete time it was there and thus makes a stronger commitment. •

Thanks to: Anne Furhman Douglas, Connie Estep, Monique Maas Gibbons, Paulette Dunn Hennum, Kittu Longstreth-Brown, Dominique Schultes.

5B | OBJECT HANDLING

DIXIE NEILSON, ILLUSTRATIONS BY CATHERINE PHILLIPS

Of all dangers to museum collections, harm done by human interaction is by far the most common. While we may design elaborate systems for preventing fire, theft, and other disasters, mere common sense and a thoughtful approach can prevent us from mishandling the objects we are entrusted to safeguard. Therefore we handle objects as little as possible and only when absolutely necessary. The General Rules section in this chapter contains object handling procedures and information applicable to most types of museum collection objects and should be reviewed before moving to type-specific instructions. It is also recommended that the sections Hazardous Materials and Proper Lifting Methods be reviewed prior to handling objects. Further readings of a more specific nature are available from sources such as the American Association of Museums, the American Association for State and Local History, and the National Park Service, as well as many other organizations in the museum community. See Bibliography in the Handling section of the Appendices for other resources.

WHO SHOULD HANDLE COLLECTIONS OBJECTS?

Those without prior training in museum object handling should not touch any object in the collection (education collection items excepted). The registrar or collections manager should have the final say in determining who may handle and move collection objects.

Museums differ on the subject of who among the staff may be permitted to handle objects. Some do not allow volunteers or interns to touch any part of the collection, while others allow supervised handling by a variety of staff members. The practices in your institution should be contained in the museum's Collection Management Policy. In all cases no one should be allowed to handle objects until he or she has been provided specific training, which may include readings, informational videos, hands-on practice with non-collection objects and a fairly lengthy period of "apprenticeship"—supervised time working with another, more experienced handler. Handling museum objects is a serious responsibility and should not be taken lightly. Case-by-case judgments on handling readiness shall be made by supervisors, taking into consideration experience, general demeanor, and attitude.

GENERAL RULES

Museum collections are made up of many types of objects and while some handling practices can be very type-specific, most procedures usually fall into just a few categories. Becoming familiar with guidelines for handling two-dimensional objects, such as paintings and works on paper, and three-dimensional items such as sculpture, furniture and artifacts, will prepare you for most object handling situations.

All objects have some handling rules in common: prepare yourself, do not rush, plan ahead, and think through your procedures before laying a hand on any object. Just as a careful driver anticipates problems on the road, so should one planning to move museum objects from place to place. Ask yourself what could go wrong and if it does, what will be your response in order to decrease the chance of bringing harm to the object.

Because we are stewards of the cultural heritage contained within our collections, handling museum objects should always be done thoughtfully and with the utmost regard for each object. Monetary value should not be a consideration; each object is a priceless part of the collection.

All objects should be vigorously protected from over-exposure to light. Light damage is cumulative;

obviously objects never regain their color nor fabrics their flexibility and strength, despite the false implication when we say an object is "resting" in storage. Unlike living creatures, objects do not improve in a resting state; their rate of deterioration is only slowed. Many studies have been done on the least damaging light levels for artistic materials. Consult a current source for the best information. Keep in mind, however, that when a work of art is too dimly lit while on view in an exhibition, visitors will attempt to get closer to see it, creating danger of a different type.

Keep all harmful materials away from the objects. Do not allow eating, drinking or smoking in any area containing collection objects. Use only pencils in work areas, and never work with tools directly above an object.

In many cases gloves should be worn to prevent transfer of oils on even the cleanest hands. Common glove materials are cotton, nitrile, butyl, neoprene and latex (the latter is used less often because of the high incidence of people with latex allergies). Cotton gloves should be changed as soon as you notice they're getting dirty. In some cases cotton may not be the best material for gloves. Where the object has a rough surface that may snag on cloth gloves, or where the object has a very slick surface that may not provide an easily graspable surface, nitrile gloves or another rubber-like material may be a better choice. In addition to protecting the object, gloves also protect the wearer. Cotton gloves may absorb toxins embedded in some objects and thus should not be used in those cases. Nitrile gloves are best when handling many objects in natural history collections. Butyl gloves provide a chemical barrier except against petroleum and other hydrocarbons and neoprene gloves are more resistant to snags, punctures, abrasions and cuts. When working with chemicals refer to the Material Safety Data Sheets (MSDS) or check with manufacturers for chemicals that you are using to identify recommended types of gloves.

Examine yourself: your hands whether gloved or not should be clean and your clothing should be free of anything that could catch on an object and scratch or tear it. To provide a snag-free surface wear a clean, bibbed apron with empty pockets. If you wear glasses use a safety strap to insure that they do not fall off while you are bending over the object. Remove jewelry including watches, dangling earrings and necklaces, and tie back long hair while you work. ID badges or chains should be removed or tucked inside your shirt. Your clothing should permit free movement without danger of dragging across your object. Shoes should be of a design and material that allow you to be stable and slip-free.

Examine your route: Know where you are going and how you will get there before even picking up the object. Make sure your pathway is clear and unencumbered. Plan how you will open doors that you will encounter on the way and avoid stairs if at all possible. Turn on lights in advance so that you have a clear view. Do not hesitate to ask someone to accompany you if you need help with these maneuvers. Assure yourself that the spot where the object will be put down is free and clear and ready to receive it. If you must travel through public areas of the museum you may wish to do so before or after open hours, or at least when there is little traffic.

Examine your object: before ever touching the object, look it over to see if there are obvious areas of concern. Gently ensure that attached parts are secure and even then do not assume that attachments can bear much weight. If possible, review existing condition reports for information about known problems. Even after satisfying yourself that the object seems stable, handle it as though it were not.

Examine your tools: Gloves should be clean and in ready supply so they may be changed frequently. Carts, flatbeds, and dollies should be clean and free of flaking or rusting paint. Carpet squares or padding should be soft, snag free, and clean.

Always carry one less object than you have hands. Only one object at a time is the rule, no matter how small.

When lifting heavier objects maintain proper posture; keep your back straight and let your leg muscles do most of the work. Good body posture prevents or reduces debilitating back problems. Use of an industrial back support belt helps reduce the risk of injury caused by repetitive motions and acts as a reminder to use proper lifting techniques. Supervisors should monitor staff lifting techniques and ensure they are not over-exerting themselves.

PROPER LIFTING

Workplace injuries of this nature are common, but are preventable with correct practices and equipment.

Do not hand objects from one person to another; set the object down and have the other person pick it up. If you are alone, resist the urge to lift or move objects beyond your capacity; wait until you have assistance.

If the size or weight of the object is such that it takes two people to carry it (generally over 50 pounds) communicate during the entire move. Discuss in advance exactly how and where each of you will hold the object and move toward your destination. Be aware of your surroundings so you do not bump into furniture or other objects, especially when your view is partially blocked by the object you are carrying. Neither of you should be permitted to walk backward while carrying the object; with careful planning this will not be necessary. Ideally, a third person should accompany the move to open doors, monitor clearance through doorways, and generally provide assistance. Keep the conversation focused on the move; this is not the time to discuss other matters.

Use a ladder, never a chair, to reach objects above head height. Make sure the ladder is secure before stepping on the first rung. If the ladder has locking wheels, make sure the lock is engaged while you are on it. Have another person below, ready to receive the object.

Carts or flatbed trucks used to move objects should have rubber wheels to provide smooth transportation. Make sure the object is fully and properly placed on the cart so it cannot slip off or protrude dangerously over the edge. If necessary, carefully strap the object down to prevent movement. To protect the object, place padding underneath the straps and do not over-tighten them.

MOVING OBJECT ON CART

Be aware of physical limitations. Do not work while fatigued and take breaks as needed. Work at a steady pace, without hurry, and stop before either your muscles or mind is worn out.

Do what you can to make lifting and carrying easier. When building crates, sand the hand-holds well, and create only rounded corners. A sharp angle on a handle will become uncomfortable after only a few moments of carrying. Do not over-pack crates, both for the safety of the objects and to keep the weight at an acceptable level. Attach skids to the bottom of the crate for use with a forklift, J-bar, or dolly.

TWO-DIMENSIONAL OBJECTS

Paintings, Framed

Framed paintings stored in a consistent environment pose fewer handling concerns than those that have been subjected to fluctuations in temperature and humidity. Nonetheless, all paintings should be handled as little as possible to avoid loss and damage. Frames do provide some protection when moving paintings, and often provide an easier way to carry and support the work.

All objects expand and contract. The amount of this movement varies with individual object types and although not ideal, in moderation it is not a cause for alarm. However, when a work of art that is framed has been subjected to wide fluctuations in temperature and humidity, a great deal of stress is put on the object. When the different materials, such as canvas, wood and paint, for example, are bound together, each continues to expand and contract at its own rate. The result of this movement may not be noticed right away, but eventually the paint may begin to flake off, supports may weaken and hardware loosen. These defects worsen if the work is not handled properly.

Canvas, which serves as a support to many paintings, is also vulnerable to brittleness, which over time can lead to distortion, loss of elasticity, and tearing.

As with any object, examine paintings visually first before touching them. Look for broken or loose frame pieces. If you can see the reverse, check that the keys (thin wedges that stabilize and tighten corner joints) are firmly in place. If there is old wire attached as a hanging device, remove it. Wires can scratch other paintings if they are improperly stacked together, and because of their brittleness and tendency to snap without warning, they should never be used to hang paintings.

Both hands should always be used in lifting and carrying framed works of art. *Never presume that the frame is stable and firmly attached.* Never lift the painting by grasping the top of the frame; it is very likely to separate from the rest of the frame body, leaving you holding the top as the rest of the work crashes to the floor. It is a difficult lesson to learn, and a completely avoidable one. Rather, with gloved hands, lightly but firmly hold both sides of the frame and lift, keeping your back straight, with your knees and legs providing the muscle. If the painting is heavy, do not attempt to move it yourself. To carry paintings, whether alone or with another person, always use two hands, one at the side in a solid place, and one on the bottom. Do not lift or carry a painting by its stretcher bar, or insert your fingers between the stretcher bar and the canvas.

SIDE CART

If possible, use a padded truck or cart to move large paintings. Be sure the work is securely on the cart; it is prudent to lash it to a padded portion of the cart. A side cart may be used to move more than one painting at a time. Never overload the cart, and make sure that the paintings are distributed evenly on both sides. Keeping paintings oriented in the direction they hang, place similar-sized works back-to-back and front-to-front on the cart. Insure that the frame from one never touches the face of another painting. To protect adjoining frames, insert an archival board or soft piece of foam rubber between them where they meet. Move only a few paintings on a cart at one time. A heavy cart may shift its weight unexpectedly, causing it to tip over. This is dangerous to both objects and the staff moving them.

When leaning paintings against the wall, place them on rubber mats or on padded blocks. Never stack paintings more than five deep and do not stack paintings that are extremely large and/or heavy. If the frame is heavily ornamented, it may not be possible to rest the painting on its frame. If gilded, the surface of the frame should not be touched. Always hold a gessoed frame by the uncarved back edge and set it on its back edge, so the gesso is not damaged.

The ideal storage method for framed works of art is hanging on screens in the direction they were meant to hang (except those with severely flaking paint, which should be stored flat while waiting for conservation treatment). If screens are not available, framed works may be stored in bins. Pad the interior of the bins with archival board and the bottom with carpet made from a material that is inert or has had sufficient time to off-gas. Framed works in bins should be stored with works of similar size and placed back to back and front to front.

To prevent unnecessary handling, print the object's title and/or accession number on two archival paper and string tags, attaching one to the D-ring (or similar hanging device) at each side. In this manner the tag will always be at hand without pulling the painting from the bin. Never allow wires on paintings. D-rings offer much more stability for a hanging piece.

When shipping framed works under glass, taping the glass will afford the work some protection. It is important to realize *that taping does not insure the glass against breaking*; it protects the work from damage from the glass shards, should it break. Do not use tape with a strong adhesive, as this will be difficult

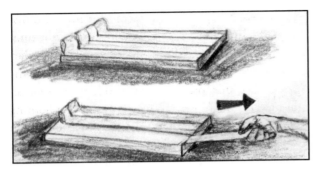

REMOVING TAPE FROM GLASS

to remove and cause delay, frustration, and breakage when unpacking the work. Some tapes are made specifically for glass taping, and come in a large variety of widths, although any low-tack tape will serve. Slightly overlap each strip of tape, covering the entire surface of the glass. Fold each end of the tape back on itself to allow for easier removal. Do not allow the adhesive side of the tape to come in contact with the frame. To remove the tape, pull each strip back gently at less than a 90-degree angle to avoid undue pressure on the glass. *Never tape Plexiglas; it will leave a permanent residue on the surface.*

Paintings, Unframed

Without the protection afforded by its frame, a painting that is unframed is at greater risk of damage from handling. Ungloved hands may leave behind fingerprints that will attract dirt and dust to the unavoidably oily residue. Varnishes are subject to harm from touch, which may necessitate overall restoration.

While not usually advised, it is sometimes necessary to carry a painting by its stretcher bar. In this case be sure that your fingers do not touch the back of the canvas, as this may cause slight indentations in the canvas that will worsen over time.

Never touch the front surface of a painting. When carrying an unframed work by its edges always wear thin gloves and use the lightest grip that will still ensure a good hold. To move a work a short distance, slip a board underneath and carry it horizontally. Be sure to orient the painting properly at the destination. Never stack works that do not have frames, and do not use any type of lashing or rope to secure them.

Textiles

Under no circumstances should a costume or any wearable textile object be worn.

Textiles must be handled, stored and exhibited with extreme caution. When exhibiting textiles, limit light levels to no more than 50 lux (5 footcandles). Always move textiles on a support such as a hanger or mannequin, and never allow the fabric to drag on the ground. Lack of support can cause stretching or tearing of the material. Some textiles cannot be cleaned due to their material and construction. Do not exhibit them in the open; enclose them in a Plexiglas or similar case.

In storage, a flat textile may be rolled on an archival tube and covered with a muslin case. Do not use plastic dustsheets because of their dust-attracting quality. Attach a large tag with a color photograph of the textile, along with its accession number, to each end of the tube to reduce handling when searching for a particular piece. Tubes may be supported on racks attached to the storage room walls. Do not store the rolls on the floor or underneath HVAC vents.

If textiles must be folded, stuff the folds with crumpled, unbuffered, acid-free tissue and store in archival textile boxes. Do not store textiles with any plastic objects, such as fashion accessories, because of damaging off-gassing, which may degrade the fabric or tarnish metal threads.

Heavy textiles should never be pierced with holes for display. Line the fabric to prevent dust from penetrating it from behind. Be sure to attach the lining loosely so it does not pull or stretch the fabric when moved. Mount the textile on a muslin-covered board and exhibit it on a slant for easy viewing without stretch damage. If the fabric must be hung, the weight should be evenly distributed along the top edge. Sew Velcro to a band of heavy material and then hand-sew this material along the top of the fabric using large stitches. Do not break the threads with your needle; rather insert the needle carefully between the threads. Do not sew by machine.

Accession numbers may be attached to textiles with cloth tags hand-sewn to the fabric, as long as it is of a loose weave.

Works on Paper

Never lift a work on paper by its edges, the weakest area of the object. Slip a thin support such as an index card or a spatula underneath to raise it enough to place a board (e.g., foam core, gator board, etc.) under it; place a clean sheet of acid-free paper on top and carry the board, not the work. If hand-carrying the work without a support board, always hold the longest sides of the paper and always use two hands. A work on paper that is held by one hand is subject to bending; in the case of a brittle work, ripping or cracking may occur where held.

If a work on paper must be turned over, use a board underneath as support; place a tissue on its surface, then another board, and turn the entire package. If the work has a very fragile surface, such as pastel or charcoal, this method is not advised.

When working with a stack of drawings never pull one out from the middle of the stack. Remove each one individually until you reach the desired one.

In storing works on paper, make archival paper folders that are slightly larger than the work, write the accession number or title in pencil on the outside of the folder in an obvious place and slip the work inside. Never write on the folder while the work is inside, to ensure that the pencil does not leave an imprint on the work. Having the number or title on the outside of the folder prevents unnecessary handling when searching for one object in particular.

Never use clips or staples on works on paper. If they are already present, remove them carefully so they do not leave impressions or rust stains. If a paper has a dog-eared corner, carefully try to unfold it. If the paper is brittle, do not attempt to unfold it, as the folded corner may tear off. Consult a paper conservator for advice or leave it as it is.

Do not roll works on paper, no matter how large. Fibers can become distorted, and inks and pigment may flake off. Works should be placed in a Solander box or supported from below and moved on a cart.

Any material that comes into contact with the work on paper, such as matting or interleaving, must be acid-free and of a high quality. Glassine is an acid-free material; however, over time it will absorb acid from contact with any acidic material. If using glassine as an interleaving material for long-term storage, change it for fresh tissue every year or so. Use an acid-detecting pen on older glassine to test for acidity.

In ideal circumstances, all stored works on paper should be matted to protect the surface of the work from direct contact with objects above it. All non-matted works should be interleaved with an appropriate material. Most works should be interleaved with buffered tissue except for blueprints, hand-tinted works, diazo reproductions, or any work with wool or silk components. Pastels and charcoals should not have any material touching their surfaces; instead, they should be stored singly in shallow boxes. When framing either of these media, do not use Plexiglas, Mylar or any plastic material which can set up a static reaction and pull the media off the surface of the work.

Paper that has been exposed to high humidity or wet conditions may be subject to mold. Foxing, a red-brown spotting, or mold may be an indication that storage conditions are too humid. Do not attempt to remove this type of stain. A paper conservator should be consulted for treatment. Mold may appear as a light gray haze on the inside of the glass in a framed work. In this case isolate the object to prevent the mold from traveling to other objects. Unframe the piece and move to a drier location. Inactive mold residue may be washed off the glass, but removal from the paper should be left to a conservator, as it may streak and permanently stain the work. Remove glass from the frame before washing. Inactive dry mold should be removed from frames, drawers, or anything with which it has been in contact. Should conditions become humid again, mold may be reactivated and cause further damage.

All works on paper should be actively protected from overexposure to light. Keep all works enclosed in drawers or boxes when they are not being used. When objects are in use, such as when performing condition reporting or examinations, keep them covered by tissue unless you are actively working on that particular object. Never leave them exposed on a worktable overnight. Whenever you leave the room, no matter how short the duration, turn off the lights. Think in terms of a 500-year lifetime or longer. Over that length of time, each small exposure to light can accumulate enough to cause significant changes.

THREE-DIMENSIONAL OBJECTS

Books

Books should be treated gently, as their appearance may mask a fragile condition. Shelving should have a smooth surface. If the sides of the shelf have holes or grooves for adjusting the shelf height they should be covered with glass or acid-free board. Bookends should cover the entire surface of the book next to it.

Books should be stored with those of like size and, if stored vertically, should remain completely so at all times to prevent sagging pages. If a book is removed from the shelf, replace it with a foam block to maintain verticality. Particularly fragile books or those of great value should be stacked horizontally with no more than three or four to a stack. Never stack open books.

Do not overstock the shelf; each book should be easily removable without excessive pulling on the headcap or spine. To remove a book from the shelf reach over the top to the fore-edge and gently pull it out. If this is not possible push the books on either side in, until you can grasp the sides of the selected book. Lift the book out, rather than dragging it.

Books with loose pages or damaged bindings should be tied with a soft cotton tape, never string or rubber bands, and sent to a conservator. Do not force a book open, nor attempt to make it lie flat by pressing it open.

When on exhibit, an open book should be kept in low light conditions. This will prevent the open page from fading at a different rate from the rest of the book. To display an open book, place supports beneath its covers. If possible, the open page should be changed every few days. To turn the pages, slip your fingers under the top corner of the page, and without bending it, run your fingers down the side and turn. If a book must be open to show a certain page, the time on view should be limited.

Books with undamaged edges may be brushed infrequently with a hog's-hair brush, to eliminate dust. Hold the closed book firmly and brush the top from the spine to the outer edge. This prevents dust from being swept into the spine. If dust has penetrated the pages, rest the open book on foam supports and brush from the inner to the outer edges. Do not attempt to clean the area of the page closest to where it is bound and do not erase marks from the pages.

Ceramics and Glass

You may use ungloved, clean and dry hands, unless the ceramic is porous or unglazed. Nitrile or other rubber-type gloves may also be used.

Gently grip ceramics by their base, never by any protruding element or lip. Examine carefully for evidence of old repairs that may weaken the structure. Because adhesives used in repairs may break down over time, use caution in these areas and be aware that not all repairs are immediately evident.

Place padding between objects when transporting them on a cart. Conservation "pillows" or "snakes" made from muslin or lightweight canvas filled with poly pellets are especially helpful in keeping objects from tipping or rolling on cart or shelves.

Do not store drinking glasses inverted on the rim. The rim is the most fragile part of the glass.

Furniture

Lift and carry furniture; do not drag, push or pull, which strains joints and may cause them to snap. Use a cart or flatbed truck for the move, if necessary. Use pads or blankets to protect fragile edges and projections from bumps during the move. Use only soft cords or cloths as straps and place pads between the strap and surface when moving. Do not over-tighten the straps, which may mar delicate surfaces.

PROPERLY LIFTING CHAIR

Never pick up chairs by backs or arms. Lift them from under the seat; carry with one hand under seat

BOOK SUPPORT

and the other supporting the back. Use the middle portion of your body as a brace only if you are wearing clothes without front buttons, zippers, or buckles, or if you are wearing a carpenter's apron with empty pockets.

Large pieces of furniture should be moved by at least two people, one on each side. If the view is obstructed, enlist another person to watch for doorways, stairs, etc., and hold doors open.

Furniture that has component parts, such as dressers, bureaus, and grandfather clocks, should be taken apart and the pieces moved separately to reduce its weight. Secure moveable parts, such as hinged drop lids, with cotton twill tape, and collapse or remove table leaves before moving. Tables should be lifted by placing fingers below the top, after determining that the top is securely attached.

Carry marble and glass tops vertically, rather than flat; the horizontal weight may cause the piece to crack or split.

Musical Instruments

Cotton gloves should always be worn in order to protect surfaces of many instruments, including polished brass and varnished stringed instruments. The varnish is considered a critical aesthetic, and unlike that of a painting, should never be removed or replaced.

When moving an instrument from one area of a building to another, especially when there are differences in room temperatures, it should be covered to prevent thermal shock. Instruments should not be dismantled for transportation unless under the supervision of a specialist, because of the risk of damaging delicate sounding parts.

An instrument should never be lifted by, nor rested upon, its keys, bridge, strings or other delicate component. Avoid storage or display near exterior walls, sources of heat, air vents, or areas where condensation may accumulate.

Adhesives, such as museum wax, should never be used to prop up an instrument in an installation or for photographic purposes.

Natural History Specimens

Because of the prevalent use of arsenic as a preservative in the past, *never allow taxidermy mounts to be used for "hands-on" demonstrations before they are tested for arsenic residue.*

Many specimens (e.g., fossils) can be extremely heavy. Lifts, webbing, or other special equipment may be necessary to move them.

The surface of some specimens, such as shells and painted ethnographic objects, may be powdery or have fugitive dyes and paints that are easily rubbed off. Insect specimens are also extremely fragile. Special care has to be taken when handling these items. It is better to move the mount or storage container than to touch the object. Transport smaller items inside boxes padded with a neutral colored material; inks in colored tissue may transfer to the objects. If these objects must be touched, wear latex or nitrile gloves.

Support all of the appendages and body of the object. For example, mounted animals may have arms and legs sticking out in precarious positions. Tails can be especially vulnerable to breakage. Birds can have fine, spindly feathers that stick out from the body and need special protection.

Bone, ivory, and antler materials are susceptible to chipping and fingerprint stains. They should be handled as little as possible. These object types may crack in low humidity conditions and thus should be protected from the heat of examination and photography lights.

Sculpture

When moving items from the rear of a storage shelf, first remove all objects from the front of the shelf so that you do not lift one object over another.

Inspect the object before touching it. Look for loose components, cracks, breaks, and areas of old repair, while being aware that not all damage may be obvious.

In general it is best to transport objects in their most stable position, usually that in which they are stored or displayed. If possible, sculpture should remain vertical in the position which best supports its weight. A horizontal placement may put stress on fragile areas. If sculpture must be laid down, insert padding underneath to support any weak areas.

When moving several items, it is easier and safer to use a cart. Objects with removable parts, such as a teapot and lid or sculpture and base should be

SCULPTURE WITH SUPPORT

separated prior to moving. Brace small or fragile objects with clean foam blocks, muslin conservation pillows, or rolled towels so that the objects do not roll around on the cart. A padded box can hold particularly fragile or small objects while in transit on a cart.

HAZARDOUS MATERIALS IN THE COLLECTION

Along with the fragile nature of many museum objects, concerns exist with toxic preservation methods sometimes used in the past and/or the inherently hazardous make-up of the objects themselves. This is particularly true in historic and natural history collections. Although it is exciting to be the one to open a crate containing new additions to the collection, possible health risks demand added caution. Protective equipment (respirators, masks, non-permeable gloves, etc.) and special procedures may be needed to handle such items. Supervisors in museums with these collections are urged to stringently enforce staff usage of protective gear. Prolonged contact with these materials or working in an area with inadequate ventilation should be prohibited.

In earlier times, taxidermy mounts, many ethnographic objects, and preserved organic archaeological specimens were treated with pesticides containing arsenic, ethylene oxide, Vapona, DDT, strychnine, mercuric chloride, naphthalene and paradichlorobenzene (mothballs). Residues from these pesticides can be absorbed through inhalation, ingestion, or absorption through the skin. These chemicals are particularly prevalent in Native American remains and artifacts and have caused serious concerns in repatriation efforts. The National Park Service reports that at least 55 different chemical compounds

and mixtures (including arsenic and mercury) may have been used to preserve their museum collections. Virtually all are irritants, and many are harsh poisons and/or carcinogens. Other concerns exist with collection objects, including explosives, asbestos, radioactivity, poisons, and pathogens. Staff involved with handling any material that may pose a health or safety risk should approach such objects with caution, information, and protection.

WHEN DAMAGE OCCURS

Despite careful handling, mishaps may occur, resulting in a damaged and/or broken object. It may be possible to prevent further harm to the object by following established procedures immediately after the incident. It is best if these procedures are included in preliminary training sessions when a calm atmosphere prevails.

Any damage should be immediately reported to the department supervisor so that incident reports and photographs may be made right away. Never try to cover up a problem; it will only prevent resolution of the situation. Blame, if any, should be dealt with after the object is properly cared for. If damage occurs on weekends or after hours, all personnel should know to notify the security staff that can oversee proper procedures. All museum staff should be aware that there are rules in place for this type of occurrence.

If the object is on loan to your museum, the lender should be notified according to instructions provided in the loan agreement. If there are no instructions, report the situation by telephone and follow up with a written report and photographs. Depending on the severity of the damage your insurance agent may also need to be notified; he or she will request copies of the damage report and photographs.

Unless further damage will result, objects should not be cleaned up or removed until the report is completed and photographs have been taken. The appropriate staff member should carefully gather up all pieces, no matter how small, and put them aside in a sealable bag if possible. Under no circumstances should repairs be attempted or pieces fitted back together on the spot. This may cause abrasion and greatly increase the chance that complete restoration will be impossible. Mark off the area where the damage happened and do not allow the public or staff to walk through it. If you need to go back to search for missing components it will be easier if the area has not been disturbed.

If the incident occurred because of improper mounts, pedestals having been placed in poor locations, or similar reasons, the situation should be remedied before the object is returned to display.

If damage has occurred during shipment, do not discard any packing material or containers that the object was in. The shipper should be notified as well; insurance claims may be negated if the company is not informed as soon as the damage is discovered. Should you notice damage to any crate or box as it is being delivered, the driver should be asked to stay on the premises until the company has been contacted.

EMERGENCY PROCEDURES

As a component of a museum's emergency preparedness plan, all staff should have at least an introduction to the principles of object handling. This can be done in conjunction with other staff training, such as fire drills, use of fire extinguishers, and other emergency techniques. Museum security guards and docents are often the only staff members present on weekends or during open evening hours. If an object is knocked off a pedestal or falls from the wall, staff should know enough to prevent further damage or loss. In holding a training session for this purpose it should be stressed that *normally non-collection staff will not handle museum objects,* but in the event of an emergency without other staff present, they may need to know what to do. Training should focus on specific object types found in your collection, and on damage mitigation (see When Damage Occurs).

When a natural disaster such as a hurricane or a flood is impending and collections need to be moved quickly, all staff may need to be involved. One person should be designated as point person so confusion is kept to a minimum. The staff should be organized into teams with at least one trained object handler on each team. Keep in mind that all staff will be under stress and calm attitudes will help to smooth the process. All workers will have personal concerns on their minds and may not be thinking clearly; encourage focused thought. Do not stay in the building longer than is safe. No matter their value, objects are objects and nothing is more valuable than human life. •

5c | Measuring

HOLLY YOUNG

Measurements are basic to curatorial and registrarial processes. They are a vital part of the initial record of an object entering a museum and serve as a base line for publication, exhibition, and storage. Size, weight, and color should be recorded systematically. Object measurements and weight are used to determine space and material requirements for exhibit cases, storage furniture, and packing crates. Measurements can help track the condition of an object subject to breakage or dimensional changes. The registrar should define a standard procedure for object measurement as part of the written procedures of the registration department to ensure consistency between individuals and through time.

Measurement Systems

Many scientific disciplines and most nations use the metric system, as do many institutions in the United States. For those institutions that use the English system, an alternative is to record measurements in both systems.

Another important issue to consider is the amount of precision necessary. Normally, metric measurements are expressed in centimeters to one decimal place (or the nearest millimeter) and English measurements in inches to within 1/16 of an inch. If a measurement falls between significant increments, the reading is rounded up to the larger measurement. If increased precision is necessary, measuring implements must be selected that are similarly fine-tuned.

The equipment used to measure objects ranges from simple linear measures to instruments that allow electronic data capture and record information directly into a computer file. The registrar selects the kind of equipment that will be most useful for the institution, based on three major considerations: the types and sizes of objects to be measured, the measurement system used, and the amount of precision necessary.

Linear measures, such as rulers, yardsticks, and measuring tapes, are the most widely available and frequently used pieces of measuring equipment. They are particularly well-suited to measuring two-dimensional objects and very large objects. Metal measuring tapes are the most durable, but have the potential to damage the object being measured. Plastic measuring tapes have the advantage of being flexible, but are easily stretched or warped, resulting in inaccurate measurements. Cloth measuring tapes and flexible fiberglass tapes are more durable than plastic and, although they can become distorted, represent a good compromise.

Calipers and osteometric boards are useful for measuring three-dimensional objects. They consist of a linear measuring scale with one stationary and one sliding arm which are used to measure the distance between two points on an object. These devices yield a more accurate measurement of a three-dimensional object than is possible using a straight rule. Digital calipers can be used to record measurements directly into computer data files. Calipers with both straight and pincer arms are useful; pincers are especially good for recording thickness at a particular point on the object.

Templates and gauges can be used for more analytical measurements, if necessary. Similarly, color can be measured using standard charts, such as the Munsell Soil Color Chart, useful for materials of geological origin. When weighing is necessary, there are a variety of electronic and spring-loaded scales and balances from which to choose. A sturdy, easy-to-calibrate triple beam balance is useful for small to medium-sized objects. Tiny objects will require a more delicate balance.

MEASUREMENT PROCEDURES

To establish institutional measurement procedures, it is prudent to work with curatorial staff in various disciplines, as they will know the standards within their fields. While inter-observer variability can never be eliminated, it can be reduced, making measurements more reliable. Keeping the equipment clean, calibrated, and in good working condition and properly storing it after use are important components of the measuring procedure. Measuring equipment should be calibrated on a regular basis, as often as needed, and should be checked before use. More sophisticated and complex equipment must be calibrated more frequently.

Use particular care when handling an object for measurement. More than simply moving an object, measuring requires a certain amount of manipulation of both the object and the measuring device. For this reason, it is prudent to remove rings, watches, bracelets, pendant necklaces, or other items that may inadvertently come in contact with the object. Hands should be free of lotion or soap residues. Cotton or nitrile gloves should be worn, as appropriate. *(See the chapter on Handling.)* Make sure that an adequate amount of space is cleared and prepared for the activity and that any necessary auxiliary materials, such as padded supports, are readily available before moving the object. When using calipers, be careful not to crush the object or damage delicate edges by applying too much pressure. To record measurements, use a pencil rather than a pen or marker, both of which can inadvertently leave a permanent mark on the object.

Two-dimensional Objects:

In general, height and width (or length) are the two basic measurements taken for flat objects. Thickness (or depth) should also be recorded for framed or mounted objects. By standard practice, height precedes width.

  •**Paintings.** For square or rectangular formats, make at least two measurements from the back of the work in each direction, one at the middle of the stretcher or panel, the other at an edge; record the larger measurement, if any variation

ALL ACCESSIONS MUST BE CAREFULLY MEASURED.
PHOTO BY LEE STALSWORTH, HIRSHHORN MUSEUM.

occurs. Record the diameter for a circular painting, and the length of two axes for oval or lozenge-shaped works. Measure the thickness of paintings on heavier supports, such as panels, and those with auxiliary supports, such as stretchers or cradles. If the frame prevents such measurements, record a sight measurement of the painting surface and the dimensions of the frame, and indicate them as such.

•**Textiles.** This category includes two-dimensional items such as flags, rugs, wall-hangings, and bedding. Simple woven textiles should be measured along the warp (stationary element) and the weft (moving element). Be clear as to whether or not fringe, borders, or tassels are included in the overall measurement; in any case, their length or width should be measured and noted separately. Hand woven pieces may have the number of warps or wefts per unit of measure. More complex pieces, such as flags or quilts, should be measured in two dimensions according to their orientation in use. If a textile has a significant pile or loft, include this as a third dimension.

•**Works on paper.** Unless otherwise indicated, works on paper are measured along the left side for height, and the lower edge for width. In addition to measuring the paper support, dimensions should be taken of the design area and plate mark, if the piece is a print. Historic documents require similar measurements, including the area covered by text. If the paper support has been hinged and matted, consider it an auxiliary support and take the measurements of the mat as well.

Three-dimensional Objects:

Generally, the overall height, length or width, and depth or thickness of these objects should be measured; take these measurements at the point of greatest dimension. It may be practical to take a few additional measurements which are specific to the type of object and which may be important to the identification, display, or use of a particular object.

•**Amorphous items.** At times, objects with odd shapes and no true orientation (e.g., clumps of charred botanical materials, clods of fired adobe, crumpled pieces of metal, slag, fire-cracked rock) must be measured. Place the object on a flat surface in its most stable position, and take measurements in three dimensions from that orientation. Record the orientation or draw a simple diagram. A weight is also useful for amorphous specimens.

•**Boxed collections.** Archival paper documents, with the exception of large format materials, are usually measured by the linear inch or foot. Large format documents, such as maps and plans, are measured by storage volume. Some repositories measure all archival collections by volume, specifically by cubic feet. This figure is determined by adding the exterior dimensions of the storage containers. Large collections of artifacts and samples that are stored in boxes are similarly measured in cubic feet.

•**Coins.** By convention, coins are measured in millimeters; if an institution uses the English system, a conversion should be made. Measure the diameter and the thickness of the coin. For coins with central perforations, give the internal dimensions of the perforation.

•**Furniture.** The measurements for furniture may be less ambiguous if expressed as height, side-to-side, and front-to-back dimensions. Since dimensions may vary, take several measurements and record the largest. In addition to the basic measurements, measuring the height and depth of seats, and the length of aprons, table leaves, and legs may assist in developing exhibit groupings and identifying particular pieces. Since furniture is susceptible to dimensional changes, areas of loss, decay, cracks, and splits should be noted and measured.

•**Historic hardware and tools.** Record the weight of hardware in addition to gauges. Indicate measurements of handles, including circumference, and working edges.

•**Natural history specimens.** A wide variety of materials falls under this classification. In addition to covering the entire spectrum of "animal, vegetable, or mineral," it includes auxiliary items such as nests, specimens in various stages of growth, and variously preserved specimens, including mounts and dried or cross-sectioned specimens. Registrars are advised to consult one of the references provided, or to look to the individual curatorial departments for guidance. In general, overall dimensions and often weight will be useful. Specimens in containers may have the container volume recorded, as well.

•**Personal items.** For items of clothing, in addition to overall dimensions, tailoring measurements are usually taken, such as inseam length or inside waistband. If a standard size is marked on the object, this can be recorded, as well. Accessories, such as hats or bags, should have careful measurements made of applied parts which may be subject to damage, especially feathers or trim. Component parts of jewelry should be measured: for example, the watchband or chain, as well as the watch itself. Measure diameters and restrictions for items of personal adornment such as bracelets or labrets.

•**Prehistoric tools.** Record basic measurements of projectile points, blades, axes, etc.; for artifacts that were originally hafted, also measure hafting features, such as grooves, holes, and tangs. The hollowed-out area of artifacts such as grinding stones or mortars should be measured. Elongated artifacts such as awls, needles, or shafts should be measured for length, and diameters or thicknesses at mid-shaft and at the base.

•**Sculpture.** Record standard dimensions; include the pedestal or other support only if it is an integral part of the sculpture. For portraits, record measurements from the proper aspect (i.e., from the depicted person's left or right, not the viewer').

•**Toys.** Record standard dimensions. Toys made of separate components should have a count of the pieces and a range of measurements given.

•**Vessels.** The objects in this category can be made from many different materials, including botanical materials, ceramic, glass, and stone. For bottles and jars, measure the height and maximum diameter; other measurements that may be taken include the orifice diameter and the neck height, where the neck is specifically delineated. Similarly, bowls should be measured for height and maximum diameter; occasionally wall thickness is measured. At least three overall measurements should be taken for eccentric forms and other vessels such as scoops or effigies.

•**Weapons.** In addition to basic measurements, record the length of the barrel and size of the bore for firearms. Weapons with a cutting edge should include measurements of the blade and haft.

Images and other machine produced/machine readable media:

•**Static images.** If matted and framed, these objects should be measured as flat works of art. If they are unframed, record the support and image size for positives. Record film size, length of strip (when applicable), and a count of the individual images for negatives. For slides and transparencies, give a count of the images and the size of the mount. As these are easily duplicable, have a policy on whether or not counts should reflect unique images or include all copies of the image.

•**Moving images.** Film and video can be measured in a number of ways, including length in feet or in playing time. Generally, the format and size of the reel or cassette are recorded.

•**Sound recordings.** Although there are many formats, including historic cylinder and wire recordings, tapes of varying sizes and formats, and disks of different media and speeds, sound recordings are generally measured as moving images.

•**Computerized information.** In addition to the above methods of measuring, computerized information can be measured by the byte. Other measures, such as the number of digitized images, should also be recorded. •

Thanks to: Laura Andrew, Noelle McClure, and Lindsey Vogel.

5D | CONDITION REPORTING

MARIE DEMEROUKAS

OVERVIEW

A good condition report is an accurate and informative account of an object's state of preservation at a particular moment in time. It provides a verbal and/or visual description of the nature, location, and extent of each defect in a clear, consistent manner. A condition report written by a registrar, curator, or collections manager (as discussed in this chapter) is not the same as a condition report written by a conservator. The former aids collections management while the latter is intended for planning and performing object treatment.

A condition report can:

- establish the exact condition of an object at the time of a loan or upon its return

- benchmark the type and/or rate of deterioration

- differentiate otherwise identical objects from one another

- document an object's condition history, providing past evidence for future problems

- set priorities for conservation care and treatment

- suggest a default monetary value on an object in lieu of an actual value for insurance purposes

- make future handlers aware of seen and unseen problems

Tools
A variety of tools help conduct object examinations.

Documentation
- soft lead pencils (pens can leave a permanent mark)
- writing paper
- examination forms
- computer
- film or digital camera

Measurement
- cloth tape measure, without metal caps (caution: some tapes can stretch)
- calipers
- clear plastic flexible ruler

Handling/Support
- clean white cotton gloves
- nitrile gloves
- acid-free, lignin-free board
- buffered and unbuffered acid-free, lignin-free tissue paper
- padded muslin rolls and blocks
- flat-bed dolly

Illumination
- flashlight
- pen or crevice light
- portable incandescent lights (e.g., a mechanic's drop light)
- ultraviolet light

Magnification
- 10x hand lens
- jeweler's loupe
- 55x microscope
- head-mounted magnifier

Miscellaneous
- hand mirror
- dental mirror
- magnet (to identify ferrous metals)
- natural hair brushes in a variety of shapes and stiffness
- probes (dentist's tools)
- tweezers
- air blower

EXAMINATION

Examine objects in a clean, secure, well-lit work area where eating, drinking, and smoking are prohibited. For small- and medium-sized objects, pad a sturdy table or desk with polyethylene foam. A padded flat-bed dolly may be useful for large objects. Cover the examination surface with clean, white, acid-free paper to help detect signs of flaking, infestation, etc.

Use cotton or nitrile gloves to handle objects. Nitrile gloves are especially important when working with ethnographic and natural history collections, since in the past many specimens were treated with fumigants and chemicals. Nitrile gloves are smooth and less likely than cotton gloves to disrupt loosely adhered paints. Follow all appropriate handling guidelines, making sure each part is properly supported. Large, awkward, or fragile objects may require several handlers. Be aware of an object's visible faults, such as cracks or tears, and potential weaknesses, such as repaired handles or brittle veneer. *(See chapter on Handling.)*

Make sure lighting is adequate to the task. General lighting, which illuminates the object overall; raking light, which illuminates at an angle; and transmitted light, which illuminates from the reverse, can reveal a variety of surface and subsurface irregularities. Use ultraviolet (UV) light judiciously to detect adhesive residues, paints, resins, etc. An X-ray uses electronic radiation to detect subsurface cracks and losses. Avoid light damage by reducing long-term exposure, filtering UV from general lighting, minimizing intense exposure, and reducing heat build-up. *(See chapter on Preventive Care.)*

To understand and identify an object's defects and weaknesses, it is important to determine its composition. Objects can be made of organic materials (e.g., bone, cotton, hair) or inorganic materials (e.g., gold, clay, flint). These materials may be in their original form, such as marble, or may have been modified, such as brass (an alloy of copper and zinc). Objects made from a combination of materials may suffer from a variety of problems, such as weak joints, dissimilar rates of expansion and contraction, or chemical incompatibility.

Damage affects an object's condition. An inherent fault, also known as inherent vice, is a weakness in the construction of an object or the incompatibility of materials of which it is composed, such as a thin handle on a heavy teapot or metallic salts added to 19th-century silks. Pests and mold, which feed on organic materials or deposits, cause biological damage as they weaken an object's structure or create problems such as riddled wood or discoloration. Physical damage is caused by mechanical stress and includes abrasions, losses, tearing, etc. Chemical damage is the result of a reaction between a material and an energy source (heat, light) or a chemical (water). It is evidenced by corrosion, tarnish, fading, etc.

Always distinguish between historic and "modern" damage or repair. Other condition-related factors to keep in mind:

- One type of damage may encourage another (e.g., embrittlement can lead to tearing).

- Some objects have important evidence of a past function (e.g., stains on a ritual blade, dried residue in a medicine bottle).

- Burial may affect an object's condition (e.g., salts efflorescing on pottery).

Whenever possible, examine objects by category (e.g., hats, bird mounts, paintings) or by types of materials (e.g., stone, paper, wool). Grouping will promote consistency, thoughtful observations, and accuracy. Determine an appropriate examination pattern, and follow it each time (e.g., top to bottom, proper left to proper right, front to back, exterior to interior).

DOCUMENTATION

An object's condition can be documented by text (physical description), sketch (rough representation), and photographic image (exact representation). A combination of these methods provides a complete account of an object's condition at a particular moment in time.

Textual documentation can take the form of a narrative or a checklist. Although some technical terminology will be needed for clarity, in general a report's language must be simple, straightforward and understandable. Condition reporting software or off-the-shelf spreadsheet programs can be used to generate and update report forms.

A condition report should include:

- identifying numbers (accession, loan, field, catalog)
- type of object
- name of artist/maker (if known)
- title of object (if any)
- date and place of manufacture (if known)
- dimensions (height x width x depth, circumference)
- number of parts
- object composition
- types of damage
- extent of damage
- location of damage
- previous repairs (historic and modern)
- dates of and reason for damage (if known)
- examiner's name
- date of examination

Digital documentation quickly captures the nature, extent, and location of damage and, when shot at a high resolution, can provide passive documentation of unnoticed problems for future confirmation. Prints serve as canvases for making notes and highlighting problem areas.

A photographic image should include:
- identifying numbers
- scale
- color chart
- date of image

Whether an object's condition is recorded on paper, on film, or electronically, make sure that the materials and methods used are archivally sound and selected for preservability. Black-and-white film is more stable than color, although modern color film is more stable than its predecessors. Digital images should be captured at a high resolution and saved using widely available, non-proprietary lossless data compression. View or modify a surrogate file, rather than the master. Process film or print digital images according to American National Standards Guidelines for longevity. Documentation should be stored in a physically secure and environmentally stable area. Electronic documentation should be refreshed every few years to prevent degradation of media and migrated as technology changes. All duplicates and back-ups must be housed separately, outside of the institution.

When writing a condition report, consider the nature, location, and extent of damage. Completely discuss one type of damage on one portion of the object before moving on, to ensure accuracy and minimize handling. Observational skills will have been honed after creating condition reports for several similar objects. Review the earlier reports and improve as necessary. Keep all reference materials (e.g., glossaries, location nomenclature) on file for future reference. Use terms consistently. Be objective and specific.

Type of Damage

What is the nature of the damage? If the examiner is trained in conservation, it may be possible to determine whether it is biological, physical, or chemical in nature or the result of an inherent fault. If the cause of the damage is not apparent, leave etiological statements to the conservator. Describe damage in terms of texture, color, shape, odor, and other physical properties, as appropriate. A glossary, whether established or constructed, can be used to assign a descriptive term to a specific condition. Speculative assessments should be indicated with a question mark.

Location

Where is the damage located? Whenever possible, use a recognized nomenclature to indicate the exact position of damage (e.g., proper left, viewer's right) or describe the damaged part of the object (e.g., hammer: face, neck, handle, grip, cheek). Sources for standards include museum nomenclatures, collector organizations and publications, product manufacturers, and reference texts. (See chapter on Data Standards.) The object itself may provide location names (e.g., the "shirt" or "face" areas on a figure in a painting, or "to the right of the handle, at the base").

A zone system (fig. 1) provides a generalized method for locating damage on two-dimensional objects. Each zone or square is labeled, such as TR (top right) or C (center), and the damage is placed within a zone. The matrix system (fig. 2), also for two-dimensional objects, is more precise, as the damage is plotted in millimeters on the x and y coordinates. The x coordinate represents the bottom edge of the object; the y coordinate represents the left edge. A stain near the top right corner of a document might be plotted as 450 mm along the x (bottom) axis and 400 mm along the y (left) axis; this is represented as (450, 400 mm). Sketches, photographs, or digital images offer location guidance for three-dimensional objects.

TL	TC	TR
CL	C	CR
BL	BC	BR

FIGURE I. ZONE SYSTEM

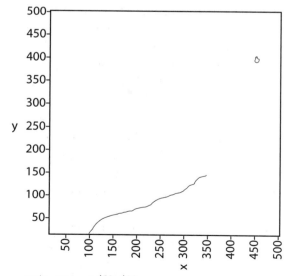

stain: center at 450, 400 mm
tear: from 100, 0 mm to 350, 125 mm

FIGURE 2. MATRIX SYSTEM

Measurements in the United States have been taken either metrically or in the English system, depending on the museum's discipline and traditions. If the English system is used, metrics should be indicated as well. Whenever possible, lay the measuring device alongside the object to avoid touching it. Other ways to describe location include:

- direction (horizontal, vertical, diagonal)
- object side (obverse/reverse, interior/exterior, proper left/proper right, verso/recto)
- range (scattered, overall)

Extent

What is the extent of the damage? Proceed from the general to the specific (e.g., "object yellowed overall, especially in BR corner"). Some damage, such as a tear or a loss, can be readily measured. Damage that cannot be conventionally measured, such as foxing or yellowing, can be described in the following standardized degrees of severity: "negligible," "slight," "moderate," "marked," and "extreme." Recognized condition standards have been established for a variety of objects (e.g., coins, stamps).

MODIFYING REPORTS

When updating reports, add new condition information next to the old, so past and present comments appear together. Include the date and the examiner's name. Unless there has been a change in condition, there is no need to repeat the same information for an object that is part of a long-term traveling exhibition. Rather, indicate that the comments provided in the initial report or by previous examiners are still applicable. Treat the condition report as a legal document; it may be used in title or insurance disputes.

Carefully review all incoming condition reports in a timely manner. If there is a discrepancy, a digital photo of the problem area can be made and promptly sent to the lender. When dealing with a large incoming collection, it's best to have two examiners: one person to read the report aloud (and make notes) and another to visually confirm the description against the object.

CONDITION REPORTING GLOSSARY

The following are some of the many terms used to describe conditions.

General Terms

Abrasion: A wearing away of the surface caused by scraping, rubbing, grinding, or friction; often superficial.

Accretion: Any external material deposited on a surface; often results from burial conditions or accidental deposits, such as splashes, drips, flyspecks, etc. (cf. inclusion).

Adhesive residue: May be from glue, paste, or pressure-sensitive tapes.

Bleeding: The suffusion of a color into adjacent materials; often caused by water or other solvents.

Chip: A defect in a surface characterized by the breaking away of material.

Crack: A surface fracture or fissure across or through a material, either straight-line or branching in form; no loss is implied. A crack may be described as blind when it stops part way, as hairline when it is a tiny fissure, and as open when it is a large fissure.

Crease: A line of crushed or broken fibers, generally made by folding. A dog-ear is a diagonal crease across the corner of a paper, parchment, textile, etc.

Delamination: A separation of layers; splitting.

Dent: A defect in the surface caused by a blow; a simple concavity.

Discoloration: A partial or overall change in color caused by aging, light, or chemical agents. Yellowing and darkening can occur, along with bleaching, the lightening of color, and fading, a loss of color or a change in hue.

Disjoin: A partial or complete separation of a joint between two members of an object, as distinguished from a crack, tear, check, or split.

Distortion: A warping or misshaping of the original shape; shrinkage may occur.

Embrittlement: A loss of flexibility causing the material (e.g., paper, parchment, leather) to break or disintegrate when bent or curled.

Gouge: A defect in the surface where material has been scooped out.

Fold: A turning over of a surface so that it is in contact with itself. The line of flexing may or may not be creased.

Inclusion: Particle accidentally bonded to the surface of an object during manufacture (e.g., ceramic, plastic, cast metal, paper).

Loss: Missing area or hole.

Mildew: See mold.

Missing element: Loss of an integral component of, or an addition or appendage to an object (e.g., handle, tassel).

Mold: Biological in nature, mold or mildew can be in the form of foxing; of colored, furry, or web-like surface excrescences; and/or of musty odor.

Patina: A colored surface layer, either applied or naturally occurring.

Pest damage: Surface loss, tunneling, holes, fly specks, etc., obviously caused by insects or other pests.

Scratch: Linear surface loss due to abrasion with a sharp point.

Sheen: A polish produced by handling; often occurs on frequently touched locations.

Soil: A general term denoting any material that dirties, sullies, or smirches an object. Dust is loose soil generally distributed on surfaces; grime is soil tenaciously held on surfaces; a smear and a fingerprint are types of local grime. A spatter or run is the result of dried droplets or splashes of foreign material.

Stain: A color change as a result of soiling, adhesives, pest residue, food, oils, etc. A diffuse stain is without a distinct boundary; a discrete stain has a distinct boundary; a liquid stain has a discrete boundary or tide-line that is darker than the general area of the stain; a centered stain has a darker or more intensely colored center within its general area (cf. foxing). In metallic staining, adjacent materials are discolored as a result of metal corrosion.

Tear: A break in fabric, paper, or other sheet material as a result of tension or torsion.

Wear: Surface erosion, usually at edges, due to repeated handling.

Painting

Painting Layers

Ground: Layer(s) of material applied to prepare a surface for painting; usually a pigment in a binding medium.

Paint layer: Layer(s) of colored pigment and binder used to make the design.

Varnish: A clear resinous film applied over the paint layer for protection and to saturate the colors.

Painting Supports: Panel, Fabric, Board

Cradle: On a panel, a system of wood or metal ribs fastened parallel to the grain, with perpendicular sliding members; used in an attempt to prevent warping

Lining: The addition of a new layer of material to the reverse of the original, using one of a number of adhesives such as wax-resin, glue, paste, or synthetic resins.

Strainer: A fixed-joint, non-expandable, wooden frame auxiliary support for fabric.

Stretcher: An auxiliary wooden-frame support for fabric that has one of several types of expandable joints to permit dimensional enlargement.

Stretcher keys: Wooden wedges used in the slots of the joints of some stretchers them mechanically.

Tacking edge: The edge of a fabric painting support that is turned over and attached to the stretcher or strainer, usually with tacks or staples.

Painting Terms

Blanching: Irregular, obtrusive, pale or milky areas in paint or varnish; not a superficial defect like bloom but a scattering of light from microporosities or granulation in aged films.

Blister: A separation between layers appearing as an enclosed, bubbled area.

Bloom: A whitish, cloudy appearance in the varnish layer caused by exposure to moisture or resulting from wax-based media. Sometimes called efflorescence.

Buckling: Waves or large bulges in a canvas from non-uniform tension around the stretcher or strainer. In paper, a soft, concave/convex random distortion.

Chalking: Loss of a paint or emulsion layer by powdering off.

Check: Splitting of wood along the grain, from the edge of a board or panel for a part of its length. Checking is usually in response to repeated dimensional change brought on by fluctuations of temperature and humidity (cf. split).

Cleavage: A separation between the paint layers and the support producing tenting (gable-like ridges) or cupping (concave flakes). Caused by the contraction of the support, forcing the paint layer up off the surface.

Crackle: A network of fine cracks found in a variety of objects including paintings, lacquers, inlays, and ceramics. The crevice has a narrow aperture and often penetrates more than one layer; the rift has a relatively wide aperture and penetrates only a single layer. A traction crackle has an "alligatored" pattern of complex branching, with wide, disfiguring apertures. Mechanical cracks resulting from a blow or pressure to the reverse, can cause a feather-like or radiating crackle pattern (bulls-eye or spider web) or the bending or creasing of a canvas (e.g., along the inner edges of stretcher bars).

Crazing: A fine system of crackling in a varnish layer, usually found in aged films in their final stages of drying and embrittlement.

Cupping: See cleavage.

Dishing: A defect in the stretcher caused by the torque of a drawn fabric. If the stretcher members are twisted out of a common plane, a shallow dihedral angle is formed at the corners. Dishing is a common cause of corner wrinkles in stretched canvases (cf. draw).

Draw: A local distortion at the corner of a painting, marked by diagonal cockling from the corner toward the center of the mount (cf. dishing).

Fill: The material used to replace areas of loss; the fill is then in-painted.

Flaking: Lifting and sometimes loss of flat areas of the surface layer.

Impasto: Thickly applied paint, often with pronounced brushwork, often a trouble spot because of cleavage or flattening during lining.

Inpainting: New areas of paint to restore design or color continuity; restricted to areas of loss.

Overpainting: Areas of repainting over existing original surface.

Split: A rupture running along the grain of a piece of wood from end to end, usually caused by exterior mechanical stress (cf. check).

Stretcher crease: A crease or line of cracks in the ground and paint layers of a painting on fabric, following the inside edges of stretcher members or the edges of cross-members. Caused by the flexing of the fabric against the edges of these members.

Tenting: See cleavage.

Warp: In a panel, the planar deformation of the support caused by changes in relative humidity.

Wrinkling: Small ridges and furrows of crawling paint or varnish caused by improper methods or materials; usually related to a non-drying medium and loss of volume in the film through evaporation.

Paper Terms

Buckling: A soft, concave/convex random distortion.

Cockling: A soft, concave/convex distortion characterized by parallel, repeated ripples, usually either horizontal or vertical.

Dimpling: A local distortion, usually in the corner, marked by a distinctly concave area; usually caused by local adhesion of the support to the secondary support.

Draw: A local distortion at the corner, marked by diagonal cockling from the corner toward the center of the mount.

Drumming: A type of matting where the support is adhered on all edges to the window mat; causes problems if the relative humidity becomes too low.

Foxing: Small yellow, brown, or reddish-brown spots on paper; caused by mold or oxidation of iron particles in the paper.

Wrinkling: An angular, crushed distortion.

Photography Terms

Ferrotyping: Glossy patches found on the surface of photos; resulting from lengthy contact with a smooth-surfaced storage enclosure, such as polyester or glass.

Frilling: Separation and lifting of the photographic emulsion from the edges of the support.

Silvering: Shiny or mirror-like discoloration in the shadow areas of a photographic image caused by the aging of excessive residual silver compounds.

Plastic Terms

Bubbly areas: A type of deterioration found in cellulose nitrate and acetate.

Odor: Smell of sulfur, camphor, vinegar, etc. Produced by the degradation of cellulose nitrate or acetate products. Strong odor indicates severe degradation.

Oozing: See sweating.

Sweating: A clear or yellow oily liquid found on the surface of a deteriorated cellulose nitrate or acetate object.

Textile Terms

Crocking: Rubbing off of color, resulting in the loss of dyestuff but not of fiber.

Fraying: Raveled or worn spot indicated by the separation of threads, especially on the edge of a fabric.

Tendering: A deterioration of threads, most common in silk. Usually caused by light, heat, uses of salt mordants, exposure to perspiration, or a combination of these.

Wood Terms

Alligatoring: Series of hairline cracks in old varnish, creating the appearance of alligator hide.

Checking: Slight gapping between wood cells that creates a checkerboard-like pattern. Found where wood is cut straight across the grain for carving, such as in a ball-and-claw foot.

Dry rot: Decay of seasoned timber caused by fungi that consume the cellulose of wood, leaving a soft skeleton that is readily reduced to powder.

Shrinkage: A loss of mass or size in response to dry relative humidity conditions.

Ceramic, Glass, and Stone Terms

Crizzling: Fine network of cracks on glass caused by hydration of the salts in the glass. Resulting from the leaching out of the excess alkali (cf. devitrification, weeping).

Devitrification: Loss of transparency in glass caused by the crystallization of the original ingredients (cf. crizzling).

Efflorescence: Powdery or crystalline crusts on the surface of stone, plaster, ceramics, etc. Formed when transmigrating water reacts with an object's chemical makeup or extraneous deposits from burial.

Iridescence: Color effect in glass or pottery due to the partial decomposition of the surface and the formation of innumerable thin scales, resulting in an uneven, flaky surface.

Powdering: A stone surface that is crumbling or pulverized.

Spalling: Shallow losses or flaking from the surface of stone or ceramic.

Sugaring: Erosion of the surface of marble creating a very granulated or "sugary" surface appearance.

Weeping: A wet, dripping surface on glass. Caused by a reaction between water and formic acid.

Leather Terms

Hair loss: Area of loose or missing fur in objects and garments made of pelts; often due to pest activity or improper processing of the hide.

Red rot: Powdery red substance found upon vegetable-tanned leather objects resulting from a chemical reaction with pollutants in the air.

Metal Terms

Corrosion: The chemical alteration of a metal surface caused by agents in the environment or by reagents applied purposely. Corrosion may only affect an object's color and texture without altering the form (bronze disease) or it may add to the form, producing hard nodules or crusts (rust). Bimetallic (or galvanic) corrosion results from incompatible metal contact.

Pitting: Small, irregular, shallow pinhole-sized losses scat-tered over the surface of metal caused by acid conditions or resulting from the casting process.

Tarnish: A dullness or blackening of a bright metal surface. •

Thanks to: authors of Basic Condition Reporting: A Handbook *(3rd edition, Southeastern Registrars Association, 1998): Sharon Bennett, Paisley S. Cato, Mary Giles, Patti A. Hager, Helen B. Ingalls, Elise V. LeCompte, Allyn Lord, Douglas McCash, Martha Tonissen Mayberry, Anne E. Motley, and Stacey Savatsky. Thanks also to Richard D. Buck, Margaret Holben Ellis, and to Rachel Vargas and the Straus Center for Conservation, Harvard University Art Museums, for additional glossary terms.*

MRM5 Museum

Condition Report for Collection Paintings/Drawings/Prints

Acc.#

Examiner _____ Date _____

Artist

Title

Medium

Stretcher/Panel Size	H	W	IN.
Sheet Size	H	W	IN.
Image Size	H	W	IN.
Frame/Mat Size	H	W	IN.

Sig./Date (how? where?)

Marks/Labels (what? where?)

Conservation Priority   1 2 3 4 5
Curatorial Priority   1 2 3 4 5

Priority Key
Conservation Priority
1 = Object in Jeopardy
2 = Not exhibitable as is
3 = Needs minor repair or cleaning
4 = Needs further evaluation
5 = Needs no work

Curatorial Priority
1 = Needed immediately for exhibit or loan
2 = Needed in future for exhibit or loan
3 = May have some need at some time
4 = Object need never see light of day
5 = Potential deaccession

DESCRIPTION	DEFECTS	REMARKS
FRAME ❑ Framed ❑ Backed ❑ Glass ❑ Plexi ❑ Unframed Other	❑ Broken ❑ Disjoins ❑ Glazing touches ❑ Artwork ❑ Paint loss ❑ Hanging devices ❑ Insecure ❑ Accretions ❑ Abrasions Other	
AUXILIARY SUPPORT ❑ Stretcher ❑ Keys intact ❑ Strainer ❑ Secured/nails ❑ Secured/plates ❑ Cradle ❑ Matted Other	❑ Keys missing ❑ Checks ❑ Infestation ❑ Adheared to backing ❑ Acidic materials Other	
SUPPORT ❑ Fabric ❑ Lined ❑ Wax lined ❑ Wood ❑ Masonite ❑ Paper ❑ Illust. Board Other	❑ Brittle ❑ Tear ❑ Hold ❑ Dent ❑ Bulge ❑ Sagging ❑ Draws ❑ Infestation ❑ Mold Other	

Form continues on back

DESCRIPTION	DEFECTS	REMARKS
DESIGN ❑ Oil ❑ Watercolor ❑ Tempera ❑ Pastel ❑ Gouache ❑ Pencil ❑ Ink ❑ Mixed Media Other	❑ Painter's lice ❑ Crackle ❑ Cleavage ❑ Cracking ❑ Buckling ❑ Flaking ❑ Powdering ❑ Loss ❑ Blistering ❑ Accretions ❑ Abrasions ❑ Soiled Other	
VARNISH ❑ Varnished ❑ Unvarnished	❑ Crackle ❑ Bloom ❑ Scratched ❑ Cracking ❑ Grime ❑ Accretions Other	

Action Taken upon Receipt:

Is further work needed? ❑ yes ❑ no

Describe: ❑ new mat ❑ new frame ❑ repair frame
❑ other (itemize)

Is professional attention indicated? ❑ yes ❑ no

Conservation Record

Date	Conservator	Treatment Given

Marks and Inscriptions:

Face

Reverse

5E | MARKING

TAMARA JOHNSTON AND ROBIN MEADOR-WOODRUFF
UPDATED AND EXPANDED FROM 4TH EDITION, EDITED BY TERRY SEGAL

INTRODUCTION

Marking or labeling museum objects with their identification numbers is an important part of the registrar's responsibilities. The primary goal in marking an object with its accession number is to provide a unique set of numbers and/or characters in order to connect an object with its documentation. Not all object marking is for the permanent collection; objects can also be temporarily marked for exhibition or while on deposit for purchase or gift consideration. Marking is one of the most basic, albeit invasive, procedures undertaken in registration. Methods and materials should be selected with care and the process should be fully understood before engaging in object marking.

This chapter will cover the following topics for object marking:

Section 1: Preferred Practices

Section 2: Choosing a method: Temporary, Semi-Permanent, or Permanent

Section 3: Recommended materials for Marking— See also Chart B

Section 4: Location and size of a mark on an object— See also Chart A

Section 5: Description of methods. Step by step instructions and alternative strategies

Section 6: Materials that should not be used

Chart A: Marking Specific Kinds of Objects

Chart B: Materials for Marking

Bibliography for further reading and current websites can be found on the Registrar's Committee Website: www.rc-aam.org

SECTION 1: PREFERED PRACTICES

Objects enter a museum's collection either permanently or temporarily, and should be marked accordingly. An object that is incorporated into the museum's collection by accession is an example of the former, while objects that are on loan to the museum for an exhibition, on deposit for potential acquisition, or part of auxiliary collections, such as education collections, have temporary status. It should be clear to anyone working with a museum collection, both now and in the future, which objects are part of the permanent collection and which are not. (For definitions of permanent collection and what an accessioned object is, please see chapter on Accessioning.

The marks themselves consist of the object's accession number, a unique identifier for that particular object and its parts (such as a, b, c). An accession number may include a catalog number, a lot number within the year of accessioning, the accession year, the museum's name, acronym or institutional id number (e.g., 1978.4, or 37-2-912, or DIA 1978.4, or 71.2008.2.112). Marking should be consistent within the institution and accession numbers should be centrally controlled by the registrar. Uncontrolled marking can lead to confusion and "double numbering" of museum objects.

Once an object has been assigned an accession number, that number should be used in perpetuity. As a rule, accessioned objects should not be re-numbered, although exceptions must be made when the accession number is a duplicate and has been erroneously applied to multiple objects. Occasional mistakes in object marking do occur, often after an inexperienced volunteer or staff member has been allowed to mark objects unsupervised. These mistakes must be corrected on the object and re-numbered, keeping in mind that all documentation should be checked and double-checked before proceeding with the re-numbering.

The need to correct mistakes brings up an important goal in object numbering: reversibility. As with any procedure performed on a museum object, all treatments should be reversible. Within the basic methods of direct application (pencil and ink, tying/attaching, sewing, or adhesive material), there are several techniques and options utilized in marking. Investigate the possible method and materials one can safely use to mark a particular object. *(See Section 3 for materials; Section 2 and 5 for methods in this chapter.)* Knowledge of the object itself and the materials of which it is made are necessary. If it is not clear what the object is made of, consult a conservator. In the absence of a conservator, use the least invasive technique of object marking

Best practice in object marking requires an experienced registrar or collections steward to oversee all object marking. A person may become experienced by first practicing numbering techniques on different types of non-museum objects in order to acquire an understanding of the effects the various methods of marking can have on different surfaces. Never practice object marking on museum objects. An experienced registrar or collections steward will understand not only how to mark an object but also where to mark an object, how big the accession number should be, and which method and materials should be used to mark the object.

As with any procedure in registration and collections stewardship, it is advisable to develop a set of written guidelines. A list of recommended supplies that are regularly stocked by the museum is also helpful for keeping a proper selection of supplies on hand. Written guidelines and consistently stocked supplies not only will allow a choice of materials and methods to suit the needs of all objects in the collection, but also will minimize the range of methods for each collection type to enable staff to develop familiarity and expertise.

Observe, inquire, investigate, and practice before beginning to mark any museum object.

SECTION 2: CHOOSING A METHOD: TEMPORARY VS. SEMI-PERMANENT VS. PERMANENT MARKING

Ideally, an object is marked by applying an accession number directly to the object so that it does not become disassociated from the object for which it is providing identification. The accession number must be secure enough that it cannot be accidentally removed, yet can be reversed in the future.

Care should be taken that neither the initial marking of the number nor the materials required for any subsequent removal of the number damage the object's surface. In view of this, permanent (i.e., irreversible) marking methods are not recommended for general use; however, there may be some situations in which permanent marks may be preferred. Generally, museums have found labeling the object directly with semi-permanent markings to be the most suitable method for marking their permanent collections. Temporary methods of marking are easily removed and are not applied directly to the object. Temporary marking, such as tying on or placing a tag with the object and marking a wrapping or storage container, are used for marking loans, temporary deposits, and any other objects that cannot be marked directly.

Even when temporary or semi-permanent marks are used, no given method can be considered completely reversible in all situations. For example, acrylic varnish base coats, used to prevent the absorption of inks or paints by the underlying object, may leave permanent discoloration on porous objects. Stitches may leave permanent holes in some textiles. Ties and tags can abrade or cut the surface of some objects. In addition, not all the products and methods have been systematically tested or in use long enough to determine their long-term effects. Such concerns must be weighed against the value of a durable mark. When in doubt about the marking material's effect on the safety of the object, consult a conservator.

Temporary Markings Methods
Temporary marking methods include tying or attaching a tag to the object, marking the storage box, sleeve, vial, etc., or placing loose labels, tags or entry receipts with the object. Temporary marking methods should

be used as a primary method for any objects which cannot be marked directly, such as:

- All loans and temporary deposits (non-accessioned items entering the museum)

- Objects that have an unstable, highly uneven, or friable surface (e.g., weathered wood, severely corroded metals) or a very powdery surface (e.g., painted ethnographic wooden objects, some leather objects)

- Very small objects, such as jewelry, coins or stamps. (Although it is possible to legibly mark tiny objects, marking coins or stamps may decrease their value.)

- Many plastic, vinyl and rubber objects

Temporary marking should be used as a secondary method for:

- All objects in storage.

- Large objects on which the direct marking is not easily located.

- Objects that are stored or displayed outdoors, such as farming or military equipment, vehicles, or sculpture. (When permanent marking is not appropriate or when semi-permanent marking media have proven not to remain stable in extreme heat or cold, moisture, and sunlight.)

Temporary Marking: Using Tags

The most common process for marking an object with a temporary number is to loosely tie a tag, marked with loan number or accession number, to the object. Use Tables 1 and 2 to select appropriate tags and ties. Consider all conditions to which the tags and ties will be exposed - weather, oil, water, chemicals, insects. Use the same archival quality materials for tagging permanent collections and loans, as temporary loans sometimes remain longer than initially anticipated. Pencil is recommended for writing the numbers on paper tags. If corrosion resistant wire or metal tags are used, both ends of the tag should be secured to prevent the tag from moving and continually abrading the object.

Tags should be placed in locations that will not be seen when the objects are on display so that tags can remain attached to the object in the gallery. If tags must be removed while objects are on display, the tags should be reattached as soon as the objects are removed from their display location. Permanently sited objects, such as large public sculptures, do not need to be marked or tagged directly as they are unlikely to be moved. The accession number can be included on a commemorative marker.

Temporary Marking: on Object Housing

If it is not possible to tag the object, the object should be placed in an archival sleeve, vial, box, tray, or small polyethylene bag, which is marked with the number; or, a loose tag or label should be placed with the object. If the object will be stored in polyethylene in a location with wide variations in temperature, several small holes should be made in the bag, or the points of the corners should be cut off the bag, to prevent condensation. Avoid other plastics, which may exude plasticizers and other harmful substances. Tags placed inside bags should be marked with pencil, not ink, as direct transfer of the ink or off gassing may damage some objects.

Temporary Marking: on Textiles

Textile fragments may have loose tags placed in their wrappings, or the numbers can be marked in pencil on the wrappings. Matted objects may have the number marked in pencil on the reverse of the mat. Framed objects may have the number marked on the backing board in pencil, or tags may be attached to the screw eye, d-ring, or metal hanger.

Temporary Marking: Fine Art Exhibitions

In the case of paintings, drawings, prints, and other framed works that are lent to special exhibitions; a label is often applied to the reverse of the protective backing. The label usually includes the loan or catalog number, the title or a description of the object, medium, artist or maker's name, and the title, location, and dates of the exhibition. This label is left on the backing when it is returned to the lender as a record of exhibition history. Labels in common use include both pressure-sensitive (self-stick) adhesive labels, as well as gummed paper labels which must be moistened with water for application. Gummed paper labels are preferred because the adhesive of some pressure-sensitive labels often deteriorates, leaving a sticky residue, or the adhesive becomes brittle;

such labels pose the risk of detachment and possible transfer to the surface of another painting or object. The adhesive can also permeate wood, leaving a permanent stain and possibly a tacky residue. Often gummed labels can be removed and reapplied if the backing board is replaced, thereby preserving the exhibition history of the artwork. Gummed paper or pressure sensitive labels should never be applied directly to the object itself.

Temporary Marking: Natural History Specimens

Some natural history specimens require special tagging considerations. Fluid-preserved specimens often have two levels of labeling. Fluid-resistant tags or labels marked with the catalog number are tied to specimens or placed inside the jar and a label with more extensive information is placed on the outside of the container. It is important to remember that tags or labels inside the jars of fluid-preserved specimens may abrade and lose their marking if they are jostled during transit, and the label on the outside of the jar will ensure that the specimens' documentation is not lost.

Vertebrate specimens may have numerous tags representing past owners or treatments. These tags usually remain attached to the specimen and a new tag is added when needed.. The existing tags may represent a variety of materials (paper, metal, wood, leather) that may or may not be archival. If it is necessary to remove such tags for any reason they should be retained in an archival object file.

Specimens may come into contact with many fluids during treatment and cleaning. For this reason, Resistall paper has sometimes been used for tags on dry specimens. However, the preferred pH range for labels in contact with proteinaceous tissues is 6.0 to 8.5 pH and the pH level of Resistall paper ranges from 4.5 to 5.2 pH. A pH neutral paper (lignin-free or 100 percent rag, not alkaline buffered) or an inert material (polyester or polypropylene) is preferred.

Alkaline-buffered paper is sometimes used for labeling dry botanical specimens because it is desirable for maintaining cellulose stability. Using buffered paper with botanical specimens should be approached with caution as the alkalinity may negatively affect non-cellulose components of plants, such as resins, and impair future study of these materials.

Semi-permanent Marking Methods

There are four main methods for marks that can be applied directly to museum objects, will not cause deterioration, and can be removed in the future. The four most commonly used marking methods (in non-living collections) are discussed in Section 5: barrier coat with ink or paint, adhered labels, sewn labels, and pencil marking.

Permanent Marking Methods

Permanent marks, although rarely used, may be considered for some types of collections. Permanent marks should not be used without careful consideration of the ramifications of permanently disfiguring objects. The location for such marks should be chosen with extreme care. Permanent marks may be useful as a deterrent to theft, as in the case of firearms. While permanent marks may decrease the monetary value of such objects, the gain in terms of security may be significant.

Examples of objects on which permanent markings may be desirable include objects used by interpreters in living history settings, such as cooking pots, utensils, and farm implements, as well as objects that are stored or displayed outdoors. There is no means of applying and maintaining a durable, reversible mark on such collections. Additionally, reproductions used in demonstration collections should have permanent numbers to prevent the objects from being identified or sold as authentic if the numbers wear off. Other examples are archeology or anthropology collections that have bone fragments or pottery shards numbering in the thousands. Such artifacts may be virtually impossible to identify, even with photography. The separation of the artifact from its identification number may destroy that object's value for future study purposes.

For this reason, natural history specimens are sometimes marked directly with permanent ink because the labor-intensive semi-permanent methods may make the marking of some objects (e.g., all bones of a bird skeleton) impractical.

Permanent marking methods for various types of objects are discussed below.

When marking authentic objects, choose the method least destructive to its surface. A discrete number applied with permanent ink may be less damaging than etching the object's surface, for example. Do not use any method that will cause future corrosion or continued deterioration of the object. Museums often use a separate prefix and/or color code to distinguish reproductions or demonstration collections from the permanent collection, and the marking should reflect this.

In the past, paper has been marked with permanent ink, or a sharpened 2H (#3) hard pencil was used to indent or emboss the paper. Many museums stamped their name or mark with ink on the reverse of prints and manuscripts to indicate ownership. This practice has been largely discontinued by museums because the marks are not reversible and the ink may migrate to the front, leaving stains on the image and causing permanent damage. Libraries or manuscript collections that wish to continue the practice of stamping materials with ink should consult the Library of Congress' publication Marking Paper Manuscripts, http://www.loc.gov/preserv/marking.html also cited in the bibliography.

Numbers can be engraved, branded, or stamped on wood. Leather, hides, and pelts can be marked with permanent ink or a stamping tool. Textiles can be marked with permanent ink. When using ink on porous materials, be sure that the ink does not bleed, thereby obliterating the number. Semi-porous materials such as bone, plastic, and ceramics, can be marked with permanent ink or can be etched or imprinted with an engraving tool or stamping tool. Non-porous or impervious materials, including metals, can be etched with a scriber or engraving tool, or the number can be imprinted with a stamping tool.

SECTION 3: RECOMMENDED MARKING MATERIALS: PERMANENT, LIGHT, COLOR FAST

Materials used to mark objects must be as chemically stable as possible and demonstrate excellent aging characteristics to ensure the longevity, long-term legibility, and reversibility of the number. The products suggested throughout this chapter were selected after reviewing the marking materials reported in current use in a 1995 survey of 205 museums. Pen tests were performed by a group of registrars and conservators

in 2006. In addition, a supplemental survey of registrars was undertaken in 2008. An effort has been made to include archival quality materials, as well as products that are easy to use, inexpensive, and readily available. It is recognized that many museums will not have the expertise or facilities for mixing chemicals. All materials discussed in this chapter are readily available on-line from conservation, archival, or art supply companies. See Chart B for details of materials.

Conservators have not reached a consensus on some of these materials, and there are pros and cons to each. New products continue to enter the market and further testing may cause some of the materials listed in this chapter to fall out of favor. Keep in mind that the performance of a commercial product may vary as formulations change from time to time. It is recommended that products be tested on non-museum objects before use. Simple tests such as exposure to sunlight, water, or solvents can be easily performed. A Material Safety Data Sheet (MSDS) can be obtained from the product's manufacturer. This is a useful way to identify materials which may be harmful to museum objects, as well as staff, as the manufacturer is required to list all toxic, flammable, and corrosive materials.

When choosing marking materials evaluate the risks to which objects, and the numbers with which they are marked, are likely to be exposed.

- Will the objects be on display for long periods of time? Light fastness of inks and paints will be a prime concern.

- Are there oils on the surface that cannot, or should not, be removed? Plastic ties and tags may be preferred in place of paper and cotton string so that the oils do not damage the tag.

- Will the objects be at risk for accidental water contact, such as overhanging water pipes or outdoor display? Waterproof materials will be desired.

- Are pests a problem? Insect resistant materials may be preferred to paper and other natural materials that provide food for pests.

SECTION 4: LOCATION AND SIZE

The number should be placed in a location that is unobtrusive while on display, yet clearly visible or easily accessible when the object is in storage. Choose an area that is unlikely to be displayed or photographed. Do not obscure maker's marks, major design elements, or old inventory numbers. Marks attached by previous owners should be retained, as they contribute to the object's history.

The number should not be applied to physically unstable surfaces, such as loose or flaking paint, or to pitted or corroded areas, as numbers will be difficult to apply and remove and may harm the object's surface. The number should not be placed in an area that receives wear, friction, or pressure from the object's own weight or its mount. With the exception of small objects with concave bottoms or objects that have ornamentation or decoration, which would make numbering elsewhere difficult or unsightly, avoid marking the bottom of an object.

Since handling of museum objects is the greatest single source of damage, the number should not be placed where excessive handling will be necessary to locate it. Large, heavy objects should be marked on the reverse near the base, not on the bottom, to avoid the need to lift or tip the object to read the number. Large paintings may be marked at diagonal corners of the frame or backing so that the number can be easily located whether hung low or high on a storage screen or wall. Rugs and other large textiles may also be marked at diagonal corners so that the labels can be easily located regardless of the direction in which the pieces are rolled for storage. If the number will not be visible in storage, an auxiliary tag should be used; the tag can be left in storage to represent the displaced object.

All detachable parts and accessory pieces should be individually marked (e.g., 1978.120A and 1978.120B). Examples might be a snuffbox and cover, a knife and sheath, or frag-ments of a broken object. The number should never be applied only to a bracket, arm, or trim piece that could become separated from the object.

Choose a consistent location on objects of the same type. When a conflict arises, the highest priority should be given to ensuring the least disruption to the object. Some objects may have no readily apparent location on which to mark the number (e.g., complex abstract sculptures, automobiles). When an object is marked in an unusual or difficult-to-find location, make note of the location in the object's file. Add an auxiliary tag if necessary.

Marks should be unobtrusive yet clearly legible. Use common sense guided by the size of the object, the location of the number, and the marking method, when determining the size of the numbers. Numbers may range from less than 1/8 inch for very small objects to 3/8 inch for larger objects. Some types of collections call for larger numbers, such as large-scale industrial artifacts or living history collections where numbers must be located in dark historic interiors. Numbers applied to areas such as backing boards of paintings, textile storage boxes, or auxiliary tags may be as large as desired, as they are not applied to the object itself or visible when on display. See Chart A for advice on placement for particular objects.

SECTION 5: DESCRIPTION OF METHODS. STEP-BY-STEP INSTRUCTION

Method 1: Barrier Coat with Ink or Paint Marks

Recommended for most three-dimensional objects. (Not recommended for paper, textiles, plastics, leathers, and fibrous materials.)

Examine the object to determine a suitable location for marking the number. See section on object location and Chart A for recommended locations. If an object is constructed of more than one material, place the number on the smoother, harder, less porous surface. Generally, mark on the back, in the lower right side of an object (if there is a back, right side).

Clean the area to be marked. The area to be marked should be clean and free from dust and surface dirt. Dust the surface with a soft, clean brush. Some objects may need additional cleaning before a number can be applied. Do not use a solvent (not even water) to clean an object without the advice of a conservator. If using a solvent, stop the process immediately should a change or "bloom" appear in the surface of the object. Never clean flaking, crazed, or unstable surfaces such as deteriorating ancient glass; consult a conservator.

Apply a base coat of clear varnish. Acryloid B72 in acetone is recommended for the base varnish. A base coat should be used on most surfaces, including non-porous ones. Ink or paint may not adhere well to smooth surfaces; some inks bead, and both ink and paint are easily abraded from non-porous surfaces. Some permanent inks are formulated to etch metal and other materials to improve their adherence, and metal oxide pigments in paints have the potential to react with the surface of metal or organic objects. A reversible varnish provides a smooth, hard writing surface and may add a measure of security for the number, as it is not readily removable without the appropriate solvent. In addition, mistakes can be corrected during the process, and numbers can be removed with a solvent at a later date without affecting the surface of the object.

Choose a varnish that is compatible (i.e., will not dissolve or damage, during application or removal) with the surface of the object to be marked. See Chart B, Tables 3 and 4, for recommended varnishes and solvent compatibility. When choosing a location for the number, keep in mind that the varnish may leave a permanent stain. Apply a neat rectangle of varnish just large enough to contain the accession number with an artist's brush. Allow the varnish to dry 10–5 minutes or until it is no longer sticky to the touch before applying numbers. Drying times will vary with the temperature and humidity levels. It could take 30–60 minutes if it is too humid and too warm. If bubbles form in the varnish, it is most likely too thick and more solvent should be added to provide a clear, smooth surface for marking.

Porous materials, such as unfinished wood, may need more than one coat of varnish or an alternative method. A thickened varnish may prevent extensive penetration into porous materials. Apply one coat of varnish at a time, allowing each coat to dry, until a discernible film is visible on the surface. While drying times vary, a thicker varnish will require a longer drying time. An alternative method of marking (such as adhesion) should be employed if the object is too porous.

Write the number on the base coat. Numbers can be written with a permanent pigment-based ink or acrylic paint using a fine-point technical nib pen, or a crow quill pen, or a fine artist's brush. Disposable marking pens, such as Pigma pens, may also be used. (See Chart B, Tables 5, 6, and 7.) Do not press too firmly when using a crow quill or metal-nibbed pen, as the nibs can cut through the base coat and scratch some surfaces. Take care not to drip inks or paints. Practice a few numbers on a test object before attempting to mark a museum object.

Choice of color is determined by the color of the object to be marked, as well as the past practice of the institution. See Chart A. Preferred practice is to use carbon black and titanium dioxide white; they are very stable pigments and should meet the needs of most collections. Dark objects are usually marked with white numbers. (Alternatively, a base coat of white can be placed on the clear barrier coat before the number is written in black but this method should only be employed if the institution has practiced this method in the past.) White numbers are commonly used on glass objects, as white is less obtrusive for display purposes.

Note on color: If another color (such as red) has been used consistently by the institution in the past, it may be acceptable to continue the practice for the sake of consistency. First check with the manufacturer regarding the light fastness of the pigment intended for use. (Red can be used successfully on many objects, except those with very dark, red, or green backgrounds; on the latter, such as patinated bronzes, red creates an optical illusion and is difficult to read. Keep in mind that many red pigments are not light fast and red numbers cannot be read by color-blind individuals.)

Using a compatible varnish, apply a topcoat of varnish over the number. Acryloid B67 in mineral spirits is recommended for the topcoat. A protective topcoat is used to prevent accidental removal of the accession number from contact with water and other solvents. It also protects against abrasion or chipping due to handling. It will help prevent number loss in the event of a disaster. Allow the number to dry approximately twenty to thirty minutes before applying a topcoat.

For the topcoat, use a material containing a

solvent that will not soften the base coat, e.g., Acryloid B67 in mineral spirits over Acryloid B72 in acetone, Acryloid B72 in ethanol over Acryloid B72 in acetone, or a water-based emulsion or dispersion over a solvent-based varnish, according to a conservator's instructions.

Load the brush with varnish and apply it in a single light stroke. The bristles float over the varnish film and will not rub the number. The topcoat should be a slightly smaller rectangle than the base coat, particularly if a different material is used. Allow the topcoat to dry thirty minutes, or until it is no longer tacky, before moving the object.

Condensed Version for Applying Marks using Method 1: "Acryloid Sandwich"

1. Examine the object to determine what materials the object is made of and the best location for marking the number. Determine which materials will be best to use to make the mark. Consult Appendices as necessary.

2. Using a soft brush or clean, lint-free cloth, clean the area to be marked.

3. Test the base coat, Acryloid B72 in acetone, and make sure it is the right consistency for a label base. It should be fluid, not too thick. Thin with acetone if it bubbles when set. Allow the base coat to dry thoroughly, approximately ten to fifteen minutes, depending on temperature and humidity.

4. Write the number on the base coat. Use a Pigma pen, quill and nib with ink, or a tiny paintbrush and acrylic paint. See appendices to make proper choice. Allow the mark to dry thoroughly, approximately ten minutes depending on the marking tool, temperature and humidity.

5. Apply a topcoat of varnish over the number. Acryloid B67 in mineral spirits is recommended for the topcoat. Allow the label to dry for at least thirty minutes before returning it to its permanent storage location.

Method 2: Adhered Labels

Adhered labels may be substituted for Method 1. Read the section on applying labels using Method 1 before proceeding with an alternative method. This method is less intrusive than Method 1. Less foreign material penetrates the surface and most of the adhesive is removed with the paper, leaving only a small amount of residue that can be easily removed.

This method is suitable for most objects and is ideal for flexible, porous, and irregular, uneven surfaces. As with Method 1, adhered labels should not be placed over unstable paint, flaking lacquer, or other or insecure surfaces.

The papers and adhesives should be chosen carefully. Commercial adhesives are not recommended because they do not provide the stability or reversibility desired for marking. Several adhesives are recommended below. If instituting an adhered label system for the first time, consult a conservator or practice the method on a non-museum object first. The label should be as small as possible and placed in an area that does not receive light exposure, as the label will cause uneven fading of the object's surface.

Method 2, Option 1: Adhered Paper Labels for Marking for a Variety of Objects

This method can be used with laser printed labels on Perma/Dur bond paper, or Japanese tissue. See also other Options below.

Advantages to using this method of numbering:

• Fewer errors because of the ability to write the number on a secondary material, rather than directly on the object.

• It is reversible.

• It is controllable.

• Can use various types of papers—including computer-generated numbers.

• Can use ink or pencil.

• Can make solutions in small batches as needed.

• No long drying times between bottom layers, number layer and topcoat.

Tools:

• Clipboard

• Japanese Tissue

• Kozo, hinging tissue, etc. depending on what is to be numbered

• Perma/Dur Bond. For printing numbers on a

laser printer or where a more opaque label and a straight cut are needed

•Acryloid (Paraloid) B-72 granules. B72 = synthetic resin, soluble/reversible with acetone.

•Acetone. Reagent grade is preferred (use a dropper to thin acetone if using small quantities such as pre-mixed bottles of B72 in acetone).

•Cellofas B 3500-SCMC (Sodium carboxymethyl cellulose), also known as "sod. CMC"

•Jade 403N (PVA emulsion)

•Krylon Clear Spray Acrylic or Lascaux Fix

•De-ionized or distilled water

•Pigma Pen

•Color Shaper

•Teflon-coated Spatula

•Dissecting Tweezers

•Tiny Paintbrushes (try a short script/liner paint brush in size 1 or zero)

•Pencil, #2 or HB

•Scalpel

•Ruler

•Scissors

•Ethafoam Block

•Silicone release paper

•Pins

•Blotting paper

•Clean cloth

Preparing adhesives:

B-72 granules should be mixed with acetone **24 hours in advance** of using so that the mixture is thoroughly dissolved. In a glass jar, dissolve 25 grams of granules in 75 ml of acetone, stir and cover. B-72 must be stored in an airtight container. Make sure the lip of the jar and lid are clean of any dissolved B-72 before sealing it, as the residue will cause the lid to adhere to the jar. If the jar is sealed shut, invert the jar so that it rests on its lid (the acetone in the solution will loosen the bond) or invert the bottle in a larger container of acetone.

Before using the B-72, add more acetone to bring the solution up to 100 ml total volume. At any time, if the solution has bubbles in it when applied, thin it with more acetone.

Mixing the proper adhesive is like cooking. It requires developing a feel for it in order to recognize a good consistency. Experiment with adhesive mixtures on practice objects before using it on real museum objects. To mix the Cellofas and Jade, begin with a 1:3 ratio (one part Cellofas to three parts Jade).

Cellofas B3500 = Sodium carboxymethylcellulose is a cellulose ether and is a weak paper adhesive; it is soluble in water and provides reversibility.

Jade 403 = Plasticized polyvinyl acetate emulsion is synthetic emulsion that gives strength to an adhesive when mixed with Cellofas. (Jade 403 on its own is not reversible with water.)

Advantages to using Cellofas/Jade: It is water-based and compatible with many materials and substrates. It is safe (no safety issues, toxic fumes, etc.), easy to use and easy to clean up. It can be used on lacquer, most plastics, and organic materials.

Note: B-72 will make Japanese tissue translucent and the number will be difficult to see on a dark colored object. For dark objects, use a heavier Japanese tissue (more opaque) with the Cellofas/Jade adhesive (which is the more opaque option) and the resulting mark will show up better on dark colored objects. Perma/Dur Bond, being the most opaque, will also show up better on dark objects.

Step-by-step instructions:

1. Gather needed tools

2. Examine the object and select an appropriate place to put the number.

If using ink on Japanese tissue, it may be necessary to size the tissue first.

3. In a well-ventilated area or outside, size the Japanese tissue with the clear acrylic or Lascaux Fix. Do not saturate the paper. Practice on scrap tissue paper first to get the feel of lightly coating the more expensive Japanese tissue. Let the tissue air-dry. Skip this step if using Perma/Dur Bond.

4. Stir up the B-72 solution and thin with

acetone as necessary. If using Cellofas with Jade, first prepare the Cellofas by mixing the powder with distilled water at a 1:3 ratio. Use a micro spatula to mix together one part prepared Cellofas with three parts of Jade.

5. Place the tissue or paper on a clipboard.

6. Use Pigma pen or pencil to write the number on the tissue. Make sure the size of the number is appropriate for the object and where it is to be placed.

7. Draw a box around the number with paintbrush wet with de-ionized water or distilled water to set up a "water tear."

8. Use spatula straight edge to pull out the number along the wet lines of the "water tear," creating many "hairs."
When printing numbers on Perma/Dur Bond, or when a straight edge is desired instead of the "hairs," skip #7 and #8 and use a scissors to cut out the number. It is recommended to round the corners to reduce lifting of the paper label.

9. Put label face down on the Silicone release paper

10. Paint the back with B-72 or the Cellofas/Jade mixture. Apply the adhesive from the middle out. Pull the hairs outward with the adhesive. If using B-72, let it tack up a bit before moving on to next step.

11. Pick up label with tweezers

12. Put label in appropriate spot, tamp down gently with the color shaper. Pull hairs out and tamp down. If using a cut number, make sure all the edges are tamped down.

13. Let the number dry before returning it to storage (Dry times will vary according to temperature and humidity conditions but generally, adhered labels should dry for approximately 30 minutes.)

Method 2, Option 2: Japanese Tissue Paper with Starch paste

Recommended for use on bark cloth, mats, and plant materials; may be used on some basketry items and leathers but this method requires weight on the paste until it dries.

1. Water-tear a small rectangle of Japanese tissue large enough to accommodate the number easily. Do not cut the tissue; it is important that the long fibers of the tissue are exposed to add strength to the bond.

2. Place the piece of tissue on top of blotting paper and carefully write the number on the tissue with ink. The blotting paper should draw off moisture from the ink and prevent bleeding. Be careful not to rip the paper fibers with the nib of the pen when writing; it is best to use no pressure at all. Allow the ink to dry thoroughly before proceeding.

3. Turn the piece of tissue over on the blotting paper and coat the back of it with wheat or rice starch paste or methyl cellulose with a brush. Use as dilute a solution of paste as possible. The blotting paper should draw off excess moisture from the paste.

4. Lift the tissue carefully from the blotting paper with tweezers and place it right side up on the object in the selected marking location. Using a stiff stencil brush, gently tamp the tissue into place to ensure good contact.

5. Place a piece of blotting paper on top of the number and gently rub it with a finger to draw off excess moisture.

6. Insert a piece of spun-bonded polyester (Reemay) between the number and the blotting paper; if the object is flat and not brittle, a weight without sharp corners or projecting points may be placed on top of the blotting paper. The Reemay will prevent the blotting paper from sticking to the number. Allow the paste to dry weighted for 10–15 minutes, then remove the weight, blotting paper and Reemay and allow the paste to dry thoroughly.

7. To remove the label, roll a slightly moistened cotton swab over the paper surface until the paper is damp. After a few moments, the label may be lifted off with tweezers.

Some materials, such as baskets, may require a paste with greater adhesion. A stronger adhesive can be made using equal parts starch or methylcellulose paste and an acrylic emulsion (See Method 2, option 1 above).

Method 2, Option 3: Printed-paper Labels Adhered with Acrylic or PVA Emulsion

Recommended for many three-dimensional objects with firm surfaces. Also very useful for small items or items with an irregular surface, since very small legible numbers can be printed with a laser printer. Use either the Century Gothic or Arial type font. Century Gothic produces the most legible number when the character spacing is expanded by .3 to .4, but it is not always available as a font option. Depending upon the font, anywhere from a 3 point to 11 point size can be used.

1. Determine the size of lettering required for the label. The lettering size depends upon the size of the item and the surface available for label placement. As a general rule, use a larger point size on large items and a smaller point size on small items. The numbers also will be clearer if the Bold feature is used. Some guidelines for smaller fonts:

a. Century Gothic point size 6 (**97-86-543**), 7 (**2009-20-1**), or 8 (**2009-20-1**) for large items.

b. Century Gothic point size 5 (**97-86-543**) for medium sized items.

c. Century Gothic point size 4 for small items.

d. Century Gothic point size 3, characters expanded by .4, might be used in extreme cases for tiny items, but it is not generally recommended.

2. Create numbers and sizes in the appropriate word processing package, load the laser printer with laser quality acid-free paper, and send the print job. Do not use labels printed on daisy-wheel, dot matrix, or ink jet printers. These types of printers do not use a stable ink fusion process. Laser printers, on the other hand, use the same xerographic process as modern photocopiers. The laser toner is composed of carbon-based ink with a stable thermoplastic polymer (polystyrene, acrylics or polyesters) that is thermally fused to the paper.

3. When labeling many items it is most efficient to create a consecutive, columnar, single-spaced list of numbers. To separate the numbers, cut the paper with scissors as close as possible along one vertical side of the numbers. Cut horizontally between each of the single-spaced numbers, then cut the paper along the second vertical side allowing the numbers to drop on the table. If possible, cut the labels with rounded, rather than square, corners. It is generally not feasible to round the corners of the smaller letter point sizes.

4. Attach the label using an under- and over-coat of either Jade 403 (PVA emulsion) or Rhoplex AC-234 (Acrylic emulsion). Jade 403 results in a thicker, less shiny coat than any of the Acrylics. Acryloid B-72 should be used with caution as the solvent will tend to "melt" printed lettering. The emulsions do not contain toxic solvents and are good choices when a fume extractor system is not in use. Do not let the under-coat dry before applying the paper label.

5. Allow the label to dry completely and lose its tack. In dry conditions (Rh lower than 30 percent), the drying process might be completed within an hour. In more humid situations (Rh higher than 45 percent), the drying process might last a day or more.

6. Before the labeling emulsion sets up or hardens, it is soluble in water. For this reason, keep a vial of water and paper towel nearby to clean the paintbrush. After drying, the emulsion is no longer soluble in water but is soluble in acetone.

7. If it is necessary to remove the number at a later date, use the tip of an acetone dipped cotton swab to dab the surface. Once the emulsion has dissolved, the paper label can be removed and replaced. For a complete removal of the label, roll an acetone soaked cotton swab over the surface until the remaining emulsion residue has been removed.

Thanks to: Elaine Hughes for her work on the printed-paper label technique.

Method 3, Option 1: Handwritten Labels Sewn with Cotton Tape or Reemay

Recommended for most textiles. Do not sew a label on textiles that are disintegrating or in very poor condition. May also be used for some basketry materials and leather objects.

Tools and Materials:

Pigma = Pen *(SAKURA Pigma Micron recommended)*

Scissors

Unbleached Cotton Tape, tight weave, 1/2"

Natural color cotton thread

Needle, size 7 or 8 for most things

De-ionized or distilled water

Orvus detergent

Clothes Iron

(Drying rack)

1. Choose a material for making the label.

Fabric tape (cotton, polyester, or linen) is usually used for making labels for costumes, rugs, tapestries, and other textile objects. Fabric tape is available in widths from 1/4 to 1 inch and wider but the 1/2 inch tape is the best choice for most labels. It is preferable to use fabric tape of varying size, appropriate for the size of the object, rather than cutting a label from fabric such as unbleached muslin. The double selvages of the fabric tape will prevent the label from unraveling. Unbleached tapes are preferred. Use a tape that is fine and tightly woven, as it will make writing the number easier.

Some museums use an inert material such as non-woven polyester (Reemay) for sewn labels. An advantage of this material is that it does not ravel at the edges and can be cut to any desired size. Reemay and related materials are purchased in bolts and are available in various weights, some of which may be abrasive to delicate fabrics. Choose a lightweight with a smooth finish dense enough to accept the number. Some conservators caution against using Pellon, another non-woven polyester, because the material has a resin finish which may be harmful to some museum objects. Only non-fusible fabrics should be used. Soft grades of Tyvek may also be used for sewn labels. Tyvek may require sealing with B72 to prevent bleeding of the ink.

2. Write the number on the twill tape. Leave about 1/4 inch on each side of the number for adhering to textile.

3. Iron the label to set the ink. Wash the label in a container using distilled or de-ionized water and Orvus detergent. Rinse several times in clear, distilled or de-ionized water.

4. Iron the label dry or let it air-dry on a drying rack.

5. Determine where the label should be placed. Turn under the cut ends of the label. Sew the label in place using the needle and thread. Sew between the threads of the textile (object) and not through the textile weave.

For Delicate or Fragile textiles:

4-mil Reemay may be used in place of cotton twill tape if the textile is delicate or fragile.

Do not iron the Reemay as it may melt onto the iron. Let the ink thoroughly dry 15–20 minutes before handling and washing. Turning under the ends of Reemay will not be necessary.

Method 3, Option 2: Typed Labels Sewn with Tyvek or Reemay

Using a Typewriter with Reemay or Tyvek for textile labels

The numbers are usually typed on non-woven polyesters such as Reemay. The Reemay is cut into sheets and fed into the typewriter like a sheet of paper. Non-correctable or one-strike carbon ribbons are recommended, as they tend to be the most durable, but they are becoming obsolete and may be difficult to obtain. Most correctable carbon ribbon impressions become tough and smudge-resistant if allowed to cure two to five days after application, but some stay soft indefinitely. Fabric ribbons are not recommended as they tend to smear continually. Do not put Reemay or Tyvek in a laser printer. To test a typewriter ribbon, type a series of sample numbers on the labeling material. Rub the numbers to see if the ink smears, and eliminate any typewriter ribbons that do. Second, rinse the tags in hot soapy water to see if the ink runs when wet. Third, rub each number while it is still wet. If the ink is fast in each of these tests, the marking material may be used.

1. Choose a material for making the label.

2. Type the numbers on the fabric. Leave about 1/4" on each side of the number for adhering to textile.

3. Wash the fabric and let it dry before cutting the tags apart.

Laundering the tags will remove acid released by some kinds of marking inks. Some museums size the label to provide a better writing surface or seal the label with varnish before and after marking the number to prevent the ink from bleeding. Sizing will result in a stiffer tag, which may be abrasive to some textiles. Sealing the tape should not be necessary if the earlier steps for testing the ink and laundering the tag are followed. If the tape is to be sized or sealed, leave the ends untreated so that they can be turned under for stitching. Reemay may be swished through an acetone bath to remove excess typewriter ink.

4. Stitch the label to the object.

Labels should be gently stitched, never attached with staples, pins, or adhesives. Select a sturdy area on the reverse side, preferably at the hem or near a strong selvage. Be consistent in the choice of location. See the "Marking specific kinds of objects" section for suggested locations for specific items. Place the stitches between the warp and weft threads of the fabric; do not pierce the threads. See Table 9 for suggested needles and thread.

While all conservators agree that the number of stitches should be limited, opinions vary as to where the stitches should be placed. Some conservators recommend stitching the tag around all four sides with a loose running or basting stitch to prevent the possibility of picking up the textile by the tag or accidently catching a finger in the tag and thereby snagging or tear-ing the textile. Other conservators recommend only a few tacking stitches at each end to avoid piercing the textile in so many places. A good rule of thumb is to evaluate the specific collection. How often will it be handled and by whom? Are the fabrics strong and in good condition or weak and deteriorating?

Select a stitching method that best meets marking needs with the least possible intrusion to the textile. For fragile textiles, such as lace, the label can be attached with a single loop of thread, leaving the tag hanging loose. Use a loop long enough for easy positioning of the tag, yet as short as possible to avoid snagging. This method can be used for small, flat items so the tag can be tucked out of sight when the object is on display. It may not be possible to tag directly some very fragile textiles, such as silks, without causing extensive damage. Alternatively, the accession number can be marked on the storage container. Permanently mounted textiles should be labeled on the mount.

Use a single strand of thread. Do not use small, tight stitches, which will cut the threads of the textile or distort the fabric. Machine-wound spool threads shrink for about a year after being unwound and may pucker the textile if the stitches are pulled tight. Begin and end the stitching with several backstitches in the label, not the textile. Do not use knots, which tend to break or disassemble or may pull through the textile creating holes. Fabric tape should be turned under 1/4 inch at the ends to prevent raveling; tack down the corners. To remove a tag, cut each stitch, taking care not to cut the textile, and carefully pull out the individual threads.

Method 4: Pencil (Various Types, See Media Type for Pencil Recommendation)

Recommended for paper and photographic materials.

1. Select a location for marking the number.
Works of art on paper, such as prints, drawings, and photographs, should be marked on the reverse side behind a non-image area at the

lower margin. The number should be consistently placed in the same corner on every object. If the object is mounted or hinged, in addition to marking it directly, mark the number with pencil on the back of the mount or on the face of the mount, below the object. This will eliminate unnecessary handling of the object to locate the number. Framed works on paper should be marked on the frame and backing in the same manner as framed paintings.

See the "Marking specific kinds of objects" section for suggested locations for other paper and photographic materials.

2. Select an appropriate pencil.

Most paper objects are marked with a medium lead pencil; hard lead can crease or dent paper, while soft lead has a tendency to smudge. Recommended grades are #2, HB, F, and H. For a further discussion of pencil grades, see Table 5. If uncertain about the performance of a particular pencil, test it on several weights and finishes of paper prior to using it to mark objects. Modern resin-coated photographic papers and other glossy papers may resist standard pencil markings. Try a #1 pencil, a Stabilo All Graphite pencil or a Berol China Marker. Do not stack objects marked with these materials without interleaving with acid-free tissue to prevent the markings from transferring to the image below, or place the items in individual acid-free sleeves.

3. Place the object on a firm surface and write gently to avoid indentation.

This is especially important for coated photographic papers, such as Cibachrome prints, on which the emulsion is easily bruised, and thin sheets, such as tissue and albumen prints, particularly if the image is printed to the edge of the sheet. Use only #2 or HB pencils, or softer, on these objects. Dull the point of a newly sharpened pencil by scribbling on a sheet of paper. Remove excess lead by blotting once, not rubbing, with a vinyl eraser.

In cases where an object cannot be marked directly see the "Temporary marking methods"

or the "Marking specific kinds of objects" sections for alternatives.

Method 5: Bar Codes and Other Technology
A small number of museums have used bar code labels or tags and RFID with varying degrees of success. Many museums find this technology to be too costly to implement because either the hardware and software are too expensive to purchase and maintain, or the amount of time it would take to apply the barcode to objects already marked is prohibitive. A number of museums have successfully used bar coding as a temporary marking method for tracking large-scale object moves. Most museum collection management database programs have bar-coding capabilities.

The most successful use has been as an auxiliary method for inventory purposes where objects are still marked directly with accession numbers. The production of bar code tags requires a computer, a dot matrix or laser printer, and an inexpensive software package. The bar code information can be printed on any type of paper or label, including acid-free stock. The number itself can be the actual catalog or accession number for the object or a dummy number. The bar code can also include the storage location for the object. Additional information, such as the culture or artist, can be included on the tag.

Reading the numbers requires a scanning device. The least expensive type is a pen scanner, which is attached to a computer and functions in place of a keyboard. This type of scanner is not recommended. as it is necessary to almost touch the bar code and the pen must remain tethered to the computer so that objects must be brought to the scanner. The more expensive hand-held scanners with a built-in keypad are preferred. The bar code can be read at a greater distance and the scanner can read upside down, sideways, and through Mylar, although reflection is sometimes a problem. The light emitted is cool.

The disadvantage with bar codes as a primary marking method is that tags can become separated from objects. With the exception of larger objects, there are no satisfactory methods of adhering the tags, which are usually larger and less discrete than a simple accession number. In addition, the bar code tags cannot be read when the scanner is out of order.

A small percentage of museums now use Radio Frequency Identification (RFID) tags, which can be as small as 1 mm x 5 mm. At present the tags are cost prohibitive for most museum applications, although the chips are used to tag small zoo animals. Bar coding is also used for animal registration. For an excellent discussion of bar-coding for museum purposes, see "Improving Collection Maintenance Through Innovation: Bar-Code Labeling to Track Specimens in the Processing Stream." http://www. msb.unm.edu/mammals/publications/Racz-2005-Gannon(Collections).pdf

Section 6: Unacceptable Marking Methods and Materials

The following materials should not be used:

Pressure-sensitive tape (including cellophane, masking, adhesive, and embossing tapes): The adhesive on some of these tapes sticks more and more tightly to the object as time passes and may become difficult to remove without strong solvents. Other tapes dry out and fall off, leaving behind a sticky residue or stain. Even if the tape does not fall off the object, it may discolor and stain the surface to which it is adhered.

Pressure-sensitive labels: The adhesive on many pressure-sensitive (self-stick) labels can deteriorate within several months to a sticky residue that penetrates paper products. Some adhesives can cause corrosion to metals around the periphery of the label. After removal these labels leave irreparable dark areas on finished wood, especially wood exposed to excessive illumination. The labels also have a ten-dency to fall off over time as the solvent in the adhesive evaporates.

Gummed (water-moistened) paper labels: The adhesives on these labels can stain and are difficult to remove from some materials. On other materials they have poor adhesive quality and are not durable. (They may be used on the reverse of painting frames, stretchers, or protective backings of framed art.)

Rubber cement: This adhesive behaves somewhat like pressure-sensitive labels and should be avoided. It can stain organic materials and tarnish metals.

Silicone products: Silicones are generally nonreversible and other marking materials will not adhere well to them.

Spray varnishes: It is difficult to control where the spray will land. In addition, the product composition may change and some materials may yellow and become brittle or difficult to remove.

Typewriter correction fluid: This material is widely used as a white base coat on dark objects. Correction fluids are white paints of varying composition; most use 1,1,1,trichloroethylene as the solvent although some are water-based. While some formulations may not harm the surfaces of objects, many correction fluids have poor durability and tend to dry out and flake as they age. Others may prove solvent resistant with age.

Nail polish: Clear nail polish once was in wide use as a base coat and topcoat. Nail polishes are usually made from cellulose nitrate, which yellows, turns brittle and shrinks with age. Modern formulas may be composed of more stable acrylic resins but may be a mixture of the two. The resin is dissolved in a mix of solvents, which may include acetone, xylene, alcohol, or toluene. The exact formula and aging properties of these polishes cannot be determined. Some polishes will peel with age, taking the accession number and part of the surface of the object with them.

Nail polish remover: Commercial nail polish remover may contain additives such as perfume, oil, dyes, and gelatin, in addition to the solvent.

Ballpoint ink: Most ballpoint inks tend to smear and can be difficult to remove with age. Many are not light fast. Some contain iron gall, which is very acidic and corrosive.

Permanent marker: Do not use unless it is on the approved list of tested permanent marking pens. Most permanent markers are not lightfast, will bleed easily, and are often acidic.

Chalks: These materials are not durable. They smear indefinitely and can be difficult to remove from porous materials without strong solvents.

Fusible iron-on fabrics: These materials should not be used for labeling textiles. The adhesives leave a residue and may damage textiles.

Metal-edged tags: The metal can corrode and stain objects.

Wire: Wires can corrode or abrade objects and may tear fragile or soft surfaces. (An exception is the use of aluminum or annealed stainless steel wire, or plastic or vinyl coated stainless steel for large industrial artifacts or outdoor use. See Table 6.)

Nails, pins, staples, screws, and other metal fasteners: Metals may corrode, thereby staining objects, cause corrosion of metal objects that they are in contact with, leave permanent holes, or cause splitting or cracking of woods and other materials. •

CHART A: MARKING SPECIFIC KINDS OF OBJECTS

ALBUMS

See BOOKS

AMPHIBIANS

See REPTILES AND AMPHIBIANS

ANIMAL HIDE

See LEATHER

ARMOR

Mark with ink or paint over a base coat inside each element, or tie an acid-free 2- or 4-ply mat board tag to the object with fabric tape, or polypropylene cord. Metal tags stamped or engraved with the number are sometimes used; however, more inert, non-abrasive materials are preferred.

BARK CLOTH

Apply Japanese tissue paper labels with wheat or rice starch paste or methylcellulose at one corner.

BASKETRY AND MATS (including bark cloth, and other fibrous materials)

These materials can be difficult to mark. Some basket fibers are resistant to the application of varnishes and adhesives, or may be too narrow for a legible written number. Mark at the center bottom of the basket or inside the rim. Choose location carefully, as varnishes and adhesives may stain porous fibers. The preferred method for marking these types of porous materials is to use an adhered label of Japanese tissue. Alternately, if it is necessary to directly mark the basket or other objects of fibrous plant material, do not apply the number directly without a varnish base coat. (Marking media can stain the objects, and inks applied directly may bleed.)

If the reeds of the basket are not long or wide enough, or will not accept the application of a base coat or adhesive, tie or sew a tag or label to the fibers. It is always a good idea to use a secondary label on these types of materials, even if a label is adhered or directly marked using a barrier coat. Use caution with fine materials such as spruce root. Label or tag mats and other flat objects at one corner.

BEADS

Number large beads on a flat, undecorated surface, if possible. Use method appropriate for the material. Place small beads in a padded, marked container. String loose beads with polyester thread and tag.

BIRDS

Number with ink on the leg or toenail. Label mounted specimens on the base near the right rear corner. Tag skeletons or number the bones directly with ink in the center or on the largest part of each bone. Attach a tag to skins around the ankle of one foot. Use non-absorbent tag and tie materials for oily skins and specimens. Label fluid-preserved specimens both on and inside the jar. Mark dry eggs with pencil or ink, usually above or below the opening. Tag nests or mark the tray holding the nest.

BONE (including cultural artifacts and art work; for natural history specimens see individual listings for specimen type)

Seal bone with varnish to prevent ink or paint numbers from bleeding or staining the object.

BOOKS
(including manuscript albums, periodicals, portfolios, scrapbooks, and sketch books)

Number with pencil on the reverse of the title page and inside the front cover at the lower right side near the spine. If the inner cover is marbleized or decorated, mark the number on the first blank page. Number all loose or weakened pages, portfolios, and containers individually. Number scrapbooks in several places, as they are often cheaply bound or in weakened condition and the pages are liable to separate from the binding. For books of moderate value, attach a bookplate bearing the number inside the front cover with starch paste or methylcellulose. For rare books, or books that are works of art in which every page is precious, insert an acid-free paper marker bearing the number in pencil. See also: MANUSCRIPTS AND DOCUMENTS, PAPER, CARDBOARD OBJECTS

BOTANICAL SPECIMENS

Attach labels to herbarium sheets or write the number in pencil on the lower right corner of the sheet. Label the vial or box containing the specimen. When type photographs are made, fasten a small scale with the number of the print to the herbarium sheet and photograph along with the herbarium labels of the institution to which the original specimen belongs. Use of alkaline-buffered paper may negatively affect non-cellulose components of plants, such as resins, and impair future study of these materials.

BRONZES

See METAL OBJECTS

BUTTONS

Mark on the reverse, if possible, using a method appropriate for the material. Store small buttons in a labeled container or attach a tag.

CELLULOID

See FILM

CERAMIC OBJECTS

Apply the number with ink or paint over a base coat in an inconspicuous place not likely to be worn by handling and not obscuring any marks. Unglazed, porous ceramics may require more than one application of the base coat. Choose the location carefully; the base coat will leave a stain. Use a thickened varnish to prevent extensive penetration into porous materials. Use a solvent-based varnish on low-fired pottery; water-based materials may dissolve the surface. Avoid marking cracked areas. Place the number where it will not be scraped as the object is set down or moved; it is often placed under the base, if recessed. If necessary, place the number near the lower edge of the back or near the base on a side not likely to be displayed. Mark vessels inside the lip. Mark pottery shards on the side without decoration, never on the break edge. Mark pottery pipes on the bottom of the bowl or on the pipe stem.

CHINA

See CERAMIC OBJECTS

CLOCKS

Number on the back of the case at a lower edge or corner. Number clocks with a hinged door inside the door as well. Use method appropriate for the material.

COINS AND MEDALS

The preferred method of marking coins is to mark the "flip" they are stored in. If coin "flips" are used for storage, use only those made of Mylar or Melinex, as they do not contain softening agents often found in vinyl flips. In addition to the coin holder, coins should also be identified with marks on the box and/or envelope in which the coin is stored. Thoroughly photo document both sides of each coin. (The same method may be applied to medals that fit in coin flips.) If a coin must be marked directly, use a barrier coat of B-72 and a very fine point archival marker. Mark on the edge or rim if possible. Do not mark coins on their obverse or reverse faces and never use permanent marks. When using semi-permanent marks on medals, number the medal in a smooth undecorated area on the reverse.

COMPACT DISCS (CDs AND DVDs)

Using an archival permanent pen, number the disc on the innermost ring or the clear inner hub or the "mirror band" of the disc, where no information is written onto the CD or DVD. Discs should never be marked on their recordable areas, and should be stored vertically in archival sleeves. For an excellent discussion of issues pertaining to CDs and DVDs, including printing and other methods of marking, see "The Care and Handling of CDs and DVDs—A Guide for Librarians and Archivists" at: http://www.itl.nist.gov/iad/894.05/docs/CDandDVDCareandHandlingGuide.pdf

CORAL

See GEMS, PRECIOUS STONE

COSTUMES AND COSTUME ACCESSORIES

Sew a label to textiles. For details on preparing and attaching the label, see Method 3: Sewn Labels. The label should not obscure any maker's labels. For items composed of non-textile materials, use method recommended for the material. Some museums choose a standard location for all garments, such as inside lower edge near the proper right side seam. See below for additional suggested locations. Standardize the location for all items of the same type. Dresses, coats, shirts, and other upper garments with sleeves: sew the label on the back neckband or, if a tag in that location would be visible on display, in one sleeve on the underarm seam or inside the cuff, usually at the left sleeve. Vests and other sleeveless garments: inside the left armhole at the side seam. Skirts, trousers, and other garments with waistbands: at the center back at the waistband. Hats: inside the band at the center back, or if no band, at another suitable cloth location; mark leather, straw, or other materials at the center inside back of the crown using a method suitable for the material, or carefully attach the label to one edge, or the reverse, of the maker's label. Stockings and gloves: inside near the top edge. Neckwear, sashes: on the underside at the center back or at one end. Flat items (handkerchiefs, scarves): at one corner. Carpetbags, muffs, purses: inside near the opening. Belts: inside near or on the buckle. Footwear with heels: mark on the bottom of the sole in the rise before the heel or on the inside face of the heel. Cloth footwear may have a textile label sewn to the inside lining at the heel end. Footwear without heels (flats, sandals, slippers): at the back of the shoe in the heel area. Umbrellas, canes: on the handle or knob or on the shaft near the handle.

DOCUMENTS

See MANUSCRIPTS

DOLLS

Number on the back of the head at the nape of the neck or, if this is not possible, on the foot. Use a method appropriate for the material. An auxiliary tag is recommended for dolls in storage so that the number may be seen without having to handle the doll. Label each item of clothing as for textiles.

DRAWINGS (including watercolors)	Mark in pencil on the reverse of the work at a lower corner. Mark two-sided drawings with separate accession numbers for each side of the work (e.g., 1991.1A recto and 1991.1B verso) on both sides. If the work is mounted or hinged, mark the number on the back of the mount or on the face of the mount below the edge of the drawing. If framed, mark the frame as for paintings.
EMBROIDERIES	See TEXTILES
ENAMELS	See GLASS OBJECTS
EPHEMERA (including greeting cards, postcards, trade cards, etc.)	Mark in pencil on the reverse in an undecorated or blank area, usually at one corner. Use a Stabilo A7 pencil or Berol China Marker for glossy papers, plastic or foil items. Mark materials with double-sided printing on the side least likely to be displayed. Mark envelopes on the reverse at a lower corner.
FANS	Mark folding fans on the reverse of the rear guard so that the number is visible when the fan is closed, but not while on display. Mark other fans on the reverse end of the handle or stick. Alternatively, apply the number on the ring if wide and sound enough. Use method appropriate for the material.
FEATHERS	Mark with ink or paint, on a base coat, on the shaft or on the bottom of the quill, or attach a tag. Items that cannot be marked directly or tagged should be placed in a marked storage container or labeled on their mounts. Natural history specimens may be marked directly with ink, if permanent marks are desired.
FILM, PLASTIC (Celluloid and vinyl)	Film can be permanently marked directly with India ink. A temporary means is usually employed by housing film in archival photo sleeves made specifically for film.
FIREARMS	Mark on the metal butt plate, if available, on the handle or stock near the butt end, or on the underside or interior of the trigger guard. Long arms and rifles: on the breech end of the barrel or near the trigger on the floor plate. Revolvers: on the cylinder, turned out-of-view while on exhibit. Powder horns and flasks: on the back edge near the opening. Use method appropriate for the material.
FISHES	Tag fluid-preserved specimens with solvent-resistant labels placed inside and also label the jar, or tie a tag through the mouth or gill opening or around the caudal peduncle (the narrow end before the tail). For skeletal material, apply the number with ink directly on the bone; use a base coat and topcoat if permanent numbers are not desired. Place small bones in labeled containers. Label mounted specimens on the mount.
FLUID-PRESERVED SPECIMENS	Place a label that is resistant to the preservation fluid inside the jar and label the exterior of the jar. Resistall paper or 100 percent linen rag heavyweight record paper marked with waterproof, alcohol resistant ink, or Tyvek embossed with solvent-resistant ink numbers or an impact printer are recommended. Do not put Tyvek in a laser printer. It should be noted that if a Tyvek tag inside

a jar of solution is abraded, the printed numbers could wear off. Additional numbering should be applied to the outside of the jar if a specimen receives significant amounts of handling, such as during study or loan.

FOSSILS

Number on a base coat with ink or paint on any smooth flat surface, or use an adhered label, but not on any part that will interfere with study. (Consult a conservator regarding fossil resins. They may be dissolved by solvents.) In the case of specimens consisting of several pieces, such as disarticulated vertebrates, mark the number on each fragment. Label microscopic invertebrates at one corner of the slide mount with ink. Store micro-fossils in labeled vials.

FURNITURE

Mark on a base coat with ink or paint or use method appropriate for the material. Use a base coat that will not dissolve or damage any finished surfaces. Avoid painted areas. Attach an auxiliary tag to large pieces in storage. Number all removable parts such as shelves, keys, etc. Commodes and chests: on the back at the bottom left or bottom right corner; mark low chests at an upper corner. Highboys and multiple case pieces: at a top corner of the lower piece and the corresponding lower corner of the upper piece. Chairs and sofas: at the back of one leg at the height of the seat, or for less visibility on display, on the inside of the leg. If a piece is completely upholstered, sew a textile label near the left or right back leg. Tables: on the underside of the top near one leg, on the apron, or on the inside edge of one leg just below the apron. Beds: on the back of the rail at the head of the bed near one leg, or on the outer edge of both legs at the head of the bed. Lamps: on the lower right hand side at the back, or on the base if there is one. Mirrors and sconces: on the reverse at diagonal corners of the frame. If the object is extremely heavy, place the number on the lower edge of the frame near one corner.

GEMS, PRECIOUS STONE

Extreme caution should be exercised when marking gems. Gems or precious stones that are hygroscopic, fragile, or porous should not be directly marked. Examples of these are opals and organic objects such as pearls, ivory, and coral. Instead of marking the object directly, mark the housing or mount for the object. See also, STONE and GEOLOGICAL SPECIMENS.

GEOLOGICAL SPECIMENS
(including gems, minerals, and rocks)

For non-porous minerals, mark with ink or paint on a clear base coat, placed so as not to obscure any important feature. Use a white primer or white numbers over the clear base coat on dark objects. Adhered labels may also be used. If the specimen is too small to number directly, place it in a padded vial or polyethylene bag on which the number is marked. Store gems in labeled, acid-free boxes or gem papers. See also STONE and GEMS.

GLASS
(including enamel)

Mark on a base coat with ink or paint. Avoid directly marking etched or frosted glass or deteriorating ancient glass, as well as areas of airbrushed or painted design. Make the number as small and legible as possible. Use white lettering on clear glass to minimize the visibility of the number when the object is on display. Place the number on the back edge of the foot if wide enough, underneath the foot if recessed, or on a lower back edge. Mark blown glass in the recessed area near the point where the glass has been cut from the rod.

GLASS, FROSTED OR PAINTED

See LACQUER

GOLD See METAL OBJECTS

HATS See COSTUME AND COSTUME ACCESSORIES

HIDE, ANIMAL See LEATHER

HORTICULTURAL SPECIMENS In addition to informational labels for the public, living plants and trees may also be marked with an accession tag. Trees with a large enough trunk may have a tag attached using a special aluminum nail driven into the bark, while smaller plants may be tagged with a stake that is driven into the ground, then wired to the plant. The tags and labels should be placed in standard locations (e.g., the south side of the specimen).

INSECTS Mark dry-pinned specimens with pencil or ink on unbuffered, acid-free paper labels that are pinned directly below the specimen. Tag fluid-preserved specimens with solvent-resistant labels placed inside the jar and also label the jar. Label microscopic specimens with ink on the slide mount.

INVERTEBRATES Use acid-free paper tags tied to the specimen for dried crustaceans. Mark mollusks with ink; use a base coat if permanent numbers are not desired. Adhered labels may also be used. Tag fluid-preserved specimens with solvent-resistant tags or labels placed inside the jar and also label the jar.

IVORIES Mark with ink or paint on a base coat of a petroleum solvent-based varnish. Use white ink or paint to number dark pieces. Some ivories resist the adhesion of varnish or adhesive. Attach a tag or mark the storage container. Do not mark portrait miniatures on ivory and other thin fragile ivories directly as they are highly susceptible to damage. See also: GEMS, PRECIOUS STONE.

JAPANNED WOOD See LACQUER

JEWELRY Mark in an inconspicuous place not likely to be abraded by handling. Use a method appropriate for the material. If the piece is very small, attach a small acid-free tag bearing the number, loop a cloth tag marked with the number around the piece, or use a small, adhered label. Do not use paper jeweler's tags with colored strings. The paper is usually acidic and the dyes in the string may run when wet. Place numbers on the backs of pendants, watch cases, charms, and fobs.

LACE Sew a textile label bearing the number at a corner or near the end of the piece with a small loop of thread or with one or two stitches on the reverse.

LACQUER Painted, lacquered, japanned, and other finished surfaces (e.g., tole ware, lacquer ware, frosted or painted glass, varnished wood). The preferred method is the Japanese tissue method with Cellofas and Jade as the adhesive. See also WOOD.

Note on Lacquer and painted surfaces: The organic solvents used as carriers for acrylic varnishes can permanently damage painted or finished objects by dissolving the surface finish; mark an unfinished area, if possible, or use a varnish composed of acrylic resins dissolved in a petroleum solvent. Mineral spirits, petroleum benzine, or related petroleum solvents are safer for more surfaces than acetone-based varnishes. Test objects carefully in an inconspicuous location to determine if the solvent affects the finish. Do not use petroleum solvents on wax or waxed surfaces. See WOOD.

LEATHER (including HIDE)	Soft, porous leathers and skins cannot be marked directly with varnish and are permanently stained by inks and paints. Do not mark these directly unless it has been determined that permanent marks are appropriate. The preferred method of marking is to attach a textile label or acid-free tag with stitches passed carefully through an existing hole in the leather or around and underneath the assembly stitches, thongs, etc., provided that the existing stitching is strong enough to withstand such manipulation, or tie to a sturdy appendage. Inert, chemical resistant tags and ties will be more resistant to tannins. See Tables 1 and 2. Sew cloth labels to linings or loop them around a strong appendage, such as a strap or belt loop. Adhered labels may sometimes be used, but consult a conservator and avoid painted surfaces. Place the number on a metal decoration or hardware if no other suitable location can be found.

Hard-finished, stiff, impervious leathers (such as rawhide) may be sealed with a base coat of a petroleum solvent-based varnish. Use a small amount of a solvent-based varnish, on a smooth, inconspicuous surface. Seal minimally, as excessive varnish may stiffen the leather and cause cracking around the varnished area. Avoid alcohol and acetone as they may cause drying or cracking. Do not use water-based materials as they will stain. Apply the number with ink or paint. |
LINENS	See TEXTILES
LIVE SPECIMENS	See ZOOLOGICAL SPECIMENS
MACHINERY	Mark on the right lower rear corner in close proximity to a manufacturer's plate, if present. Attach an auxiliary tag with non-absorbent oil resistant materials on large artifacts.
MAMMALS	Mark bones with ink in the center of the largest part of the bone or near the proximal end of long bones. Mark skulls with ink on the cranium and the mandible. Use a base coat unless permanent numbers are desired. Limit the marking of skeletal material to bones that can be easily and legibly labeled. The numbering is done on the most completely ossified portion of the bone, as marking materials will spread in porous bone, particularly from immature mammals. Use a thickened varnish on very porous bone. Keep small bones in numbered containers. Number mounted specimens on the mount near the base of the right rear leg or at the back edge. Number small skins in ink on the reverse, on the inner part of the neck or near the leg, or tie a tag to the ankle of the right rear leg. Number large skins on the reverse or use a label attached through a natural opening that is unlikely to tear, such as the eyes or nostrils; perforate large skins with a three-cornered awl in the middle of the lower back. Attach specimen labels or tags of heavyweight permanent record paper, 100 percent cotton or linen rag, with a cotton or linen thread or tie. Use non-absorbent oil-resistant tags and ties on oily specimens. Tag fluid-preserved specimens with a fluid-resistant label placed inside the jar or attached to a rear ankle of the specimen, and also label the jar.

MANUSCRIPT ALBUMS	See BOOKS
MANUSCRIPTS AND DOCUMENTS	Write in pencil on the reverse or blank side of the document near an upper or lower corner. In cases where an object cannot be marked directly (e.g., an illuminated manuscript with decorative elements extending to the edge of the paper on both sides), mark an acid-free storage sleeve or box with the number. A stamped ink identifying symbol is used for some manuscript collections but is not generally recommended for museum collections. For complete information, see the Library of Congress's Preservation Leaflet 4, "Marking Paper Manuscripts," cited in the bibliography.
MARBLE	See STONE
MASKS	Number on the inside or reverse near the bottom. Use method appropriate for the material.
METAL	Mark with ink or paint, on a solvent-based acrylic base coat, in an inconspicuous place. Avoid areas of corrosion and painted decoration. Use a solvent-based varnish on unfinished metals. Water-based materials may initiate corrosion at the application site. Water-based acrylic emulsions may be used as a base coat on finishes that are not water soluble; however, these media will not re-dissolve in water when dry. Organic solvents or mechanical methods needed for future removal may damage the surface. Avoid the use of commercial artist's acrylic media on copper, brass, or sterling silver, as they may contain ammonia which will stain the metal. Ammonia may also etch resinous coatings. Do not use materials containing ammonia on copper-based metals (including sterling silver). Mark flatware on the back of the handle so as not to obscure hallmarks. If flatware is to be exhibited with hallmarks up, place the number on the other side. If the piece is too small for numbering, attach a tag bearing the number or place the object in a self-sealing polyethylene bag or other container that is marked with the number. Make one small hole in polyethylene to prevent condensation. Use soft ties and tags to avoid scratching. See also: COINS AND MEDALS, MACHINERY, TOOLS, VEHICLES AND WEAPONS.
MINIATURES, PAINTINGS	See IVORY
MINERALS	See GEOLOGICAL SPECIMENS and STONE
MUSICAL INSTRUMENTS	Mark on a base coat with ink or paint. Avoid areas that will be worn if played. Mark pianos and harpsichords as for commodes and chests (FURNITURE). Mark string instruments on the back of the heel at the base of the neck, or on the back of the body near the base. Mark wind instruments on the underside along the shaft. Mark horns on the stem near the mouthpiece or inside the bell. Many instruments have a lacquer coating which will be dissolved by solvent-based varnishes. Use a petroleum solvent or water-based material. Do not use materials containing ammonia on copper-based metals (including sterling silver).

NATURAL HISTORY SPECIMENS

See listings for specific types of specimens. For more information contact the Society for the Preservation of Natural History Collections (SPNHC).

PAINTINGS

Never write a number on, or apply a label to, the face of a painting or the reverse of a canvas. Paintings are marked on the reverse of their frames, protective backings, and supports, such as stretcher bars or panels. If the stretcher or panel is covered by a protective backing, the number is marked on the backing in the same location that it would be marked if the stretcher or panel were visible. The number can be marked on the backing with pencil or ink according to the standard practice of the institution. Ink is easier to read. For exhibition loans, a gummed paper label is sometimes pasted on the protective backing or stretcher bars. Some paintings, such as miniatures on ivory, contemporary paintings with no frame or stretcher, or reverse paintings on glass, may pose numbering problems. If in doubt as to the appropriate method for a particular piece, use a temporary method, or consult a conservator. Ivory miniatures are often thin, translucent, and extremely fragile. It is generally recommended, therefore, that the accession number not be applied directly to the ivory. If the miniature is framed or mounted in a case or locket, the number should be applied to one of these supports. If the miniature is unframed, the number can be marked on its storage box. Consistently mark objects in the same location, e.g., upper right corner of the frame and panel. Mark large paintings at opposing diagonal corners so that the number can be easily located whether the work is hung high or low on a wall or storage screen. This is not necessary in the case of small works. If both sides of an object are in view (such as a two-sided painting—a painting on both the recto and the verso), mark the number on the bottom edge at one corner. See also: SCROLL PAINTINGS.

PAINTED WOOD AND OTHER PAINTED SURFACES

See LACQUER

PAPER AND CARDBOARD OBJECTS

Mark with pencil in an unobtrusive place. See Table 5 for information regarding pencils. Place paper items on a firm surface. Write gently to avoid indentation. Mark pamphlets as for books or mark on the back cover at one corner. Mark sheet music on the reverse at one corner, and also mark individual loose pages. Three-dimensional paper objects may be tagged. See also: BOOKS, DRAWINGS, EPHEMERA, MANUSCRIPTS AND DOCUMENTS, and PRINTS.

PEARL, MOTHER OF PEARL

See GEMS, PRECIOUS STONE, and SHELL

PHOTOGRAPHS

Mark lightly with pencil on the reverse, preferably in a non-image area at a corner of the lower margin. Mark all items consistently in the same corner. See Table 5 for information regarding pencils. If the photograph is hinged in a mount, place the number on the unhinged end. Also number the mount and, if framed, mark the frame as for paintings. Some modern photographic papers resist pencil; place in a labeled archival sleeve; or try a #1 pencil, Stabilo All pencil, or Berol China Marker. In the latter case, interleave photographs with acid-free tissue to prevent transfer of the marking material. Do not use alkaline-buffered materials in contact with cyanotypes or color photographs. For cased tintypes, ambrotypes, and daguerreotypes, apply the number on a base coat with ink or paint, on the lower back of the case by the hinge, or tag the object. Do not attempt to disassemble cased photographs without the advice of a conservator. Uncased tintypes, ambrotypes, and daguerreotypes are not usually marked directly; place in a labeled container.

Photographic negatives cannot be labeled with pencil, but can sometimes be labeled directly with inks such as India ink for film. The number should be placed on the non-emulsion side in a non-image area. Since such areas are usually very small, it is difficult to write the number legibly without the aid of magnification. More commonly the number is written in pencil on an archival storage sleeve before the negative is slipped in.

PLASTICS, VINYL, AND RUBBER

Most plastics may be damaged by solvents and moisture. The most damaging solvents are acetone and toluene; alcohol and mineral spirits will damage some plastics. Mark on a non-plastic component if possible. Mark numbers on plastic directly with acrylic artist's paints. Tag with acid resistant tags and ties (Teflon, polyester, polypropylene). Some plastics give off acids as they deteriorate which can damage paper and cotton tags and ties. Plastics can be numbered directly with a Berol China Marker or Schwan-Stabilo All Stabilo pencil, although the numbers may not be durable. A second (temporary means) of marking should be employed.

When dealing with plastic objects, it may not be possible to identify which type of plastic is present; there are many types of plastic and each has its own specific chemistry. In addition, many plastic objects have painted or printed surfaces, and the marking media that is safe for the plastic may not be safe for the surface treatment and vice versa. To complicate matters, some plastics resist the adhesion of varnishes and adhesives; however, they may be stained by the dyes and pigments in marking media if a base coat is not used. Therefore, it is difficult to make specific recommendations.

Solvents should be avoided. The solvents used as carriers for acrylic resin varnishes, such as acetone and toluene, may dissolve the surface or cause stress cracking or crazing, or may affect the gloss finish or surface texture of plastic objects. Acrylic resins dissolved in mineral spirits pose the least possible risk for most plastics, although caution is still advised. Some petroleum solvent blends may contain a small percentage of other solvents.

Base coats of water-based acrylic or PVA emulsions are not a safe choice, as older plastics, such as cellulose nitrate, may be damaged by moisture. Water-based materials can also initiate stress cracking upon application or over time. In addition, these materials are not reversible in water when dry, and stronger solvents or mechanical methods, which may damage the plastic, will be necessary for their future removal. Also, the numbers may not be durable as these emulsions have a tendency to peel over time. Oil paints are not recommended, as both the oils and their solvents can soften or otherwise damage some plastics with long-term contact.

The following marking alternatives are suggested for plastics and rubbers:

1. Mark a non-plastic component if possible
2. Tie a tag to the object and/or mark its storage container
3. Mark hard plastics and rigid rubbers directly with a Berol China Marker, Stabilo All pencil, or acrylic paint. (See Table
5.) Keep in mind that these numbers may not be durable.
4. Mark the object directly with pigmented ink or India ink for film. Consider this method permanent, as it may stain the plastic or rubber.

PORCELAIN

See CERAMIC OBJECTS

PORTFOLIOS — See BOOKS

POTSHERDS — See CERAMIC OBJECTS

POTTERY — See CERAMIC OBJECTS

PRINTS — Mark lightly with pencil on the reverse, preferably in a non-image area at a lower corner. If the print is hinged in a mount, place the number on the unhinged end. Also number the mount and, if framed, mark the frame as for paintings.

RAWHIDE — See LEATHER

REPTILES AND AMPHIBIANS — Attach tags to the larger parts of skeletal specimens or write the numbers with ink directly on each bone. Use a base coat if permanent numbers are not desired. Do not mark small bones directly if the numbers will obscure study features; store them in labeled containers. Attach tags to skins and skulls through a natural hole or opening if strong enough. Tag fluid-preserved specimens with a solvent-resistant tag tied to a leg or around the neck, and also label the jar. Mark dry eggs with ink above and below the opening.

REPRODUCTIONS — See section above on Permanent Marks.

RESIN — Treat the same as lacquered or painted surfaces.

ROCKS — See GEOLOGICAL SPECIMENS

RUBBER — Use water-based products, such as acrylic paint, on rigid rubber objects. Do not use acetone. Flexible rubbers are difficult to mark directly, as marking media tend to flake or peel. Mark on a non-rubber component, attach a tag, or write the number directly with a Berol China Marker. Mark the number directly with India ink for film but consider the numbers permanent on light colored objects. Enclose rubber objects in polyethylene bags or film labeled with the number (use a sulfur scavenger to absorb harmful gases; available from conservation materials suppliers), and isolate from other media since many rubber formulations contain sulfur compounds which can damage adjacent materials through direct transfer or off-gassing. Most rubber products are adversely affected by oils and hydrocarbon solvents and some by alcohol. Synthetic rubbers vary as widely as plastics in their properties. Take care when using inks as they often contain metallic elements that may cause degradation of the rubber. Rigid rubber objects may be marked with acrylic paint or other water-based materials. Base coats and top coats of solvent-based acrylic varnishes are not recommended as they may not adhere well and the solvents may attack the rubber, fillers, or colorants. Flexible rubber objects are difficult to mark directly as marking media have a tendency to peel. For an outstanding and extensive discussion of the properties

	of rubber, see the article by Sharon D. Blank, "Rubber in Museums: A Conservation Problem." Marking is covered briefly at the end of the article. http://www.aiccm.org.au/index.php?option=com_content&view=article&id=687:rubber-in-museums-a-conservation-problem&catid=55:1998-iccm-bulletin-volume-14-no-3-a-4&Itemid=44
RUGS (including tapestries)	Sew a textile label to reverse diagonal corners so the number is easily found when the rug or tapestry is rolled. Attach a tag to the roll's tie.
SCIENTIFIC INSTRUMENTS	Mark on a base coat with ink or paint in an inconspicuous place near the base, or use an adhered label. Number all removable parts. Number instruments that have revolving parts and revolve the part to the far side when exhib-ited. Metal parts may have a shellac coating, which could be damaged by solvent-based varnishes.
SCRAPBOOKS	See BOOKS
SCREENS	Mark on a base coat with ink or paint on a lower edge on the back of the frame, near an outside corner, where it can be seen when folded.
SCROLL PAINTINGS	Mark on a base coat with ink or paint on one knob of the scroll; also mark the box. Attach an acid-free tag to the cord at the opening end of the scroll.
SCULPTURE	Use a method appropriate for the material type. For sculpture in the round, apply the number at the lower rear base or, if there is no base, in an inconspicuous place not likely to be worn. Mark removable pedestals at the lower rear. Mark relief sculpture on the bottom edge, not the back, where it can be seen without lifting or moving the object. For unusual objects, such as complex abstract sculpture, note the location of the number in the object file and attach an auxiliary tag in storage.
SHELL	Mark on a base coat with ink or paint in an inconspicuous place not likely to be worn by handling. Natural history specimens may be marked directly with ink. Adhered labels may also be used. See also: INVERTEBRATES, GEMS, and PRECIOUS STONE
SHOES	See COSTUMES AND COSTUME ACCESSORIES
SILVER	See METAL OBJECTS
SKETCH BOOKS	See BOOKS
STAMPS	Not usually marked directly, although the number is some-times written lightly in pencil on the back. Direct marking may lower the monetary value of stamps. More commonly, place the stamp in an acid-free envelope or sleeve, which is labeled. Number

	mounted stamps with pencil on the back of the mount and on the hinge beneath the stamp.
STONE	Some stone, such as marble, is semi-porous and easily stained. Use the Japanese tissue method or if marking directly on the stone, use a base coat, especially on sculpture and cultural artifacts. See also: GEOLOGICAL SPECIMENS and GEMS
TABLEWARE	Use a method appropriate to the material. Mark the number under a recessed foot or on one side at the base, and on the inside of lids. Individually mark all removable parts. For flatware, see: METAL OBJECTS
TAPESTRIES	See RUGS
TERRACOTTAS	Mark on a base coat with ink or paint. Extremely porous items may need more than one application of the base coat. Use a thickened varnish to prevent extensive penetration of the varnish. Choose the location carefully, as the base coat will leave a stain. Use a solvent-based varnish, as water-based varnishes may dissolve or damage the surface. Place the number where it will not be scraped as the piece is set down or moved. It may be placed under a recessed base, if the piece is small, or at the lower edge of the back. Mark roundels or medallions on the back or on the bottom edge.
TEXTILES (flat textiles, including draperies, embroideries and linens)	Sew a textile label at one corner on the reverse of small pieces, preferably along a hem or selvage. Label large textiles at opposing corners so the number is easily located when rolled. Tie a tag to the roll's tie. When textiles are wrapped on tubes or mounted on boards, also mark the support. Attach tags to fragile textiles with one loop of thread between the weave of the fabric as for lace. Do not sew a label directly to very deteriorated textiles. Label or tag fragile mounted textiles on the mount only. Draperies and curtains: sew on the reverse lower left or right corner of each panel; if very sheer, sew on the reverse but on the outside corners where it will be less conspicuous. Bed coverings and quilts: sew on reverse diagonal corners. Pillow cases: sew inside the left corner of the bottom half on or near the hem. Decorative pillows: sew on the reverse lower left or lower right corner. Flags, banners, and pennants: sew on the reverse side at the top of the hoisting edge. See also: COSTUME AND COSTUME ACCESSORIES
TOLE WARE	See LACQUER
TOOLS	Mark on the butt end of handles, along the shaft, or on the bottom edge of the head. Mark planes at the back of the stock; mark wedge and iron. Use method appropriate for the material.
VEHICLES	Mark at the lower right rear corner of the body or stern or on the rear axle. Use method appropriate for the material. If a manufacturer's plate is present, mark the number in close proximity to it. Attach an auxiliary tag if the direct marking is not easily located.
VINYL	See FILM and PLASTICS

WATERCOLORS	See DRAWINGS
WEAPONS (including those with long shafts such as arrows, clubs, harpoons, knives, and spears)	Place the number on the handle of clubs and tomahawks near the butt end, on the shaft of arrows, and on the inside end of bows. Number swords and knives on the blade below the counterguard or hilt, or at the base or butt end of the handle. Use method appropriate for the material. See also: FIREARMS
WOOD (including lacquer)	Mark on a base coat with ink or paint in an inconspicuous place not likely to be worn by handling. Very porous wood may require more than one application of the base coat. Choose the location carefully, as the base coat will leave a stain. Use a thickened varnish to prevent extensive penetration into the wood. Avoid finished or painted surfaces or use a base coat that is compatible with, i.e., will not dissolve or damage, the finish. Varnishes dissolved in a petroleum solvent will be safe for more finishes than acetone but do not use petroleum solvents on waxed surfaces. Water-based products, such as acrylic paint or artist's acrylic matte or gloss medium, will be safer for more finishes than solvent-based varnishes, but may not be as durable and will require a solvent or mechanical methods for future removal, which may damage the finish.
ZOOLOGICAL SPECIMENS (Live Specimens)	Live animals have specific issues for marking. Each category of animal is marked in a standard way according to guidelines set out by the Association of Zoos and Aquariums. (See: "The importance of animal identification and registration for collection management" at http://www.eaza.net/magazine/download/64_AnimalIdentificationandRegistration.pdf) Methods include tags, bands, tattoos, radio frequency identification (rfid) tags and ink. The "transponders" or chips are usually inserted at the right shoulder or under the neck. For the most recent standards contact the Association of Zoos and Aquarium (AZA): http://www.aza.org/

CHART B: MATERIALS FOR MARKING

TABLE 1: BARRIER MATERIALS FOR BASE COATS

Material	Uses/Comments
Acryloid B67	An acrylic resin; can be purchased in pellet form or as a 40 percent solution in mineral spirits from conservation suppliers. Dissolve it in mineral spirits or a related petroleum solvent, not toluene or xylene. Reversible in mineral spirits; may yellow slightly over time. The resin may need to be thinned with mineral spirits periodically as the solvent evaporates. **Do not use on wax or waxed surfaces.**
Soluvar, Liquitex	A commercial varnish composed of Acryloid B67, possibly combined with another acrylic resin, Acryloid F10; may yellow slightly over time. Easily obtained and ready to use. Reversible in mineral spirits, as well as stronger solvents such as acetone, xylene, and toluene. Mineral spirits are safer for more surfaces than acetone or toluene. The gloss version is recommended. The matte version may cloud if successive layers are used and contains other additives including a small amount of methyl alcohol. Thin with mineral spirits or a related petroleum solvent. **Do not use on wax or waxed surfaces.**
Acryloid B72	An acrylic resin; can be purchased in pellets, as a 40 percent solution in toluene from conservation suppliers, or as a 25 percent solution in acetone. The most stable acrylic resin used by conservators. Disadvantages are that its least toxic solvent is acetone and it is reversible only in acetone, xylene, or toluene, which may damage some surfaces. For lower toxicity, dissolve it in acetone, not toluene, or in an ethanol/acetone mix (at least 10 percent acetone). The resin may need to be thinned periodically as the solvent evaporates. **Do not use on plastic, painted or lacquered surfaces.**
White base coats	White acrylic artists' paints, or white paints made by adding titanium dioxide pigment to B67, Soluvar or B72, can be used as a base coat on dark objects. They should be applied over a clear base coat to avoid leaving a white "ghost" on the object.
Acrylic emulsions	These white, water-based materials turn clear when dry. They are available commercially at art supply stores as acrylic medium; manufacturers include Golden, Liquitex,, and Aqua-tec,. They are not as durable as the previously listed materials. Acrylic emulsions are also available from conservation suppliers (Rhoplex AC-337 is one example). Soluble in ethanol or acetone, not water, when dry. **Some water-based emulsions may contain ammonia, which should not be used on copper-based metals (copper, brass, bronze, sterling silver) as it will stain the metal. Ammonia may also etch resinous coatings. Do not use water-based materials on objects that are dissolved or damaged by water.**
Polyvinyl acetate (PVA)	There are a wide variety of PVAs, both solvent-based and water-based. Solvent-based PVAs are soluble in ethanol or acetone when dry. The water-based emulsions are soluble in water when wet, but can be difficult to remove even with stronger solvents (e.g., acetone, toluene) when fully cured. Removal of the base coat at a later date may not be possible without causing damage to the surface of the object. They are white in liquid form but turn clear as they dry. (Elmer's glue is a PVA emulsion.) PVAs can be hygroscopic and may turn white or swell with moisture contact, causing damage to some surfaces, including plastics. They may soften or become sticky in warm temperatures. Most release acetic acid when degrading, which corrodes lead and plastic. Most PVAs are not recommended as a base coat. Acrylic resins are preferred. However, Jade 4037, a water-based PVA emulsion, performed well in pH testing conducted by the Canadian Conservation Institute (CCI). It is reversible in acetone. Observe cautions regarding acetone.

TABLE 2: SOLVENTS

Most solvents are flammable and highly volatile, i.e., they evaporate rapidly and vapors quickly fill an enclosed space causing both fire and health hazards. In addition, **all solvents (and marking materials containing solvents) are toxic to some extent; u**se them only in well-ventilated areas. Keep bottles tightly capped when not in direct use and wipe up spills immediately. Avoid skin contact and wash hands frequently. Keep a **Materials Safety Data Sheet (MSDS)** on site for all solvents and marking materials. Do not attempt to remove varnishes from the surface of an object without the advice of a conservator. If a white "bloom" develops on the surface of an object, discontinue use immediately.

Materials	Uses/Comments
Acetone	Acetone is used to thin and prepare varnishes (including B-72), clean brushes, and remove varnishes. It is used in commercial nail polish and nail polish remover. It will harm most finished surfaces and plastics. **Do not use on plastics, resin, lacquered, or painted surfaces. Do not use acetone on moisture-sensitive materials such as ivory, wood, or leather as it may cause excessive drying or cracking.** *More toxic* than alcohol or petroleum solvents.
Alcohol	Alcohol, including ethanol (ethyl alcohol) and isopropanol (isopropyl or rubbing alcohol), can be used to remove some inks and varnishes, including B72. **It will damage shellac finishes on wood and historic metal objects and some plastics. Do not use alcohol on moisture-sensitive materials such as ivory, wood, gems, or leather as it may cause excessive drying or cracking.**
Mineral spirits	A petroleum distillate used to dissolve B67 and to thin Soluvar,, mineral spirits can be used to clean brushes or remove base coats and top coats of these materials. Mineral spir-its are sold at hardware stores as paint thinner. Check the label and look for a product that is labeled "pure mineral spirits." Similar petroleum solvents may also be used (e.g., heptane, petroleum benzine, Stoddard solvent, naphtha). **Do not use on wax or waxed surfaces.**
Naphtha	Naphtha is a common name for the industrial solvent Petroleum Ether. Other names include benzine, X-4, or Lingroin. Chemically, naphtha is a mixture of straight-chained hydrocarbon-ethers, straight chained alkanes, as well as some aromatic hydrocarbons. Should be used only in well-ventilated areas. **Do not use on wax or waxed surfaces.**
Petroleum Benzine Petroleum Ether	See Mineral Spirits and Naptha.
Toluene	It is *very toxic* and not recommended for use outside a laboratory setting. Used for preparing varnishes, toluene may be found in small amounts in commercial paint thinners and nail polishes. **Will harm finished surfaces and plastics.**
Xylene	Xylene is in the toluene family. Some disposable marking pens contain xylene. (See *Ink and Paint Chart* for tests on disposable pens.) **Will harm finished surfaces and plastics.** It evaporates more slowly than toluene but is also *very toxic.*

TABLE 3: WRITING MATERIALS

Material	Uses/Comments
Pen and Ink	Crow quill pens or fine steel-nib technical pens, such as Rotring or Koh-I-Nor Rapidograph pens, are recommended for applying ink numbers. A variety of nib sizes (e.g., .25 very fine, .35 fine) can be used for different size numbers. Crow quill pens can be used to write with acrylic paint as well. Exercise *caution* with metal tipped pens so as not to scratch the object, splatter, or drip ink. The ink should flow well enough to write without pressing down. If rapidograph pens clog, try shaking the pen or dipping the tip in water. Pens should be cleaned frequently. See chart below for inks and paints to use with pens.
Brush and Paint	Very fine sable or camel's hair artist's paint brushes (000-00000) are used to write numbers. Slightly larger brushes can be used to apply base coats (0-1). Larger brushes also may be used to paint numbers on large objects such as vehicles or machinery. Brushes should be cleaned frequently. See chart below for paint recommendations.
Ink and Paints	See Table 4 Below.
Berol China Markers	Can be used to write directly on plastic, foil, and resin-coated photographs. Easily abraded, hard to keep a sharp point. Can be used in black or white.
Schwan-Stabilo All Stabilo pencil	Can be used to write on glossy surfaces, including resin coated photos, glass and plastic. Standard pencil size and hardness, easier to keep a fine point than a Berol China Markers. May abrade. Schwan-Stabilo All Stabilo, a water-soluble pencil which will mark clearly, densely, and legibly on any transparent, glazed surface (acetate, glass, metal, photo, film, etc.). Wipes off with a damp cloth on smooth surfaces and erases on paper. #8052 Titanium White; #8008 Graphite; and #8046 Black.
Drawing or Writing Pencils	Writing pencils are graded Nos. 1, 2, 2.5, 3, and 4, which reflect the degree of hardness of the lead, with No. 1 being the softest. Drawing pencils have a broader range of desig-nations. Medium-grade pencils are used for marking numbers on paper objects. No. 2 writing pencils are recommended, as well as drawing pencils graded HB, F, and H (listed from softest to hardest). HB = No. 2, F and H = No. 2.5. The No. 2 or HB pencils are recommended for most paper as they will leave a dark mark with less pressure on the pencil point. They may smear slightly if rubbed. Numbers can be blotted gently one time, not rubbed, with a vinyl eraser to remove excess lead. The harder grades (F and H) are less likely to smear but may indent the paper if applied too forcefully. A No. 1 may be used on some glossy papers, but check for smearing.

TABLE 4: INK AND PAINT

Desired ink qualities are as follows: quick drying, acid-free, light fast, good adhesion, abrasion resistant, fluid resistant (i.e., "permanent"), able to write well on a variety of porous and non-porous surfaces. Each pen tested claimed some "archival qualities" or were already being used by collections staff in museums across the country. The disposable pens were tested against India Ink applied with a metal nib pen and black acrylic paint applied with a tiny, natural bristle, size 0 paintbrush.

Inks containing a mineral pigment rather than a dye are recommended for light fastness. Inks which contain carbon are very light fast. To date, more than one type of ink or paint is needed for a variety of object marking. Pens continue to come onto the market and formulas occasionally change for ink manufacturers. Some pens contain alcohol, xylene or other solvents which may damage some surfaces. It is recommended that the ink be periodically tested before using it for semi-permanent or permanent marking. The chart below provides a starting point for choosing an ink or paint for marking. A variety of types were tested in 2006. India Ink and Acrylic Paint are still highly recommended but are not as easy to use as the disposable pens. Pens and inks will continue to be tested by the Registrar's Committee and future results will be published; see the RC-AAM website for updates.

Pen	Claim	Quality of cover	Lightfast	Smear Test 1 (various dry time* on poly plastic)	Smear Test 2 (various dry time* on metal with B-72 base)	Acryloid Sandwich: B72 base with B67 topcoat	Fabric test for bleeding: unbleached muslin and cotton tape
Pigma Micron by Sakura	"Pigma Micron pens are acid-free and archival, making them ideal for any application requiring precision and permanence. Pigma ink will not feather or bleed, even through the thinnest paper. Pigma ink is derived from a single pigment to ensure color consistency, and is fadeproof against sunlight	Fairly consistent coverage.	No noticeable fading after one month or one year.	Smeared completely after 5 minutes and 10 minutes of drying time. Smeared significantly after 15 minutes of dry time. Not a good choice for plastic.	Pigma Micron: Completely wiped away after 5 minutes and after 10 minutes of drying time. Smeared after 15 minutes of drying time. Must let ink dry at least 30 mins.	Mark was allowed to dry for 15 minutes before applying B67 topcoat and did not smear. Longer (15–30 min.) dry time recommended for this ink.	Marks highly legible on muslin; marks sufficiently legible on cotton tape. Best results with heat set.

Pen	Claim	Quality of cover	Lightfast	Smear Test 1 (various dry time* on poly plastic)	Smear Test 2 (various dry time* on metal with B-72 base)	Acryloid Sandwich: B72 base with B67 topcoat	Fabric test for bleeding: unbleached muslin and cotton tape
	or UV light. Pigma inks will not clog or dry out like most mechanical pens."						
IDenti-Pen Dual-Point Marker by Sakura in black	"One fine-point bullet shaped fiber tip and a finer, plastic tip for details. For paper products and non-porous surfaces such as metal, glass, tools, sporting goods, test tubes, photographs, plastics, CDs and wood. Permanent, waterproof, low odor, bleed-proof on most papers, are built for heavy use. The alcohol solvent, dyestuff colorant ink will mark on nearly any surface including slick PVC and polypropylene sheet protectors."	Excellent, opaque coverage.	No noticeable fading after one month or one year.	Smeared slightly after 5 minutes. Smeared significantly less after 10 to the point that it was difficult to tell whether it had. Did not smear after 15 minutes. Smeared negligibly after 10 minutes of drying time. Did not smear after 15 minutes of drying time. Dry time=15 minutes	Smeared slightly after 5 minutes. After 10 minutes, ink was set and it did not smear.	Excellent results. No smearing on any surfaces. Held up the best on Volara.	Significant bleeding on muslin and cotton tape.

Pen	Claim	Quality of cover	Lightfast	Smear Test 1 (various dry time* on poly plastic)	Smear Test 2 (various dry time* on metal with B-72 base)	Acryloid Sandwich: B72 base with B67 topcoat	Fabric test for bleeding: unbleached muslin and cotton tape
Permapaque, opaque paint markers by Sakura, in black	"Archival quality ink – chemically stable, waterproof, and fade resistant. No smears, feathers, or bleed-through on most papers. Odorless, quick drying and non-toxic. Works well on standard scrapbook papers and vellum. Best on: canvas, plastic, metal, glass, wood crafts, ceramics, pottery."	Contrary to its name, coverage was not opaque and was inconsistent.	Opaque black coverage dissipated after one month; very slight fading. After one year, the result remains the same, no worse.	Smeared slightly after 5 minutes of drying time. Did not smear after 10 minutes of drying time. Dry time=10 minutes	Smeared slightly after 5 minutes. After 10 minutes, ink was set and it did not smear.	Slight abrasion to the mark from the application of the B67 topcoat. Otherwise no smearing.	Marks are not legible. Point of pen is too thick to make appropriate sized marks. Additionally, marks bleed on cotton tape.
Microperm Ultra fine point by Sakura	"Used to make precise long-lasting marks on test tubes, circuit boards, diamonds, cellophane, wood and glass, plastic, metal, or wherever there is a need for waterproof ink that will write on non-porous surfaces. Chemically stable. Low odor and fulfills	Good, consistent coverage.	No noticeable fading after one month and one year.	Smeared slightly after 5 minutes of drying time. Smeared negligibly after 10 minutes of drying time. Did not smear after 15 minutes of drying time. Dry time=15 minutes.	Smeared slightly after 5 minutes. After 10 minutes, ink was set and it did not smear.	Excellent results. No smearing on any surfaces.	Slight bleeding on muslin and on cotton tape.

Pen	Claim	Quality of cover	Lightfast	Smear Test 1 (various dry time* on poly plastic)	Smear Test 2 (various dry time* on metal with B-72 base)	Acryloid Sandwich: B72 base with B67 topcoat	Fabric test for bleeding: unbleached muslin and cotton tape
	non-toxicity requirements. Permanent adherence to most surfaces. Fine line nib with a protected tip that will not split. Writes on diamonds, glass, wood, cellophane, plastic, glossy sheets, CDs, photographic and x-ray film, paper, metal. Alcohol based cleaners will remove ink from non-porous surfaces."						
ZIG, The Opaque Marker in Black	"Will cover all colors and also boast an extraordinary smooth ink flow. Permanent, acid-free, lightfast, waterproof, non-bleeding and opaque."	Good, consistent coverage.	No noticeable fading after one month or one year.	Smeared completely after 5 minutes of dry time. Smeared completely after 10 minutes dry time. Smeared significantly after 15 minutes of dry time. Dry time is approx. 20 mins. Not a good choice for plastic or ethafoam products.	Completely wiped away after 5 minutes and after 10 minutes of drying time. Smeared after 15 minutes. Not a good choice for marking on a B-72 basecoat.	Mark smeared on all surfaces tested. Does not set up and dry on the B72 in acetone.	Numbers illegible. Point is not conducive to writing on textiles.

Pen	Claim	Quality of cover	Lightfast	Smear Test 1 (various dry time* on poly plastic)	Smear Test 2 (various dry time* on metal with B-72 base)	Acryloid Sandwich: B72 base with B67 topcoat	Fabric test for bleeding: unbleached muslin and cotton tape
Sanford's Sharpie, black permanent marker, ultra fine point	"Permanent on most surfaces, Fade and water resistant, Quick-drying ink, AP certified nontoxic formula".	Somewhat translucent cover quality. Fair coverage.	Significant fading after one month. Fade to gray after one year. No lightfast. Not recommended.	Smeared slightly. Smeared slightly after 10 minutes. Did not smear after 15 minutes. Dry time=15 minutes. Not archival.	Smeared slightly after 5 minutes. Did not smear after 10 minutes of drying time. Not archival.	Slight smear on smooth surface objects such as glazed ceramics. Not archival.	Bleeds significantly on muslin, bleeds less on cotton tape. Not archival.
India Ink (black) with metal nibbed pen	"Semi-flat black finish on most surfaces. Waterproof, opaque, permanent, fadeless and acid-free."	Good, consistent coverage.	No noticeable fading after one month or after one year.	Smeared negligibly after 5 minutes of drying time. Smeared negligibly after 10 minutes of drying time. Did not smear after 15 minutes. Dry time=15 mins	Ink was set after 5 minutes of drying time. Retest at 10 minutes produced no smearing.	Excellent results. No smearing on any surfaces.	Bleeds on muslin and cotton tape. Difficult to mark on textiles with metal nibbed pen.
Acrylic Paint with brush (Carbon Black or titanium dioxide white) Only black was tested in 2006. If red is necessary, vermillion or cadmium reds have been tested in the past and hold up as well as black and white.)	Liquitex: "The high pigment load produces rich-brilliant, permanent color." G: "Pure colorants mixed with 100 percent acrylic emulsion providing excellent permanency and lightfastness without fillllers, extenders or opacifiers." Both have mineral pigments.	Good, consistent coverage.	No noticeable fading after one month or one year.	Smeared negligibly after 5 minutes of drying time. Did not smear after 10 minutes. Dry time=10 mins	Paint was set after 5 minutes of drying time. Retest at 10 minutes produced no smearing.	Excellent results. No smearing on any surfaces. Top coat prevents abrasion that might normally occur with acrylic paint marks.	Difficult to mark on textiles with paint brush. Marks barely legible, even with skilled hand.

Pen	Claim	Quality of cover	Lightfast	Smear Test 1 (various dry time* on poly plastic)	Smear Test 2 (various dry time* on metal with B-72 base)	Acryloid Sandwich: B72 base with B67 topcoat	Fabric test for bleeding: unbleached muslin and cotton tape
TRIA pen, Letraset	An inexpensive, refillable disposable pen. Golden fluid acrylic paints and India inks can be used to fill the pens, which also have replaceable tips.	Tested in a 1988 study by Rose M. Wood & Stephen L. Williams and was not highly rated. Preliminary tests in 2006 showed the pen to be difficult to work with.	Not tested in 2006.	Not tested in 2006.	Not tested in 2006.	Not tested in 2006.	Not tested in 2006.
Pilot, SCA-UF	Permanent, ultra fine point, no xylene; writes well on most non-porous surfaces, high bleeding potential on paper and textiles; soluble in alcohol; porous plastic tip. Fair light fastness.	Tested in a 1988 study by Rose M. Wood & Stephen L. Williams and was recommended.	Not tested in 2006.	Not tested in 2006.	Not tested in 2006.	Not tested in 2006.	Not tested in 2006.
Other Ink: Rotring Black (Artist Pen with choice of nibs)	Ability to write well on a variety of porous and non-porous surfaces.	Good consistent coverage; noted for being quick drying and light fast; abrasion resistant.	Not tested in 2006. But was rated highly in a 1986 study by Stephen L. Williams and Catherine A. Hawks.	Not tested in 2006.	Not tested in 2006.	Not tested in 2006.	Not tested in 2006.

Pen	Claim	Quality of cover	Lightfast	Smear Test 1 (various dry time* on poly plastic)	Smear Test 2 (various dry time* on metal with B-72 base)	Acryloid Sandwich: B72 base with B67 topcoat	Fabric test for bleeding: unbleached muslin and cotton tape
Pelikan drawing ink, Black (disposable technical pen)	"The metal-sheathed porous point lays down black, documental, acid-free ink smoothly."	Good consistent coverage; noted for being quick drying and light fast; abrasion resistant.	Not tested in 2006. But was rated highly in a 1986 study by Stephen L. Williams and Catherine A. Hawks	Not tested in 2006.	Not tested in 2006.	Not tested in 2006.	Not tested in 2006.
Chinese white ink or titanium dioxide white ink or "fluid" acrylic artist's paint	White inks and paints should not be used in Rapidograph pens as they clog the pens but may be used with a nibbed pen.	Not tested in 2006.	Not tested in 2006.	Not tested in 2006.	Not tested in 2006.	Not tested in 2006.	Not tested in 2006.

Table 4. *Note that dry times are comparable for the all pens tested (in 2006) on a particular day in the spring time, inside a building in eastern Pennsylvania. Dry times are relative to the working environment. Dry times will vary for each pen depending on the relative humidity and temperature in which the objects are marked. Test the drying time at each marking session before assuming a medium is dry.

*Note: To test a marker on fabric, write or type a series of sample numbers on the labeling material. Rub the numbers to see if the ink smears, and eliminate any pens or ribbons that do. Second, rinse the tags in hot soapy water to see if the ink runs when wet. Third, rub each number while it is still wet. If the ink is fast in each of these tests, the marking material may be used.

TABLE 5: TAGS

Material	Uses/Comments
Acid-free card stock	100 percent cotton rag or lignin-free, pH neutral tags are recommended for general use both to protect the object and to ensure the longevity of the tag. Tags can be purchased with cotton string ties or made from card stock. A pH testing pen can be used to check acidity. Rounded corners are preferred to prevent piercing delicate surfaces. Not waterproof or oil resistant. Alkaline-buffered materials are not recommended for use in contact with some objects, including cyanotypes, color photographs, and proteina-ceous materials, as they are thought to hasten the degradation of these objects. 100 percent linen rag heavyweight permanent record paper is sometimes used for fluid-preserved specimens. **Can be laminated in plastic for outdoor use.**
Reemay	Non-woven polyester; inert; acid resistant. Used as drop tags or for textile labels. Insect resistant.
Tyvek	Spun-bonded polypropylene; stiff and soft varieties. Water, oil and chemical resistant. May be used for fluid-preserved specimens (marked with solvent resistant ink or an impact printer). Insect resistant in general usage. (Consumed by dermestids.) Good for outdoor use. Soft varieties are sometimes used for tagging textiles and baskets. Tyvek Brillion can be used in an ink jet to print label and barcodes. ***Do not put Tyvek in a conventional laser printer that uses heat to seal the ink to the page. See DuPont website for update on applications of Tyvek.***
Resistall paper	Coated or impregnated with melamine; recommended for labels placed inside jars containing fluid-preserved specimens (alcohol or formaldehyde), pH 4.5-5.2. Rounded corners are preferred to prevent piercing delicate surfaces.
Metal	Limited use. Aluminum tape (non-adhesive) or aluminum sheets can be used to make tags for large industrial artifacts and machinery. The numbers can be embossed with a DYMO labeler or metal stamp, or an impression can be made with a pencil or knitting needle. Other types of metal tags are **not** recommended. Relatively soft but may scratch. Secure both ends of tag.
Teflon tape	Non-adhesive, can be marked with a DYMO labeler (the tape must be .015 cm thick and 1 cm wide). Water, oil and chemical resistant. Use for tagging plastics, which give off acids as they degrade. Insect resistant.
Mylar	Clear, inert; sharp edges. Round corners. Water and oil resistant. Insect resistant.
Plastic corrugated board	Water and oil resistant. Brand names include Coroplast, Primex, Cor-x. **Good for outdoor use or for large machinery.** Insect resistant. May have sharp edges.
Formica	Carved or etched. Water, oil and chemical resistant. **Good for outdoor use.** Insect resistant.

TABLE 6: TIES

Material	Uses/Comments
Thread/string	Un-dyed or natural cotton thread or string can be used to attach small tags. Polyester thread is more durable but may be too strong for use on fragile materials. Do not use jeweler's tags with colored strings; dyes may run when wet.
Fabric tape	Cotton, linen, polyester. Use to tie string tags onto large objects or mark with the number directly and loop around an object. Non-abrasive.
Cord	Un-waxed polyester or polypropylene cord can be used for large objects or strong materials such as suits of armor. Shoemaker's supply companies carry 2, 3, and 4-ply polyester cords. Cotton cord is soft and non-abrasive but is not as durable. Nylon cord has a short lifetime and is not recommended.
Polyethylene straps or ties	Plastic "zap straps" (such as those used to tie garbage bags) and thinner ties with male/female ends can be useful for objects which have oily surfaces. Cloth or thread ties wick oils into paper or cloth tags. Inert and relatively non-abrasive, these materials can be used in outdoor situations although prolonged sunlight exposure may cause deteriora-tion of the plastic ties and straps with long-term usage. They can be obtained from plastics suppliers. Use polyethylene, not nylon. Insect resistant.
Wire	Limited use. Annealed stainless steel, Monel or aluminum wire may be used to attach aluminum tags to large-scale industrial objects or vehicles. Aluminum wire may corrode in outdoor conditions. Stainless steel will discolor but will be corrosion-resistant. **Caution: wire can scratch; use only in situations where other materials would not suffice. Wire can also be covered with surgical tubing or heat-shrink polyethylene tubing.** Vinyl-coated stainless steel cable, with the ends secured by a crimp connector, can also be used. Vinyl coated cable is softer and less prone to scratching until the vinyl deteriorates. Do not use PVC (off-gassing causes deterioration) wire or insulated copper (due to corrosion problems associated with the copper).
Teflon or PTFE dental floss	Teflon, a trade name for a polymer known as polytetrafluoroethylene, also known as PTFE. Other dental floss is made from nylon, which deteriorates. Teflon/PTFE resists water, oil and chemicals. Use to tie tags on oily specimens, such as birds, or oily or greasy objects. **Use only unflavored and unwaxed dental floss.** May cut soft or fragile surfaces. Insect resistant.
Teflon thread tape	Non-adhesive plumber's tape; chemically inert and soft; can be used to tie tags onto objects with fragile surfaces. Water, oil and chemical resistant. Good for ties for plastic, rubber and leather objects which may cause cotton thread or string to deteriorate. Insect resistant.
Tyvek #1422	Chemically inert; soft; no fibers. Water, oil and chemical resistant.

TABLE 7: ADHERED LABELS

Material	Uses/Comments
Acid free paper	Labels can be made from 100 percent rag, lignin-free, or acid-free paper. Acrylic emulsions (Rhoplex AC-337) and PVA emulsions (Jade 4037) are used to adhere labels. See discussion of PVAs in Table 4. The number can be written with ink or printed with a laser printer. Use laser quality acid-free paper. Do not use labels printed on a daisy, dot matrix, or ink jet printer. Solvent-based adhesives such as B72 can also be used on solvent resistant surfaces but will remove type printed with a laser printer. Use solvent resistant ink or try a dot matrix or ink jet printer. For the least intrusion to porous objects apply the adhesive to the label, then apply the label to the object. **Do not use on friable or painted surfaces.**
Japanese tissue paper	Wheat or rice starch paste or methyl cellulose is used to adhere Japanese tissue paper labels. Used for bark cloth, baskets, wood objects with uneven surfaces, and occasionally leather. Heat or solvent reactivated tissue can be used for materials, such as leather, which cannot tolerate moisture (Rhoplex AC-2347 adhesive). Consult a conservator. Starch paste may attract pests. **Do not use on friable or painted surfaces.**

TABLE 8: SEWN LABELS

Materials	Uses/Comments
Fabric tape	Unbleached cotton twill tape is recommended for textile labels. Plain woven cotton, linen or polyester tape may also be used. Sizing is sometimes used to stiffen or seal the tape but is not generally recommended. The number is written with ink. The ends are turned under 1/4" before sewing.
Reemay	Labels may be cut from non-woven polyester interfacing. The numbers are written with a typewriter.
Tyvek	Soft grades of Tyvek are sometimes used for making textile tags. Numbers are written with ink. *Do not put Tyvek in a traditional heat set laser printer.* Tyvek 1073 B is recommended. Round corners. The following advice is from the DuPont website on Tyvek (2009): INK-JET PRINTING: Tyvek can be ink-jet printed for addressing and bar coding. For optimum performance, solvent-, oil-and wax-based inks are recommended. Selected, pigmented water-based inks can provide satisfactory performance by using special settings. When doing high-quality graphics, an ink-jet coated Tyvek must be used. SCREEN PROCESS : Tyvek can be printed on hand, automatic and rotary screen presses in sheet and web form for signs, banners and other decorative uses. When conveyor ovens are used instead of room-temperature drying, high-velocity air will aid drying and carry away the solvents. Sheet temperature should be kept below 175°F (79°C), with tensions below 0.75 lb/lineal in (1.4 N/cm) to avoid shrinking and mis-registration in multi-color web printing. When using UV-cured screen inks, cooling is required to prevent sheet distortion or shrinking due to the heat generated. (See website for further details on screen process inks for Tyvek.)

TABLE 8: SEWN LABELS, *continued*

Materials	Uses/Comments
	LASER PRINTING (NON-IMPACT): Conventional laser printing is not recommended on Tyvek because of the temperatures involved in the printing units. For the same reason, Tyvek should not be used in electrostatic copiers. However, Tyvek can be used with the newer cold lasers (which generally have a fusing temperature below 200°F [93°C]).
Threads	THERMAL TRANSFER: All hard structure styles of Tyvek are compatible with thermal transfer printing. Tyvek Brillion is recommended for bar code printing. All three types of ribbons can be used; however, under harsh conditions or in outdoor applications a wax/resin ribbon is recommended.
	Cotton thread (#50 or #60), un-dyed and unbleached is preferred (white is acceptable), is recommended for sewing labels on textiles. Ideally, the strength of the thread should be equal to or less than the strength of the fibers of the textile so that the thread will not tear the textile if the tag is snagged. Cotton/polyester or polyester thread may be used for very strong fabrics but may tear fragile textiles. Silk threads deteriorate quickly and are not recommended. Silk thread is also very slippery, and stitches may pull out easily. Dark, colorfast thread may be used for stitching tags on dark-colored objects if the stitches will be visible on display. Test the thread to make sure that the color does not run when wet.
Needles	Fine, sharp pointed needles (#8 quilting in between, #9-10 crewel, #10-#12 sharps) are recommended for medium and fine textiles. Small size tapestry or ball-point needles are recommended for sewing labels on textiles with a heavier, open weave. A sharp pointed needle can be blunted with fine sand paper.

5F | PHOTOGRAPHY

SCOTT HANKINS

Photography plays an important role in collections management. For registrars, object photographs can serve as visual documentation of the collection, provide detailed views of an object's condition, record the scene of an incident and the resulting damage, or supply an appraiser with the information needed to asses an object's value. In addition, other departments in the museum use object photographs in a variety of ways. Marketing and public relations departments use them for exhibition banners, brochures, posters, and newsletters. Exhibition designers incorporate images into their designs and use them as a visual layout for planning. Museum educators include object photographs in lesson plans and public programming.

ASSESSING PHOTOGRAPHY NEEDS

Before turning off the lights to start shooting, it is important to understand how photography is used in the institution and how it relates to the mission and long-range goals. What types of photography does the museum currently have? How is existing photography used, and how will it be used it in the future? What space is available for photo shoots for object photography? What financial resources can be allocated to photography? Whether the institution is just starting to photograph its collection or object photography has been an ongoing function, it is important to answer these four questions when considering the role it plays in the museum.

Begin with an examination of the types of photography the museum already has. Most museums have a mix of several different types because they incorporate new photographic technologies while maintaining the previous methods as long as is practical to do so.

COMMON TYPES OF OBJECT PHOTOGRAPHY

Color transparency. A positive color photographic image on a clear film base. Sizes range from 35 mm color slides to 8 x 10 inch (203 x 254 mm) sheet film transparencies.[1]

Color negative. A negative color photographic image on a clear film base. Sizes range from 35 mm color slides to 8 x 10 inch (203 x 254 mm) sheet film transparencies.

Black-and-white negative. A negative, colorless photographic image on a clear film base. Sizes range from 35 mm color slides to 8 x 10 inch (203 x 254 mm) sheet film transparencies.

Print. A positive black-and-white or color image created from a negative or a printout from a digital print. Prints usually are made on paper and vary in size. A typical size for a print is 8 x 10 inches.

Digital image. An electronic photograph taken with a digital camera or scanned from an original document. It is composed of pixels, the smallest units displayed by computer monitors. Each pixel is assigned a tonal value (black, white, a shade of gray, or color) and is stored in binary code (zeros and ones).[2]

After determining the types of photographs in the museum, assess who uses them and how. Object photography is utilized primarily by the museum's registrar to document the collection visually and enhance the records. Whether the photographs are black-and-white prints placed in the object files or digital images attached to the museum collections database, a visual record helps with all aspects of collection management. Other uses include distribution for reproduction by outsiders and the museum's marketing and public relations departments, use in commercial products for the museum shop, posting on the museum's website, and incorporation into the exhibition design process and educational programs and materials. While these are not all of the possibilities, they show the depth of uses possible in a museum.

After assessing past and current uses, determine how photography will be utilized in the future by examining the institution's long-range goals and strategic plan. Are there uses that no longer fit the museum's needs? Are there new uses that should be incorporated into the museum's plans? Maybe the museum aims to make its collections management database available online, necessitating a digital image of every object it owns. Maybe it plans to include a picture of recent acquisitions in its newsletter. If the exhibitions department has been photographing objects for its designs, it may be easier and more effective to use existing object photographs. Whatever uses are provided in the photography plan, it is important that they relate to the museum's long-term goals.

Like all programs and operations, photography requires space. A good photography space requires three things for success: enough room to house the photography equipment, adequate size to accommodate the object(s) to be photographed, and the capability of being completely dark. Ideally, photography should be done in a rectangle-shaped, windowless room with a large width, height, and depth that can become completely dark. This type of room allows for multiple set-ups. However, if such a room is not available, compromises are possible. Photography can be done nearly anywhere, although each space will have its own advantages and disadvantages. The best way to think about the size and amount of space needed for photograph is to consider the sizes and types of objects in the collection. A collection consisting of works on paper will have different photography space needs from a collection of large-scale paintings and sculptures. If options are limited and a dedicated space is not available, be creative and consider all of the spaces in the museum. Galleries are often suitable for photography because of their size; they can accommodate a large number and variety of works and photography equipment. An auditorium

may provide another good alternative; the stage typically is roomy enough to accommodate most types of photography. Another possible space for photography is the storage area, although the types and arrangement of furniture may limit its usefulness.

The final and probably most important thing to consider is the budget. The amount of money available for object photography will dictate what can be accomplished. Whatever amount the institution is able to invest in photography, it should be used to fulfill the goals of the institution.

ANALOG OR DIGITAL

After completing a review of the museum's photographic needs, determine the type of photographs that meet them best. Currently, two types of photographs are used in museums: analog and digital. An analog photograph is film based and "has a continuous scale of tones, with unbroken gradations from light to dark."[3] A digital photograph is electronic based and consists of an amount of solid toned pixels.[4] Most museums have a combination of both analog and digital photographs; each has its own advantages and disadvantages.

ANALOG

The origins of film trace back to the beginning of photography itself. Film-based photography was invented in the 1880s when a gelatin emulsion that suspended light-sensitive silver salts was created and applied to roll film. This new film made photography quicker, easier, and accessible to the masses.[5] Until recently, film was the only form of photography available to museums and was versatile enough to serve many uses. Unlike the films of the 1880s, films today come in many varieties and sizes. These films can produce a positive or a negative image. They can record and reproduce images in both color and black-and-white and come in a variety of sizes.

Transparencies

A transparency or color transparency is a positive color photographic image on a clear film base.[6]

Transparencies are one of the most common forms of analog photography found in museums. The main reason for their popularity is their versatility. Transparencies can be used as aids in lectures or scanned to create digital images. They come in various sizes, from 35 mm to 8 x 10 inches.

Negatives

A negative is the opposite of a transparency, a negative image on a clear film. Negatives are another common form of analog photography found in museums. While most negatives are black-and-white, color negatives are also available. Like transparencies, negative film comes in variety of sizes, from 35 mm to 8 x 10 inches.

STORAGE OF ANALOG PHOTOGRAPHY

Proper storage of film is very important because it ensures its longevity. There are two important factors to consider regarding storage of analog photography: climate and material. The ideal conditions for film storage are 68°F and 30–40 percent RH. However, if those standards cannot be achieved, store film in a climate with low and stable temperature and relative humidity. High and fluctuating temperature and humidity can accelerate deterioration. Film can be stored in either plastic or paper enclosures. Suitable plastic enclosures are made of uncoated polyester film, uncoated cellulose triacetate, polyethylene, and polypropylene. Suitable paper enclosures are both acid free and lignin free and available in both buffered (alkaline, pH 8.5) and unbuffered (neutral, pH 7) stock. In addition, paper enclosures must pass the ANSI (American National Standards Institute) Photographic Activity Test (PAT).[7] While either paper or plastic enclosures are acceptable, plastic enclosures are preferred because they allow for easier viewing—due to their transparency—and, therefore, reduced handling. Both paper and plastic enclosures should be stored in archival acid-free boxes. Also, when placing film in an enclosure, be sure the emulsion side (dull side) does not rest against a seam. The emulsion side should always be against the smooth side.

DIGITAL

Digital photography, as we know it today, began with the recording of television images onto magnetic tape. "In 1951, the first video tape recorder (VTR) captured live images from the televisions cameras by converting the information into electrical impulses (digital) and saving the information onto magnetic tape."[8] Then in the 1960s, digital imaging developed further with help of the U.S. government and advances in computers. Signals from spy satellites and space probes were converted from analog to digital, and, taking advantage of new computer advances, NASA employees were able to enhance those images. Around the same time, the private sector was working on digital imaging as well. In the 1970s, "Texas Instruments patented the first film-less electronic camera."[9] Also at this time, "Kodak invented several solid-state image sensors that 'converted light to digital pictures' for professional and home consumer use."[10] This led to the release of "products for recording, storing, manipulating, transmitting, and printing"[11] and "the first worldwide standard for defining color in the digital environment of computers and computer peripherals."[12] With standards and a system of delivery in place, digital photography became available to consumer use, and the switch from analog to digital began.

RGB and CMYK

RGB and CMYK are two color models used in digital imaging. RGB is an additive color model created in the 19th century and was based on the trichromatic color vision theory.[13] The three primary colors—red, green, and blue—are added together in various ways to reproduce a broad array of colors. "The main purpose of the RGB color model is for the sensing, representation, and display of images in the electronic system, such as televisions and computers."[13] But digital photography was not the first time the RGB color model was used in photography. It also is found in analog color transparencies. The top layer of the transparency is sensitive to blue light, the middle layer is sensitive to green light, and the lower layer is sensitive to red light.[14]

CMYK is a subtractive model used in color

printing. In the CMYK color model, cyan, magenta, yellow, and key (black) are "used to partially or entirely mask certain color on a typical white background."[15] During printing, "the three primary colors are half toned, or printed less than full saturation."[16] This process of half toning is achieved by "printing tiny dots of a color in a pattern small enough for the human eye to perceive a single color."[17] Without the half-toning process, printers would print color as solid blocks and would be limited to only six colors: the three primary colors themselves, and three complementary colors produced by layering two of the primary colors.[18] The fourth primary color used in CMYK printing, key (black), is added separately, instead of mixed. There are two reasons for this: cost and quality. Since black is heavily used in printing, it is cheaper to add black ink separately instead of buying additional cyan, magenta, and yellow for mixing. As for quality, black ink purchased separately has a better overall quality when compared to black ink made from mixed colors.[19]

File Formats

A digital image can be saved in a variety of file formats, each of which has advantages. When picking a file format, consider three things: how much loss is acceptable, how will the images be used, and how much storage space is available. The amount of loss in a digital image is determined by the algorithm used to compress the image. Some algorithms discard no information, others discard some information, and others look for recurring patterns and replace each occurrence with a short abbreviation in order to reduce an image's file size.[20] This amount of loss also determines how the image can be used and how much storage space it will require. Here are some common files formats and their advantages and disadvantages.

TIFF. A very flexible format that has no loss. The details of the image storage algorithm are included as part of the file. In practice, TIFF is used almost exclusively as a lossless image storage format that uses no compression at all.[21] Images stored in this file format are very large and not good for the Internet because of their overall size and lack of support. The TIFF file

format is good for archival storage and requires a lot of storage space.

JPG. An optimized format that has loss, JPG works by analyzing images and discarding kinds of information that the eye is least likely to notice.[22] Images stored in this file format vary in size but are much smaller and require less storage space than TIFFs; they are ideal for the Internet. JPG images degrade every time they are opened; thus, they are not recommended for archival storage.

PNG. A lossless format that looks for patterns in the image that it can use to compress file size. The compression is exactly reversible, so the image is recovered exactly.[23] Images stored in this file format are larger than JPGs and smaller than TIFFs. They are good for the Internet, if a lossless image is required. The PNG file format also is good for archival storage and requires less storage space compared to a TIFF.

RAW. An image output option available on some digital cameras. It is similar to a TIFF in that there is a little loss to the file. The problem with the RAW format is that each manufacturer creates its own, and without the manufacturer's software the user may not be able to view the image. However, some graphics applications can read other manufacturers' RAW formats.[24] The RAW file format is not good for the Internet or archival storage and requires a lot of storage space.

Storage of Digital Images

Each method varies in size and cost and requires maintenance and upgrading. When determining which storage method is right for a given situation, consider the identified uses and needs and the budget. For photographs that are to be used for in-house documentation, a combination of CDs, DVDs, and hard drives might be the best storage method. To incorporate images into a collections management database and make them available online, a server would better fill the need. In addition, as technology changes, the method of storage may need to be upgraded or changed completely. For example, floppy disks used to be the main method of digital storage but, as technology improved, the disk size has changed and old, large disks no longer can be read. Another example is the CD-ROM. While CD-ROMs are still used widely today, DVDs offer more storage room. Furthermore, a Blu-ray disc offers more storage room than a conventional DVD. But Blu-ray disks are entering the market slowly, and it remains to be seen if people will be willing to buy new Blu-ray players or drives for their computers. Regardless of the storage method chosen, be mindful of changes and upgrade as needed. Otherwise, there is a risk that the storage method will become obsolete or out of date and ultimately unusable.

Common Digital Storage Methods
- Floppy disk
- CD-ROM
- DVD
- Internal/external hard drive
- Server

COLOR MANAGEMENT

In both analog and digital photography, color management is a very important factor; without it, photographs will reproduce incorrectly. In analog photography, proper color management is dependent on two things: correct exposure and proper processing. To ensure the exposure is correct, photographers use a technique called bracketing: after determining the correct exposure, a photographer will shoot subsequent photographs a half-stop change higher and lower. Bracketing allows for error and provide a range of photographs to determine which one is best. The second criterion for analog color management is proper processing. Without it, the film will be developed incorrectly and become unusable. Many things can go wrong during the development process; photographers understand the potential problems, shoot backup copies, and develop them at different times, increasing the chances of obtaining at least one good photograph.

In digital photography, color management begins with the color model in use: RGB (the color model used for digital capture and display) or CMYK (the color model used for printing). All digital images are taken in the RGB color model and are device dependent "in that each different device detects and reproduces the amount of Red, Green, and Blue differently."[25] These differences are noticeable when transferring images from one device to another. To correct this problem, the International Color Consortium (ICC) was formed in 1993 "to create a universal color management system that would function transparently across all operating systems and software packages."[26] To accomplish this, the ICC created color profiles. A color profile "is a file that describes how a particular device reproduces color; that is, it describes the device's color space."[27] For example, when images are transferred from camera to computer, the computer reads and converts the information into defined colors based on its color space. If the camera's color space is different from the computer's, the colors in the resulting images will be different. Color profiles are used to correct this problem. The color profile describes the color space used by the camera to the computer, which then converts the information it receives into the correct colors. The result is a new image that looks as similar to the original image as possible.[28] In the picture below, the different color spaces within the RGB model are compared according to the amount of color in visible spectrum they cover.

There are several different color spaces in the RGB mode; the two most common are sRGB and Adobe RGB. Microsoft and Hewlett Packard (HP) created sRGB to ensure color was represented consistently on monitors, devices, and the Internet. It has become the standard color space for the Internet and can be found in most medium- to low-level devices. The Adobe RGB color space was created by Adobe to show the most colors achievable on a CMYK printer on a RGB monitor. Since all printers use the CMYK color model, the Adobe RGB color space greatly increases the ability to edit and print digital images accurately.[30]

Another tool for ensuring color accuracy is the color separation guide for color and for black-and-white film. The guide for color film consists of nine color control patches with two saturations of each patch. The colors represented on the patch are red, green, blue, cyan, magenta, yellow, black, white, and three-color. These are the colors used in film layers and in the development process. The guide for black-and-white film consists of a gray scale (20 steps in 0.10 density increments between 0.0 [white] and a practical printing black of 1.90 density). For digital photography, the color guide consists of a checkerboard array of twenty-four 2-inch scientifically prepared colored squares in a wide range of colors used for calibrating and evaluating color reproduction systems. In addition to the colors mentioned above, this guide includes natural colors such as human skin, foliage, and blue sky. These guides should be included in all object photography. While including the guides is not always easy and for certain objects can be very difficult to work into the image area, they are necessary to ensure color accuracy, especially when sending photographs to third parties for reproduction.

WHICH IS BETTER: ANALOG OR DIGITAL?

Ideally, an object photography collection should consist of both analog and digital photography. A museum with an established object photography collection already has a mix of analog and digital photography. However, a museum starting to build one likely will have mostly digital photography because photographers are shifting toward that format. While there are several reasons for this shift, the main driving factor is industry support. For example, Polaroid discontinued film production and switched to digital products only. The Polaroid camera (an instant photography technology) allowed a photographer to see the image and make adjustments before shooting to film. Photographers who had been accustomed to shooting 4 x 5 transparencies consequently became reluctant to continue to do so. Now, without the ability to preview and adjust the image, photographers are hesitating to shoot film because there are fewer labs to process it, which increases the cost. As labs continue to abandon film processing, it will become harder and harder to develop film, resulting in less film purchased. As demand drops, so will the supply, leading to increased prices and fewer sellers. While there will always be a market for film, it will be smaller, with less industry support.

With less industry support and fewer photographers working in analog, digital photography will become the dominant format for object photography. Digital photography is cheaper, quicker, and easier to use. Despite these advantages, however, digital photography is not yet perfect. The first digital cameras were released in 1991, compared to analog photography, which started in 1826. Despite much progress, digital photography is still early in its life. And as research and technological advances continue to develop, problems with digital photography will be resolved. It is hard to say at what point in time analog photography will become obsolete for object photography; that will depend on the ability of each institution to purchase and develop analog film.

FREELANCE PHOTOGRAPHER

The crucial decision before shooting starts is who will do the work, a freelance photographer or a staff photographer. There are many types of photographers, commercial, fine art, and fashion to name a few. In addition, photographers come in a wide range of experience and expertise. Most object photographers are freelance or independent photographers, and their clients consist of museums, galleries, and private collectors. When deciding to hire a freelance photographer, several issues must be considered.

The first issue is the method of photography: analog or digital. While most freelance photographers can work in both methods, there are some who work in only one or the other. Finding a photographer who can address the institution's needs is very important. The second issue is who handles the post-shoot work. For analog photography, who will be responsible for having the film developed? For digital photography, who will be responsible for editing and color management? While most freelance photographers develop their own film or do their own post-production work, it is important to determine which party is responsible for this work up front. The third issue is who owns the photographs. If a photographer is working in analog, he/she most likely is bracketing or shooting several copies at different F-stops to eliminate errors. While it is common for freelance photographers to hand over all copies to the museum regardless of quality, some prefer to keep the "bad images." It is important for a museum to obtain all of the images, regardless of their quality. Arrangements with freelance photographers working in digital must specify whether the photographer can keep a copy or if he/she must delete all files once the final versions have been delivered. The fourth issue is equipment. Will the freelance photographer be expected to use his or her own equipment or will the museum provide all or some of it? Most freelance photographers will bring their own cameras and lights to a photo session. However, there are some large-sized accessories (paper backdrops, tables, special mounts) that museums usually own and let photographers use.

The fifth issue, one of the most important, is copyright. Who will retain the copyright to photographs? Any photographs done by a freelance photographer should be considered "work for hire," meaning that the museum is the sole copyright owner. Under U.S. copyright law, this arrangement must be stated in writing and agreed to by both parties. If it is not, the photographer may claim to own the copyright and distribute copies of the photographs with the institution's permission. Any agreement should include to the following language:

> *Work for Hire.* You agree that all original works prepared by or for you in the performance of the services for the Sample Art Museum shall be "works made for hire," and the Sample Art Museum will own such works and all copyright and all other intellectual property rights therein. For any original works of authorship prepared by or for you in the performance of this agreement that, under the copyright laws of the United States, may not be considered works made for hire, you agree at the request of the Sample Art Museum to convey and assign all copyright interests that may subsist in any documentation developed by you to the Sample Art Museum. This provision shall survive the termination of this agreement.

The issue of copyright is especially important if the photographer keeps the bad copies of the film or retains a copy of the digital images. Most freelance photographers who work with museums do not do this, but some sell images as another source of income. Thus, it is important to identify the institution as the sole copyright holder.

The final issue is whether the museum will require the photographer to carry liability insurance. For example, the museum hires a photographer to photograph an exhibition, and a visitor trips over the power cord of one of the lights, is injured, and decides to sue. Who is responsible, the museum or the photographer? Accidents will happen, and part of the museum's risk-management strategy should be to determine whether responsibility lies with the institution or with the freelance photographer.

Staff Photographer

While most of the issues related to hiring a freelance photographer also apply to staff photographers, there are differences. The issue of photography format will be the same regardless of the photographer hired. While most photographers can work in both digital and analog methods, there are some who work only in one or the other. The second issue, the post-shoot work, becomes a responsibility of the staff photographer. If the staff photographer is to work in analog, ensure that there is a film supplier and a lab accessible to the museum and consider the impact that buying and developing the film will have on the budget. For example, if the nearest supplier and lab are out of state, there will be an increase in mailing costs, in addition to the cost of the film and processing. If the staff photographer works in digital photography, he/she will require office workspace and a computer for the editing and color management. A photographer with experience in editing and color management may be difficult to find and expensive to hire.

With a staff photographer the issue of ownership is clear. Since the staff photographer is an employee, all of the photographs are the property of the museum, regardless of format. The fourth issue of equipment will become the responsibility of the museum and, again, cost of purchasing and maintenance will become a consideration.

Equipment Required for a Staff Photographer
- Camera
- Cable release

- Easel
- Copy stand
- Lighting kit
- Film
- Color separation guides
- Seamless (backdrop paper)
- Computer
- Scanner
- Tripod
- Light stands

The fifth issue, copyright, is also clear with a staff photographer. Under U.S. copyright law, the employer owns the copyright of any employee's work. There are circumstances in which an employer will not own the copyright, but in such cases, ownership is agreed upon in advance and established as part of the employer's intellectual property or human-resource policies. The final issue of liability insurance is also clear with a staff photographer; it is the responsibility of the museum. A staff photographer should be treated as all other employees with regard to liability, and this also should be covered in the museum's human-resource or risk-management policies.

CONCLUSION

Object photography can play a very important role in an institution, from documenting the collection to use in marketing and public relations materials. It is important to determine the role object photography will play in the institution. Whether photographing collection objects in analog or digital format or hiring the services of a freelance photographer or employing a staff photographer, the goals and uses of the museum's photography program must be well defined and incorporated into the long-range plan and budget. Doing so ensures that the money invested in object photography goes toward the fulfillment of the institution's mission. •

NOTES

1. DocuSource on NC, LLC., "Education Materials for Digital Printing: Glossary." http://www.docusourceofnc.com/pages/techtips/glossary.php (accessed on November 24, 2008).

2. Vintage Image Craft.com, "Craft Glossary Your Guide to Crafting Tools and Terms" (Glendale, Calif.: Brayerson Publications). http://www.vintageimagecraft.com/craft_glossary.html (accessed on November 214, 2008).

3. Barbara London and John Upton, Photography: Sixth Edition (New York: Addison-Wesley Educational Publishers, Inc., 1998), 255.

4. Ibid.

5. Ibid., 342–46.

6. DocuSource on NC, LLC.

7. The Library of Congress, Preservation Section, "Caring for you Photographic Collections." http://www.loc.gov/preserv/care/photo.html (accessed on January 29, 2010).

8. Mary Bellis, "History of Digital Cameras." About.com, The New Times Company. www.inventors.about.com/library/bldigitalcamera.htm (accessed on November 7, 2008).

9. Ibid.

10. Ibid.

11. Ibid.

12. Ibid.

13. Wikimedia Foundation, Inc., "RGB Color Model." http://en.wikipedia.org/wiki/RGB_color_model (accessed on November 24, 2008).

14. Michael W. Davidson, "Photomicrography, Troubleshooting, Photomicrography Errors, Color transparency Film Processing Errors," *Molecular Expressions Optical Microscopy Primer.* Mortimer Abramowitz, Olympus America Inc., and The Florida State University, August 1, 2003. http://micro.magnet.fsu.edu/primer/photomicrography/chromeprocerrors.html (accessed on November 24, 2008).

15. Wikimedia Foundation, Inc., "CMYK Color Model." http://en.wikipedia.org/wiki/CMYK (accessed on November 24, 2008).

16. Ibid.

17. Ibid.

18. Ibid.

19. Ibid.

20. Rick Matthews, "Digital Image File Types Explained." Wake Forrest University. http://www.wfu.edu/~matthews/misc/graphics/formats/formats.html (accessed on November 24, 2008).

21. Ibid.

22. Ibid.

23. Ibid.

24. Ibid.

25. Wikimedia Foundation, Inc. "RGB Color Model." http://en.wikipedia.org/wiki/RGB_color_model (accessed on November 24, 2008).

26. ——, "ICC Profile." http://en.wikipedia.org/wiki/

ICC_profile (accessed on November 24, 2008).

27. Adobe Systems Incorporated. "TechNote: ICC profiles in Photoshop 6.0 and later." http://kb.adobe.com/selfservice/viewContent.do?externalId=321382&sliceId=1 (accessed November 24, 2008).

28. Wikimedia Foundation, Inc. "sRGB." http://en.wikipedia.org/wiki/SRGB (accessed on November 24, 2008).

29. ——, "Image: Colorspace.png." http://en.wikipedia.org/wiki/Image:Colorspace.png (accessed on November 24, 2008).

30. ——, "Adobe RGB color space." http://en.wikipedia.org/wiki/Adobe_RGB_color_space (accessed on November 24, 2008).

Colletions Management I | HYPOTHETICALS

1

An accession number's most important quality is its uniqueness.

To what extent can or should an accession number also convey information about the object (its source, the transaction, etc.)?

Is an accession number meant to signify something more than a tool for tracking?

2

Your museum receives as a gift a purse containing matching accessories: a wallet and comb. The purse is also inside of its original felt storage bag. The curator wants to accession the storage bag as well as the purse and its contents.

How do you number this gift?

Is the storage bag part of the purse, or a separate object?

Do all four elements create a set?

Are the purse and its contents one object with four parts?

3

In what circumstances might wearing gloves while handling art not be the best practice?

In what circumstances are gloves indispensable?

4

Do you take measurements in the English or metric system?

Why?

5

You need to measure the diameter of a large circular sculpture.

How do you proceed?

What's the best way to get an accurate measurement?

6

To what extent do you note inherent flaws while taking a condition report?

7

An exhibit is about to close at your museum. You have limited gallery space, so you plan to pack loans for return shipment in your storage area. Your conservator, however, wants to complete outgoing condition checks in the gallery; he can see the objects better while they are still on the wall or on their pedestals.

How do you respond?

8

Older accession marks are not always easy to remove.

What can you do when a number must be removed (because the piece has been deaccessioned, or the number proves to be wrong), but the removal process might end up damaging the piece?

9

You have been asked to oversee the numbering and marking of an acquisition of 3000 pieces of china.

What steps might you take to organize this project?

How can you ensure that all pieces are numbered correctly and marked consistently?

10

Is there any reason still to use film photography?

11

You must photograph for an exhibition catalog a mobile that hangs in your gallery, 20 feet in the air.

How do you proceed?

5G | PREVENTIVE CARE

GENEVIEVE FISHER

From the moment of their creation, all objects are vulnerable to physical deterioration. This process can be mitigated by careful handling[1] and by storage in clean, environmentally appropriate conditions. It has been estimated that a lack of proper routine maintenance is responsible for 95 percent of conservation treatments; the remaining 5 percent result from inappropriate handling Museums seek to preserve their collections in ways that are environmentally safe and sustainable and economically prudent. Preventive care, also called preventive conservation, is the most cost-effective strategy. It is defined as the mitigation of deterioration and damage to cultural property through the formulation and implementation of policies and procedures for the following:

- appropriate environmental conditions
- handling and maintenance procedures for storage, exhibition, packing, transport, and use
- integrated pest management (IPM)
- emergency preparedness and response
- reformatting/duplication

Conservation is the profession devoted to the preservation of cultural property for the future. Its activities include examination, documentation, treatment, and preventive care, supported by research and education. Along with staff conservators, museums may use the expertise of freelance professional conservators, regional conservation facilities, and conservators from museums that provide outside services. For institutions requiring outside assistance, the Foundation of the American Institute for Conservation of Historic and Artistic Works (http://aic.stanford.edu/public/select.html) provides a referral system that identifies conservators by specialties, services provided, and geographical area.

In institutions with permanent conservation staff, the responsibility for monitoring as well as treating objects may be the province of conservators. Nevertheless, registrars and collections managers should be fully informed about preventive care practices.[2] They may take the lead in museums without permanent conservation staff. Indeed, a museum's collections maintenance program will meet the greatest success when all staff, including building maintenance and cleaning crews, understand and support its goals. In addition to widely available published resources, guidance about environmental risk assessment and mitigation is accessible online through the Canadian Conservation Institute (www.cci-icc.gc.ca), Image Permanence Institute (www.imagepermanenceinstitute.org), and New England Document Conservation Center (www.nedcc.org).

THE ENVIRONMENT

Long-term preservation of collections is affected by relative humidity, temperature, light, air pollution, and pests.[3] Responsible collections management should adopt a holistic approach to the preservation environment that balances the collections' needs and priorities, capabilities of the facility's mechanical and structural systems, and institutional resources and values.[4] Traditional environmental requirements of temperature at 70°F +/-2°F and humidity at 50 percent +/-5 percent are generally accepted among museums, and an ability to demonstrate adherence to this standard may be necessary to secure loans from many institutions. Recent research, however, particularly by the Image Permanence Institute and the Canadian Conservation Institute, supports a nuanced, performance-based approach to preservation, with a focus on flexible guidelines rather than rigid specifications, and changes may begin to appear in institutional standards in the future. Greater attention has been directed towards the long-term storage environment and seasonal fluctuations, instead of primarily towards short-term variations. Because of the different components of composite objects and the mixed character of museum collections, no single environmental condition will be ideal for all collections or even all components of an object.

Changes in standards for environmental control should be done thoughtfully, taking into consideration the physical structure of the museum, the care of collections, the concerns of lenders, and the current and changing state of research and accepted professional practices.

Environmental conditions can cause three types of damage:

1. *Chemical deterioration* is the result of a chemical reaction. Chemical reaction rates, and hence deterioration, increase with higher temperature, increased concentration of reactants, and increased relative humidity.

2. *Biological deterioration* is caused by living organisms such as molds, insects, and bacteria. These agents become more active at higher temperatures and relative humidity.

3. *Mechanical deterioration* results from movement of the object's components, either due to the amount of water absorbed by organic materials or to thermal expansion of inorganic materials. As the object changes size and shape, cracking, splitting and warping result, causing additional damage to surfaces and joins. In a mixed collection, fluctuations in relative humidity cause more mechanical damage than changes in temperature.

TEMPERATURE

Sources of improper temperature include sunlight, climate, electrical incandescent lighting, building mechanical systems, and inadequately controlled transportation conditions. The traditional temperature target of 70°F +/-2°F has been called into question by research indicating that this specification reflects human comfort, rather than collection needs. Damage due to chemical sensitivity, physical change, and biodeterioration, while not preventable, can be slowed down by ensuring that collections are not stored at improper temperatures (Michalski

2009b). Generally, the preservation of collections will be extended with increasingly low temperatures. For example, the deterioration of materials such as furs, paper archives, and textiles is reduced by storage at 41–50°F (5–10°C).[5] Cellulose nitrate film, which can ignite at temperatures above 106 °F (38°C), should be isolated and stored below freezing.[6] The longevity of acetate- and polyester-based media and photographic and inkjet prints also can be extended by maintaining collections at freezing temperatures.

Temperature control involves considerations of energy cost, environmental impact, and sustainability. Ideally, the environment should be stable, as fluctuations in temperature affect relative humidity. However, recent research[7] indicates that the preservation benefit of temperature stability has been overrated, causing museums to expend resources unnecessarily. Changes in both temperature and relative humidity should occur gradually as the seasons change. Acclimatization in an intermediary space is necessary when moving cultural materials between cooler storage spaces and warmer collections use areas.

RELATIVE HUMIDITY

Relative humidity (RH) may be defined as the proportion of the amount of water vapor in a given quantity of air compared to the maximum amount of water vapor that the air could hold at that same temperature, expressed as a percentage. As air temperature increases, so does its capacity to hold moisture. Therefore, as temperature goes up, the RH goes down and vice versa. These two measurements generally are considered together. Research by the Image Permanence Institute indicates that heat and moisture are the primary rate-controlling factors in almost every form of decay.

The appropriate RH for any object is the range at which change is minimized. In the past, a stable RH level of 50 percent +/-5 percent was sought for mixed collections. However, conservation research has demonstrated that the large expenditures of resources necessary to achieve such tight RH control bring only modest prevention benefits to humidity-related deterioration[8] and can inadvertently produce other environmental problems.[9] Today, any specification must be understood less as a rigid target and more as a range of tolerance for certain types of materials. Many museum objects are composed of multiple materials and, in order to provide a good environment for the entire object, the ideal conditions for a certain constituent may be compromised. A high RH (above 60–70 percent) can produce mold growth on organic materials, leaching of salts from unglazed ceramics and fossils, and rapid corrosion of metals. Hygroscopic (readily taking up and retaining water) materials—such as bone, wood, ivory, paper, textiles, parchment, basketry, animal hides, and some adhesives—will expand with increasing RH, resulting in overall dimensional changes. Absorbed salts in porous archaeological materials also can be activated. When RH decreases, these materials will give up moisture and dissolved salts, causing efflorescence and spalling. Conversely, a low RH (below 40–45 percent) produces desiccation, cracking, and embrittlement in organic materials, such as wooden objects, furniture, panel paintings, furs, and lacquers. Unstable glass alternately "sweats" when the RH exceeds a critical level (~55 percent) and "crizzles" when the critical RH is too low (~40 percent).

Preservation metrics, which translate temperature and RH information into numerical estimates of collection decay risk, allow cultural institutions to assess the preservation quality of their storage environment for different types of collections. Using a software program to model environmental readings collected by a proprietary data logger, the Image Permanence Institute has developed a general quantitative model of organic decay, called the Time-Weighted Preservation Index (TWPI). This index supports a strategic assessment of risks to the collections and cost/benefit approaches and can be used to adjust environmental conditions to maximize collection life. The International Organization for Standardization (ISO) recommends environmental conditions for specific types of photographic, audio, and digital media (www.iso.org). However, since most museums hold a range of such media, frequently incorporating hygroscopic housings or mounts, the Image Permanence Institute has developed an

assessment tool, the Media Storage Quick Reference (www.imagepermanenceinstitute.org/shtml_sub/MSQR.pdf), to help museums determine proper storage environments for specific media.

Maintenance of stable RH is desirable, as extreme and rapid fluctuations ("cycling") can result in damage by changes in shape and size, chemical reactions, and biodeterioration of materials comprising an object. Seasonal extremes in RH, which produce greater damage than short-term events, should be minimized. The rapidity with which an object attains moisture equilibrium with the ambient relative humidity will be determined by the object's constituent materials and its size, mass, and structural configuration. Small fluctuations, such as those occurring within diurnal cycles, are generally less important to big-picture preservation planning but can still result in damage.

LIGHT

Light is radiant energy that permanently damages light-sensitive materials by catalyzing degradation reactions. The type (proportion of ultraviolet and infrared light), intensity (amount of illumination), and duration of light affect an object's condition.

Radiant energy can be characterized by where its waves fall on the color spectrum. Three types of radiation affect the condition of objects:

1. Visible radiation, measured in lux or foot-candles (fc), provides illumination. Visible light can be monitored through the use of a light meter.

2. Ultraviolet (UV) light, invisible short-wave radiation, is the most damaging component of the light spectrum. A UV monitor can be employed for determining the amount of UV radiation as microwatts/lumen (mw/lm).

3. Infrared (IR) or long-wave radiation manifests as both heat and light.

Light fades pigments; causes yellowing, weakening, and disintegration of materials; and can heat an object to an improper temperature. Damage is cumulative and cannot be reversed. The traditional recommended light level for sensitive materials—including textiles, botanical and zoological specimens, pigmented objects, works on paper, and organic materials such as feather, furs, and skins—is no more than 50 lux or 5 fc. Moderately sensitive materials, such as oils and acrylics on board and composite inorganic objects, should be exposed to light levels of not more than 150 lux or 15 fc. The traditional levels recommended for the least light-sensitive materials, such as stone, ceramics, metals, and glass, are not more than 300 lux or 30 fc. Care should be taken at these higher light levels to avoid the generation of excessive heat.[10] An estimate of damage that an object might sustain from exposure to a particular intensity of light and length of exposure can be calculated from an ISO Blue Wool standards card or the Canadian Conservation Institute's light-damage slide rule; a similar assessment for photographic collections is based on a simple algorithm.[11]

Daylight is most hazardous to objects because of its intensity and high UV and IR components. The amount of daylight entering a building should be reduced by shutters, curtains, or blinds. Additionally, excessive UV radiation from daylight can be mitigated by covering windows and skylights with UV-blocking film or with UV-filtering specialty glass or acrylic sheet filters.

At the reduced levels appropriate for object safety, natural lighting appears gloomy and, during evening hours and in windowless areas, must be supplemented by artificial lighting. A museum's lighting scheme may require a combination of artificial sources. Determining the most appropriate supplementary light sources requires balancing costs against risks. Conventional incandescent lamps, such as the ordinary household light bulb, emit very little UV radiation but generate considerable heat. Fluorescent and tungsten-halogen lamps (quartz lamps) emit undesirably high levels of UV radiation, although housing bulbs with UV-filtering sleeves or behind acrylic diffusers reduces the received amount of this radiation. Compact fluorescent lamps, which last longer and offer better color rendition than traditional fluorescents, still require UV-filtering. Mercury or metal halide high-intensity discharge (HID) lamps should not be installed.

In exhibition areas, indirect lighting providing general illumination is often combined with direct light to accent specific objects. Fiber-optic lighting, which transmits light through glass or acrylic fibers, does not discharge infrared or ultraviolet light and, when designed with an external light source, does not produce heat build-up within the case. Unacceptable light levels in exhibits can be addressed by installing movement-sensitive light switches and by limiting the amount of time light-sensitive objects are on display. In addition, the object itself can be shielded by a fabric covering over the case exterior. Storage areas can be evenly illuminated by indirect light that is bounced off a light-colored ceiling. While high-pressure sodium HID lamps might be appropriate for a storage setting due to their low UV emission, low-heat generation, and low-operating costs, they are too intense and pose color-rendition problems when used for direct lighting purposes.

While acknowledging the traditional guidelines for light exposure detailed above, some museums now attempt to balance deterioration from light exposure against the need for visibility by developing a lighting policy that addresses criteria for an acceptable rate of fading, assesses object sensitivities, considers visibility, appraises available lighting equipment, and determines display time.[12]

CONTAMINANTS (GASES, LIQUIDS, AND SOLIDS)

Contaminants damage all objects through disintegration, discoloration, and corrosion. Chemically reactive and porous materials are particularly vulnerable to such deterioration. Pollutants can reach objects through airborne delivery or contact with contaminated material, or the pollutants may be intrinsic to the object itself (Tétrault 2009).

Gaseous pollutants—primarily sulfur dioxide (SO_2), nitrogen dioxide (NO_2), and ozone (O_3)—can catalyze deleterious chemical reactions. Ozone, for example, which comes from photocopiers and electrostatic air purifiers, produces a chemical reaction that breaks down both inorganic and organic materials. Other pollutants cause metals to tarnish. Objects incorporating intrinsic pollutants, such as wool, sulfur-based compounds, or polyurethane foam, can cause damage to themselves by off-gassing.[13]

Particulate pollutants, such as pollen and dust, fibers, and soot, can enter the museum through open windows and doors, through unfiltered ventilation systems, or via people's clothing and bodies. Interior particulate pollutants can be generated by construction and maintenance activities and cigarette smoke, among other sources. Particulates leave a disfiguring and abrasive layer on objects that must be mechanically removed.

Moisture and oils from human hands will stain organic materials and corrode metals. As a regular part of object handling, staff should be encouraged to wash their hands and required to wear appropriate gloves. Objects should be enclosed or palletized to minimize the need for direct handling.

The primary response to potential damage from pollutants is the minimization or elimination of contact, either by creating a physical barrier between the object and pollutants or by chemically altering the rate of deterioration through increased exposure to reactive compounds.[14] Air-filtration systems clean incoming air of its particulate and gaseous contaminants.[15] For further protection, individual objects can be stored in neutral tissue or untreated cotton or linen under polyethylene sheeting or in boxes constructed of acid-free corrugated board. Storage housings for acidic materials can incorporate an alkaline buffer to neutralize acidity Additional protection against environmental pollutants and byproducts of deterioration not neutralized by alkaline-buffered storage material is afforded by a molecular trap, either activated carbon or zeolites.[16] Potential off-gassing by cleaning materials, paints, and varnishes should be reviewed before collections are exposed to these substances. Storage and display materials should be tested in advance for potential off-gassing and adequate time built into schedules to allow required chemical curing of materials to occur. More fundamentally, the rate of deterioration can be slowed by protecting collections from improper levels of temperature, relative humidity, and light.

PESTS

Pests such as insects and rodents feed on the organic constituents of objects and their storage materials.

In addition to the grazing damage caused directly by pests, consequential wastes foul objects and attract additional pests. Many institutions follow an IPM program.[17] The components of an IPM program include monitoring, identification, inspection, habitat modification, good housekeeping, treatment action, education, and evaluation. Pest activity should be monitored by visual inspection and by recording contents of pest traps at regular intervals. If an infestation occurs, material should be isolated, treated, and cleaned. Future infestations can be prevented by:

- inspecting objects brought into the museum
- quarantining any objects suspected of or exhibiting insect activity
- controlling the sites at which pests enter the museum
- removing pest attractants, such as food residues, pest carcasses, and mold
- establishing environmental conditions (cool, dry, good air circulation) inhospitable to pests

Positive pest management can prevent the enormous costs of remediating an infestation; mitigate staff illnesses caused by exposure to molds, mildews, and other allergens; and obviate expensive conservation treatments for damaged collections. Chemical pesticides pose risks to museum personnel and objects[18] and are not recommended unless absolutely necessary. The long-term effects of the residue of chemical pesticides, both upon objects and humans who will handle them in the future, should be fully considered.[19] Non-chemical alternatives currently employed by conservators include subjecting infested materials to freezing or modified atmospheres (decreased oxygen, increased carbon dioxide, or introduction of inert gases) for periods sufficient to destroy all stages of the insect's life cycle.

COLLECTIONS CONTAINERS LARGE AND SMALL: FROM THE BUILDING TO THE STORAGE BOX

Registrars and collections managers should work with facility managers and administrators to promote a shared understanding about the importance of the physical plant and mechanical systems in promoting appropriate collections care. Equipment that fails or is operated improperly poses a risk to collections preservation. Energy efficiency, the ability of the building and its mechanical systems to modify the outdoor climate, preservation requirements, and human comfort all need to be balanced. Prohibiting collections storage and exhibition from environmentally compromised areas of the building, most typically the basement and attic, mitigates the risk of damage. Decisions about how and where to house collections can inexpensively enhance preservation. Improper RH levels can be avoided by locating storage units away from exterior walls and elevated above cool floors. Proximity to heating units should be avoided. Museums that include buildings as part of their collections have an additional problem: The external environment, against which most of the collections are protected by the structures housing them, is in these cases in direct contact with the collection itself.

Microenvironments can be produced to maintain desired temperature and RH levels within small areas. In exhibition cases, humidity can be buffered or reduced through the use of silica gel, a porous, non-crystalline form of silica[20] or saturated salts.[21] These materials must be properly conditioned in order to be effective. In storage, a quantity of cellulosic materials may be incorporated into the object's container in order to buffer fluctuations in RH and temperature.[22]

RECORD KEEPING

Temperature and relative humidity should be constantly monitored in storage and exhibition areas with the use of properly calibrated and maintained data-gathering instruments, such as recording hygrothermographs, dosimeters, data loggers, or other sensors. Building-wide records of environmental conditions, including pest activity, should be retained. Condition information, including treatment records and traveling condition reports, should be incorporated into an object's permanent file. Visual images should supplement textual records. Full and accurate record keeping is of crucial importance when an

object has been treated with pesticides, such as arsenic and ethylene oxide, which are themselves hazardous to humans. Monitoring the conditions in which an object is housed enables museum staff to determine whether the environment considered to be suitable has been realized and to assess its effect upon the object. Ideally, data analysis enables museum staff to predict the occurrence and severity of biodeterioration and mechanical damage and to quantify the rate of chemical damage. These records will contribute to the development of a performance-based collections-care model incorporating general conservation and object-specific assessments, environmental and storage upgrades, and conservation management. •

NOTES

1. Randolph 1987, p. 3

2. Untch 2006

3. Appelbaum 1991; Lull 1995

4. Grattan and Michalski 2009; Weintraub 2006

5. Thomson 1986, p. 45

6. NFPA 2007; Wilhelm 1993

7. Michalski 2009b

8. Michalski 1994; 2009a

9. Weintraub 2006

10. Lull and Merk 1982a, p. 20; 1982b, p. 9

11. Von Waldthausen 2003

12. (Michalski 2009c; Weintraub 2006).

13. Grzywacz 2006; Tétrault 2009

14. Hatchfield 2002; Tétrault 2009

15. Thomson 1986, pp. 133–35, 156–58

16. Rempel 1996

17. Kingsley et al. 2001; Pinniger 2001; Strang 1994; Zycherman 1988

18. Webster 1990

19. Odegaard and Sadongei 2005

20. Lafontaine 1984

21. Creahan 1991a, 1991b; Piechota 1992

22. Piechota 1978

5H | STORAGE

LYNN SWAIN, REVISED AND UPDATED BY REBECCA BUCK

INTRODUCTION

Most museum collections are held in storage. Museums often report that only 2 to 5 percent of their collections are on exhibit; the number of objects or specimens that can be shown is dependent on size of the collection, exhibition space, conservation funding, and discipline. House museums with stable collections might show a large percentage of their holdings while art museums with large collections and limited exhibition space show few objects. Science and archaeological collections often number in the hundreds of thousands, and most are held for research. Those objects that are not shown rest in storage.

As professional museum positions have evolved, storage issues have become a concern primarily of collections managers and registrars as well as curators and conservators. There must be a good team approach to these issues, and there must be clarity about the various tasks associated with storage. The collections management policy for each institution should clearly state which staff position has primary responsibility for care and development of storage areas, for maintenance, and for inventory. This allocation of responsibility generally is determined as much by the size and history of the collections and the density of workers in various departments as it is by accepted standards.

For many museums with limited funds, sophisticated cabinets and unlimited acid-free boxes may seem unattainable. Yet even the biggest and most well-funded museums struggle with storage issues as larger collections often create larger problems. Without good storage, collections are neither safe nor accessible, and their lifetime is shortened. In most cases a course of gradual improvements consistently implemented can make a dramatic impact on the life span of objects.

The goals of good storage are to protect and preserve collections. Disasters, environmental factors, physical damage, and problems caused by poor-quality storage materials all can be mitigated or prevented with adequate planning and information. This chapter provides guidance in storage methods, materials, and equipment.

STORAGE AREAS

Collections storage should be located in an area separate from all other activity, removed from exhibition, preparation, and general administrative functions. In the best of worlds, storage space will not be at the top of the building or in any area below grade. Spaces should not have mechanical systems—electrical, air, or water—running through them. There should be no windows, and areas should be isolated enough to be easily secured. They should be located in an area that is privately accessed from the outside, through a loading dock and prep area, and from the inside, through corridors or doors leading to preparation and exhibition space.

Many museums have a centralized storage area. A growing number of museums use separate warehouses or buildings away from the main museum as offsite storage or for storage of less frequently needed objects, but such facilities present difficulties with access, monitoring, and security. In addition, insurance companies are demanding greater control over offsite areas than they have in the past. Some museums develop open (or visible) storage areas where collections can be viewed by the public, although the practice may mean an increase in light, dust levels, and environmental problems. Depending on the space available, separate rooms or areas within buildings can be used for discrete portions of the collections. Historic house museums sometimes adapt spaces like attics or closets into storage for smaller objects. Careful consideration should go into such adaptive uses, however, to avoid pipes, windows, and skylights as well as the heat, humidity, infestation, and disaster potential of attics and basements.

Large, centralized storage areas, whether in the museum or an offsite location, usually are divided into areas by material type. It is efficient for access and for consistent and modular storage development to store all like objects together: all paper, all paintings, all large flat textiles, etc. Within material categories, objects may be grouped by type (e.g., costumes, rugs, and laces under textiles) or arranged by size, geographic origin, cultural area, or accession number. Scientific collections are stored by their discipline-specific classification system (e.g., taxonomically for biological collections, by mineral families for mineral collections).

For fire and security reasons, storage areas also should be divided into discrete rooms. In addition to physical efficiency, it is easier to adjust environmental control if like objects are stored together. Some museums store objects by curatorial discipline, for instance, all Native American objects together, all textiles or decorative arts together. There has been a gradual change toward centralized storage by object and material type in many museums, but the issues are institution-specific and need to be addressed by all members of the collections team.

Accessibility of objects in storage is critical. Each storage area, from room to bank of cabinets to individual drawer, should be clearly labeled with its contents. Positioning objects in storage with their accession numbers, labels, or tags visible and maintaining up-to-date inventories greatly facilitates access and minimizes object handling. The old adage of "a place for everything and everything in its place" helps with accessibility and inventory as well as protects objects.

STORAGE FURNITURE

Each collections room should be outfitted with the furniture and materials that will safely store the objects that will be placed in that area. Most collections may be properly stored in closed cabinets or on open shelving with dust and light covers. Sliding

racks are available for paintings and racks also often are used for collections of weapons. Flat textiles either are rolled or stored folded in drawers; costumes may be padded and stored in boxes or drawers, but many are padded and hung. Paper objects may be placed in folders and then into modular boxes, or they may be matted, boxed, and placed in cabinets or on shelves. Three-dimensional objects present unique challenges that have to be resolved by creative staff members.

Outfitting a Storage Area

•Review the objects to be stored, including material type, sizes, numbers of objects.

•Check literature for currently preferred storage methods, furniture, and object housing.

•Visit museums with similar collections, particularly those that have recently renovated storage areas, to learn good and bad points of storage types.

•Consult with conservators who are clear about pros and cons of various storage options.

•Develop a storage floor plan with furniture. If using companies with museum storage expertise, get more than one plan with price proposal.

•Plan staff responsibilities and the time needed for implementation.

•Order storage furniture and materials needed to store specific objects.

Storage areas often are developed incrementally using these same steps. Upgrading or developing new storage is time-consuming and expensive, and must be carefully planned. Seeking out local, state, and national funding sources is vital.

Metal cabinets are available with sulfur-free, heavy-duty gaskets, to keep out dust, and with filtered vents, if air circulation within the cabinet is desired. Cabinet interiors may be designed with modular shelving and drawers or hanging options to meet the needs of many types of small to mid-sized objects. Preferred cabinets are painted using an electrostatic process to avoid the problem of paint solvents off-gassing and harming the objects stored inside. Wood and wood-composite shelving and cabinets are considered less than optimum because of the acids they contain. If wood storage must be used, it should house only objects made solely of wood, stone, ceramic, or glass; in addition, shelves and drawers should be lined, preferably with Mylar.

Stable storage environments can be created without a central climate-control system. Closed cabinets with good sulfur-free gaskets provide a considerable buffer from exterior environmental fluctuations. Individual acid-free boxes can add another layer of insulation. Silica gel conditioned to a specific relative humidity (RH) can be used in individual drawers or cabinets to minimize and will slow down changes in the RH. These microclimate techniques can be used to meet the humidity needs of special materials, even within a climate-controlled situation. Striving for RH stability at the microclimate level is one of the most important goals of good storage.

Pollutant problems also can be mitigated without a centralized air-filtration system. Closed cabinets can minimize dust problems, but certain types of materials stored together in a closed environment can react with each other (e.g., sulfur, a component of natural rubber, will corrode silver). Dust covers on individual open shelves are a low-cost method for minimizing exposure. Covers can be made of cotton muslin if air circulation and reduced light are important, or they can be made of an inert plastic film, like polyethylene sheeting, if reduced air movement and visibility of objects on the shelves is a higher priority. Plastic films should be checked often since they can cause condensation and mold problems. Dust covers should not touch or rest on objects.

Museum-specific storage equipment has advantages over commercial storage units designed for other purposes. Some are specifically designed to handle particular types of collections. Large racks on wheels or tracks are available for paintings and other framed artworks or oversized wall hangings. Large rollers can help prevent the stress caused by folding quilts and other flat textiles. Zoological fluid-preserved collections should be stored in an appropriate preservative in airtight jars and then placed on sturdy shelving with light covers. Safes or vaults are available for high-value and fire-sensitive objects, although floors may need special reinforcement to support their weight. Oversize objects, like farm

wagons, sculptures, or mounted elephants, can be stored in open shelving in a warehouse.

When space is at a premium, cabinets and storage units can be mounted on compactor tracks, which eliminate the need for aisles between every bank of cabinets or shelves, thereby effectively doubling the amount of usable space in a given area. Staff working near compactor units and stacked cabinets need to pay extra attention to safety to prevent accidents.

Several manufacturers specialize in museum storage equipment, with a good deal of variability in price. Storage cabinets can range from several hundred to several thousand dollars depending on their size, material, paint finish, airtightness, and arrangement of drawers or shelves.

STORAGE MATERIALS

Specialized storage materials can be used to support and pad objects to protect them from bumps and snags caused by overcrowding, vibrations, or internal structural failure. *(See chapter on Preparation.)* Within each storage unit, each three-dimensional object should have a place to stand or lie by itself on a shelf or in a drawer, rather than be stacked or crowded with others in the same compartment. Adequate padding and supports should protect objects from collisions and vibrations caused by walking or by retrieving other objects. Objects being hung should be supported in more than one place to prevent the weight of the object from tearing the edges away from the hanger. Individual boxes can add an extra layer of microclimate insulation and make moving objects easier.

The types of materials and supplies used in storage can directly affect collections. Many commonly used office supplies do not have archival qualities. Unknown materials should not be used. Unless materials have been tested and proven to be inert, they place the collections at risk. Use storage materials recommended by a conservator for specific collection situations.

Storage Materials to Avoid
•Cellophane tape dries out, and the adhesive creates stains.

•Cotton wool can snag on rough textures and be impossible to remove.

•Foam rubber and urethane foam produce fumes that deteriorate objects; they are also flammable.

•Masking tape contains an adhesive that is not easily removable.

•Metal paper clips, unless they are made of stainless steel, rust and stain.

•Nail polish and polish remover can cause adverse chemical reactions.

•Paper products must be carefully checked. Some office paper, paper towels, cardboard, and cigar boxes are highly acidic.

•Most plastics (e.g., kitchen plastic wrap, dry-cleaning bags) contain chlorinated compounds and plasticizers that give them flexibility; these compounds can migrate out and harm objects. In addition, materials trapped in airtight plastic wrap may mold or mildew.

•Rubber bands crumble as they deteriorate.

•Rubber cement stains.

•White glue can become acidic and is not reversible.

•Wood products (especially unsealed) produce damaging acids.

Tested and Recommended Storage Materials

•Acid-free paper products (e.g., tissue paper, writing paper, photocopy paper, file folders, archival boxes) may be either buffered or unbuffered. Unbuffered paper has a neutral pH and is used for housing photographs, textiles, and most other types of objects. Buffered paper is impregnated with calcium carbonate, giving it an alkaline pH. Used for storing paper objects, it absorbs the acids they emit and keeps the micro-environment from becoming dangerously acidic for a longer period of time. All paper products will gradually acidify over time, so even acid-free storage materials need to be replaced after a period of years. Boxes and trays in modular sizes designed to fit standard cabinet drawers can be used to house a wide variety of objects.

•Cotton fabrics and threads may be used; they should be washed to remove sizing chemicals. Linen also may be used.

•Plastic paper clips do not rust and stain, but they easily bend and distort paper. Use with care.

•Polyester batting can be used for all sorts of padding projects; it is particularly good with textiles.

•Polyester film (sometimes called by the brand name Mylar) is used in paper preservation and as a vapor barrier.

•Polyethylene microfoam (often referred to as Ethafoam, the brand name of the Dow Chemical Company version) is an inert foam which comes in a variety of thicknesses. It has a multitude of uses in the storage environment, from lining drawers and shelves (usually 1/8" or 1/4" thicknesses) for padding and slip protection to cutting special mounts or cradles (2" or thicker).

•Polypropylene bags come in a multitude of sizes, with or without zip closures, and are useful for containing all sorts of small objects. They should be ventilated to prevent condensation.

•Special adhesives based on methyl cellulose or wheat or rice starch, which are water soluble and non-toxic.

•Special envelopes and mounts are available for many objects; these include coin envelopes, frames, gem papers, and doll stands.

Conservationally sound storage materials are available from a variety of specialty suppliers. In some areas, museums have banded together to form purchasing cooperatives to buy supplies at discounted rates. Storage materials should be kept in a clean and environmentally friendly place separate from collections, such as a preparation area.

ENVIRONMENT

Environmental stability involves temperature and RH. Fluctuations in either cause stress to collections materials by forcing them to expand and contract on a microscopic level. This stress eventually wears out the collections. Keeping the temperature and RH as stable as possible in storage areas is one of the most critical ways to prevent deterioration.

Each type of material has traditionally had an optimum temperature and RH range based on its chemical composition. *(See chapter on Preventive Care.)* General solutions to temperature and RH problems usually begin by monitoring levels and fluctuations with hygrothermographs. Although expensive, these instruments are necessary to determine base levels and demonstrate improvements after changes are made. To function optimally, they must be calibrated as recommended by the manufacturer. Museums with small budgets may be able to borrow one or fund the purchase through a conservation grant. Data loggers are a newer and somewhat less expensive technology for monitoring environmental conditions.

A centralized HVAC (heating, ventilation, and air conditioning) or climate-control system can maintain temperature and RH at constant levels. Historic house museums may face a challenge to retrofit their buildings without destroying the historical integrity and generating structural challenges by installing HVAC. The building may need RH levels different from those required by the artifacts stored within them. Seasonal changes may be resolved by slowly increasing the HVAC output to minimize damage to both the structure and its artifacts. Optimally, collections storage should be placed in a separate building or wing that can be climate controlled without confronting these issues. At the room level, humidifiers or dehumidifiers can be used to bring RH closer to optimum levels.

Pollutants also cause gradual deterioration in storage. They come in many forms—from dust to cigarette smoke to off-gassing from chemicals in cleaners or preservatives. Corrosive gasses may also be generated by certain storage materials or even the objects themselves. Common culprits are unsealed wooden shelving (especially plywood and composite wood products), paints and solvents, and acidic paper products. Sealing the building to minimize the intrusion of dust and fumes is one way to reduce pollutant problems. Developing an air-filtration system, often as part of the HVAC unit, is another.

Regular housekeeping by staff trained in handling objects provides inspection of materials for possible problems.

Pests come in many forms, from insects to small mammals, such as rodents, and they infest organic collections of all types; some are dangerous to humans as well. Routine fumigation can add levels of toxic chemicals to the collections. Current theory recommends the integrated pest management (IPM) approach, based on intensive monitoring of sticky traps for insects and other traps for rodents, locating and eliminating pest entrances and attractors based on the monitoring, banning food in collections areas, and, as a last resort, chemical treatment. Treatments always should be carried out with the advice of a professional conservator or pest manager. *(See chapter on Integrated Pest Management.)*

Light levels should be kept low in storage areas to protect against both intense visible and ultraviolet (UV) light, which can cause fading or trigger chemical reactions. Light damage is permanent and irreversible but easy to prevent by keeping objects in the dark. Eliminate windows in storage, or black out existing windows. Use banked lighting systems, and turn off lights when the storage area is not in use. Closed cabinets minimize exposure of objects while staff members are working in the storage area. Light levels can be monitored with a relatively inexpensive light meter, which small museums may be able to borrow from larger institutions nearby or from a state museums organization. Fluorescent bulbs have a high UV output and should be fitted with filters. Halogen bulbs generate significant heat in confined areas, which can trigger or exacerbate chemical decay. Often a little ingenuity in rearranging light placement, using different types of bulbs, and adding filters can minimize the potential for light damage.

SECURITY

Security against theft and vandalism is a critical component of all good storage areas. Art objects and jewelry are often thought of as theft concerns, although other objects—such as prints in 19th-century magazines, military paraphernalia, autographed documents, certain minerals, and insects of value to collectors—may be vulnerable. High-profile, "professional" theft is rare, but casual theft is always a possibility. A large proportion of theft in museums is carried out by employees.

Museums should start with good hiring practices, using criminal-background checks for all employees who interact with collections. This should include any interns and volunteers who work in collections areas and all maintenance personnel who are assigned work in vulnerable areas. As increased national security protocol has developed, post 9/11, staff should be aware that they also might have to undergo background checks as well.

Procedures for monitoring access to storage are important. Staff should be logged into storage by key-card systems, key-control logs, or sign-in sheets in the storage area. Sign-in sheets should be used in conjunction with other systems, and all visitors to storage, whether scholars or people installing or repairing systems, should be logged in.

A key-control system must be established to determine who has access to storage. Curators, conservators, collections managers, and registrars who need to work with collections should be able to obtain access easily, but unauthorized personnel and members of the public should not. Often restricted access is achieved by keying separate storage areas with different but related locks. Staff needing access to one storage area have a key that works only in that lock, while registration or security staff members who need access to many areas have a master key. Key lists should be kept by security, and keys should be turned in when staff members leave at the end of the day. If keys are lost or stolen, locks should be changed immediately.

Key-card systems with computer monitoring are considered more secure than hardware systems and allow the tracking of persons entering and leaving storage. It is important, regardless of the method chosen, to have written policies and a clear line of command protecting access to storage.

Physical changes to storage areas can improve security. Storage should be designed with a minimum of entrances and exits, so access can be easily monitored. If a building is retrofitted for storage, eliminate unnecessary doors and block all windows. Alarm systems can generate an alert if unauthorized entry or departure has taken place. Often these can be low-cost magnetic contacts on normally unused doors and windows. A vault should be available to protect high-value objects from theft and valuable documents from fire.

Monitoring the use of storage is critical to security. Closed-circuit video systems can be installed either inside or at the entrance to storage areas. It is best to develop a separate work space outside the storage area for researchers to study collections. If researchers are permitted directly into storage areas, staff should personally oversee them at all times. Visitor logs should be kept to track who uses which parts of the collections. Good records of who had access to storage may help track a thief or vandal if such an event occurs. Regular inventory procedures add to security by identifying missing or damaged objects and locating misplaced objects in a timely fashion.

RISK

Handling places objects at a much higher risk of damage than when they are sitting still on a shelf or in a drawer. *(See chapter on Handling.)* Staff should be trained in appropriate techniques for handling the range of objects in the collections and in the use of moving equipment. Precautions include padding lifts and dollies; moving small, fragile objects on carts instead of carrying by hand; lifting objects from underneath by the sturdiest part; and taking extra time and care when on ladders or stairs. If each object can be stored in its own box, the box can be lifted out of a drawer, and direct contact with the object can be avoided. Easily visible labels or accession numbers also minimize handling needs. Since most inks are not easily removed, limit writing implements in storage and research areas to pencils only.

HOUSEKEEPING

Housekeeping in storage areas should be given special consideration, and drawing up a housekeeping plan indicating tasks to be undertaken at specific intervals can be helpful. For security and handling reasons, collections management staff may prefer to perform these duties rather than delegate them to the janitorial staff. Staff cleaning storage areas should be trained in the concerns of each particular collection. Collections areas should be cleaned regularly to minimize dust and potential pest attractants. Material Safety Data Sheets (MSDS) should be reviewed and cleaning solutions should be chosen carefully to avoid accidental introduction of corrosive or dangerous chemicals. When maintenance workers are required to be in storage areas, staff with collections responsibilities should oversee the workers.

WORK AREAS

Under ideal circumstances, separate areas physically distinct from the rest of storage should be established for several purposes: temporary storage for processing objects in transit, a place for researchers to study the collections, and a space for keeping storage supplies. Office supplies and cleaning materials should be isolated from collections storage.

Temporary storage for processing objects moving into or out of the museum should be maintained at the same RH as the exhibition or storage areas to which the objects will proceed next. Allow sufficient time for the objects to equilibrate to the climatic conditions inside the museum building. The general rule-of-thumb is 24 hours, but lenders may specify other timelines. This time should also be used to monitor arriving objects for signs of pest infestation. If pests are discovered, objects should be sealed and treated before the problem can spread to other parts of the collections.

DISASTER PREPARATION

Disaster preparation for large- or small-scale disasters or emergencies, whether natural or manmade, is covered elsewhere in this book, along with more detailed information on preventive care. *(See chapter on Disaster Preparation.)* Storage-specific issues of disaster prevention include many building maintenance concerns. Install monitoring and alarm systems for fire, smoke, water, and intruders. Be aware of water pipes running through storage and avoid placing objects beneath them. Keep objects elevated off the floor in case of water leaks in the area. Store objects in closed cabinets to keep out leaking water and to provide shelter and insulation in case of fire. Mount storage furniture on vibration-dampening pads in earthquake-prone areas. Install emergency lighting and have flashlights handy. Train staff in the locations and uses of emergency systems.

Fire-suppression systems should be installed in storage areas. Current thinking recommends a water-sprinkler system with air-charged pipes. The air in the pipe prevents water leaks and gives a time delay to stop the system if a false alarm is triggered. In most instances, the potential fire damage, possibility of the fire spreading, and smoke damage are considered higher risks than water damage from the sprinkler system, but this should be evaluated carefully for each particular collection with input from local fire officials and conservators. Mist systems also should be considered. Fire extinguishers should be positioned regularly throughout the building and staff instructed in their use.

CONCLUSION

Ideal storage—with each object in an individually labeled, acid-free box, in a drawer within a metal cabinet, inside a climate-controlled room, in a well-maintained building—may seem like a daunting goal, but each layer of protection increases the longevity of an object. As conservators learn more about the nature of museum materials and what causes them to deteriorate, the definition of good storage changes as well. Federal grants, such as those available from the National Endowments for the Arts and Humanities, the National Science Foundation, and the Institute of Museum and Library Services, can help pay for a conservator's assessment of storage situations and for implementing improvements on a matching fund basis. The primary storage goal is always to do no harm and to protect and preserve collections for future generations. •

MAUREEN McCORMICK

The creation and maintenance of a reliable, accurate, and up-to-date inventory is critical to the mission of any museum and is worth the often sizeable investment of museum resources—human and otherwise—in what is an admittedly Sisyphean task. Despite the demands of exhibitions, outgoing loans, insurance-policy renewals, shipping arrangements, and indemnity applications, it is essential to find the time to create and maintain an inventory of the institution's collection.

Never before have museums been held to such high standards of transparency and best practices. The American Association of Museums (AAM) recently published *National Standards & Best Practices for U.S. Museums,*[1] which summarizes and codifies decades of wisdom collected from the hundreds of museums that have elected to go through its rigorous peer-review accreditation process. Among the 38 "Characteristics of Excellence for U.S. Museums (in translation)" are the following from section IV, Collections Stewardship (paraphrased):

- know what stuff you have
- know where it is
- take good care of it

First and foremost, an accurate inventory of a museum's collections underpins its fiduciary imperative to hold its collections for the public trust. However proprietary we may have come to feel about the objects in "our" collections, they are not ours; they are not even "our museum's." These objects belong to current and future generations and, as such, are not ours to lose track of or misplace. Therefore:

> Registrars, through the records maintained, are accountable for the objects in custody of their museums and must be able to provide current information on each object, its location, status, and condition.[2]

We document our collection objects in order to preserve them and to make them accessible to the public. An accurate and current inventory supports preservation by:

- identifying objects that require conservation
- identifying objects that require improved storage conditions in order to prevent or mitigate deterioration
- documenting the location and movement history of an object for security purposes
- documenting the collection in the event of a catastrophic loss

Knowing what we have and where we have it is, of course, essential to making our collections accessible to the public. Moreover, an inventory:

- enables and invites research on the collection
- identifies poorly or undocumented objects so that they may be better researched and documented
- may be required by law (e.g., NAGPRA)[3]
- may provide an opportunity to digitize the collection

From a purely pragmatic standpoint, a reliable inventory, or the process of conducting an inventory:

- facilitates day-to-day management of the collection
- complies with institutional audit requirements, especially if the museum is part of a larger institution, such as a university
- identifies missing objects so that appropriate action may commence
- "starts the clock ticking" for museums in states with legislation to address old loans or objects found in the collections (*see chapter on Old Loans*)
- provides an opportunity to review object

movement procedures and put protocols for best practices in place

•engenders confidence in the museum on the part of donors, lenders, and other constituencies

TYPES OF INVENTORIES

The most comprehensive inventory is called, variously, a complete inventory, a 100-percent inventory, a wall-to-wall inventory, or a baseline inventory. Whatever term is preferred, the goal of a complete inventory is to document the location of every object that is in—or is *supposed* to be in—the museum's custody. This survey will include not only objects in the permanent collection but also objects that are owned by the museum but not accessioned (e.g., study collections), objects in temporary custody, and long-term loans. Likewise, a complete inventory will confirm the location of objects that are out on short- or long-term loan, in commercial offsite storage, or otherwise off-premises for official purposes. The benefit of a complete inventory is that it can be authoritatively reconciled (or justified) against the museum's records, identifying 1. records for which no object was located, and 2. objects for which there is no documentation (see Reconciling the Inventory, below).

A partial, or section-by-section, inventory is limited in its scope to some logical unit, such as objects on display, objects in one particular storage area, or high-value objects. Gallery reinstallations and storeroom renovations present good opportunities for conducting partial inventories. Although valuable, and certainly better than no inventory at all, partial inventories, by definition, cannot be definitively reconciled against museum records.

A random, or spot inventory, is very limited in scope. Its goal is to verify the location of a representative sampling of objects, thereby checking the reliability of a museum's location records. An ongoing program of random spot inventories also may act as an effective deterrent to insider theft.

The rest of this chapter is concerned primarily with planning for and implementing a complete collections inventory, as this is the most complex and labor intensive type; many of the principles also are applicable to partial and spot inventories.

PLANNING THE INVENTORY

Every minute spent in planning an inventory will save hours in its implementation. The first step is to determine its purpose and scope and to articulate this succinctly in writing. Questions will arise, and decisions will have to be made throughout the course of the inventory; a carefully conceived project plan will guide the effort and keep it on track. A good place to start is with the Collections Management Policy (CMP), which ideally includes an affirmative statement that the museum will inventory its collections on a regular basis, will offer general guidelines on the appropriate frequency and type of inventory (e.g., weekly or monthly random inventories; annual section-by-section inventory to achieve 100 percent every five years; 100-percent inventory every 10 years at minimum, etc.), and will detail what actions will be taken with respect to missing objects and undocumented objects. If the museum does not have a CMP or it is hopelessly out of date or incomplete, the chapter on collection management policies in this book, the excellent chapter on the subject in Marie Malaro's *A Legal Primer on Managing Museum Collections*,[4] and *Things Great and Small: Collections Management Policies* provide help in drafting or updating a policy, which must then be approved by the museum's governing authority. An institutional imperative is critical to the ultimate success of the admittedly unglamorous and laborious inventory process and goes to the important work of building institutional support.

Unless a museum's collection is very small, a complete collections inventory almost certainly will constitute a disruption in its day-to-day operation and will divert staff and financial resources away from other activities. Success will depend in large part on the cooperation of many, if not all, of the museum staff. It is important, therefore, to have "top-down" support from the governing authority, museum director, and curatorial departments, and a well-crafted CMP can be a great ally. A planned building expansion or renovation project, the move of all or a significant portion of the collection to temporary or new quarters, or preparing for AAM accreditation can be good (and hard to argue against) catalysts for conducting a complete inventory. Similarly, an inventory can be piggy-backed onto an institutional push to digitize and put collections online.

Once an inventory project has philosophical support, it is necessary to establish the practical support—staff, time, and money—needed. Begin by defining what will constitute a standard inventory record. In general, a basic inventory record should be as concise as possible and include at least:

- the accession or other unique inventory control number

- "tombstone" information about the object (artist/maker, title/description, medium)

- current location

- inventory staff member(s) and date

Depending on the goals and scope of the inventory, it may also include:

- a brief condition assessment

- direct digital-image capture

- dimensions (new or confirm existing)

- an assessment of storage needs (storage mount, backing, new hardware, etc.)

Obviously, the more ambitious the inventory is in its scope, the more time and resources it will require. However, the additional investment required to broaden the scope of the inventory may repay itself many times over in the long run. For example, if a collection move looms in the near or mid-term future, taking or confirming measurements or bar coding at the time of the inventory would be well advised.

Next, factor in planning assumptions.

- Will it be possible to close galleries or "freeze" storage areas?

- Will it be possible to impose moratoria or limit activities such as exhibitions, outgoing loans, etc.? Or must the museum continue business as usual during the inventory?

- Is it possible to divert and dedicate existing staff to the inventory? Hire dedicated term staff? Rely on interns and volunteers?

- Does a record for each object in the museum's custody exist in its collections management system (CMS), or will retrospective data entry be required?[6]

- Is there enough "elbow room" in the storage areas to allow for objects to be examined and documented in situ, or will objects need to be moved out of storage? Can non-storage space (e.g., a gallery that can be secured) be designated as an inventory area for collections that can easily be moved (e.g., Solander boxes of works on paper)?

- Will the inventory attempt to include accessories, such as object mounts and frames?

- If the inventory will include direct digital capture, what quality of images will be made? ID quality only? Publication quality? How many images will be taken of three-dimensional objects?

Consider also strategy and methods.

- Will inventory data be entered directly into the CMS (e.g., is the museum wireless and does it have or can it purchase laptop computers)? Or will checklists be generated from the CMS (by location, collection, etc.), annotated, and inventory data retrospectively entered?

- Will inventory staff be trained for one task only (e.g., art handling, data entry, digital photography), or will they be cross-trained?

- Will bar codes or other inventory technologies, such as RFID (radio frequency identification be used? (See sidebar on Bar Codes.)

- How will unnumbered or otherwise unidentifiable objects be documented?

- What equipment and materials are already on hand? What will need to be purchased?

Once these and other variables specific to the collection and museum have been pinned down, it is time to conduct one or several trial runs through representative sections of the collection. Track how long it takes to inventory Solander boxes full of matted works on paper versus large pieces of furniture versus paintings on display in the galleries versus the drawers full of dinosaur bones. Do not forget to take into account the time necessary to process digital images, download bar-code readers, etc. This exercise almost certainly will bring to the fore questions not previously considered and otherwise make obvious any false assumptions in the plan. Problem solve. Conduct more trial runs. Eventually it will be possible to extrapolate an accurate estimate of how long the inventory might reasonably take. This timetable can always be condensed by dedicating more staff or modifying other planning assumptions.

PREPARING FOR THE INVENTORY

With a basic strategy established, there is still much to be done before embarking on the actual inventory.

Conduct retrospective data entry, if necessary. Is there an electronic record for every object in the permanent collection or custody? Are the data sufficiently systematized to produce reliable queries and reports? If not, it would be advisable to address this situation before beginning the inventory.

Design queries and data-entry screens. If object location and other data are to be entered directly into the CMS, and if the CMS is typical of today's complex off-the-shelf systems, a custom-designed data-entry screen that includes only the fields pertinent to the inventory will speed up the inventory significantly. If the museum does not have staff capable of designing such a tool, the software vendor can do so, and the cost will be money well spent.

Design forms and reports. If instead of direct data entry the plan is to annotate lists generated by the CMS, design these queries and reports. Again, the CMS vendor should be able to assist if in-house expertise does not exist.

Organize storage. A logically organized and tidy store area also will speed up the process and minimize risks to collection objects and inventory staff.

Create a location authority for all storage and gallery locations. Physically label all locations where practical to do so. The location authority should be hierarchical and detailed, for example see below.

If the CMS accommodates controlled vocabulary drop-down menus, employ this capability to ensure consistent location descriptions. Assign and limit the authority to create new locations to two or three inventory staff members.

Develop thorough written guidelines and protocols for inventory staff. These guidelines should include:

- documentation rules and vocabulary authorities
- art-handling procedures
- condition-assessment guidelines and nomenclature
- how to document objects with multiple components
- how or whether to document object accessories
- how to document objects without numbers or other identifying information

Hire or train staff or volunteers. Traditional best practices suggest that inventory staff work in teams of two or three: an art handler; a reader, who refers to and verifies or amends current object record; and a scribe. The potential advantages of this model are efficiency, enhanced security against insider theft, quality control, and boredom prevention, especially if team members are cross-trained in all functions and can rotate roles. Training team members for one function only may result in inefficiencies when team members are out sick or on vacation. Too large or too specialized a team may also result in the hurry-up-and-wait syndrome with one or two team members standing idly by while others work, resulting in

Building	Museum	Museum	Offsite Storage
Room	**Painting Storage**	Gallery	Storeroom 1
Storage / Display Type	**Painting Screen**	In-wall case	Cabinet D
Storage / Display Unit	Screen 47	Case 28	Drawer 7
Other	Left side		

both inefficiency and boredom. Experiment with the number of team members and configuration of functions to find the best fit for the collections.

CONDUCTING THE INVENTORY

After all the planning and preparation, the inventory itself should be a relatively straightforward process. Inventory staff should proceed systematically through all galleries and storage areas, inspecting and documenting objects and their locations. In other words, matching objects located to object records and not vice versa. Doing otherwise may result in your overlooking objects that are undocumented or not cataloged.

One common approach is to use the CMS to generate lists of objects by location, which then can be verified or amended during shelf inspection. At the end of each day or week, or upon completion of a particular storage unit/area, update the CMS accordingly. This assumes, of course, that one is not starting entirely from scratch and that the CMS contains more object records with locations than not. If this is not the case, choose instead to generate lists by curatorial area or object type and annotate this list with object locations as the inventory progresses. Entering or verifying locations directly into the CMS will eliminate or minimize the need to produce hard-copy lists. Instead, queries by location or object type can isolate pertinent object records.

Identify and tag, or physically isolate, objects that pose problems such as illegibly or incorrectly numbered objects, double numbers, missing numbers, missing records, and missing components. Staff should not become bogged down attempting to solve these problems during the inventory proper. Either address these problems as a team at the end of each day, week, or month, or assign this duty to a project manager or designated staff member working in tandem with the inventory staff.

RECONCILING THE INVENTORY

In a perfect world, an inventory will result in a one-to-one correspondence of objects to records. More likely, the inventory will result in a group of records lacking objects and a group of objects lacking records. In a nearly perfect world, there will be a one-to-one correspondence between these two groups, and each undocumented object will match with a record for which an object was not found (e.g., accession numbers have worn off, the objects were never marked with their accession numbers in the first place, labels identifying loan objects have disappeared, etc.). Unfortunately, even after this match-up has been done and the objects have been marked *(see the chapter on Marking)* and returned to storage, there likely still will remain the vexing problems of missing objects (those "lost in inventory") and undocumented objects.

Again, the CMP should offer guidance on what actions to take in response to these problems. Museums are generally wary of advertising the fact that collections objects are missing. Wishful thinkers hope that the objects will turn up eventually, and the publicity-averse may worry about accusations of negligence or, worse, malfeasance. While most specialist fine art insurance policies will honor claims made for objects lost through "mysterious disappearance," few museums are likely to file such claims as doing so would likely have a negative effect on renewal terms and premiums. As a result, some museum decision makers may conclude that there is nothing good to be gained by transparency in this area. However, without timely, documented due diligence, a museum may not be able to recover works of art that surface years after a loss is discovered. It almost always will be in a museum's best interest to err on the side of transparency and pursue any suspected loss aggressively.[7]

Undocumented objects that are discovered in the course of an inventory and which cannot be reconciled against existing museum records constitute the complementary problem: objects found-in-collections (FIC). Because the museum has no evidence that it holds title to FIC objects, these exist in a collections-status limbo that limits how they may be used, cared for, or disposed of. For a discussion of strategies for dealing with FIC objects, see the article entitled Found in Collections in Section 3, as well as *Collection Conundrums: Solving Collections Management Mysteries.*[8]

MAINTAINING THE INVENTORY

The museum staff have conducted a complete inventory and have painstakingly reconciled it. They have taken appropriate action with respect to missing objects and have documented all FIC objects. To ensure that the significant human and financial resources invested in the inventory were justified, systems and procedures must be put in place to maintain an accurate, real-time inventory of the collection.

The formula for maintaining an accurate inventory is simple: *record object movement at the same time an object is moved + update collection records as soon as possible thereafter + do so 100 percent of the time = accurate inventory.* However, until RFID becomes ubiquitous, or new technologies emerge that track object movement passively, all approaches to location and inventory control ultimately will rely upon, or be thwarted by, the human beings that move objects.

Record the move. The staff member who moves the object should record at a minimum the following information at the time of the move:

- accession or unique inventory number of the object
- old location
- new location
- date of move
- name of person moving the object

A museum also may seek to capture additional information, such as:

- object description
- reason for move
- estimated return date

The object-movement record can be made in as many ways as there are objects to move:

- a handwritten notation in a bound object-movement log specific to every storage area and authorized art handler
- a carbonless or photocopied form designed for this purpose, with one copy left in place of the object, one copy traveling with the object, and one copy being filed or used to update the collections record

- entry into a PDF form or spreadsheet designed for this purpose (this method is only practical if there is a computer dedicated to this purpose in each storage area)
- entry directly into the museum's CMS (again, only practical if there is a dedicated computer in storage)
- via bar-code reader (see sidebar on Bar Codes)

Update collections records. Generally the registrar or collections manager is responsible for updating collections records with object movement data at some appropriate interval. Weekly updating might be sufficient for the small museum with minimal object moves, whereas daily data entry or bar-code downloads would be advisable for larger institutions or during busy exhibition installation periods.

Do so 100 percent of the time. Here is where best laid plans often go awry. It is the rare museum that can claim sufficient staff or hours in the work day to implement best location and object-movement control practices at all times. However, the chances of doing so are improved by the following measures:

- Limit access. It is worth stating the obvious: the fewer staff members that have access to and the authority to move collection objects, the smaller the margin of error in maintaining an accurate inventory. The museum's CMP or procedures manual should specify which staff members may handle and are authorized to move works of art, and what level of training is required. The duty to maintain accurate object location records, and the attendant accountability, should be made an official part of these staff members' job responsibilities.

- Make it easy. Overly complicated and burdensome procedures will not be practiced consistently or at all, so tailor procedures to suit the institution, collections, and programs. Maintaining a handwritten logbook may be perfectly adequate for a small museum or historic house in which two or three staff members typically move 10 objects per week, but not for a major metropolitan museum in which hundreds of objects are moved each day by scores of art handlers. Develop procedures for tracking object movement with the staff members that move the objects; they are the greatest resource and ally. Write these procedures down, share them widely, and review and revise them often.

•Make the time. As in most areas of life, a task can be done quickly, or it can be done accurately. Build time into the daily workflow to allow those who move objects to record object movement, and for those who manage collections data management to update object records. Be relentless in the education of colleagues about the importance of maintaining an accurate inventory and sooner or later everyone will experience firsthand the wonder of an accurate inventory: the object sought will be right where it is supposed to be.

The devil is in the details. —*German proverb*
God is in the details. —*Ludwig Mies van der Rohe (1886–1969)*

You decide! •

NOTES

1. *National Standards & Best Practices for U.S. Museums,* commentary by Elizabeth E. Merritt. Washington, D.C.: American Association of Museums, 2008.

2. *Code of Ethics for Registrars.* The Registrars Committee of the American Association of Museums. Accepted and endorsed 11 June 1984.

3. www.nps.gov/history/nagpra/

4. Malaro, Marie. *A Legal Primer on Managing Museum Collections.* Washington, D.C., and London: Smithsonian Institution Press, 1998.

5. Simmons, John E. *Things Great and Small: Collections Management Policies.* Washington, D.C.: American Association of Museums, 2006.

6. For the purposes of this chapter, it shall be assumed that your collection records are automated. If this is not the case, doing so might arguably be of higher institutional priority than conducting a complete inventory, with location being one of a constellation of core data fields. At this time there are enough affordable options available for even the small, underfunded museum.

7. See "Inventory Procedures and the Reporting of Missing Objects," Malaro, pp. 409–11.

8. Buck, Rebecca, and Jean Allman Gilmore. *Collection Conundrums: Solving Collections Management Mysteries.* Washington, D.C.: American Association of Museums, 2007.

BAR CODES: TRUE OR FALSE?

A bar code is an optically machine-readable representation of data, most commonly in the form of a series of parallel lines of varying widths and distances from one another.
A: *True. Bar-code technology originally was developed to automate the checkout process in grocery stores.*

Barcodes are printed on labels that are affixed directly to museum objects.
A: *False. Bar codes are printed on labels that are affixed to archival tags or labels that may be attached to a museum object, but which are removable. Alternately, the bar code may be printed on a card that is kept in proximity to the object in storage or on display. In addition to associating bar codes with museum objects, all locations (shelf, drawer, painting screen), storage containers or conveyances, and even the art handler must similarly be associated with a unique bar code.*

Bar-code technology is currently the most effective data-management tool available to museums for maintaining an accurate inventory.
A: *Arguably true, but bar-code technology is only as accurate as collections records are.*

Bar-code technology is magic!
A: *False. Like all technology, it is only as reliable as the human beings who use it correctly and consistently.*

Bar codes replace the permanent marking of objects with their accession numbers.
A: *False. Bar codes are ephemeral in nature and may be separated from their associated object intentionally (e.g., when the object is put on display) or inadvertently.*

There is much more information available in print or online than could ever be squeezed into this sidebar.
A: *Absolutely true!*

By the time you finish reading this, bar-code technology will be obsolete.
A: *Hopefully, this is not entirely true, but certainly emerging technologies, such as RFID, may eclipse its use as a data-management tool.*

5J | PREPARATION

CLAUDIA JACOBSON

Once a museum artifact or specimen has made the journey from acquisition to accessioning documentation, it is ready to be prepared for integration into the collections. Preparation methods depend on whether the initial location will be storage or exhibition, but future use is also a consideration, and the material also may be needed for loans and research. In preparing an object for any of these activities, the goal is to ensure the best possible long-term preservation of both its physical and chemical condition and its connection to documentation through current and potential uses. To do so requires an understanding of the nature of the material, its condition, and the types of deterioration to which it is susceptible.

Each discipline and type of material has its own requirements, methods, policies, and procedures. What may be appropriate for a rabbit skin in a zoology collection might be quite different in an anthropology collection; its use is as a study skin or taxidermied specimen would impose still other demands. Most preparation activities require specialized knowledge and training and use of conservators or preparators. Staff (including volunteers) without such expertise may acquire additional training, but it is important to keep actions within one's level of skill and knowledge, to document such activities, and to call in professionals when needed.

All preparation activities should be based on common principles of collections care. For example:

- Use stable, non-reactive materials with collections.

- Use reversible, non-damaging materials and procedures.

- Provide proper support, housing, and environment.

- Document all activities affecting collections.

- Retain the association of objects and their documentation.

- Consider each specimen's unique nature.

- Take into consideration museum conditions and potential situations in which objects may be placed.

- Respect the integrity of the object, its research potential, and the role it may still play within its originating culture.

Collections are not simply brought into the museum and placed on a shelf. Preparation begins as soon as something is acquired for the institution, whether it is acquired as a donation or collected in the field. Use of the proper field techniques will assist in long-term preservation. New acquisitions and incoming loans that are susceptible to pests should be bagged, quarantined, examined for signs of infestation, and treated if necessary. It may be desirable to test for substances, such as arsenic, which may have been used as a preservative and may pose a problem for the staff, limit their usage, or require specialized storage. All objects, especially organics, should be carefully and continually monitored for possible infestation.

Remedial preparation also may be necessary when an object or specimen goes on exhibition or loan, moves to a different storage location, or experiences a change in some aspect of its original preparation. Conditions that pose a hazard to an object's long-term preservation should be corrected if that can be done without damaging the object. Objects that are matted, framed, or mounted should be examined to ensure that the matting materials are archival and that the technique is appropriate. An acidic, inappropriate, worn, fragile, or inaccurate catalog label may make it necessary to re-mark the item, following proper guidelines *(see chapter on Marking)*. Such activity should be documented and the removed label filed with other documentation. If an old label is adhered to or information is written directly on an object, he services of a conservator may be necessary to remove it.

Objects may need additional housing beyond that provided by storage furniture. *(See chapter on Storage.)* Boxes and other enclosures can provide a better environment, additional support, and surface protection and can limit handling, facilitate movement, and enable safe access to the collection. Objects also may require special support and mounts. Needs may change, especially if an object goes from storage to exhibition or transit, but it is desirable that the support system be usable in all situations, if possible.

In determining the need for additional enclosure, bear in mind the following:

•Does it need protection from dust or touch (beyond your existing storage/exhibit environment)?

•What kind of environment must be provided?

•Is light or relative-humidity control important?

•Is there a need for pest protection or a microenvironment?

•What is the potential for off-gassing of materials?

When assessing support, consider these questions:

•Can the object support itself without deforming?

•Is handling a problem and would a support facilitate safer handling?

•Are there stress points which need to be alleviated?

•Will new stress points be created when function is changed?

MATERIALS AND METHODS

All materials used with museum objects, whether by direct contact or environmentally, must be benign both to the collection and to personnel. In general, this means using acid-free (neutral pH) materials that will remain stable over a long period of time and do not have components that release damaging gases or become sticky as they age. Nor should they have dyes that can bleed if wet. Simple tests can identify some unsuitable materials. Materials for construction should be sturdy enough to provide proper support and suit the object needs. The design should be simple and easy to use. Mechanical closures and attachments are preferred. If needed, adhesives should also be acid free, stable, and kept away from the objects or used with a barrier. Conservators can be consulted about materials and can test materials under consideration for preparation. *(See chapter on Storage for more detailed information.)*

COVERINGS

Enclosed storage cabinetry is ideal for most objects. However, if such equipment is not available, open cabinetry can be simply covered or objects bagged. Especially large items, such as furniture, dinosaur bones, and farm equipment, may best be protected with a covering, which provides protection from dust and water leaks and buffers changes in relative humidity. Fabric (e.g., unbleached muslin) is washable, allows air circulation, and is opaque and inert; it should be washed before use with a mild soap without fabric softener and rinsed twice. Polyethylene sheeting (or bags) is relatively stable, translucent, waterproof, and low cost. However, it generates static electricity and must not be used in proximity with flaking or loosely attached surfaces. If the surface is fragile or prone to crushing, coverings should not touch objects but should be supported by a framework of safe materials, such as closed-cell foam (e.g., Ethafoam) or other inert materials. Care should be taken to avoid the creation of an unfavorable microenvironment of high relative humidity or air pollutants inside such an enclosure.

CONTAINERIZATION

Boxing objects is a cost effective alternative to other types of housing. Boxes must be sturdy enough to bear the weight of the contents without deforming and, if stacked, must bear the weight of items on top. Handling devices (e.g., handles, straps) must be effective or not used at all.

Time and material costs influence whether to buy or make enclosures. Pre-made boxes are more expensive than sheet goods, but the size of the project, availability of staff and time for production, and end quality and uniformity are also factors. Consider purchasing boxes in a limited number of "standard" sizes suitable to the collection and storage furniture. Boxes also can be manufactured to fit preexisting storage systems or unique collection needs. Additional padding or support can be added to provide cushioning or to prevent movement within the box.

Containers made of paper products provide some relative-humidity buffering but will deteriorate if wet. Stable plastic containers provide water, vapor, and some insect protection. Properly sealed and used with packets of silica gel, they also can provide a microenvironment. Regular plastic sheeting, such as polyethylene, is not completely vapor proof and air tight. Newer plastics (e.g., clear Escal or opaque Marvelseal) are, however, and bags can be made of these materials in which one can create an anoxic environment by the use of oxygen-scavenging material or a humidity-controlled environment with silica gel.

Large or heavy materials may require the structural stability provided by wood and metal containers. However, wood emits harmful, acidic gases, some of which appropriate paint or other coatings decrease but do not eliminate. Wooden containers, especially those used for long-term storage, must be lined with a vapor barrier such as an aluminum or plastic laminate and stored in well-ventilated areas. Rather than baked enamel, metal storage containers should be made of stainless steel or anodized aluminum or should be electrostatically pigment or powder coated.

ENCLOSURES

Enclosures such as mats, folders, encapsulation, and frames are used for flat or shallow items—e.g., paintings, works on paper, and flat textiles—that need surface protection and support. The type of enclosure depends on the stability of the object's surface, the flatness of the object, the volume of material, and the available storage space as well as time and money.

Folders are simple and quick to make and a good choice for large, flat items such as maps. Folders can be made by folding in half a piece of acid-free stock that is large enough to enclose the object along with a margin and heavy enough to support it. Matting provides excellent protection, but more labor is involved, materials are more expensive, and a fair degree of training and practice is required. Some museums use the services of commercial framers.

A mat is composed of a window mat and a backing mat, hinged together along one side. A window cut in the top mat allows examination yet limits touching. Double-window mats, where one or both windows have Mylar or fine netting attached for support, reveal both sides of the object. The surface of the window mat must project above the surface of the object being matted and can be augmented by spacers or multiple mats. For artwork, photographs, or archival materials, the object is held in place either by hinging it to the back mat board or by affixing corner mounts or rails. An interleaving sheet should be placed between the work and the window mat for protection during storage but removed before framing. For textiles, the backing board is covered with padding (e.g., polyester batting) and covered with washed muslin to which the textile can be lightly sewn along one edge; care must be taken to use a thread softer than the textile. Consult a conservator when mounting fragile textiles. Using standard-sized mats and frames throughout the collection makes mounting exhibitions easier and less costly. Matted objects usually are stored in special drop-fronted boxes (Solander boxes) or in map cases. Do not overstack materials prepared this way.

FRAMING

Frames provide surface protection, support, and a method of hanging, and often are an integral part of the work. Whether to use an existing or a new frame is a collections care, curatorial, and aesthetic decision. Existing frames can have artifact status in their own right, so careful consideration must be paid to replacing or modifying an old frame.

The frame must fit the work. The painting should not touch the frame directly; narrow velvet ribbon applied to the rabbet edge (frame side) will protect painting edges from abrasion. A backing board of stable, non-reactive material (such as foam core or Coroplast) attached to the frame provides buffering and keeps fingers and dust away from the back of the work. There should be room for expansion between the work and the rabbets. The frame for a paper object should be deep enough to accommodate glazing, a mat, separator, or barrier between the work and the frame or glazing (if used), the artwork, the back mat, and a protective backing board. If the frame is not deep enough, it may be built up on the reverse. Mending plates or other devices attached to the frame hold the package together under slight pressure. Taping around the perimeter of the backing board and frame prevents dust infiltration. Place a label with basic information on the backing, not on the work itself.

Whether to glaze and what material to use (glass, non-glare glass, Plexiglas, ultraviolet (UV)-filtering Plexiglas, Lexan, or Tru Vue Optium) depends on curatorial, collections care, and safety concerns. Traveling glazing should be UV-filtering acrylic, but if the artwork is a pastel or other friable surface, then glass is preferred due to static generated in plastics. Newer materials such as Tru Vue Optium provide UV-filtering and non-breaking anti-glare qualities without static or distortion. If glass is used, it must be taped in transit to hold glass fragments in case of breakage and prevent damage to the artwork and other contents of the container.

If the painting is to be hung, hanging hardware (e.g., D-rings, eye screws, security hangers) strong enough to hold the weight of the painting should be attached to the frame; avoid stringing a single piece of wire across the back of the frame. Old hardware may be weak and inappropriate and usually should be replaced. Works stored in a rack rather than hung should have any protruding mounting hardware or picture wire removed to prevent snagging and scratching.

SUPPORTS AND MOUNTS

Supports and mounts provide form and stability and alleviate stress, thereby preventing distortions, creasing, and eventual structural damage. Supports also facilitate the transportation of objects. Their design is determined by the object and how it will be stored or exhibited. A successful support is not overly complex, is easily removable, provides as much visual access as possible, and does not apply stress on the object by either insertion or removal. With space at a premium, it is also space conservative. It need not be elaborate and may be as simple as crumpled acid-free tissue or a pillow or snake made of muslin filled with polyester batting. Items that are prone to collapse—for example, soft baskets, moccasins, shoes, bags, and items of clothing—should have internal support, such as acid-free tissue, a fiber-filled pillow, or custom support fitted to the size and shape of the item. A simple storage mount can support a hat by lifting it up and supporting the whole rim from beneath. If the object is not stable at rest, like a round-bottom ceramic, a ring of Ethafoam can be constructed to give it support and keep it from moving.

Preparing artifacts and specimens for exhibition requires careful analysis of the needs of both the object and the exhibit design. Ideally, objects on exhibit should have mounts to keep them from moving if the case is bumped or there is earth movement. In earthquake-prone areas, earthquake mounts are critical for most artifacts, both on exhibit and in storage, to prevent them from movement and breakage.

Exhibit supports or mounts need not be invisible but should not be visually intrusive or obscure important details of the object. Areas of contact must be located at stable points and properly distributed for the weight. The mount also should eliminate or distribute stress on the object to avoid the weight of the object from resting on a few vulnerable areas. Inert barrier material should be placed between the object and the mount. In storage, an object may lie flat in a drawer; for exhibit, it may be desirable to have it shown vertically or as if in use. The condition of the piece may allow this, but only if a proper exhibit mount is made for it. While, many successful mounts can be purchased or made with mat board, polyethylene foam, covered "L" hooks, or other easy-to-use materials, certain pieces may require the services of a mount maker skilled in metalworking or Plexiglas construction.

CLOTHING AND TEXTILES

Clothing and textile collections often are soiled with dirt, grime, food stains, and perspiration, all of which are damaging to the collections and attractive to pests. Cleaning most of these textiles should be done only by or under the supervision of a conservator. The fragile and flexible nature of textiles requires padding or special supports. Garments that are stable enough to be hung safely should be placed on padded hangers. Cotton straps sewn into the inside waistband can help to redistribute the weight of heavy skirts to the hanger. Textiles stored flat (e.g., beaded dresses, fragile textiles) should have folds padded to prevent creasing. If flat textiles can be hung for exhibition, Velcro or a pocket for a rod may be sewn to the reverse and used for hanging. Textiles may need the additional support or protection of a muslin backing.

MANNEQUINS

Exhibiting clothing on mannequins is often desirable, but commonly used store mannequins are rigid, and their size and contemporary fashion proportions are not suitable for historic period clothing. Such mannequins are difficult to dress, put stress on garments, and are often aesthetically unsatisfactory. The ideal mannequin is soft bodied, flexible, and custom designed to fit the garment being displayed without stress; it should provide support throughout the garment. Some mannequins are made with flexible, jointed appendages and may be posed.

If hard-bodied mannequins must be used, one smaller than needed should be selected and covered with muslin or stockinette to provide a barrier. The covering can be padded as needed for form and support with polyester batting. Attention must be paid to the method by which the mannequin itself is supported. If the mannequin is to wear shoes from the collection, the support cannot come up through the bottom of the foot. Nor should the weight of the mannequin rest on the shoes.

SPECIAL PREPARATION TECHNIQUES

Some collections, especially those with natural history specimens, need specialized methods of preparation. Often, the majority of these collections are for research and seldom exhibition. Preparation begins at the time of collection and has a great deal to do with long-term preservation. Processes focus on preservation of scientific data and maintaining research potential; however, as with any museum collection, the most stable and long-term materials and preservation techniques should be selected.

ANTHROPOLOGY COLLECTIONS

Ethnographic collections. Increasingly, collections staff interact with the cultures that created the objects in determining their care. Cultural representatives may make arrangements with museum staff to prepare objects for storage or exhibition in their own ways. These may include the use of cornmeal, tobacco, or herbs; special ceremonies; the orientation of objects within the museum; or other preparations in order to follow native beliefs.

Archaeological collections. The stability and need for special preparation methods are determined by their archaeological and storage environments. While some can be quite stable, others may require treatment to remove salts absorbed while buried or placement in a controlled environment to prevent further damage. Previous preparation techniques, such as use of unstable adhesive to reconstruct ceramics, also can cause problems. These may now be failing and require either removal or additional supports.

NATURAL HISTORY COLLECTIONS

Botanical collections. Specimens are prepared for storage by pressing and drying plant parts, usually in the field. They then are prepared for storage at the museum by adhering or attaching them to a large sheet, along with documentation, and placing them in folders. These folders are arranged systematically into metal cabinets. Material too bulky for herbaria sheets, such as wood samples, is placed in separate packets that can be attached to an herbarium sheet or put into boxes.

Paleontological material. Such collections can range from dinosaurs to small invertebrates that have been released from a matrix in an acid bath. The latter are likely to have been field jacketed (placed in a plaster, burlap, and structural support) upon excavation and are very large and heavy. Supports must bear the specimen's weight, prevent it from collapsing, and assist transportation, often with mechanized equipment such as forklifts.

ZOOLOGICAL COLLECTIONS

Techniques and materials—including drying, fluid preservation, skeleton preparation, tanning, taxidermy, and consolidation—change constantly; new preparation methods include freezing, slide production, scanning electron microscope (SEM) preparations, and tissue and DNA samples. It is not uncommon for parts of the same specimen to be preserved in different ways; maintaining the documentation link between them is critical.

Zoological "dry" collections. These include study skins, skeletons, and mounted and pinned collections. Study skins are prepared by defleshing, drying, and stuffing to restore the original form. Skeletal collections are cleaned in a number of steps to remove the flesh and fats and often employ dermestid beetles for the final cleaning.

Mounted (taxidermied) specimens. Careful consideration is needed to decide to make a taxidermied mount. The process of preparing one destroys much of the research use of the specimen due the treatment and chemicals involved. The skin is tanned, usually commercially, and a variety of materials are used to reproduce the animal body. These usually are supplemented by metal wires or armatures to lend support, and the ability to position the mount. Fillers, modeling compounds, and pigments reproduce lost or shrunken features and colors.

Freeze-drying. Useful for making exhibition mounts, the whole specimen is positioned and placed in a freeze-dryer, which removes the water content through sublimation. Unfortunately, a freeze-dried mount is very attractive to dermestid infestations. Since most of the activity takes place inside the body cavity and can be well advanced before being noticed, monitoring is critical.

Invertebrates. Insects and other invertebrates are prepared for storage by the technique of pinning. The specimen is dried and positioned with an entomological pin inserted through the body, through cataloging labels, and into the bottom of a special storage box with a tight-fitting, glass-topped lid.

Zoological "wet" collections. A wide range of specimens is preserved in fluid. Specimens are "fixed" in formalin as soon as possible after death to halt enzymatic processes, then transferred for long-term storage usually to 70-percent ethyl alcohol (ethanol), which preserves research potential. Today, other liquids are being investigated but ethanol is still preferred. Usually they are stored in glass jars with tight fitting lids but are still prone to evaporation, so the fluid levels of wet collections must be regularly checked and maintained.

LIVING COLLECTIONS

Living collections have their own challenges, but many of the same preparation principles apply. Collections management must not only maintain the collections' well-being but also, in some cases, foster reproduction. Many museums, arboretums, and botanical gardens maintain living collections for research and education. Some museums are frequent recipients of zoo animals that have died. In these cases, it is important to be informed of any potentially hazardous infections, pest problems, etc., as these can affect both the staff and other collections and preparation techniques. Antibiotics, for instance, can affect dermestid cleaning.

CONCLUSION

A number of specialized books and articles have been written on the preparation of museum collections, especially in the field of natural history. This field changes rapidly as research progresses on the best long-term care of these collections. Keeping up to date in new techniques and materials and the status of research in preparing collections is critical in order to provide the best possible care for collections. Equally important is documentation of past and current practices so the changes can be tracked and proper decisions can be made in the future. •

Collections Management II | HYPOTHETICALS

1

Discuss the pros and cons of old-style "flat-line" temperature and humidity as opposed to newer concepts of flexibility.

2

You're asked to keep an exhibition of hand-colored prints up for a six-month period instead of the originally scheduled three months. Then the most prestigious museum in the region asks you to loan the exhibition of prints to them for an extra three months.

What are your concerns and how do you approach consensus with curators, educators, and the director about the situation?

3

Your storage areas are—

　1. below grade

　2. cramped

　3. filled with objects in card-board boxes

　4. filled with wooden shelves holding the cardboard boxes

　5. without a consistent location identification scheme.

What do you tackle first?

Why?

How do you work through each problem?

4

Write a grant proposal to upgrade the storage of your quilt collection. Go through the steps that are necessary to develop the project.

5

You're working through your first complete inventory.

How do you ensure that the information will be kept current when it is done?

How often should you do spot inventories?

6

You have inherited a decorative arts collection of over 4,000 pieces—with only five percent accessioned and numbered. You have files and files of records, but cannot relate them readily to the other 95 percent of the collection.

Develop a plan that includes inventory to gain intellectual access to this collection.

7

Should a museum that has over 5,000 works on paper from American, European, Asian, and African sources develop a standard system for matting in a few specified sizes (for instance, 16 x 20, 22 x 28, 30 x 40 and oversize—modular matting)?

Whether you answer yes or no, you must work out a storage scheme that will simplify location tracking and inventory.

5K | MOVING AND RIGGING SAFETY

DAVID RYAN

Museums—with their many disciplines, wide-ranging exhibitions, and varied permanent collections—often need to move heavy and awkward objects. There are taxidermied elephants and giraffes, stagecoaches, boats and fire carts, slim, unbalanced Puryear sculptures, marble goddesses and large DiSuvero works, Chinese beds and Victorian tables, huge paintings, and crate after crate after crate.

Safety is the most important and overriding consideration for any rigging or heavy moving task. Although the object being moved may be very valuable, there is nothing more valuable than human health and safety. The tragic death of artist Luis Jimenez in a rigging accident in 2006 reinforces the potentially deadly nature of some of these operations.

Humans are all equipped with intuition—the gut feeling about things that defies explanation but should never be ignored. If something doesn't seem right, it probably isn't. The careful move planner will trust that gut feeling and call an immediate halt to any moving project that does not feel comfortable or inspire confidence. Hindsight is 20/20, but one cannot undo a process after someone is hurt.

The number one rule in moving is to leave an escape route. It is one thing to steady a crate as it is being lifted or moved. It is something else entirely to try to keep one from tipping over once it has started to fall. Get out of the way as soon as possible. Never allow any body part to be trapped between an object being lifted or unexpectedly falling and an immovable surface.

Personal protective equipment should be used when lifting and moving. Good quality gloves will protect hands from splinters that come from crates, exhibit furniture, and pallets. Steel-toed shoes and boots can help protect toes from heavy objects inadvertently falling on them. Back braces, when worn for heavy lifting tasks, remind the lifter to keep a straight back. Any personnel in the vicinity of overhead lifting should be wearing a hardhat.

RIGGING

Rigging enables the lifting of a heavy object, such as a sculpture, a piece of equipment, or a large artifact. Outdoors, rigging usually employs a truck-mounted crane. Indoors, a forklift, a chain hoist, or block and tackle may be put to service. The hoist may be attached to an "A" frame gantry or to a structural element of the building.

While rigging is a specialty that requires training and experience beyond most registrars' expertise, it is important to grasp the concepts, understand some of the terminology, know when to call in the experts, and be able to get a sense that contractors know what they are doing. References can be invaluable, but in a remote location where there is only one local crane company, a registrar must be able to evaluate whether its personnel can handle the job satisfactorily.

Determining the weight of the object to be moved is the first step. This information may be readily available via a shipping document, a label on the object, catalog information, or design drawings. More often than not, the weight will be unknown and must be estimated by measuring to determine cubic footage and consulting a chart similar to the one below that gives the weights of various materials per cubic foot.

Based on the weight of the object, equipment must then be sized to lift the object within the appropriate safety margin. The crane or other lifting engine should be located as closely as possible to the load, as lifting capacities decrease dramatically with distance. The rigger will use a chart that calculates the capacity of the crane based on distance and boom angle to properly size the crane.

Safety margins are typically 3 to

CHAIN HOIST

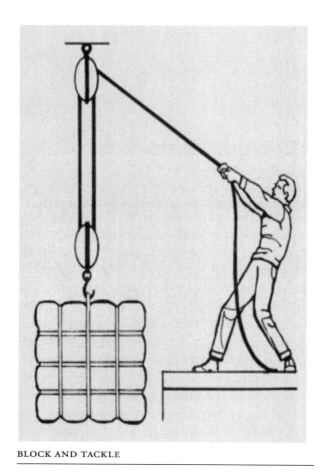

BLOCK AND TACKLE

1. That is, the capacity of the lifting engine and the capacity of the slings or chains or cables and hardware being used are rated at 3 times the actual weight of the object. Such a large safety margin is necessary

because the capacity of a crane is calculated when a load is very close to the body of the crane and the boom is retracted. This capacity decreases with the distance a boom is extended and the angle lowered. An error is possible in calculating the actual weight of the object or the capacity of the crane with the boom extended and lowered. Although the hardware should be regularly inspected, some may have been overstressed or may be sub-standard and below its rated capacity. The operator might be less than smooth with his lift, putting an additional strain on the equipment and hardware. It is better to be safe than sorry.

Rigging to lift directly above the center of gravity is a key element in a safe lift. If the center of gravity is off to one side, the load will swing dangerously to the center when it is lifted. Any load swing of more than 5 degrees requires that the load be lowered and re-rigged. The center of gravity of the object should be below the pick or lifting points; otherwise, the load will flip when lifted.

Loads are often lifted with slings. Sling selection will be based on the size and type of load from the three basic types of slings: chains, wire rope, and synthetic web. In most museum settings, synthetic web slings are used, as chain and wire rope slings have the potential to damage surfaces.

Alloy steel chain slings are strong but must be carefully inspected prior to each use. Individual links can become stretched as evidenced by an inward

WEIGHTS OF COMMON MATERIALS IN POUNDS PER CUBIC FOOT

Wood		**Masonry**		**Miscellaneous**	
Oak	54	Brick	128	Clay	120
Pine	34	Concrete	144	Loose Earth	94
Walnut	41	Concrete (reinforced)	150	Glass	160
		Marble	169	Ice	58
Metals		Stone	158	Mud	102
Aluminum	165			Wet Sand	128
Brass	535	**Liquids**		Tar	75
Copper	560	Alcohol	49		
Iron	480	Gasoline	42		
Lead	710	Oil	58		
Steel	490	Water	62		

LIFTING A 17-TON BOULDER WITH THE PICK POINT INCORRECTLY PLACED BELOW THE CENTER OF GRAVITY. COURTESY: THE COLORADO SPRINGS MUSEUM

THE 17-TON BOULDER AFTER IT FLIPPED, ABRADED THROUGH A STRAP, AND CAME CRASHING TO THE GROUND. COURTESY: THE COLORADO SPRINGS MUSEUM

bend to the oval of each link. Attached hooks should be inspected for any cracks, twisting, or excessive wear to the bearing surfaces. Both the chain and hooks should be free of gouges or nicks. Any of the above mentioned defects should be cause to remove the chain sling from further service.

Wire rope slings are composed of individual wires that have been twisted together to form strands. These too must undergo a visual inspection prior to use. Slings should be rejected for various reasons including an excessive number of broken strands, severe corrosion, localized wear, kinks, bird caging (strand that has become unwrapped and bulged outward), or damage to the end fittings.

Synthetic web slings are commonly made of nylon, polypropylene, or polyester. The advantages of this type of sling are its strength, load protection (grips the load without marring the surface), and shock absorbency. Slings should be rejected prior to use if they exhibit burning or melting, snags, tears, cuts, or broken stitches. Some manufacturers build

in a red indicator layer below the surface. As the upper layer is stressed and tears, this layer will show through. Immediately reject any sling showing these red indicator fibers.

Sling angle is an important aspect. If two or more slings are attached to a central point, a sling angle less than 45 degrees places a great stress on the slings and hardware, reduces the rated capacity, and can be dangerous.

Occasionally a spreader beam will be used as part of the sling setup. This effectively distributes the load across the beam. If a spreader beam is used, it must be sized properly and its weight included in the weight of the load calculations.

Hitches are the configurations used with slings to attach the hoisting engine hook to the sling and attach the sling to the load. An experienced rigger will know which hitch is most appropriate to use, based on the load. This is akin to the knots used by an experienced mariner. These hitches include the single vertical hitch, bridle hitch, single and double basket hitches, double wrap basket hitch, and the single and double choker hitches.

MOVING CRATES AND EXHIBIT FURNITURE

Most moving projects involving crates or exhibition furniture depend on human power as the lifting engine. These occur frequently in a museum setting and require certain procedures and equipment in order to be done safely and efficiently.

Most traveling exhibits are housed in crates that arrive by truck, must be unloaded and moved to an unpacking area, and are reloaded at the end of the exhibit. Many museums store a majority of their collections off-site and regularly move objects from storage to museum and again to storage.

The tools most commonly used for this activity are four-wheel dollies, commonly known as furniture dollies or piano moving dollies, and two pieces of leverage equipment: two-wheeled hand trucks and J-bars.

Furniture dollies consist of two hardwood crossbars equipped with swivel ball-bearing casters mounted on each end. Above these wheels and perpendicular to the crossbars are two padded bumpers mounted on each end. These can be covered with either rubber or carpet.

FURNITURE OR PIANO DOLLY

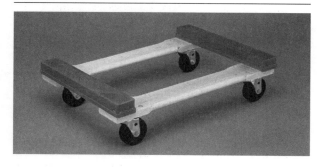

A good quality dolly is well worth the expense. These dollies typically have a capacity of 800 to 1200 lbs. A local moving company will know the source of such equipment and may be able to order them at a wholesale price. Large casters with soft rubber wheels are the best. The more uneven the surface to be traversed, the more important are larger diameter

casters and softer wheels. A small caster with a hard plastic or hard rubber wheel will give satisfactory results only on a very smooth surface.

Padded rubber surface bumpers minimize the shifting of the load when rolling over an uneven surface or transitioning over a threshold. The carpeted variety tends to slip much more under these circumstances.

Carpeted dollies are designed to protect fragile surfaces such as the finish on a piece of furniture. However, unless these dollies are used only for furniture, it is a good idea to provide further protection by placing additional padding between the carpeted bumper and the furniture. In a busy museum, these dollies are often used for crates and other items, leaving dirt and grit embedded in the carpet.

A general rule of thumb is that a healthy strong human can lift no more than about 100 pounds. This must be done properly, however. Lifting should be done with the legs while keeping the back straight. Backs can be injured by lifting as little as 25 pounds, if done improperly. Part of all training in object handling should be a demonstration of correct techniques for lifting.

The proper way to move a crate is to tip it up on one end, center a dolly underneath, and lower it onto the dolly. On light to medium crates, this is normally done with one or two people lifting one end of the crate. If the crate is very heavy, the principle of leverage can be used. A two-wheel hand truck catching underneath the edge of the crate with the front edge of the platform of the hand truck adds mechanical advantage to lifting the end of the crate.

Pulling back on the handle will lift the edge of the crate off the ground. Never apply more force on the handle than one person can muster, as this will overload the capacity of the equipment. The handle can be pulled as far down as the floor if necessary to allow a dolly to be placed underneath the crate. The bumper of the dolly should be placed as far back as necessary to center the dolly under the center of the crate, with bumpers perpendicular to the crate, and should be held up under the load (at an angle with hands underneath the cross-bars) as the load is brought down onto the dolly.

If the crate is too heavy to be lifted by one person

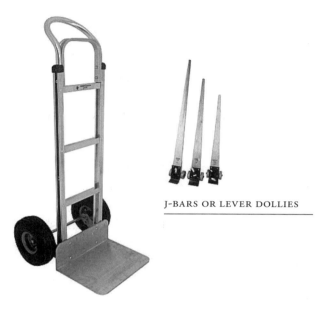

J-BARS OR LEVER DOLLIES

HAND TRUCK

using a hand truck, a J-bar or lever dolly can be used instead. This is a long (about 5 feet) hardwood handle attached to a steel plate with a slight upward bend to it. Steel wheels are attached to each side of this plate. The leverage principle is the same as with a hand truck, but the J-bar has a much larger lifting capacity. If the lift is not high enough for a dolly, 2 x 4 chocks (blocks of wood) can be placed under the crate, the crate lowered onto the chocks, and a new "bite" taken with the J-bar farther up under the crate.

Communication is key to the safety of this operation. The person handling the hand truck should announce to any helpers "Going up" or something similar when lifting the crate. The person placing the dolly should wait until all upward movement has stopped before doing so. This person should then announce "Come on down" or something similar to signal the lifter to begin lowering the load. The lifter should then announce "Coming down" or something similar before beginning to lower the load.

Moving crates through doorways or openings requires particular care. Always think about an escape route should the crate be tall and tippy. Steady the crate but don't try to stop it from falling if it is on its way down. Fingers need an escape route as well. Fingers and hands can be crushed by a heavy crate bumping into a doorway, if hands are wrapped

around the edge. Move carefully and deliberately to avoid these mishaps.

When you have reached the place to unload the crate from the dolly, exercise the same care and attention as in lifting and placing the dolly. Be particularly vigilant about the location of feet to avoid crushing a foot or toes under a heavy crate as it is placed on the floor. Communicate at all times to remain safe.

Exhibition furniture is moved in much the same way as crates. Common sense requires that artifacts first be removed from an exhibit case or pedestal. Exhibit pedestals and portable walls can be constructed in such a way that the cross braces that span the bottom underneath just above the toe kick are spaced so that the bumpers of the furniture dolly fit just to the outside of these braces, allowing the dolly to be solidly "locked in" under the pedestal when rolling it into position.

USING A FORKLIFT

Using a forklift is not rocket science, and anyone who is a reasonably good driver can learn how to operate a forklift safely. Ideally someone who is familiar with forklift operation should train other users in its safe operation. A good "final exam" is to unstack and re-stack a pile of six pallets one at a time without spilling a cup of coffee sitting on the top pallet.

Unlike a car, a forklift steers from the back wheel, requiring considerable operating familiarization; a slight move of the steering wheel will produce a rather abrupt turn. This feature enables the forklift to turn in very tight and confined spaces but creates a tendency to wobble back and forth when traveling long distances. For this reason, and because the load may obscure the view forward, some operators choose to travel in reverse (looking over their shoulders) if moving an extended distance.

The first step in lifting something with a forklift is to adjust the width of the forks. Most forklifts have adjustable forks that slide back and forth to accommodate lift points of various widths. The forks are very heavy, however, and it often takes two people, one slightly lifting the fork at the far end and the other pushing on the back end, to slide them into position.

Forklifts have two adjustments to the forks that are controlled by the operator: raising and lowering the forks and tilting the forks forward and back. After manually adjusting the width, the next step is to lower the forks to just above ground level and tilt them forward until they are level. Drive forward slowly until the forks are under the load and the load is as close to the back of the forks as possible. The next step is to lift the forks and consequently the load and make sure that the load is stable. Then the forks should be tilted back slightly to ensure that the load will not slide off the end of the forks.

Never allow anyone to ride on the forks or to have their hands anywhere near the frame that the forks attach to when raising or lowering the forks. Drive to the destination slowly and with the load riding as low as possible. Upon reaching the destination, slowly straighten the forks to a level position, lower the forks, and back out slowly. It helps to have a spotter who can tell the operator when the forks have reached a level position, as the operator may have his view obstructed by the load or the front of the fork frame.

A forklift can also be used in conjunction with nylon slings to lift an object from the top. In this case the forks are pushed together and one loop of the sling is placed over both forks and pushed as far back on the forks as possible in order to prevent the loop from sliding off the front of the forks and to provide lift directly over the center of the object. This is most often done in an outdoor setting as the frame of the forks is often too tall to clear the ceiling inside. Beware of this height problem if attempting this lift inside a building.

Whenever the driver leaves the seat of the forklift, level the forks and lower them to the ground. This precaution insures that no one will trip over the elevated forks, and acts as an added emergency brake.

PALLET JACKS

A pallet jack is essentially a small human-powered forklift. It differs from a forklift in that the forks are fixed (not adjustable for width), lift only about 6 to 8 inches off the ground, are raised by pumping the handle, and are lowered with a lever that releases

hydraulic pressure. They are used mostly for moving pallets around in an indoor setting but are occasionally useful for moving heavy objects that are not on a pallet.

A pallet jack is often carried in the back of a truck to enable the driver to roll a pallet to the back edge of the truck where it can then be lifted out of the truck with a forklift.

The pallet jack has small diameter steel rollers that pivot down from the fork that contains them, thus raising the forks. Occasionally a pallet will be constructed with a cross piece of wood attached under the pallet in a direct line with the wheels of the pallet jack. In this situation, pumping the handle to raise the forks forces the pallet apart from within rather than raising it off the ground. The solution is to back out the pallet jack slightly until an open space is encountered for the wheels.

PULLING A LOAD

On rare occasions there may be a need to pull a load a short distance in order to gain access for a piece of equipment to do the lifting. An example may be a heavy crate that is towards the front of a truck and must be pulled towards the back before a dolly can be placed under it. This is commonly done with a chain or cable wrapped around the crate and pulled with a forklift.

PALLET JACK

This can be a very dangerous operation and requires extraordinary caution. If a cable breaks, it can recoil with such force as to cause grave bodily injury and even death. The most likely path of this recoil is directly back towards the source of the pulling power. It can, however, whip out to the side as well.

Cable is much more likely to recoil than a chain, so the choice should be a chain. The chain should be attached as low to the ground as possible. All personnel should be away from the path of the chain, at least 1 1/2 times the length of the chain. As an added precaution, a packing blanket should be draped over the chain while pulling. This will reduce the amount of energy in any recoil, should it occur.

DESIGN IT TO MOVE

Inevitably, everything in the museum will move at least once and probably more than once. Why not design in a convenient way to move it?

In the past, this was part of the design process. Large industrial artifacts, even very old ones, were usually designed with moving pick points in mind. Large engines and motors almost always have lifting eyes and loops attached at convenient places.

A thoughtful sculptor might design an element of the piece that can be removed and temporarily replaced with a lifting eye for ease of lifting and moving. Another might design a piece that can be moved with a forklift with slots at the base that can accommodate the forks.

If given a choice, ask for all large incoming artifacts, sculpture, and equipment to be delivered on pallets. This will make the job of unloading and moving much easier.

As mentioned earlier, exhibition furniture should be designed so that it can be easily and efficiently moved. If the museum's mission calls for collecting or exhibiting large artifacts and sculpture, buildings should be designed to accommodate the moving of these pieces. Doorway dimensions, elevator dimensions, and lift capacities should all be large enough to make moving tasks simple and routine.

Rigging and moving are necessary tasks that all museums undertake. As these activities hold inherent danger to people and artifacts, using common sense and doing it safely is a goal that all should strive for.

GLOSSARY

A-frame Gantry A framework similar in appearance to a child's swing set consisting of an "A" shaped framework on each end and a crossbar between them at the top. Used for lifting by attachment of a chain hoist or a block and tackle to the crossbar.

Bird Caging A defect in a wire rope sling whereby the wire strands become unwrapped and bulge outward and look similar to a bird cage.

Block and Tackle An arrangement of pulleys and lines that increases hoisting power for lifting heavy loads.

Chain Hoist A system of gears that allow a slight pull on a continuous chain to lift a heavy load with little effort.

Lifting Eye A hardened steel loop that bolts onto a piece of equipment and is used to hook a lifting mechanism to in order to lift the equipment.

Pallet A platform, usually constructed of wood, on which a number of packages or pieces may be loaded to facilitate handling. Usually the pallet is constructed so that it has space underneath it to permit lifting by mechanical equipment.

Pick Point Also known as lifting point—the actual point where the lifting power is applied. It can be a lifting eye or the point at which a sling is attached to the load.

Spreader Beam A rigid beam hanging from a crane hook and fitted with a number of anchor points at different spots along its length used to spread out the load when lifting. •

5L | PACKING AND CRATING

BRENT POWELL, WITH JOHN MOLINI AND T. ASHLEY McGREW

INTRODUCTION

Packing and crating of art and artifacts involves numerous players. Thoughtful pre-planning, design and construction of crates, and proven packing techniques are employed to protect the objects from the rigors of handling and transit. Whether the object is traveling within the museum, across town, across country, or overseas, all parties involved must work cooperatively to ensure its safety.

This chapter offers a strong basic understanding of packing and crating art and artifacts for transport. Consultation with packing experts from the institutional, commercial, and conservation fields always should be considered to ensure all potential methods and materials are considered.

RISK ASSESSMENT AND PACKING DESIGN

Ongoing technical developments in conservation studies combined with the cumulative practical knowledge of experienced museum packers have helped determine the best packing methods and safest materials to use. Registrars and commercial shipping agents have added to the knowledge about which combinations of transport and technical design will maximize safety. *(See chapter on Shipping.)*

PRE-PLANNING RISK ASSESSMENTS: WHO, WHAT, WHERE, WHEN

The registrar, in consultation with curators and conservators, conducts a risk assessment before arrangements are made for packing and shipping. This assessment entails careful and complete examination of the object, knowledge of the environmental conditions during transit, review of the facility report to evaluate when and where it will be displayed, and consideration of how the object will be mounted or installed at the final destination. These assessments determine the needs of the object and dictate the in-house or contractor personnel necessary to ensure the successful execution of these requirements.

Information gathered from the pre-planning risk assessment determines the design of the crate and internal packing. Consideration of transport options and the facility report ensures that the design, size, and weight of the crate can be easily managed by all parties involved and helps decide the type of equipment required for ease of movement and special handling or installation needs, including rigging and mounting. Storage requirements and the best method of safely unpacking and then repacking the object for its continued journey or return shipment also can be addressed. All these factors help create a budgetary picture, which must be approved and supported.

Only experienced personnel with knowledge of museum standards should do the handling and packing. New materials under consideration should be researched and tested before being used with museum objects. It is imperative to understand the properties of materials, what type of protection they offer, and what type of interaction they may have with the object they are meant to protect. Improper use of materials can cause damage to the object.

Several designs and materials may be appropriate for packing a certain object. When in doubt, always seek advice from experienced colleagues or ask a conservator to review the design and methods.

When contracting with a commercial firm, take the time to establish a working supervisory dialogue. Provide accurate instructions and measurements, and include drawings if a specific packing solution is required.

GENERAL GUIDELINES FOR PACKING MUSEUM OBJECTS

Carefully examine the inherent properties of each object to ensure that it is structurally stable. If there are questions about the object's stability, consult a conservator, or seek the opinion of someone more familiar with the object.

When deciding on the design and construction of the packing and crating, keep the risk assessment in mind: who will transport, receive, and handle the object; the object and its inherent properties; the destination; and when the transit will occur.

Design crating and packing to protect the contents within the container against movement, shock, vibration, and abrasion. Sealed, waterproofed, and insulated containers must be constructed to retard and stabilize humidity and temperature fluctuations.

Build the appropriate container—case, box, or crate—to support the internal packing components for the rigor of transport. Always design the packing so that the person unpacking it can easily understand the design. Mark all removable packing components with written descriptions or related markings for the repacking of the objects. A superior design uses as few loose components as possible to minimize potential component loss and mistakes in repacking.

Document the packing methods with photographs or simple diagrams, and place these instructions inside the lid of the case or packing manuals. Language-specific instructions should be considered for international shipments. Packing systems that provide superior visibility ensure more informed and safer handling.

CRATE DESIGN AND CONSTRUCTION

The standard packing crate is a six-sided box constructed to withstand the rigors of transit and protect the contents from impact, puncture, and weather. Plywood and wood are the most commonly used materials. Aluminum and particle- or fiberboards also have been used, although these materials may require special tools for cutting and may add cost and weight.

Materials

Generally, construction- or exterior-grade plywood (4' x 8', 1/2" or 3/4" thick) is used. It is relatively inexpensive, fairly easy to cut, and has acceptable levels of strength. Because formaldehyde is used in the manufacturing process, off-gassing is a concern, as is moisture. Lining the interior is recommended. Tyvek, Marvelseal, Nomex, and plastic sheeting all work. Avoid waterproof papers. Some contain tar, and all off-gas.

MDO (Medium Density Overlay, 4' x 8', 1/2 or 3/4" thick, also referred to as exterior or marine grade) has become the material of choice for many. Each sheet is coated with a waterproof paper, available on one side or two. Unlike construction-grade plywood, MDO has far less formaldehyde. That feature, combined with the paper coating, eliminates the need for a liner. Its composition resists warping, cuts cleanly, and has high and consistent levels of strength.

Wood Product Treatments

All woods, soft or hard, used in packaging and shipping must be compliant with ISPM 15, an International Standards of Phytosanitary Measure developed by the International Plant Protection Convention. This measure originated with the European Union in response to the spread of the North American Pinewood Nematode, an insect that causes pine-wilt disease. It states that all soft- and hardwoods must be heat treated (HT) to a core temperature of 132 degrees Fahrenheit for 30 minutes. To be in compliance, all packages, crates, and cases assembled using these woods must display the American Lumber Standard Committee bug-free quality mark. This mark, more commonly known as the "bug stamp," is leased monthly to individuals, companies, and institutions based on their compliance. Compliance requires purchasing HT-marked lumber from approved lumber mills or vendors, keeping records of HT stock bought and used, and submitting to monthly on-site inspections. The stamp is required on opposing faces of assembled packages, crates, and cases. It is the only stamp recognized and accepted around the world. As an alternative to heat treatment, ISPM 15 allows fumigating cases with methyl bromide.

Manufactured woods (those manufactured with heat, glue, and pressure, such as plywood) currently do not need certification. Cases and crates made completely of manufactured wood must be marked with the letters NC (for non-coniferous) and the initials of the country of origin. For example, NC/US means Non-coniferous/United States. More information may be obtained via phone or e-mail from USDA/APHIS/Export Services, 301-734-4382 and the American Lumber Standard Committee, 301-972-1700, alsc@alsc.org.

Case Construction

Starting with the walls, the two most common construction types are simple pine planks and plywood with 1" x 4" pine battens along the edges. Pine planks are joined using a simple butt joint. Walls composed of plywood and pine can be joined using either a butt joint or a lap joint.

The butt joint is the simplest in both method and description: one edge butted against the backside end of the other edge forms the corner. A lap joint, on the other hand, requires setting the edges of the plywood and pine so that the materials "lap" over each other; plywood covers plywood and pine covers pine. While a butt joint provides an acceptable level of strength, it can be compromised. High impact can knock it out of square or split the pine. Lap joints, on the whole, are more durable with greater levels of strength and tolerance for abuse.

Like walls, two types of lid and back are commonly constructed: a simple plain sheet or one fitted with pine battens along the edges. Battens that run horizontally, vertically, or both, depending on size and need, can be added for greater structural integrity. The lid and back can sit flush on the edge of the wall or be recessed so that, like a lap joint, plywood covers plywood and pine covers pine.

Handles and feet or skids are always recommended. While the former are obviously for lifting, the latter serve a dual purpose. Besides allowing safe and easy access for the blades of a forklift or pallet jack, skids reduce the points of contact between the bottom of the crate and the floor of a truck, thus reducing the amount of vibration transmitted during transit.

Assembly: Screws, Nails, Staples, and Carpenter's Glue

Glue not only strengthens the bonds between the materials, it helps seal the joints against moisture and vapors. Running a bead of latex acrylic caulk or a silicone-based product along the interior seams provides additional protection. A word of caution: if choosing a product that contains silicone, make sure to read the label or specific material data sheets.

There are three ways to seal a crate: screws, a bolt-closure system, or one of several types of latches. Screws are relatively inexpensive and fairly durable. They are great for one-way or two-way transit. They are not recommended for multi-venue exhibitions. Bolt-closure systems, or variations of them, are extremely durable, especially if the bolt and bottom plate are tempered (a process that uses extreme heat and cooling during manufacturing that makes the metal strong, but not brittle) or made from cold-rolled steel. Tempered and cold-rolled steel components reduce the chances of the bottom-plate threads to strip out and the bolts to snap. Bolt-closure systems can be purchased from vendors such as Masterpak or manufactured at a local tool-and-die or machine shop. Obviously, bolt-closure systems cost more than screws, but their reusability far outweighs the initial cost.

Latch systems have the advantage of requiring no special tools to open. When properly installed, they provide a consistent and even pressure on the gasket. However, the disadvantage is compromised security. Because fewer latches are used on a crate—compared to screws or bolt closures—the gasket can be easily damaged during transit. Latches are also costly and difficult to install correctly and can break if improperly installed or handled.

Exteriors should be marked with dimensions, weight, cautionary symbols, and directional markings. Of course, a shipping label is necessary, but never list the contents of the container. While painting the case or crate is not necessary, it does improve the appearance and provides a vapor and moisture barrier. If reusing crates, an application of a fresh coat of paint or a touchup provides a clean surface for remarking.

Types of Crates

One-time/one-way crate. This is a very simple crate for sending an object one-way only. It is usually destroyed after one use.

Two-way crate. This case is built to send the object there and back but not to withstand extensive travel.

Touring crate. This container is built to stand up to a multi-venue tour, usually with reusable fastening hardware on the lid. It is built to withstand abuse from handling and is weather and, usually, water resistant.

Breakaway crate. This is a case that is built with removable sides and top, leaving a pallet with the object on it.

Slat crate. This crate uses a minimal amount of wood and does not have solid sides, which consist of slats instead of sheets. While the sides are not solid, if needed they can be lined with poly sheeting, cardboard, or Coroplast. A slat crate can be constructed with a solid bottom of plywood with 1" x 4" pine battens along the edges supported by feet or skids (for 3-D objects). Or it can be a simple pine collar with slats running vertically (for 2-D works; also known as a travel frame). These crates can be used within a solid wooden crate, such as an end loader or breakaway, or as a stand-alone container.

TYPES OF INTERNAL PACKING

Brace pack. This basic packing style for 3-D objects holds objects in place by simple wooden braces (typically 2 x 4s or T-braces), which are secured to the walls of the crate or inner crate. The most basic method secures the braces in place with screws driven through the outside of the crate. Better versions secure the braces to blocks permanently attached to the inside of the crate walls. It is critical to label and "key" each brace accurately to allow for proper repacking.

Cavity-pack/foam cut-out. The object fits into a space cut or made to conform to the shape of the object. Cavities can be lined with tissue or soft inert fabric.

Contour bracing/yokes/guillotines. This method generally is used for medium- to large-sized 3-D objects. Braces are made the same size as the crate's interior.

Braces for smaller objects are made of Ethafoam. Larger or heavier objects require padded plywood braces. The yokes or guillotines are formed by cutting the shape of the object out of the brace and then cutting them in half. Braces generally are oriented on horizontal planes on different levels, designed to be in contact with the most stable portions of the object. The front half of the braces are held in slots created by two strips of wood or foam so that when the front of the crate is removed, they can slide out. The back part of the brace should be glued or screwed into place to help stabilize the container. To be effective, the braces must be cut very accurately to avoid uneven distribution of shock to the object.

Foam-lined box. The object, often wrapped in poly or Bubble Wrap, is placed into a box lined with foam that does not fit the contour of the object; the voids are filled with material such as tissue paper, newsprint, or scraps of foam.

Double-crating. An inner container stabilizes the object by limiting or eliminating movement and providing a sub-environment. The cushioning takes place between the inner and outer containers. The outer container provides a rigid shell, and its design helps define how it will be handled.

Slot style. A traditional style of packing for multiple, usually 2-D, objects, and this method allows each object to be unpacked as needed without handling the others in the crate. Individual usually framed) objects fit into their own slots, and the ability to move directly from crate to wall and the same in reverse makes for efficient and safe installation, minimizing handling of the object. Lining the slots with non-abrasive material that eliminates the need to wrap each individual object and minimizes handling enhances this packing technique. Larger objects generally are placed in side-loading crates, while smaller objects—especially works on paper—are usually packed in top-loading crates.

T-frame slots. This method incorporates multiple travel frames in a single crate, lowering crating costs and creating a more stable crate footprint than a single-painting crate. Travel frames make it easier to wrap large pieces in a vertical position, thus avoiding stress to the canvas when laying it flat.

Drawer or rack style. This sideways slot-style crate, in which individual boxes slide into the crate like drawers, provides a particularly effective method of packing traveling exhibitions containing many small 3-D objects. Each box can be removed individually, and its contents can represent the objects contained in an individual gallery or a case within a gallery.

Sliding tray. This style of packing uses rigid trays that slide out of a side-opening crate. Multiple slide-out trays may be placed at different heights within the same crate, or a single tray may be located at the bottom for larger objects. Especially with multiple trays, objects may be braced or strapped directly onto the tray. Single trays often are used in combination with yolk-style braces to facilitate loading and unloading.

Tray-pack. Objects, usually 2-D, are placed onto a flat tray typically made of cardboard, Fome-Cor, or Gatorboard and surrounded by foam on all sides cut to a depth slightly higher than the object. Trays then can be stacked on top of each other in a crate with the foam supporting the weight of the layers above it. Trays always should be stacked with the smallest-sized or multiple small objects toward the bottom of the crate, not the other way around. Placing the largest on the bottom puts the bulk of the accumulated trays (and weight) above the tray with the broadest span, increasing the potential for sagging.

SOFT PACKING

The term "soft packing" can be defined as a method of packing an object with materials that give the object structural protection without the conventional means of a hard-shell (wooden) crate. Soft-packing designs and materials usually are meant for a one-time handling or transport need, differing from the more elaborate multiple-use packing designs and materials used in museum loan or touring exhibitions.

Several types of handling needs can be met by soft-packing designs and techniques:

•internal movement of objects within a facility
•regional shipments between different museum sites, local lending institutions, or to and from a collector's home

•hand carrying airline shipments for domestic or international transit

The decision to use soft-pack designs should not be made solely on the criteria of cost and time; a conservator, packer, and registrar or collections manager should be consulted before a final decision is made. The risk-assessment issues need to be thoroughly researched, discussed, and weighed so that all basics of safely moving the object are properly covered.

Internal Movement within the Museum

Soft packing is a convenient and very effective method of transporting objects within the museum facility. Basic cardboard or plastic corrugated boxes or baskets can act as containers to handle the objects which are wrapped or nestled within materials placed in the container. Materials need to support, cushion, and protect the objects from abrasion as the container is moved and handled. Materials commonly used include tissue, Bubble Wrap, polyester batting, polystyrene beads in plastic bags, and sand bags, to name a few.

Containers can be moved on carts, platform flatbeds, dollies, hand trucks, and pallets with ties, bracing, or strapping to secure these containers to the equipment. Equipment such as "sided carts" can be padded to make the cart a handling container. Custom-made pallets can be built that will properly support large or bulky objects.

Regional Movement between Museum Sites, Local Institutions, and a Collector's Home

Regional movements include transfers which involve a roundtrip journey that will take less than a normal working day. Because the transit will occur outside the museum-controlled environment, packing considerations will include temperature and humidity changes, shock and vibration, and the method of transportation.

If an object is subject to temperature or humidity fluctuations, buffering materials can be added to the support materials to help stabilize humidity and temperature fluctuations. Entire containers can be wrapped with polyethylene sheeting to create a vapor barrier and a sealed environment, if needed.

Object containers, such as cardboard boxes or plastic tubs, should be strong enough to be securely tied, strapped, or braced to the interior of a truck or van. Containers can be secured in a similar fashion inside the trunk of a car or securely strapped to the car seat using the seat belt or additional ties.

Hand carry airline shipments for domestic or international transit

Hand carrying objects is a practice that has fallen out of favor over the last decade because of stringent security practices implemented by the U.S. Transportation Security Administration (TSA) and other airline security operations around the world. Standard practices in the past, such as purchasing individual seats or placing hand-carry containers in overhead compartments, is no longer deemed reliable or guaranteed. Airport security or airline staff can take arbitrary measures that might remove the object from the courier's control and supervision during the flight.

However, if the object requires a hand-carry transit, the container must be structurally sound and comfortably portable for the person carrying it. The shell must be made of durable material, double-walled corrugate, or wood, or be a piece of hard-sided luggage. The protective shell will safeguard it from being crushed or broken in handling, especially if the container is moved from the courier's supervision to the cargo bay of the aircraft. The container must be designed to be easily opened, if required by airline security, and re-secured for the remainder of the journey.

CREATIVE ALTERNATIVES

Not every museum object can be neatly contained in a box or case. Due to the unique nature and size of many objects, it is often necessary to devise creative packing alternatives. Oversized objects can be addressed in several ways. The truck itself can become a container for large objects, with the loaded truck driven onto a cargo plane for shipment. Airplane pallets can be modified or specially constructed to accommodate large objects. Special cradles or supports can be constructed to transport large cases at angles that will permit them to ride steadily within airplanes or trucks. Airplane containers can be used as a protective external structure for objects safely positioned within. Containers can be delivered to the museum where museum staff can load them and design internal bracing for the contents.

Flatbed trucks often are used with simple frameworks and tarps to transport odd-shaped objects. When wrapping them is not possible, objects can be suspended within trucks or containers.

Using a sea container is similar to using the truck as the box. Objects placed inside sea containers must be braced for movement in all directions. Research standard practices in proper dunnage (that is, packing material used to cushion cargo on a ship) packing or bracing, or consult a shipping agent who is familiar with loading artworks into sea containers to determine the best methods.

Moving large numbers of objects down the hall or across town to an off-site storage facility can be addressed in a number of creative ways. Trays can be used to carry numerous objects that are either wrapped or divided from one another by padding. Trays can be stacked on moving carts that can be rolled onto trucks and secured for short trips. A variety of carts can be padded with tissue, cotton batting, sandbags, etc., and used to transport objects. There is no single correct way to pack museum objects. Common sense and experience must apply to packing, along with keeping up on new materials and methods. Continued dialogue among packers, registrars, conservators, and vendors will help to protect collections more effectively.

PACKING MATERIALS

Materials used for packing art and objects possess a wide variety of characteristics. Understanding these characteristics and matching them with the needs of the object and the conditions under which it will be exposed are fundamental aspects of packing and object care.

When objects are particularly sensitive (for example, metals and some kinds of photography) or will be kept inside their packaging (multi-venue traveling exhibitions or packing that doubles as storage) care must be taken to use only archival materials. Most of these materials are the same ones that are listed as storage materials. For shorter-term packing (most situations), normal packing materials such as cardboard and Bubble Wrap are adequate for most objects. Under these circumstances, the next level of protection is provided simply by the correct choice of the material that comes into contact with the surface of the object as well as the quality of the barrier material used between object and the rest of the packing materials.

Backer rod. This form of polyethylene foam is extruded into rods with a smooth outer skin. Usually round and gray in color, this material is used in the place of rolls of tissue in the folds of textiles. A white, triangular backer rod is also available for use as wedges or blocks on trays and storage mounts.

Blankets. These are packing blankets or pads commonly used by moving companies to cushion and protect the surface of furniture and other large objects. They must be clean and should be used with an intermediate material (e.g., tissue, Tyvek, or plastic sheeting) between the pad and the object itself. They are also helpful in mitigating vibration when placed under soft-packed objects. They can be reused if kept free of dirt, oils, and tape residue.

Blue board. This material is either single- or double-walled archival and acid-free cardboard. It can be used for boxes, trays, or mounts that may be built for storage as well as transit. Most common is a blue-gray color, but it is available in white and a white-blue combination.

Bubble Wrap. This common material consists of two layers of polyethylene, polyvinylidene chloride, or polyvinyl chloride films, which are quilted to create air-filled compartments. Air is injected into circles (1/4" to 2" in diameter), making bubble sizes typically 3/16", 5/16", and 1/2". It comes on rolls of different widths and lengths, perforated and un-perforated. The material is inexpensive and tear resistant, but bubbles will deflate over time. Some versions (e.g., Aircap) have an additional layer of nylon designed to prolong the life of the bubbles. Some varieties are treated to be static resistant (pink) or fire resistant (green). The bubble side of this material can leave circular marks if put next to a delicate surface and, therefore, should not be placed in direct contact with artwork.

Cardboard. Corrugated sheets come in various sizes and weights. Cardboard boxes, envelopes, and other packages can be constructed as a shell for the object. Inexpensive and easy to use, this material is subject to moisture breakdown, may be very acidic, and should be restricted to short-term use only.

Cellulose wadding. Often called Kimpak (now Versapak), this material consists of layers of soft, tissue-like paper, sometimes with a Kraft-paper backing. It is available in rolls and a variety of widths (12" to 48") and thicknesses (1/8" to 1/4"). It is not archival, but it has good cushioning and vibration-dampening qualities, especially when used in layers. Highly hygroscopic in a sealed environment, it can help mitigate changes in relative humidity (RH). It is inexpensive and can be recycled with paper.

Corrugated polystyrene sheeting (Coroplast Polyflute). This translucent or white material may be used alone in soft packing or in combination with wood to make durable lightweight containers. Commonly used for making sides of transit frames, it is widely used for storage trays and boxes that may also function well in transit as inner containers.

Dartek. This thin, transparent, cast nylon film breathes and is hygroscopic. It can be used to wrap objects and makes an excellent see-through dust cover for objects in storage.

EPS (expanded polystyrene) board. This form of Styrofoam is smoother and more rigid than the more readily recognized "beadboard." This material comes in a variety of thicknesses in 4'x 8'sheets and is usually blue in color. It is used to provide thermal insulation in crates and boxes. It also provides some cushioning but can crush on initial impact.

EPS (expanded polystyrene) peanuts (Pelspan). This common packing material should be used with caution, if at all. Heavy objects, especially, can shift and settle inside their containers. This disadvantage can be best mitigated by placing small quantities very loosely into bags. The thinner the material the bag is made of, the better the pellets can conform to the shape of the object—its best characteristic. The bag prevents scattering while handling, which creates static-attracting dirt and debris. This kind of material also is called loose fill. Its ability to provide cushioning is limited and unpredictable compared to foam.

Fome-Cor. This product consists of sheets of a styrene foam sandwiched between paper sheets; it comes in thicknesses between 3/16" and 2" and usually is sold in 4'x 8' sheets. This material can be used like cardboard, providing a cleaner appearance and surface, but it is more expensive. It, too, should be reserved for short-term use only, unless an acid-free Fome-Cor7 is used.

Gatorfoam. These sheets are similar to Fome-Cor but are denser and more rigid, and the facing is less prone to tearing.

Glassine. A glazed, semi-transparent paper, glassine typically is used to wrap paintings and other artwork or for interleaving works on paper. It is available in an acid-free version. It should not be reused for wrapping because creases caused by unwrapping create an abrasive surface.

Hot (melt) glue. This product is used for adhering cardboard, Ethafoam, Volara, and other packing materials in crates and boxes. Some approved types can be used for storage mounts.

Marvelseal. This material is plastic with a layer of metal suspended inside so that it acts as an extremely effective vapor barrier to protect objects from pollutants and changes in humidity. For the most effective barrier, it can be easily bonded to itself with heat. In packing, it often is used as a crate liner. It can be used in soft packing to provide stable sub-environment for objects like works on paper. It also is used extensively in storage and display applications to protect objects from off-gassing of wood products in storage or materials used in display-case construction.

Microfoam. This material is a trademarked name for thin polypropylene foam. It can be identified by its obvious layers fused together with widely spaced "dimples."

Microfoam. This term is broadly used to refer to a wide range of polyethylene foams, such as Ethafoam 221. It has a smoother skin than polypropylene. Thinner versions may be used to wrap complex forms. Thicker versions can be used to cover padding where it comes into contact with object surfaces or as a material for tray or shelf lining.

Minicell (chemically cross-linked polyethylene). This material has the same characteristics as Volara, only it is available in greater thicknesses. Most commonly used in 2-pound form, it can be used for cushioning pads or storage mounts.

Muslin. This plain-weave, cotton fabric should be unbleached and unfinished or desized, and washed in hot water prior to use. In packing, this material is primarily used with textiles. In storage, it is used as an opaque dust cover.

Mylar, Melinex. This 100 percent polyester film is a chemically stable polymer with a neutral pH. It provides a barrier in packing to keep objects from contact with non-archival materials and often is used in the form of envelopes or sleeves for paper objects.

Newsprint. Inexpensive and widely available, this old-fashioned material is still effective for use as dunnage (fill material) in soft packing. Crumpled up and stuffed around objects wrapped in plastic or Bubble Wrap, this material is for one-time, short-term use only.

Pellon. This is a 100-percent nonwoven polyester that is usually 1/8" to 1/4" thick. A thicker polyester batting, known as bat garrett, is also available for padding.

Plastic sheeting (low-density polyethylene [LDPE]). This is the most commonly used plastic for wrapping artwork. Used both for soft packing and for creating a sub-environment inside boxes and crates, it provides a barrier against abrasion, dirt, and moisture. While the common thickness for wrapping paintings is 4 mil, it is also made in 2-, 3-, and 6-mil thicknesses. "Virgin poly" is a term used for pure polyethylene containing no recycled materials. This allows for production methods that do not require the excessive use of plasticizers and slip agents (talc-like material).

Plastic sheeting (high-density polyethylene [HDPE]). This less commonly used plastic film has less stretch but greater strength per mil. Because it comes in much thinner weights, it conforms better to 3-D objects, and it places less pressure on delicate ones.

Polyethylene foam (Ethafoam, Polyplank). This is

polyethylene plastic, which is expanded into foam, made up of many tiny, closed cells or bubbles filled with air. It is widely used in cavity packing objects, mounting forms, and padding in crates. It is inert as long as it is free of additives. Ethafoam is the best-known variety of this material and comes in different densities; 2.2 pounds is the most common.

Polyurethane-ester foam. This open-celled foam—usually a charcoal gray—is used for cushioning and thermal insulation. Positive attributes of this foam also include superior vibration mitigation and a more forgiving cushioning curve (easier to calculate) than many other foams. Urethane foams are characteristically less chemically stable than some other foams (polyethylene, polypropylene). Breaking down when exposed to moisture, heat, and UV light, they can produce harmful by-products. The ester-based urethane foam is more stable, however, than the similar, more common (and cheaper) ether-based foam. As a rule, avoid polyurethane–ether foams.

Silica gel. Used in packing, display, and storage to stabilize relative humidity, this form of silica (the same material that is the main ingredient of common sand) comes in granules and beads. It is composed of many open cells that create a very large amount of surface area on a microscopic level. This makes it possible for it to wick away or absorb excess moisture in the air. Some gels can be conditioned to specific humidity levels to help maintain relative humidity in a sealed environment.

Stretch wrap (linear low-density polyethylene [LLDPE]). This variation of polyethylene often passes Oddy or off-gassing testing for archival stability, but because some types have a coating, it should not come into direct contact with the object. It is commonly used to hold in place packing blankets that have been wrapped around large objects. It also provides an extra layer of protection when applied to the outside of crates, and it can be used to secure objects in some packing systems. Note: Stretch wrap should not be confused with shrink wrap, which actually shrinks with the application of heat and often is made of PVC, usually inappropriate for use in proximity to art objects.

TAPES

Blue painters tape. This preferred variation of masking tape offers a higher quality, less aggressive adhesive that is less likely to tear Tyvek used in wrapping. It is more expensive but more stable than standard masking tape.

Double-sided tape. As the name indicates, this product has adhesive on both sides of the tape. Use only archivally safe varieties (3M #415) in proximity to artwork.

Duct tape. This tape is strong and easy to use; it is very durable. Because it off-gasses, it should be for temporary use only.

Filament tape. This translucent, reinforced strapping tape is very strong. It is good for short-term use to strengthen cardboard boxes.

Linen tape. This woven, gummed tape is pliable; the adhesive is acid free and is activated with water. Use this tape with archival board for making boxes, especially where they also may act as long-term housing for storage.

Packing tape. This economical tape has strong adhesion and a high-strength plastic back, primarily used for sealing cartons and plastic sheeting. Some versions of this common tape are backed with a PVC plastic film (an unstable material that can be prone to breakdown and off-gassing) and rubber-based adhesives, which vary considerably and will fail over time—short-term use only! Other packing tapes are backed with polypropylene and use acrylic-based adhesives. Both materials can make this a better choice for use where tape must perform over a longer period of time.

Reinforced paper tape. This gummed, water-activated product is a very strong, waterproof tape that provides superior closure over the long run for cardboard boxes.

Tyvek tape. Tape with an archival, acrylic, pressure-sensitive adhesive applied to one side that can be used with archival board to make boxes.

Tissue. Tissues come in a range of types, textures, and forms: packing tissue, acid-free tissue, and buffered tissue. These vary from crisp, more structural tissue for stuffing out voids in boxes to soft "lens-type" tissues used with textiles to storage tissues used for interleaving. For packing purposes, start by looking at the physical characteristics called for (soft or stiff, roll or sheet). Consideration of chemical or off-gassing issues largely is related to the duration of exposure. It is important to consider that most packing is for the short term. While the use of acid-free tissue in many packing applications appears prudent, such thinking must be tempered by the realization that it can also be wasteful of the limited resources allocated to object care in most museums. Of course, when dealing with artwork made of highly sensitive materials (for example, some photographic prints or uncoated metals), refer to the product information available and check its appropriateness for use in long-term storage. Even then, realize that the best tissues must be replaced in time.

Twill tape. A 100 percent cotton, woven, non-adhesive tape which comes in different thicknesses and widths, twill tape is used for a number of purposes, most of which are related to attaching or securing parts of objects (for example, lids or mounts) or pieces together. When used for storage, specify unbleached instead of white.

Tyvek. This spun, fiber-bonded olefin is composed of high-density polyethylene fibers that are bonded together under pressure and intense heat. It is very strong and resists tearing, chemicals, and mildew. It is good for providing moisture protection and a clean surface. Although advertised as waterproof, this material breathes, preventing it from being a true vapor barrier. "Hard" Tyvek has a slick surface and can be used in storage applications and as a crate-liner. Soft-structured Tyvek (or "softwrap") can be identified by a pattern of dimples that make the material more pliable. This version is used as a contact-wrapping material, to cover pads and cushion braces, and to line cavities cut into foam.

Velcro (hook-and-loop fastener). This material is a good solution for securing lids of inner boxes where they will be opened and closed repeatedly. It also may be used to secure lightweight objects in some crating systems. It is commonly sewn to textile gussets for display purposes.

Volara. This is very fine-celled, cross-linked polyethylene foam with a smooth surface. It can be bonded to other polyethylene foams with heat or hot (melt) glue and often is used to pad objects where they come into contact with rough or hard surfaces. •

IRENE TAURINS

Choosing a method of transportation requires consideration of the museum object. This includes but is not limited to value, size, historical or cultural importance, condition, fragility, rarity, state of packing, crate and shipment size and weight, timetable, and expense. The best method offers the highest level of control to the object. Clear documentation and instructions must then be given to the carrier.

SHIPPING BY LAND

Types of Vehicles and Carriers

When using commercially available carriers, find a company experienced in transporting museum collections; recommendations on reputable carriers are best sought from other registrars. If museum specialists are unavailable, moving companies that specialize in handling delicate electronic equipment, using vans with air suspension systems and climate control, are a next best alternative.

Common carriers (also called regular-route motor carriers) are not generally used for shipments of fragile or high-value material. However, for heavy or bulky shipments of moderate value, they provide an economical method. This service usually involves considerable handling or "cross-docking," which is the transfer of cargo from truck to dock to truck, one or more times.

Types of Trucking Services Available

Exclusive use. This service deals exclusively with one institution's cargo, with all stops and deliveries defined by that institution. This is door-to-door delivery service. Exclusive use affords maximum control in timing and security. The registrar chooses the day, time, and route and can make arrangements for special guards or museum couriers to accompany the shipment. This, naturally, is the most expensive service.

Last on, first off (LOFO). Other freight may be on the truck, but the LOFO shipment is guaranteed to be the last freight loaded and the first unloaded. There is slightly less control of the timing and slightly less cost than with exclusive use. This is a uniquely American service, not available in Europe.

Expedited use. With this service, the shipper specifies a certain finite range of dates during which your shipment as well as other freight is loaded on the vehicle; each shipment has a reserved space. This service is less expensive than exclusive use.

Shuttle service. This service is defined as "less than truckload lots" (LTL) or smaller "space reservation" with no special time or route restrictions. Shuttle service is the least expensive method and can be safe, but in some cases, it may be more time consuming. Ask for the details of the route and whether your cargo will be off-loaded or "cross docked."

Features to Consider

The major features to consider when booking a trucking service include air-ride suspension, double-driver teams, and climate control. Air-ride is available on larger vans and trucks and provides a cushion of air to absorb road shocks. Double-driver teams protect the freight if one of the drivers becomes ill or tired and allow the truck to be supervised at all times, including during rest stops. Climate control can include full-range temperature and humidity control where exact settings are determined by the kind of objects shipped; however, most climate control is temperature control only, which may be adequate for certain objects. Ideally, the driver monitors and controls the climate from the cab; some trucks are equipped to generate a graphic record of conditions during the trip. Ask vendors to specify what services they provide.

Another feature to consider is an adequate interior strapping or tie-in system. The truck should be equipped with sufficient furniture pads, dollies, and other equipment such as a J-bar. The truck also should have lockable doors and a security system. If the load is heavy, if there is no loading dock, or if the loading dock at either end is inadequate, a lift gate on the truck is needed to ease the crates on and off the truck.

Depending on the service required, it may be wise to choose a company that provides drivers who can double as handlers and packers, although not every company provides this service. This feature is particularly useful when picking up objects from private collectors who may not have the ability to pack their own objects. Other services to consider when booking a truck are extra security or the ability to accommodate a courier on the truck or in a follow car. These requests should be discussed fully when booking the shipment.

Good communication and understanding are important, both when booking and also during the transit. For long-distance or sensitive trips, make certain that the driver can be reached via cellular telephone and that the owner or dispatcher of the company is available during off-hours in case of emergency. Some companies track their vehicles via two-way satellite communications, in-route status reports, and on-board computer tracking.

Truck size and equipment availability vary among carriers. The size of the shipment may determine the choice of carrier. If the load is small in size, it may be best and more economical to transport it in smaller ("straight") trucks or vans, which run from 12 to 24 feet. The smaller trucks also can be equipped with air-ride and climate control with varying degrees of sophistication. Height is often a determining factor in the size requirement of the truck; discuss your height requirements fully before booking a truck.

Some transports require larger (30 to 51 feet) vans and tractor trailers. The determining factor is the size of the shipment, particularly height and volume, but other considerations include the distance to be traveled and the need for sophisticated climate control. Tractor-trailer doors vary in height, usually between 105 and 117 inches; more specialized high-cube vans have an interior height up to 125 inches. To determine equipment needs, provide all shipping dimensions to a vendor before booking.

Trucking companies offering interstate transport were governed by the Interstate Commerce Commission (ICC) until January 1, 1996. Although the Interstate Commerce Commission is no longer a regulatory body, its guidelines are often still used for classifications, rules and regulations, rates, mileage guides, and the services offered by interstate moving companies. The Department of Transportation (DOT) is now the main regulatory body that regulates safety in interstate transit. Each state also has intrastate regulations. Companies operating motor vans or trucks within a city or state are generally subject to the approval of regulator bodies in each city and state. The conditions under which shipments are accepted by carriers appear on the bills of lading issued to shippers. It is a good practice for registrars to read the back of the bill of lading (see Documentation, below).

It is also common and safe to engage non-commercial carriers, such as a museum- or staff-owned car, van, or small truck, to transport museum objects. The main advantage is that the handling is completely under the control of the museum. Care should be taken to balance the needs of the object against the potential hazards of vulnerable vehicles, lack of cushioning systems, and inadequate climate control. The same rules for commercial vehicles also should apply here. For security, two people should travel in a car. It is best to have a cellular phone in case of emergency. Always let other museum staff know the full route, schedule, and itinerary. Be sure the vehicle is large enough to permit the object to ride safely; tie downs or other devices may be necessary to secure it from shifting. *(See chapter on Couriering.)*

Freight services offered by the railroads are not generally used for museum shipment as the ride on the tracks has too much vibration. The train, however, is an acceptable mode of transport for objects that can be hand carried.

SHIPPING BY AIR

Airlines offer the most rapid means of transportation for long-distance domestic and foreign shipments. Ideally, all arrangements for the air shipment of valuable and fragile museum objects should be handled by museum personnel or by reliable agents. These personnel or agents must be able to supervise all movements from shippers to airports, through terminals into planes, from planes, to and through terminals, and from terminals to final destinations. Supervision at cargo terminals is especially advisable to ensure the safe handling at airport assembly areas active with loading and unloading equipment. The 9/11 Commission Act of 2007 passed by the U.S. Congress includes a mandate that by August 2010 all cargo tendered for transport on passenger aircraft will be required to be screened by the air-transport industry. While complying with current Transportation Security Administration (TSA) regulations, Museums should consult their shipping agents to determine the best procedures to use to avoid the opening of crates at the airport.

Types of Aircraft

Different types of aircraft have certain limitations for carrying freight. Although "all cargo" planes afford the most control, they have been drastically reduced in number and are therefore not readily available to every destination. However, the size of the freight may necessitate the use of planes with larger door openings. Freight more than 63 inches high can fit only in an aircraft with main-deck (the upper part of the aircraft generally reserved for passengers) cargo capacity, such as all-cargo or "combi" aircraft. All-cargo flights do not generally take passengers, but arrangements can be made to allow a courier aboard. Combi flights are part passenger and part main-deck cargo, with doorways high enough to take oversized freight. It is generally easier to engage an agent to arrange cargo flights.

When using passenger flights, wide-bodied aircraft such as Boeing 747s and 767s, Douglas DC10s, Lockheed L1011s, Airbus 340s, and other airbus models are best because their cargo space is large enough to permit the loading of containers and pallets. Wide-bodied passenger planes generally can accommodate freight up to 63 inches in height. Containers are large receptacles, usually metal, of different configurations, depending upon the size of the aircraft. Always inspect containers before loading for holes and dents that could allow leaks. Pallets are low, portable platforms, usually metal, on which cargo is placed and built up to conform to the aircraft size. When shipping museum objects, ask the airline crew to place polyethylene plastic sheeting on the floor as well as over the entire build-up on the pallet or around the interior of the container to protect the cargo in case of rain or other inclement weather. The pallet also must be tied down with special straps to keep it stable. Care should be taken in the orientation of crates on the pallet to minimize the effects of stress on the contents during take-off and landing. Beware, also, of including potentially hazardous materials on the pallet.

Smaller aircraft, such as Boeing 707s and 727s and Douglas DC8s and DC9s, cannot accommodate containers or pallets. Cargo must be loaded loose, so there is significantly more handling and risk of mishap. Individual pieces are loaded and unloaded on a conveyor belt. If you do not have wide-bodied service to your destination, it is probably best to truck the objects rather than use air freight. If trucking is not possible, very careful supervision is recommended.

Services

Air freight rates apply from airport to airport. Delivery to and from airport terminals can be arranged by the airlines at additional cost, but this is not recommended for museum collections because airport trucks do not follow museum standards (single drivers, non-air-ride, non-climate trucks, no means of securing the cargo within). If possible, make your own pickup and delivery arrangements or have door-to-door transportation arranged by reliable agents.

A registrar can book directly with an airline without the use of an agent. In this case, it is advisable to call the cargo terminal and personally talk to the cargo manager to explain your requirements, e.g., the freight must be "booked to ride," that is, made a priority shipment guaranteed for the flight, and museum personnel must be able to supervise the containerization and palletization of the cargo and to remain with it until it is on the plane and airborne. The cargo manager can complete an air waybill for you to sign. Get the name of the person who will be the cargo manager on duty during the time of your delivery and flight, and make contact with that person before you arrive.

Air freight services will also arrange to transport door to door. There is a loss of control in this type of shipping, as freight is often bundled together with other freight that may not be as sensitive. It is best to use air-freight services for only the sturdiest and best-packed objects. If air freight is the only option, establish a good relationship with plenty of personal contact and communication.

Freight forwarders can be used for both domestic and foreign shipments to book the shipment, complete an air waybill, communicate effectively with airport personnel, and provide supervision. (See below, International Shipping and the Use of Agents.)

Good supervision is important to ensure the safe handling of collections at the airport. Supervision is necessary to be certain that a crate is properly placed in a container or on a pallet, that it is secure, and that it is not shipped with hazardous materials. Optimally, you or your agent should follow the freight onto the tarmac and witness the loading onto the aircraft. In today's high-security climate, it has become more difficult to get beyond the "yellow line" at cargo terminals, and therefore it is important that your agent have full security clearance to supervise. Full supervision includes staying at the airport until your flight is airborne for at least 20 minutes. On rare occasions flights are returned to the ground after takeoff, and someone should be available in this case.

A freight-forwarding agent or cargo manager can help with flight planning. Also, the Official Airline Guide (OAG) Cargo Guide (www.oag.com) is published monthly, lists almost all flights available for cargo, and provides information necessary for advance planning of your shipment. A quarterly supplement gives plane sizes and container and pallet capacity information.

Cargo managers can provide information about the availability and schedules of planes that will meet the requirements of shippers. They must be told the sizes and weights of the boxes when asked to reserve space on the desired flight.

Always book on a nonstop flight. If a nonstop is unavailable, a flight with stops but without a change of plane is the next best routing. If a flight must stop en route, emphasize and receive assurances from the cargo manager that your freight will not be off-loaded. Avoid flights that have plane changes; if you cannot, it is advisable to contact an agent in the stopover city to supervise the transfer of the freight.

INTERNATIONAL SHIPPING AND THE USE OF AGENTS

It is best to engage a customs/freight forwarder for export and import of museum objects. The proper documents are important, and communication is essential when choosing a customs/freight-forwarding agent. For international shipments, museums generally engage customs brokers, freight forwarders, and cargo agents who are specially trained and licensed in importing and exporting. Customs brokers not only arrange for international transportation but also make certain that shipments comply with all import and export regulations. They prepare the documents required by the U.S. Customs Service and the customs offices of other countries. They can provide supervision, an important service that will actually see the shipments through all the processes of handling and customs. (See above and chapter on Export/Import.)

Freight-forwarding agents or other specialized museum agents also offer help in arranging transportation, including pickup and delivery, and, if desired, packing of museum shipments. Care should be taken to select agents who are well informed about the policies and requirements desired by a museum.

SHIPPING BY SEA

Ocean transportation is not recommended for most museum objects because of the lack of control in scheduling and handling. For extremely bulky and sturdy objects, it may be an economical but slow solution. It is complicated by the fact that many documents are required, both by the carriers and by the governments of the United States and foreign countries. Museums generally engage ocean freight forwarders to handle these shipments.

TSA Certified Cargo Screening Program

Adapted from Masterpiece information sheet; used with permission.

The 9/11 Commission Act of 2007 that was passed by Congress included a mandate that by February 2009 the air-transport industry would be required to screen at least 50 percent of cargo tendered on each air waybill for transport on passenger aircraft. By August of 2010 the requirement will become screening of all cargo tendered for transport on passenger aircraft. There is also a possibility that cargo for all-cargo aircraft will require the same type of screening in the future. The proposed regulations indicate that screening will have to be done by X-ray, swabbing, or physically opening each piece of cargo. The airlines will not have enough equipment or time to do all the required screening. To avoid total chaos, the TSA has proposed that freight forwarders and shippers be allowed to organize and conduct this screening of cargo before delivery to the airlines. The TSA is currently doing this through the Certified Cargo Screening Program (CCSP).

The CCSP allows freight forwarders, third-party locations such as fine art warehouses, and shippers, in limited situations, to become certified cargo-screening facilities (CCSF), based on security standards outlined by the TSA. Further information, as it is updated, can be found online. See www.tsa.gov or write to CCSP@dhs.gov.

Shipping by U.S. Mail and Air-express Service

Shipment by mail is not recommended for valuable or fragile objects because of transit and handling hazards, the Postal Service's limitations on the size and weight of packages, and the limited value for which underwriters are willing to insure mail shipments. For small shipments of replaceable and non-fragile objects of low value, parcel post may prove economical and convenient. It is common practice, for example, to send some natural history specimens by mail. If mail shipment is used, special care should be taken to see that containers are strong enough to ensure protection from the weight of other parcels, from pressure and friction, and from climatic changes and repeated handling.

When shipping by mail, it is often best to use express mail. This method offers the fastest delivery and, therefore, the least amount of handling. The other options in descending order of preference are registered mail, certified mail, numbered mail, priority mail, and regular mail.

Air-express companies offer a wide range of services, from small air-cargo agents who use commercial carriers and contract truckers to major forwarders who own their own planes and trucks. Their small-package services have size limitations that are marked on their air waybill or are readily available by telephone. With good packing, this kind of service can be an effective option for transport, with the understanding that there will be a great deal of handling. Again, the fastest service is preferable in order to limit handling and time spent on loading docks and in warehouses.

Other advice when using express-mail service is to ship early in the week in order to avoid weekends. Use only services that can provide tracking and require signatures of delivery. Pack well, address the package clearly, and mark it "Fragile." Most important, develop a relationship with one or two local forwarding companies, and try to elicit their help and understanding of your special needs.

Insurance/Indemnity and Loan Agreement Considerations

When deciding on the best shipping method to use, always keep in mind that guidelines from your insurance carrier, indemnity application, or loan agreement must be considered and honored. Shipments must be properly insured. In most cases the insurance should be through the museum policy. Carriers assume only a limited liability, unless excess value is declared. A shipper making an excess declaration is, in effect, purchasing insurance coverage through the carrier. *(See chapter on Insurance.)*

DOCUMENTATION

The general rule of documentation when shipping is to always obtain a signature of receipt when transferring possession of a museum object. Always read what you are signing for when your signature is requested. Receipts, bills of lading, and air waybills are contracts between shippers and carriers as well as receipts for the material accepted for shipment.

The bill of lading is a legal document, and your signature in theory releases the shipper from any liability for damages discovered at the time the cargo is received. Always examine the crate or package for any damage and never sign for a damaged package. Always use a disclaimer phrase such as "Condition unchecked, contents unknown" or "We are signing for the receipt ONLY. By signing this document, we are NOT issuing a clean bill of lading." •

Thanks to: David Epstein, James Conroy and the late Jim Ikena.

5N | IMPORT AND EXPORT

RACINE BERKOW

GUIDELINES FOR INTERNATIONAL SHIPPING

Museums and galleries, both large and small, exchange works with their colleagues abroad. Once the loan has been negotiated and the terms and conditions approved, the physical process of exporting the work from one country to another follows. Although international exchange is becoming a part of many museum activities, there is still much confusion, misunderstanding, and lack of information about proper procedures. If the parties involved have not had previous experience with international transport, the first step might be to call a museum that has done international shipping and ask for a referral of an international transportation agent. It is always good to contact more than one company to get competitive bids in order to be assured of getting the best service and the best price.

Information on export from the United States and the return import covered below is relevant for the United States only and may vary slightly from port to port within the U.S. The following information regarding procedures may change, and the museum should check with its own agent to verify procedures at the port of entry or departure that the museum is using.

EXPORT FROM THE UNITED STATES

Museum X (U.S.) is lending a very important work from its collection to Museum Y (overseas). The terms of the loan have been agreed to, the object has been prepared, and the shipping date approaches. It has been agreed that a courier must accompany the work. Museum X has arranged for the work to be crated by a crating company that uses wood packaging material that meets international standards and has the appropriate international stamps on it.

Museum X has secured the assistance of an agent to arrange the shipping or has agreed to work with the agent selected by Museum Y. In order to plan properly, the following information must be supplied to the agent by Museum X:

Schedule. When must the work be at the final destination? What dates are best for the courier, for installation?

•*Airline.* Is there a preference of an airline? Has Museum Y secured airline sponsorship? If so, what are the special instructions for the export agent?

•*Crate Dimensions and Weight.* This information is essential and must be correct. It determines the type of aircraft on which the object must be booked and will determine the final flight schedule. For air transport, the dimensions should be given L x W x H, in accordance with IATA regulations. The height should always be last. It is also important for the agent to know if the crate can be turned or transported flat.

•*Special Requirements of an Object and Courier.* Who is responsible for payment? What are the cost considerations? Is it okay to consolidate with other shipments or send as a partial shipment? Is there a particular agent overseas that Museum Y wants to use, or can Museum X's agent consign the shipment to an agent of their choice?

•*Service Requirements.* Museum X should also inform the agent if trucking services, armed guard services, special security, or airport supervision is required.

All details of the shipment should be discussed. The agent will offer guidance, since he or she is familiar with museum protocol and the shipping of museum objects.

It is usually up to Museum X to prepare a commercial or pro-forma invoice. It must contain the following information and be on museum stationery:

Shipper:	Name and address
Consignee:	Name and address
Inventory:	Artist (Maker)
	Title (Object Name), Date
	Media
	Dimensions
	Value
Purpose:	For exhibition? For sale?
	For examination?

Declaration and Signature:

If antique, it must be certified as more than 100 years of age. If for an exhibition and return, it should be so stated.

Documentation should be given to the exporting agent at least three days prior to export. It is customary practice for the exporting agent to e-mail, at least 48 hours prior to the arrival of the shipment, the pro-forma invoice, the waybill, and a shipper's letter of instruction to the overseas agent receiving the shipment. If there are paperwork problems they can be sorted out prior to the arrival of the artwork.

There are different information requirements for different countries. Certain objects require special documents and/or photographs. The agent will advise about these requirements; however, Museum X must supply the proper documentation and accurate information. After the museum has given the agent all necessary information, it becomes the agent's responsibility to book the shipment, prepare appropriate export documentation, make the necessary arrangements with the airline to allow warehouse access, provide trucking to the museum's specifications, provide security (if required), and coordinate arrangements with the overseas agent for Museum Y. The export agent may also procure the courier's ticket or make arrangements for the courier to board a cargo flight. The export agent, as needed, will also arrange security access. At this point, it is best for Museum X to allow the agent to do his or her job unencumbered; it becomes problematic if both the museum and the agent call the airline, truckers, etc.

The export agent will work with the information supplied by Museum X in the following way:

•*Schedule.* The agent will try to work within the requested schedule, but the museum must leave enough time for unforeseen events. Flights do get canceled, weather conditions can be a factor, civil unrest does occur, airplanes do break down, and airlines do change equipment. These factors are beyond the agent's control. Allow a couple of days' leeway. Airline schedules change from month to month. Many airlines will not take freight bookings more than two weeks in advance. It is good to start planning early, but the booking cannot be finalized until the airline schedule is confirmed and it is assured that the correct type of aircraft for a particular shipment will be utilized on that date.

•*Airline.* Different airlines have different rules and regulations. The export agent will do everything possible to arrange airline access for the courier to watch all the stages of placing the cargo on pallets and ramp access. It must be stressed here that even though this object may be the most important piece in the museum's collection, to the airline it is only a small box representing a minimum of revenue and a maximum of hassle. It is critical that the courier follow airline rules and procedures. Allow the agent to negotiate with the airline. The agent has a working relationship with the airline and understands the airline's restrictions. Most of all, the museum must not make unreasonable demands on the airline unless it is prepared to pay for them. For example, if the work must be secured in a particular way inside a container, and the airline is not allowed to load other freight touching the museum's crate, be prepared to pay for the entire container. Above all, it must be stressed that it is a privilege, not the right of the museum, to be a guest in the airline's cargo area; this is a live operation with heavy equipment in motion. The courier must cooperate with the airline and the agent for the move to be successful and to proceed without damage to the artwork or personnel.

•*Crate Dimensions and Weight.* If the information provided is not correct, the agent may not make the proper booking arrangements. For example, crates higher than 64 inches must be booked on freighters or combi (combination passenger/freighter) aircraft.

Special Requirements for Object and Courier

If the agent is advised about the object's fragility or special temperature/humidity needs, then all precautions will be taken (e.g., climate-controlled vehicles for long truck rides both in the U.S. and overseas). Also, if the packing is particularly complicated or the crate difficult to manage, the agent will make sure that the overseas agent knows what to expect and has the proper equipment available upon arrival at the foreign port. Special arrangements for the courier are another story. Your agent's primary concern is the proper handling and safety of the artwork. Your cargo agent is glad to supply your courier with his/her plane ticket and will make sure that he/she is met on the other side and has a place to stay. However, your agent does not want to, nor should he, be involved with the courier's personal agenda and vacation planning. Your agent will be glad to help the first-time courier do his/her job, but the museum must be wise enough to select a courier with flexibility, stamina, maturity, interpersonal skill, and the good judgment not to antagonize customs, airline, and transport officials.

•*Payment/Cost Consideration.* These factors should be clearly defined before the shipment takes place. As the details and parameters of the shipment change, so do the costs. For everyone's protection, it is best to have everything in writing. However, there are times when unforeseen circumstances necessitate schedule changes and may cause costly delays. Shipping is not an exact science, and the museum should allow a budget cushion to cover contingencies.

IMPORT

Assuming that the loan has arrived safely at Museum Y, it will eventually be time for Museum Y to return Museum X's loan. All arrangements will be reversed. There will be additional paperwork. In general, works valued at more than $1,250 require a formal entry filed with U.S. Customs. An individual or corporation may clear its own shipment; however, this clearance is a time-consuming and sometimes complicated process, depending on what commodity is being imported. In order to facilitate the process, one often hires a customs broker.

In the case of a returning artwork, proof of exportation will be required to avoid the merchandise-processing fee, which is levied on all imports.

A bond might also have to be posted. In order for the import agent to do his job properly, it is important that there be either a pro-forma invoice from the museum or shipping invoices from Museum Y. These documents must be transmitted to the U.S. agent. If Museum X wants to pick up the returning work as soon as it is available after arrival, the entry documentation must be submitted to U.S. Customs prior to the arrival of the flight. The entry package cannot be submitted for release until the aircraft is "wheels-up" in the foreign country. If the airline participates in the AMS (automatic manifest system) and all the documents are in order, the shipment will be released electronically by U.S. Customs by the time the aircraft touches down.

The customs agent arranges warehouse access, trucking, and security for the returning shipment, according to the museum=s requirements. The agent can have access to the shipment between one and six hours after landing. Depending on what time the plane lands, the shipment and courier may arrive at the museum quite late. It is, therefore, important that the museum have adequate personnel to help unload the truck or allow the agent to hire sufficient labor to handle the shipment properly. These arrangements can be quite costly and must be budgeted.

QUALIFICATIONS FOR AGENTS

•*Import-Licensed Broker.* The brokerage company should be licensed by U.S. Customs. To obtain this license, the company has been investigated and meets the fiscal, organizational, and security requirements as described in the "Customs Regulations of the United States of America." A licensed individual who has passed an examination and whose background has been investigated must be responsible for running the day-to-day operations of the company. The company must have a valid permit to operate in a particular port of entry or can be approved to file entry in any port in the U.S. The company must also be bonded.

Many companies perform import services in conjunction with a licensed broker. However, by law, the importer must be allowed to have contact with the broker directly.

Working with a licensed company guarantees that one is working with a corporation that meets very stringent legal standards. In order to maintain its permit, the company must continue to comply with the most recent customs regulations. Should the company not perform in an acceptable manner, the client has the right to redress under specific procedures within U.S. law.

EXPORTS—IATA MEMBER—TSA APPROVED IAC (INDIRECT AIR CARRIER)

The agent should be an IATA (International Air Transport Association) forwarding agent. In the U.S. this means that the agent has been endorsed by the CNS (Cargo Network Services, an IATA company). Although many companies arrange export through IATA agents, working directly with an IATA agent will assure the following:

•The agent issues his or her own air waybills in-house and books directly with the airline. The documents are not issued or processed in any way by an intermediary party.

•The agent or someone in the company has successfully passed both a written and oral examination of worldwide regulations and procedures that govern air cargo transport.

•The agent's handling warehouse has been investigated and complies with international standards.

•The agent meets the worldwide financial and security standards for necessary IATA endorsement.

•As a TSA (Transportation Security Administration) approved IAC (Indirect Air Carrier), the company must be in compliance with all TSA mandates and policies.

SECURITY ISSUES

Since 9/11, the TSA has been formed to secure passenger and cargo safety. This agency operates under the Department of Homeland Security. The TSA has been mandated by Congress to implement a screening process for cargo and is responsible for all aspects of airport security. All TSA protocols for cargo and access within secure areas of the airport must be explicitly followed. This is non-negotiable. The agent should be up-to-date about these policies and procedures and will provide guidance. In addition, there may be a TSA-certified person within the museum who might be able to assist with cargo screening.

Although regulations and criteria differ from airport to airport, the agent should have an airport identification pouch. At Kennedy Airport in New York, for example, the company and those individuals who have a Port Authority ID have been approved by the Port Authority Police to have access to some controlled areas. This ID must be worn conspicuously when working at the airport. In addition, the agent should have a U.S. Customs ID in order to have access to customs controlled areas; it must also be worn conspicuously in conjunction with the Port Authority ID. Having these badges indicates that the agent is bonded by U.S. Customs and meets airport security standards.

In some instances it might be possible for airline access to be arranged by the agent directly with the airline. Certain airlines will only allow access under the Escort Principle. They will assign an airline staff member to escort their clients while in the cargo area.

Import and export of museum materials are complicated matters. The agent chosen should have all the right credentials, and must also meet the museum's needs in terms of quality of service and price. In order to accomplish this, the museum must specify what is wanted, and museum staff must be realistic about what the agent can actually do or not do. The agent and museum must work together as a team, with mutual trust and respect, for the international exchange to be a successful experience. •

50 | COURIERING

A courier provides a chain of custody when an object is shipped from one institution to another. The courier is a representative of the owner of the work; s/he may be a staff member of the lending institution, an independent contractor, or a staff member of a sister institution sharing the task.

There are many good reasons for museums to send a courier when objects travel locally, nationally, and internationally. Museums may make the decision to have a courier accompany a shipment when shipping is not direct, when an object has a high value or is very fragile, when customs have to cleared, or when the object has special installation requirements. The destination could be down the block, or a trip could easily last 30 to 40 hours with combined surface and air transportation. Couriered shipments may be soft-packed, crated, or packed in a special case for a hand-carry.

The events of Sept. 11, 2001 (9/11), have drastically changed the way we transport museum objects. New phrases such as tarmac security, boarding security, and TSA (Transportation Security Administration) were not everyday vocabulary before that date. New security requirements and systems are established continually to counter perceived threats. It is important to know these changes and how they affect museum objects in transit, and a freight forwarder or agent is the best source of current information.

During the initial stages of loan approval, the borrower should immediately be advised of the need for and purpose of a courier. Reasons for using a courier for a loan may be the object's fragility, monetary value, historical or cultural value, museum policy, installation requirements, political considerations, or simply the complexity of the shipment. These trips are most frequently made by a member of the lending museum's staff. It is important to select the appropriate person for this task since there are many factors to consider and different expertise may be needed for different shipments. Qualifications for the task include knowledge of packing, crating, art handling, condition reporting, etiquette in a trucker's personal residence (the truck), and airline procedures, as well as being a quick thinker when plans go awry. The importance of being in good health at the start of a journey cannot be underestimated. Accommodating a courier imposes tremendous expense on the borrower. The lending institution should be sensitive to these costs and consider sharing a courier with another lender from the same area, especially if the two lenders have the same standards and are in agreement as to the shipping plans.

Hiring a security person, in addition to a courier, may be necessary for different aspects of a complex trip, especially if the courier must be separated from the shipment at any time. In some cases two couriers may be needed. The assistance of a forwarder or agent in booking the freight and courier are essential for international shipments. The agent is no longer allowed in the passenger terminal, but security services can be hired through the agent to supervise boarding of both courier and object on the plane. These combined services are also useful for complex domestic shipments.

PREPARATIONS

There are differences between domestic and international shipments, especially the paperwork! The proforma invoice (stating the catalog information on the work(s) with purpose for shipment) should include name and address of consignee, forwarder, value of work(s), and crate size and weight. This should be signed by a representative of the shipping institution and given to the forwarder/agent prior to the international shipping date.

The following documents are needed for any trip:

- recent condition report with photograph, and knowledge of how the object is packed and repacked

- copies of loan agreement, evidence of insurance, and pertinent correspondence

- health certificate, permits, licenses, if applicable

- list of representatives at borrowing institution, staff home or cellular telephone numbers, and contact information for forwarder/agent, if applicable

- names of hotels and reservation information en route and at final destination

- names and telephone numbers of and instructions for connecting with personnel meeting the courier at final destination

- e-ticket or airline ticket, updated passport, cash, travel checks, and/or museum credit card

- names and telephone numbers of truck drivers and/or security guards at both ends of the trip

One sheet of paper with all these names, telephone numbers, and other pertinent information together for easy reference is one of the greatest tools the courier will have. Provide an extra copy of this sheet to be placed in the courier's luggage.

Information on the exact route to the destination should be verified and confirmed with the driver(s), and details should be revealed to staff members and others on a "need to know" basis only. Keep in mind that this information is confidential in nature.

A courier should wear respectable, comfortable clothes and shoes and be prepared to climb steep ladders and stairs, sweat in the sun, and freeze in the warehouse breezeway. He or she must be prepared to carry luggage up and down stairs, and so should pack lightly. It is prudent to have snacks and water in a carry-on bag, although the water will be taken away by airport security; empty the container beforehand and refill it on the other side of the checkpoint.

Visit the lavatory just before boarding a vehicle. Facilities at airport cargo areas are available "sometimes." Use good judgment and prepare for a long wait between stops.

AIR SHIPMENTS

The truck shipment should arrive at the airline cargo area well in advance of the cargo close-out time. A single crate or an entire exhibition should never be left unattended. Observe unloading and count each item. Staying with the shipment at all times may be impossible, and this is where hired tarmac security comes in. The shipment can be accompanied until it is taken to be palletized at the cargo area of the airport. The courier must respect the rules at each cargo area, as restrictions vary. Airlines no longer permit a courier to observe the packing of a pallet or container unless this takes place beyond their designated "yellow" line, which cannot be crossed; the forwarder or agent will be able to observe the palletization or containerization. Airline personnel should be informed ahead of time to place crate(s) on pallets in the correct orientation, and confirm that only non-liquid, non-flammable materials and nothing that would pose a risk is placed next to the museum's shipment. Crate(s) should be completely covered with plastic sheeting and the final netting should secure the entire pallet. The courier should record the pallet and/or container number. If the plane is not an all-cargo flight, the courier will be taken by the agent to the terminal. Hired tarmac security personnel will stay with the shipment until it is loaded unto the plane, and the courier must be informed that the cargo is on board before boarding plane. Exchanging cell phone numbers enables the tarmac security person and the courier to maintain direct contact.

SURFACE SHIPMENTS (TRUCK, VAN, CAR, TAXI, TRAIN)

Many of the rules of air shipment apply to the transport of objects in a vehicle. In general, the courier must ensure continuous supervision; monitoring the shipment is easier when traveling by vehicles than when moving through airports. For all types of vehicles, supervise the loading and unloading of the items, check the number and condition of the cases, and sign the appropriate release and receipt upon leaving the point of origin and arriving at the final destination. Upon arrival, the driver must wait until the courier and shipment are safely inside a secure area before departing. If a vehicle breaks down and the shipment is small enough to handle, seek out another means of transport that would safely and securely complete the transit. Waiting for a replacement truck and transferring all the crates need the same attention as when first loaded.

Truck. Advance permission must be obtained from the shipping company for the courier to ride in a commercial truck. If the truck does not have an extended cab for a passenger or living area, the courier may have to sit between the two drivers to enable the co-driver to assist with the trip. Before departure, verify the best and agreed-upon route; verify that the side and back doors are secured and sealed; verify, if necessary, that the police of each state have been warned that a convoy is passing through their jurisdiction, especially if firearms are carried. Finally, verify that the required climate control is set for monitoring during the trip. Remember that a single crate or an entire exhibition should never be left unattended, and a courier and/or a second driver should take turns staying in the truck during rest stops. Alternatively, the courier may travel in a follow car with a shipping agent or security escort; the same rules apply.

Van or private car shipments can be delivered directly, resulting in less handling and less change in temperature and climatic conditions. Staff who use their own vehicles should have insurance that covers the use of the car for official business. Official cars are suitable only for smaller items that can travel safely packed. Meeting a courier with a hand carry is a good example. The courier should never be the driver of a vehicle, in case of a problem; the courier should stay with the shipment and the driver should be the one to seek help if there is a breakdown.

Taxis should be used only for small items on short and direct routes and should be ordered, not hailed in the street. Insist that the driver wait until the courier and the items are safely in the building before leaving.

Train. Carrying larger or high-value exhibitions may require the presence of two couriers. Although this is not a common way to ship cargo in the U.S., trains are frequently used in other countries.

HAND CARRIES

When accompanying an item as a hand carry or hand-luggage, the courier should travel "first" or "business class" to take advantage of extra services provided by the transport carrier in placing the item in a safe, secure location. Only small and portable items should be hand-carried. Avoid over-packing, as the courier may have to unpack and repack during an inspection at security. Simplicity in packing allows someone to view the item without handling. It may be necessary to purchase an extra seat next to the courier into which the object can be strapped with a seat belt extension. Advance planning will assure that this extra room is available and may also provide for a cheaper ticket. If applicable an agent should book the courier's seat, especially if clearance formalities are required and coordination of the courier's arrival must be arranged. The trip may involve customs formalities at ports of entry and exit and can involve long delays that an agent will be able to ease. Return trips without the object should be coach class.

UPON ARRIVAL

The borrowing institution should arrange hotel accommodations and provide the courier, upon arrival, the cash per diem for expenses as previously agreed. Keep a copy of the receipt that is signed for this payment. The borrower should make any adjustments to the travel arrangements if travel condition change or delays occur.

Upon arrival, the courier should inspect the location of where the item(s) will be temporarily stored and assess the area and method of display. After the items have acclimatized, the courier will supervise unpacking, complete a thorough condition check, comparing the item with original document, and observe installation. Should a change in the object's condition occur, photograph these changes in case they are to be given to your insurance company. Obtain a written agreement for any treatment that may be required. Agree in advance where the object will be stored or handled if the exhibition area is not completed before the courier departs. Have the borrower sign a receipt of delivery to verify that all conditions agreed upon are in force. Inform the lending institution that the object has arrived safely and of the circumstances of the object's condition.

RETURN SHIPMENT

The borrowing institution must make similar preparations for the return trip: secure advance reservations and bookings and work out details, such as trucking company, flight plans, hotel, per diem, time of departure, personnel and staff information, etc. Such preparation ensures that the courier's work will be completed as quickly and smoothly as possible. Details and documentation must be completed before the courier leaves on the trip. Again, the courier's travel without an object should be coach class unless otherwise agreed. Returning with the object(s) has the same requirements described above. Be aware that the time lapse between trips could also mean a seasonal change, posing differences in climate conditions. Plan ahead for these changes and dress accordingly.

After the object has arrived at its final destination and has been unpacked and condition checked, the borrowing institution should be informed that the work has arrived safely. Signing the borrower's receipt of delivery will close out this portion of the loan. •

CODE OF PRACTICE FOR COURIERING MUSEUM OBJECTS

Courier Policy

The consideration for using a courier is based on certain primary facts:

Certain museum objects are of a fragile nature, whether by construction or formation, size, materials used, deterioration by age or abuse, and/or require special handling or installation techniques.

Certain museum objects are irreplaceable, rare and unique, politically or culturally sensitive, of extreme artistic, historical, scientific worth, or are of extreme value for other reasons.

Certain shipping routes may prove dangerous to fragile museum objects because such routes expose the object to careless handling, excessive movement, changing and/or extreme temperatures, and other human and/or natural hazards.

Lending and borrowing museums must agree that:

The museum that owns the object may determine that a courier is necessary to lessen the hazards inherent in the object itself, and may specify the transportation methods and/or the route to preserve the object from loss by damage or theft and/or to assure that the object will not receive such wear as would cause future problems in the museum's efforts for preservation.

Both the lending and the borrowing museum are fully cognizant of and in accord with the limitations and requirements of third parties to the loan (such as insurance companies, transport companies, and forwarding companies) and are in agreement about which museum will take responsibility for actions not covered by such third parties.

The lending and borrowing museums accept that:

The care of museum objects is the top priority in the shipment, except in life-threatening situations.

The requirement of a courier will be established and agreed upon by the lending and borrowing museum by the time the loan agreement is signed and accepted.

The courier, acting as the agent of the lending museum, has full authority to act in protection of the object until the object is officially released to the borrowing museum.

Therefore:

The courier designated must be a museum professional (understanding the condition of the object and its special requirements, familiar with packing, trained in handling, and, as applicable, experienced with transport procedures) in whom the lending museum reposes complete trust for execution of all courier-related duties.

The museum that selects the courier is, in effect, bonding that person for knowledge of the problems of the object and of the transit, for ability to withstand the rigors of travel, and for taking full responsibility for protecting the object.

The courier will be made aware of and understand the responsibilities entrusted to him/her, and of all known or possible hazards that might be encountered in transit.

The lending and borrowing museums must agree in advance on costs related to the courier, on which museum shall pay for them, and on the method of reimbursement for expenses whether foreseen or unforeseen.

The shipment of a museum object will not become the basis for unrelated travel or activity.

Courier Procedures

Who Selects a Courier?

The decision to select a courier should be made in consultation among the director, curator, registrar, and conservator, or by one of these, in accordance with authority specified in museum policy.

Who Is Qualified to Be a Courier?

Directors, curators, registrars, conservators, and, in certain cases, senior preparators, should be the only people eligible to serve as couriers. People who serve as couriers must be those who are experienced in handling museum objects.

The courier must possess certain qualities: firmness, patience, stamina, and the ability to make intelligent decisions quickly. If the object is to be hand-carried, the courier must have the physical strength to do so. The courier should not carry any luggage while hand-carrying an object. He/she must possess packing skills, be able to make condition reports and effectively use a camera, and be familiar with shippers, brokers, customs, surface transportation, and airport and airline procedures.

Borrower and Lender Agreements and Responsibilities

The agreement to courier an object should be included as part of the loan agreement or a separate written agreement. If the lender has special requirements (that the object be a hand-carry, that it travel flat, that armed guards be required from the door of the aircraft to the door of the museum, that first-class travel is necessary, that an extended stay by the courier at the borrower's institution is required, or special installation instructions), these should be stipulated in writing at the outset. The borrower should clearly outline its courier procedures regarding all flight details or surface arrangements, arrival, unpacking, condition reporting, and installation, as they apply. All arrangements should be understood by all parties well in advance of the shipping date, including back-up plans for sudden schedule changes. Hotel accommodations and terms for daily expenses should be clearly set forth as part of the formal agreement. It is incumbent upon both borrowing and lending museums and their appointed couriers to make every effort to adhere to cost-effective planning and implementation of courier expenses.

Arrangements

The borrowing and lending institution registrars or loan officials make the arrangements for the loan and courier in accordance with accepted practice and the loan agreement.

The registrar or borrower's representative must meet the courier upon delivery. The courier must know exactly where he/she is to be met when arriving. For international shipments, the borrower's customs broker must be at plane-side if possible to supervise off loading while the borrower is bringing the courier to cargo to meet the broker and shipment. The borrower should not move the shipment until the courier is present unless an emergency develops. The borrower's broker must make incoming customs clearance arrangements so that the objects are not jeopardized at the airport by having their crates opened for inspection. The borrower must provide suitable vehicles to get the courier and shipment from the airport to the museum, and provide personnel at the museum to help off load the truck. If courier and object are in separate vehicles they should travel in tandem.

Once the courier is satisfied that the object is safely stored, the borrower should assist the courier in getting to his/her hostel, and should inform the courier how and when to return to the museum to unpack the object. Twenty-four hours should be designated for object acclimatization. The borrower should provide help to unpack, prepare, and install the object as necessary, and should initial the courier's condition report.

The borrower must provide secure storage for the courier's objects. The borrower must recognize that the courier has authority over the object until the courier is satisfied with its disposition. The courier should act cooperatively with the borrower's staff and accommodate shipping arrangements and installation schedules.

Accompanied Shipment

An accompanied shipment is one in which a courier agrees to oversee other museum loans in the same shipment, but is not responsible for overseeing packing, unpacking, or making condition reports. Museums and couriers should have a written agreement regarding the accompaniment of their or other objects, clearly stating what the courier is expected to do about other objects, with respect to both responsibility and authority.

Responsibilities of the Courier

The courier constitutes a continuous chain of accountability for the object, from the hands of the lender to those of the borrower. The implication is that the courier can take efficient, rapid, on-site action to preserve the object from, or through, high-risk situations in transit. Secure and expeditious movement of the object can reduce high risk to lower levels of risk.

Responsibilities to the Object

The courier is responsible for witnessing and supervising packing, unpacking after the acclimatization period, transportation and examination of the object at the beginning and end of shipment.

The courier must stay with the shipment, physically and personally or via constant contact with centers of authority in direct control of the shipment (e.g., customs brokers) where physical presence by the courier is restricted.

The courier must do all that may be necessary to keep delays or possibilities of delays to a minimum. The courier is responsible for anticipating, solving, and reporting unforeseen problems. In the event of a major change in weather, for example, the courier must decide whether it is advisable for the shipment to proceed.

The courier must have no conflicting obligations or reasons for couriering the object. The courier's family/friends must not travel with the couriered shipment; the courier must not be required, requested, or allowed to visit other locations for personal or museum matters before the object is safely delivered; and the schedule of shipment of the object must not be forced to meet appointments or to ease the courier's trip at the expense of the object.

Skill, Knowledge, and Abilities

The courier must understand and uphold the museum's standards as stated in institution policies. The courier must have vocational knowledge, founded upon practical experience in museums, to understand how these policies relate to real-life circumstances. The courier must also understand the performance expectations of the borrower.

The courier should join in the pre-evaluation of shipment difficulties: dropped cases, fork-lift hazards, major temperature and humidity variations, palletization and containerization problems (e.g., objects that were wet, excessively heavy, or loose in the container with museum crates), insecure strapping, unscheduled unloading, etc.

The courier must have knowledge of the object's construction techniques, material, and condition, and must understand the sensitivity of materials and techniques to the varying conditions of transit. He/she must be able to recognize condition problems that require examination or treatment by a conservator.

The courier must know exactly where the object is going, to whom, and by what means, including alternate/back-up routes if schedules are delayed, altered, or canceled.

The courier should have available from his/her institution or from the borrower:

- a copy of the loan agreement
- business or home addresses, telephone and telex numbers of principals (both borrowers and lenders)
- schedules of transit, including alternates
- insurance restrictions, and a copy of the certificate of insurance
- crate numbers, sizes, weights, and object checklists
- handling instructions
- condition reports
- photograph(s) of the object(s)
- copy of the customs invoice

The courier should leave an itinerary with the registrar's office.

The courier should be prepared in advance for delays, cultural differences in conducting business, language barriers, international telephone and telegraphy procedures, possible strikes, and different local and national holidays.

The courier must understand and appreciate the support functions, procedures, restrictions, and authority of carriers, forwarders, customs agents, airport security, lenders and borrowers. The courier must understand the extent of his/her own authority and responsibility, and ascribe neither too little nor too much authority to someone else.

The courier must have a sound knowledge of government regulations that can limit or curtail courier actions (e.g., restricted entry).

Information should be given only to priority

individuals directly involved in the transit of the object and with a justified need to know. The courier should not tell them anything more than is necessary for them to do their job.

The courier should have some knowledge of shipping, including under-seat sizes, storage areas on board aircraft, and how to seal truck and container locks properly.

The courier must record any container numbers for crated objects, should know position numbers within aircraft, and be seated on the aircraft loading side to watch for unscheduled unloading of crates.

The courier must secure identification of anyone taking crated objects before releasing the crates. The courier must obtain an authorized signature and date on receipts.

The courier must carefully read and understand every document or receipt before signing it, requesting translations when necessary.

The courier must take neither alcohol nor medication that might in any way impair his/her physical mobility and/or ability to make decisions.

The courier should keep accurate accounting of expenses, including copies of all receipts.

Responsibility to the Borrower
The courier must know the borrower's requirements.

- The courier is representing his/her institution and as such should conduct himself/herself fairly and ethically.

- The courier should expect to travel coach class unless hand-carrying an object.

- The courier should not make last-minute changes of plan unless essential to the shipment, but if necessary then the borrower should be immediately notified.

- No arrangements should be made that would cause unnecessary risks, complicated timetables, or extra expense. •

Collections Management III | HYPOTHETICALS

1

A very large sculpture is arriving at your museum. The piece is not heavy and does not require rigging, but it is so big it cannot fit through the loading dock elevator; it must be carried up the steps of the museum and through the front door. The weather is cold and icy.

What steps must you take to ensure the sculpture is carried safely into the museum?

2

You must send an exhibition of 100 objects packed in 30 crates to a city 500 miles away.

What are your options? Arrive at the safest and most efficient method of shipping the exhibition at the lowest possible cost.

3

A prominent overseas artist requires the use of a taxidermied bird specimen as a prop in an installation piece commissioned by your museum.

What steps are involved to ensure that the work can be collected and packed safely, be exported and imported legally, and be exhibited at the museum without risk to your collections and staff?

4

Decide whether to send a courier with—

1. a painting that is traveling from Cleveland to Berlin.

2. a sculpture that needs to be rigged, going from Philadelphia to Washington.

3. a delicate 19th century doll going from Vermont to Boston

4. an original historical document that is traveling from Los Angeles to Japan.

What criteria do you use? Defend your decisions.

SECTION 6 | **RISK MANAGEMENT**

6A | RISK MANAGEMENT OVERVIEW

PAISLEY S. CATO AND SEAN TARPEY

Risk management is an integral component of museum operations, although many of these operations are frequently initiated and managed as independent tasks. This section discusses briefly the concept of risk management as it applies to the management and registration of museum collections. Some of the most common operations that registration staff might be involved with are described more extensively. These operations include disaster planning, security and fire systems, integrated pest management, and insurance.

Publications by R. R. Waller and S. Michalski apply risk management methods as decision-making tools for preventive conservation operations in museums. In his 1995 chapter, entitled "Risk Management Applied to Preventive Conservation," Waller defines risk as "the chance of an undesirable change occurring," and risk management as "the application of available resources in a way that minimizes overall risk." Staff responsible for museum registration should be directly involved in formulating and implementing the basic steps that result in strategies to minimize overall risk to the collections.

The steps for formulating a risk management approach include:

- identification of all risks and assessment of the potential magnitude of each

- identification of strategies to eliminate or mitigate risks and determination of the costs and benefits of each

- setting priorities and establishing a plan for implementation of the strategies, periodic evaluation, and revision or modification

As a result of this process, an institution may determine the need to transfer the assumption of risk through the use of insurance. This situation occurs when the institution identifies limitations on its ability to mitigate potential risk to the collections.

Risks to collections can be grouped according to 10 basic types, as summarized by Waller: physical forces, fire, water, criminals, pests, pollutants, light and radiation, incorrect temperature, incorrect relative humidity, and custodial neglect. Waller and Michalski discuss ways to assess and rank the potential magnitude of each type of risk. This step is an essential precursor to the identification and development of mitigation strategies. As identified in their respective papers, there are five stages for controlling risks, and within each stage, there are eight possible levels of control. The five stages are:

- avoid the source
- block the agent
- detect/monitor the agent
- respond to mitigate the problem
- recover from the problem or treat the result of the problem

The eight levels of control that must be considered for each stage include: location, site, building, room, cabinet, specimen, policy, and procedure. These parameters can be analyzed for a particular collection, resulting in a matrix of possible strategies for mitigation. As noted in Waller's 1995 paper, the type of risk is categorized as potentially catastrophic, severe, or mild/gradual, and then assigned appropriate levels of control. These levels are ranked relative to their importance in mitigating the risk. From this type of assessment, staff determine the costs and benefits of these controls, set priorities, and create a plan to ensure implementation of the controls.

It is important to understand the risk management framework in order to place other functions in perspective. Why should a museum implement an integrated pest management program? Or develop emergency preparedness plans? Or assess the extent and quality of fire and security systems? In all cases, it is to minimize the overall risk to the collections. There will be limitations on the resources a museum has available. The museum may decide to transfer the risk, through insurance, to a commercial business. •

6B | INSURANCE

SEAN TARPEY AND PATRICIA J. HAYES, UPDATED BY DEBORAH PEAK

It has been said that there are no accidents, only events that result from a failure to plan properly. Risk management is the "proper planning," that is, the recognition, analysis, and control of risks. Once the risks have been identified, it is possible to deal with them one by one. Some risks may be avoided by taking measures to eliminate them (e.g., hire guards, update or install electronic security system to protect objects from vandalism). Other risks may have levels of acceptance (e.g., without sufficient numbers of guards, expect a level of damage each year). Risks may be managed by transferring the consequences of them to others (e.g., purchase insurance to pay for possible damage), although insurance companies do expect and include conditions in policy language that insured parties are responsible for protecting the covered property against loss or damage. In the absence of such protections, insurers may impose higher deductibles or not insure for those unprotected perils, shifting a part of the risk back to the insured museum.

It is not always possible to isolate all of the risks to museum collections, and it is even more challenging to decide how to handle each hazard. Seek expert advice in isolating and categorizing potential perils. Some easily identified risks include inadequate record-keeping, handling, transportation, and environmental hazards such as fire, water, smoke, pollution, and loss of climate controls. More complex analysis may be required to identify exposure to theft and vandalism and hazards involving exhibition and storage. Policies and procedures should be reviewed and strategies developed to eliminate and minimize threats. Insurance must be purchased to cover borrowed objects and should be purchased to protect the museum's permanent collection.

Insurance should be integrated into the risk management program. Its purpose is to offer financial protection by insulating the museum from catastrophic monetary loss. The extent of the collection covered and the dollar amount of coverage can vary. The insurable interests generally include the current market values of all objects owned by the museum (i.e., the permanent collection), all property owned by others on loan to the museum (i.e., long term or temporary loans), and other property such as a historic site that is significant to the museum's mission. The amount of insurance coverage will by necessity have a monetary limit. A loss or blanket limit option is allocated as needed and provides coverage for any property under the museum's "care, custody, and control" without regular inventory reports to the insurance company. If not already appraised, the current market value of the lost or damaged object(s) prior to loss will be determined. In the case of damaged object(s) the insurance company will pay the costs and expenses of repair/restoration and any resultant loss in value after restoration, as agreed upon between the insured and the company. In the case of loans, the value is that stipulated in the loan agreement.

Most recent museum policies avoid the tedious task of reporting and are based on well-considered limits of liability. A museum's limit is usually calculated to reflect a probable maximum loss (PML) as established by the senior staff of the museum and endorsed by the governing board. The probable maximum loss is usually large enough to cover the loss incurred should one distinct area of the museum suffer a catastrophe. Total destruction of a storeroom, a wing, or—in the case of a small museum—the entire structure may be used to determine probable maximum loss. One should envision the worst possible disaster in that area (e.g., 100-year flood, long burning fire). When calculating this figure, it is important to remember that all property owned by others for which there are binding loan agreements (requiring the museum to maintain insurance coverage) will account for the first dollars paid out in any catastrophic loss. Examine the loss limit frequently, especially in a time of rapid collection growth, volatile art market, or increased exhibition activity. A loss limit sufficient for an entire storage vault a decade ago might be absorbed by a single item today. Separate limits may need to be established for objects in transit, on loan to other locations, and on exhibition loan. The premium will be based upon the likely limits of exposure for the year.

Scheduled policies will pay only for losses of or damage to the objects listed on the schedule, and for the dollar amount stated on the schedule. This type of policy is extremely labor intensive for museums with active collecting and exhibition programs. All incoming loans with values and coverage period must be submitted in advance to the company. Each new acquisition and object arriving for purchase consideration, gift, or bequest must be immediately and accurately assigned a value and be reported to the company. Any subsequent fluctuation in the value of individual objects must be reported to the company. The premium will be based upon reported values. This type of policy is not generally used except when special exhibitions are insured separately from a museum's main policy. The scheduled policy is cumbersome and runs the risk of being inadequate if an inventory or schedule is not updated on a regular basis.

Once the degree of acceptable risk has been established, it is time to meet with insurance representatives. Contact a museum insurance specialist, a professional well versed in issues affecting museums. This will result in several beneficial side effects. The contact person will have a clear understanding of questions or concerns. A fine arts specialist will not try to shoehorn the exhibition program into a policy designed for manufacturing. The better the reputation of the agent and underwriter, the more at ease lenders will be. The policy can be tailored specifically to the museum's needs, and premiums may be lower with a fine arts insurer than with a multi-purpose insurance agent.

REQUEST FOR PROPOSAL

Insurance policies may be purchased from a broker or an independent agent. The independent agent has access to all insurance markets and the underwriters who represent them, and will canvass the market to help the museum find the underwriter and policy best suited to the museum's situation. The agent will then work with staff and negotiate with the underwriter to be sure the coverage meets the museum's expectations. For this service, the agent will receive a percentage of the premium. As noted above, insurance companies that have traditionally insured fine arts and have solid museum relationships should be sought. It is also important that the proposal provide the insurance company's AM Best's Rating Guide and financial size category including an explanation of these ratings. For example an A++ is the highest (superior) rating, B and B- are fair, C++ and C+ are marginal. Many agencies will not use insurance markets with ratings of B or higher.

When reviewing insurance needs, put together a request for proposal (RFP). The bidding process serves several functions. First, it allows the museum to complete a self-assessment. The museum should examine the elements of the current insurance program and collections procedures (collections management, written statements, loan practices, security, climate control, packing, storage, hiring and training of personnel, etc.). Second, it allows the museum to get outside opinions about risk. As part of the bid packet, the museum should submit a facility report and expect a site visit from the insurance company and/or agent. The museum will learn its deficiencies and its strengths in the process. Be prepared to discuss in detail exhibition plans for the next several years and address plans for overseas loans, building plans, and many other activities. Unless there is a substantial change in the museum's operations or insurance company rating/financials (something the broker should let you know), it is recommended that the bid process take place every 3 to 5 years.

Once the policy is bound, the agent should continue to work with the museum on several issues: risk management, management of the allocations of coverage, and the need for temporary additional coverage for loans or exhibitions. A special exhibition with unusually high values detracts from the coverage provided to the permanent collection. In this case, it may be necessary to purchase additional coverage in the form of an endorsement to the policy or a separate exhibition policy.

POLICY CONTENT

The museum policy is a form of inland marine insurance, derived from the earliest insurances available for items in motion—those easily transported from one place to another. The policies vary, but most contain many similar clauses. It is important to become familiar with insurance terminology; much of it is very specific to the insurance industry. A reputable insurance representative will not hesitate to answer questions and clarify concepts if asked.

PROPERTY

•Property Insured. The policy should specify classes of property such as permanent collection, loan collections (including long-term and short-term loans), items on purchase approval, and objects in which the museum has an insurable joint interest. This may also include promised gifts and bequests. Some policies may cover special exhibitions organized by the museum, including objects on loan, in transit, and at other venues.

•*Categories of Materials.* In addition to specifying classes of property, the policy should describe the categories of materials in the collections as follows: collectible objects of every kind and description including but not limited to paintings, drawings, etchings, photographs, prints, manuscripts, rugs, furniture, statuary, antiques, armor, bronzes, rare books and coins, glassware, marbles, pictures, porcelains, potteries, sculptures and tapestries; antique paneling, ceilings, floors, frescoes and murals in rooms known as "period room," including Oriental rooms, cases, frames, glazing, shadow boxes, pedestals, and other display equipment; scientific specimens; all other bona fide works of art and objects of rarity, historic value, cultural interest, or artistic merit. Do not impose a test of artistic merit or value; objects accessioned into the collections should qualify since the intellectual tests have been passed during the acquisition process. The most important wording for insured property is "not limited to." If too much is described without those words included, there is no coverage for items not shown on the list.

•*Property Excluded.* This section of the policy lists categories of property not covered by the policy, such as the building, mechanical systems, office furniture, and other non-collections property. These properties should be covered under a separate policy. Valuable papers are generally covered under another commercial non-fine art property policy as they deal with the museum's administrative processes. Special library collections, archives, and manuscripts can be insured under a fine art policy as long as they are historic, rare, of cultural or historic merit, and not readily available for public use.

•*Valuation.* The valuation clause is the key to the policy. Valuation may be scheduled, but most annual museum policies today are loss/blanket limit policies based on the current market value at the time of loss or damage. A schedule policy means that an inventory detailing the value of each item must be reported to the insurance company on a periodic basis. If an object is omitted from the list, or the value is incorrectly stated, the museum will not receive adequate reimbursement for the object. The amount paid in a loss will follow the list of record. Fair market value, with an agreed upon policy limit, is often the preferred option. Ideally, the value for an object involved in a loss should already be pre-determined by the museum maintaining updated values with an appraisal or other professional source (i.e., auction prices). The value can, however, be determined by an appraisal after the fact, making the need for good photographs and records evident. The exception is for objects on loan to the museum, and in this case the prevailing loan agreement should state the value agreed to by the owner of the object and the museum.

•*Appraisal.* Read this clause of the policy very carefully. Should a loss occur, the museum and the insurance company must agree on the value of a total loss, or on the resulting loss of value and cost of restoration in the case of damage to an object. Failing that agreement, the insured and insurance company each obtain an appraiser at their own expense; an appraiser is hired to determine the value. If an agreement still is not reached, many insurance policies call for the selection of various referees. Courts and judges are alluded to in the wording of the policy.

•*Loans.* Property of others in the museum's "care, custody, and control" is usually governed by the terms of a loan agreement signed by the owner and by the registrar or director of the borrowing institution. It is best that the museum countersign after the lender has indicated his valuation on the agreement. Some argue that a museum should verify the owner's stated value, perhaps by obtaining an independent appraisal. Naturally, extraordinary values need to be questioned and considered, but a museum is not in the business of verifying values; the issue continues to be debated. If the value is extraordinary, do not countersign; renegotiate the loan. The agreed upon value is a meeting of the minds. This value will be the payoff figure should a total loss occur, and it must be realistic.

LOCATION

•*Off Premises.* The blanket of coverage will extend beyond the front doors or shipping dock. Works in the permanent collection lent to exhibitions, at the regional conservation lab, or at the mount maker's shop will be covered under this section of the policy. Check the policy wording carefully, especially the territorial limits, which may stipulate the U.S. and Canada, the congruous United States and Canada (may not include Hawaii), or worldwide; the policy should clarify the locations or restrictions on locations that are covered. If the coverage is restricted and it is necessary to send an object outside the territory

covered, it will be necessary to arrange for extra coverage.

•*Transit.* The policy should include a limit on insurance coverage for objects in transit. Examine the museum's shipping history and arrive at a value limit for objects in transit based on the highest value shipped during the past year(s) or anticipated shipments. You can have your insurance agent/broker negotiate an increased transit limit if necessary to avoid repeated requests for increases. Since premiums are generally based on premises limits, it is wise to negotiate a high transit limit.

PERILS AND EXCLUSIONS

Circumstances in which a loss is not covered must be explicitly stated in the policy. Although one might ideally prefer a policy that covers all perils, many types of coverage are available only with expensive premiums. Sections describing exclusions and restrictions should be analyzed carefully and discussed with the agent to determine the likelihood of the peril relative to the museum's collection. Request the removal of restrictions that will inhibit the museum's mission. Each peril is ultimately negotiable, but the dollar cost in premiums may be too steep to be acceptable.

•*Standard Exclusions.* Examples of policy exclusions are acts of war; nuclear reaction; wear and tear; gradual deterioration; moths; vermin; inherent vice; damage sustained due to or resulting from any repairing, restoration or retouching process; insurrection; rebellion; government seizure; perils of customs quarantine; and illegal transportation. It is quite common to have certain types of shipments restricted, such as regular mail unless first class registered; or dollar limits might be placed on the use of overnight express carriers. Loans to politically sensitive cities or countries might be restricted, as might loans to earthquake prone regions. Terrorism may be an exclusion on the policy, offered for an additional premium or automatically included by the insurance company. Refer any questions regarding terrorism to your agent/broker.

•*Lost in Inventory.* This section might include language concerning unexplained or "mysterious" disappearance. The insurance company does not want to be responsible in the first year of a new policy for the unexplained losses of the past 50 years. Some policies will state that losses for objects not physically identified and recorded within a stated number of years be excluded. Many agents will not write a policy for an institution that does not have an up-to-date inventory.

•*"Wall to wall"* Coverage. Such coverage implies that the object is covered from the moment it is removed from its normal resting place, incidental to shipping; through all phases of packing, transfer, consolidation, exhibition, and repacking; until it is returned to the original resting place, or the place designated by the owner, and the museum's involvement is finished. Coverage thus includes damage to the object from the first instant it is touched until the loan is officially terminated. Termination should be in writing, preferably by receipt, and should note that the owner has accepted the object in a condition that is acceptable. If arrangements for further museum involvement are made (for instance, the museum agrees to have someone reinstall the work a week or month later), a written release should be obtained when all involvement is finished.

Terms, Duties, Limits, Liabilities

•*Terms.* The terms of the policy define the parameters for premiums, record-keeping, reports, and notices. The policy specifies the amount and payment terms of the premium. The museum will be required to maintain accurate, comprehensive records of the collection; this may entail photographs of the most valuable objects. The policy may include the address to which all formal correspondence (notice of loss, etc.) should be mailed.

•*Duties of the Insured.* The policy stipulates that the museum agrees to use the best professional judgment and practice with respect to packing, handling, security, and fire safety.

•*Loss.* Once the insured is aware of or has discovered an incident resulting in loss or damage to insured object(s), the insurance agent should be notified. A claim may need to be filed within a specific time to be valid; check your policy for any specific time frame in which the loss must be reported. Once a claim is paid, in the case of a total loss, the insurance company will have the right to take title and possession of the object, should it be recovered. The best policies give the museum the right-of-first-refusal to purchase the object back.

•*Additional Insured.* Owners of loan objects and temporary borrowers of insured property can be added to the insurance policy as "additional insured" as required in the loan agreement. Packers and shippers not employed by the museum but hired as fee-for-service providers are generally not covered. Anyone requesting to be named as an additional insured on the museum's policy must have his name added to the policy by means of an endorsement. This will provide him with some legal protection.

•*Limits of Liability (amount of coverage).* These limits are the maximum amount of insurance dollars to be paid in any one loss occurrence, in any number of categories. Limits will be set on premises, at any other location (which may be worldwide or restricted to North America), and per conveyance while in transit (by car, truck, plane, etc.). Limits will be for the total of all costs, whether partial or total loss, salvage fees, or other covered expenses.

•*Probable Maximum Loss.* Most museums are unable to afford the cost of insuring to full market value. It is much more common to assess the risks and settle upon a probable maximum loss value in case of a single event or incident on premises (loss of a gallery or wing, single storage vault, or floor), in transit, and at any other location.

•*Deductibles.* These are monetary amounts for which the insured is responsible to pay on each loss to which the deductible applies. The insurance company pays the remaining amount of each covered loss. A deductible should only apply to property owned by the museum. The loan collection should not have a deductible, nor should objects in transit. Deductibles may range from a few dollars to many thousands of dollars and will be reflected in savings to the museum's premiums. In order to maintain a low loss record, agents frequently discourage frivolous claims (i.e., claims of less than a few hundred dollars).

•*Legal Liability.* The policy will pay, within established limits and subject to restrictions, amounts the museum shall be legally obligated to pay if a loss occurs to an object in the museum's care that the museum has been instructed not to insure (as when a lender elects to maintain his own insurance coverage and a waiver of subrogation has not been received). This refers to legal costs incurred should someone agree to maintain his own insurance, then attempt to collect from the museum in the event of a loss. Some policies state a specific limit of liability, while others do not; if not stated, the limit is the policy limit.

•*Other Insurance.* Should another policy or national indemnity coverage be in effect at the time of the loss, the policy may limit payment to the amount not paid by the other insurance. The museum cannot collect twice on a single loss.

•*Insured Not to Assume Liability.* This clause directs the museum not to assume voluntarily any liability on behalf of the insurer. In other words, the museum should not make any promises for the insurance company. The museum must also agree to assist the company in resolving claims if requested.

OTHER PROVISIONS

•*Loss Buy Back.* This provision states the terms by which the museum can purchase recovered property. If the object is recovered after the museum has cashed the insurance check, the object belongs to the insurance company according to the terms of the policy. However, by this provision the museum may repurchase the object from the insurance company. Commonly, the museum pays the same amount that it initially received, plus expenses incurred in recovering the object; some policies include interest as well, and some allow the current market value of the object to be the buy-back price. Some policies also stipulate a time limit. This clause varies from policy to policy.

When a damaged object is deemed to be a total loss and the claim has been paid by the insurance company, the museum may "purchase" the piece from the insurer for the newly adjusted fair market value if it believes there is still some merit in keeping the object in the collection.

•*Pairs and Sets.* If the museum has a set of six objects and one is lost due to theft or damage, the museum may not want the other five. The museum will have the option under this clause of turning over the remaining portion of the set to the insurance company; the museum will then receive the full value of the set.

•*Subrogation.* This clause states that the insurance company, in return for paying a claim, takes the museum's rights to any possible legal action. Should the museum have reason to take action against an individual or company (for example, a deliberate act of vandalism by a known individual), the insurance company may ask to have the museum's right to action transferred to the company. The insurance company will then try to collect all or part of its expenses from the responsible party. A waiver of subrogation is intended to convey to a borrowing institution a pledge that the insurance company will not sue the borrower to recoup expenses in the event of a loss. Most insurance companies will not subrogate against a nonprofit entity.

•*No Recourse.* A no recourse clause states that the insurance company will not try to sue or collect from the museum's packers, crate makers, shippers, or others, with some possible exceptions.

•*Endorsements.* These documents constitute formal changes to the details of the policy. They may adjust the limits, extend territories, name additional insured, or cover special temporary exhibitions for specified dates. Endorsements are also called riders.

•*Certificates of Insurance.* A certificate of insurance is issued to lenders or borrowers, depending on the loan situation. This document is a proof of insurance for information purposes and is not a legal document. A lender or borrower may be named as an additional insured, or a waiver of subrogation may be specified on the certificate of insurance. If this is done, similar language should be placed in the loan agreement, the document that actually governs the transaction. Although not a legal document, the certificate of insurance must reflect the current policy terms and conditions. Anything agreed to that is outside of the policy will be the responsibility of the insured. Refer any such requests to your agent/broker, who may have to negotiate with the insurance company.

temporary storage or mobile equipment needs, such as portable climate control facilities and freeze-drying units. If immediate action is required to minimize or avoid continued destruction, the museum's policy should provide the funds. •

CLAIMS

Reporting procedures is critical when handling a claim. Should a loss occur, start taking notes immediately. Your fine arts broker/agent should have a claims reporting form that will list the pertinent information needed to report a claim to the insurance company. Gather information and put it in writing as soon as possible. Take photographs of damage, collect environmental data, and take statements from witnesses. Notify the museum's agent by telephone and in writing; the agent will contact the claims representatives. In case of suspected theft or vandalism, contact the appropriate authorities (police, Federal Bureau of Investigation, etc.).

If the nature of the loss is catastrophic, the insurance company will respond by sending members of its staff or assign an independent fine art loss adjuster to assist on site. Your broker/agent should provide you with an insurance company or loss adjuster contact and claim number. Keep this information handy for quick reference and response. The priority must be to contain the loss and prevent further damage. These representatives should be able to authorize funds as needed to hire additional security or provide

6C | EMERGENCY PREPAREDNESS PLANNING

PAISLEY S. CATO AND ANNE FURMAN DOUGLAS

WHY?

Emergencies happen, so museums need to plan and prepare for responding to the emergency. With advance thought and preparation, staff can prevent or mitigate extreme damage to collections. A museum emergency preparedness plan focuses on preparing for and mitigating the damage from catastrophic events that endanger people and collections. In addition to the objects in its collection, as a public space, a museum is responsible for the safety of visitors and employees.

The project of writing a disaster preparedness plan may be given priority for other reasons. Accreditation by the American Association of Museums indicates a museum's adherence to accepted professional standards and to public accountability. An institution's emergency preparedness plan is considered a critical element during the accreditation and re-accreditation processes. Museums that are part of a larger organization (e.g., a college, university, or corporation) may be required to develop an emergency preparedness plan as part of an overall commitment to safety.

The primary objectives of emergency planning are to identify risks in order to anticipate and, if possible, to avoid emergencies; to retain control when an emergency occurs; and to mitigate potential damage as quickly as possible. Surprise is often a key feature of an emergency, and no museum professional would want or plan to experience a disaster. Emergency preparedness plans focus on responsibilities and procedures to be implemented during and after an emergency. Key to minimizing the impact of an emergency is the anticipation and prevention of potential risks.

Anticipation requires determining the likelihood of various risks and emergencies, evaluating both the environment and the facility; by determining the most likely risks, staff can plan and anticipate what to do with the collection in case the event occurs. Planning details will include, for example, communication lines, lists of materials and tools needed, and procedures for moving the collections. Prevention is always preferred, but of course that is feasible only to certain degrees; once a risk is identified, corrective actions should be taken as soon as possible.

Emergencies get rapidly and progressively worse if they are not dealt with quickly in a productive manner. A recoverable situation can become a total loss if the response is not swift and correctly implemented. Established procedures and an existing supply of materials can significantly reduce the damage to objects during this vulnerable period.

WHAT?

The specifics of an emergency plan must be written down. Time passes, people forget, and staff members change. The idiosyncrasies of the institution, collection, and staff must be considered when determining the format and content of the plan. While the process of developing a plan requires research and compilation of a variety of information, the final format needs to be easy to understand and use. A "quick response" version of the plan should be easily accessible to all staff so that each individual has pertinent contact information and procedures instantly available.

Resources that are helpful in developing a plan include: information on the Heritage Preservation website (http://www.heritagepreservation.org/programs/TFPlanPrepare.html); *Building an Emergency Plan: A Guide for Museums and Other Cultural Institutions* (http://www.getty.edu/conservation/publications/pdf_publications/emergency_plan.pdf); and the *Field Guide to Emergency Response*, published by Heritage Preservation. Agencies in several states and at several universities have developed guides as well; these frequently include state or regional resource listings (e.g., *Generic Disaster Plan Workbook*, http://calpreservation.org/disasters/generic/index.html).

The plan should contain sections that incorporate the following:

- potential risks
    - a. identification of greatest risks and problem spots
- contacts and responsibilities
    - a. chain of command
    - b. individual responsibilities
    - c. duties of response coordinator
    - d. administration's responsibilities
- initial assessment and immediate responses
    - a. evacuation procedures
    - b. floor plans
- assessment of damage and mitigation plans
    - a. documentation
    - b. collection salvage priorities
    - c. how-to steps for initial responses to various material types
- supply checklist and suppliers
- resource contacts for specialty services
- emergency preparedness and response for specific disasters
- maintenance checklist
- forms
    - a. damage assessment form
    - b. post-disaster report form
- bibliography and resources

How?

The mechanics of producing an emergency preparedness plan will vary from institution to institution; there must, however, be support from top level administrators as well as support staff for the plan to be successful. To create a successful, useful emergency preparedness plan, the process of writing the document should involve staff members who will implement the procedures. These individuals need to have familiarity with the procedures and, in some cases, may need additional training to implement them effectively.

Large museums may form committees and subgroups to accomplish the task; small museums may have one or two people write the plan. With either structure, one person must lead the project to completion. Once written, the job of regularly reviewing, updating, and otherwise maintaining the plan must be assigned to a specific person or group. Emergency planning is an ongoing process; resource listings and responsibility assignments need periodic updating. Training and drills must take place at least annually for a plan to be useful.

The first step in writing an emergency preparedness plan is analysis and research. If the museum has a parent institution (e.g., university, city, county), an initial step is to read and analyze that organization's emergency plan. In theory, that plan should contain basic procedures and resource information that may be helpful, and the museum can tailor its own plan to fit within the bigger perspective. Many cities and communities have developed emergency response plans, so a museum should have a copy of that plan as a guide for developing its own preparedness plan.

Identify and assess potential risks and hazards. Assessment tools may include the institution's general conservation survey, which will have identified risks as part of the assessment process. If that assessment is not current, self-assessment checklists have been developed by several organizations and can be obtained online or at minimal cost. Information from this assessment should be used to complete projects that will prevent damage before the emergency can happen. If projects cannot be completed due to cost or time, awareness of the risk will help the planning team develop procedures should the emergency occur.

Information about natural disasters is available through the U.S. Geological Survey's Natural Hazards Gateway (http://www.usgs.gov/hazards/). Included is information about the seven major types of natural disasters that may impact museums: earthquakes, floods, hurricanes, landslides, tsunamis, volcanoes, and wildfires. Refer to the Declared Disasters by Year or State website at FEMA (http://www.fema.gov/news/disaster_totals_annual.fema) to assess the recent history of major disasters for your region.

With information from this research step,

itemize the disasters that may affect your building or collection. Rank them according to likelihood, and envision the worst-case scenario in each situation. What damage would each disaster cause? Consider both localized and widespread disasters. Is it likely that your institution might be needed by the community as a temporary command post or hospital?

Part of the research phase includes locating pertinent resources and suppliers. Resource information includes the obvious (police, fire, emergency response teams) but also the less obvious for sources of materials for mitigation response (e.g., dehumidifiers, oversized fans, etc.). Some regions host coalitions of cultural institutions that have developed caches of supplies for emergency purposes. Some supplies need to be purchased and held on-site in strategic locations. An emergency supply cart, or multiple carts, can be effective for holding supplies and small equipment that should not be used for other purposes.

Identify priorities for rescue of collection objects and documents. While this needs to be completed collection by collection, there also needs to be an institutional priority listing. Time is usually an issue in responding to an emergency, so the tough decisions of prioritizing need to be made in advance.

Priorities will also guide the team in pulling together information on how to handle different types of collection materials. This information is not intended to serve as a full recovery resource but rather as a guide for initial handling, allowing responders to carefully remove objects from continuing risks. Often, this information is valuable for reminding responders what not to do.

Identify which staff members will be needed to respond to a major disaster and what individual responsibilities will be. Decide who has the right personality to direct the recovery effort. This does not have to be, and often should not be, the museum's director. Assign specific jobs to specific people so that everyone knows exactly what is expected. Such advance planning can prevent chaos in an emergency. Distribute "telephone trees" to those staff members whose presence will be essential in an emergency. Schedule training sessions and annual reviews of the plan.

The format of the final product should be a practical, useful one. A sectioned three-ring binder allows for easy updating. The core committee may have an extensive binder, but there should be a small, short, easy-to-read, response guide for all staff. Remember that the staff member who first responds to an emergency situation may be neither a member of the emergency preparedness committee nor a trained collections care staff person.

Complete a draft of the emergency preparedness plan, and make it available for review and comment by the entire staff. At least one copy of the final version should be in each office, and the head of each department should receive another copy to keep at home or in a car. The plan must be required reading for all new employees.

A schedule for reviewing the plan, inspecting supplies, and on-going staff training should be established. Mock disasters, quizzes, and videos can make staff training both fun and informative. As disasters happen around the country in a year, use the occasion to review your plan with other staff under a structure of "what if that had happened here?" The written emergency preparedness plan should always be considered a work in progress and undergo regular evaluation and updating. •

6D | EMERGENCY RESPONSE AND RECOVERY

PAISLEY S. CATO

An efficient, focused response to an emergency situation can significantly reduce the potential damage to collections. The first few hours and days are critical to mitigate damage caused by the emergency and, just as importantly, to prevent additional damage resulting from well-intentioned but incorrect actions taken.

In addition to the response, which might in fact take several days, weeks, or even months, there is a recovery phase during which a series of salvage and rehabilitation activities occur. The recovery phase can take years but is marked by a consistent, controlled process with carefully thought-out and executed actions.

Emergencies range from relatively small, localized situations to catastrophic events affecting a widespread region. Some aspects of the staff response, however, apply to all sizes of emergencies and to all steps taken during the response and recovery phases: assess and maintain safety, encourage calm and deliberate action, and start planning the next steps. Safety for staff and visitors is always an over-arching concern. In the initial response to an emergency, during evacuation, consciously look for hazards: frayed or loose electrical wires, fallen objects that might trip someone, broken glass, etc. Guide staff and visitors away from hazards as evacuation continues. Staff should not re-enter the emergency area until cleared to do so by professional emergency responders (fire, police, etc.). Upon re-entering the area, consciously look for hazards and proceed only if safely equipped to do so. While this approach seems one of common sense, we all know professionals whose first thought of safety will be for the objects and specimens, not the people!

"Calm and deliberate" should be the mantra for staff response. Responding in a calm manner helps defuse the anxiety and instinctive rapid response to an emergency. Too frequently a frantic, rapid response results in mishandling of objects and increased level of damage.

Start planning for the next steps of response and recovery. In a catastrophic emergency, access to collections may be significantly delayed; in a minor emergency, access should be delayed intentionally, at least long enough to assess the situation and think ahead to the next steps that are the appropriate response for this particular situation.

Basic steps in the response to an emergency include:

- implement emergency notifications
- secure area
- identify source of problem
- notify insurance contact
- assemble response team
- conduct initial assessment for hazards and damage
- document
- protect priority collections
- stabilize temperature and humidity
- plan the next steps
- gather supplies, equipment
- contact and initiate specialized services
- set up and implement salvage areas
- document, communicate, coordinate

Notify relevant emergency services such as fire department, police, and ambulance, as well as the institution's response team leader. Secure the area affected by following institutional plans for evacuating staff and visitors and ensuring safety. Prevent re-entry until it is clear that hazards are not present. Identify the source(s) of the problem; take corrective action only if it is safe to do so. Notify the insurance contact and begin to document the damage. Note taking is helpful, but photos and videos are essential. Assemble the response team, and make assignments specific to this emergency. Complete an initial assessment for hazards and damage and begin a more thorough process of documenting what happened and the conditions. Reinforce in all responders the need to remain calm and to proceed with deliberation, not with frantic, haphazard tasks.

Implement the plan for protecting at-risk collections with the highest priority. This may involve covering collections to prevent further damage or bringing in specialized services for stabilizing temperature and relative humidity. This is one of several response steps for which advance research and planning facilitate significantly the speed and efficiency of the response. The response period is not when one should spend time researching and locating services.

With the initial assessment of damages, the extent and type of collections affected, and the areas of the institution affected, plan the next steps in the response to guide decisions on the resources needed. The initial response needs to remove (or protect) as much of the collection as possible from imminent danger, and then a salvage or recovery plan should slow or stop deteriorating agents. There is never one clear path that will solve all the salvage issues, so flexibility with periodic re-assessment is essential. While it is possible to train staff in some basic methods for handling and salvaging materials so as to stabilize the objects, expert knowledge will be necessary at points during the recovery to assess methods as well as the condition of individual objects. Basic problems will likely include damage due to water: too much, contaminated, salty, muddy, heated, mold-inducing, corrosive. Other common problems involve air-borne pollutants (soot, ash, noxious gasses), broken objects, pests, or unknown hazardous materials.

Designate staff, supplies, and equipment needed and set up a salvage area to begin the salvage and recovery phases. Reinforce the need for continuing documentation, communication, and coordination among respondents and administration. Salvage and recovery plans require flexibility, informed decision-making, and revision as the work continues.

Recognizing that the recovery phase can extend many weeks, months, or even years depending on the nature and extent of the emergency; communication with administrators is critical to manage and obtain adequate resources. Good photographic documentation will help with fundraising efforts, whether grant-based or from individual donors.

A number of resources referenced in the previous chapter on planning for emergencies contain useful information for responding to and recovering from emergencies. A practical tool that all museums should have on hand is the *Field Guide to Emergency Response* (Heritage Preservation, Inc., 2006). It should be used as part of a more extensive planning process but also serves as a quick guide to remind responders what to consider.

The *Field Guide to Emergency Response* contains a useful description of the roles and responsibilities for response team members:

- response team leader
- emergency responder liaison
- health and safety coordinator
- security and facilities coordinator
- administrative and financial coordinator
- supplies and equipment coordinator
- communications coordinator
- assessment coordinator
- documentation coordinator
- salvage coordinator

Small organizations can use the descriptions of key responsibilities to help organize their response plan, assigning the key issues to appropriate staff, volunteers, or outside providers. The reality of emergencies is that the issue will be there regardless of the size of the institution; the scale may be different but the problem has to be dealt with.

The best response to an emergency is carried out by individuals and organizations that have completed advance research, planning, and training. Resources are available to help, but it is incumbent on the institution to start long before the emergency occurs; if an emergency occurs, response team members are supported by the plan and reinforcement to remain safe and calm, and to act deliberately. •

6E | SECURITY SYSTEMS AND FIRE PROTECTION SYSTEMS

PAISLEY S. CATO

Control of some risks to collections may be handled through a variety of security and fire protection systems. In the overall framework of risk management, these systems are the museum's response, ideally to block or prevent the threat; in the event that total prevention isn't possible, these systems serve to mitigate the effect of the threat. Critical to the effectiveness of security and fire prevention systems is the set of policies and procedures implemented by staff. Physical components are essential, but if personnel do not consistently and correctly follow procedures, the physical components can be useless. While it is beyond the scope of this section to provide extensive descriptions of various systems, it is important to understand the basis for policies, procedures, and equipment to implement these systems.

SECURITY

To safeguard collections from theft and vandalism, one can consider the general levels of risk control described in Waller's framework (1995), that is, location, site, building, room, cabinet, and specimen. Keller and Willson's chapter, "Security Systems" (1995), provides a similar listing for consideration: grounds, public area, gallery (exhibit areas), offices, work space, storage, and vault. Initially, one must determine the primary problems or risks faced at each level and, subsequently, the appropriate methods for mitigating the risk. The process of identifying security risks at each level applies regardless of the institution's size, whether a small, single building or a large, multi-building complex.

Protection begins with the design of the landscaping and structure relative to its position in a neighborhood. Most staff members have little control over design and location and must focus instead on mitigating the risks that come with the building.

The ultimate security of an object depends on

several levels of protection, beginning with effective policies and procedures that are developed and implemented by staff. Security systems are comprised of both human and equipment components. Staff formulate and implement policies and procedures; equipment is used to monitor events that may pose risks to the security of the collections and to alert humans to breaches of security.

Keller and Willson propose, in their 1995 article, three factors that affect and determine museum security: access control, parcel control, and internal security. Control of who has the authority to enter and leave the building and individual spaces within the building is essential. Building level control starts with who can enter when, at which entrances. Careful consideration must be given to where individuals may travel within the building and whether an individual can enter an area unaccompanied or in the presence of others. Policies for access need to apply to all levels of staff, trustees, and volunteers as well as contractors, service personnel, and guests. Policies must clarify when these groups are permitted to enter and what they may or may not carry in and out; procedures should specify how those policies are to be implemented.

Security equipment can be used to implement the policies (e.g., key controls on 24-hour clock), to detect events that indicate a failure to follow the policies (e.g., intrusion detection systems), and to summon police or guards in such events. The equipment is effective, however, only if they support the policies and procedures and if the equipment is used consistently and correctly.

In addition to security at the facility, the security of collections in transit must be addressed. Procedures should exist for reviewing each loan or object transport with respect to security. Consideration should be taken not only for the physical packing parameters but also for the chain of custody that might be required; the latter varies greatly with the method of transport. Documenting and monitoring the implementation of these procedures is essential.

Keller and Willson stress that internal security is provided by hiring honest people and by providing deterrence for dishonest behavior. Achieving these goals requires routinely doing fingerprint and/or background security checks, not only for staff but also for volunteers. It also involves training to improve awareness among staff and volunteers of the security of the collections and how to handle situations involving potential security breaches.

An effective security system is structured to the museum, its staff, and its level of resources. The Director and Trustees need to provide an adequate level of resources for equipment and training as part of their fiduciary responsibility for protecting the institution's collections.

The following checklist enumerates issues to consider when establishing security systems. The chapter in the *NPS Museum Handbook*, Part I, entitled "Museum Collections Security and Fire Protection," provides a good overall introduction to security systems. The chapter includes a useful table that describes the types of intrusion detection devices (what each is, what it detects, where it should be located, and what its limitations are). In addition to further reading, staff should consult security experts and insurance representatives; both can provide assessments, information, and recommendations directly relevant to the institution.

CHECKLIST OF ISSUES TO CONSIDER FOR SECURITY SYSTEM COMPONENTS

Policies and Procedures

Staff authority for security program
- Position responsible for program
- Additional positions to assist

Access restrictions (who, where, when)
- Who has authority to determine access levels

Procedures to allow access
- Key control
- Opening/closing procedures for museum

- Opening/closing procedures for individual spaces

Procedures to monitor access
- Sign in/out
- Passes
- Identification badges

Procedures for inspection of packages (in and out)

Procedures for reporting and documenting events
- For theft, vandalism, intrusion, etc.

Emergency response procedures

Staff and Volunteers

Background security checks during hiring process

Formal security staff
- Visible, professional
- Contract agency or use in-house staff

Staff training and awareness

Drills for emergency responses

Drills to test security systems and procedures

Equipment

Purpose of equipment
- Intrusion detection
- Tampering detection
- Interruption of building systems (e.g., power)
- Contact with people to initiate response

Types of contact systems (examples)
- Telephone
- Radio
- Remote monitoring/notification

Types of detection systems (examples)
- Magnetic contact
- Photo electric ray
- Ultrasonic
- Sound
- Motion
- Infrared
- Weight/press
- TV monitor/closed circuit

Test systems routinely

Fire Protection Systems

Fire safety programs also rely on a combination of human and mechanical components. Either one alone is not a sufficient safeguard, yet each brings essential elements to the program. In a 1995 article, Wilson identifies five elements of a basic fire safety program:

- Policy development and enforcement
- Staff training and selection
- Equipment selection and location
- Inspection and maintenance
- A fire emergency plan

Policies and procedures set the framework for the fire safety program. They establish who in the institution has primary authority for establishing and implementing the program. They should clarify the responsibilities of other staff positions in support and implementation of fire safety programs. Procedures for fire prevention and safety must address clearly the situations that pose risks to the collections. These situations include, for example, exhibit production, conservation labs, research labs, staff and catering kitchen facilities, building equipment, etc. In other words, almost every function and space in the museum is subject to risks from fires. Staff involved with each different functions and areas should work with the safety officer to establish appropriate procedures for fire prevention as well as response to fires.

Staff training must be a continuous process if the institution is to minimize its risk from fires and fire damage. Volunteers should also receive training to improve their awareness of the need for prevention and appropriate responses. Wilson (1995) suggests a number of issues in which staff should receive training:

- How to recognize and correct fire hazards

- General housekeeping standards to improve prevention

- Compliance with regulations (e.g., smoking, fire doors)

- How to store, use and dispose of hazardous materials

- How to notify fire department and museum staff

- How to evacuate building and perform other duties in response to fires

- Practice using portable fire extinguishers

- General information about automatic sprinkler systems and location of control valves

Sources for staff and volunteer training can be found in any community. The local fire department usually has one or more individuals available to provide training for agencies in its region. Departments generally welcome opportunities to tour facilities they might have to protect and to develop training sessions for staff of such institutions.

Fire protection equipment includes detection systems, signaling systems, and extinguishing systems. Selection and location of the most appropriate equipment for the facility should be done in consultation with an expert. Selection of equipment should involve a thorough discussion of the maintenance needs over time, because equipment that is not regularly maintained will not respond adequately if an emergency arises.

Detection systems respond to one or more of the following: smoke, heat, sprinkler water flow and flames. The detection system should trigger a signaling system that is monitored continuously by an individual responsible for dispatching appropriate response personnel. It is important to have a person available to receive the signal on a 24-hour basis if the risk due to fire damage is to be minimized. The *NPS Museum Handbook*, Part I, chapter, "Museum Collections Security and Fire Protection," includes a table that describes the types of fire detectors available.

Automatic sprinkler systems comprise the most common and most effective means of suppressing a fire. As Wilson states in his 1995 article, these systems "are designed to detect fires at the point of origin, cause the sounding or transmission of alarms, and control or extinguish the fire." Types of automatic sprinkler systems include: wet pipe, pre-action, on-off, and dry pipe. Halon automatic systems, which are no longer available, have been replaced by other waterless systems such as FM-200.

Occasionally all fire prevention efforts fail. Thus, it is imperative that the museum have a response plan to mitigate potential damage from fire, smoke and water. Staff need to undergo emergency drills to be comfortable with individual roles and responsibilities. Resources must be available to respond to the crisis. *(See chapters on Emergency Preparedness Planning and Emergency Response and Recovery.)*

A fire safety program requires a staff that is aware and trained to prevent and respond to fires. Even if a registrar is not directly responsible for designing a fire safety program, he or she should be active in the development and implementation of policies, procedures, and training programs for both staff and volunteers. •

6F | Integrated Pest Management

ALBERT GREENE AND NANCY L. BREISCH

All buildings need pest control, but museums are among the facilities presenting the greatest challenges for this service. Like schools, hospitals, and zoos, collections of specimens, art, and artifacts are considered "sensitive," with precious, irreplaceable contents requiring constant protection from damage. Since many of the traditional chemical methods characterizing pest control since the 1950s are themselves potentially harmful either to the collections or to human health, the task requires considerable expertise.

Museums are at risk from four overlapping categories of pest problems:

Stored Product and Fabric Feeders.

Many different insects, most of them small beetles or moths, feed on a wide array of dry, organic materials. Common examples include carpet and hide beetles *(Dermestidae)*, drugstore and cigarette beetles *(Anobiidae)*, spider beetles *(Ptinidae)*, and clothes moths *(Tineidae)*. Because they are virtually ubiquitous, can easily escape detection, and are often introduced as eggs on new acquisitions, these insects are usually the most important pest threats to collections.

Wood Destroying Insects.

As in the above category, members of this group tend to be extremely cryptic. Items made of wood and other types of cellulose may arrive in a museum already infested by several different types of beetles, most commonly powderpost beetles *(Lyctidae, Bostrichidae, and Anobiidae)*, furniture and deathwatch beetles *(Anobiidae)*, and bark and timber beetles *(Scolytidae)*. Some of these insects are capable of reinfesting additional dry, seasoned wood upon emergence. In addition, termites and powderpost beetles damaging structural wood in buildings can spread to stored cellulose objects under some circumstances. A particularly insidious invasion route for subterranean termites is through settling cracks or inadequately sealed expansion joints in concrete floor slabs, from which they can access material directly above without detection.

General Feeders.

Several very common types of pests, including cockroaches, silverfish, crickets and rodents, are general feeders that may damage many different materials by feeding or defecation. These pests are much more readily detected than those in the first two categories, and tend to be problems in other areas of a museum in addition to the collections.

Nuisances and Health Hazards.

Most buildings harbor numerous animal species that cause little damage to property but are considered undesirable because they annoy, disgust, or frighten the human occupants. The majority of ants, flies, and spiders found indoors fall into this group. However, many nuisance pests also present a continuum of more tangible health risks (bites, stings, and disease transmission), the severity of which depends greatly on individual circumstances.

Detailed discussions of pests associated with buildings are provided by Bennett et al. (2003) and Mallis (2004). Several primers on pest biology and identification written specifically for museum personnel are also available (Appelbaum, 1991; Harmon, 1993; Pinniger, 1990; Zycherman and Schrock, 1988), and collection staff should have a working knowledge of the major groups. Unfortunately, insect identification is notoriously difficult, even for those with some specialized training. There is often no substitute for a professional entomologist if a specific determination is critical. It is far more important for collection managers to understand the general principles of modern pest control, which

369

should be applied as an ongoing process even in the absence of immediate pest problems.

THE PROCESS OF INTEGRATED PEST MANAGEMENT

Objectives

Modern pest control has evolved into a complex, specialized discipline that is often termed integrated pest management, or IPM. Those responsible for implementing this process should be aware of three principal objectives:

Protection of Property.

Although this is the obvious *raison d'être* for IPM in a museum, it is important to realize that effective pest control for collections and the structures that house them goes far beyond either killing bugs or applying pesticides.

Protection of Health and Safety.

The transformation of pest control from an almost exclusively chemical-based activity into modern IPM has been driven by widespread concerns over the potentially harmful effects of pesticides. Although pests themselves can sometimes be a serious threat to both human and environmental health, the public expects building managers to control them without compromising either indoor air quality or the safety of food consumed on the premises. In particular, children are considered to be at much greater risk from any sort of toxic substances than are adults.

Legal Compliance.

The use of pesticides in workplaces is governed by a bewildering array of laws and regulations. At a minimum, museum staff responsible for pest control should be thoroughly familiar with the label and Material Safety Data Sheet (MSDS) for every pesticide used in the facility, whether applied by contractor or in-house staff. The label is more than a set of directions; it is a strict, legal commandment. If pesticides are stored in the building (almost never a good idea), there are often specific state-mandated requirements for

security, fire protection, and signage. Other pesticide-related edicts that may apply under some circumstances or in some jurisdictions involve pesticide applicator certification for personnel and associated record-keeping requirements, posted notification prior to pesticide use and similar right-to-know actions, locally mandated prohibition of certain pesticides, and accommodations for chemically sensitive individuals in compliance with either state law or the Americans with Disabilities Act of 1990. When in doubt about any aspect of pesticide law, consult your state pesticide regulatory agency.

Strategy

What exactly is IPM and what are its basic ground rules? Every pest management professional has a slightly different definition of the term, but there is a general consensus that any control program can legitimately be called IPM if it emphasizes the following three elements:

Prevention.

This is the single most important pest management concept. IPM strives for "built-in" control solutions by minimizing or eliminating the resources that pests need to enter or live in a particular area. Like all preventive maintenance processes, IPM's fundamental assumption is that it is cheaper, safer, and more effective to anticipate and protect rather than continually react to chronic breakdowns. Pest control in the modern sense thus signifies control of pest access to critical areas, control of pest habitat and shelter ("harborage"), and control of pest food and water. It is an environmental manipulation strategy that attempts to make direct control of the pests unnecessary.

Least-Toxic Methods.

Although modern pest control tries to emphasize physical methods such as exclusion, sanitation, and inspection, there are some situations where chemicals must be used as well. Furthermore, pests are famous for occasionally circumventing even the best preventive efforts. When this occurs, direct, corrective measures are essential, and pesticides frequently are the most efficient tools at hand. Despite the widely held misconception that IPM is a pesticide-free methodology, the discipline regards these chemicals with pragmatism if they are necessary to achieve its objectives. What distinguishes IPM from old-fashioned pest control practices are the principles that least-toxic methods are tried first and that all pesticides are considered to be, at least in theory, temporary measures only. The overall program aims to reduce both pesticide use through alternate control techniques, and pesticide risk by favoring compounds, formulations, and application methods that present the lowest potential hazard to humans and other non-target organisms.

Systems Approach.

The characteristic of IPM most difficult to convey to the uninitiated is its extraordinary scope and diversity. Even a building that does not house delicate, precious objects is subject to many different types of pests that enter through, live in, and feed on a bewildering variety of resources. Aging structures in need of repair are even more vulnerable. Factor in the additional burden of safeguarding collections, and the difficulties of museum pest control would seem to be almost insurmountable. The secret to an IPM program's success, as well as its greatest challenge, is effective coordination with all other relevant programs that operate in and around the building. Plans and procedures involving design and construction, repairs and alterations, custodial and solid waste management, food service operations, landscape maintenance, etc., should all be guided in part from a centrally developed pest management perspective. Unless the IPM process truly incorporates activities throughout its surrounding infrastructure, it can never achieve optimal results.

Contracting for Expertise

For many institutions, particularly those with a history of pest problems, modern pest control is not a task that can be delegated to generalists. Experience has shown that personnel whose primary responsibilities and training are in other areas will simply not have the time, talent, or inclination to manage a meaningful control program. IPM is an expert-dependent process. The specialists who practice it most effectively in museums have a thorough knowledge of facilities management procedures, pest biology, pesticides, and alternative control technologies adapted to a wide variety of collection types. Normally, the curatorial or preservation staff carries out many of the routine, common-sense components of pest control that directly affect the objects under their care. However, most institutions periodically require two types of expert assistance:

- consulting entomologists
- pest control companies

Common situations requiring the services of a professional entomologist involve discovery of an unknown pest or type of damage, technically difficult pest problems, the need for impartial recommendations on specific control products, or the need for an expert witness or advisor in a pesticide-related legal issue. At the very least, a museum's actions for developing and implementing an upgraded IPM program should be guided and reviewed by a knowledgeable expert who can also provide the necessary staff training.

In the field of pest management, the term "entomologist" takes on an expanded meaning. "Applied biologist" would be more appropriate, since a consultant's expertise usually encompasses mammals and birds in addition to invertebrates. At a minimum, credentials include at least a bachelor's degree in entomology and the title "board certified entomologist" (BCE), conferred by the Entomological Society of America's professional certification program. As with any sort of technical specialist, recommendations from colleagues and a review of the candidates' referral lists is probably the best method of selection. Additional recommendations for consultants can frequently be obtained with a call to the entomology department of the nearest state university.

Unless the museum is extremely small or unusually free of pests, a consulting entomologist may not be able to provide all the specialized help needed to suppress pests adequately. It is particularly important that the IPM program for the collections include, or at least be coordinated with, routine pest control service for the entire building. From a pest manager's point of view, the overall structure is both reservoir and portal for pests entering into the collection areas. Perfunctory "spraying" of this surrounding habitat serves no protective function whatsoever and is now considered to be an unacceptable risk to the health of children and other pesticide-sensitive individuals.

A consulting entomologist may be able to recommend a local pest control firm or, ideally, may be associated with one. Worst case scenarios follow when pest control manpower for a building is provided by a facilities manager who is interested in little more than cost. At a minimum, the contract's technical specifications should include the following items:

•Pesticide applicator certification of all on-site personnel. Although passing the state-administered exam for certification is no guarantee of technical competence, personnel who have done so generally represent a considerable investment in training on the part of their employer. Do not accept uncertified technicians "working under the supervision" of a certified applicator.

•Clear statement of pests included and excluded. Standard contract language lists common pests to be controlled (e.g., "cockroaches, ants, flies, spiders, rats, mice . . . and all other pests not specifically excluded"). Typical exclusions are non-routine pests that require specialized skills and equipment (such as termites, birds, and mammals larger than rodents), that are usually contracted for separately.

•No scheduled pesticide treatments. This provision directly contradicts what many building managers and tenants think that an "exterminator" should do. However, it is inspection for pests that should be rigidly delivered by schedule, not pesticide application.

•Conservative and incisive pesticide use. Pesticide use should always consist of the least hazardous materials, most precise application techniques, and minimum quantities of material necessary to achieve control. Solid, paste, or gel bait formulations should be used whenever possible. Conventional sprays or dusts should be applied only to crevices, and even then only in

exceptional circumstances. Labels and MSDS sheets should be provided for all products used.

•Service frequency by need. Service frequency should reflect what is necessary to achieve program objectives and varies from on-call only to temporary daily service for severe infestations. Scheduled monthly visits are typical for property with minimal pest problems, weekly for larger, older buildings in urban core areas. In general, it is better that service for non-public space be delivered during normal working hours to maximize interactions between pest control technician and staff. There should also be a contractual provision for same-day emergency service.

PREVENTIVE TECHNOLOGY AND PROCEDURES

The Preventive Approach

Regardless of the type of building in which they occur, pest problems and their resolutions tend to follow a logical progression of events: detection, identification, correction, deterrence, and evaluation. The degree and effectiveness with which each stage is accomplished varies according to the resources applied to them and the general approach of the pest control process. In the most neglected, unplanned, and reactive programs, detection of a pest problem is made either by an unsuspecting patron in the cafeteria or by the staff's discovery of significant damage in the collections; identification of the pest is too superficial to be of much use in selecting optimal control strategies; the immediate corrective response is either unfocused or too narrow in scope; "deterrence" signifies merely a scheduled repetition of corrective efforts; and evaluation is mainly concerned with immediate costs.

With a preventive approach, an ongoing inspection protocol will be in place and detection is more likely to be made at an early stage of infestation; there will be an established procedure to obtain rapid and precise identification; immediate corrective responses are therefore more likely to be safe, efficient, and effective; the "deterrence" stage will be characterized by an informed analysis of the problem to select or refine the best feasible protective actions; and evaluation will be an ongoing process that attempts to improve all aspects of the system with a bearing on the problem. IPM is very much a "Total Quality Management" approach to pest control in the sense that it tries to be continually anticipatory. Collection staff should be an integral part of a team that develops and implements IPM procedures for the institution.

Following is a review of three basic types of procedures for reducing a building's vulnerability to pest problems. Unfortunately, the preventive aspect of IPM is often its most frustrating administrative challenge. Despite being simple in conception, these actions are often quite difficult to implement consistently and sustainably.

INSPECTION

All meaningful pest control begins with inspection. In museums, this includes continual monitoring of collections, careful examination during the quarantine period for new (i.e., potentially infested) acquisitions or returned loans, and routine surveillance of the general facilities and grounds. The process of inspection is by far the cheapest form of insurance against unexpected pest damage and other pest-related liability. Following are five components of a basic inspection program. Occasionally, these may need to be augmented with more specialized technologies, such as the use of x-ray equipment to examine wooden objects suspected of harboring borers.

Visual.

The best form of inspection is simply looking. Scheduled, systematic reviews of all areas and items at risk are ideal. At the least, constant vigilance by personnel trained to recognize pest signs should be part of the culture of any museum staff. All that is required is an eye for detail and a mental image of about a dozen out-of-place items: termite tubing and shed termite wings; the tiny piles of fine powder or sawdust-like "frass" produced by insect feeding; fresh exit holes from cellulose objects; the shrimplike cast skins of dermestid beetle larvae; rodent,

cockroach, and spider droppings; and insect bodies or body parts.

Sticky Traps.

The humble cardboard sticky trap has become the symbol of modern pest monitoring. Liberal use of these simple tools should be part of all indoor pest control programs. Inexpensive, easily concealable, and capable of immobilizing any flying or crawling bug that touches them, sticky traps constantly yield surprises in even the tightest and cleanest of buildings.

Pheromone Traps.

A rapidly expanding surveillance technology, these compact devices lure in stored product and fabric feeding pests by means of synthetic, species-specific attractants. They are primarily employed in warehouse and market facilities, but any museum that includes textiles or natural history specimens would greatly benefit from their use. At present, not all pheromone-based trapping products are equally effective; consult an entomologist for up-to-date recommendations.

Expert Identification.

An essential part of any early warning system is skilled interpretation of the results. Are the unrecognizable insects on the sticky trap significant pests or merely incidental intruders? Is the trapped rodent a resident house mouse or invading deer mouse? Are the shed wings from subterranean or drywood termites? Distinctions that appear trivial to the layperson often distinguish between totally different types of problems requiring unique control solutions.

Record-Keeping.

As with any other program, record-keeping is a necessary evil for pest control surveillance. Obviously, the emphasis should be on the "necessary." Schooled in a data-oriented discipline, consulting entomologists tend to recommend IPM reporting and logbook systems that border on the obsessive. Records of inspection and trapping results often prove invaluable for detecting patterns and trends in a facility's pest problems, but the goal should always be to match record-keeping with actual needs.

EXCLUSION

The fortress concept is at the heart of the preventive approach to pest control. Regardless of location, a museum can be thought of as a vaulted island in a sea of vermin. In fact, the facility-as-leaky-boat is one of the oldest IPM metaphors; traditional pest control confines itself to bailing, while IPM concentrates on plugging the leaks.

Sealing is an important technique. Filling or screening gaps is fundamental to reducing pest access into a structure, from one part of a structure to another, and to harborage (protected hiding and living space) within the facility. The same sealing principles apply to the building envelope as to the display or storage envelope that ideally surrounds all vulnerable objects in the collection. Remaining gaps must be smaller than the target pests, and the protective barrier must be resistant to pest chewing.

Museum professionals usually are familiar with available types of pest-resistant display and storage systems. They tend to be less knowledgeable about what specifically can be done to improve the security of their outer perimeter. Active sites of pest entry into a building are universal and include under doors, around window frames, and through chases and other penetrations for utilities, weep holes in masonry, damaged or poorly screened vents, window air conditioning units, floor drains, and so forth. There are now so many different types of caulks, polyurethane foams, quick-setting cements, rubberized membranes, and weatherstripping materials to seal every type of opening and adhere to every type of building material that consultation with a maintenance or construction specialist is often essential for pest-proofing projects. The pest control industry itself increasingly employs an arsenal of specialized products for these purposes, such as finely screened weep hole plugs, stainless steel drain inserts, and rolled copper mesh for rodent exclusion. Even mundane items such as window screening or hardware cloth may be all that is necessary to provide a critical barrier to pest access.

Pests do not live out in the open. Most need darkness and seclusion to survive. "Harborage" signifies not only cracks and crevices but also any protected habitat created by fixtures, furniture, equipment, boxes, and other seldom-moved objects that enable small species to escape detection. Museums by their nature are "harborage-intensive" facilities, and pest control guidelines for the reduction of clutter in office buildings may not be realistic where collections are accumulated, curated, and displayed. The design of the storage room and equipment directly affects the museum's ability to control pests. However, other than "less is better," the most universal housekeeping and storage rule is to keep items off the floor and away from the walls as much as possible. This facilitates visual inspections and reduces the risk of damage by pests such as termites and mice.

A second rule mandates the use of air conditioning to produce as cool and dry an environment as practicable for storage and display areas. Although this will not totally discourage museum pests, insect activity generally increases in warm (above 20°C), moist conditions.

Most aspects of structural or landscape design that tend to promote pest problems are unchangeable either for historic, aesthetic, or monetary reasons or because they were purposely selected for their function. A classic example is raised flooring, one of the greatest gifts to indoor pests ever developed, that is unfortunately also the most efficient means for housing dense arrays of telecommunication and computer cabling. Cafeteria serving and preparation islands also are often designed with enclosed, hollow bases that keep out dropped food and other debris but frequently serve as impregnable hiding places for rodents and cockroaches.

Nevertheless, opportunities do arise during renovation or retrofitting projects to make meaningful improvements in design if knowledgeable pest management specialists are consulted in the early stages. Such changes do not have to be elaborate. A facility plagued by flying insects entering through the outer doorway might benefit greatly from the installation of an air curtain unit or (even better) a well-sealed vestibule. If most of these insects are drawn to lights around the building at night, there is an entire sub-specialty of pest control that deals with exterior lighting. Relamping from bright white mercury vapor bulbs or incandescent floodlights to lower wattage yellow sodium vapor or halogen lights, partially shielding or redirecting the lights away from doorways and vents, slightly delaying the onset of lighting at dusk to avoid the peak flight time of certain midges, and the use of bright "decoy" lights at the property's edge to lure insects away from the primary structure have all been successfully used for pest deterrence.

Landscapes can often be altered more readily than buildings. In general, problems with rodents and many types of nuisance species are increased by extensive plantings of dense shrubs or ground cover, particularly if these are close to the structure's foundation. Ivy covering exterior walls is an especially critical "attractive nuisance" from a pest control point of view. Excessively watered or poorly drained grounds, especially in drier climates, are also guaranteed to promote local pest populations. In cases where dense surrounding plantings cannot be modified, the creation of a bare strip of pavement or crushed rock bordering the foundation may reduce pest entry.

Bird-proofing of buildings, particularly historic structures, is another highly specialized branch of modern pest control. In addition to choosing an anti-roosting system that is durable, effective, and discreet, there are often equally important concerns with avoiding physical damage to the building and minimizing adverse public relations. An abundance of technologies are available. Three that should be avoided are scaring devices such as plastic owls or giant eye patterns (birds soon become used to them), repellent gels (eventually discolor and may permanently damage masonry), and ultrasonic or other electronic "pest repellent" products (totally worthless).

"Porcupine wire" is the generic name for modular arrays of protruding spikes or coils that are usually effective against pigeons if properly installed, but may actually promote nesting by smaller birds. They tend to be aesthetically unacceptable for sites in the public view but may be useful for concealed applications. Electrically charged wire is another traditional system that has been prone to frequent breakdowns as the hardware ages as well as to masonry damage where the insulators are attached. However, newer refinements have eliminated many of the older products' flaws.

At present, the two leading technologies for bird deterrence on historic structures or any high-visibility site are "pin and wire" systems and tensioned netting. The former consists of non-electrified stainless steel wires tightly strung at different heights along projecting structural elements such as ledges, lintels, sills, and string courses. The wires are supported by slender steel pins inserted into mortar joints. Tensioned netting installations consist of various types of synthetic net fabrics, stretched taut by peripheral cables across recessed elements such as niches, colonnades, and coffered ceilings. Although employing technically simple hardware, both of these systems require a high level of skill and experience to be installed correctly.

SANITATION

For maximum effectiveness, procedures that deny pests access and shelter must be combined with those that deny them food. Once again, it is not unusual for museum staff to devote most of their attention to the immediate protection of organic collection items while neglecting far more extensive (but more mundane) sources of pest nourishment nearby. For example, a natural history museum continually treating its displays for dermestid beetle infestations may have accumulated enough organic debris in flooring cracks or under carpeting to sustain a reservoir of thousands of these insects. Similarly, it makes no sense to trap mice out of a gift shop while they are continually replenished because of poor sanitation in the adjacent snack bar.

It is also essential for employees to realize that many common, apparently inedible materials are actually extremely rich food resources for some pests. An excellent example is the widely used, biodegradable packing nuggets composed of cornstarch that superficially resemble Styrofoam but are highly attractive to general feeding pests such as cockroaches. "Sanitation" in an IPM context means the same pest-proof storage practices for this type of product as for more obvious food substances.

Cleaning is a vital activity. Careless treatment of food throughout a building is one of a pest manager's greatest headaches, since most personnel consider any sort of cleaning to be an unpleasant, tedious chore. Furthermore, contracted or in-house custodial programs tend to emphasize relatively superficial cleaning operations and rarely focus on the most critical types of sanitation from a pest's point of view. Any accumulation of edible residue on surfaces or in crevices where food is stored, prepared, consumed, or discarded puts a facility at risk for pest infestation.

To a certain extent, newer types of more efficient technologies can compensate for the human propensity to postpone or neglect meaningful "deep" cleaning. The best example is compact, electrically powered, pressure washing machines for the removal of grease and debris in food service facilities, trash holding areas, garbage receptacles, floor drains, and similar locations. However, offices and laboratories must still depend on essentially the same type of procedures applicable to residential kitchens. There is no substitute for strictly enforced staff policies on proper food storage and cleanliness around pest-prone appliances such as coffee machines, microwaves, and refrigerators.

Solid waste must be managed with an integrated perspective. Garbage and food-laden trash is stored twice in a building, first in small local receptacles throughout the structure and finally in larger containers emptied by a private or municipal contractor. This material represents a concentrated resource for many general-feeding and nuisance pests that is unequaled anywhere else in or around the facility. From a public health standpoint, a waste management program must effectively concentrate, isolate, and secure food debris before removing it from the premises as rapidly as possible.

Public and staff trash receptacles and beverage container recycling bins should ideally incorporate sturdy, disposable plastic liners that are replaced with every pickup. Although these receptacles are typically designed more for ease of use than security, models with tightly sealing, foot-pedal operated lids (such as those used for medical waste) are recommended for disposal of food remains in offices. Food should be strictly banned from all collection display, storage,

and preparation areas. Procedures should be in place for periodic inspection and cleaning of receptacles and trash collection carts, particularly those used for wet garbage and recycled beverage containers.

Centralized waste storage equipment should, at a minimum, be mouse-proof. This is generally defined as being constructed of steel and having no gaps greater than one-quarter inch. If rodent infestation in trash-holding areas is a problem, the traditional garbage cans or dumpster should be replaced with a self-contained compactor. These pest resistant machines are watertight, range from 1 to more than 40 cubic yards in capacity, and are available in horizontally or vertically compacting models. They are normally leased from a waste hauling contractor.

CORRECTIVE TECHNOLOGY AND PROCEDURES
Action Thresholds

Despite the most thorough preventive efforts, it should be taken for granted that pests will eventually be detected somewhere inside the facility. Following identification, there should be rapid selection of the best corrective response. However, long before these events occur, every curatorial staff should have resolved the fundamental policy issue of exactly when corrective procedures will be implemented. That is, how many pests must be observed in a given situation before they are deemed a problem? This numerical decision point is termed the "action threshold" for a pest.

In many cases, all it takes is one pest specimen to justify the expense of treatment. Often, only a sign is necessary, such as a cast skin of a dermestid beetle larva in a display case or fresh mouse droppings on a desk top. An important principle is that action thresholds are site-specific. A few dermestid adults (which feed on pollen) on the window sills may not be cause for concern, particularly during the summer months.

There is sometimes considerable dispute over the justification for prophylactic treatments of collection items that are highly susceptible to cryptic feeding damage by pests. When the desired action is either limited in scope (e.g., for newly acquired or returned material that normally would be quarantined) or nontoxic (e.g., freezing), the issue is primarily one of time and expense. However, when a corrective procedure such as a slow-release fumigation becomes a routine preventive operation, museum management must factor public health risks into their cost/benefit analysis.

Following is a brief review of the most widely used, proven methods for killing or removing pests that infest museums. Technologies that are still mostly experimental, such as the use of microwave or gamma radiation, are omitted. Similarly, although the application of heat above 50°C has been successfully used to control insects in some circumstances (e.g., herbaria, and in general is far more efficient than freezing for the majority of pest species), this procedure is potentially harmful for many specimens, art, or artifacts.

Vacuums

The use of small, canister-type vacuums for routine structural pest control operations has increased greatly in recent years. One of the most common applications is for initial "cleanouts" of cockroach infestations in desks, lockers, appliances, and other sites prior to pesticide treatment. At the same time, the machine's narrow nozzle can efficiently remove food remains and other organic debris lodged in crevices that serve as a food reservoir for these insects. Precision vacuuming of collection storage and display areas is also an excellent preventive measure to reduce accumulated organic material such as hair and lint that feed stored product and fabric pests. Additional corrective uses include elimination of spiders and webs, rapid disposal of swarming termite and ant reproductives, and the capture of many other nuisance invaders.

Traps

Flying Insect Traps.

Despite the marketing literature that accompanies them, most insect traps are more practical as monitoring, rather than control, tools. An important exception is the wide variety of products for eliminating flying insects inside buildings. The most versatile and effective type, although also the most conspicuous and expensive, are electrically powered units combining ultraviolet lights that attract the pests and replaceable sticky sheets that immobilize them. One variation employs a harmless low-voltage pulse to maximize capture by stunning the insects (not to be confused with the older type of "bug zapper" electrocuter traps intended for outdoor use). Several models have the form of decorative, wall-mounted sconces for discreet use in food service and other sensitive public facilities, although, in general, smaller units are much less effective. Virtually every type of flying indoor insect pest, including many incidental invaders, is susceptible to these devices.

Rodent Traps.

Trapping is usually more desirable than rodenticide bait for the control of rats and mice inside structures since poisoned rodents often die and decompose in inaccessible locations. Traditional snap traps with expanded triggers are still the preferred tool in most situations. Windup multiple-catch mouse traps can be very efficient in commercial kitchens or other areas with relatively dense infestations. Although effective under some circumstances, glue boards tend to allow more escapes than snap traps and have become controversial because of the extreme suffering inflicted on the immobilized animals. All rodent traps must be concealed in locations out of the public view, protected from accidental disturbance, and checked regularly.

Freezing

With an increasing number of museums concerned about the cost, regulatory, and safety issues associated with conventional fumigation procedures, freezing has become the preferred substitute for treatment of many types of infested (or potentially infested) specimens and artifacts. The ideal facility consists of a walk-in, humidity-controlled chamber capable of flash freezing its contents down to -40°C. Commercial meat lockers and refrigerated trucks with these specifications are available for rent, although still well beyond the financial resources and practical needs of many smaller institutions. Collection staff must therefore be familiar with the general protocols for successful freezing treatments to evaluate the suitability of available equipment.

It is critical to consult a professional familiar with freezing specific objects, since the process may damage certain woods, bone, leather, paint, finishes, and other materials. Many types of natural and artificial adhesives lose their bonding properties under extremely low temperatures. However, the primary technical challenge for any object is protection from ice during freezing and condensation during thawing. Unless a controlled humidity chamber is used, items should always be enclosed in airtight, polyethylene bags or similar containers. Depending on the fragility of the specimen or artifact, various procedures can be used to minimize the possibility of damage, such as partial evacuation of air before sealing, inclusion of a water absorbing material (such as silica gel) inside the bag, or even vacuum packing. A gradual return to room temperature over a period of 24 hours is recommended at the end of the treatment. Most museum pests will be killed after 48 hours at -25°C, well within the capability of a good quality, modern chest freezer if not packed too densely. However, some species may require much longer freezing times and lower temperatures. It is important that the items reach the pest-specific target temperature as quickly as possible, since gradual cooling may promote greatly increased cold tolerance by insects. The most hardy pests (e.g., powderpost beetles, particularly the egg stage) generally require a protocol of freezing to at least -35°C within several hours, storage at this temperature for 1–2 weeks, a gradual thaw to room temperature, then refreezing for at least several days.

Inert Gases

Due to the potential damage that freezing may cause to a broad range of fragile materials and objects composed of multiple, closely combined materials, there has been extensive research into another category of "alternative" control methodologies in which specimens at risk are placed in an enclosure with a modified atmosphere that is either anoxic (almost totally oxygen deprived) or has a high concentration of carbon dioxide. Noticeable deterioration of most substances does not occur with any of the various methods, and control effectiveness is on a par with both freezing and conventional chemical fumigants. However, length of treatment may be considerably longer, often over a week and up to several weeks in some circumstances. As might be expected, all types of inert gas treatment have their own operational complexities and consultation with a knowledgeable specialist is essential. The field has been reviewed in depth by Selwitz and Maekawa (1998).

The simplest and most widely used method of oxygen deprivation is to seal small items inside plastic bags along with packets of powerful "oxygen scavengers" that absorb oxygen from air by converting iron to iron oxide. The bags are constructed out of laminated films fabricated specifically for low oxygen permeability. They can be purchased premade but are frequently fashioned by conservators on a customized basis with heat sealing equipment. Oxygen purging may be enhanced by the introduction of nitrogen or argon from pressurized cylinders. Larger quantities of material are more efficiently treated in a more permanent rigid or flexible chamber scaled to the needs of the institution. In another variation, the inert gas is continually passed through bags or a reusable container to keep oxygen levels reduced. Particularly with this type of "dynamic" system, humidification of the extremely dry compressed gas is essential to avoid damaging the treated items.

Pest control with elevated carbon dioxide levels has not been as popular as anoxia, but has gained numerous adherents for several reasons. It is generally cheaper for high-volume treatments in large chambers, the precise concentration of gas is not as critical, sealing tolerances are less stringent, and humidification is often unnecessary. At this time, it is primarily used by larger institutions by means of proprietary equipment.

Conventional Fumigation

Although often incorrectly applied to any insecticidal space treatment, the term "fumigation" strictly refers to the use of a toxic gas (as opposed to aerosol or mist formulations) for pest control. The procedure is used extensively to treat entire structures for wood-destroying pests and food storage facilities for stored product pests. In a museum, fumigation on a more limited scale is a traditional method to treat items that actually or potentially contain pests that are highly cryptic or deeply embedded. Although rapidly falling out of favor, conventional fumigants are still employed for infested items that cannot be subjected to freezing temperatures, where inert gas technology is unavailable or impractical, or when treatment must be acccomplished within an extremely limited time frame.

On the other hand, fumigants present many drawbacks. Chamber fumigation is a highly specialized and expensive technology requiring extensive training and skill. Unlike freezing and oxygen deprivation, it is usually performed as a contracted, rather than in-house, service. Matching fumigant to material is critical, since many substances can be seriously damaged if the wrong product is used. The two remaining conventional fumigation chemicals (phosphine and sulfuryl fluoride) are broad-spectrum, extremely toxic poisons that must be handled with great care. Conversely, despite the lethality of fumigants in general, the eggs of many beetles are remarkably resistant to harm, accounting for the majority of fumigation failures involving museum items. And of course, as with all corrective technologies, fumigation has absolutely no protective value.

Operationally, fumigation of museum objects can be divided into two basic procedures: chamber fumigation and slow-release fumigation. Chamber fumigation, using a specially designed vault or chamber to confine a toxic gas, is the safest and most effective type of fumigation. Slow-release fumigation uses chemical solids that gradually release a gas for pest control and are thus categorized as "passive" fumigants. None can penetrate very far into most materials. All are now considered to be potentially severe, chronic, and acute health hazards and should no longer be used by the museum community (e.g., PDB, Naphthalene, DDVP).

Indoor Pesticides

The role of conventional pesticides as routine corrective solutions for pests of public buildings, particularly "sensitive" ones such as museums, has steadily diminished in recent years. In general, almost any liquid or dust insecticide applied with air pressure out of a nozzle is now considered to be a weapon of last resort where exceptional measures are required. These products have a long history of excessive and haphazard use by the pest control industry. Even with special "crack and crevice" application equipment they are intrinsically difficult to confine to precise areas. When used in close proximity to collections, virtually all compounds have the potential to damage some materials with which they come into contact.

At present, the general category of nonvolatile insecticide baits is clearly the best choice for corrective cockroach and ant control in museums. Active ingredients of these products all have extremely low mammalian toxicities. Formulated into solids, pastes, and gels, they are either protected inside small, plastic containers or applied in limited amounts with devices resembling syringes or miniature caulking guns. Discreet and nonintrusive in the indoor environment, they have become indispensable for those concerned about the effects of "spraying" on collection items and public health.

In contrast, rodenticide bait and tracking powder formulations are not recommended for routine use inside buildings because of the potential odor problems of poisoned animals that cannot be retrieved. Decomposing carcasses behind walls also serve as breeding sites for numerous species of insect pests. In addition, most types of rodent bait attract stored product beetles. Rodent tracking powder presents the same disadvantages as residual insecticidal dusts in that it is difficult to contain and may become a hazard during future renovation work.

Structural Infestations of Wood Destroying Insects

Termites, powderpost beetles, and other wood destroying insects cause a multitude of problems for facilities managers beyond threatening the structural integrity of buildings framed with wood. Even concrete and steel buildings are susceptible to damage in fibrous insulation and sheathing, furring strips, trim, paneling, and hardwood flooring. Museums are particularly at risk from structural infestations spreading to stored documents and collection items composed of cellulose. In addition, swarms of winged termite reproductives accidentally emerging indoors from subterranean colonies beneath a slab can severely disrupt operations, even though the insects themselves are completely harmless.

Wood destroying insect control is one of the most complex, specialized, and expensive areas of pest management and is undergoing a rapid expansion of its technology. Unless there is an in-house employee with up-to-date expertise in this discipline, museums are strongly advised to consult a professional entomologist prior to committing to any specific course of action. •

Appreciation to Virginia Greene for valuable discussions, suggestions, and insights from behind the scenes.

6G | REGISTRARS AND SUSTAINABILITY

An Introduction to the Issues and a Call for Action

LEA FOSTER WARDEN AND SARA FRANTZ

At first people refuse to believe that a strange new thing can be done. Then they begin to hope it can be done. Then they see it can be done. Then it is done and all the world wonders why it was not done centuries ago.
—Frances Hodgson Burnett

INTRODUCTION

Registrars are uniquely positioned to take a leadership role in fostering sustainable behavior both within their institutions and in the profession at large. First, registrars are trained to analyze and address actions that may affect the preservation of collections. Their awareness of the connections between behavior and its intentional and unintentional consequences is a vital resource for understanding and implementing sustainable practices. Secondly, the purview of a registrar's job is vast. Duties span many departments, requiring efficient communication and collaboration. A registrar's relationships with colleagues allow him or her to approach an interdepartmental project with a broad point of view, an attribute complementary to the sustainability paradigm. As detail oriented, collaborative decision-makers, registrars have the potential to increase the sustainability of their institutions.

In order to engage in a dialogue regarding sustainability, the terms *green* and *sustainable* must be defined. In reference to the environment, the notions of *green* and *sustainable* share a similar objective: to protect and conserve natural resources. *Green* generally refers to an end result, such as, does this product or action have a benign or positive effect on the environment? *Sustainability* instead reviews an entire system and the relationship between systems—a more holistic approach. One concise definition of *sustainable* is meeting the needs of the present without compromising the ability of future generations

to meet their needs.[1] An action is rated by whether or not it maintains an amicable balance among its economic, social, and environmental components—a triple-weighted scale. Therefore, a product may be *green*, but ultimately not *sustainable*. Biodegradable plastic, for instance, can be considered green because it degrades under certain conditions relatively safely, but it is not sustainable because more fossil fuels are consumed to manufacture biodegradable plastic than traditional polymers. *Green* products or actions are a step in the right direction, but *sustainability* is the ultimate goal.

Sustainability has become relevant within the framework of climate change. Climate change is the result of humanity's perspective that nature is a force to be dominated or controlled. The Industrial Revolution, for instance, was based upon a perceived endless supply of "natural capital" and "neither the health of natural systems, nor an awareness of their delicacy, complexity, and interconnectedness, [were] part of the industrial design agenda."[2] Humanity has spanned the globe, building structures and using resources at a faster rate than can be replenished. Furthermore, the loss of natural habitat coupled with species extinction continues to occur at a rapid pace. The stress humanity has placed upon our fragile ecosphere is alarming. Museums play a role in this natural resource drain; standard museum operations such as the maintenance of stable microclimates and exhibitions do impact the environment.

There is growing support, both nationally and internationally, for sustainable initiatives within the museum profession. First, a number of publications are available that discuss museums and sustainability in the areas of outreach, education, exhibit design, lighting, and food service. A recent addition to the resource list is *The Green Museum: A Primer on Environmental Practice*, by Sarah Brophy and Elizabeth Wylie. Second, it is now typical for museum conferences to include some element of environmental responsibility both in program content as well as event administration. At the 2008 American Association of Museums meeting, 102 people signed up for the newly formed professional interest committee, PIC Green. The British Museum's Department of Conservation and Scientific Research hosted a one-day meeting in 2009 entitled "Going Green: Towards Sustainability in Conservation." Lastly, there are a number of online resources such as the Green Design Wiki, the Green Museums Wiki, and GreenExhibits.org.

LEED (LEADERSHIP IN ENERGY AND ENVIRONMENTAL DESIGN)

Building green museums is perhaps the most publicized initiative within the profession. Green building methods originating from the design and engineering fields are being adopted for the construction and renovation of museums and exhibits. Many museums are also seeking LEED (Leadership in Energy and Environmental Design) certification. The LEED program was developed by the United States Green Building Council to promote design and construction practices that reduce the industry's negative environmental impact and establish guidelines for those practices. One subset of the program is LEED for Existing Buildings (EB): Operations and Management (O&M). This program was designed to implement sustainable operations and maintenance practices to reduce the environmental impact of existing buildings. The program specifically addresses the following areas: sustainable purchasing, waste stream management, green cleaning, energy performance, indoor environmental quality, and site management techniques for pests, storm water, landscaping, and lighting.[3]

GREEN COMMITTEES

Creating a green committee that uses LEED-EB O&M guidelines is an excellent starting point to implement sustainable operations at a museum— even if certification is not an objective. However, it is important to tailor initiatives to the specific institution in question. In *Fostering Sustainable Behavior: An Introduction to Community-Based Social Marketing,* Doug McKenzie-Mohr and William Smith provide insightful strategies for instituting behavioral changes. The authors note the importance of determining the barriers and benefits of a particular sustainable behavior. Since non-communal, drastic alterations typically do not result in long-term change, establishing an open forum within a museum, in which sustainability goals are defined and potential barriers and benefits are explored, is vital to accomplish successful behavioral changes. Staff members will have varying opinions and knowledge levels about today's environmental problems and it is important to establish an atmosphere of respect and collaboration.

The interdepartmental nature of the registrar's position gives him or her the opportunity to take a leadership role in forming a green committee. A green committee will be most successful with the participation and collaboration of all departments. The committee's responsibility may include rethinking current needs, systems, and methodologies, and setting future goals and pathways to achieve those goals. Potential results of a "Green Team" include: economic savings, diminished use of resources including water and electricity, the formation of mutually beneficial partnerships with service providers, a reduction in museum consumption and waste, and improved standing amongst constituents and colleagues.

Registrars will find useful information in the aforementioned resources concerning energy efficient technologies and green consumer products to help launch green committee initiatives. However, much work is still needed both to consolidate and to build upon data specifically geared for the registration department. Further research into new products and procedures, such as green archival products and alternative lighting strategies, is needed in order to develop new standards. Opportunities abound for museum studies students and established professionals alike to research and collaborate with service providers to develop, test, and apply alternative methods and materials. The following discussion, therefore, should be seen as one installment in a portfolio the authors believe will continually develop as museums bring their behaviors more in line with environmental sustainability. The topics included range from complex undertakings such as modifying lighting and climate control systems to more mundane tasks such as purchasing office paper.

As previously noted several museums are now building green and seeking LEED certification. One key component of LEED certification is the installation of, or upgrade to, energy efficient lighting and climate control systems. The guidelines also promote the use of natural light and passive ventilation as ways to reduce energy consumption. Although these ideals do not completely conform to the standards of object preservation, there are ways to mix passive systems and energy efficient technologies to reduce a museum's energy consumption.

LIGHTING

Electric lighting, for example, accounts for more than a third of all electricity consumed for commercial use in the United States.[4] Encouragingly, "due to soaring electricity prices and ever-growing environmental concerns about energy consumption and waste disposal, lighting is experiencing a technology revolution."[5] Museums' challenge with lighting has always been controlling the negative effects of light upon objects, which must be exposed to light in order to be viewed, yet light damage is cumulative and cannot be reversed. Light exposure can cause fading, darkening, yellowing, embrittlement, distortion, and stiffening. The type of light and duration of exposure are important factors in light damage: illuminance plus time equals total exposure. The light spectrum is divided into three sections: ultraviolet (UV), visible, and infrared (IR). Most damage to artwork is caused by the UV and the violet/blue and green end of the visible light spectrum. Damage is also caused by IR wavelengths, which produce heat. Since sunlight is full spectrum light, it is the most damaging to light-sensitive objects.

Typically, museums use halogen or metal halide track lighting in galleries, and fluorescent lighting in collection storage areas, all of which require filtering. Many types of filtering materials are available to protect objects from light damage; however, it should be

noted that the "shelf life" of filtering materials varies from manufacturer to manufacturer. This museum lighting paradigm has begun to change, however, based upon advances in lighting technology and the growing need to control the cost of lighting. The following presents four lighting alternatives: LED, fiber optics, hybrid solar, and diffused natural light.

LEDs (light emitting diodes) are the most promising new light source that may have application within the museum setting. LEDs consume one-fifth as much energy as a conventional bulb and last 100 times longer. They are illuminated by the movement of electrons in a semiconductor material, which is typically aluminum-gallium arsenide. As the electrons move, photons are released—the most basic units of light. LEDs can be used in place of incandescent lights and can be dimmed without changing the color of light emitted—unlike incandescent lights, which become yellow. Although LED lighting is currently more expensive than incandescent lighting, its low energy usage makes it a cost effective alternative in the long-term. LEDs also produce no UV light and little heat, which makes them ideal for illuminating objects.[6] LED lighting, as an alternative lighting source, is still in its infancy.[7] The main drawback to full-scale implementation is initial cost and mediocre CRI (color rendering index.)[8] While there are LED products specifically designed for museum or display use, it may take some time before fixture manufacturers begin to offer a large selection of LED products for the highly specialized needs of museums. In the meantime, rigorous LED research and development continues.[9]

Fiber optic lighting, also known as remote source lighting, uses plastic or glass fibers to distribute light. The fibers can be side emitting, which means the fiber itself is lighted, or end emitting, which means the light is conducted to an attachment at the end of the fiber. The benefit to using fiber optic lighting is that the heat source is removed from the end of the fiber. The Lighting Research Center at Rensselaer Polytechnic Institute notes that: "[p]utting the light source outside of a secured enclosure, such as a display case of costly objects, means the display area doesn't have to be opened for servicing."[10] Although fiber optic lighting offers creative solutions, it has some drawbacks. Glass fibers dissipate UV light, but plastic fibers require UV filtering. The longer the length of fiber, the more loss of light occurs at the endpoint. Furthermore, severe bending of the fibers will result in extreme light loss, a consideration in configuring fiber placement. Finally, if environmental benefits were not factored into the cost benefit analysis, overall energy cost savings may not offset the expense of implementation.[11]

Hybrid Solar Lighting (HSL) is one of the newest technologies in the lighting field. HSL uses solar power and fiber optics to channel sunlight into an enclosed space while simultaneously directing IR light to a concentrating thermo-photovoltaic cell that converts it into electricity. Sunlight is tracked throughout the day using a parabolic dish. Sensors are used to maintain a constant level of illumination by supplementing sunlight with traditional electric light in special hybrid lighting fixtures.[12] Since hybrid solar lighting pipes sunlight directly to the light fixture, this newly discovered process is far more efficient than photovoltaic cells, which convert 15 percent of sunlight into electricity and then change the electricity back into light, resulting in the use of only 2 percent of the original sunlight. As with all fiber optic cables, the longer the cables are the more light they lose.[13] Since the incoming natural light is full spectrum sunlight, light fixtures specifically designed for exhibiting objects and filters may make this technology applicable for museums in the near future.

Lastly, museums have experimented with natural light use in galleries. By diffusing direct sunlight and creating complex systems that track and control sunlight, museums can take advantage of natural light while simultaneously avoiding the harmful effects of ultraviolet rays. A report by David Behar Perahia on the use of daylight in museums cites several institutions in Europe and the United States that have successfully integrated architectural designs that use natural daylighting. The Menil Collection in Houston, Texas, uses a system of ceiling louvers, skylights, and large windows that allow for diffused full spectrum natural lighting in the galleries. The Beyeler Foundation in Basel, Switzerland, has a glazed ceiling that also employs the use of louvers and brise-soleil.[14] Brise-soleil, an ancient architectural shading technique, appears to be experiencing a revival and is used in the new wing of the Milwaukee Museum of Art and will be incorporated into the proposed Louvre Abu Dhabi in the United Arab Emirates.

Ultimately, advances in lighting technology may produce a suitable compromise between the needs of objects and museum visitors. A report produced by The Getty Museum Lighting Research Project noted that "[w]hen applying light damage mitigation techniques simultaneously to maximize conservation, compromises are necessary—display times are limited, and light levels may be so low that they challenge perception through skewed color rendering and reduced detail."[15] David Behar Perahia attributes this challenged perception caused by inadequate lighting to museum fatigue, a well-known phenomenon identified by Benjamin Coleman in 1916.[16] Author David Clinard states that "traditionally, color quality has been and still is one of the most critical concerns for displaying art objects."[17]

Creative lighting strategies throughout a museum building benefit an institution's budget, staff, visitors, and collections. The use of motion sensor lighting and dimmers reduce both object exposure time (thus slowing deterioration) and energy use (thus lowering electricity bills). Other forms of non-traditional lighting such as the Solatube, a lighting strategy that redirects sunlight down a reflective tube and diffuses light within an interior space, can incorporate natural light into non-art spaces such as offices, cafés, museum stores, or meeting rooms, creating a more appealing atmosphere for staff and visitors. LEDs, fiber optic lighting, hybrid solar lighting, and natural light have the potential to benefit museum objects as well as the earth's natural environment.

HVAC (HEATING, VENTILATION, AND AIR CONDITIONING)

Energy consumption can also be reduced by addressing museums' climate control systems. Museums use twice as much energy as typical office buildings because while office buildings typically cool, heat, and illuminate from 9 a.m.–5 p.m., Monday through Friday, museums often have extended hours and maintain constant climate control for collections.[18]

Museum HVAC systems are complex, require constant monitoring, and are one cause of museums' excessive energy use.

A typical HVAC system adjusts air temperature and humidity. In a museum air is first heated or cooled (the cooling removes humidity from the incoming air if needed), then humidified by water heaters or boilers before entering the galleries or art storage areas. Within this system the air passes through three filters: the first filter removes large particulates, the second filter removes fine particulates, and the carbon filter removes vapors. All of these processes are controlled by a central computer system. Clearly, HVAC systems use a great deal of resources and electricity.[19, 20]

Yet, even within an HVAC system, opportunities to reduce waste and decrease costs exist. The Nevada Museum of Art, for example, is currently considering alternative methods of performing air handler carbon filter change-outs. Presently, carbon filters are changed every 12 to 18 months. The old filter, made up of plastic, metal, cardboard, and carbon, is disposed of in its entirety. Alternatively, the carbon could be exchanged for fresh carbon and the used carbon could be sent to a reclaiming company for reactivation (discharging of the contaminants) so that it could be reused.[21] In addition to saving money and keeping filters out of landfills, this method would establish a waste-free recycling system for carbon.[22] This is one example of how creative thinking can reduce the overall cost of operating HVAC systems.

Temperature and humidity guidelines currently utilized by museums also offer energy and cost reduction possibilities. The mechanisms of decay for objects can be attributed to three situations in humidity and temperature control: too low, too high, and too much fluctuation. The resulting damage can be chemical, mechano-physical, or biological.[23] Most museums follow the guidelines for humidity and temperature control as presented by Garry Thomson in The Museum Environment, published in 1978. Thompson recommends a narrow humidity range of ± 4 percent or 5 percent humidity. However, Thompson states that "[t]he tolerance usually quoted of ±4 or 5 percent RH is based more on what

can be expected of an air-conditioning plant than on what exhibits can actually stand without deterioration, which is not known in any detail."[24] Despite his forthright admission of how he obtained his guidelines and their potential lack of accuracy, museums have adhered to his ranges, sometimes even implementing stricter guidelines of ±2 percent.

Research published in 1994 on the specific properties of materials by Marion F. Mecklenburg, Charles S. Tumosa, David Erhardt, and Mark McCormick-Goodhart of Conservation Analytical Researchers (CAL) widened the range of humidity control to 50 ±15 percent.[25] Although the results were considered highly controversial at the time, gradual acceptance has yielded the current Smithsonian-recommended ranges of 45 percent ± 8 percent RH and 70° ± 4°F. Applying these guidelines nationally could result in significant energy savings. Mecklenburg, Tumosa, Erhardt, and McCormick-Goodhart note that "[o]ngoing implementation of the new guidelines in Smithsonian museums resulted in cost savings of $2.7 million in just the second half of 2006 (out of $32 million total energy costs for all of 2006), and $1.5 million in the first quarter of 2007."[26] Additionally, allowing for seasonal drift to occur (a slow adjustment in the humidity and temperature set points to allow for seasonal change) could result in monetary savings by maintaining an environment that correlates more closely to outside temperature and humidity. The building envelope (the separation between the interior and exterior environments of a building) must also be considered, especially in older buildings, because introducing high humidity into the air can cause condensation to develop within the building envelope, which can then freeze and cause accelerated deterioration of the façade—thereby promoting mold growth. If acceptance of the Smithsonian-recommended temperature and humidity ranges, including seasonal drift, were to replace current rigid humidity and temperature control limits, museums could incur substantial savings from diminished energy usage while still maintaining safe environmental controls for the objects within their care.

MATERIALS AND PRODUCTS

Alongside lighting and HVAC systems there are other operations under a registrar's purview that could become more environmentally friendly. One way to review daily tasks is to apply the familiar "Reduce, Reuse, Recycle" mantra, maximized by a fourth "R"—rethink. Ask questions related to the three R's when deciding how best to accomplish a project: What is the minimal amount of material needed to properly store, display, or ship an item? Will waste be generated from the action and are there systems in place to store, recycle, or dispose of that waste properly? Is this product needed for long or short-term use? Answers to these incremental questions will often reveal sustainable alternatives, and such analysis is far more manageable than detangling the web of issues posed by the question, "What are the economic, social, and environmental costs to executing this task?" The following will discuss potential products and practices registrars should explore to align their departments with the goals of sustainability.

As indicated previously, there are differences between purchasing green versus sustainable products. Locating a collection care product that balances the triple weighted scale of sustainability—economy, society, and environment—is difficult in today's global economy. Comparisons between raw materials, such as tree versus plant based papers, are dependent upon specifying the geographic location and manner in which the resource is grown, followed by how it is processed, where and by whom. For example, one group of people state that the agricultural plants hemp and kenaf, both rapidly renewable resources, have high yield rates, require minimal amounts of fertilizer, and have lower lignin contents than trees—thus requiring fewer chemicals in the pulping process. A different group of people state that tree plantations certified by the Forest Stewardship Council (FSC) prevent soil erosion, provide habitat for more species, and typically apply fertilizer once every crop rotation (7 years) compared to once a year with annual agricultural crops.[27] Common among all groups is an argument against over-consumption and monocultures, and agreement that even the greenest pulp mill generates some form of pollution.

Ultimately, product choice is an act of compromise. However, if consumption is warranted—having first taken "Reduce, Reuse, Recycle, and Rethink" into account—it is important to support companies that have made the effort to incorporate some form of sustainability rather than none at all. The following will place the tasks of purchasing archival products, and packaging and shipping loans under the lens of sustainability.

Plant and tree fibers are key ingredients in many archival materials. Sustainable alternatives to conventional paper products and textiles are available to other markets, but further effort is needed to bring appropriate products to the museum profession. It is possible to produce organic, non-bleached cotton cloth and to produce ANSI certified archival paper from 100 percent post-consumer content without the use of chlorine.[28] Why, then, are these products not available in standard archival catalogues? Understandably, there are concerns within the profession that deviations from approved standards may ultimately harm collections. However, if museums recognize their responsibility to educate and promote sustainability in the public sphere, it is irresponsible to ignore the world's environmental problems behind the scenes. Alternative products should be tested and everyday practices should be reviewed to determine their environmental impact.

Registrars could begin taking responsibility for their departments by asking vendors if sustainable alternatives are available. The more the profession requests sustainable alternatives, the more industries will seek them out to maintain and build their customer base. As of this writing B- and E-fluted corrugated boards distributed by Gaylord Brothers are made with post-industrial waste.[29] These products meet the same archival standards as corrugated board made from single stream pulp. However, Gaylord does not advertise the products' environmentally friendly aspect due to concerns over a potential reduction in sales. This is a good example of the importance archival vendors place on consumer trust and how the industry could be encouraged to seek sustainable alternatives with collaboration and support from registrars.

The archival industry is considered a niche

market. Due to its small size and specific product requirements the industry is not able to withstand economic forces from larger competing markets. Suppliers struggle to maintain product quantity and quality as mills close down, merge, or move overseas.[30] However, the archival industry's small scale may lend itself to the support of smaller localized farms, manufacturers, and businesses. For example, Vision Paper, a company in New Mexico, has been working with local farmers since 1990 to grow the rapidly renewable plant, kenaf, for paper production at mills with strict environmental standards. Several of Vision Paper's products are archival. Over the past five years the mills that produced Vision Paper products have closed, and the specialty mills still available are priced too high and cannot meet the company's specifications. Rather than admit defeat, Vision Paper is in the process of forming its own pulp and paper mill, buying used machines at favorable prices from other mill closures.[31] The potential for creating a sustainable, archival market, integrating local suppliers such as Vision Paper, could increase with support and demand from the museum, archive, and library professions.

Switching from traditional products to green products does not necessarily solve the sustainability issue, however. Product change does not equal behavior change. For instance, using bio-composite board or FSC certified wood products for crate exteriors instead of traditional plywood does not reduce the amount of natural resources consumed and wasted. It is the system in which crates are used that is unsustainable—not the crates in and of themselves. While it is important to incorporate more sustainable and green products and methods into the profession, such alternatives lose their luster if used within an inefficient and wasteful system. As with product choice, registrars could fill an important leadership position by fostering the development of new norms through collaborative research with service providers.

LOANS AND TRAVELING EXHIBITIONS

Loans and traveling exhibits are two systems managed by registrars. These systems have an admirable, educational mission but consume physical and financial resources in a single-use manner, producing a significant amount of museum waste. Three pitfalls of the current loan system that make it unsustainable are: a lack of support to facilitate the reuse of packaging and crating materials, the inefficient and polluting manner in which loans are transported, and the lack of environmental responsibility when creating and disposing of museum generated products.

The Guide to Organizers of Traveling Exhibitions: 2003 Edition lists 110 exhibit agencies serving museums nationwide. The amount of materials consumed and discarded each year is enormous if one considers that the 40 current SITES (Smithsonian Institution Traveling Exhibition Service) exhibitions require more than 400 crates, and ExhibitsUSA's 30 exhibitions require 240 crates.[32] Crating and packaging is expensive and a large amount of museum resources are used to fund loans. Results from a 2007 online survey show that out of 105 participating institutions, 29 reported ordering a total of 426 crates in 2006 for a cost of $412,108. Unfortunately, disposal fees are inexpensive, and once-valuable materials are routinely thrown away with no regard to the associated environmental costs.

There is a significant price difference between purchasing new crates and retrofitting used crates. Results from the aforementioned survey show that 30 participants reported retrofitting 510 previously used crates for a total of $38,563. This equates to an average of $75.62 per crate instead of an average $967.39 per newly built crate.[33] Therefore, retrofitting crates not only reduces waste but also saves a significant amount of money. The argument could be made that costs associated with storage and transporting empty crates would decrease any monetary savings. However, before adequate feasibility studies have been undertaken and a true lifecycle analysis between reusing and building new crates occurs, it is premature to assume that crate retrofitting would not yield savings.

In order to facilitate reuse, crates must be stored. The National Gallery of Art retains a large collection of crates (approximately 300) that are stored and managed by a local fine art shipper. The museum typically retains medium-sized crates for versatility of reuse and as a rule does not use a crate if it is more than 12 inches bigger than the artwork in any one direction. Although neither the museum nor shipping company keeps track of the number of times crates are reused or which ones are used the most, the museum estimates that 95 percent of single object loans travel in retrofitted crates, at a third less than the cost of a new crate.[34] For those institutions that cannot afford storage, a cooperative warehouse system could be developed, managed, and collectively funded by local or regional museums. Crates could be leased, with resulting funds returning to the cooperative or to the proprietary museums. Alternatively, an independent third party could purchase, warehouse, and either lease or sell materials, similar to a construction salvage center. Art handling and exhibition companies could form similar partnerships and devise ways of profit sharing when resources are needed by clients outside of the contractor's immediate service area. While such systems would not satisfy every situation, they would reduce the production rate of new materials and provide a means for organizations to retain valuable resources. This model could also be followed for commonly used and discarded exhibition support materials beyond crates.

It is important to note that the European museum community has successfully instituted a crate leasing program. Several European crate companies have designed reusable crates, especially for two-dimensional works.[35] In general fine art crating companies in the U.S. do not believe a leasing system would be efficient due to the country's larger size and museum density differences in comparison to Europe. However, a modified system that approaches leasing from a regional perspective and promotes cooperation among independent crating companies should be explored in America if museums wish to carry out loans in a more sustainable manner.

Transport is the second aspect of loans that makes them unsustainable. Traveling exhibitions equal greenhouse gas emissions. Just one SITES exhibit, "The Burgess Shale: Evolution's Big Bang," traveled 20,044 miles, producing 38 tons of carbon dioxide. This is equivalent to 80 barrels of oil, and 6.3 passenger vehicles traveling 12,000 miles per year.[36] If traveling exhibitions are to continue, the field must develop alternative methods to rotate

and transport them. Currently, where and when an exhibit travels is the outcome of variables presented by both the exhibit and the borrower. The content, cost, and size of an exhibit generally determine the borrower and hence the location, while the borrower's internal exhibit schedule—which may or may not be planned in advance—typically determines the dates. These variables often cause exhibits to travel great distances back and forth across the country. A new system in which lenders direct how exhibitions circulate based on geography, not time, could be developed. Exhibit companies often advertise works-in-progress to judge interest levels. This business strategy could be a means to establish schedules based on the location of interested borrowers. Exhibit brochures could indicate when a particular exhibition would be available in a certain region. Such a system would continue to allow advanced planning for both lender and borrower but would reduce the frequency of long-distance round trips.

In conjunction with improved scheduling methods, exhibits could be transported using more energy efficient technologies. For example, low to moderate security exhibits, especially those that do not contain collection items, could travel by train. Comparisons between highway and rail transport have shown it is more economical to use trains for distances beyond 500 miles.[37] On average, railroads are three times more fuel efficient than trucks; railroads move a ton of freight an average of 404 miles on a single gallon of fuel. The U.S. Environmental Protection Agency (EPA) estimates that for every ton-mile, a typical truck emits roughly three times more nitrogen oxides and particulates than a locomotive.[38] Museums and art handling companies should consult with the railroad industry to explore current options and encourage the development of equipment and services that would facilitate a variety of museum shipments. Fine art transport companies could therefore expand their services to include intermodal transport. When highway transport is necessary, support should be given to companies that use energy efficient technologies such as vehicle idling reduction initiatives and auxiliary power units that reduce greenhouse gas emissions.[39] The EPA's website lists transport companies (rail, truck, and intermodal) that are a part of their

Smartway Transport Partnership Program.

Finally, museum loans and exhibitions produce vast amounts of waste. Again, reuse is rare due to a lack of storage space, and the true cost of land-filling our waste is masked by inexpensive disposal fees. Recycling packaging components, which for the purposes of this essay means implementing a secondary use for a material, is rarely practiced. There are bins for soda bottles and office paper; why not foam and metal? There are regionally based online recycling communities such as Freecycle, why not "Museumcycle"? Ely Inc., an exhibit and museum service company based in Maryland, is recognizing the need for reuse and recycling in the museum profession. On the company's website there is an "Ely Recycle" web page where museums can post exhibit frames, crates, and other items for sale, trade, or donation.

There are options to reduce the amount of waste generated from loans. Scott Carlee of the Alaska State Museum stated the following about resource-saving practices in his museum:

We probably do more than most museums just because it is so expensive to get materials shipped up here. Therefore material is more precious to us than to most museums. We will take apart a crate and reuse the wood for some other task or we will take apart exhibit walls and make crates out of them. For our traveling exhibits we have reusable crates that were custom-built for the shows that travel. We reuse whatever we can and when something just can't possibly be used one more time it is disposed of in a land-fill. All burnable wood is usually given to someone to burn in their wood burning stove for heat. The biggest drawback is space to store the material before we can reuse it.[40]

Museums in the lower 48 states should perhaps adopt an Alaskan state of mind when it comes to the life cycle of museum-generated products. Redesigning crating and packaging systems to increase recycling is a necessity. For instance, gluing crate joints in addition to using typical metal fasteners impedes the break-down of crates. Wood from crates has been used by art organizations and businesses for sculptures and cabinetry or as fuel in ceramic kilns or furnaces. The use of cardboard instead of Coroplast™ or Gatorfoam would increase the percentage of packaging material that can enter the conventional recycling stream. Before purchasing a product, a registrar should determine whether or not the manufacturer has a recycling program. Sealed Air Corporation, the manufacturer of both ETHAFOAM and Bubble Wrap®, for instance, has a mail back recycling program. Materials sent back to one of their seven receiving facilities is reprocessed within the company or by an outside company. DuPont has a similar mail-back recycling program for Tyvek®. Additionally, pack-and-ship centers frequently welcome packing supplies to support their operations, and the cleanliness and integrity are often not an issue.

CONCLUSION

Many museums and service providers are adopting green and sustainable practices. For example, Atthowe Fine Art Services uses solar panels on the company's roof, biodiesel in its fleet of vehicles, and recycles cardboard, wood, foam, and bubble wrap. In September 2008, the California Academy of Sciences opened the doors of its new museum, which is on track to achieve LEED Platinum certification. The building includes a 2.5-acre living roof, 60,000 photo voltaic cells, denim insulation, and natural lighting from skylights and exterior walls of glass. The academy has an official statement on sustainability approved by its board of directors as well as a green team. Initiatives developed by the academy's green team have altered many routine operations and include the elimination of plastic bottles at all staff meetings; the reuse and recycling of packing supplies; bulk ordering; and the elimination of anti-bacterial soap, which is harmful to marine life. In the past year, the academy recycled nearly 80 percent of its garbage.[41] These institutions and individuals have taken a leadership role in the sustainable movement and their efforts will help facilitate sustainable practices across the profession.

As stewards of the past, present, and future, registrars must continually assess how products created for and by museums affect the world. They can update accepted standards of collection care and management to reflect environmental stewardship and take a leadership position in forming and managing a green committee within their institutions. Registrars can be active participants in the pursuit of a sustainable future by being open to new technologies, working with service providers to bring new products to the market, and collaborating with colleagues throughout the museum world. •

NOTES

1. World Commission on Environment and Development. (1987). *Our Common Future*. New York: Oxford University Press.

2. McDonough, William and Michael Braungart. *Cradle to Cradle: Remaking the Way We Make Things*. North Point Press, New York, 2002, p. 26.

3. United States Green Building Council. *LEED® for Existing Buildings: Operations & Management*. p. 4, accessed at https://www.usgbc.org/ShowFile.aspx?DocumentID=3617, October 11, 2008.

4. U.S. Department of Energy, *Solar Lighting Basics*. accessed at http://www1.eere.energy.gov/solar/sl_basics.html, October 18, 2008.

5. McKenzie, James and Majd Zoorob, "Design Considerations for Intelligent Color-changeable LED Luminaires." LEDs Magazine, Oct 2008, p. 33. accessed at http://www.ledsmagazine.com/magazine/pdf/0810, October 11, 2008.

6. Lighting Design Lab, *Advantages of LED Lighting*. accessed at http://www.lightingdesignlab.com/articles/LED_fund/led_advant.htm, September 19, 2008.

7. Krieger, Sari, "Bright Future: Thanks to Improved Technology, LED's May be Ready to Take Off." *The Wall Street Journal*, September 15, 2008. accessed at http://online.wsj.com/article/SB122123942429828649.html?mod=ITPWSJ_20 , September 17, 2008.

8. McKenzie, James and Majd Zoorob, "Design Considerations for Intelligent Color-changeable LED Luminaires" LEDs Magazine, Oct 2008, p. 33. accessed at http://www.ledsmagazine.com/magazine/pdf/0810, October 11, 2008.

9. Lighting Design Lab, *Disadvantages of LED Lighting*. accessed at http://www.lightingdesignlab.com/articles/LED_fund/led_disadv.htm, September 19, 2008.

10. Lighting Research Center, "Lighting from Afar." *Rensselaer Polytechnic Institute*, no. 3 (1998). accessed at http://www.lrc.rpi.edu/programs/Futures/LF-RemoteSource/index.asp, September 21, 2008.

11. Lighting Design Lab, *Introduction to Fiber Optic Lighting* accessed at http://www.lightingdesignlab.com/articles/fiberoptic/intro_fiber.htm, September 21, 2008.

12. U.S. Department of Energy, Solar Energy Technology Program, *Solar Lighting Research and Development*. accessed at http://www1.eere.energy.gov/solar/sl_research_development.html, October 18, 2008.

13. U.S. Department of Energy, Solar Energy Technology Program, *Solar Lighting*. accessed at http://www1.eere.energy.gov/solar/solar_lighting.html, September 19, 2008.

14. Behar, David, Dr. Capeluto Guedi, and Professor Levin Michael. *Light in the Art Exhibition Space*. Faculty of Architecture and Town Planning, Technion Israel Institute of Technology, Haifa Israel. May 2007.

15. The Getty, *Museum Lighting Research*. accessed at http://www.getty.edu/conservation/science/lighting/index.html, September 15, 2008.

16. Perahia, David Behar, Ph.D. Technion Israel Institute of Technology (Haifa, Israel). Telephone interview by author, April 15, 2007.

17. Clinard, David. "Show & Tell: Museum Lighting." *Architectural Lighting* 17 (April/May 2002): 59.

18. Brophy, Sarah, and Elizabeth Wylie. "It's Easy Being Green: Museums and the Green Movement." *Museum News,* September/October 2006, p. 39.

19. Elliot, Garth. Chief Engineer, Nevada Museum of Art. Interview by author, February 13, 2007.

20. Sugarman, Samuel C. *HVAC Fundamentals*. Lilburn, Georgia: The Fairmont Press, 2005.

21. The granular carbon reactivation process renders saturated carbon into reusable carbon through thermal reactivation. The spent activated carbon is treated in special kilns with steam that are devoid of oxygen at 850° C or more in order to release organic compounds. The volatized organics are destroyed in the furnace's afterburner. Volatile inorganics are then removed by a wet chemical scrubber. A complete description can be found at http://www.water.siemens.com/SiteCollectionDocuments/Product_Lines/Westates_Carbon/Brochures/reactivated_carbon_q_and_a.pdf.

22. Elliot, Garth. Chief Engineer, Nevada Museum of Art. Interview by author, October 6, 2008.

23. Brokerhof, Agnes W. *Applying the Outcome of Climate Research in Collection Risk Management*. accessed at http://www.padfield.org/tim/cfys/mm/brokerhof/brokerhof.pdf, November 11, 2008.

24. Erhardt, David, Charles S. Tumosa, and Marion F. Mecklenburg. *Applying Science to the Question of Museum Climate,* November 2007, p. 13. accessed at http://www.padfield.org/tim/cfys/mm/erhardt/erhardt.pdf, September 15, 2008.

25. Originally named Conservation Research Laboratory (CRL), it was renamed Conservation Analytical Laboratory (CAL) in 1963 and was renamed in 1998 as Smithsonian Center for Materials Research and Education (SCMRE). It is currently named Museum Conservation Institute (MCI).

26. Erhardt, David, Charles S. Tumosa, and Marion F. Mecklenburg. *Applying Science to the Question of Museum Climate,* November 2007, p. 15. accessed at http://www.padfield.org/tim/cfys/mm/erhardt/erhardt.pdf, September 15, 2008.

27. The Forest Stewardship Council (FSC) is an international organization that has established policies and standards to protect forest ecosystems. http://www.fsc.org/en/. "Paper Listening Study", Conservatree.org. accessed August 25, 2008

28. ANSI, American National Standards Institute oversees the creation, promulgation and use of thousands of norms and guidelines. Cascades Fine Papers Group includes Rolland Enviro100 which is made of 100% post-consumer waste that is processed chlorine free in a plant that uses biogas and is certified Permanent Paper by ANSI.

29. Post-industrial waste is leftover material created when manufacturing a product. This type of waste can be collected to be used in-house or by an outside party to make a similar or different product. In contrast post-consumer waste is material that has been used by a consumer and discarded at a recycling center such as used newspapers, plastic bottles, or aluminum cans.

30. Dolores King, Product Manager, Gaylord Brothers; interview with author (Warden) August 25, 2008

31. Vision Paper www.visonpaper.com accessed August 31, 2008

32. Of the 40 exhibits advertized in "Update: Smithsonian institution Traveling Exhibition Service Catalogue of Exhibitions 2008–2009" only 35 list crate quantities for a total of 390 crates.

33. Twenty-nine museums reported ordering a total of 426 new crates in 2006 for a cost of $412,108, which averages to $967.38.

34. Johnnie Mizell, interview with author (Warden) March 2007; Sally Freitag, Chief Registrar, National Gallery of Art, email correspondence (Warden) September 26, 2007

35. Hasenkamp, 2-D and 3-D crates www.hasenkamp.com; Turtle Box by Hizkia Van Kralingen, Netherlands, www.turtlebox.com also www.vankralingen.com; Pegasus Packaging Crate by Helicon: The Conservation Specialist, Netherlands, www.helicon-cs.com

36. The average tractor trailer, fully loaded, gets 6 miles per gallon. Carbon Dioxide data was calculated using The Greenhouse Gas Protocol Initiative's Sector Tool, CO_2 Emissions from Transport or Mobile Sources, http://www.ghgprotocol.org/calculation-tools/all-tools; and the U.S. Environmental Protection Agency Greenhouse Gas Equivalencies Calculator; http://www.epa.gov/solar/energy-resources/calculator.html both accessed November 8, 2008.

37. H. Conlon, Hub Group, Inc., interview with author (Warden) April 5, 2007

38. "Overview of U.S. Freight Railroads" National Atlas of the United States, accessed at www.nationalatlas.gov, October 20, 2008.

39. Environmental Protection Agency, SmartWay Transport Partnership http://www.epa.gov/otaq/smartway/index.htm

40. email correspondence (Warden) April 19, 2007

41. The California Academy of Sciences www.calacademy.org accessed October 20, 2008

Risk Management | HYPOTHETICALS

1

The museum hires a well-established and respected art service company to pack and ship a very fragile group of ceramics from a lender's home to the museum for exhibition. They are also contracted to help install the works in the exhibit. Everything is overseen by the museum's registrar. A vase is broken in the home of the lender and a ceramic sculpture turns up with hairline cracks at the time of de-installation.

Define a process of reporting, and discuss interactions with the lender, insurance company, and the art handling company.

2

You're on a panel to hire the new security director.

Define the optional talents and experience you're looking for and discuss your department's interactions—current and best— with security.

3

You are looking for new off-site storage space. You visit different sites to check their security, climate control, etc.

What specific factors will you consider from the point of view of disaster mitigation?

4

Outline a plan and schedule for integrated pest management within your museum. Include a log for tracking and reporting problems and basic reference materials that should be available to staff.

5

A river that runs close to your museum has risen to record-breaking heights, and experts predict that it will continue to rise and flood in a matter of days. The water is seeping through walls as well as through the back-up floor drains, so your precaution of keeping things off the floor level has not saved the day. When you get a call from your security force, water is approximately an inch deep; shelves containing rare books and print boxes are involved as well.

Go through the steps needed to respond to the emergency and then to mitigate the damage.

6

Work out an actionable follow-up plan to keep the situation outlined in 5 from happening again.

7

Your insurance broker has advised you that your insurance premiums might be lower if your disaster plan had a more thoroughly detailed chapter on fire prevention.

What must you consider in order to revise?

8

You work at a historic house museum located in a downtown urban area. You have just learned that an office building next to your museum is planning a major renovation.

What are your possible risks and how will you mitigate them?

SECTION 7 | ETHICAL AND LEGAL ISSUES

7A | ETHICS FOR REGISTRARS AND COLLECTIONS MANAGERS

REBECCA BUCK

Registrars and collections managers are daily confronted with complex situations that demand ethical responses. These often lead to thoughtful discussions and the need for calm responses in situations that might easily build and become areas of major dissonance in an institution. It is often up to the registrar to keep the institution on a straight course and alert those involved when questionable situations arise. It is sometimes up to the registrar to be the referee. It is always up to the registrar to maintain highest standards of personal integrity.

The best legal stance offers only the lowest level in a series of standards; museums must rise above the legal bar and try to hold to the highest of ethical standards, lest they be charged with (among other things) feeding the chain of looting, selling off their collections to cover operating expenses, giving their reputations up to commercial enterprises, or becoming centers of entertainment when they should, by virtue of their missions, be educators. The constant dance with acquisitions, exhibition funding and exhibition design, marketing, development, maintenance, special events, human resources, and educational activities requires careful choice of battlefields and firm responses when necessary. Vigilance, creativity, and good humor have to be part of the registrar's arsenal.

The Registrars Committee Code of Ethics is undergoing revision as *MRM5* goes to publication. The updated version of that code will appear on http://www.rcaam.org when it is adopted. Below is a compilation of collection ethics statements from major museum professional organizations: AAM, AAMD, AASLH, and ICOM.

SELECTED FROM THE AMERICAN ASSOCIATION OF MUSEUMS CODE OF ETHICS FOR MUSEUMS
Adopted in 2000

http://www.aam-us.org/museumresources/ethics/coe.cfm

The distinctive character of museum ethics derives from the ownership, care, and use of objects, specimens, and living collections representing the world's natural and cultural common wealth. This stewardship of collections entails the highest public trust and carries with it the presumption of rightful ownership, permanence, care, documentation, accessibility, and responsible disposal.

Thus, the museum ensures that:

•collections in its custody support its mission and public trust responsibilities

•collections in its custody are lawfully held, protected, secure, unencumbered, cared for, and preserved

•collections in its custody are accounted for and documented

•access to the collections and related information is permitted and regulated

•acquisition, disposal, and loan activities are conducted in a manner that respects the protection and preservation of natural and cultural resources and discourages illicit trade in such materials

•acquisition, disposal, and loan activities conform to its mission and public trust responsibilities

•disposal of collections through sale, trade, or research activities is solely for the advancement of the museum's mission. Proceeds from the sale of nonliving collections are to be used consistent with the established standards of the museum's discipline, but in no event shall they be used for anything other than acquisition or direct care of collections.

• the unique and special nature of human remains and funerary and sacred objects is recognized as the basis of all decisions concerning such collections

• collections-related activities promote the public good rather than individual financial gain

• competing claims of ownership that may be asserted in connection with objects in its custody should be handled openly, seriously, responsively and with respect for the dignity of all parties involved.

THE ASSOCIATION OF ART MUSEUM DIRECTORS

(http://www.aamd.org) allows non-members access to position papers. Included are:

Art Museums and the practice of Deaccessioning, 11/2007

Art Museums and the Restitution of Works Stolen by the Nazis, 06/2007

Art Museums and the International Exchange of Cultural Artifacts, 01/2002

SELECTED FROM THE AMERICAN ASSOCIATION FOR STATE AND LOCAL HISTORY STATEMENT OF PROFESSIONAL STANDARDS AND ETHICS

Adopted June, 2002

http://www.aaslh.org/ethics.htm

Historical Resources
Historical Resources including Collections and other evidence of the past, provide the tools through which we interact with the past and are the bedrock upon which the practice of history rests. In fulfillment of their public trust, historical organizations and those associated with them must be responsible stewards of the collections within their direct care and are challenged to be advocates on behalf of the historical resources within their communities.

A. Association members shall give priority to the care and management of the collections within their care and always shall act to preserve their physical and intellectual integrity.

B. Institutions shall manage historical resources, including collections, in accord with comprehensive policies officially adopted by their governing authorities.

C. Collections shall not be capitalized or treated as financial assets.

D. Collections shall not be deaccessioned or disposed of in order to provide financial support for institutional operations, facilities maintenance or any reason other than preservation or acquisition of collections, as defined by institutional policy.

E. Historical resources shall be acquired, cared for, and interpreted with sensitivity to their cultural origins.

F. It is important to document the physical condition of collections, including past treatment of objects, and to take appropriate steps to mitigate potential hazards to people and property.

In addition to its code of ethics, AASLH has position papers posted on the following topics:

The Capitalization of Collections

When a History Museum Closes

Repurposing a Historic House

SELECTED FROM THE ICOM CODE OF ETHICS FOR MUSEUMS

The *ICOM Code of Professional Ethics* was adopted unanimously by the 15th General Assembly of ICOM in Buenos Aires, (Argentina) on 4 November 1986. It was amended by the 20th General Assembly in Barcelona (Spain) on 6 July 2001, retitled *ICOM Code of Ethics for Museums,* and revised by the 21st General

Assembly in Seoul (Republic of Korea) on 8 October 2004.

http://icom.museum/ethics.html

Section 2. Museums that maintain collections hold them in trust for the benefit of society and its development.

Principle: *Museums have the duty to acquire, preserve and promote their collections as a contribution to safeguarding the natural, cultural and scientific heritage. Their collections are a significant public inheritance, have a special position in law and are protected by international legislation. Inherent in this public trust is the notion of stewardship that includes rightful ownership, permanence, documentation, accessibility and responsible disposal.*

ACQUIRING COLLECTIONS

2.1 Collections Policy

The governing body for each museum should adopt and publish a written collections policy that addresses the acquisition, care and use of collections. The policy should clarify the position of any material that will not be catalogued, conserved, or exhibited (See also 2.7; 2.8 .)

2.2 Valid Title

No object or specimen should be acquired by purchase, gift, loan, bequest, or exchange unless the acquiring museum is satisfied that a valid title is held. Evidence of lawful ownership in a country is not necessarily valid title.

2.3 Provenance and Due Diligence

Every effort must be made before acquisition to ensure that any object or specimen offered for purchase, gift, loan, bequest, or exchange has not been illegally obtained in or exported from, its country of origin or any intermediate country in which it might have been owned legally (including the museum's own country). Due diligence in this regard should establish the full history of the item from discovery or production.

2.4 Objects and Specimens from Unauthorised or Unscientific Fieldwork

Museums should not acquire objects where there is reasonable cause to believe their recovery involved the unauthorised, unscientific, or intentional destruction or damage of monuments, archaeological or geological sites, or species and natural habitats. In the same way, acquisition should not occur if there has been a failure to disclose the finds to the owner or occupier of the land, or to the proper legal or governmental authorities.

2.5 Culturally Sensitive Material

Collections of human remains and material of sacred significance should be acquired only if they can be housed securely and cared for respectfully. This must be accomplished in a manner consistent with professional standards and the interests and beliefs of members of the community, ethnic or religious groups from which the objects originated, where these are known (See also 3.7; 4.3.)

2.6 Protected Biological or Geological Specimens

Museums should not acquire biological or geological specimens that have been collected, sold, or otherwise transferred in contravention of local, national, regional or international law or treaty relating to wildlife protection or natural history conservation.

2.7 Living Collections

When the collections include live botanical and zoological specimens, special considerations should be made for the natural and social environment from which they are derived as well as any local, national, regional or international law, or treaty relating to wildlife protection or natural history conservation.

2.8 Working Collections

The collections policy may include special considerations for certain types of working collection where the emphasis is on preserving cultural, scientific or technical process rather than the object, or where objects or specimens are assembled for regular handling and teaching purposes (See also 2.1.)

2.9 Acquisition Outside Collections Policy

The acquisition of objects or specimens outside the museum's stated policy should only be made in exceptional circumstances. The governing body should consider the professional opinions available to them, and the views of all interested parties. Consideration will include the significance of the object or specimen including its context in the cultural or natural heritage, and the special interests of other museums collecting such material. However, even in these circumstances, objects without a valid title should not be acquired (See also 3.4.)

2.10 Acquisition by Members of the Governing Body and Museum Personnel

Special care is required in considering any item, either for sale, as a donation or as a tax-benefit gift, from members of governing bodies, museum personnel, or the families and close associates of these persons.

2.11 Repositories of Last Resort

Nothing in this *Code of Ethics* should prevent a museum from acting as an authorised repository for unprovenanced, illicitly collected or recovered specimens and objects from the territory over which it has lawful responsibility.

REMOVING COLLECTIONS

2.12 Legal or Other Powers of Disposal

Where the museum has legal powers permitting disposals, or has acquired objects subject to conditions of disposal, the legal or other requirements and procedures must be complied with fully. Where the original acquisition was subject to mandatory or other restrictions these conditions must be observed, unless it can be shown clearly that adherence to such restrictions is impossible or substantially detrimental to the institution and, if appropriate, relief may be sought through legal procedures.

2.13 Deaccessioning from Museum Collections

The removal of an object or specimen from a museum collection must only be undertaken with a full understanding of the significance of the item, its character (whether renewable or non-renewable), legal standing, and any loss of public trust that might result from such action.

2.14 Responsibility for Deaccessioning

The decision to deaccession should be the responsibility of the governing body acting in conjunction with the director of the museum and the curator of the collection concerned. Special arrangements may apply to working collections (See also 2.7; 2.8.)

2.15 Disposal of Objects Removed from the Collections

Each museum should have a policy defining authorised methods for permanently removing an object from the collections through donation, transfer, exchange, sale, repatriation, or destruction, and that allows the transfer of unrestricted title to the receiving agency. Complete records must be kept of all deaccessioning decisions, the objects involved, and the disposition of the object. There will be a strong presumption that a deaccessioned item should first be offered to another museum.

2.16 Income from Disposal of Collections

Museum collections are held in public trust and may not be treated as a realisable asset. Money or compensation received from the deaccessioning and disposal of objects and specimens from a museum collection should be used solely for the benefit of the collection and usually for acquisitions to that same collection.

2.17 Purchase of Deaccessioned Collections

Museum personnel, the governing body, or their families or close associates, should not be permitted to purchase objects that have been deaccessioned from a collection for which they are responsible.

CARE OF COLLECTIONS

2.18 Collection Continuity

The museum should establish and apply policies to ensure that its collections (both permanent and temporary) and associated information, properly recorded, are available for current use and will be passed on to future generations in as good and safe a condition as practicable, having regard to current knowledge and resources.

2.19 Delegation of Collection Responsibility

Professional responsibilities involving the care of the collections should be assigned to persons with appropriate knowledge and skill or who are adequately supervised. (See also 8.11.)

2.20 Documentation of Collections

Museum collections should be documented according to accepted professional standards. Such documentation should include a full identification and description of each item, its associations, provenance, condition, treatment and present location. Such data should be kept in a secure environment and be supported by retrieval systems providing access to the information by the museum personnel and other legitimate users.

2.21 Protection Against Disasters

Careful attention should be given to the development of policies to protect the collections during armed conflict and other human-made or natural disasters.

2.22 Security of Collection and Associated Data

The museum should exercise control to avoid disclosing sensitive personal or related information and other confidential matters when collection data is made available to the public.

2.23 Preventive Conservation

Preventive conservation is an important element of museum policy and collections care. It is an essential responsibility of members of the museum profession to create and maintain a protective environment for the collections in their care, whether in storage, on display, or in transit.

2.24 Collection Conservation and Restoration

The museum should carefully monitor the condition of collections to determine when an object or specimen may require conservation-restoration work and the services of a qualified conservator-restorer. The principal goal should be the stabilisation of the object or specimen. All conservation procedures should be documented and as reversible as possible, and all alterations should be clearly distinguishable from the original object or specimen.

2.25 Welfare of Live Animals

A museum that maintains living animals should assume full responsibility for their health and well-being. It should prepare and implement a safety code for the protection of its personnel and visitors, as well as of the animals, that has been approved by an expert in the veterinary field. Genetic modification should be clearly identifiable.

2.26 Personal Use of Museum Collections

Museum personnel, the governing body, their families, close associates, or others should not be permitted to expropriate items from the museum collections, even temporarily, for any personal use. •

Printed with permission from AAM, AAMD, AASLH, and ICOM.

7B | COLLECTIONS ETHICS

ILDIKO POGANY DeANGELIS

INTRODUCTION

Registrars have an important role in promoting and maintaining the integrity of the museum's collection management. A Registrar's duty is to ensure that all acquisitions, management and care processes, as well as deaccessions, are properly handled and documented. No one now doubts that sound museum collection management policies are essential to perform these functions effectively. Registrars, therefore, must be advocates in their museums for the establishment of such policies, and must monitor these policies, once they are established. To be effective, museum-specific collection management policies should be drafted with special regard to the needs of particular collections and with provisions that are consistent with the law and ethical codes promulgated by museum professional organizations and relevant discipline-based groups.[1]

Basic legal requirements together with professional ethics codes provide the backbone for our collection management policies on which Registrars rely daily for guidance and support. A first step in formulating prudent policies is to know both what the law and our ethics codes require for sound collections management. Requiring conduct that is only consistent with existing laws is not enough. Our ethical standards should require us to do more. As Professor Marie Malaro explained over a decade ago,[2] the goal of ethics codes is to maintain the integrity of our museums in the eyes of the public. Ethics codes must aim higher than what the law requires. They are concerned with even the appearance of impropriety, not only actual wrongdoing. They should require transparency and accountability in the collection management process.

In the past decade or more, we all have been forced to relearn the importance of ethics codes that aim for a higher standard. Our largest and best

museums have had to return valuable collection objects acquired under policies that were grounded on legal technicalities. But the loss of collections is not the whole story and perhaps not the primary lesson. As noted author Stephen Weil wrote, "no museum is an island"—one museum's reported wrongdoing will come back to haunt all museums. Aside from inviting further restrictive regulation, the bigger issue for the museum profession is public confidence or, simply put, *trust*. If public trust in museums is eroded, museums stand to lose support from those on whom they must rely. As public charities, museums receive a majority of their donations, both funds and collection objects, from the very people they are potentially alienating. If there has been any doubt in the past about the value of solid ethical standards or the power of negative public opinion in their absence, we need only examine the recent history of museum acquisition practices.

ACQUISITION ETHICS: A CASE STUDY

It is safe to say that in the last decade there has been a sea change in how museums go about collecting cultural property, due in large part by a major shift in public opinion. This situation is not surprising, as the arts sections of daily newspapers for years were replete with stories of past alleged museum wrongdoings in the collecting arena. Those of us in the collections management profession read these articles with open-mouthed incredulity and fear that public confidence in all museums will erode. Such a reaction is not out of line, given that 1) a former American antiquities curator was indicted in Italy for conspiracy for allegedly trafficking in looted antiquities; 2) several of our largest and most prestigious art museums have returned significant collection objects that were allegedly looted and removed illegally from their countries of origin; and 3) several more American museums have been negotiating restitution agreements with foreign governments for return of undocumented material.

These revelations of missteps in the acquisition of antiquities and archaeological materials in particular lead one first to question the effectiveness of the ethics codes that guided our collecting practices. Or was the problem one of failed implementation? In fact, both the standards and their implementation were problematic and they will be examined in turn.

A. Ethics Then: Weak Standard

Even a brief examination of relevant professional codes of ethics in place during the last two decades reveals that often standards required little more than what U.S. law dictated at the time. But during the same period, U.S. case law evolved with respect to protections offered for objects clandestinely removed from countries of origin. For example, the definition of what constitutes "theft" under federal law has been expanded to include objects protected by foreign patrimony laws that declare all cultural property state-owned. Anything, including cultural material without any documentation, removed without an export permit from one of these countries may be considered stolen. The law is thus fluid and evolves through court precedents. As discussed below, collection objects that may have been found legally present in the United States in one court case may be held illegal in the next with a slightly different set of facts or with a broader reading of the law by a judge sympathetic to righting a perceived wrong. Following stricter ethical guidelines, rather than the letter of the law, offers museums a safe harbor and an effective form of risk management as laws change. Ethical acquisition standards passed by a handful of museums in the early 1980s requiring museums to pay attention to foreign law restrictions, not only U.S. law, ended up protecting their reputations and their collections.

Surprisingly, the Registrars Committee of the American Association of Museums' ("RCAAM") *Code of Ethics for Registrars* ("RCAAM Code"), dating back to 1984, is not very specific on the issue of "acquisition ethics."[3] It makes no mention of the goal, enunciated in the hallmark UNESCO Convention on the Means of Prohibiting and Preventing

Illicit Import, Export and Transfer of Ownership of Cultural Property of 1970 ("UNESCO Convention"),[4] for museums, through prudent acquisition practices, to aid the preservation of the world's cultural heritage at risk from looting and pillage. This is surprising because the extended public debate on implementation of this Convention in the United States[5] in the 1970s and the early 1980s did much to bring to the attention of the museum community the problems inherent in the international art market, emphasizing how important it is for museums in particular to avoid encouraging illicit trade. Perhaps the RCAAM membership believed that codes established by other museum professional organizations would guide their museums in this regard.[6] Such reliance on others may have been misplaced.

Aside from a handful of American art-collecting institutions such as the Smithsonian in 1973, the Harvard Museums in 1972,[7] most major museums active in the art market did not publish ethical codes or acquisition policies specifically for their museums in keeping with international efforts urged in the UNESCO Convention. The codes promulgated by American professional organizations show that some efforts were made, but with a bias towards not unduly tying the hands of our museum curators wishing to collect in the international art market.

As early as January 1973 the Association of Art Museum Directors (AAMD)[8] issued a resolution urging its members to cooperate fully with foreign countries to prevent the illicit traffic in works of art.[9] This resolution confirmed the belief of the AAMD that art museums should refuse to acquire objects in violation of the relevant laws "obtaining in the countries of origin." Yet the Code of Ethics published in 1981 by the AAMD did not go so far. The AAMD Code included a provision declaring it to be unprofessional for directors of art museums to:

> "knowingly acquire . . . any art objects which have been stolen . . . in contravention of the applicable laws of its country of origin or any exporting countries and/or contravention of international treaties and international conventions."[10]

In other words, if an object considered for acquisition is determined to have been "stolen,"[11] an art museum director was instructed not to acquire it for the museum's collections.[12] In addition, by limiting acquisition to objects *known* to have been stolen, the AAMD 1981 Code left the door open for acquisition of objects without traceable documentation or scientifically excavated "find-spots." In this way, the AAMD mirrored a "presumption of innocence" approach: assuming objects available for acquisition in the art market were innocent until proven stolen. Underlying this approach is the belief that antiquities without provenance can still provide important aesthetic, cultural, and educational value in the permanent collections of museums.[13] But the risk in this approach is that presumed innocent objects may later be proven guilty, in that they were obtained as a result of destructive looting or other wrongful activity.

By the time the 1992 revision of the AAMD Code was published, the reference to compliance with foreign laws was removed. Instead, the new acquisition guidelines looked essentially only to what U.S. law directed. If the object was legally in the United States (as judged under U.S. law), presumably art museum directors were free to acquire it.[14] In other words, the object need not be considered "stolen" if taken in violation of a foreign patrimony law because U.S. courts would probably not recognize blanket foreign state-ownership laws.[15] Apparently, in the 1990s, no one considered the risk of being prosecuted in a foreign court. Even if someone had considered this possibility, the risk may have been viewed as negligible, as proof required to track the movement of objects from foreign jurisdictions to the museum's display cases was highly unlikely to surface. Foreign courts may have also seemed remote to stay-at-home curators buying locally from international dealers. In addition, perhaps no one considered that another court might later find that indeed foreign patrimony laws do prove legitimate ownership and export without permission constitutes a theft under U.S. Federal law.[16] In sum, the 1992 AAMD Code did little more than guide directors to avoid criminal penalties (with a narrow reading of what our criminal laws required), not to set higher standards by which to earn public confidence.[17]

The American Association of Museums' ("AAM") Code of Ethics set out broad principles only, with little guidance in how the principles need to be elaborated and implemented at the museum level. Given the broad range of collecting organizations that are its members, the AAM Code expects individual museums to promulgate their own codes to suit the needs of their collections and organization types. However, in the AAM Code, museums were instructed to ensure that an acquisition activity (along with disposals and loans) "respects the protection and preservation of natural and cultural resources and discourages illicit trade in such materials."[18] In addition, by the early 1990s, the AAM Accreditation Commission also had released a "Statement on Cultural Property" urging its members to adopt collections management policies that articulate acquisition criteria. The thrust of this document, however, was to warn museums that they have an obligation to the public trust not to return objects to claimants of lawful ownership unless they are rightful and fact-based.[19]

In addition, to the writer's knowledge, no professional organizational code of ethics in the museum field, until very recently, specifically addressed the following key points:

(i) what steps should be taken to investigate the origins of objects proposed for acquisition;

(ii) what types of documentation of clean legal title should be required; and

(iii) whether undocumented objects without provenance should be collected at all, and if so, under what limitations.

Admittedly, independent inquiry and key documentation about objects considered for acquisition would have been out of step in the art market where the "don't ask, don't tell" practice was firmly in place. However, such requirements would have imposed higher standards on dealers or collectors wishing to sell or donate to publicly supported institutions. Knowing that object histories are easily forged, requiring that the inquiry be "independent" and not simply relying on information provided by the seller would have provided museum buyers with an additional level of protection. Instead, many American museums were seemingly content to protect themselves from financial damage when buying objects with little or no histories by requiring written warranties from "reputable dealers" who could be forced later to pay up, if it should prove necessary to invoke warranties.[20]

A major flaw in the practice of acquiring objects with little or no provenance is explained in part by the term "undocumented." If an object cannot be traced because there are no documents describing its origin or history of ownership, there would be no evidence to prove theft, illegal export, or looting. But what if documentation is later found? This is exactly what happened in the recent Italian investigations that brought down the "house of cards" antiquities art market and, in turn, our major art museums that were active in it.

B. Ethics Then: Weak Implementation

But as weak as our professional acquisition ethical standards may have been, these codes were not even implemented through museum-specific policies. Aside from the few museums mentioned earlier, for large museums active in the art market, acquisition policies, if they existed, were not made public.[21] Similarly, museum acquisition documentation files were generally not open for public examination in most large museums. By contrast, a few pioneer museums declared their acquisition records open for public inspection as early as 1973.[22] For the majority of our museums, the goals of openness, accountability, and transparency were apparently sacrificed for the freedom to acquire objects directly or indirectly from an art market that operated under much different standards.

AAM required a museum to have ethics policies (including collections management policies) in place as a condition of accreditation. Having an ethics code in place is recommended but not a condition of membership in AAM.[23] As only a small percentage of our museums are accredited, many museums may remain without any meaningful museum-specific internal ethical guidance. Moreover, even if an ethical code is in place, there is no independent professional body to monitor whether the provisions are implemented. Ethics codes generally are self-enforced and susceptible only to peer pressure within the profession.

How can a registrar operate to protect the museum and its collections without a clear policy to guide her?[24] Although the current RCAAM Code notes that "registrars should encourage and assist in their formulation" and "[i]n the absence of written museum policies registrars should develop written procedures for use by their departments to ensure compliance with traditional but oral museum policies." The RCAAM Code should go further and require Registrars to advocate openly, not only "encourage," the establishment of museum-specific guidelines on how acquisitions for the collections and other major collecting functions are handled, and specify clearly the roles and responsibilities of registrars in the establishment and monitoring of these processes.

C. Ethics Now: The Revised Codes

In 2004, the AAMD published comprehensive new guidelines on acquisition of archeological materials and ancient art. These new guidelines were issued after the groundbreaking decision in the *U.S. v. Schultz* case involving a dealer indicted for theft of an object owned by Egypt under its patrimony laws, and after an announcement of the indictment of an American curator in Italy. The 2004 guidelines tightened the requirements for art museums, yet they still did not require compliance with foreign export regulations, nor did they prohibit the acquisition of undocumented materials if the acquisition did not provide a "direct and material incentive to looting" or illegal excavation judged by the amount of time the object has been out of the country of origin (the suggestion was 10 years).[25]

Less than four years later, the AAMD came out with the even stricter revised July 2008 guidelines now in effect.[26] Meanwhile several major art museums were subject to restitution claims by foreign governments and major pieces were being readied for return. In the same month, AAM also published its first detailed guidelines to its member museums that own or acquire archaeological material and ancient art not originating in the United States.[27] Both of these guidelines establish 1970 (the date UNESCO Convention was signed) as the threshold year for the application of more rigorous standards. No museum should acquire any archaeological or ancient work of art unless research indicates that the work left its country of modern discovery legally after 1970. Both require rigorous research on provenance before acquisition and to obtain documentation with respect to an object's history.

In the past, the principle touted by many was that in the absence of evidence that undocumented property has been looted, why should we assume every object is guilty until proven innocent? That principle has been overturned. Evidence of legality both under U.S. and foreign laws is required for any object not within the borders of the United States as of 1970. Evidence must be found that either the work left the country of origin before 1970 or it was legally exported from that country after 1970. In my opinion, based on the history of the Italian investigation, the strong links between illegal looting and subsequent museum acquisitions of antiquities cannot be denied. Undocumented objects are now assumed suspect until proven otherwise, in spite of their aesthetic, cultural, and educational value.

The justification given for the new revised 2008 guidelines by the AAMD is that "museums evolve their professional practices as the world changes" and that we are entering "a new era of collaboration with archaeological and other organizations to devise new, effective ways to safeguard heritage resources worldwide." The incoming President of the AAMD stated that "We also believe it is important to go beyond the letter of the law in considering acquisitions of antiquities and ancient art, and the acquisitions of these works must be responsible and ethical as well as legal."[28]

The new guidelines also recommend that museums require or make "rigorous effort" to acquire documentation of legal export and import for any such work. The AAMD guidelines established a webpage where museums acquiring such art post their acquisitions promptly after purchase for public inspection. As of February 2009, only one work of art had been so listed.[29] The AAM guidelines go one step further. They urge museums to "make serious efforts to allocate time and funding to conduct research on objects already in their collections where provenance is incomplete or uncertain" and to "make available the known ownership history of archaeological material and ancient art in their collections."[30]

Finally, both guidelines urge museums to establish acquisition policies and provenance research practices consistent with these guidelines and to make such policies publicly available. Several of our major museums that were burned by recent restitutions already include such provisions. It is time for the remaining museums to follow suit.[31] Registrars should lead the way in this effort by formally incorporating the need for advocating such policies in the RCAAM Code of Ethics.

CONCLUSIONS

One might note that we have come full circle since the first acquisition policies established by a handful of U.S. museums in the early 1970s. Our current professional guidelines nearly 40 years later mirror standards set in those early policies. Those few museums that took the call to action seriously through tough ethical guidelines that respected the international goals of the UNESCO Convention saved themselves from major controversy in the interim. One key lesson could be learned from this history. Ethics codes should anticipate problems and require behavior that merits public confidence and do not merely respond to public pressure after widely publicised scandals. We need to look to other areas of our professional activities and see which ethical standards should be adjusted before major problems force us to do so.

One area may be the special relationship reported in the press between museums and donors of collections. Museum curators have reportedly furnished assistance (as part of official duties) to major donors for purposes of building private collections, sometimes over a number of years. Museum staff have also organized dedicated exhibitions of private collections, and museums have published accompanying catalogues at the museum's expense, often only in hopes rather than with firm a commitment that the collections would ultimately be donated to the museum.[32]

These practices should be openly and rigorously questioned by our profession. Not surprisingly, according to published accounts, collectors/donors (who may also be trustees) routinely benefit from museum resources with special services not otherwise available to the general public.[33] It is time that the museum community re-examine closely the relationships with private collectors in the realm of museum collecting activities.

The impropriety in these relationships can lead to unexpected consequences. An Italian prosecutor charged a major American art museum curator of "collection laundering" based on the alleged relationship between the curator and donors of a collection that was largely without provenance.[34] Specifically, he alleges that the curator instructed the donors to purchase antiquities with faulty provenance, with the understanding that these objects would be later acquired from them by the museum. The allegation is that this interim step of ownership in a large domestic private collection would help to cleanse provenance of these objects, especially if the suspect objects were later published in the museum's catalogue. In the Italian prosecution's view, a museum curator would not agree to do special favors for a private collector (consulting on acquisitions, organizing a dedicated exhibit, and publishing a catalogue) unless a prior agreement for the donation/purchase of the collection were in place. It would be difficult to explain to this prosecutor or indeed anyone looking at this issue why an American museum might provide such favors to private collectors based on the mere hope of a future donation.

Another area ripe for reconsideration is the use of proceeds from the sale of deaccessioned objects. In this era of global financial crisis, many struggling museums may be tempted to follow the lead of some universities that recently sold valuable works from their museums to raise money for operating funds. Some have suggested that museums pledge their collections for loans to continue operations. Others, that museums should sell shares of time in their valuable collection objects to donors who would be free to take the works home for a portion of the year equal to their percentage of ownership. These are extremely troublesome developments that need the attention of policy makers. Registrars, as stewards of the collections, should make their voices heard loud and clear in the upcoming debate over these and many ethical issues that are bound to appear on the horizon. •

NOTES

1. Museum-specific policies focus the often broad ethical guidelines provided by professional groups, such as the American Association of Museums. The principles must be adapted in context to serve that museum's specific mission and types of objects in its collections. A one-size-fits-all collections management policy does not exist and each policy, not unlike a pair of eyeglasses, must be "individually prescribed and faithfully used." Malaro, Marie C. *Legal Primer on Managing Museum Collections.* 2nd ed. Washington D.C.: Smithsonian Press, 1998. 46.

2. Malaro, Marie C. *Museum Governance: Mission Ethics Policy.* Washington D.C.: Smithsonian Press, 1994.18.

3. The 1984 RCAAM Code of Ethics for Registrars states: "Registrars should be aware of, and not contribute to, the violation of tax, wildlife, import, or other laws and regulations governing acquisition of objects by their museums and other institutions with which they are involved." http://www.rcaam.org/ (accessed February 9, 2009).

4. The UNESCO Convention's Article 7(a) urged member nations to control by domestic law the acquisition policies of museums within their borders. However, the history of the negotiation and ratification of the Convention shows that Article 7(a) would be interpreted by the United States to apply only to institutions whose acquisition policy is subject to national control under existing domestic law (for example, museums controlled by government agencies, such as the Department of Interior museums and museums of the Armed Forces). See Bator, Paul M. 1988 *The International Trade in Art.* Chicago: University of Chicago Press (Midway reprint) 104. As the Convention was awaiting the passage by an act of Congress for implementation in the United States, a handful of museums and some museum professional groups established voluntary ethical policies in keeping with 7(a). The U.S. law implementing the UNESCO Convention took over a decade to pass.

5. From 1970 to late 1982 the debate continued until Congress passed The Convention on Cultural Property Implementation Act in December 1982 as Title II, Pub. L. 97–446, 19 U.S.C. Secs. 2601–2613) Convention on Cultural Property Implementation Act (CPIA).

6. For a selected but comprehensive list of ethical codes used by the museum profession, see American Association of Museums. *Information Center Fact Sheet: Standards and Best Practices for Museums.* Washington D.C.: American Association of Museums, 2008. http://www.aam-us.org/museumresources/ic/musref/loader.cfm?url=/commonspot/security/getfile.cfm&PageID=30932 (accessible to AAM members only, accessed February 9, 2009).

7. See the Harvard University Statement on Acquisitions (January 1972) and Smithsonian Institution Policy on Museum Acquisitions (May 1973) reproduced in Malaro, Marie C. *A Legal Primer on Managing Museum Collections.* 2nd ed. Washington D.C.: Smithsonian Press, 1998. Figures IV.1 and IV.2. The first museum to announce an acquisition policy of this nature was the University of Pennsylvania Museum on April 1, 1970. Others included the California State University at Long Beach, The Field Museum, Southern Illinois University, Washington State

Museum in Seattle, Peabody Museum in Salem, Massachusetts, Arizona State Museum in Tucson, and the Utah Museum of Natural History. See Bator, Paul M. 1988 *The International Trade in Art*. Chicago: University of Chicago Press (Midway reprint) note 144. Notably absent from this original list are major private art museums. To my knowledge, there have been no studies to evaluate the implementation of these early policies. Some of these few collecting organizations obligated themselves to make good faith inquiries into the provenance of objects offered for acquisition, professed to greatly limit acquisition of objects without provenance, and declared that they would not collect objects suspected to be stolen or illegally exported from their countries of origin. Not surprisingly, these museums also did not play a major role in the ensuing acquisition scandals of the last two decades.

8. The AAMD's membership consists of 190 active members who serve as directors of art museums, mostly in the United States but also several from Canada, and Mexico. The Association maintains a ceiling of 200 active members. Its broad purpose is to support its members in increasing the contribution of art museums to society. http://www.aamd.org. (accessed February 10, 2009). It publishes a Code of Ethics for its membership discussed below.

9. The AAMD resolution was adopted on January 23, 1973, and published in an article, "The AAMD Takes a Stand," *Museum News* (May 1973), 49. A close version of the same resolution appeared as a Joint Professional Policy on Museum Acquisitions published in *Museum News* (September 1973), 46, which was signed by representatives of the AAMD, American Association of Museums, the College Arts Association, the International Council of Museums, the Archeological Institute of America, the American Anthropological Association, and the Society of American Anthropology.

10. Association of Art Museum Directors, 1981, "A Code of Ethics for Art Museum Directors As Adopted by the Association of Art Museum Directors," published in *Professional Practices in Art Museums: Report of the Ethics and Standards Committee*. New York: Association of Art Museum Directors. ("1981 AAMD Code")

11. Presumably stolen in the traditional sense of taking wrongfully from a known rightful owner or in the broader sense of removing from a country in violation of so-called "patrimony laws" that declared cultural property state-owned.

12. Note, however, nothing in this 1981 AAMD Code provision expressly required an art museum director to abide by *export controls* of foreign nations. Absent such a prohibition, objects lacking legitimate export permits from their countries of origin could be acquired for art museum collections. Foreign export regulations attempt to control the removal of cultural property located within the country's borders, and as urged by archaeologists, typically smuggled objects are looted material headed for the international art market. Why this limitation? Perhaps because foreign export laws are not enforceable under U.S. law. In other words, a foreign export law may have been broken, but U.S. law has not. Also justifying lack of compliance with foreign export controls is the belief that export regulations of source countries are in effect an embargo on trade as export permits are rarely, if ever, issued. As implemented, such foreign export controls were argued to be contrary to U.S. policies that support free trade in cultural goods. In sum, the AAMD policy tracks what U.S. law would require, in large part.

13. By contrast, the position of archaeologists shared by source nations is that an unprovenanced antiquity of museum quality can be presumed to be the product of illicit looting. Acquisition by museums of unprovenanced objects fuels such activity that leads to the irretrievable loss of knowledge and destruction of sites (including other less market desirable objects) resulting from unscientific excavation. The term "provenance" refers to information on the history of an object. This includes its creation, the trail of ownership, exhibition, and publication. "Provenience" is a term used to define a work's archaeological find spot. An object's provenience is a part of its provenance. Urice, Stephen K. (2007) "Antiquities as Cultural Property: Dealing with the Past, Looking to the Future –An Introduction," *ALI/ABA Legal Issues of Museum Administration Course book* (Philadelphia: ALI/ABA), 26, 25, n2. "Unprovenanced" objects are those that come with no information about their history.

14. Association of Art Museum Directors, 1992, "A Code of Ethics for Art Museum Directors As Adopted by the Association of Art Museum Directors," published in *Professional Practices in Art Museums: Report of the Ethics and Standards Committee*. New York: Association of Art Museum Directors. ("1992 AAMD Code"). The 1992 AAMD Code declared that it is unprofessional for art museum director members: "(C) To acquire knowingly or allow to be recommended for acquisition any object that has been stolen, removed in contravention of treaties and international conventions to which the United States is a signatory, or illegally imported into the United States." Note that this provision refers to U.S. laws and treaties and conventions as limited by U.S. laws only. Why were we now less concerned with foreign ownership laws? A district court case that was decided three years before the AAMD issued this revised policy may have influenced this change. See note 13.

15. In *Peru v. Johnson*, 720 F. Supp. 810 (C.D. Cal. 1989), *aff'd sub nom., Peru v. Wendt*, 933 F.2d 1013 (9th Cir. 1991), the court held that the national laws of Peru declaring public ownership of all undocumented cultural objects were not sufficiently clear as to provide notice to U.S. citizens required under the due process clause. This decision was often cited for the proposition that broad foreign patrimony laws that declared all cultural property to be state owned would not necessarily be recognized as valid proof of ownership by U.S. Courts. By relying on this case regarding Peruvian law as precedent, museum decision-makers may have concluded (with some risk) that foreign patrimony laws generally could be ignored after an object had entered the United States and come under U.S. jurisdiction.

16. In addition to foreign prosecutions, a major shift in U.S. law has now left the door open for prosecutions under U.S. federal law of theft.

In addition to foreign prosecutions, a major shift in U.S. law has now left the door open for prosecutions under U.S. federal law of theft. In *United States v. Schultz*, 178 F. Supp 2nd 445 (S.D. N.Y. 2002) *aff'd* 333 F3d 393 (2nd Cir. 2003), *cert.*

denied 157 L.Ed. 2nd 891 (U.S., 2004), an antiquities dealer named Schultz was indicted in New York under the federal National Stolen Property Act ("NSPA") for one count of conspiring to receive stolen property. The property at issue was Egyptian antiquities illegally removed from Egypt after the 1983 law that vested ownership of all undiscovered antiquities in the national government. The U.S. court held that foreign patrimony law of Egypt would be given credence. The court concluded that "[w]e see no reason that property stolen from a foreign sovereign should be treated any differently from property stolen from a foreign museum or private home" for purposes of federal criminal theft law. 333 F3rd at 47. Commentators note that following *Schultz*, U.S. courts will be left to determine the applicability of potentially over 100 different foreign patrimony statutes, many dating back to the early 20th century. It is argued that short of a court case, museums may not know whether a country's law is valid or not.

In the civil law context, the *Schultz* criminal case has additional implications. Title to undocumented antiquities can be subject to challenge by countries of origin in civil cases brought in the United States basing ownership on patrimony laws. The burden on a source country seeking restitution in a civil case is to prove ownership via the patrimony law and removal of the state-owned object across its borders after the ownership-vesting statue was enacted. No proof of guilty knowledge of the law is required. A first major change regarding compliance with foreign laws followed this development through guidelines issued by the AAMD in 2004.

17. The AAMD published a new version of its Professional Practices in Art Museums in 2001. In that document, for the first time, there is a provision directing investigation of provenance as a step in the acquisition process: "The director must ensure that best efforts are made to determine the provenance of a work of art considered for acquisition." (Paragraph 18) In addition, in 2004 and again in 2008 the AAMD issued new specific guidelines that are discussed below.

18. American Association of Museums, *Code of Ethics for Museums*, Washington D.C.: American Association of Museums 1993, 2000.

19. American Association of Museums *Statement on Cultural Property* (accessed at http:www.aam-us.org March 17, 1999) This document is no longer available on AAM's website as it has been replaced by new standards released in July 2008 discussed below.

20. The J. Paul Getty Museum was the first large art museum actively buying in the art market that departed from replying on the AAMD Code alone by publishing its own museum-specific acquisition policy for antiquities in 1987. This was over 14 years after the Smithsonian and Harvard museums passed their UNESCO-inspired policies. From 1987 to 1995, the Getty policy required warranties from dealers that included warranties of clean title, of legal export, and that all other customs and patrimony laws, regulations, and requirements of all relevant countries had been met. As long as a dealer was willing to sign the museum's warranty, only two additional inquiries were prescribed: Getty staff was directed to notify potential countries of origin about proposed acquisition and also to run a check

through a stolen art database. J. Paul Getty Acquisition Policy for Classical Antiquities, November 13, 1987. Notifying countries of origin has been criticised as an ineffective substitute for conducting provenance research or requiring the seller to provide provenance documentation. Many objects in the market are undocumented and neither the countries of origin or so-called stolen art databases are likely to have information about them. The Getty issued a revised policy in 1995 that dropped the need to contact countries of origin and limited itself to acquiring only "known collections" by requiring a so-called "provenance by publication." Object must have appeared in a publication as of November 1995 to be considered for acquisition. This policy led to Getty's acceptance of the controversial Fleischman Collection that met the "provenance by publication" requirement through an earlier museum catalogue published by the Getty itself. Objects from this collection, many of them lacking any other form of documentation were subject to restitution claims and several were returned to Italy. Subsequently in October 2006, the Getty announced a significantly strengthened art acquisition policy that commits the Getty to "further developing its collection according to the highest ethical standards and in compliance with all applicable laws."

The revised policy adopts November 17, 1970, the date the UNESCO Convention was signed, as the key date for determining whether an ancient work of art or archaeological material can be considered for acquisition. The Getty's previous policy required objects to be from "established, well-documented collections" and published before 1995. See a further discussion of new ethical guidelines below. http://www.getty.edu/news/press/center/revised_acquisition_policy_release_102606.html (accessed February 10, 2009)

21. One major art museum released its policy for the first time only in late 2008. See note 31 below. Those few museums that did pass meaningful acquisition policies in the early 1970s in keeping with the goals of the UNESCO Convention went much farther than the demands of museum professional codes in the next decades by requiring good faith inquiries into the provenance, greatly limiting acquisition of unprovenanced objects, and declaring that they would not collect objects suspected to be stolen or illegally exported from their countries of origin. See note 7 above.

22. See note 7 above.

23. In the early 1990s the AAM Task Force commissioned to re-write the AAM Code of Ethics originally suggested that adherence to the AAM Code of Ethics should be made a condition of membership for museums wishing to join the AAM. This provision was dropped in the final version adopted in 1994.

24. Registrars Committee of the American Association of Museums, Code of Ethics for Registrars 1984. http://www.rcaam.org/ (accessed February 9, 2009).

25. For a discussion of the reach of these guidelines, see DeAngelis, Ildiko. "How Much Provenance is Enough: Post Schultz Guidelines for Museum Acquisition of Archaeological Materials and Ancient Art," in *Art and Cultural Heritage: Law, Policy and Practice*, edited by Barbara Hoffman. Cambridge: Cambridge University Press, 2006. 398—08.

26. http://www.aamd.org/newsroom/ documents/2008 ReportAndRelease.pdf, (July 4, 2008). (accessed February 10, 2009).

27. http://aam-us.org/museumresources/ethics/upload/Standards%20Regarding%20Archaeological%20Material%20 and%20Ancient%20Art.pdf (July 2008) (accessed February 10, 2009).

28. http://www.aamd.org/newsroom/ documents/2008ReportAndRelease.pdf, (July 4, 2008).

29. http://aamdobjectregistry.org (accessed February 5, 2009).

30. http://aam-us.org/museumresources/ethics/upload/Standards%20Regarding%20Archaeological%20Material%20 and%20Ancient%20Art.pdf (July 2008) (accessed February 9, 2009).

31. See the strengthened Getty policy issued in 2006 discussed in note 20 above. A moratorium on the acquisition of undocumented antiquities was also declared by the Indianapolis Museum of Art (IMA) on April 16, 2007, which will remain in effect while the IMA "evaluates and reframes" its current policies on the collection of antiquities and ancient art. "We hope it will be a small step towards stemming the tide of illegal excavation or clandestine removal of accidentally discovered objects from countries the world over," said IMA Director and CEO Maxwell Anderson in an internet posting on Apr. 30, 2007. The IMA subsequently adopted the changes outlined in the new 2008 AAMD guidelines. So did the Metropolitan Museum of Art. In June 2008 the Executive Committee of the Board of Trustees of The Metropolitan Museum of Art formally accepted the AAMD 2008 Guidelines on the Acquisition of Archaeological Materials and Ancient Art, and on November 12, 2008, the Board of Trustees adopted a revised Collections Management Policy incorporating those guidelines. http://www.metmuseum.org/press_room/full_release.asp?prid={85EDA1CD-A74C-447A-9D2A-1494592D9256} (accessed February 10, 2009).

32. Silver, Vernon 2006 "Money and Power at the Met." *Bloomberg Markets* April: 138-146; Darraby , Jessica. "To Have and To Hold." *California Lawyer* 26(5): 22–28.

33. Silver 138–146.

34. DeAngelis, Ildiko P. Interview: Italian Prosecutor Paolo Ferri in Rome, Italy, March 2007. *Yearbook of Cultural Property Law 2008.* ed. by Sherry Hutt and David Tarler. Walnut Creek, California: Left Coast Press., 2008.17–18, 25–27.

ALISON EDWARDS

Museums' critical role in promoting scholarship and preservation has inclined museum leaders, and the museum-going public, to regard museums as a place where civic and social discourse is somehow kept apart from issues of belief and the sacred. Yet a resurgence of interest in spirituality and belief across societies, and a renewed commitment to traditions and symbolic artifacts by many living traditions in the United States and throughout the world, now confronts curators and directors with the reality that the items in their collection have never lost their religious significance. . .

Lawrence E. Sullivan
Stewards of the Sacred: Sacred Objects, Religious Culture, and the Museum as Social Institution, Harvard Center for the Study of World Religions, 2001[1]

Most museums are regarded as secular spaces. However, a significant percentage of museum collections worldwide have religious significance; many of these objects are considered sacred by living religious communities.[2] Museum collections also contain many objects that may be culturally sensitive, including funerary objects, human remains,[3] objects of cultural patrimony, or other artifacts that are highly charged due to their historical relevance.[4]

When museums serve as the repository for sacred objects, sacred and secular space and experience intersect. Examples of this intersection include (but are not limited to) the demand for repatriation of sacred objects, the veneration of sacred objects in public galleries, loan agreements that allow sacred objects in museum collections to be used in religious ceremonies and then returned to museum storage, care protocols for sacred objects in museum collections involving restricting access to objects or other special conditions, and conservation practices that avoid methods that can desecrate sacred materials.

Sacred objects have been acquired by museums in many ways. Some were made by artists who intended them to be collected, displayed and even venerated in museums.[5] Some are still owned by religious organizations but cared for by (or loaned to) museums; in these instances the objects are frequently taken out of the museum for ceremonies and then returned to the museum for specialized storage, research, or display purposes.[6] Some sacred objects were sold or donated to museums by religious organizations. Some were stolen. And some sacred objects and human remains have come to be in museum collections through painful and violent historical circumstances, including acts of religious suppression, war, and genocide.[7]

After sacred objects and human remains entered U.S. museum collections, museums often reflected dominant-culture bias in their treatment of these sacred artifacts.[8] Museums' treatment of sacred objects in ways that are offensive to practitioners and violate cultural practices has led in many cases to demands by groups affiliated with these objects—from governments to religious institutions to individuals or families—that they be returned or handled with heightened sensitivity.

Museums must respond ethically to demands for reform regarding the disposition of sacred objects, some of which entered museum collections under questionable circumstances. However, defining what is sacred or culturally sensitive, who the affiliated groups are, and who can speak for an affiliated group can sometimes be difficult. Very fundamental questions—about the mission of museums, the meaning of the term religion, and the definition of a religious community—are implicated. Primary among them are:[9]

1. What is sacred—or integral and essential—to a culture?

2. Who has the expertise—or the right—to determine that?

3. What specific legal rights and basic rights must be considered when addressing these questions?

4. What process—of inclusion, consultation, partnership, representation—should be instituted to ensure that these basic rights are met?

Developing procedures for the care and disposition of sacred or sensitive objects must engage these four questions.

This chapter will explore these questions by discussing precedents for the care of sacred and culturally sensitive objects from four sources:

1. *Museum-specific policies* for the care of sacred objects in museums[10] and policy guidelines including the Association of Art Museum Directors' (AAMD) *Draft Sacred Objects Principles and Guidelines*. This chapter will discuss sample policies from select museums in the U.S., Canada, and Australia. These museums have advanced experience in developing new policy and practices for the care of sensitive collections due in part to laws governing indigenous groups' rights in their respective countries. Two are national museums—the Smithsonian National Museum of the American Indian and the National Museum of Australia—with monumental collections of Native American material culture, amassed in part as a result of past governmental policies. A third, Harvard's Peabody Museum of Archaeology and Ethnology, is a university museum with one of the largest collections of Native North American material. Two of the museums are Native American/First Nation institutions: the Alutiiq Museum and Archaeological Repository and the Woodland Hills Cultural Centre. It is unusual for museums to have developed or published internal policies for the care of sacred or sensitive objects. The selected policies were published and in some cases developed as part of a five-year research project focusing on museums and religion at Harvard's Center for the Study of World Religions. All recognize cultural or religious knowledge and outline institutional processes for determining the disposition of sacred materials involving consultations and partnerships with affiliated groups. These policies may be valuable models for other institutions seeking to develop their own internal policy. A broader survey of museum policies worldwide, including, for example, sample policies from Asia, Africa, or Latin America, is beyond the scope of this short chapter.

2. *The 1989 National Museum of the American Indian Act (NMAI Act) and the 1990 Native American Graves Protection and Repatriation Act (NAGPRA)*. These laws are discussed in detail in the chapter entitled "Complying With NAGPRA" by Timothy McKeown *et al*. These two laws recognize the violation of Native Americans' civil and human rights to equal protection for gravesites and religious freedoms.[11] The laws also recognize cultural knowledge and expertise in defining sacred materials, and they require Native representation through consultations during an inventory process to identify sacred materials in museum collections and potentially return them to Native tribes. The laws define four categories of sensitive materials: Native American human remains, funerary objects, sacred objects, and communal property (Echo-Hawk, 2004; Pepper Henry, 2004; West, 2004).

3. *International laws, resolutions, and codes of ethics addressing cultural property issues* are outlined in depth in Ildiko DeAngelis's chapter in this volume. These laws, resolutions and codes outline basic rights and legal rights that, if violated, can lead to the repatriation of sacred or culturally-sensitive objects to affiliated groups. These laws, resolutions and codes mandate at least minimum museum compliance in regard to sacred objects.[12]

4. *Innovations in the care and conservation of contemporary art* are discussed in depth in the chapter "Documenting Contemporary Art" in this volume. Some approaches to the care of sacred materials that have been deemed radical have direct corollaries in the field of contemporary art. In particular, conservation practices in contemporary art museums similarly seek to preserve the conceptual integrity of a work as a priority above precisely preserving the physical work. Similarly, when caring for sacred

materials, the cultural integrity of an object may be preserved as a priority above the strict preservation of the physical object.[13] In both cases museum staff recognize the expertise, authority and intent of the work's maker/affiliated group, and in both cases processes for discerning such intent include extensive consultations.

The specific examples of policy and related practices discussed in this article may be relevant and useful in other museum settings. However, these policies and practices should not simply be transplanted to another museum without conducting new consultations, guided by the above principles and specific to the sacred or culturally sensitive objects in the museum's collection. Each museum must work in partnership with groups affiliated with sensitive collections in order to define its own policy.

What is Sacred—or Integral or Essential—to a Culture?

Museum staff should not attempt to define what is sacred for a group. Rather, staff must seek to work with legitimate representatives of established traditions to determine what objects are sacred, integral, or essential to a living culture or religion.[14] With that said, concepts and working definitions can be helpful orientation points in the complicated project of understanding what is sacred and what is culturally sensitive. Examples from museum-specific policies, museum codes of ethics, U.S. laws, and the cultural heritage and comparative study of religion literature follow.

To begin, sacred objects frequently fall into the larger category of cultural property, which Sherry Hutt defines as

> . . . the tangible and intangible effects of an individual or group of people that define their existence, and place them temporally or geographically in relation to their belief systems and their familial and political groups, providing meaning to their lives.
> . . . Cultural property is so central to personal identity that the International Conference on Cultural Property at the United Nations termed it 'ethnocide' to withhold or destroy cultural property.[15]

Within this larger category of cultural property, some objects are also considered to be *sacred*. Sacredness or holiness is a cross-cultural concept . . . which followers of every tradition understand and describe differently. In many theologies sacredness can be understood as spiritual power.[16] Spiritual power thus permeates or resides within sacred objects. Sacred objects can be understood in many religious traditions to connect human beings to a sacred reality; the object of such power is therefore treated with care. In many theologies the mishandling, or desecration, of sacred objects can cause harm, either to those handling the object or in some cases to those individuals connected to the object, whether or not they are involved in the mishandling of the object.[17]

The process of consecration provides important insight into the nature of sacred objects. Consecration can take many forms. It can encompass (but is not limited to) one or more of the following processes:

- *Formal consecration by a religious authority.* Objects can be consecrated by a religious authority, such as a priest, who performs rituals or blessings.

- *Sacred symbolism.* Sacred symbolism can be employed by an artist to create a sacred object. Or an object that is not man-made, like a stone or tree, can be recognized for its inherent sacred symbolism.

- *Ritual creation.* An artist can ritually prepare him or herself before creating a sacred object or perform sacred rituals during the act of creating the object; the artist's intention and prayer is one way of consecrating the object.

- *Relationship to a sacred place or time.* Objects can be consecrated because they originate from or traveled to a sacred site. Or materials may be gathered to represent significant places and times and combined in containers, such as amulets.

- *Veneration.* In some cases, objects have been deemed consecrated because people have used them in prayer; these cases do not always include religious authorities.

- *Human remains.* In some cases human remains are considered consecrated because they housed the soul or spirit of a human being. Relics are the remains or partial remains of spiritual leaders, sacred for example in many Christian and Buddhist traditions. Some traditions consider all human remains sacred, not only those of revered individuals, which is often the case in Native North American religions.

As previously noted, museum staffs should not seek to define what is sacred to any religious group *for* that religious group. However, museum representatives can develop definitions and guidelines in partnership with affiliated communities. In practice, working definitions for sacred and culturally sensitive materials give institutions and communities a starting point from which to begin conversations about sensitive collections. Several examples are presented below from the NMAI Act and NAGPRA, museum-specific policies, and codes of ethics:

The NMAI Act (as amended) and NAGPRA. These laws both define sacred objects as follows:

Sacred/ceremonial objects means items that are specific ceremonial objects needed by traditional Native American religious leaders for the practice of traditional Native American religions by their present-day adherents.[18]
[43 CFR 10.2 (d)(3)].

The laws also provide definitions for funerary objects, cultural patrimony, and human remains. See McKeown et. al in this volume for a detailed discussion of these definitions.

Museum-specific policies. The National Museum of Australia's Policy on Aboriginal and Torres Strait Islander Secret/Sacred and Private Material defines sacred objects, along with "secret" and "private" materials:

Secret/sacred material: objects, including photographs, and related knowledge or information that is restricted in the sense that only certain categories of people can see the objects or be privy to the knowledge or information. All references to "secret/sacred material" in this policy should be taken to refer to Aboriginal or Torres Islander secret/sacred material.[19]

"Guidelines for the Spiritual Care of Objects" from the Alutiiq Museum in Kodiak, Alaska states that:

All objects require respectful treatment to maintain their integrity and please their sua. As such, the guidelines include provisions for the spiritually sensitive care of all objects in the museum's holdings. In addition, however, the Alutiiq Museum recognizes four classes of religious items that have the potential to be considered sacred. These objects were identified with the help of oral histories, anthropological research, and historical accounts and do not necessarily represent a complete list of sacred items. Furthermore, not all items from each context are necessarily considered sacred. Each object must be individually evaluated to ascertain its cultural context and potential meaning.

1. Ceremonial items: Objects used in religious practices that were specifically designed to interact with the spirit world, particularly those used in the winter hunting festivals. This category of objects includes masks of all sizes (plank masks, portrait masks, and maskettes); musical instruments (drums and rattles); and some ceremonial clothing (parkas, headdresses, dance belts, jewelry).

2. Shamanic tools: Objects used in the performance of shamanic tasks, such as healing, communicating with the spirit world, and foretelling the future. This category of objects includes shamans' dolls, amulets, whistles, rattles, and clothing (belts, aprons, bracelets, headdresses).

3. Whaling gear: Objects used by whalers in preparation for and execution of the hunt. This category of objects includes preparatory gear (model boats, tools for making aconite poison), hunting amulets, hunting tools, and special clothing (pointed hats, rattles). This category may also include any materials from a whaler's cave.

4. Church artifacts: Objects used in the practice of Russian Orthodoxy, including crosses, icons,

Bibles, grave markers, vestments and other religious furnishings.

Codes of Ethics. The Association of Art Museum Directors' Sacred Objects Principles and Guidelines defines sacred objects as follows:

> In general, sacred works of art are venerated objects created for use in ritual or other ceremonial activities and needed by present-day adherents of a traditional religion to continue the practice of their religion.

All of the above definitions serve as a starting point for identifying sacred materials and should be expanded and interpreted in consultation with appropriate religious or cultural representatives. (A discussion of how to identify such representatives follows.)

Who has the Expertise—or the Right—to Determine What is Sacred—or Integral or Essential—to a Culture?

An affiliated group can be broadly understood as a cultural or religious tradition from which the object emerged and which continues today as a living tradition. Within that definition, it is important to recognize the right of religious and cultural groups to define their own beliefs and practices. These may in some cases have evolved from specific beliefs and practices of the past. Religious practices evolve and change over time, just as institutional practices do. For example, notions of conservation and related best practices in museums have radically changed over the last century.[20]

Collections management staff can play a central role in identifying affiliated groups. In some cases a group may initiate contact with the museum regarding sacred objects of interest to them that are known to be in the museum's collection. In other cases museum staff may discover potentially sensitive material in the collection and initiate contact with a religious or cultural group.

A first step is always to consolidate, organize, and review existing documentation in order to determine the provenance of an object or gaps in documentation that require further research. As a second step, should the provenance for the object prove to be incompletely documented, museum staff may

conduct new research, guided by models presented in a discussion of inclusive practices, to follow.

What Specific Basic Rights and Legal Rights Must be Considered When Addressing These Questions?

The following rights must be considered when addressing the disposition of sacred objects in museum collections:

Human rights are generally understood as those guaranteed to an individual simply by being born, not those granted by a nation to its citizens. They include the right to life and liberty; freedom of thought and expression, including religious freedom and cultural continuity; and equality before the law. For example, removing objects from a community that people need in order to continue religious or cultural practices without their consent interferes with their right to religious freedom, a human right that in the U.S. is protected by the Constitution. Such removal also violates the human right to cultural continuity, protected by international resolutions such as the United Nations Declarations on Human Rights and on the Rights of Indigenous Peoples. Although the latter has not yet been signed by the U.S., it must remain an important guide for museum practitioners.

Civil rights are those guaranteed by laws of various nations, including laws that offer protections for the categories of human rights listed above. Civil rights movements thus seek the human right to equal protection under national laws. Equal protections for religious freedom or for the protection of gravesites from looting are violated if one group is treated differently, as has historically been the case in the U.S. for African Americans, Native Americans, and many other groups.

Property rights. Property rights apply to individuals, groups, and institutions and are protected by the U.S. Constitution and the U.N. Universal Declaration on Human Rights. The involuntary alienation of an artifact from a community, family, or individual or otherwise questionable provenance may violate property rights. Equally, an object improperly repatriated to the wrong party would be in violation of property rights.

Intellectual freedom. Intellectual freedom is a human right protected by the *Universal Declaration of Human Rights.* Article 19 of the Declaration states: "Everyone has the right to freedom of opinion and expression; this right includes freedom to hold opinions without interference and to seek, receive, and impart information and ideas through any media and regardless of frontiers." This right has been cited by some opponents of repatriation who seek access to artifacts and human remains.

There is much disagreement regarding the interpretation—and prioritization—of how these rights apply to the disposition of sacred objects in museum collections.

Some argue that:[21, 22]

•Sacred objects or objects of cultural heritage within museum collections should be seen as the common inheritance of humanity, not the property of any one group, since cultural and political boundaries shift over time.

•Western "encyclopedic" museums can often provide greater access to objects of cultural heritage than can museums in countries of the objects' origin and Western museums can also frequently safeguard these objects more successfully than can countries of origin.

•Museums are able to successfully serve, above any one political agenda, as the stewards of cultural heritage on behalf of all groups. Diverse representation in museum staffs or boards of trustees is not required to fulfill this role. [23]

•The meanings of objects change over time and thus no one interpretation should take precedence.

•To determine protocols for the disposition and care of sacred objects based upon their religious or cultural meaning elevates the right to religious freedom for a few over the right to intellectual freedom of the academic community as well as the education of the general public.

But others argue the reverse:[24]

•Not everything belongs equally to everyone; often specific groups can claim primacy in their relationship to specific sacred objects and objects of cultural heritage, and these relationships are verifiable and justified.

•Museums have not always been ethical in their treatment of cultural groups due to their treatment of affiliated sacred objects. This treatment has in some cases violated human rights and civil rights protected by the Constitution, U.S. laws, and international resolutions.

•Much museum bias has been due to museums' excluding cultural groups from their decision-making processes as partners, consultants, or members of museum staffs and boards of trustees.

•In cases where scientific and academic interests conflict with Constitutionally-protected human rights, human rights should take precedence.

•Institutional best practices continue to evolve and must be updated. Museums must recognize past abuses and reform practices when necessary to promote social justice.

•It is true that cultural and political boundaries shift over time. Yet it is also frequently true that Western museums promoting this argument have more distance from disputed objects of cultural heritage than nations requesting the return of such objects.

•Only a very small percentage of objects amassed in Western encyclopedic museums, on average 5% or less, are on display. Objects in storage are generally not accessible to the public.

•It is contradictory for Western museums to claim that they are better able to safeguard objects of cultural patrimony than non-Western museums when Western nations may have influenced the atmosphere of risk (such as is the case with the frequently cited example of the Baghdad Museum, made vulnerable due to the invasion of Iraq by a coalition of Western nations).

Clearly, it can be difficult to determine what is sacred or essential to a culture or individuals belonging to a particular cultural group and who has a right to make such a determination. Yet just as clearly, not everything is equally the common inheritance of all people. It is inherently contradictory to argue on the one hand that Western museums should not be encumbered by cultural politics and do not need to be inclusive in their practices and on the other hand that these museums can serve as the stewards of and repository for cultural heritage on behalf of all groups. These arguments incorrectly cast Western museums' stewardship as a neutral position rather than one of many implicated by the term "cultural politics."

In practice, museum staff must work in partnership with the appropriate representatives of cultural groups to determine if human or civil rights were violated in the acquisition and subsequent treatment of sacred objects, if any laws were violated, and if the continued alienation of the object or institutional treatment of the object violates others' human or civil rights. Where this is the case, such rights can reasonably be judged to outweigh property law or a museums' fiduciary responsibility to the public trust. This can mean privileging the human rights of affiliated groups when applicable over unrestricted access to sacred objects, or access without consent, by non-affiliated groups.

What Process—of Inclusion, Consultation, Partnership, Representation—Should be Instituted to Ensure that These Basic Rights are Respected?

Key precedents for inclusive processes for the care of sacred objects are found in the NMAI Act and NAGPRA, museum-specific policies for the care of sacred objects and associated knowledge, and corollaries in the care and preservation of contemporary art. These precedents all address the following issues: how to conduct *consultations*, access to sacred or sensitive collections and associated knowledge, developing and administering *care and exhibition protocols,* and repatriation. I have thus organized my discussion of inclusive processes using the above themes.

Consultation

Although NAGPRA mandates consultation, in practice this mandate has been variously or generally ignored, conducted poorly, and (though in far too few cases) conducted successfully with benefits to all involved. Elements of successful consultations

identified in the post-NAGPRA repatriation literature[25] include the following points:

•Consult with official representatives of an affiliated or affected group, not any member of the group. NAGPRA requires museums to consult with tribes' political leadership. Whenever possible, initiate contact with affiliated groups; do not wait for them to contact the museum. If feasible, meet with group leaders in their offices before they visit the museum. This demonstrates a commitment to establishing a relationship with parity.

•Recognize cultural expertise and knowledge in the research and documentation process. NAGPRA recognizes oral histories and other forms of cultural knowledge.

•Provide delegations with documentation of potentially sensitive collections prior to a consultation to allow groups to prioritize their review of objects.

•Develop complete documentation of consultations. Museum staff should attribute recommendations made by specific representatives to the individual speaking, not to the group as a whole. Museum staff should discuss issues of confidentiality with groups prior to a consultation so that restricted information is not recorded inappropriately. For example, some information could be deemed inappropriate for inclusion in a museum's database at all; some can be entered if access is restricted to certain individuals identified in advance by the museum and cultural group. And in some cases audio or video recording proceedings, including songs, prayers or chants, might be fully or partially restricted.

•Accommodate rituals, ceremonies, and other cultural practices during meetings or as requested during a consultation:

    a. Rituals can be appropriately represented as cultural practices if there are legal concerns regarding conflicts of church and state.

    b. Staff may voluntarily participate in ceremonies if invited to do so but must never be required to participate, which would violate their rights.

Museum-specific policies reviewed for this article[26] are in agreement with the literature cited above on how to conduct consultations properly. All affirm that consultation is required to fulfill the museum's mission.[27] All agree that museum staff must recognize the expertise of a cultural representative to identify sacred or sensitive objects. Sven Haakanson, Jr., who received his Ph.D. in anthropology from Harvard University and returned to his hometown in Kodiak to direct the Alutiiq Museum, emphasizes the role of traditional leaders in identifying and interpreting sacred materials:

> We asked Elders if they could translate the word "sacred" into Alutiiq and Mary Haakanson suggested arinaartuq, "that which is important within and deserves respect." The word itself suggests that sacred is not just the object, but what is embodied in it by the makers and Creator. This is very important to understand and respect. However, it requires an Elder to teach us the importance and significance of an item beyond our respect for that item.[28]

Further, all of the policies agree with the following recommendations for successful consultations.

Prior to a museum visit:

•Delegations should be provided with full documentation from the museum's files, including accession records and affiliated archives, of potentially sensitive items and asked which objects or categories of objects are of most interest to them.

•If the representative of the group is a political rather than a religious leader, he or she should be advised that it may be helpful to include religious leaders in the consultation.[29]

•Delegations should be made aware of museum staff's responsibility to the museum with regard to documenting the consultation. Let the delegation know if and how they can share information that will not be recorded, and ask how to identify what information is for the record and what is restricted.

•Delegations should be fully briefed on any risks involved due to the use of pesticides and other toxic conservation methods on objects in the collection.

    a. Pesticides and other toxins create risks for people who may use or wear the object in ceremonies.

    b. Delegations should be advised of the options for testing collections for toxicity, as these tests may also be seen as desecration.[30]

Questions museum staff should ask prior to a consultation include:

•Will the delegation use photography? If so, what equipment will be used? Delegations should be advised that flash photography should generally be no less than ten feet from objects, if applicable. If the group plans to use video, describe the light conditions in the area of the museum where the consultation will take place (or improve the lighting).[31]

Questions during a consultation should include (beyond the obvious identification of objects and their origin, meaning, and use):

•What objects may be displayed or used for educational purposes?

•Are any of the objects essential to ongoing religious practices?

•Are there recommendations for how objects should be stored?

•Does the community wish to borrow objects for ceremonial purposes (this could include objects that will later be repatriated or objects that will remain in the museum collection)?[32]

In the field of contemporary art, as discussed by Mark Schlemmer in this volume, consultation methods for working with living artists often parallel methods for consulting with communities and sacred materials. Recommended practices of use to our discussion include:

•Consultations should include "multiple voices in conducting the interview" including artist, curator, conservator, technician, art historian, art-handler, registrar, etc.."

•During consultations, incorporate access to the object, whether in storage or installed in the museum galleries. If the work is installed in a public gallery the installation and accompanying interpretation can be approved or critiqued.

•Preferred methods for documenting consultations include a) using questionnaires; b) recording detailed notes; and c) photographing, audiotaping or videotaping interviews and on-site consultations that include access to the work. Videotaping and photography should focus on the artist and artwork, not museum staff. This documentation must necessarily exceed the documentation of media (i.e., should not be limited to the object itself) and include the conceptual foundation of the work.

Access

Museum-specific policies for the care of sacred or sensitive material balance the need for increased access for communities to sacred or sensitive material[33] with the need to protect sacred or sensitive material from inappropriate contact or handling. When dealing with esoteric material culture or knowledge, in some cases museums may properly act to restrict access to information or objects. This increased access to sensitive objects for affiliated communities may occur while seeking to decrease access for others.[34] Not all information is meant to be accessible to all. This is true for institutions that are responsible for individuals' medical records or, in museums, financial information related to institutional donors. Therefore, as previously noted, when conducting consultations museum staff should inform traditional religious leaders that they should not share restricted information that they would not want included in museum records. Information that is sensitive but deemed necessary to share with the museum can be restricted to certain staff members' access through a tiered access database. For example, at the NMAI:

> There are circumstances when Native representatives provide confidential and/or sensitive information that is not intended for wide distribution to staff or public, including the location of burial sites of human remains and funerary objects repatriated

by the museum, the contents of ceremonial bundles, and the disclosure of ritual or ceremonial activities associated with collections in the museum's possession. (The database) provides a way to control access to sensitive collections information through a hierarchy of controls.[35]

Museums should therefore:

•Tier access to sensitive information in museum databases so that not all staff may access certain records, as is the case, for example, with museum donors' financial records.

•Maintain essential knowledge needed for the ongoing care of sensitive collections at an institutional, not individual, level. Individual staff may leave the institution, taking critical knowledge with them.

•Segregate sensitive collections in storage areas if this tactic is recommended in consultations.

•Tag sensitive collections in the museum's databases with a warning that alerts staff of care and handling methods. Such warnings can be used without revealing sensitive knowledge regarding why objects require this status. When objects should properly be handled by one gender or another in accordance with cultural protocols, this information should be shared in the records and staff asked to comply on a voluntary basis.[36]

•If requested, abstain from publishing images of sensitive objects or related information in print or on the Internet if this would violate religious practices or is otherwise offensive to the community.

•Designate staff to oversee specialized care of collections.

•Respect the wishes of affiliated communities regarding researchers' or others' requests directed to the museum asking for access to sacred or sensitive collections. Many museums refer such requests to the community for their approval before granting access.[37]

•Respect the wishes of affiliated communities regarding conservation practices. Some conservation methods may desecrate sacred materials. (Many museum conservators have developed new conservation methods that are both effective and culturally appropriate.)[38]

In sum, as Sven Haakanson notes:

As we learn and understand that we are dealing with sensitive knowledge, we move the recordings and/or objects into a restricted access area; do not use this information in our publications; inform our staff about restrictions and the sensitive nature of an item; document this process so we know why this information should be restricted. (This need not be detailed; simply indicating that it is 'sensitive information, only for other Natives' may be sufficient).[39]

Developing and Administering Care Protocols

When caring for sacred objects in general, museum staff must not take on the role of a surrogate for traditional religious leaders. Rituals and other ceremonial interactions should always be performed by a religious leader designated by the affiliated group.

Protocols for the care of sacred objects are primarily designed to minimize staff interactions with powerful, potentially dangerous objects, in order to keep these objects in a dormant stage. Indeed, when religious leaders do perform rituals and ceremonies in museums, as they regularly do at the Smithsonian National Museum of the American Indian (NMAI), such ceremonies are often designed to bless and protect staff from risks due to their proximity to powerful objects and to keep collections safe from disturbances that might inadvertently activate them.

Care protocols for sacred objects are thus often intended to isolate or protect sacred material from inappropriate contact. These protections can include, but are not limited to, handling restrictions, the burning of offerings, adding offerings to storage, placing objects in alignment with the cardinal directions, and gender separation in storage.[40] Many objects are deemed too powerful to be handled by non-initiates. These objects are frequently stored in segregated areas with warnings attached to alert staff of the handling restriction. Other objects are placed in certain alignments in storage or separated from

objects that should not be in proximity to them.

Offerings may also be added to storage areas or used in ceremonies in museums. If offerings are to be burned, ideally an area for this purpose, either inside or outside the museum, can be designated. When a designated space for burning offerings is inside the museum, as is the case with the Harvard Peabody Museum of Archaeology and Ethnology and the NMAI, fire systems are coordinated with the facilities department to allow smoke in a segregated safe area without setting off alarms.

To track a complex array of care protocols at the Harvard Peabody Museum of Archaeology and Ethnology, three statuses are applied in the collections database: a) collections: handling consideration; b) collections: care consideration; c) exhibits: exhibit consideration. An authority record is also created; the "consideration field" in the database is filled in with the appropriate tag—handling, collections, or exhibits consideration, as noted above. Staff then use the "remarks" field to add descriptions or explanations regarding the status consideration and how to proceed.[41]

Offerings added to the collection are not accessioned but are tracked differently in the database.

. . . all offerings are entered into (the database) and given a tracking number that identifies it as an "unaccessioned item that resides in the storage area and is identified in the database." This is similar to the museum's tracking of other items such as high-end exhibit mounts and documentary photographs. Staff members needing additional information about the offering can retrieve the pertinent details from the database as needed.[42]

The physical organization of offerings is also a consideration:

Unique storage containers are used in most cases in order to visually segregate the offerings from accessioned collections. This prevents the accidental moving or inspection of the item during standard collections management work in the storage areas. Acid free, archival-quality cardboard boxes that are a different brand from other storage containers are used. These standard box sizes also allow the museum to more easily facilitate the planning of the quantity and type of offerings before the actual event. Offerings are generally placed in the open box adjacent to or in the vicinity of specific collections. Paper or plastic bags, if feasible, are sometimes used to conform to the museum's integrated pest management program.[43]

Once in storage, offerings may require upkeep.

The specific storage conditions and specific uses of the offerings are discussed with tribal representatives during consultation visits. The repatriation department works with collections management to permanently place the object in storage and to instruct the relevant museum personnel as needed. The collections management department also proactively monitors when and if museum activities may affect the offerings or their related collection. Annual checks are also made of the objects to insure their integrity and storage.[44]

Additional institutional structures can assist those staff who have responsibility for the care of sacred material in communicating essential information to other staff. For example, in addition to disseminating guidelines for handling sensitive objects and issuing care protocols through the database, care requirements can be discussed at staff meetings and communicated through the museum intranet or memoranda.[45]

Special considerations for sacred materials also impact exhibition practices. As outlined in the NMAI policy:

Religious and ceremonial objects shall be exhibited and displayed only with the consent of the culturally affiliated group. Before displaying religious, ceremonial, or potentially sensitive material as part of exhibitions or public programs, curators should consult with interested and concerned parties and shall consider and be guided by their views in determining the methods of display. Planning of exhibitions—form and content—shall be done in consultation with Native American representatives of the tribe and/or culture involved to assure historical and/or cultural accuracy in the presentation of all information and materials, and to avoid desecration, insensitive treatment, and inappropriate interpretation of religious or ceremonial materials.[46]

Repatriation

If a community requests the return of sacred or sensitive material, factors that must be taken into consideration are, as previously noted:

•Were individual or group rights violated by the objects' removal from the community?

•Was the material stolen or sold under duress?

•Were existing laws, ethical standards, or regulations violated in its acquisition?

•Is the object essential to the continued traditional religious or cultural practices of the community?

In addition to ethical considerations, practicalities may apply. For example, the NMAI policy allows for the repatriation of "duplicate or abundant objects."[47] Finally, whether or not documentation of repatriated objects is retained by a museum varies, depending on the needs of the affiliated group.[48]

Example in Practice: Tibetan Buddhist Altar

The question of how to present religious material in the secular context of a museum has been much debated in the last few decades, after identity politics prompted a reassertion of the authenticity of certain spiritual traditions, and scholars insisted that performance has often constituted the meaning of ritual art.

The matter may seem purely academic for anyone committed to the modernist divide between art and religion. But a belief in the active agency of sacred things has many implications. It is fire that burns beneath bitter repatriation disputes, and in places like India or Africa it shapes the very concept of what a museum is.

The Museum for African art is one of the few museums in Manhattan to regularly and seriously bring secular and sacred together in a gallery. But Newark has been doing so for years—for Christian art too—thus placing itself in the vanguard.

—Holland Cotter[49]

The Newark Museum is regarded as a leader among other major art museums in the U.S. for developing innovative practices for the care and interpretation of sacred materials in museums. Importantly, the museum's practices extend beyond the requirements of U.S. laws addressing Native North American material to address religious material culture from religions throughout the world, including Christianity, Buddhism, and Islam.[50] As Director Mary Sue Sweeney Price notes:

> Since its founding in 1909, the Newark Museum has embraced the richness of world cultures, as well as cultural difference and cultural connection, through the presentation of devotional art in a broad context of use and practice . . . (The fact that) directors and curators in the institution's history did not shy away from the religious or devotional interpretation of objects, or "denature" them by placing them on pedestals far removed from their previous use has made for a unique history.[51]

The museum's much-celebrated Tibetan Buddhist altar adds to our understanding of several principles of consecration outlined earlier, including multiple levels of consecration over time and how sacred traditions evolve within a strong, living tradition. The case of the Tibetan Buddhist altar also illustrates how to use the principles previously outlined to determine the disposition of sacred materials and how these can enhance the museum's research and educational functions. These principles include *recognizing cultural knowledge and authority, accommodating religious practices, developing special care protocols for sacred materials, and developing sustained, long-term relationships with affiliated groups.*

And finally, the case of the altar also illustrates how both religions and museums endure as institutions yet change fundamental practices over time.

The Newark Museum holds one of the world's finest collections of Tibetan material culture. In 1935, American artists constructed an altar to contextualize the presentation of Buddhist objects in the collection to the public.[52] Although the 1935 altar was never consecrated and was constructed by non-Buddhists, the power of its symbolism and the significance of the objects presented through it inspired veneration by museum audiences and recognition by Tibetan religious leaders, including members of a Tibetan trade delegation in 1948 and His Holiness, the 14th Dalai Lama, in 1979 and again in 1981. As Valrae Reynolds, former Senior Curator and Curator of Asian Art at the Newark Museum, notes:

> From this first Tibetan delegation in 1948 up to the present day, the Museum actively contacted and hosted members of the Tibetan community. These visits effected more than good will; they contributed to the research and documentation of the collection, and they communicated the significant responsibility the Museum held as a steward for sacred Tibetan material culture.

In the mid-1980s the museum determined that the breadth and significance of the collections warranted a major gallery renovation. Building upon past practices and relationships, museum staff involved Tibetan communities in the planning for the new galleries, including high-level religious specialists, local community groups, and internationally-recognized scholars.[53]

In the resulting discussions with religious authorities, it was decided that the existing altar had been consecrated through veneration by lay audiences and should be formally deconsecrated before being dismantled. The deconsecration ceremony was held, and the elements of the altar were saved so they could be enclosed in the new altar soon to be built.[54]

The Tibetan advisors worked closely with the Museum's designers to develop the architectural elements for the new altar. In addition, the museum commissioned a contemporary Tibetan artist,

Phuntsok Dorje, to paint the altar and surrounding space. His work and choice of iconography were also guided by the Tibetan advisory groups.

The sacred symbolism employed by the artist and in the design of the space itself is a first layer of consecration. A second level of consecration was provided through enclosing the remnants of the previous altar in the new altar frame. As a third level of consecration, sacred images were first chosen and then reconsecrated by religious advisors for use in the altar. Tim Wintemberg, now Director of Exhibition Design, designed the altar as his first project at the museum 20 years ago:

> Along with the design of the altar to display and store sacred texts, and the appropriate symbols that *Phuntsok* Dorje was going to paint, there was also a consideration of what objects would be most appropriate to place onto the altar. After going through the collection, the religious advisors determined that a particular Shakyamuni Buddha image was the most auspicious and the most correct figure to put in this altar. . . . Unfortunately the Buddha had been opened up . . . some generations past, to determine what the contents were inside the image. Of course we stated, in the label later, that this would no longer be done, since it would violate the sanctity of the consecrated object. In the reinstallation the image was re-consecrated and the portions of the old contents from the original consecration were displayed, at the monks' request, so that people could understand how museum practices had at some level changed over the decades.[55]

To reconsecrate the image, the monks assembled new prayers and elements to be enclosed in the statue and invited the Museum staff to contribute elements to be included in the image; this inclusive gesture both adhered to and adapted past practices. The staff contributed gold, coral, volcano ash, and other items that were used in the reconsecration. Prayers were first handwritten, then reduced in an approach that similarly continued an established tradition while also reflecting change due to the incorporation of new technologies:

> Inside the image is . . . a red obelisk shaped piece, the "life tree" (srog-śin),[56] placed inside the hollow of the image. . . . And around that were packed, densely packed, bundles of prayers on scrolls, rolled very, very tightly. . . . (T)hey actually wrote out the prayers and then . . . the prayers were, I think, grouped by different organ types or different attributes that were important.
>
> . . . (I)t resembled an arrangement of tightly-rolled prayers in a layered representation of the body of the Buddha. . . . (T)hese written prayers were Xeroxed to reduce them and then Xeroxed to reduce them again so that they became almost micro-sized type, barely visible. . . . [That let them] incorporate many times more iterations of the prayers than they would have been able to by just hand-writing. . . . It was analogous to, if you spin a prayer wheel . . . numerous times, each time you spin that, that prayer is then going up and out. By having more revolutions inside these prayer bundles reiterating the same prayer over and over and over again, it was adding more resonant strength to it.[57]

Importantly, not all aspects of the consecration of the image included museum staff. At certain points the monks worked alone and this was not documented.

Given the solid relationship between the museum and the Tibetan religious communities, and because of the collection's religious significance, His Holiness the 14th Dalai Lama performed the next level of consecration: the consecration of the altar as a whole. It also provided the occasion for the first meeting between His Holiness the 14th Dalai Lama and South African Bishop Desmond Tutu, who joined him and the museum's Tibetan advisors for the ceremony at the museum on September 23, 1990.

> Assisted by ritual masters, lamas, and attendants, the Dalai Lama first made three prostrations and presented a white katak, a silk

scarf which is the traditional Tibetan greeting symbolizing primordial purity. The first flame was lighted in a special golden butter lamp. Next, prayers were chanted: the mantra of interdependent origination (to "set the stage" for the ceremony, placing it in the context of universal Buddhist truths), taking refuge in the Buddhas, arousing compassion for all sentient beings, and making the Universal Mandala offering. Grain was tossed between chants to make the prayers "true" and "solid." The potent emblems of Tantric Buddhism, the dorje and bell (power and wisdom), were held in special positions. The central moment of the ceremony was an invocation to the Buddhas to enter the altar and stay there. These prayers were repeated three times, reminding the Buddhas that they have promised to stay in this world to teach enlightenment to all and to not enter final nirvana until this task is completed, especially here at this altar.[58]

The altar thus illustrates multiple levels of consecration over time, beginning with the enduring sacrality of the collection and the accrued sacredness of the previous altar, then the inclusion of sacred architectural symbolism and iconography, veneration, the incorporation of sacred elements in consecrating rituals, including the elements of the old altar following its deconsecration, and finally a formal consecration by well-established religious authority, His Holiness the 14th Dalai Lama.

This process reflected both the continuation of a museum and an established, living tradition as well as adaptations to both religious and institutional practices. Ultimately these adaptations reflect a balancing of old and new that, in Wintemberg's words, led to "a feeling that together we were sort of building a new situation, a new altar, a newly consecrated space, a newly consecrated image." The process reflected tradition "as a thriving cultural phenomenon."

CONCLUSION

The examples of policy and practices presented in this chapter for the care of sacred and culturally sensitive collections illustrate four key principles:

1. They recognize affiliated cultural groups' human and civil rights, including the right to cultural preservation.

2. They respect cultural or religious knowledge.

3. They outline inclusive institutional processes for determining the disposition of sacred materials involving consultations and partnerships with affiliated groups.

4. They seek to preserve the cultural integrity of sacred or sensitive objects.

Approaches to preserving the cultural integrity of a sacred artifact must stress the importance of accommodating religious practices, developing sustained, long-term relationships with affiliated groups, consulting with these affiliated groups regarding the object's disposition, documenting these interactions when appropriate (while respecting restrictions on esoteric information, if any) and devising repatriation, care, exhibition, research and archival practices consistent with the cultural importance and purpose of the object.

The specific examples of policy and practices discussed in this chapter may be relevant and useful in other settings but cannot simply be transplanted to other museums without new consultations specific to the objects at hand. Each museum can use the above guiding principles to develop its own internal policy specific to its collections. Museum leaders and staff cannot develop policy on behalf of, but in isolation from, the communities they seek to represent and serve through new research, exhibitions, programs and publications.

While it is true that American museums are not legally bound to negotiate with cultural groups to return sacred objects or to develop new care protocols, unless a specific law or international agreement applies to that case, a concern for social justice and ethics should lead them to do so. Museums must recognize human and civil rights issues related to objects in their care, acknowledge the sometimes painful historic circumstances that brought sacred materials into museums, and recognize cultural knowledge as they conserve, research, exhibit and interpret sacred and sensitive objects. As institutions that generate knowledge, not simply act as store-houses for information, museums must preserve the cultural integrity of sacred objects, occasionally even above the preservation of the physical object. To preserve a sacred object in violation of its meaning is not preservation, as we can also understand by looking to precedents in contemporary art.

The care of sacred and culturally sensitive objects in museum collections is thus not only about preserving the cultural or conceptual integrity of an object in balance with its physical integrity. It is about the responsibility of museums to engage and interpret the past and present in ways that are ethical and promote both knowledge and justice. •

NOTES

1. Much of the source material for this chapter is drawn from the research programs of the Religion and the Arts Initiative (RAI) at Harvard's Center for the Study of Religions from 2000-2004 and the RAI's museum partners the Smithsonian National Museum of the American Indian, the Alutiiq Museum and Archaeological Repository, the Woodland Hills Cultural Centre and Harvard's Peabody Museum of Archaeology and Ethnology. I am grateful to the then Center Director Lawrence Sullivan, to the directors and staff of our partner museums cited throughout this chapter, to the RAI's senior and research fellows, guest speakers and authors, faculty advisory committee, teaching fellows, staff and team of research assistants, and I am grateful to the Newark Museum's director and my colleagues for their generosity, insight, and in some cases comments on this draft. Any errors in representing their work are my own.

2. Although there can be no single definition for the term *sacred,* some scholars and religious leaders have set forth working definitions for specific aspects of the broader concept of sacredness; these are discussed later in this chapter.

3. In some traditions funerary objects or human remains are also considered sacred.

4. Objects that bear testimony to genocide, such as those related to the Holocaust, although terrible to face, may serve an essential role in memorializing those who lost their lives. Museums treat such materials with heightened sensitivity, including, in some cases, restricted access to or ritual care of the objects. Both religious and nonreligious groups may feel that relics of events such as the September 11, 2001, terrorist attacks on the World Trade Center should be treated with reverence.

5. For example, Robert Wilson's *14 Stations,* exhibited at MASS MoCA in 2001–03, is a version of the Christian Via Crucis or "Way of the Cross." The work was originally commissioned for the Oberammergau Passion Play in 2000. The consecrated Tibetan Buddhist altar commissioned by the Newark Museum is another example, discussed in detail later in this essay. See Mary Sue Sweeney Price's discussion of living altars in the Newark Museum in her essay "Embracing the Spiritual at The Newark Museum," in *Stewards of the Sacred,* ed. Lawrence E. Sullivan and Alison Edwards (Washington, DC: American Association of Museums; Cambridge, MA: Harvard Center for the Study of World Religions, 2004).

6. See, for example, Yutaka Mino's essay "Care of Religious Materials," in *Stewards of the Sacred,* 100, describing how temple-owned artifacts are stored and conserved in Japanese museums. Also see Gerald T. Conaty's chapter "Glenbow's Blackfoot Gallery: working toward coexistence" in *Museums and Source Communities,* eds. Laura K. Peers and Alison K. Brown (New York: Routledge, 2003), 227-241.

7. See David Hurst-Thomas, *Skull Wars: Kennewick Man, Archaeology, and the Battle for Native American Identity* (New York: Basic Books, 2001).

8. See Suzan Harjo, "Native Peoples' Cultural and Human Rights: An Unfinished Agenda," *Arizona State Law Journal* 24, no. 1 (1992): 321–28.

9. These four questions as a framework are taken from Alison Edwards, "Native American Social Movements and Museum Reform: A Legislative History for the National Museum of the American Indian (NMAI) Act and the Native American Graves Protection and Repatriation Act (NAGPRA)," qualifying paper, Harvard Graduate School of Education, 2008.

10. Reproduced in *Stewards of the Sacred,* 129-210.

11. Since first contact, Native American sacred objects and bodies have been collected through wars and as a result of governmental laws and policies outlawing the practice of Native American religions. Although the U.S. Constitution's First Amendment protects United States citizens' rights to religious freedom, Indians were not granted citizenship until the Indian Citizenship Act of 1924, enacted as part of assimilation policy at that time (see Stephen Cornell, *The Return of the Native: American Indian Political Resurgence* [New York: Oxford University Press, 1988]). Throughout the nineteenth century and into the mid-twentieth century, Native religious ceremonies were outlawed, and religious objects were confiscated during raids by government and church officials; many of these objects were sold or donated to museums. As noted by Suzan Harjo in "Native Peoples' Cultural and Human Rights," 322: "In 1894 and 1904, the United States Department of the Interior issued Regulations of the Indian office, specifically outlawing Native religious practices."

12. DeAngelis further argues that such museums must develop internal, museum-specific policies that exceed the requirements of existing laws and resolutions.

13. See Miriam Clavir, *Preserving What is Valued: Museums, Conservation and First Nations* (Vancouver: UBC Press, 2002).

14. See Nancy Rosoff's chapter "Integrating Native Views into Museum Procedures: Hope and Practice at the Smithsonian National Museum of the American Indian," in *Museums and Source Communities,* 72-80.

15. See Sherry Hutt, Caroline Meredith Blanco, Walter E. Stern, and Stan N. Harris, *Cultural Property Law: A Practitioner's Guide to the Management, Protection and Preservation of Heritage Resources* (Washington, DC: American Bar Association, 2004), xi.

16. There are many differing conceptions of what sacred means. See writings by Mircea Eliade in *Symbolism, the Sacred, and the Arts,* ed. Diane Apostolos-Cappadonna (New York: Crossroad, 1985), or the discussion of the components of sacred space in Lawrence E. Sullivan, "The Disintegration of Primordial Worlds and the Recombinant Nature of Ritual Space," Vivens Homo 8, no. 2 (Rivista Teologica Fiorentina) (July–December 1997): 237–54.

17. See James Pepper-Henry, "Challenges in Maintaining Culturally Sensitive Collections at the National Museum of the American Indian," in *Stewards of the Sacred,* 107.

18. Additional related definitions include: "Traditional religious leaders are individuals recognized by members of an Indian tribe or Native Hawaiian organization as responsible for performing cultural duties relating to the ceremonial or religious traditions of that Indian tribe or Native Hawaiian organization based on the tribe's or organization's cultural, ceremonial, or religious practices. While many items, from ancient pottery sherds to arrowheads, might be imbued with sacredness in the eyes of an individual, this definition is specifically limited to objects that were devoted to a traditional Native American religious ceremony or ritual and which have religious significance or function in the continued observance or renewal of such ceremony."

19. See National Museum of Australia, "Policy on Aboriginal and Torres Strait Islander Secret/Sacred and Private Material," reproduced in *Stewards of the Sacred,* 187.

20. See Douglas Greenberg, "Conservation and Meaning," in *Stewards of the Sacred,* 41–45.

21. See, for example, Neil McGregor, "Oi, Hands Off Our Marbles!" Sunday Times (London), January 18, 2004, and Michael Brown, Who Owns Native Culture? (Cambridge, MA: Harvard University Press, 2003). See also James Cuno, Who Owns Antiquity?: Museums and the Battle Over Our Ancient Heritage (Princeton, NJ: Princeton University Press, 2008).

22. Proceedings of the May 10, 2006, American Art Museum Directors symposium "Antiquities and the World's Shared Heritage: The Value of Museums," held at the New York Public Library, included remarks by Philippe de Montebello, then director of the Metropolitan Museum of Art: "The insistence for keeping objects at their sites, also shows lack of concern for broad access, as most of these, let's face it, they're in remote locations. . . . As you well know, the Metropolitan returned to Turkey in 1993, a group of spectacular West Anatolian pieces in precious metals, the so-called Lidian Treasure dating back to the sixth century BC. It turned out

to have been illegally excavated from a site in or near Ushak in the 1960s. . . . In an April 20 article in the Turkish press, the chief officer of the Ushak culture and tourism department stated . . . : 'In the past five years, 769 people visited the museum in total.' . . . We also display as a group, the Nimrod ivories excavated by the Met, along with our colleagues from the British Museum and shared through partage with the museum in Baghdad. . . . Tragically, most of these ivories have almost certainly been irretrievably damaged in Baghdad by poor storage conditions and their inaccessibility to get them out in time during the chaos that ensued after the coalition forces invaded in 2003."

23. Speaking at the same symposium, Kwame Anthony Appiah, a philosopher and cultural theorist based at Princeton, remarked: "So that now we have a system whose—which looks like its point is to stop the movement of culture across national boundaries. It looks like many of the regulations that have been either proposed or actually enacted through UNESCO recently seemed to have behind them the thought that every object . . . is the expression of some national geist and it should live at home with its geist. . . . And the effect of the current system of international regulation is in many cases, have made things worse than they would have been if things had just been left to the sort of random forces of the market . . . and in thinking about what's sensible and practical, we need to bear in mind the real circumstances of say, the National Museum of the Sudan in Khartoum or the National Museum of Ghana in Accra, which has very few resources, cannot protect the objects, and furthermore we don't have the bureaucratic resources in those places simply to implement these regulations. . . . There was once an encyclopedic museum in Kumasi in Ghana where I grew up. It was destroyed by the British when they conquered us and the objects were looted. I'm not an enthusiast for looting, but if we wanted to try again to do what the Ashanti king who did that, tried to do, one of the main obstacles to our doing so would be a bunch of UNESCO regulations, and this is a great irony I think since the king of Ashanti who started that museum, did so because he was inspired by the story of the British Museum."

24. Both excerpts are from the transcript of the proceedings in an email from the American Art Museum Directors to the author, June 23, 2009.

25. James Cuno writes: "Often those who claim that art museums are always contingent and at best discursive also claim that . . . if museum visitors do not see what they like and who they 'are' it is said that they feel excluded from the museum and what it represents. This argument holds that people who do not see themselves represented in the works of art on view, or whose social or ethnic category is not represented on the museum's executive staff or board of trustees, or who are not perhaps familiar with the formality of the museum's architectural style are, this argument holds, intimidated by and have no access to the qualities of the works of art on view, and feel excluded from the museum itself. Nothing in my experience suggests that this is true. When I first went to an art museum as a college student in my twenties (and as a first-generation liberal arts university student of

a military family, I was hardly privileged over others in my preparation for museums) I felt free to enjoy, engage with, even identify with anything on view. Nothing seemed inaccessible to me." "Why Art Museums are Essential," in *Stewards of the Sacred,* 37.

26. See especially Robert E. Bieder, *Science Encounters the Indian, 1820–1880: The Early Years of American Ethnology* (Norman: University of Oklahoma Press, 1986); Thomas Bilosi and Larry Zimmerman, eds., Indians and Anthropologists: Vine Deloria, Jr. and the Critique of Anthropology (Tucson: University of Arizona Press, 1997); Patty Gerstenblith, "Cultural Significance and the Kennewick Skeleton: Some Thoughts on the Resolution of Cultural Heritage Disputes," in Claiming the Stones, Naming the Bones: Cultural Property and the Negotiation of National and Ethnic Identity, ed. Elazar Barkan and Ronald Bush (Los Angeles: Getty Research Institute, 1992), 371; Greenberg, "Conservation and Meaning"; Kenn Harper, Give Me My Father's Body: The Life of Minik, the New York Eskimo (New York: Washington Square Press, Pocket Books, 1986); Jack F. Trope and Walter R. Echo-Hawk, "The Native American Graves Protection and Repatriation Act: Background and Legislative History," Arizona State Law Journal 24, no. 1 (1992): 35–78.

27. See, for example: Bruce Bernstein, "Repatriation and Collaboration—The Museum of New Mexico," Museum Anthropology 15, no. 3 (1991): 19–22; Kathleen Sabinoff Fine-Dare, *Grave Injustice: The American Indian Repatriation Movement and NAGPRA* (Lincoln: University of Nebraska Press, 2002); Amy Lonetree and Amanda J. Cobb, eds., *The National Museum of the American Indian: Critical Conversations* (Lincoln: University of Nebraska Press, 2008); Judith Ostrowitz, "'Concourse and Periphery': Planning the National Museum of the American Indian," American Indian Quarterly 29 (summer–fall 2005): 384–425; W. Richard West, "The National Museum of the American Indian: A Prototype for the 21st Century?" Archiv für Völkerkunde 50 (1999): 115–23.

28. From Harvard's Peabody Museum of Archaeology and Ethnology, the Alutiiq Museum and Archaeological Repository, the National Museum of the American Indian, Woodland Hills Cultural Centre, and the National Museum of Australia. Full text for these policies is reproduced in *Stewards of the Sacred.*

29. As summarized in the National Museum of the American Indian's repatriation policy statement of February 19, 1991: "During the inventory process and following its completion, the Museum will consult widely with Native peoples. The Museum will disclose all relevant information pertaining to collection objects identified in the inventories, and curatorial staff will be available to respond to additional requests for information. Physical access to materials will be provided as requested. In addition, a special area will be made available for Native American peoples to view or otherwise inspect their culturally affiliated materials. Every effort will be made to reach agreement through informal consultation and cooperation. Where issues remain after good faith discussions,

those pertaining to human remains, funerary objects, and other objects covered by this policy will be referred to a special Review Committee established by the Board of Trustees." Reproduced in *Stewards of the Sacred,* 148.

30. Sven Haakanson, Jr. "Understanding Sacredness: Facing the Challenges of Cultural Change," in *Stewards of the Sacred,* 127.

31. From the National Museum of the American Indian document "Culturally Sensitive Collections Care Program," reproduced in *Stewards of the Sacred,* 137.

32. Ibid., 141

33. Ibid., 139

34. Haakanson, "Understanding Sacredness," 164.

35. "Access to the collections for viewing, study, the performance of ceremonies, and other purposes for Native American people shall be allowed to the maximum extent." National Museum of the American Indian, repatriation policy statement, 151.

For example:

"Public access to collections for research, study, or viewing purposes may be restricted if such access offends the religious or cultural practices of Native Americans." Ibid.

 "[We must handle] Elders' knowledge respectfully and honorably by: asking them what we can and cannot share with the public and other Natives; restricting access to the information, if they request that this be done; sharing what they teach us with the public and giving proper credit." Haakanson,"Understanding Sacredness," 127.

36. See Pepper-Henry, "Challenges in Managing Culturally Sensitive Collections," 110.

37. Ibid., 112, 109.

38. See the National Museum of Australia's "Policy on Aboriginal and Torres Strait Islander Secret/Sacred and Private Material," reproduced in Stewards of the Sacred, 190; and the Woodland Cultural Centre's Museum Policies, revised December 12, 2003, reproduced in ibid., 208.

39. See, for example, Ann Drumheller and Marian Kaminitz, "Traditional Care and Conservation: The Merging of Two Disciplines at the National Museum of the American Indian," in Preventative Conservation, Theory, Practice, and Research: Preprints of the Contributions to the Ottawa Congress, 12th–16th September, 1994, ed. P. S. Ashok Roy (London: International Institute for Conservation of Historic and Artistic Works, 1994), 58–60; and Miriam Clavir, Preserving What Is Valued: Museums, Conservation, and First Nations (Vancouver: University of British Columbia Press, 2002). See also National Museum of Australia, "Policy on Aboriginal and Torres Strait Islander Secret/Sacred and Private Material," 192, which states that the museum will conserve sacred objects only with permission from the affiliated community.

40. Haakanson, "Understanding Sacredness," 127.

41. See Patricia Capone and Diana Loren, "Stewardship of Sensitive Collections: Policies, Procedures and the Process of

their Development at the Peabody Museum," in Stewards of the Sacred, 170; National Museum of Australia, "Policy on Aboriginal and Torres Strait Islander Secret/Sacred and Private Material," 188.

42. See Harvard Peabody Museum of Archaeology and Ethnology, "Policy and Procedure for Implementing Special Considerations for Care and Handling of Collections," reproduced in Stewards of the Sacred, 177.

43. Ibid., 178.

44. Ibid.

45. Ibid.

46. See Pepper-Henry, "Challenges in Managing Culturally Sensitive Collections," 111.

47. National Museum of the American Indian, repatriation policy statement, 150.

48. Ibid., 147.

49. National Museum of Australia, "Policy on Aboriginal and Torres Strait Islander Secret/Sacred and Private Material," 195.

50. Holland Cotter, "Museums Look Inward for Their Own Bailouts," New York Times, January 11, 2009.

51. Price,"Embracing the Spiritual at the Newark Museum," 71.

Ibid.

52. Valrae Reynolds, Tibetan Buddhist Altar (Newark, NJ: The Newark Museum, 1991), 9.

53. Reynolds, Tibetan Buddhist Altar.

54. Ibid., 11.

55. Tim Wintemberg, unpublished interview with Alison Edwards, the Newark Museum, December 12, 2008, 1.

56. For a detailed discussion of Tibetan Buddhist consecration ceremonies and elements including the srog-śin, see Valrae Reynolds, Amy Heller, and Janet Gyatso, The Newark Museum Tibetan Collection, vol. III, Sculpture and Painting (Newark, NJ: The Newark Museum, 1986), 56–59.

57. Wintemberg, interview, 2

58. Reynolds, Tibetan Buddhist Altar, 29.

Ethics | HYPOTHETICALS

How do you handle the following situations?

1

You're the new curatorial assistant on the staff. The curator you work for is taking you on a tour of the complex. In a damp basement room of the historic house are remnants of the once fine natural history collection. The curator picks up an old glass display of butterflies on cotton batting sandwiched between two pieces of glass. He says that this is the type of thing that should be deaccessioned. You say, well, we still have parts of this collection, and this seems to be in fairly good shape. The curator says, no, it isn't, and smashes the panel on the floor. Now, he says, it can be deaccessioned.

2

You are invited to give a short talk at a board meeting. After the talk, you watch in astonishment as the director tells the board that there wasn't enough money for the last exhibition, and they should vote to reallocate the restricted funds. They do—and one of the unrestricted funds is the money gained from deaccessioning.

3

As the loan officer, you keep close watch on courier trips. One of the curators insists that he be the courier to Germany. You go over all of the necessary information with him, letting him know what needs to be done. He refuses to give you a written report when he returns. Three months later, when the second courier goes to pack up, you find that the curator has left no notes, no condition reports, and no packing information.

4

You have a constant battle with the administration about renting space in the museum. Now you find that a 500-person dinner party is being given in the most value-intensive galleries at the museum. You protest but are told that the money is absolutely necessary. You walk through on the day of the event and find a microphone dangling over a statue. People are placing tables close to other sculpture. After the event you find a butter knife under one of the bases and splash marks where the cleaning table has been set up.

5

The director of your art museum collects art. He insists on storing a new purchase of his in the museum's storage area before you have arrived. Shortly after that he insists that the museum truck deliver it to another storage area of his choice.

6

You find a colleague smoking in a storage room in the basement of the historic house, stomping out the butts on the wooden floor.

7

You have just learned that a prominent board member has used his museum ties to get better deals on purchasing art.

Should you intervene? If so, how do you do it?

7D | COPYRIGHT

CHRISTINE STEINER

This chapter provides a broad overview of certain aspects of U.S. copyright law. Because of the limitations imposed by the nature of this publication, this brief chapter will address in depth the following topics—the exclusive rights of a copyright owner, the duration rules, and the concept of fair use.

For detailed or additional information, please consult *A Museum Guide to Copyright and Trademark* (available at www.aam-us.org), which addresses the complex intellectual property issues embedded in every aspect of museum practice. The work introduces copyright and trademark principles for the museum community. Its five chapters serve equally for those who want a general understanding of copyright and trademark in a museum-specific context and for those who need an answer to a specific question or issue. Chapter 1 addresses copyright law—what it is (and is not), its requirements, duration, and limitations. Chapter 2 deals with trademark law—what it is, why it matters, how to use it. In chapters 3 and 4, two increasingly significant issues for museums—the World Wide Web and licensing—are treated in depth. Chapter 5 highlights international protection matters, critical today because museums no longer operate in a comfortable world of relative isolation.

Please note that the *Guide* and this chapter are not intended as a substitute for legal advice, but rather to provide information to assist museum professionals in the performance of their duties. Specific intellectual property issues may require more in-depth treatment, and some may require the assistance of counsel. The author urges readers to consult the *Guide* in combination with this chapter.

INTRODUCTION

Intellectual property rights—particularly copyright and trademark—have always been relevant for museums in their multiple roles, as they build and pre-serve collections, conduct research and interpret the collections for the public, organize exhibitions, and provide educational programs and services. What specific properties would be considered *museum* intellectual property? Why are intellectual property issues especially significant for museums today?

Museums use works created by others, and at the same time they create original works; own collections in trust for the public (images, objects, specimens, documents, databases); sell products; and license their names for reproductions of objects and images. As educational institutions, museums are also entitled to fair use of the copyrighted work of others. A working knowledge of the basic principles of intellectual property is essential if museums are to respect and maintain the legal relationships that define and govern these various roles.

Commonly grouped under the rubric of "intellectual property," separate and distinct protection regimes govern the traditional categories—copyrights, trademarks, patents, and trade secrets. The brief definitions developed by the U.S. International Trade Commission are helpful in distinguishing these terms of art:

• A *copyright* is a form of protection provided by a national government to creators of original works of authorship including literary, dramatic, musical, artistic, and certain other intellectual works.

• A *trademark* is any word, name, symbol, or device, or any combination thereof, adopted and used by a manufacturer or merchant to identify his goods and distinguish them from those manufactured or sold by others.

• A *patent* is a grant issued by a national government conferring the right to exclude others from making, using, or selling the invention within the national territory.

•A *trade secret* is information, including a formula, pattern, compilation, program, device, method, technique, or process, that derives independent economic value, actual or potential, from not being generally known, and not being readily ascertained by proper means, by other persons who can obtain economic value from its disclosure or use, and is the subject of efforts that are reasonable under the circumstances to maintain its secrecy.

Under U.S. copyright law, a work is protected (i.e., it is "under copyright") or it is in the public domain. Works in the public domain are freely available for use by others because there is no copyright owner of these works. Some works are in the public domain because Congress excluded certain categories for public policy reasons. These are "any idea, procedure, process, system, method of operation, concept, principle, or discovery, regardless of the form in which it is described, explained, illustrated, or embodied in such work." Congress also made ineligible for protection works of the federal government. Other works have been ejected into the public domain because the copyright lapsed for failure to comply with copyright formalities, and, of course, works enter the public domain when the copyright has expired by passage of time.

What is Copyright?
The Copyright Law of the United States, codified in Title 17 of the United States Code, states that copyright protection subsists "in original works of authorship fixed in any tangible medium of expression, now known or later developed, from which they can be perceived, reproduced, or otherwise communicated." These three elements—originality, authorship, fixation—are threshold requirements of copyrightability and initiate inquiries: Is the work original or a derivative? Is there an author? Is the work fixed in a tangible medium? If the work was created in the course of employment, it is likely a "work made for hire," in which case the employer is the creator and therefore the copyright owner.

Assuming the work is eligible for protection, and the courts counsel that the standards for creativity need not be high, the authors (or other copyright owners to whom rights may have been transferred) are granted exclusive rights in and to their creative properties. Copyright is described as a "bundle of property rights," and it is indeed akin to physical property. Copyright can be owned, sold, leased, and borrowed and, like real property, it has owners, licensees, and trespassers. These exclusive rights are the right to reproduce, adapt, distribute, publicly perform, and publicly display the works, and these rights can be understood as follows:

Reproduction. This is the right to make copies of the work. It prevents one who is not the copyright owner from making exact or substantially similar copies without permission. Copies are defined in the Act as "material objects, other than phonorecords, in which a work is fixed by any method now known or later developed, and from which the work can be perceived, reproduced, or otherwise communicated, either directly or with the aid of a machine or device. The term 'copies' includes the material object, other than a phonorecord, in which the work is first fixed."

Adaptation. This is the right to prepare derivative works based on the original copyrighted work by transforming the original or altering it in some manner. This can take the form of a reproduction of, say, a collection item in a different medium for sale in the museum shop, or a translation, a musical arrangement, dramatization, a video, and the like. Derivative works are challenging because one must determine whether there are sufficient original elements for the work to garner its own copyright; even if so, the copyright extends only to the added elements.

Distribution. The distribution right gives the copyright owner the right to control the initial public distribution of copies of the work by sale, rental, lease, or loan. The owner can determine the timing of distribution, the number of copies to be distributed, the place of distribution, and the like. The distribution right is subject to an important limitation, known as the first sale doctrine, which provides that one who owns a copy of a protected work is entitled, without the authority of the copyright owner, to sell or otherwise dispose of the possession of it. (Note, however, Congress excepted computer software and sound recordings from the first sale doctrine; for these properties, permission of the appropriate copyright owner is required to rent, lease, or lend software or recordings, with certain exceptions for nonprofit educational institutions and libraries.)

Public Performance. This is the right to control the listening to or viewing of a copyrighted work. Under the Copyright Act, three types of public performances can be distinguished: 1) a performance at a place open to the public; 2) a performance by transmission to a place open to the public; and 3) a performance to an audience that may be separated in time, place, or both. Many activities taking place in public spaces of museums are public performances requiring the owner's permission when copyrighted works are involved. Music in connection with an opening, or background in the restaurant, or an exhibition transmitted for viewing by persons in geographically dispersed locations or at different times could constitute a public performance. The *Guide* contains a fuller explanation of this right, including the role of performing rights organizations for music performance, and the *Guide* should be consulted for questions concerning public performance.

Public Display. The copyright owner has the exclusive right to display the copyrighted subject matter (except sound recordings). The right of public display applies to the exhibition of original works of art and to their reproductions, because a "copy" includes any material object in which the work is fixed. Where a museum acquires a work but not the copyright (generally the case in museum practice), the Copyright Act places an important limitation on that exclusive right, allowing the owner of a copy of a copyrighted work to "display that copy publicly, either directly or by the projection of no more than one image at a time, to viewers present at the place where the copy is located." This public display right extends only to the immediate physical surroundings of the work. Without express authorization, the museum would not be permitted to project images of the work into other galleries or to multiple computer workstations over a local area network, or transmit the copy of the work over computer networks for

viewing at multiple locations—unless that use is a fair use, discussed later in this chapter.

How Long Does Copyright Last?

Copyright subsists from the moment of creation until expiration of the statutory duration, regardless of whether the property lies dormant or is so popular that it is used, adapted, and reproduced on a daily basis. Congress enacted the first U.S. copyright legislation in 1790. Since then, there have been four general revisions and many amendments of the copyright law. For much of the 20th century, the Copyright Act of 1909 provided the basic structure for protecting creative expression in the United States. Congress overhauled the copyright law when it enacted the Copyright Act of 1976, which took effect on Jan. 1, 1978. However, the 1909 act rules continued to apply generally to works that were published or registered before Jan. 1, 1978. Finally, since 1976, there have been several significant amendments to the copyright law, including the Digital Millennium Copyright Act of 1998. And in 1998 Congress passed the Copyright Term Extension Act, which added 20 years to the previous "life plus 50" duration of copyright. The matter of "orphan works," works for which the copyright owner cannot be determined or located following a diligent search, is one of great concern for museums in light of the scope and scale of museum holdings. The museum community has been actively engaged in shaping legislation pending before Congress; as of this writing, no law has been enacted and the Copyright Act has not been amended.

For museums, custodians of works produced under both laws, a working knowledge of the principles and rules of both the 1909 and 1976 acts is important. The publication rules were strict under the 1909 rules and, especially for pre-1978 works, it is also important to understand the distinction between "published" and "unpublished" works. The Copyright Act defines publication as "the distribution of copies or phonorecords of a work to the public by sale or other transfer of ownership or by rental, lease or lending... A public performance or display of a work does not of itself constitute publication."

Current copyright duration rules discussed in this section are summarized here.

Works Created on or After Jan. 1, 1978
For works created on or after Jan. 1, 1978, copyright protection subsists from the creation of the work and lasts for the life of the author plus 70 years (previ-

ously 50 years). In general, protection lasts until the end of the calendar year 70 years after the author's death. Copyrights in works of joint authorship (other than works made for hire) last until the end of the year of the 70th anniversary of the last surviving author's death. Anonymous or pseudonymous works (if the name of the author is not revealed) and works

Copyright Term	Pre-1999	New
Subsisting (pre-1978) copyrights	28 years, + 47-year renewal term = 75 years	28 years, + 67-year renewal term = 95 years
Works created on or after January 1, 1978	Life of the author plus 50 years	Life of the author plus 70 years
Joint works	Same as above, measured from life of last surviving author	Same as above, measured from life of last surviving author
Anonymous and pseudonymous works and works made for hire	75 years from publication or 100 years from creation, whichever expires first	95 years from publication or 120 years from creation, whichever expires first
Works created but not published before 1978	Same as post-January 1978 works, but term expires no earlier than December 31, 2002

If work is published before December 31, 2002, term shall not expire until December 31, 2027 | Same as post-January 1978 works, but term expires no earlier than December 31, 2002 (no change from previous law)

If work is published before December 31, 2002, term shall not expire until December 31, 2047 |
| **Presumption as to author's death** | After 75 years from publication or 100 years from creation, whichever expires first; the author is presumed to have been dead for 50 years if Copyright Office records do not indicate that the author is still living or died within the past 50 years | After 95 years from publication or 120 years from creation, whichever expires first; the author is presumed to have been dead for 70 years if Copyright Office records do not indicate that the author is still living or died within the past 70 years |
| **Termination** | Pre-1978 grants may be terminated during 5-year period commencing 56 years from date copyright was first secured | If previous termination right has already expired and was not exercised, copyright owner has a new termination right during 5-year period commencing 75 years from date copyright was first secured |

Source: David Carson, General Counsel, U.S. Copyright Office

made for hire are protected for 95 years (previously 75 years) from the date of first publication, or 120 years (previously 100 years) from the date of creation, whichever is shorter. Nothing in the 1998 term extension law restores copyright protection for any work that fell into the public domain prior to Oct. 27, 1998, the effective date of the legislation.

Unpublished Works Created Before Jan. 1, 1978

Museums are also the custodians of a vast body of unpublished works such as diaries, letters, and manuscripts, many of which date to the 18th or 19th century. Many museum professionals (and lawyers alike) are surprised to learn that these works may still be protected under federal copyright law. For works created before Jan. 1, 1978, but never published or registered as unpublished works with the Copyright Office before that date, the same duration rules discussed above apply, with two important differences. First, the earliest date that copyright could expire for works in this category was Dec. 31, 2002 (if the work remained unpublished). Second, to encourage publication, the copyright term for such works was extended through Dec. 31, 2047 (if the work was published before Dec. 31, 2002).

Works Created and Published Before Jan. 1, 1978

The rules for determining copyright term for works created and published before Jan. 1, 1978, are much different and much more complex. For many years to come, museums will need to be familiar with the old rules, which remain applicable to many works in museum collections. The general rule for works created under the 1909 Copyright Act was that copyright protection began on the actual date of publication (or the date of registration for unpublished works) and lasted for 28 years, subject to a renewal term of 28 years, for a total potential term of 56 years.

To apply these rules for works created or published before Jan. 1, 1978, a museum must bear in mind three fundamental differences between the old and current copyright laws. First, under the 1909 act, the copyright term was measured from the publication or registration of the work and not from the creation of the work. Second, copyright lasted for a definite number of years rather than the indefinite period measured by the life of the author and a fixed number of years. Third, the copyright term included a mandatory renewal feature. Failure to comply with any of the formalities of publication associated with notice or renewal could eject the work in the public domain.

Renewal of Works Created and Published Before Jan. 1, 1978

In theory, the renewal feature of the old copyright law was a mechanism to give authors and artists a chance to regain their copyrights after 28 years. In practice, renewal often operated as a trap for unwary copyright owners. To maintain copyright protection during the second, or renewal, term, the copyright owner had to file a renewal application with the Copyright Office during the 28th year of the initial term. Failure to comply in a timely manner with these strict requirements meant that the work fell into the public domain.

In the 1976 revision of the statute, Congress abolished the two-term system. However, it retained the renewal feature for works copyrighted before 1978 and still in their initial terms before Jan. 1, 1978. If the owner complied in a timely manner with the renewal requirements, there were substantial benefits. The copyright owner could get a renewal term of 47 years (bringing to 75 years the total possible period of protection for renewed copyrights). But if the copyright owner was unaware of or failed to comply with the renewal requirements, copyright in the work would be lost forever.

In 1992, in part to prevent such forfeitures of copyright, Congress eliminated the mandatory renewal registration requirement, automatically extending the second term for works copyrighted between Jan. 1, 1964, and Dec. 31, 1977. The renewal term for works in this category was automatically extended to 47 years. In 1998, Congress added another 20 years of protection to works in the 47-year renewal term, bringing the total possible term of protection for works in their renewal term to 95 years from the date copyright protection was originally secured (either through publication or registration). The 1992 renewal legislation also provided a number of important incentives to encourage owners to file renewal applications, the most significant of which,

431

for museums, is that those permitted to make a derivative work based on the original work during the first term of the copyright must obtain a new license to use the work after the first term.

Copyright Restoration

In 1994, Congress implemented international trade treaties that for the first time covered certain intellectual property matters. The new law had a significant potential impact on museums, as copyright was restored in certain foreign works that had previously entered the public domain in the United States for failure to comply with certain formalities under U.S. copyright law. With little or no warning, a substantial number of such foreign works—many previously used by museums in good-faith reliance on their public domain status—were again protected by copyright.

Copyright restoration rules are quite complex, usually requiring a museum to consult with a specialist. Still, museums should be familiar with the basic framework governing the eligibility of foreign works for copyright restoration in the United States and the rights and remedies for infringement of restored copyrights, including the special rules for reliance parties.

To decide whether a foreign work is eligible for copyright restoration in the United States, the following steps should be followed:

1. determine whether the work originated in an eligible source country;

2. determine whether the foreign work is still under copyright in its source country;

3. determine the period of protection for the restored work;

4. determine the identity and rights of the owners of the restored copyright;

5. determine whether the museum qualifies as a reliance party.

To qualify for restoration, the work must originate in a country (other than the United States) that is a member of the Berne Convention or the World Trade Organization (WTO), and given the large number of nations included in these categories, works published in the last 70 years almost anywhere

in the world may now qualify for copyright restoration in the United States. Because of the level of complexity and the potential exposure, this area is of particular concern for museums. The discussion in the *Guide* addresses these issues in more detail, including assessing the five steps enumerated above, the status of renewal parties, the consequence of renewals and term extension legislation, the importance of the Copyright Office NIE (Notice of Intent to Enforce) publications, and rules for derivative works created by a reliance party based on an underlying foreign work in which copyright has been restored. Please consult the *Guide* and Copyright Office publications for additional information.

WHAT IS FAIR USE?

Fair use—an equitable doctrine that balances the rights of a copyright owner with those of society—speaks to specific uses of copyrighted works that are considered fair under the Copyright Act. Museums are both users and creators of works, and they may find themselves taking potentially competing positions on fair use issues.

The tension between an owner's financial and security interests and society's legitimate access to intellectual property led Congress to incorporate and codify a growing body of case law when it revised the Copyright Act in 1976. Fair use strives to ensure that an author's exclusive bundle of property rights will not hinder the very creativity the law was designed to foster. The doctrine recognizes that new works draw inspiration from older works and that productive use of older works promotes the progress of science, arts, and literature. Fair use permits certain good-faith uses that, in other contexts, would be infringement. The Copyright Act identifies such uses including criticism, comment, news reporting, teaching, scholarship, and research. And there are certain other fair uses (e.g., parody) that are not listed in the statute.

Fair use is a case-by-case determination. An activity may qualify in one instance as fair use, while it would be an infringing activity in another context. The fact that a work is intended for an educational purpose does not automatically make it eligible for the fair use exception. For example, educational publishing is a large segment of the publishing market and, while its audience is educational users, it is a commercial activity that relies on obtaining permission to use the copyrighted materials of others. Museum rights departments fulfill many textbook requests at commercial rates, and would never consider these uses to be fair uses. Similarly, a number of museum activities are not eligible for the fair use exception although they are designed for educational purposes.

The U.S. Copyright Office's informational circular on fair use acknowledges that the distinction between fair use and infringement is unclear and not easily defined. It provides examples of activities that courts have regarded as fair use: "quotation of excerpts in a review or criticism for purposes of illustration or comment; quotation of short passages in a scholarly or technical work, for illustration or clarification of the author's observations; use in a parody of some of the content of the work parodied; summary of an address or article, with brief quotations, in a news report; reproduction by a library of a portion of a work to replace part of a damaged copy; reproduction by a teacher or student of a small part of a work to illustrate a lesson; reproduction of a work in legislative or judicial proceedings or reports; incidental and fortuitous reproduction, in a newsreel or broadcast, of a work located in the scene of an event being reported."

Fair use in the context of objects and images is even more uncertain. Not only must one determine and apply the fair use test, with all its nuances and inconsistencies, but one must do so without a settled body of fine art-specific case law and in light of new challenges presented by electronic media. The growth of the Internet has been accompanied by a liberal interpretation of both freedom of speech and the fair use exception. The ease and speed of downloading and manipulating images, and the mass of unrestricted images on the Internet, lull many users into assuming implied licenses to copy, print, and distribute Internet materials. Some liken transmitting copyrighted materials via e-mail to sharing the newspaper or showing a picture to a friend. Computer networks and bulletin boards compound infringement because distribution is quick, easy, and inexpensive.

In the 1976 Copyright Act, Congress articulated the test for determining whether a particular use is fair:

1. the purpose and character of the use, including whether such use is of a commercial nature or is for nonprofit educational purposes;

2. the nature of the copyrighted work;

3. the amount and substantiality of the portion used in relation to the copyrighted work as a whole; and

4. the effect of the use upon the potential market for or value of the copyrighted work.

These criteria cannot be evaluated in isolation as a mathematical formulation, but rather the test is a "totality of the circumstances" analysis. Although the flexibility inherent in the test often leaves users and providers unsure of whether the contemplated use is a fair use, these factors guide a case-by-case determination.

A. The Purpose and Character of the Use

Generally speaking, nonprofit uses will receive more protection than for-profit uses. However, if the use is for profit, but serves primarily as news reporting, comment, criticism, or education, then the purpose and character of the use may be deemed worthy of fair use consideration. An overarching concept is that the copyright owner should benefit from any use of his or her copyrighted work that generates profits. While the commercial use of copyrighted work tends to weigh against a finding of fair use, and nonprofit use tends to weigh in favor, there is nothing conclusive about these presumptions. Important is whether the use of a protected work "adds something new" to the work, transforming "raw material" into "new information, new aesthetics, new insights and understandings," or what has been recognized as "transformative" use.

B. Nature of the Copyrighted Work

Depending on the type of copyrighted work that is being used by another, access may be more or less important to the public interest. Access to works of scholarship is considered more important from a social perspective than access to fictional works, and therefore more latitude will be granted for copying factual works.

Further, the market perspective may be considered. For instance, if a work is published with the intent that it be used in a specific way, copying the work for that same use will be afforded less protection because allowing the copying may undercut the market for the work.

Finally, a court will consider whether a work is unpublished in order to recognize an author's interest in first publication. But the copyright law itself informs the analysis by reminding that use of an unpublished work may be fair, depending on the four-factor analysis. This consideration would more likely arise in the literary context, e.g., quoting unpublished letters, but it could be relevant in the visual arts context. In European moral rights analysis, the "right of divulgation" protects an artist's absolute right to determine when and how a work is published; in U.S. law, by contrast, a use might be a fair one, whether or not the work has first been published by the creator.

C. The Amount and Substantiality Used

In determining whether a fair use defense is appropriate, a court will consider the amount and substantiality of what has been copied from the underlying work. The court may consider what proportion of the work has been copied, and/or how important the copied portion is to the work as a whole. That is, the analysis is both a quantitative and qualitative one, examining how much is too much. Generally, the greater the amount taken, the less likely it is that a court will find the use fair. But how much is too much? This is not a mathematical formulation, and there are no absolute quantitative and qualitative rules. Sometimes even a small amount taken may be unfair if the borrowed material is the "heart" of the work. A work of visual art is generally viewed as a whole, and borrowing "more than necessary" is often difficult to assess. Taking the entire work does not necessarily mean that the new use is not a fair one because the test examines *all* the factors.

D. The Effect of the Use Upon the Potential Market

This final factor in determining whether the use of another's copyrighted work qualifies as fair is the commercial import of the use. Financial incentives encourage the creation of new works. When a copyright owner objects to another's use of the copyrighted work on the basis of the negative impact such use has on the owner's market, the owner need not show actual harm—potential harm is sufficient. Under this factor, a court may evaluate actual market harm caused by the particular actions of the alleged infringer and also the adverse impact on the potential market for the original. In analyzing the effect on the potential market for the original, courts are to consider traditional, reasonable, or likely markets, and should consider also the availability of a "convenient, reasonable licensing system" in evaluating the marketplace effect of the use.

WHAT ARE TYPES OF FAIR USE?

In addition to the activities identified in the Copyright Act as fair (i.e., criticism, comment, news reporting, teaching, scholarship, and research) other uses of copyrighted works enjoy fair use protection. These include uses that transform the underlying work, including parody, appropriation and other recognized categories.

Transformative Use. Transformative use means that the new work does more than simply recast the original work to create a derivative work. Instead, the creator uses the underlying work to make a different work that stands on its own as an original expression. It is often difficult to determine whether the new expression adequately transforms the underlying work, and the outcome will depend on analysis of all the facts of the use.

Parody. Parody is by nature transformative. A parody involves using someone else's work, in whole or in part, for the purpose of humor, ridicule, comment, or the like. A work parodying another will likely use some distinguishing features of the original work in order to make a clear association between the original and the parody. It is through this association that the parody achieves its purpose of commenting on the original work.

While parody as fair use presents another area of highly subjective and fact-intensive analysis, the courts have attempted to craft some guidelines. From the cases decided to date, several elements emerge for determining whether parody will be found to be fair use:

1. a parody must comment on the original work;

2. a parody should only include as much of the original material as is needed and not enough to confuse the consumer or public, or dilute the commercial value of the original; and

3. a parody should not seek to replace the original in the marketplace.

Appropriation Art. Appropriation art, by its very nature, uses the work of another in a different context. The appropriated or borrowed work may be protected by copyright or trademark. The purpose of the use is to alter or comment on the meaning or intention of the original work, and it may take the form of reproducing a single image, or incorporating many images into a compilation or collage. Appropriation is not always enthusiastically received by the creator of the original work. Andy Warhol, for example, was often embroiled in claims by photographers that he had misappropriated their photographic images. Appropriation art is an important means of expression for visual artists. It is equally certain that controversies will continue to arise with regard to the appropriation of works. The guidelines for free speech, fair use and the first sale doctrine provide some boundaries for the ongoing discussion and resolution of such matters.

CONCLUSION

An understanding of the law governing copyright is not an end in itself. It is the necessary predicate knowledge upon which museum professionals can set institutional policy and make informed judgments about specific issues. Important steps toward a comprehensive approach include a carefully crafted copyright statement for staff and volunteers that addresses such issues as work for hire and appropriate use of museum materials; a rights and reproductions policy for outside users that articulates appropriate uses and applicable fees; and a trademark policy that identifies properties eligible for trademark protection. The policy should also squarely address departmental en-

forcement responsibility within the institution.

Museums make policy decisions in every department: Who has access to the collections? Who has permission to reproduce items from the collections? May sponsors use the museum name and images, and if so, how? Should the donor be consulted if the museum plans to make a commercial use of a donated object? Should the museum require transfer of copyright when acquiring a work in its copyright term, or is a nonexclusive license more appropriate? When and how should a museum negotiate with artists' rights societies? Who "clears" rights that the museum does not own, the museum or the third-party user? When a museum has conducted an adequate but unsuccessful search for the copyright owner, what next? When is it appropriate to institute litigation against infringers, and how aggressive should the museum be? It will reasonably be expected that museums will approach management of intellectual property differently depending on the nature of the institution, its mission, structure, size, location, print and electronic outreach activities, product development, and a host of other factors.

The law reflects a balance of competing interests, but professional ethics may articulate a duty above the minimum threshold of the law. Museums have the right to decide how, when, and by whom collections information is used, and they have the responsibility to exercise that right in an even-handed manner. Museums also have the responsibility to respect the intellectual property of others. Activities undertaken without permission, such as systematic photocopying of copyrighted works, duplicating videotapes, copying single-user licensed software, and other undetected and unreported infringement—without a favorable case-by-case fair use analysis—have no place in museum practice. Museums must establish policies to vigorously monitor copyright and trademark issues in-house. The principles outlined in this chapter and more fully developed in the *Guide* will provide the necessary guidance. •

(This chapter is excerpted from *A Museum Guide to Copyright and Trademark*, 1999, copyright American Association of Museums. The author recognizes Michael Shapiro's contribution to the copyright portion of that work.)

7E | PHOTOGRAPHIC SERVICES AND RIGHTS AND REPRODUCTIONS

MARY F. HOLAHAN, UPDATED BY BETHANY ENGEL AND JENNIFER HOLL

Museums are among the world's richest sources of images for reproduction in printed and electronic media. Dissemination of reproductions of objects in museum collections advances the educational mission of the museum and may generate income. Before undertaking any reproduction services, museums must determine what, if any, legal limits exist to reproduction and distribution of images in their collections. That is, museums must know if, and to what extent, they own the copyright to collection objects and photography of collection objects.

Copyright is a complex legal issue, governing a wide range of created works, including, but certainly not limited to, paintings, drawings, photographs, sculptures, films, video, and musical and literary works. It may also extend to non-utilitarian works of craft and design. The complexity of United States and international copyright laws is such that museum professionals with responsibilities in the area of rights and reproduction should have current source material available for reference, such as Marie C. Malaro, *A Legal Primer on Managing Museum Collections,* 2nd Edition (Smithsonian Institution Press, Washington, D.C., 1998), and Christine Steiner, ed., *A Museum Guide to Copyright and Trademark* (Michael Shapiro & Brett I. Miller, Morgan, Lewis & Bockius, American Association of Museums, 1999). They should also keep current, through professional publications and conferences, with changing laws pertaining to copyright, especially in the rapidly developing area of electronic media. *(See chapter on copyright.)*

If the museum does not own copyright or does not have a non-exclusive agreement with a copyright holder, images may be provided with the explicit understanding that the client requesting image use is responsible for procuring copyright release.

Once a museum has established that it has the right to grant permission to reproduce images in its collection, it should maintain close control over the process through appropriate contracts. If the collections photographer is not a staff member of the museum, a contract specifically giving rights in the photographs of objects to the museum should be entered into with the photographer. (See discussion in chapter on copyright about "work for hire.")

Several basic conditions should govern the permission to reproduce photographs of art and artifacts in the museum collections:

•The request must be made in writing.

•Reproduction rights are granted on a non-exclusive basis only for one usage in one North American publication, one edition, and one language; permission to publish in each subsequent edition or reprint must be obtained in advance.

•Special permission must be granted for world rights and additional languages.

•All reproductions must be made from photographic materials supplied by the museum; these materials remain the property of the museum.

•Unless the museum agrees otherwise in writing, each object must be reproduced unaltered and in its entirety; the reproduction must be full-tone black and white or full-color and must not be bled off the page, printed on color stock or with colored ink; nothing may be superimposed on the image; when a detail is used, the word detail must appear in the caption with the complete credit line, along with the full image elsewhere in the publication.

•The reproduction must be accompanied (directly under the reproduction, on the facing page, on the reverse, or in an index or list of illustrations) by the full caption and by credit lines as provided by the museum.

•The museum must see the proposed layout and

proof before color reproduction is approved.

In addition, the museum should include a statement alerting users of its photographic materials to certain legal ramifications. Such a paragraph should include the following:

> The museum makes no warranties or representations and assumes no responsibility whatsoever for any claims against applicant or museum by artists, their agents, estates, or by any parties in connection with the reproduction of works of art in the collections of the museum. The applicant agrees to indemnify the museum and hold it harmless against any and all such claims, including copyright infringement claims, royalty or fee demands and/or actions, including the costs thereof, arising as a result of the applicant's reproduction of the works of art in the museum's collections. Any and all royalty payments or other requirements specified by the copyright owner of such a work must be paid or honored by the publisher or agent requesting reproduction permission.

Most museums charge for the services of providing photographic materials and granting the right to reproduce, usually required in advance in U.S. currency, international money order, wire transfer, or by credit card. The client must provide two gratis copies of the publication to the museum. A photographic and reproduction fee schedule should clearly set forth the costs for each service, including:

Photography (Color and Black and White)

- photographs from existing negatives
- photographs for which a negative must be made
- color transparencies (ordinarily rented for three months)
- slides
- digital images (either sent to client on CD or retrieved via a secure ftp site or online folder maintained by the museum)

Reproduction

- rights for one-time editorial use
- license agreements
- royalty agreements (license and royalty agreements require special contracts defining the limits of usage and fee arrangements)
- image resolution restrictions for CD-ROM and related electronic media

Fees (Sliding Ccale)

For-profit clients:

- film, video, advertising
- book jackets, magazine covers, album/CD covers, calendars
- illustrations in books, textbooks, journals, magazines
- website usage (or e-book editions)

Not-for-profit clients:

- museums and other not-for-profit organizations/ publications
- scholars
- university-level students

Shipping Costs

Charged to client's account on museum-specified carrier

While many large museums have fully staffed rights and reproduction offices, smaller museum often rely on the registrar to handle these services. Some museums contract with commercial services such as Art Resource or Bridgeman Art Library for handling rights and reproductions requests. It is in the museum's interest for all staff to be fully aware of the complexity of rights and reproduction services and to consult with legal counsel when developing such services. ●

Thanks to John Magill.

ANITA M. DIFANIS

AAMD is not qualified to give legal or accounting advice. The information below is correct regarding federal law to the best of our knowledge as of the date of issue, but should not be relied upon; if there is doubt or conflict a legal advisor or accountant should be consulted. The information below, although not exhaustive, is intended to provide basic knowledge about some issues so users may ask more informed questions of their professional advisors. This document is intended for distribution only to AAMD members.

Please remember there may be local or state laws governing some of the issues listed below; be sure to check with local authorities.

DEFINITIONS

1. *Appreciated property* is property that has increased in value over the last price paid. For example, if a collector purchases a work of art in 2000 for $5,000 that today is worth $10,000, he owns a work of appreciated property.

2. *Fair market value* is the price a willing buyer will pay to a willing seller in an arm's-length transaction.

3. *In-kind gifts* are gifts of objects (e.g, art, books, furniture, and land)—tangible things rather than cash or securities.

4. *Related use or exempt use* is the IRS designation for the purpose(s) for which museums have been granted their tax-exempt status. Exempt use purpose can generally be equated to the museum's mission.

5. *Related use or exempt use gifts* are those given to an institution where they will be used to further the mission of the institution. For example, giving a work of art to a museum is usually a related use gift since it furthers the mission of the institution; however, giving a work of art to a soup kitchen is not a related use, since the soup kitchen's mission is to serve meals, not show art. Related use gifts are tangible personal property for which the donee (but not artists who donate their own work) generally may take a fair market-value deduction.

6. *Tangible personal property* is any property other than land or buildings that can be seen or touched, including works of art, furniture, books, jewelry, paintings, and cars. Land and buildings are not tangible personal property—they are real personal property and governed by different tax rules.

TAX ISSUES FOR MUSEUMS

Form 8282—Disposing of Donated Works of Art in Less than Three Years

If a museum disposes of (sells, trades, exchanges or gives away) a donated work of art for which the donor took a deduction of more than $5,000, in less than three years after receipt, the museum must file IRS Form 8282 reporting to the IRS within 125 days of the disposition; a copy must also be sent to the donor. The museum is required to use the property for three years in order for the donor to receive a deduction equal to the fair market value. Or the museum must provide both the donor and the IRS with certification, signed under penalty of perjury, that testifies:

1. that the work of art was related to the mission of the museum;

2. how the property was used and how such use furthered the mission of the museum;

3. the intended use of the property by the museum at the time of the donation;

4. that such intended use has become impossible or infeasible to implement.

If the museum sells or otherwise disposes of the work in less than three years without filing a certification, the donor's charitable deduction is reduced from fair market value to cost basis.

Whether or not a work is accessioned plays no role in the three-year rule.

The three-year rule is effective for contributions made and tax returns filed after Sept. 1, 2006. A $10,000 penalty will be imposed for knowingly misidentifying property as related to the mission of the museum.

TAX ISSUES FOR MUSEUMS

1. *Auctions.* Taxpayers who donate works of art to an auction (even though the proceeds will be used to support the museum's tax exempt purpose) may only deduct their basis—what they paid for the work, not the work's fair market value. Fair market-value deductions can only be taken for works of art donated for exempt use. Therefore, artists who donate their own works can deduct only the cost of materials, and collectors can deduct only what they paid for the work; neither can deduct appreciated value.

The taxpayer who purchases a work of art at auction cannot deduct the purchase price from his taxes unless he paid above the fair market value. For example, if a work being sold at auction is advertised to have a fair market value to $1,000 and is purchased for $1,000, the taxpayer deducts nothing. If the $1,000 work sells for $2,000, the taxpayer may deduct $1,000 from his taxes.

2. *Donations of Works of Art.* Deductions for gifts of art are limited to 30 percent of the adjusted gross income, but can be carried forward for five years.

3. *Fair Market Value Deduction.* Taxpayers who donate tangible, personal property to a museum—a work of art—may take the fair market value deduction. (This rule does not apply to artists who donate their own work.) The work must be related to the exempt purpose of the museum. For example, the donation of a rare set of books on archeology donated to a contemporary art museum would not likely be

an allowed deduction since the exempt purpose of the contemporary art museum is to collect and exhibit contemporary art.

If the work is valued over $5,000 a qualified appraisal must be attached to the taxpayer's income tax return. If the donor cannot take the entire deduction in the year the gift is given, it can be carried forward for five years. Museums should avoid giving appraisal advice except to offer a list of qualified appraisers, if appropriate.

Any taxpayer whose returns are audited—for whatever reason—and who has donated a work of art valued at $20,000 or more will automatically be referred to the IRS Art Advisory Panel, which will determine if the art deduction was warranted.

4. *Fractional Gifts.* Effective Aug. 17, 2006, the provision for making fractional donations of works of art changed. A donor may now give a museum partial ownership in a work of art with the remainder ownership to be completed within 10 years or the donor's death, whichever occurs first.

The donor, after receiving a qualified appraisal, deducts from his income tax the fair market value of the initial fraction given; he can also carry forward his deduction for five years, but can only deduct 30 percent of his gross adjusted income in any given year. When the donor gives subsequent fractions, after receiving a qualified appraisal, he may only deduct the lesser amount (either the first appraisal or the current appraisal); as a result, if the work has increased in value the donor cannot take an increased deduction. Donors must file IRS Form 8283, which includes description of property (and percentage interest donated, if a fractional gift), and a qualified appraisal that must be repeated for each additional portion of ownership the donor gives to the museum.

The museum is obligated to take "significant physical possession" of the work within the 10-year period.

If a donor has given a fraction before the effective date of Aug. 17, 2006, a subsequent fraction given after the effective date starts the clock on the new provisions described above. In other words, the first fraction donated after the effective date is treated like the first fraction: the donor gets a qualified appraisal and may deduct the fair market value that corresponds to the ownership interest being transferred. From that point forward the gift must be fully given within 10 years or death, deductions for subsequent fractions given are at the lesser amount and the museum must take total possession no later than the end of the 10-year period and must take "significant physical possession" of the gift during the 10-year period.

5. *Hold Work of Art One Year Before Donating.* Donors must hold a work for one year after purchase before it can be donated for a fair market value deduction. •

7G | APPRAISALS

SONJA TANNER-KAPLASH

About 400 years ago, the verb *apprize* (now appraise) first came into common use and meant "to judge or estimate the quality or worth of." Its synonym, evaluation (or valuation), is a later addition from the French *evaluer*. Each of these words denotes an indication, an estimate, or an opinion—professional and informed, but an opinion nevertheless—the validity of which is directly related to the appraiser's knowledge and experience and is most clearly demonstrated by a written statement of the facts upon which the valuation is based.

While the idea of "worth" includes aspects such as authenticity, historical importance or association, condition, quality, rarity, and market demand, it is invariably the matter of monetary value that is the major concern of museums, which generally have substantial in-house expertise in the former areas.

WHY APPRAISE?

Museums seek appraisals for many reasons. Most frequently museums need to update (or create) an inventory for insurance purposes, but occasionally they need assistance to set a value upon an outgoing loan, to confirm the purchase price of a new acquisition, to document a proposed deaccession, to satisfy requirements for federal indemnification, or to support an application for public funding or grants.

While U.S. museums do not become directly involved in arranging appraisals of gifts for which donors receive income tax benefits, this is not the case in other jurisdictions such as Canada. In such situations, the museum must be conscious not only of its own liability but also of that of its donors, since appraisals can become a pivotal point in litigation. Few situations sour the museum/donor relationship more surely than a tax investigation, which affects both repeat donations from the same source and the attitude of prospective donors.

MUSEUM POLICIES

Since the appraisal process offers some potential for problems, the governing authority of the museum must ensure that appropriate, approved, written policies and procedures are in place and followed.

The concern of the museum is to ensure that competent, reputable, arm's-length appraisers are selected, and that the appraisal document can withstand close scrutiny. The museum must act, and be seen to act, honestly and impartially when obtaining an appraisal so that the transaction is conducted in a businesslike and consistent manner.

Policies should determine under what circumstances in-house appraisals by curators are appropriate, and when and how an acceptable outside appraiser will be chosen. In keeping with the ICOM Code of Professional Ethics, most museums prohibit staff from evaluating objects for a third party on museum time and/or premises; this restriction protects both the museum and potential donors.

The board must also determine its position regarding museum staff who work as appraisers *in their own time,* since the clients of such individuals may assume that they are acting as a representative of the museum. Policies may prohibit outside appraisal work for employees or may require full disclosure of such activities to ensure that conflict of interest situations do not arise.

METHODS OF APPRAISAL

Ideally an appraisal should be based upon a physical examination of the object(s) by the appraiser; when this is not possible, photographs may be used. However, a valid appraisal cannot be based upon a verbal description only; the appraiser must see the subject material, either in the original or by means of a good photograph. Museums should be especially wary of the "telepraisal" businesses that have advertised widely in the past.

Photographs should show several different views of the object, as well as any positive or negative characteristics that may affect values. It is important to illustrate features such as wear, damage, the extent of restoration or old repairs, maker's marks, manufacturing defects or other irregularities.

The photographs, preferably taken by a professional photographer, should be accompanied by a detailed written description, including dimensions, material, technique, condition, and any other relevant source information known to the museum that might affect values.

PRICING SOURCES

Numerous standard, published references can assist the museum in evaluating its own collections. Curators will be familiar with the *catalogue raisonné* and academic publications, but these rarely report current prices. Other, more helpful publications range from price guides or catalogs of specialty collections (such as coins or maritime objects), to general books on "collectibles" or "Americana"—as well as the more conventional classifications of antiques or fine art. Many are updated annually and report prices from a variety of sources.

Periodical publications range from glossy, coffee table magazines, to serious journals, trade publications, and (often short-lived) newsletters aimed at particular interest groups. These provide current pricing information, either directly as listings or articles, or indirectly through advertising or reports of sales.

Certain dealers circulate price lists of objects available for sale ("dealer lists") to former clients and other interested parties. Major auction houses advertise forthcoming sales by means of illustrated catalogues, which show reserve prices for each object or lot; after the auction, the final selling prices are also provided to catalogue subscribers.

These references are the backbone of the published, and therefore public, information available to museum staff upon which in-house evaluations of similar objects in the museum collection may be

based. However, museums often decide to hire an outside appraiser when an object is beyond the area of expertise of a specific curator or curatorial department or is of particular importance.

Many curators and other professionals in the natural science and archaeological fields are adamantly opposed to the monetary valuation of specimens, believing that this process encourages the illicit trade in such materials. However, there is no doubt that these objects are bought and sold on the open market. Museums with such collections are usually unwilling to forego an insurance claim in the event of a major loss; in addition, they routinely provide values of such objects for outgoing loans. The insurance industry recognizes a method of valuation for this type of material that provides an ethical and practical solution: a calculation of the cost of a field trip to gather or excavate such material again. Clearly this method makes the most sense when the museum has recent records of similar field trips to use as a guide. It can be a lengthy calculation based on a large number of variables, but it provides an idea of the monetary worth of such collections. Museums would be wise to discuss this methodology with their insurers before undertaking a major valuation project.

WHO APPRAISES?

Locating a competent appraiser is not always an easy task, since this occupation is not licensed or regulated in any formal way. It is important to find someone who is already knowledgeable about the type of material under consideration. Few people are truly expert in a wide range of fields, and the "generalist appraiser" must either spend considerable time researching a particular object or provide a less than satisfactory appraisal.

Although private collectors, writers, and academics often have considerable expertise and access to published price information and may be perfectly acceptable appraisers, most appraisers are commercial dealers. The close liaison between appraisers and dealers can be advantageous in that the sales experience of the latter enhances the expertise of the former.

SELECTING AN APPRAISER

The museum could begin the selection process by securing recommendations from colleagues at other institutions. In addition, private collectors, insurance brokers, banks, or trust companies in the community may have had experience with various appraisers and their work. Directories published by the various professional associations of dealers and appraisers also provide a starting point.

When the museum first contacts likely candidates, it is appropriate to check the appraiser's credentials. For example, request information on the appraiser's background and qualifications to appraise a specific type of material. Determine how that expertise was obtained, whether by means of academic study or from experience working in an auction house or for a specialty dealer.

Inquire about membership in professional organizations, and go one step further to ask exactly what that membership signifies. Some professional appraisal associations have rigorous membership requirements and act as self-regulating bodies that set standards for training and business practices, administer examinations, discipline members, and publish monographs. Others are open to anyone who pays the membership fee. Membership in a professional organization that requires a minimum number of years of experience, successful completion of competency tests, sponsorship by existing members or character references, observation of a strict code of ethics, and accreditation and re-certification of members at regular intervals may be a meaningful indicator of an appraiser's qualifications. However, membership in an association is not an automatic indication of competency, and lack of membership may be equally meaningless.

Try to learn something about the appraiser's business, the length of time it has been in operation, the specialties of the staff, whether the owner or proprietor completes the appraisal personally, or turns it over to a junior staff member. It is especially important to learn if the business maintains a resource center and subscribes to relevant publications or data banks and if it maintains current, well-organized records of private sales for reference.

Finally, ask the appraiser to provide references, usually previous clients, and, if possible, a credential package of background information about the business and the individual; ideally, this packet should include a sample of a typical appraisal document. At this time, it is appropriate to discuss the fee structure and to ask for an estimate of the final cost of your appraisal. Should an appraiser be unwilling to undertake a particular project because she or he considers it beyond her or his area of expertise, do not insist. Instead, respect the appraiser's professionalism and honesty and attempt to locate another suitable individual.

CONFLICT OF INTEREST

Occasionally, a museum may be obliged to eliminate an otherwise competent appraiser because she or he is not sufficiently "arm's length" from the proposed transaction. To avoid conflict of interest situations, the museum should make inquiries as to whether the appraiser has any past, present, or future interest in the object being appraised and if the individual has any other relationship with the museum.

Essentially, museum policies must ensure that the appraisal process is as objective, professional, formal, businesslike, and well documented as possible. These are all elements that may be overlooked in friendly, personal relationships.

For example, an individual who is also a museum trustee should not be commissioned to do appraisal work for the same museum. Perhaps the museum intends to deaccession an object purchased some years ago from a dealer; most organizations have policies in place that require an advance appraisal of material proposed for disposal, and in such a case, it would be inappropriate to commission the *same* vendor to appraise the same object again.

IRS regulations (Publication 561, "Determining the Value of Donated Property") also state that an appraiser who derives the bulk of her or his income from a particular source (i.e., a museum) has a relationship similar to that of an employee and may not be considered a "qualified" appraiser.

LETTER OF COMMISSION

After checking references and deciding upon the best candidate, the museum should provide the appraiser with a formal letter of commission that confirms any earlier discussions and outlines the services the museum expects. The letter should identify the date by which the work is to be completed, confirm the basis on which the fee is to be calculated, provide for a personal inspection of the object by the appraiser, and specify that the value required is identified as "fair market value." The objects to be appraised should be listed with a detailed description and accompanied by photographs, if necessary.

FAIR MARKET VALUE

In much the same way as there are many different places and prices at which an item may be purchased, there is also a range within which an item is appraised. To some extent this reflects the appraiser's own experience and position in the field. For example, specialty dealers, perhaps located in a fashionable and expensive area of a major city, sell an object at a different price level than the auction house that is not obliged to keep a large selection of stock on hand for long periods of time. A decorating firm may pay a price for an attractive fragment or damaged piece that a serious collector would never consider.

Even an auction price may be the result of a bidding duel. However, "fair market value" does have a specific meaning. The IRS defines it as "the price at which the property would change hands between a willing buyer and a willing seller, neither being under any compulsion to buy or sell, and both having reasonable knowledge of relevant facts." This definition eliminates distress or liquidation sale price, as well as the bargain purchased by a knowledgeable buyer from an unwitting vendor.

For significant or highly valued pieces, some museums secure more than one appraisal from different dealers and appraisers and average the figures either as a simple numerical average or according to a formula set out in their policies.

INSURANCE VALUE

In the past, appraisers often created an "insurance or replacement value" for objects being appraised for insurance purposes. These prices were usually considerably higher than fair market values. The rationale was that in the event of a claim, the insured party would not delay purchasing a replacement or wait for a "good buy," but would be anxious to purchase a comparable item immediately—probably at the highest retail price—in addition to accumulating some travel and other costs. In reality, insurance companies and their adjusters rarely accept highly overblown values as the basis for settlement of a claim. An adjuster may seek additional opinions regarding the lost or damaged articles and recommend that the claim be settled for a lower and more realistic amount—something closer to "fair market value." In the meantime, the client (museum or private collector) has paid higher than necessary premiums for inflated insurance coverage, perhaps for a number of years.

ASSESSING THE WRITTEN APPRAISAL DOCUMENT

The format and appearance of the appraisal document reveals a great deal about the choice of appraiser. The client (the museum), the appraisal business, and the individual responsible for the work (owner, partner, employee, or independent contractor) should be clearly identified. The credentials of the appraiser, particularly private individuals (such as collectors, authors or academics, perhaps without a business letterhead), should be set out in the body of the document. Anyone else involved in the appraisal process should be identified; reputable appraisers often consult colleagues, and the major auction houses employ specialists who travel to different branch locations for special assignments.

The appraisal should be dated and indicate the date upon which the material was viewed, and where. A detailed description of each item should include its condition, dimensions, medium, technique, characteristics, title, date, and attributions to an artist or maker if applicable, information on exhibit history, previous owners and authenticity, along with an itemized value.

Since the IRS considers that the appraiser's opinion is never more valid than the facts upon which it is based, the appraisal should show evidence of an analysis of the many variables. References to values or prices should be given. Few appraisers seem willing to state in writing that "I sold a comparable object last month for $X"—although this would be the simplest solution. Therefore, it is all the more essential that the value be corroborated by information from other sales—and auction house prices are most frequently cited. In order to justify the value, the appraiser may, for example, include statements on the standing of the artists/makers in their profession, and within a particular school or movement. The appraisal might also refer to sales of other comparable artist/makers, and consider size and subject matter, as well as the current economic state of the art market.

Each page should be totaled, with a final total on the last page. Check the addition: an amazing number of arithmetical errors creep into long appraisals of many objects. Finally, the document should be signed in the original by the appraiser (not "per" another party) and should list memberships in any appropriate professional associations.

If the documentation does not meet these requirements, do not hesitate to return it for adjustment. It may not be appropriate for the museum/client to question the values, but it is certainly valid to question the evidence used to substantiate the appraisal, should it seem inadequate.

The time to correct an inadequate appraisal is immediately—before it is paid for; if there are questions later, it is often too difficult for the appraiser to reconstruct a complicated and unrecorded line of reasoning.

APPRAISAL COSTS

Until 1984, appraisal costs were almost always based upon a percentage of the total value of the appraised material. This formula provided such incentive for overblown appraisal values that, in the U.S., it was finally deemed unacceptable for IRS purposes, and was replaced with a flat fee or a *per diem* or hourly rate fee. Other jurisdictions followed suit. Although Canadian legislation does not require this pricing formula, museums and other clients have encouraged it, and it now widespread.

A well-substantiated appraisal may require extensive library research, travel to the client's premises, and consultation with colleagues in the same or different firms. For these reasons, the hourly or daily pricing mechanism provides a more accurate reflection of the actual amount of work required and allows the client to receive several estimates before making a final choice of appraiser.

Museum clients should be aware that the appraiser will also charge back any expenses, and it is wise to ask for an estimate in advance of both expenses and time required to do a certain piece of work.

Museums should not seek or accept "courtesy," free, or reduced-price appraisals. Some dealers offer this service as a goodwill gesture, but clients should be wary. Occasionally, the appraiser may be invited to defend his or her opinion to insurers or the tax authorities, and it is inappropriate to expect a professional to undertake this responsibility without a fee.

More suitable methods of reducing appraisal costs could be a cooperative venture with neighboring institutions to hire an appraiser for a day or two a month to work at various museums in the area. Another alternative is to pay an annual retainer to an appraiser that the museum uses frequently. In such an arrangement, the appraiser makes an agreed number of visits to the museum during the year to appraise several objects at once. Even these yearly fees could be shared with nearby museums that use the services of the same type of specialist on a regular basis.

For insurance purposes especially, it is advisable to have current appraisals on hand; for a modest fee, most appraisers will periodically update an evaluation that they have completed in the past.

APPRAISALS FOR INSURANCE PURPOSES

To arrive at a sensible value for the limit of liability, many museums simply take last year's "total" and add a percentage increase for appreciation. However, this technique is of little assistance to the organization tackling its first insurance purchase. In addition, a surprising number of museums have used the "best guesstimate" for so long that no one remembers how it was calculated in the beginning!

Limited human and financial resources will inevitably prohibit individual appraisals of every item in the museum collection. The sheer size of the task can be discouraging. One approach is to break the project down into several smaller components and spread it out over a period of time. Think of collections valuation as an ongoing process that becomes more refined and easier each year.

First priority should be placed upon items of high intrinsic and monetary value and those destined for outgoing loans in the immediate future. With these priorities met, the rest of the collection can be appraised gradually.

Objects of high intrinsic value are those collections that are of special significance to the museum—perhaps because of their rarity, uniqueness, or association with local or regional history. These objects may be of relatively low monetary value but extremely difficult to replace. They were probably produced in limited numbers and would be of limited interest elsewhere. This is the material that the museum will have the most difficulty appraising and replacing if necessary, so it is essential to identify it and set it aside for future attention.

Objects of high monetary value can be grouped into appropriate "value ranges," which will vary from museum to museum. A major institution may have many objects in a top value range of $200,000 to $250,000, whereas the small community museum may select $4,000 to $5,000 as a top value range in which there are only a few objects. For most organizations, the bulk of the collections will be in the lower value ranges.

Using value ranges or "schedules" (as the insurance industry labels them) to group collections saves time because it avoids the need to identify an exact value for each item immediately. Calculate the total of each schedule by using an average; for example, 10 items in a range of $3,000 to $5,000 are calculated as 10 x $4,000 = $40,000.

In the first year or two of the valuation process, available resources should be concentrated on identifying objects in the highest ranges. Adjustments will take place over time as objects are valued more accurately and moved into more appropriate categories. Eventually, the museum may introduce additional, intermediate ranges. The lowest schedules, with the largest numbers of objects, may still be something of a "guesstimate" at first; with few exceptions, these are the value ranges that can be refined and researched last. •

Legal Issues I | HYPOTHETICALS

1

A museum commissions a local artist to paint panels for an upcoming exhibition. There is, however, no written contract. The curator decides to do a publication that will include not only the finished panel, but also photographs of the artist working on it. She wants an accession number and a credit line.

Is the panel the property of the museum?

Who owns copyright?

Can a picture of the artist be published?

How would a contract have clarified the situation?

2

List and discuss the common contracts that a registrar might be involved with.

3

A photo containing a 1910 portrait by G. P. A. Healy, owned by the Sample Museum, has appeared in a *New York Times* ad for the ABC Investment firm. The ad shows the painting sitting on an easel in a sidewalk setting with a caption beside it. After some research the museum finds that a reproduction of the photograph was used in the set and that no permission had been sought.

What is the copyright status, and what steps might the museum take?

4

A request has been made to publish photographs of the following. Give the copyright status of each:
- Robert Motherwell painting, 1963
- Egyptian statuette, date?
- Paul Cézanne painting, 1898
- Unknown artist, landscape, dated 1920
- Edward Steichen photograph, 1929
- Hopi bowl, 1950s

5

A donor wants to divide a gift into two parts—each part contains several objects—so that he may take a deduction in both 2010 and 2011. He decides this after you have received the collection. He also says he wants to deal with the paperwork only once, so he asks that all of the paperwork be forwarded to him.

Since you have the intent and the delivery, which of the following do you do?

1. Send him completed paperwork for both years, dating 2011 as January 1 and sending it without a museum signature on the 2011 forms?

2. Ask him to sign a loan agreement and/or a promised gift form for the 2011 donations and send him only the 2010 gift paperwork?

3. Return the 2011 material and note that the gift should be addressed in January 2011.

6

A museum takes in a donation for an educational collection and intends to hold and use it for at least three years. After six months of use, it's destroyed.

What do you need to tell the donor and the IRS about the sequence?

7

You receive an appraisal from a donor when he sends an 8283 form to be completed by the museum, and you note that the value of the object is far too high when compared to like objects you are aware of.

Do you have a legal or ethical obligation to intervene with the donor?

If so, how do you approach the issue with the donor?

7H | COMPLYING WITH **NAGPRA**

C. TIMOTHY MCKEOWN, AMANDA MURPHY, AND JENNIFER SCHANSBERG

The Native American Graves Protection and Repatriation Act (NAGPRA) was enacted on Nov. 16, 1990, to formally affirm the rights of lineal descendants, Indian tribes, and Native Hawaiian organizations to custody of Native American human remains, funerary objects, sacred objects, and objects of cultural patrimony that are in the control of federal agencies and museums. In enacting this legislation, Congress and the president acknowledged that over the course of the nation's history, Native American human remains and funerary objects have suffered from differential treatment as compared with the human remains and funerary objects of other groups. They acknowledged that objects needed for the practice of traditional Native American religions had been acquired without the voluntary consent of an individual or group that had authority of alienation. They acknowledged the failure of American law to recognize concepts of communal property traditionally and still in use by some Indian tribes. They also made it a federal offense to sell, purchase, or use profits from Native American human remains, funerary objects, sacred objects, and objects of cultural patrimony in certain situations. The primary sources of information on NAGPRA are the statute itself [25 U.S.C. 3001 et seq.] and its implementing regulations [43 CFR 10]. See: http://www.nps.gov/history/nagpra/MANDATES/INDEX.HTM

WHO MUST COMPLY?

All federal agencies and museums receiving federal funds, except the Smithsonian Institution, are required to comply with the statute and regulations. The statute defines federal agency as any department, agency, or instrumentality of the United States. This definition includes all components of the executive, legislative, and judicial branches of the United States government that either manage land or hold collections of Native American human remains, funerary objects, sacred objects, or objects of cultural patrimony.

Federal mandate requires all federal agencies to complete summaries and inventories of Native American collections in their control and ensure compliance regarding inadvertent discoveries and intentional excavations conducted as part of activities on federal or tribal lands. Federal agencies are responsible for the appropriate treatment and care of all collections from federal lands being held by nongovernmental repositories, including those excavated or removed under the authority of the Antiquities Act [16 U.S.C. 431-433], the Reservoir Salvage Act [16 U.S.C. 469-469c], section 110 of the National Historic Preservation Act [16 U.S.C. 470h-2], and the Archaeological Resources Protection Act [16 U.S.C 470aa-mm]. Federal agencies are subject to enforcement actions by aggrieved parties under 25 U.S.C. 3013 of NAGPRA.

A museum is defined specifically in the statute as any institution or state or local government agency (including any institution of higher learning) that has possession of, or control over, Native American human remains, funerary objects, sacred objects, or objects of cultural patrimony and receives federal funds. Museums are subject to civil penalties for failure to comply with provision of the statute under 25 U.S.C. 3007 and 43 CFR 10.12.

The term "possession" as used in this definition means having physical custody of such objects with sufficient legal interest to lawfully treat them as part of the museum's collection. Generally, a museum would not be considered to have sufficient legal interest to lawfully treat human remains, funerary objects, sacred objects, or objects of cultural patrimony on loan from another individual, museum, or federal agency as part of its collection.

The term "control" means having a legal interest

in human remains, funerary objects, sacred objects, or objects of cultural patrimony sufficient to lawfully treat them as part of the museum's collection. Generally, a museum that has loaned human remains, funerary objects, sacred objects, or objects of cultural patrimony to another individual, museum, or federal agency is considered to retain control of those objects.

The phrase "receives federal funds" means the receipt of funds by a museum after Nov. 16, 1990, from a federal agency through any grant, loan, contract (other than a procurement contract), or other arrangement by which a federal agency makes or made available to a museum any aid in the form of funds. Procurement contracts are not considered a form of federal assistance but are provided to a contractor in exchange for a specific service or product. Federal funds provided for any purpose that are received by a larger entity of which the museum is part are considered federal funds to the museum. For example, if a museum is part of a state or local government or private university that receives federal funds for any purpose, the museum is considered to receive federal funds. NAGPRA applies to certified local governments. Tribal museums are covered by the statute if the Indian tribe of which the museum is a part receives federal funds through any grant, loan, or contract (other than a procurement contract).

The Smithsonian Institution is not subject to NAGPRA because it responds to a different piece of legislation. The National Museum of the American Indian Act [20 U.S.C. 80] was passed in 1989 and established separate repatriation requirements for the Smithsonian. Legislation to apply some of the NAGPRA terms and procedures to the Smithsonian was introduced in 1990 and eventually became law in 1996.

Private individuals and museums that do not receive federal funds and are not part of a larger entity that receives federal funds are not required to comply with the act.

In Summary:

•Most federal agencies must comply with provisions of the statute. Federal agencies are responsible for collections in their possession as well as those excavated or removed from federal land but currently in the possession of a non-federal repository.

•Any institution that receives federal funds—either directly or indirectly—and has possession or control of Native American human remains, funerary objects, sacred objects, or objects of cultural patrimony must comply with provisions of the statute.

•The Smithsonian Institution must comply with the National Museum of the American Indian Act, which imposes requirements similar to those found in NAGPRA.

What Objects Are Covered?

The statute applies to four types of Native American cultural items: human remains, funerary objects, sacred objects, and objects of cultural patrimony.

Human remains means the physical remains of a body of a person of Native American ancestry [25 CFR 10.2 (d)(1)]. The term has been interpreted broadly to include bones, teeth, hair, ashes, or mummified or otherwise preserved soft tissues. The statute makes no distinction between fully articulated burials and isolated bones and teeth. The term applies equally to recent and ancient Native American human remains. The term does not include remains, or portions of remains, freely given or naturally shed by the individual from whose body they were obtained, such as hair made into ropes or nets. This exclusion does not cover any human remains for which there is evidence of purposeful disposal or deposition; for example, in some Native cultures fingernail and hair clippings are purposefully buried or hidden to keep them away from witches. For the purposes of determining cultural affiliation, human remains incorporated into funerary objects, sacred objects, or objects of cultural patrimony are considered to be part of that object. This provision is intended to prevent the destruction of a funerary object, sacred object, or object of cultural patrimony that is culturally affiliated with one Indian tribe but incorporates human remains culturally affiliated with another Indian tribe. Human remains that have been repatriated under NAGPRA to lineal descendants, Indian tribes, and Native Hawaiian organizations include complete and partial skeletons, isolated bones, teeth, scalps, and ashes.

Funerary objects are defined as items that, as part of the death right or ceremony of a culture, are reasonably believed to have been placed intentionally at the time of death or later with or near individual human remains. Funerary objects must be defined by the preponderance of the evidence as having been removed from the specific burial site of an individual culturally affiliated with a particular Indian tribe or Native Hawaiian organization or to be related to specific individuals or families or to known human remains. The term "burial site" means any natural or prepared physical location, whether originally below, on, or above the surface of the earth, into which, as part of the death rite or ceremony of a culture, individual human remains are deposited. Burial sites include rock cairns or pyres that do not fall within the ordinary definition of gravesite [43 CFR 10.2 (d)(2)]. Items made exclusively for burial purposes are considered funerary objects even if there are no associated remains. Items that inadvertently came into contact with human remains—such as historic enamelware or glass fragments found in prehistoric burial contexts due to erosion or other natural processes—are not considered to be funerary objects. Certain Indian tribes, particularly those from the northern plains, have ceremonies in which objects are placed near, but not with, the human remains at the time of death or later. These items should be considered as funerary objects. The regulations distinguish between "associated funerary objects," for which the human remains and funerary objects are in the possession or control of a federal agency or museum, and "unassociated funerary objects," for which the human remains are not in the possession or control of a federal agency or museum. This distinction is only relevant for determining whether to provide information to the culturally affiliated Indian tribes or Native Hawaiian organization in a summary or in an inventory format. Associated and unassociated funerary objects that have been repatriated under NAGPRA to lineal descendants, Indian tribes, and Native Hawaiian organizations include beads of various types; pottery jars, bowls, and sherds; tools and implements of wood, stone, bone, and metal; trade silver and other goods; weapons of many types, including rifles and revolvers; and articles or fragments of clothing.

Sacred objects are defined as specific ceremonial objects needed by traditional Native American religious leaders for the practice of traditional Native American religions by their present-day adherents. Traditional religious leaders are individuals recognized by members of an Indian tribe or Native Hawaiian organization as responsible for performing cultural duties relating to the ceremonial or religious traditions of that Indian tribe or Native Hawaiian organization based on the tribe's or organization's cultural, ceremonial, or religious practices. While many items, from ancient pottery sherds to arrowheads, might be imbued with sacredness in the eyes of an individual, this definition is specifically limited to objects that were devoted to a traditional Native American religious ceremony or ritual and that have religious significance or function in the continued observance or renewal of such ceremony [43 CFR 10.2 (d)(3)]. Sacred objects that have been repatriated under NAGPRA to lineal descendants, Indian tribes, and Native Hawaiian organizations include medicine bundles, prayer sticks, pipes, effigies and fetishes, basketry, rattles, and a birch bark scroll.

Objects of cultural patrimony are defined as items having ongoing historical, traditional, or cultural importance central to the Indian tribe or Native Hawaiian organization itself, rather than property owned by an individual tribal member. These objects are of such central importance that they may not be alienated, appropriated, or conveyed by the culturally affiliated Indian tribe or Native Hawaiian organization at the time the object was separated from the group [43 CFR 10.2 (d)(4)]. Objects of cultural patrimony that have been repatriated under NAGPRA to Indian tribes and Native Hawaiian organizations include a wolf-head headdress, a clan hat, several medicine bundles, and ceremonial masks of varying types.

An item may be considered an object of cultural patrimony as well as a sacred object. These categories are not mutually exclusive. Items fitting both categories that have been repatriated under NAGPRA include Zuni War Gods, a Sun Dance wheel, ceremonial masks of several types and functions, and a tortoise shell rattle.

It should be stressed that the definitions of human remains, funerary objects, sacred objects, and objects of cultural patrimony simply define the applicability of the statute and do not in any way attempt to restrict traditional concepts of "sacredness" or "patrimony."

IN SUMMARY:

•The statute applies to four specific categories of Native American objects: human remains, funerary objects, sacred objects, and objects of cultural patrimony.

•These four categories are not mutually exclusive.

WHO MAY MAKE A REPATRIATION REQUEST?

Within the NAGPRA context, repatriation means to return or restore the control of human remains, funerary objects, sacred objects, and objects of cultural patrimony to the lineal descendant or culturally affiliated Indian tribe or Native Hawaiian organization. Cultural affiliation is defined as a relationship of shared group identity that can be reasonably traced historically or prehistorically between a present-day Indian tribe or Native Hawaiian organization and an identifiable earlier group. Cultural affiliation is established when the preponderance of the evidence—based on geographical, kinship, biological, archeological, linguistic, folklore, oral tradition, historical evidence, or other information or expert opinion—reasonably leads to such a conclusion [43 CFR 10.14 (c)]. The regulations provide certain individuals and organizations the opportunity to request the repatriation of Native American human remains and cultural items. Lineal descendants, Indian tribes, and Native Hawaiian organizations may request the repatriation of Native American human remains, funerary objects, and sacred objects. Indian tribes and Native Hawaiian organizations may request the

repatriation of objects of cultural patrimony. The criteria needed to identify who has standing to make a repatriation request are outlined below.

Lineal descendant is defined by regulation as an individual tracing his or her ancestry directly and without interruption by means of the traditional kinship of the appropriate Indian tribe or Native Hawaiian organization or by the American common law system of descendance to a known Native American individual whose remains, funerary objects, or sacred objects are being requested [43 CFR 10.2 (b) (1)]. The necessity of a direct and unbroken line of ancestry between the individual making the request and a known individual is a high standard, but one that is consistent with the preference for a disposition or repatriation to lineal descendants required by the statute. Reference to traditional kinship systems is designed to accommodate the different systems that individual Indian tribes and Native Hawaiian organizations use to reckon kinship. A lineal descendant need not be an enrolled or otherwise affiliated member of an Indian tribe or Native Hawaiian organization. Lineal descendants may request human remains, funerary objects, and sacred objects. The statute does not authorize repatriation of objects of cultural patrimony—which by definition are controlled by the Indian tribe or Native Hawaiian organization as a whole—to lineal descendants.

Indian tribe is defined as any tribe, band, nation, or other organized Indian group or community of Indians, including any Alaska Native village, as defined in or established by the Alaska Native Claims Settlement Act [43 CFR 106 et seq.], which is recognized as eligible for the special programs and services provided by the United States to Indians because of their status as Indians [43 CFR 10.2 (b)(2)]. This definition was drawn explicitly from the American Indian Self Determination and Education Act [25 U.S.C. 450b], a statute implemented since 1976 by the Bureau of Indian Affairs to apply to a specific list of eligible Indian tribes and Alaska Native villages and corporations. The decision to use the American Indian Self Determination and Education Act definition of "Indian tribe" precludes extending applicability of the same terms in NAGPRA to non-federally recognized Indian groups that have been terminated, that are current applicants for recognition, or have only state or local jurisdiction legal status. There are over 760 Indian tribes and Alaska Native villages and corporations that are eligible to make repatriation requests under the regulations. The current list of Indian tribal contacts is available on the Native American Consultation Database kept by the National Park Service [http://www.nps.gov/nacd/].

Native Hawaiian organization is defined as any organization that: 1) serves and represents the interests of Native Hawaiians; 2) has as a primary and stated purpose the provision of services to Native Hawaiians; and 3) has expertise in Native Hawaiian affairs. The statute specifically identifies the Office of Hawaiian Affairs and Hui Malama I Na Kupuna O Hawai'i Nei as being Native Hawaiian organizations [43 CFR 10.2 (b)(3)].

Non-federally recognized Indian groups do not have standing to make a direct repatriation request under the statute. That is because these groups, though they may comprise individuals of Native American descent, are not recognized as eligible for the special programs and serviced provided by the United States to Indians because of their status as Indians. Human remains in federal agency or museum collections for which a relationship of shared group identity can be shown with a particular non-federally recognized Indian group are considered "culturally unidentifiable." Federal agencies and museums that hold culturally unidentifiable human remains may request the Native American Graves Protection and Repatriation Review Committee to recommend disposition of such remains to the appropriate non-federally recognized Indian group. Details of this process are available from the manager, National NAGPRA Program, National Park Service, Washington, D.C.

IN SUMMARY:

•Human remains, funerary objects, and sacred objects may be claimed by lineal descendants, Indian tribes, and Native Hawaiian organizations.

•Objects of cultural patrimony may only be claimed by Indian tribes and Native Hawaiian organizations.

•Non-federally recognized Indian groups do not have standing to make a direct claim under the statute.

COMPLIANCE WITH NAGPRA

There are eight specific ways that a museum might fail to comply with NAGPRA:

1. sell or transfer any human remains, funerary object, sacred object, or object of cultural patrimony without complying with the statute

2. fail to complete a summary of collections that may include unassociated funerary objects, sacred objects, or objects of cultural patrimony

3. fail to complete an inventory of human remains or associated funerary objects

4. fail to notify culturally affiliated Indian tribes or Native Hawaiian organizations within six months after completion of the inventory

5. refuse to repatriate human remains, funerary objects, sacred objects, or objects of cultural patrimony to a lineal descendant or culturally affiliated Indian tribe or Native Hawaiian organization

6. repatriate human remains, funerary objects, sacred objects, or objects of cultural patrimony prior to publishing a notice in the *Federal Register*

7. fail to consult with lineal descendants or affiliated Indian tribes or Native Hawaiian organizations

8. fail to inform recipients that items have been treated with of pesticides

A museum that receives a Notice of Failure to Comply from the Department of the Interior has 45 days to take corrective action or to request an administrative hearing.

What Is the Registrar's Role?

Registrars in federal agencies and museums containing or collecting Native American items have a wide range of responsibilities that affect acquisition, accessioning, information management, care, and deaccessioning collection objects. NAGPRA influences all of these activities.

Webster's dictionary defines *acquire* as "to come into possession or control of." Federal agencies and museums may acquire objects by gift, field collection, or purchase, and most are destined for accession into their permanent collections. Objects may also be acquired for study collections, decoration, or sale in the gift shop. Since NAGPRA could potentially apply to any Native American object acquired by the museum or federal agency, all acquisitions should be reviewed in light of NAGPRA's summary, inventory, and repatriation requirements.

Summaries are written descriptions of collections that may contain Native American unassociated funerary objects, sacred objects, or objects of cultural patrimony and must include, at a minimum, the following information:

- an estimate of the number of objects in the collection or portion of the collection

- a description of the kinds of objects included

- reference to the means, date(s), and location(s) by which the collection or portion of the collection was acquired, where readily ascertainable

- information relevant to identifying lineal descendants, if available, and cultural affiliation

The statute originally required the summaries be completed by Nov. 16, 1993. New or supplemental summaries are now due within six months of acquiring control of new collections or federal acknowledgement of a new Indian tribe, and within three years of an institution receiving federal funds for the first time

"Inventory" has a very specific meaning in NAGPRA. Inventories are item-by-item descriptions of human remains and associated funerary objects and must include, at a minimum, the following information:

- accession and catalog entries: acquisition information, including name of source, if known, date, means, and location of acquisition

- description of the human remains and associated funerary objects

- a summary of the evidence used to determine cultural affiliation or lineal descent

A NAGPRA inventory is not just a list of objects. It must be completed in consultation with the culturally affiliated Indian tribe(s) and Native Hawaiian organization(s) and represent a decision by the museum or federal agency identifying the lineal descendant or culturally affiliated Indian tribe(s) or Native Hawaiian organization(s). If cultural affiliation of human remains with a particular individual, Indian tribe, or Native Hawaiian organization cannot be established pursuant to the regulations, the human remains must be considered culturally unidentifiable. Pending publication of 43 CFR 10.11 addressing the disposition of culturally unidentifiable human remains, institutions must provide information regarding such human remains to the manager, National NAGPRA Program. In addition, federal agencies and museums must retain possession of the culturally unidentifiable human remains unless legally required to do otherwise or recommended to do otherwise by the secretary of the interior. Museums and federal agencies may request recommendations from the secretary regarding the disposition of culturally unidentifiable human remains prior to final promulgation of 43 CFR 10.11.

The statute originally required that the inventories be completed by Nov. 16, 1995. New or supplemental inventories are now due within two years of an institution's acquiring control of new collections or federal acknowledgement of a new Indian tribe and within five years of an institution receiving federal funds for the first time.

In addition to the above requirements, the registrar should make sure that all donors, collectors, and sellers are aware of the possible consequences under NAGPRA. Donors should be informed that their gifts could potentially be repatriated. Field collectors should be made aware of the importance of documenting an object's provenance, particularly those aspects of an Indian tribe or Native Hawaiian organization's traditional property law related to the alienation of the object. Donors, collectors, and sellers should be informed that it is illegal to sell, purchase, use for profit, or transport for sale or profit Native American human remains, or, in certain situations, funerary objects, sacred objects, or objects of cultural patrimony. Requiring payment of admission to view such objects constitutes a use for profit.

Accessioning is the process by which an object formally becomes part of the collection. This is the time for the registrar to obtain as much information about the objects as possible from the donor, collector, or seller. It often is not possible to obtain this information later. The information obtained during accessioning can greatly enhance the importance of the object, as well as make NAGPRA compliance much easier. Collection objects are merely interesting "stuff" without information on who, where, and for what purpose the objects were originally acquired. This documentation constitutes the most readily available evidence needed to determine cultural affiliation of Native American human remains and cultural items—something required under NAGPRA. Acquisition information is also of critical importance in documenting that a new item was originally acquired with the voluntary consent of an individual or group that had right of alienation, hence providing clear title to the item. A federal agency or museum that can prove "right of possession" is not required to repatriate human remains or cultural items to a lineal descendant or culturally affiliated Indian tribe or Native Hawaiian organization.

Documentation is critical for complying with NAGPRA. Professional standards require periodic review of the collection and related records. The process of NAGPRA compliance, however, has made it clear that the Native American collections housed in many federal agencies and museums unfortunately lack documentation. NAGPRA, along with regulations on the curation of federally owned and administered archaeological collections [36 CFR 79], has provided the impetus to review Native American ethnographic and archeological areas of the collection in detail.

NAGPRA also provides federal agencies and museums with an important source of new information: consultation with Indian tribes and Native Hawaiian organizations themselves. The NAGPRA summary process is intended as an initial step to bring Indian tribes and Native Hawaiian organizations into consultation with a federal agency or museum. Such consultation is required after completion of the summary. Inventories, on the other hand, must be completed in consultation with Indian tribes and Native Hawaiian organizations and represent a decision by the federal agency or museum as to the cultural affiliation of particular human remains or associated funerary objects. Consultation demands more than a letter. It involves a dialogue in which information is shared and, at a minimum, should be conducted over the telephone. Face-to-face consultation, while providing greater satisfaction and understanding to the parties, is not always financially feasible.

Museum officials have discovered completely unexpected things about their collection during conversations with Indian tribal representatives and traditional religious leaders. For example, a large U.S. natural history museum hosted a visit of traditional religious leaders to view the collections. As the men toured the facility and read through the catalog, they were excited to notice the mention of a peach pit game. Museum personnel had no idea this particular "game" was sacred to the tribe. Because the religious leaders visited the museum to examine the collection, and share their knowledge of the sacredness of the game, the museum gained valuable documentation. It may be possible to answer cataloging questions about some Native American cultural items with a simple telephone call or e-mail.

Much of the information conveyed to registrars and other museum officials during consultation is extremely sensitive. Many religious leaders are reluctant to explain the sacredness of particular objects because the knowledge is not for everyone. Registrars should be aware of any Freedom of Information Act legislation that may apply to their institutions and not promise more confidentiality than they are able to deliver. The registrar can only provide confidentiality to the extent allowed by law.

The registrar should take special care in

documenting any treatment of human remains, funerary objects, sacred objects, or objects of cultural patrimony with pesticides, preservatives, or other substances that represent a potential hazard to the objects or to persons handling the objects. This information must be reported to the recipients of repatriated items [43 CFR 10.10 (e)].

NAGPRA also has an impact on the future care for collections. Registrars, if they aren't already collections managers, are often involved with collection managers and conservators in the design and control of collection storage areas. There are situations in which Native American human remains, funerary objects, sacred objects, or objects of cultural patrimony that can be claimed by culturally affiliated Indian tribes or Native Hawaiian organizations remain in museum storage areas. Depending on the circumstances—and after consultation with the culturally affiliated Indian tribe or Native Hawaiian organization—the registrar may wish to recommend special storage requirements.

For example, a small historical society had in its collection human remains that had been identified, through consultation, as being culturally affiliated with a particular tribe. Consultation was completed in mid-winter when the ground was frozen. During their consultations, tribal and museum officials agreed that the remains would stay at the historical society until such time as they could be buried. The human remains were wrapped in deerskin, the material traditionally used to wrap the remains of ancestors, and special precautions were taken to protect the rest of the collection against pests that might be attracted to the deerskin. Through consultation, the interests of both the culturally affiliated Indian tribe and the museum were successfully accommodated.

Handling refers to human intervention when moving an object from one place to another. While registrars and conservators have stringent rules for how objects should be handled, sometimes Native American religious or traditional practices justify a modification of handling rules. For example, smoking is forbidden in many collection areas for fire as well as conservation concerns. Many Indian tribes, however, purify areas by burning sage or tobacco. In certain circumstances, museums have allowed

purification ceremonies after taking necessary precautions. Some sacred objects and objects of cultural patrimony may be imbued with powers that create handling restrictions of their own. Many tribes send teams of male and female elders on consultation visits because some objects might be affiliated with a specific male or female society and thus are not to be touched or in some cases even seen by members of the opposite sex.

NAGPRA repatriations usually involve use of some sort of packing and may also include shipping. The statute requires that the return of a cultural item be in consultation with the requesting lineal descendant or Indian tribe or Native Hawaiian organization to determine the place and manner of delivery of such items. Registrars and other museum personnel must remember to consider tribal and individual sensibilities with regard to the return of human remains, funerary objects, sacred objects, and objects of cultural patrimony. In general, a well-made shipping container, designed in consultation with the culturally affiliated recipient, should be adequate for repatriation. An often-told repatriation horror story culminates with the box containing the bones of an Alaska Native ancestor disintegrating upon arrival at its destination as the tribal elders watched aghast. Before shipping, the relevant federal, state, and local statutes covering the transport of human remains must be checked.

Objects in museum collections are often photographed as a matter of course. Some Indian tribes and Native Hawaiian organizations believe that certain items should not be photographed. Although photography is not prohibited under NAGPRA, it is a good policy and good public relations—especially in the case of objects or remains that are scheduled for repatriation—to consult the culturally affiliated groups prior to scheduling a photo shoot.

Once a valid repatriation claim has been received, the registrar is responsible for documenting the process of permanently removing the item from the collection. Regulations require federal agencies and museums to adopt internal procedures adequate to permanently document the content and recipients of all repatriations [43 CFR 10.10 (f)(1)]. Regulations also require that repatriation must occur within 90 days of receipt of a valid claim [43 CFR 10.10 (a)(3) and 10.10 (b)(2)]. Although a registrar may initiate the deaccessioning process, a higher authority such as the board of directors or trustees usually must authorize the actual deaccession. There have been instances in which a board has been reluctant to authorize the deaccession of human remains, funerary objects, sacred objects, or objects of cultural patrimony. Remember that NAGPRA is the law and the secretary of the interior is authorized to assess civil penalties on any museum that fails to comply. If an Indian tribe or Native Hawaiian organization presents evidence of cultural affiliation and explains how an object fits a NAGPRA category and the institution cannot prove that it has right of possession to the object, the object must be repatriated. Deaccessioning procedures may need to be revised to comply with the regulatory requirements. On the other hand, there have been instances in which a museum or federal agency has been too quick to repatriate without sufficient evidence of cultural affiliation, lineal descent, or whether the object fits one of the statutory definitions. Repatriation under NAGPRA without sufficient evidence hurts everyone by distorting the consultation and repatriation process.

A federal agency or museum may not repatriate human remains, funerary objects, sacred objects, or objects of cultural patrimony prior to publishing the required notice in the *Federal Register*. A published notice is part of the due process requirement and ensures that all interested lineal descendants, Indian tribes, and Native Hawaiian organizations that may not have been previously consulted are aware of the decision. Information regarding publication of *Federal Register* notices is available from the manager, National NAGPRA Program, National Park Service, Washington, D.C.

A registrar must also consider NAGPRA when evaluating disposition options. A museum or federal agency may not transfer title to human remains, funerary objects, sacred objects, or objects of cultural patrimony to an individual or institution that is not required to comply with NAGPRA. Native American objects may be transferred to another institution that is regulated by NAGPRA, but culturally affiliated Indian tribes and Native Hawaiian

organizations should be notified in advance of the transfer.

THE FUTURE

Museum professionals—and registrars in particular—must remember that NAGPRA is forever. New collections, new applications for federal funding, newly recognized tribes, new research and opinions on cultural affiliation are all reasons for registrars to reexamine NAGPRA continually. If your institution has been required or is currently required to comply with NAGPRA, consider evaluating your collections management policy and procedure documents to make compliance with NAGPRA part of them.

Today's registrars can help those who will take their places by focusing on documentation. Now, more than ever, a well-documented collection is important. It is inevitable that some repatriation claims will result in legal suits, and some already have. In such situations, federal agencies and museums must be able to provide evidence of good faith actions. Registrars can help their institutions by assuring that accession and deaccession records are clear and complete with the maximum amount of information noted, all sources identified, and all actions documented.

Questions regarding the applicability of NAGPRA to certain situations should be addressed to the institution's lawyer or to the manager, National NAGPRA Program, National Park Service, 1201 I St. N.W., 8th floor, Washington, D.C. 20005. •

SOURCES

United States Code

1906   Antiquities Act [16 U.S.C. 431-433]

1960   Reservoir Salvage Act [16 U.S.C. 469-469c]

1966   National Historic Preservation Act [16 U.S.C. 470h-2]

1973   American Indian Self Determination and Education Act [25 U.S.C. 450b].

1976   Alaska Native Claims Settlement Act [43 U.S.C. 1601 et seq.]

1979   Archaeological Resources Protection Act [16 U.S.C. 470aa-mm]

1989   National Museum of the American Indian Act [20 U.S.C. 80]

1990   Native American Graves Protection and Repatriation Act [25 U.S.C. 3001 et seq.]

United States Code of Federal Regulations

2008   Curation of Federally-Owned and Administered Archeological Collections [36 CFR 79]

2008   Native American Graves Protection and Repatriation Act [43 CFR 10]

Webster's New College Dictionary

1989   Merriam-Webster, Inc., Springfield, Mass, 9th Ed.

71 | BIOLOGICAL MATERIAL: FISH, WILDLIFE, AND PLANTS

WILLIAM G. TOMPKINS, ELAINE L. JOHNSTON, AND JULIE L. HAIFLEY

INTRODUCTION

Consider the following scenarios:

• A donor offers your museum approximately 1,500 salvaged dead bird specimens, including whole carcasses, bones, and other parts.

• Your museum is borrowing a group of Kayapo headdresses for exhibition from a museum in Brazil.

• A staff ornithologist is importing scientific study skins from a museum in Peru.

• A private trophy hunter donates an imported jaguar hide and skin acquired by sport-hunting.

• You are receiving a shipment from the People's Republic of China of unidentified herbarium specimens.

• An upcoming international traveling exhibition includes a contemporary sculpture containing trumpet corals.

• Your zoological park is shipping a live golden lion tamarin to a zoo in France as a breeding loan.

• A staff research scientist is importing frozen tissue samples collected in the field from an elephant in Nepal.

If any of these situations sound familiar, museum staff should know the applicable laws and permit requirements concerning fish, wildlife, and plants.

The purpose of this section is to outline federal laws and regulations concerning fish, wildlife, and plants, and to assist registrars, collections managers, curators, and scientists in determining if, when, and how to apply for federal permits that allow an institution to engage in activities that are regulated under these laws. This is a general guide and is not intended to be definitive; therefore, the specific laws

and regulations should be reviewed prior to undertaking regulated transactions. In addition, wildlife laws and regulations are periodically amended. Museum staff should refer to the actual text of relevant laws and regulations as well as consult with the appropriate regulatory agency to ensure compliance with current rules. This section only addresses federal laws, including the Endangered Species Act, which implements the Convention on International Trade in Endangered Species of Wild Fauna and Flora (CITES). It is important to comply with all state and local laws as well. Check with state and local authorities to determine if there are any applicable laws.

BACKGROUND

Trade in endangered, threatened, and otherwise protected wildlife has had a destructive effect on the world's flora and fauna. In an effort to curtail activity harmful to the population of certain species, the United States and other nations have entered into international treaties and have passed domestic laws designed to preserve and conserve the world's species and their habitats. These laws limit and often ban specified activities involving protected species. Under certain conditions, exceptions to prohibited activities are allowed by regulation or permits for purposes such as scientific research, public display, enhancement of species propagation, or survival of the affected species.

Federal regulations concerning possession, disposition, and transportation of animals and plants are complex, and compliance can be daunting. Current regulations broadly govern commercial activities involving a relatively small number of the world's species. However, such regulations significantly affect the museum community. Permits may be required when:

•collecting, especially field collecting

•acquiring collections through gift or purchase

•lending or borrowing

•arranging collection exchanges

•transporting objects across U.S. state boundaries, across any foreign borders, or on the high seas

It is important that museum staff be aware of the various laws when museum activities involve protected species. Museum staff who have authority to collect, acquire, dispose, loan, or transport wildlife or plant specimens or objects containing wildlife or plant parts or products are responsible for determining whether the particular species is protected and ensuring that the museum's activities are in compliance with any applicable laws and regulations. Lack of compliance with wildlife laws, whether unintentional or a knowing violation, may result in delays, seizure, and confiscation of specimens, personal liability for civil and criminal penalties including fines or imprisonment, and damage to personal, professional, and institutional reputations.

Collections management policies should establish an institution's standard of responsibility regarding compliance with all applicable laws, including wildlife laws and regulations. The policy should establish authority and assign responsibility to approve, document, and ensure compliance with all legal requirements for transactions involving protected species. The institution should also clearly address the delegation and responsibility of collecting authority regarding field research. Internal procedures should provide guidance for staff conducting research and collection activities regarding the acquisition, importation, exportation, and transportation of wildlife and plants and the necessary accompanying documentation.

Frequently, museum staff do not realize that some items in their collections contain plant or animal parts or products protected by various federal laws. These laws prescribe that certain requirements be followed in order to acquire, take, possess, dispose, transport, import, or export specimens or articles containing plant and animal parts or products.

Under these laws, many of the routine practices of museum collection activity require a permit or compliance with other regulatory requirements. Such laws generally apply to live or dead specimens of the protected species, as well as objects made in whole or part of protected species. No matter how small the article or how very little of a specimen consists of wildlife parts, the wildlife laws may apply (e.g., blood, tissue, DNA samples). A valid permit is required before commencing any prohibited activity concerning a protected species. Prior to such transactions, it is advisable to review the laws and regulations relating to each activity.

Many species are protected under more than one law. Any transaction involving protected species must be in compliance with the requirements of all laws under which a particular species is protected. In some cases, it is possible to file a single permit application that fulfills the requirements of the multiple laws affecting the species. Contact the appropriate regulatory agency for guidance.

Wildlife laws are written very broadly and authorize that specific regulations be promulgated. Federal statutes are cited as volume number, United States Code, and section number, e.g., 18 USC § 42. Government agencies publish regulations that implement laws in the Code of Federal Regulations (CFR). The Code of Federal Regulations is a codification of the general and permanent rules published in the *Federal Register* by the departments of the executive branch and agencies of the federal government. The code is divided into 50 titles that represent broad areas subject to federal regulation. The regulations are cited as title number, Code of Federal Regulations, part or section number. Title 50—Fish and Wildlife—contains most federal regulations regarding wildlife and plants. For example, migratory birds are listed in 50 CFR Part 10, endangered and threatened wildlife in 50 CFR Part 17, marine mammals in 50 CFR Part 18. Each volume of the CFR is revised at least once each calendar year. The code is kept up-to-date by the *Federal Register*, which is published daily. These two publications should be used together to determine the latest version of any given regulation. The latest versions of these publications may be found at http://www.gpoaccess.gov/uscode/ or http://www4.

law.cornell.edu/uscode/ and http://www.gpoaccess.gov/cfr/index.html or http://cfr.law.cornell.edu/cfr/

The Department of the Interior's U.S. Fish and Wildlife Service (USFWS) has the primary responsibility to enforce federal wildlife laws that protect most endangered species, including some marine mammals, migratory birds, fishes, and plants. The USFWS also carries out U.S. enforcement obligations of certain international agreements affecting protected wildlife and plants. For the most current information on species under the jurisdiction of USFWS, go to http://www.fws.gov/. Other federal agencies have enforcement authority for certain laws and regulations discussed in this chapter, as described below.

HELPFUL HINTS FOR OBTAINING PERMITS UNDER FEDERAL WILDLIFE LAWS

1. Before Beginning the Permit Process

•Identify knowledgeable staff and museum permit procedures.

•Establish authority and assign responsibility to approve, document, and ensure compliance with legal requirements for all transactions involving protected biological material

•Identify the species involved to the most accurate taxonomic classification reasonably practicable (be species specific, including the scientific name, common name, and country of origin); seek expert advice if necessary.

•Determine which laws cover the species and the permit requirements under each applicable law.

•Determine the provenance of the object or specimen (compile supporting documentation).

•Determine the intended uses and purposes.

•Know the type of transaction (e.g., purchase, gift, loan etc.).

•Know the location where the permitted activity is to occur.

•Know the point of origin, destination, and all intermediary stops for any shipment of wildlife specimens.

•When field research or collecting in a foreign country is involved, staff must be aware of and comply with applicable wildlife laws and permit requirements of the foreign country.

•Foreign collecting and exportation / importation permits should be obtained for research materials well in advance of a proposed research project.

•Live materials may require additional permits through the Animal and Plant Health Inspection Service (APHIS), U.S. Department of Agriculture.

2. Permit Process

•Begin the permit process as soon as possible, thereby allowing sufficient time for the processing of permit applications and unforeseen delays.

•When filing a permit application, be as complete and detailed as possible.

•To expedite the permit process, consider sending the complete permit application by express mail or certified mail for proof of delivery.

•If an item qualifies for an exception, contact the federal or state agency for the required application and assistance.

•Under some circumstances, import and export of museum collections may be facilitated by a customs broker. Brokers are often familiar with permit requirements and can ensure compliance with the necessary procedures and documentation. Remember that the institution remains ultimately responsible.

•Couriers and shippers must know the permit requirements of the shipment, and the institution should have a system for monitoring their compliance.

•Maintain all records documenting importation, exportation, transportation, and subsequent disposition. Retain copies of all materials relating to permit application. It may be helpful to have multiple copies of the application and required documentation during shipment and clearance.

•Keep informed of new regulations by checking

the *Federal Register* and agency publications.

•If any questions arise as to whether a permit is required, or concerning the permit process or other related questions, contact the appropriate federal or state agency. Build a cooperative relationship with the local USFWS special agent and/or regional office.

3. Reporting

•There are procedures for using the permit that may include reporting, recording, declaration, and/or notification requirements. These requirements and instructions are often on the face of the permit or attached to it. Pay close attention to these instructions and any attachments that accompany the permit.

•It is the responsibility of the institution to make sure that timely annual reports or renewal applications are submitted.

•Any person accepting and holding a federal permit consents to and allows the entry at any reasonable hour by agents or employees of the permitting agency upon the premises where the permit activity is conducted. Federal agents or employees may enter such premises to inspect the location of any plants or wildlife kept under the authority of the permit and to inspect, audit, or copy any books, records, or permits required to be kept.

SUMMARY OF FEDERAL LAWS PROMOTING CONSERVATION OF WILDLIFE AND PLANTS

1. Lacey Act
18 USC § 42; 16 USC§ 3371, et seq.; 50 CFR Part 14
http://www4.law.cornell.edu/uscode/html/
uscode18/usc_sec_18_00000042----000-.html

The Lacey Act is the oldest and most comprehensive wildlife law in the United States. First enacted in 1900, the Lacey Act has been amended several times and its application expanded greatly. The Lacey Act Amendments of 1981 extended the protection of the act to all species of fish and wildlife, whether or not

they are considered endangered or threatened. The Lacey Act also applies to plants but only to species indigenous to the United States and its territories that have been listed on a CITES appendix or pursuant to any state law protecting species threatened with extinction. The act establishes a single, comprehensive basis for federal enforcement of state, foreign, Indian tribal, and federal wildlife laws. The Lacey Act provides the legal authority for detailed regulations that implement the statute. (Lacey Act provisions requiring humane treatment of live animals and protection against injurious species are discussed separately below.)

The Lacey Act prohibits the importation, exportation, transportation, sale, receipt, acquisition, or purchase of any fish, wildlife, or plant that was obtained or transported in violation of any law, treaty, or regulation of the United States or any Indian tribal law. Under the Lacey Act, it is illegal to import, export, or transport in interstate commerce any container or package containing any fish or wildlife, unless the container or package has previously been plainly marked, labeled, or tagged in accordance with regulations issued pursuant to the act. Making or submitting false records, labels, or identifications of fish, wildlife, or plants may also violate the Lacey Act. The importer or exporter of record may be held responsible for non-compliance of its agents, such as shippers, couriers, or brokers, if the importer or exporter has not provided adequate instructions or taken appropriate steps to ensure compliance by the agent.

Regulations implementing Lacey Act requirements for importing, exporting, and transporting wildlife are found at 50 CFR Part 14. Major provisions of the regulation that relate to importing, exporting and transporting collection material include:

a. Designated Ports:
Except when otherwise provided by permit or specific regulation, all regulated wildlife shipments must enter and leave this country through specific U.S. Customs designated ports. Special ports have also been designated for certain shipments to or from Alaska, Puerto Rico, U.S. Virgin Islands, and Guam. Special port exception

permits may be issued for scientific purposes, to minimize deterioration or loss, or for economic hardship.

b. Declaration of Wildlife Imports and Exports:

At the time of importation or prior to exportation of regulated wildlife shipments, importers or exporters must file with the USFWS a completed Declaration for Importation or Exportation of Fish and Wildlife (Form 3-177). This is not a permit, but a declaration or report form that must be submitted to the USFWS Law Enforcement Office at the port of entry. In addition to submitting hardcopies, the USFWS has developed an online system for filing Form 3-177.

c. Exceptions:

•Dead, preserved, dried, or embedded scientific specimens imported or exported by accredited scientists or accredited scientific institutions for taxonomic or systematic research may enter or exit through any U.S. Customs port or may be shipped through the international mail system. This exception does not apply to wildlife that requires a permit to be imported or exported (e.g., an endangered species), or to specimens taken as a result of sport hunting.

•Any article (other than scrimshaw) more than 100 years old that is composed in whole or in part of any endangered or threatened species and has not been repaired or modified with any part of an endangered or threatened species after Dec. 28, 1973, may be imported at any U.S. Customs port designated for such purpose.

d. Inspection and Clearance Requirement:

•Regulated wildlife shipments imported into the U.S. must be cleared by a USFWS agent before they can be released from customs. Regulated wildlife shipments to be exported from the U.S. must be cleared by USFWS before they are packed in a container or loaded onto a vehicle for export. To obtain clearance, the importer or exporter must make available to the USFWS agent all shipping documents; all permits, licenses,

or other documents required under the laws and regulations of the U.S. or of any foreign country; the wildlife being imported or exported; and any documents and permits required by the country of export or re-export of the wildlife. USFWS and customs officers may detain and inspect any package containing regulated wildlife, including all accompanying documentation, upon importation or exportation.

•A USFWS or customs officer may refuse clearance of imported or exported regulated wildlife upon reasonable grounds to believe: a federal law or regulation has been violated; the correct identity and country of origin has not been established; any permit, license, or other documentation required for clearance is not available, is not currently valid, has been suspended or revoked, or is not authentic; the importer or exporter has filed an incorrect or incomplete declaration form; or the importer or exporter has not paid any fees or penalties due.

e. Marking Requirements:

All regulated wildlife imported, exported, or transported in interstate commerce must be marked on the outside of the container with the names and addresses of the consignor and the consignee. An accurate identification of the species and the number of each species in the container must accompany the shipment.

2. The Endangered Species Act

16 USC § 1531 et seq.; 50 CFR Part 17
http://www4.law.cornell.edu/uscode/16/ch35.html

The Endangered Species Act (ESA) of 1973 is the most comprehensive U.S. law for the preservation and protection of species that have been determined to be in danger of extinction. The Endangered Species Act was designed to prevent the extinction of native and foreign species of wild flora and fauna. The law also provides for protection of the "critical" habitats of protected species.

The act defines an "endangered" species as any animal or plant that is in danger of extinction. A "threatened" species is defined as any animal or plant that is likely to become endangered within the foreseeable future. A procedure has been established under the ESA by which the USFWS determines whether a species should be listed as endangered or threatened. The determination is published in the *Federal Register* and the lists of endangered and threatened species are compiled annually in the Code of Federal Regulations. The Endangered Species List is found at 50 CFR § 17.11. The Threatened Species List is found at 50 CFR § 17.12. For current information on a given species, contact the appropriate agency with jurisdiction over the protected wildlife or plant in question.

a. Prohibitions Under the ESA

The act prohibits a wide range of activities and transactions with respect to endangered species. By regulation these prohibitions have also been extended to threatened species. The prohibitions apply equally to live or dead animals or plants, their progeny, and parts or products derived from them.

The act and implementing regulations prohibit:

- importation into or exportation from the U.S. of any endangered or threatened species

- taking any endangered or threatened species within the U.S. or on the high seas (the term "take" means to harass, harm, pursue, hunt, shoot, wound, kill, trap, capture, or collect, or to attempt to engage in any such conduct)

- possessing, selling, or transporting any species taken in violation of the act or regulation

- delivering, receiving, or transporting any endangered or threatened species in connection with interstate or foreign commercial activity

(for loans and gifts, lawfully taken and held endangered and threatened species may be shipped interstate as a bona fide gift or loan if there is no barter, credit, or other form of compensation or intent to profit or gain)

- selling or offering for sale endangered or threatened species in interstate commerce
(sales of legally acquired endangered or threatened species that take place entirely in one state are not prohibited by the ESA but may be regulated under applicable state laws)

b. Permits Under the ESA

Under certain conditions, scientific and educational activities may qualify for permits allowing activities that are otherwise prohibited. See http://www.fws.gov/permits/. Permits may be issued for prohibited activities for the following purposes:

- Endangered species permits may be granted for scientific purposes or to enhance the propagation or survival of the affected species, and for "incidental takings" or economic hardship.

- Threatened species permits may be granted for scientific purposes; the enhancement of propagation or survival of the affected species; zoological, horticultural, and botanical exhibition; educational purposes; or special purposes consistent with the act.

c. Exemptions

Certain situations may be exempt from the prohibitions of the act. In these exempt situations, a permit is not required. The burden of proof that the specimen or activity qualifies for an exemption lies with the person engaging in the relevant activity. All supporting and authenticating documentation must be maintained with the specimens, particularly when they are in transit.

- *Pre-Act Wildlife.* The prohibitions applicable to ESA species do not apply in the case of wildlife, except for African elephant ivory, held in captivity or in a controlled environment on a) Dec. 28, 1973, or b) the date of publication in the *Federal Register* for final listing of the species as endangered or threatened, whichever is later, provided that the wildlife has not been held in the course of a commercial activity. An affidavit and supporting documentary evidence of pre-act status is required.

- *Antiques.* Objects or specimens more than 100 years old, composed in whole or in part of any endangered or threatened species, that have not been repaired or modified since Dec. 28, 1973, with any part of a listed species, are exempt from the ESA prohibitions. The import and export of such antiques is allowed only through a designated port and must be accompanied by authenticating documentation.

•*Alaskan Natives* may take or import endangered or threatened species if such taking is primarily for subsistence purposes and is not done in a wasteful manner. Non-edible byproducts of lawfully taken species may be sold in interstate commerce when made into authentic native articles of handicrafts and clothing.

•*Seeds from Artificially Propagated Threatened Plants.* No permits are required for interstate or foreign commerce, including import or export, of seeds from artificially propagated specimens of threatened plants. The seeds must be accompanied by a label stating that they are of cultivated origin.

•*Captive-Bred Wildlife.* USFWS regulations provide exceptions that allow importing, exporting, taking, and interstate commercial transactions—including delivery, receipt, and sale—of certain living endangered and threatened species, provided the purpose is to enhance the propagation or survival of the species. The regulation covers only living animals that are not native to the U.S. The regulations prescribe detailed requirements for registration of captive breeding programs and other conditions that apply to captive breeding of protected species.

d. Enforcement

Both the U.S. Fish and Wildlife Service (USFWS) in the Department of the Interior and the National Marine Fisheries Service (NMFS) in the Department of Commerce enforce the Endangered Species Act. By agreement between the USFWS and NMFS, the jurisdiction of NMFS has been specifically defined to include certain species, while jurisdiction is shared in regard to certain other species. USFWS is the primary agency that administers the ESA and has jurisdiction over most wildlife and plants. For the most current information on species under the jurisdiction of USFWS, go to http://www.fws.gov/. For information on species under the jurisdiction of NMFS, go to http://www.nmfs.noaa.gov/.

3. The Convention on International Trade in Endangered Species of Wild Fauna and Flora
16 USC § 1531 et seq; 50 CFR Part 23
http://www.cites.org/

The Convention on International Trade in Endangered Species of Fauna and Flora (CITES) is an international wildlife treaty that regulates the import and export of endangered and threatened animal and plant species. The USFWS oversees CITES implementation in the United States, which became a party to the treaty in June 1975. The convention, with more than 175 party nations, protects more than 33,000 species of plants and animals by establishing import and export restrictions on wildlife threatened by international trade. The United States implements CITES through the U.S. Endangered Species Act.

The animals and plants protected by CITES are divided into three lists called appendices. Amendments to species listed in the CITES appendices are published in the *Federal Register* and listed on the CITES website. A species may be listed in any one of the three appendices, depending on the degree of protection deemed necessary.

•Appendix I includes species threatened with extinction that are or may be affected by trade.

•Appendix II includes species that are not necessarily under present threat of extinction but may become so unless strictly regulated.

•Appendix III includes species for which a country party to CITES has internal regulations to prevent or restrict exploitation and needs the cooperation of other parties in control of trade.

a. Prohibitions

The U.S. laws implementing CITES prohibit the import, export, or re-export of CITES-listed species without the required permits and also forbid the possession of any specimen imported, exported, or re-exported into or from the United States in contravention of the convention. All living and dead specimens and all readily recognizable parts and derivatives are subject to the prohibitions. Note that there are some exceptions for plant parts and derivatives.

Some species protected under CITES also are protected by other U.S. laws under which permit requirements may be more stringent, such as the U.S. Endangered Species Act, African Elephant Conservation Act, Marine Mammal Protection Act, Migratory Bird Act, Eagle Protection Act, and the Lacey Act. Permit applicants must satisfy the requirements of all laws under which a particular species is protected.

b. Permits Under CITES

Permits are required to import or export wildlife or plants listed in Appendix I, II, or III. There are different permit requirements for importing and exporting CITES-protected species, depending on which CITES appendix the species fall under. Re-export certificates are required for the export of specimens that were previously imported, including items subsequently converted to manufactured goods. Permits are issued by the management authority of nations belonging to CITES. Similar documentation is required from designated authorities of countries that are not members of CITES. Permit application procedures and issuance criteria are found in 50 CFR Part 23.

c. Exceptions

Although CITES provides exceptions relating to some wildlife or plants listed in CITES appendices, those species may also be subject to regulation under other U.S. laws. An exception provided under CITES does not necessarily allow activities that are prohibited under other U.S. laws.

CITES permits may not be required under the following circumstances:

•*Pre-Convention Specimens.* Wildlife or plants held in captivity or a controlled environment prior to listing of the relevant species in a CITES appendix do not require import or export permits. Pre-Convention Certificates are required to prove that a specimen comes within this exception.

•*Captive-Bred Certificate/Certificate for Artificially Propagated Plants.* No CITES permit is required if the specimen is accompanied by a Captive-Bred Certificate or Certificate of Artificial Propagation from the country of origin, stating that the wildlife was bred in captivity.

•*Scientific Exchange Program.* Scientific institutions may register with the CITES Secretariat to facilitate importation and exportation of accessioned specimens as non-commercial loans, donations, or exchanges between CITES-registered institutions.

•*In-Transit Shipments.* When a shipment is merely transiting a country, no import or export permits issued by that country are required, as long as the wildlife remains in customs custody. This may vary from country to country. For example, specimens listed under the Endangered Species Act generally may not transit the United States.

4. Marine Mammal Protection Act

16 USC § 1361 et. seq.; 50 CFR Part 18 subchapter C

http://www.nmfs.noaa.gov/pr/laws/mmpa/

The Marine Mammal Protection Act (MMPA), enacted in 1972, protects all marine mammals, dead or alive, and their parts and products, including, but not limited to, any raw, dressed, or dyed fur or skin. The protected species include whales, walruses, dolphins, seals, sea lions, sea otters, dugongs, manatees, and polar bears. The taking, possession, and transportation of northern fur seals for scientific research and public display is regulated separately under the Fur Seal Act.

a. Prohibitions

The act prohibits the unauthorized taking, possession, sale, purchase, importation, exportation, or transportation of marine mammals and their parts and by-products. The MMPA also authorizes the establishment of moratoria and a quota system for determining how many individuals of a marine mammal species can be taken without harm to those species or population stocks.

b. Permits Issued Under MMPA

Permits are granted for purposes of scientific research, public display, incidental taking, commercial fishing, and enhancing the survival or recovery of the species or stock. Permit application procedures and issuance criteria are found at 50 CFR § 518.31 and 50 CFR Parts 220-222.

c. Exceptions

•*Pre-Act Specimens.* The prohibitions of MMPA do not apply in the case of marine mammal specimens or articles consisting of, or composed in whole or in part of, any marine mammal taken on or before December 21, 1972. To establish pre-act status, it is necessary to file an affidavit with the agency responsible for the management of the species in question.

•*Alaskan Natives* may take marine mammals for subsistence purposes or for purposes of creating and selling authentic native handcrafts and clothing to be sold in interstate commerce.

•*Marine Mammal Parts.* Collection of certain dead marine mammal parts by beach collecting may be authorized, provided specific conditions are met.

•*Salvaging Specimen Material.* Regulations allow the utilization of specimen material salvaged from stranded marine mammals by authorized persons. Such salvaging must be only for the purposes of scientific research or the maintenance of a properly curated, professionally accredited, scientific collection and must be reported to the appropriate regional office of the NMFS.

d. Enforcement

By agreement, the MMPA is jointly administered by the USFWS and NMFS with jurisdiction specifically defined to include certain species. USFWS issues CITES permits for marine mammals under the jurisdiction of NMFS.

5. Migratory Bird Treaty Act

16 USC § 703-712; 50 CFR Parts 13 and 21
http://www4.law.cornell.edu/uscode/16/ch31.html

The Migratory Bird Treaty Act (MBTA), enacted in 1918, covers any migratory bird, any part, nest, egg, or product made from a migratory bird, part, nest, or egg. The act is administered by the U.S. Fish and Wildlife Service. Protected birds are listed at 50 CFR 10.13, go to http://www.fws.gov/migratorybirds/

a. Prohibitions

The act prohibits the taking, possession, import, export, transport, sale, purchase, barter, or offer for sale of any migratory birds, and the nests or eggs of such birds, except as authorized by valid permit.

b. Permits Under MBTA

•Permits may be issued for banding and marking migratory birds.

•Permits may be issued to import and export migratory birds.

•A scientific collecting permit is required before any person may take, transport, or possess migratory birds, their parts, nests, or eggs for scientific research or educational purposes.

•Permits may be issued for other purposes, such as taxidermy, waterfowl sale and disposal, falconry, raptor propagation, and degradations control.

c. Exceptions

•Possession or transportation of specimens acquired on or before the effective date of protection of the species under the act does not require a permit. Import, export, barter, purchase, or sale of pre-act specimens is prohibited without a permit.

•The MBTA provides a general exception to permit requirements for public museums, public zoological parks, accredited institutions of the American Association of Zoological Parks and Aquariums (AZA), and public scientific or educational institutions to acquire by gift or purchase, possess, transport, and dispose of by gift or sale lawfully acquired migratory birds. The specimen must be acquired from or disposed of to a similar institution, federal, or state game authorities, or the holder of a valid possession or disposal permit.

•The MBTA regulations, except for banding and marking permits, do not apply to the bald eagle or golden eagle.

6. Eagle Protection Act

16 USC § 668; 50 CFR Part 22

http://www4.law.cornell.edu/uscode/16/668.html

The Eagle Protection Act (EPA) protects bald (*Haliaeetus leucocephalus*) and golden (*Aquila chrysaetos*) eagles, alive or dead, their parts, nests, or eggs. It was first enacted in 1940, and amended in 1962 to include golden eagles. It is administered by the USFWS.

a. Prohibitions

The act prohibits taking, buying, selling, trading, transporting, possessing, importing, or exporting eagles or their parts, nests, eggs, or products made from them.

b. Permits Under EPA

Permits may be issued for taking, possession, and transportation of bald or golden eagles, their parts, nests, or eggs, for scientific, exhibition, and Indian religious purposes. No permits are allowed for import or export, sale, purchase, or barter of bald or golden eagles.

c. Exceptions

A permit is not required for possession or transportation of bald eagles lawfully acquired before June 8, 1940, or golden eagles lawfully acquired before Oct. 24, 1962. Pre-act specimens, however, may not be imported, exported, purchased, sold, traded, or bartered or offered for purchase, sale, trade, or barter.

7. African Elephant Conservation Act

16 USC § 4201-4245

http://www.fws.gov/international/laws/aeca_fv.html

In an effort to assist in the conservation and protection of African elephant populations, the United States passed the African Elephant Conservation Act (AECA) in 1988. This act works in conjunction with the CITES Ivory Control System to protect the African elephant and eliminate any trade in illegal ivory. Currently, the African elephant is listed in Appendix I of CITES and as such any import or export for other than commercial purposes must be accompanied by valid CITES documents.

a. Prohibitions

The act prohibits:

- the import of raw African elephant ivory from any country other than an ivory-producing country (any African country within which is located any part of the range of a population of African elephants)
- the export from the United States of raw ivory from African elephants
- the import of raw or worked ivory from African elephants that was exported from an ivory-producing country in violation of that country's laws or the CITES Ivory Control System
- the import of worked ivory from any country unless that country has certified that such ivory was derived from a legal source
- the import of raw or worked ivory from a country in which a moratorium is in effect

b. Exceptions

- Worked ivory may be imported for non-commercial purposes if the item was acquired prior to the date CITES applied to African elephants (Feb. 4, 1977) and is accompanied by a valid pre-CITES certificate.
- Articles more than 100 years old may be imported or exported for non-commercial and commercial purposes under a pre-CITES certificate, provided they have not been repaired or modified with elephant ivory on or after Feb. 4, 1977. Proof of antiquity must be provided.

8. Wild Bird Conservation Act

16 USC § 4901; 50 CFR Part 15

http://www4.law.cornell.edu/uscode/16/4901.html

The Wild Bird Conservation Act (WBCA) was enacted in 1992 to limit or prohibit the importation of exotic birds to ensure that their populations are not harmed by trade. The act assists wild bird conservation and management in the countries of origin by ensuring that trade in species is biologically sustainable and is not detrimental to the species. The WBCA is administered by the USFWS.

a. Prohibitions

The act prohibits the importation of any exotic bird in violation of any prohibition, suspension, or quota on importation and the importation of any exotic bird listed in a CITES appendix that is not part of an approved list, if the bird was not bred at a qualified facility. The WBCA authorizes the establishment of moratoria or quotas for import of certain exotic birds.

b. Permits Under WBCA

Permits to import protected species may be issued if the importation is not detrimental to the survival of the species, and is for scientific research, zoological breeding or display, or cooperative breeding programs designed to promote the conservation and maintenance of the species in the wild.

SUMMARY OF LAWS APPLICABLE TO INJURIOUS SPECIES AND PROTECTION OF LIVE ANIMALS

The laws discussed above are generally intended to promote the conservation of wildlife and plant species. Activities of museums, and especially zoos and acquaria, may also be affected by laws designed to protect against potential damage caused by injurious species or to protect live animals. These laws can be quite complex and are discussed very briefly here. Institutions that conduct activities with live animals or potentially injurious species should become familiar with these laws.

1. Lacey Act

18 USC § 42; 16 USC § 1378(d); 50 CFR Parts 14 and 16

a. Injurious Wildlife

The Lacey Act, other aspects of which are discussed above, prohibits the importation, transportation, or acquisition, without a permit, of any wildlife (or their eggs) designated as injurious to the health and welfare of humans; to the interests of forestry, agriculture, or horticulture; or to the welfare and survival of wildlife resources of the U.S. The species listed as injurious wildlife are found at 50 CFR Part 16, subpart B. Permits are available for importation of such injurious wildlife for zoological, educational, medical, or scientific purposes. The permit requirements do not apply to the importation or transportation of

dead scientific specimens for museum or scientific collection purposes.

b. Humane and Healthful Treatment of Live Animals

The Lacey Act also prohibits the transport of wild mammals or birds to the U.S. under inhumane or unhealthful conditions. Detailed rules for humane and healthful transport required under the Lacey Act are set forth at 50 CFR Part 14, Subpart J.

2. Animal Welfare Act

7 USC § 2131; 9 CFR Parts 1-4

http://www.nal.usda.gov/awic/legislat/awa.htm

The Animal Welfare Act (AWA) was enacted in 1966 to regulate the use of warm-blooded animals for research or exhibition purposes or as pets, ensuring that they are provided with humane care and treatment. The AWA regulates aspects of transportation, purchase, sale, housing, care, handling, and treatment. Regulations provide for the licensing or registration of animal dealers, exhibitors, operators of animal auctions, research facilities, carriers, and intermediate handlers. The Animal and Plant Health Inspection Service (APHIS) of the Department of Agriculture is the agency responsible for administering the act.

3. Public Health Service Act

42 USC § 216, 264-272; 42 CFR Parts 71-72; 21 CFR Parts 1240 and 1250

http://www4.law.cornell.edu/uscode/42/ch6A.html

The Public Health Service Act (PHSA) was enacted in 1944. One of the purposes of the act is to prevent the introduction, transmission, or spread of communicable diseases from foreign countries to the United States or between states. It authorizes the surgeon general to promulgate regulations necessary to carry out this purpose. Under this authority, restrictions on importation and movement of turtles, rodents, bats, psittacine birds, and non-human primates have been implemented. Permits may be issued to engage in regulated activities for exhibition, educational, or scientific purposes. The Center for Disease Control (CDC) in Atlanta is responsible for implementing the act.

4. APHIS Authorization Act /Animal Quarantine Regulations

21 USC § 101-136; 9 CFR Parts 75, 82, 92, 93 - 94, 98, 130

http://www4.law.cornell.edu/uscode/21/ch4.html

The Animal and Plant Health Inspection Service (APHIS) Authorization Act provides authority to protect the U.S. livestock, poultry, and agricultural industries against infectious or contagious diseases. The act regulates the importation and exportation of certain animals and animal products into the U.S. that are or have been affected with or exposed to any communicable disease. Permits may be issued to import or export covered species and may impose quarantine requirements and other protective measures. The Animal and Plant Health Inspection Service (APHIS) is responsible for implementing the act.

ENDANGERED SPECIES IN AN ART MUSEUM?

At first glance, one might consider an art museum an unlikely place for U.S. Fish and Wildlife problems to occur. With the possible exception of ivory, many materials requiring special consideration when importing or exporting works of art might be overlooked by even a conscientious museum staff member. For example, a silver dagger with a skin-covered handle, a tortoise shell hair ornament, or a hat adorned with colorful feathers could present potential problems if imported from a foreign country without proper documentation.

As in other endangered species situations, the time to begin asking questions is at the very beginning of any transaction involving importation or exportation. Since the export documents must originate with the foreign country, sometimes it is necessary to alert the appropriate museum officials of the need to begin the application process. In the case of one exhibition coming to the Smithsonian's National Museum of African Art from Europe, it was necessary to go through the exhibition catalogue and identify potential problems based on materials listed by each entry. A list of "problem objects" was then provided to the organizing institution, which

initiated the paperwork while the exhibition was still on its premises. Many questions arose about the types of materials involved, requiring correspondence with lenders, curators, and CITES officials. When the time came to ship the exhibition to the United States, the requisite documents had been obtained and the importation proceeded smoothly.

Not so fortunate was the purchaser of a 1920s Erard piano in Paris. A concert pianist, the new owner arranged for air shipment of the instrument back to the United States, only to have it seized by U.S. Customs agents upon its arrival because it did not meet the requirements for exemption under the African Elephant Conservation Act. In spite of the owner's protests, the ivory was eventually stripped from the keys, a sad event for all concerned [*New Yorker*, Feb. 22, 1993].

What other types of materials could be subject to CITES enforcement? For works of African art, the most common are skin and fur products, feathers, claws of mammals or raptors, primate parts (hands, feet, and tails), tortoise shell, and other types of shells. Coral, which is often used in Asian works of art, such as inlaid boxes and writing instruments, is another potential problem, as is rhinoceros horn, which is used in Chinese drinking vessels as well as in ceremonial dagger handles made in Yemen. Certain types of hardwood, such as mahogany and rosewood, could also require CITES permits.

After identification of potential problem materials, the next step is to determine specific identification, including both the common name and the scientific name of each material. This step can be very straightforward or may require consulting an expert or scientist. In one instance of a Kongo *nkisi* containing unidentified feathers, the assistance of a well-known British specialist was needed to determine that the feathers in question were from a domestic fowl and therefore not subject to CITES. In a similar situation, the crowned eagle feathers adorning a mask from Zaire were easily identified as *Stephanoatus coronatus* by the foreign lending institution, which then applied for the required permit. If only the common name is known, one may consult the CITES Appendices for the scientific name.

Perhaps the most critical information in deciding

whether one needs an export/import permit or a pre-convention certificate is the date the object was made or collected. For many African works, the date of manufacture is unknown, although it may sometimes be assumed to date from the period of Western colonization. One solution to the dating issue is to request an examination of the lending institution's accession records. If the object has been recorded as being in the collections of a museum before 1973, then one can be assured that it is pre-convention. However, U.S. Fish and Wildlife may still require an "Expert's Affidavit." To qualify as an expert, the individual must be over 21 years of age, state his or her years of experience in the field, and swear before a witness that he or she has carefully examined the object(s) in question. The witness may be another museum staff member; the affidavit does not have to be notarized. A description of each object, including an approximate date of manufacture, must accompany the affidavit (e.g., Anthropomorphic face mask. Wood, pigment, animal hide, and hair [monkey, *Colobus abyssinicus uelensis*], Zaire, probably 20th century [collected 1952-1956]).

An exhibition date or a publication date may also be used to prove pre-convention eligibility. Authenticating documentation must accompany the shipment. A statement by the affiant, such as the following, must also be included: "To the best of my knowledge and belief, the aforementioned objects were created before 1973 and have not been repaired or modified with any part of an endangered species on or after December 28, 1973. (50 CFR 14.22) They are therefore pre-Convention and are exempt under the Endangered Species Act of 1973 (15 USC 1531–1543)."

Another type of exemption that may be useful for shipping purposes is the "Exception to Designated Port." Such an exception may be made for a single shipment or for a series of shipments over a specified period of time. Unless there are special circumstances precluding their use, all wildlife shipments must enter and leave the United States through a designated U.S. Customs port. Availability of direct flights, loan requirements of institutional lenders, the need for continuous supervision by museum professionals to prevent deterioration or loss, or undue economic hardship all may be grounds for an "Exception to Designated Port." In case of economic hardship, the applicant must provide a cost comparison for inland freight, customs clearance, bonding, trucking, associated fees, etc., between the designated port and the non-designated port. An exception may also be granted for scientific purposes, although this factor would not be applicable in an art museum.

In addition to federal Endangered Species law, some states have more restrictive laws. To determine whether a particular state has endangered species law(s), one should check with the appropriate state conservation agency prior to the transaction.

In summary, one must anticipate CITES issues well in advance of international shipping in order to allow sufficient time for research and obtaining the necessary permits. The advice of experts, including CITES officials in both exporting and importing countries, can be invaluable in preparing complete documentation. Determining the date of manufacture is of primary importance. Finally, one should consider obtaining a waiver of port, if advantageous, and make sure all endangered species laws, both state and federal, have been reviewed for compliance. •

Thanks to Kim Saito, Suzanne B. McLaren, and Kristin L. Vehrs.

7J | Contracts

SUZANNE QUIGLEY, EDIT AND UPDATES BY MARY DOWD

Contracts are legally binding agreements between two or more parties detailing the responsibilities and obligations of each party. Some contracts are more formal in appearance than others and are often developed from "boiler plates"—forms with blanks to be filled in. In a "Letter of Agreement" contract the points to be agreed upon are articulated much as they are in the contract format, while the document itself may not appear quite as formal. Museums should have a legal review process for all contracts into which they enter.

Many registrars have occasion to deal with several kinds of contracts. Although registrars should not, on their own, write contracts, they often work on contract drafts for legal review, and they are asked to read contracts to be certain that all elements relating to registrarial work are covered. It is best, in the first instance, if the registrar provides a thoughtful list of needs for an attorney to include in a contract.

The most common contracts of concern to registrars are exhibition contracts, personal services contracts, and computer contracts. Although an insurance policy is not traditionally thought of as a contract, it too has clauses that are agreed upon. An insurance policy is a guarantee of service exchanged for money, in the eventuality of a claim. Because insurance policies have standard clauses, they should also be considered contracts.

Exhibition Contracts

Exhibition contracts of the "boiler plate" variety have several standard clauses. Most important to the registrar are the clauses that cover his or her responsibilities to the exhibition:

- the schedule of venues
- design and installation
- security and climate control
- packing, transport, and couriers
- condition and conservation
- insurance
- the attachments, which often include a detailed checklist

Exhibition Contract Outline

1. Introduction

   a. state exhibition name

   b. name the parties

   c. name the document as an agreement

2. Organization and Content

   a. cite object list as Exhibit A

   b. have consulting committee (optional)

   c. prohibit deletions/additions unless written agreement

   d. state organizer's responsibility for obtaining all loans

   e. state organizer's responsibility for overall organization

   f. authorize organizer to remove an object for reasonable cause

3. Schedule

   a. list venues and dates

   b. state that changes must be made in writing

4. Design and Installation

   a. name design committee of curators at each venue (optional)

   b. assign responsibility for exhibition furniture, alarms, mounts, labels, didactic panels, etc.

5. Security and Climate Control

  a. overall facility

    1) fire prevention and detection systems requirements

    2) heating, ventilation, and air conditioning standards

    3) security systems requirements

  b. temporary storage, staging area, exhibition space

    1) security requirements

    2) climate control standards

    3) staffing requirements

    4) object-handling standards

  c. exhibition area

    1) humidity requirements

    2) temperature requirements

    3) exposure restrictions (heat, light, air sources)

    4) light levels, UV protection standards

    5) food, drink, and smoking restrictions

6. Packing, Transport, Couriers

  a. assign responsibility for packing, shipping, customs

  b. state minimum number of days before and after exhibition allowed for shipping

  c. indicate that organizer may designate courier(s) (optional)

    1) assign responsibility for courier expenses

    2) state whether expenses will be reimbursed or prepaid

    3) state whether expenses to be paid on receipts or per diem

  d. assign unpacking/repacking responsibility and standards

7. Condition, Condition Reports and Conservation

  a. assign responsibilities for the following:

    1) outgoing condition reports and book

    2) photographs

    3) signatures

  b. prohibit unframing and photography

  c. specify hanging mechanisms, mounts, and case requirements

  d. prohibit treatment without written permission, except in an emergency

  e. require immediate notification of organizer's registrar upon loss or damage

8. Insurance

  a. describe coverage, usually all risk, wall-to-wall

  b. participants co-insured or waiver of subrogation

  c. organizer will handle all insurance claims, etc.

  d. damage in transit or on premises (take photos), notify organizer's registrar

    1) documentation

    2) save all packing materials

    3) notify carrier

  e. if loss not covered by insurance, liable if negligent

9. Immunity from Seizure (optional)

  a. international loans coming to United States

  b. exhibition in another country

10. Catalog

  a. describe

  b. assign pre-production costs (optional)

  c. indicate number provided free to venues

  d. state number venues must purchase at what price

11. Didactic Materials

  a. indicate what will be provided: wall labels, text panels, etc.

  b. indicate format: available as panels, on

computer disk, etc.

c. state whether foreign language translation will be available (optional)

d. list materials available for sale from organizer

e. state that materials produced by venues are subject to approval by organizer

12. Education Adjunct

a. media programs

b. must show/use

c. distribution rights rest with organizer

d. cost is in total exhibition fee (optional)

e. format delivered per agreement with venues

13. Publicity, Promotion, Photography, Reproduction

a. each venue responsible for publicity

1) media may tape in exhibition

b. available for publicity and educational only

1) press release

2) black and white photos

3) color transparencies

c. photography by public prohibited

d. venue will give to organizer N copies

1) installation views

2) black and white photos during public hours

3) all printed matter produced

4) reviews

5) attendance statistics

e. extra requested materials at borrower's cost

f. all materials produced by venue using images must:

1) give full catalog information on artwork

a) artist name

b) title, date

c) medium

d) name of lender (as provided)

e) name of photographer

2) no cropping, bleeding, printing in color other than black and white, nothing superimposed

14. Financial Arrangements

a. participants agree to pay per schedule

1) N1 upon signing

2) N2 upon receipt at museum

3) N3 upon close

4) shipping pro rata (optional)

5) shared costs per attached schedule (optional)

b. no responsibility for financial loss at a venue

c. local costs and staff time venue's responsibility

d. shared costs invoiced by organizer (optional)

e. purchase of items for sale subject to another agreement

15. Sponsorship and Credit Lines

a. all to abide by sponsorship requirements

b. credit lines acknowledge funding

1) approved by organizer

2) use in all promotional literature

c. additional local sponsors credit line

d. organizer's credit line

e. sponsorship of opening events

16. Cancellation

a. if organizer cancels, venue gets refund

b. if venue cancels

1) full fee

a) unless another venue found

b) termination fee

2) if force majeure, then just settlement of costs

17. Miscellaneous

a. N articles + N exhibits equal entire

agreement

b. exhibition available to all without discrimination

c. agreement supersedes any other

d. agreement cannot be assigned unless in writing

e. governing law

18. Signatures, Dates

19. List of Attachments

a. object list

b. loan agreement forms (optional)

c. shared cost budget (optional)

d. catalog budget (optional)

e. insurance package (optional)

f. payment schedule (optional, if written into contract)

g. corporate sponsor agreement (optional)

PERSONAL SERVICES CONTRACTS

Registrars often have to deal with personal services contracts. These contracts might apply to the services of a mount maker, a private conservator, a freelance registrar, a freelance photographer, temporary data entry staff, etc. Before entering into a personal services contract, the registrar should consult the museum's legal advisors to determine whether the employment situation meets the IRS definition for independent contractor or whether the individual should be hired as a regular, part-time, or casual employee. If counsel determines that a contract is appropriate, it is essential to indicate that the job is a work-for-hire; work-for-hire is carefully defined under copyright law and has been interpreted by the courts. It is important, for instance, to be certain that a photographer hired to take pictures of the museum's objects for a catalog does not have ownership of all negatives, slides, transparencies, or prints. The copyright to the photos for such work should also lie with the museum. The contract should state that the photographer does not have the right to use

the negatives at a later date for his or her own purposes or have the right to sell the negatives.

In addition, the terms of employment must be spelled out, including to whom the contractor is to report, the schedule for completion of the work, an outline of the compensation agreement, and a clear indication of the status of the contractor with regard to worker's compensation, holiday and sick pay, etc., as determined by the legal advisor's review. Usually a contractor is also required to maintain and provide proof of insurance and to accept an indemnification clause, wherein it is stated that the contractor will hold harmless the museum and all its parties for any liabilities that might arise from negligence, wrongful acts, breaches, failures, etc. An outline of issues to consider in a personal services contract follows below.

PERSONAL SERVICES CONTRACT OUTLINE

1. Engagement

a. contract for hire

b. subject to terms outlined here and in performance of services specified

c. reports to

d. schedule for completion of work

e. agreement to bring professional skills and adequate time to job

2. Compensation

a. agreement of amount

b. terms of payment

c. discussion of fringes (applicable or not)

d. reimbursement for out-of-pocket expenses as agreed, with documentation

3. Status

a. independent subcontractor; not employee or agent

b. museum not liable for
   1. worker's comp
   2. pension
   3. holiday/vacation/sick pay

4. personal injury insurance

5. personal property insurance

c. shall not incur obligations on behalf of museum

d. shall have the right to perform services for others

4. Other Terms

a. agree to maintain own insurance and furnish proof thereof

b. information gained through job confidential except to the extent necessary to do the job

c. agree to be bound by the terms of the contract

5. Indemnification

a. agree to indemnify, hold harmless all museum parties for liabilities, etc., arising out of services, including negligence, wrongful acts, omissions, breaches, or failures

6. This agreement is governed by the laws of the state of X

7. signatures, dates

8. attachments

a. itemization of services to be rendered

COMPUTER CONTRACTS

As is the case with all contracts, computer contracts protect both the vendor and the museum. Whether a museum buys a packaged system (pays for license to use it) or contracts with a programmer to write a program, computer contracts can be difficult to understand. Some of the main clauses in a computer contract include:

•clarification of the functions the software is expected to perform

•the type of support the museum can expect from the vendor

•the number of persons who may use the system (if a multi-user site license, the number of concurrent users allowed)

•the nature and duration of maintenance that will be provided

•the nature and duration of support provided by the vendor

•the schedule for implementation and acceptance of the system

•the frequency and cost of periodic upgrades and charges

•the amount of training, a description of the documentation

•fees and associated costs

Other contractual considerations are data conversion, post-installation modifications, and the cost of future program modifications after acceptance. It is particularly important to spell out exactly who owns the software, especially the source code. If the programming is done as a work-for-hire, then the source code is owned by the museum. If the program is written by a vendor, generally he or she will retain all rights to the source code.

The negotiation of an escrow agreement for the source code is advisable. An escrow agreement is a side agreement (but can be incorporated into the main contract) guaranteeing the museum access to the source code should the vendor's business fail or should there be breach of contract on the part of the vendor. When the source code is held in escrow, it is held by a third (neutral) party in the event that the client museum might find itself without any possibility of support from the vendor.

A computer contract should also contain a warranty clause and a termination clause. If the museum does not fulfill its responsibilities, (e.g., non-payment or unauthorized redistribution), the vendor has the right to terminate the museum's license to use the software.

The individual responsible for preparing a contract should obtain examples of similar contracts from other institutions. Several examples of contracts, as well as checklists of issues to consider, are included in recent study guides for ALI-ABA courses, *Legal Problems of Museum Administration*. If the museum has no purchasing officer who routinely reviews and processes contracts, it is advisable to have contracts reviewed by the museum's lawyer to ensure accuracy and clarify liability issues. Contracts for specialized services require more extensive research, drafting, and review before they can be processed.

COMPUTER CONTRACT OUTLINE

1. Delivery

a. definition of software

b. license agreement

    1) number of users

    2) number of locations

c. delivery and payment

    1) schedule for delivery

    2) schedule of payment

d. client responsibility

    1) hardware compatibility

    2) operating system compatibility

2. Maintenance and Support

a. initial maintenance period

    1) discovery of problems

    2) corrections supplied

    3) telephone support

    4) elective modifications, refinements, enhancements, etc.

b. extended maintenance period, including period of tech support (subject to separate agreement)

c. implementation

    1) museum's obligation to load modifications

3. Ownership of Software

a. definition of vendor's rights

b. agreement by museum to protect vendor's rights

4. Warranties

a. indemnification of museum by owner

b. non-conformance of product to documentation

    1) notification by client

    2) termination of license by client

    3) deferment of payments to vendor

    4) client receives escrowed materials

5. Termination

a. breach of contract

    1) declaration of unremedied period

    2) written notice of reasons

        a) failure to pay

        b) bankruptcy

b. termination of license

    1) if vendor is in breach

        a) license is allowed the client

        b) client receives escrowed materials

    2) if client is in breach

        a) license is terminated

        b) software must be destroyed

6. Miscellaneous

a. scope of the agreement

b. additional software purchases from vendor fall under same agreement

c. assignment of rights by either party only by agreement of both parties

d. governing law

e. all notices in writing

f. use of client's name by vendor

7. signatures, dates

8. attachments

a. implementation schedule

b. training schedule

c. extended annual maintenance agreement

d. source code escrow agreement •

Legal Issues II | HYPOTHETICALS

1

During an inventory of your museum's holdings the collections manager finds several slivers of bone stored with some lithics. Outline the steps you should take to determine what the bones are, where they have come from, and how to report them in order to maintain compliance with NAGPRA.

2

Describe a consultation process to determine actions related to the large group of Algonquin unassociated grave artifacts that your museum holds.

3

Your curator of Native American Arts wishes to acquire a headdress that contains feathers of an endangered species (not eagle). The feathers were legally obtained by the current owner.

How do the following situations affect the acquisition's process and legality?

- •The headdress is more than 100 years old.

- •The headdress is less than 100 years old.

- •The headdress is offered as a gift.

- •The headdress is offered by a vendor in Canada.

- •The headdress is offered by a vendor within your state.

- •The headdress is offered by a vendor who is also the artist and who is a Native Alaskan.

4

How does the above situation change if the object in question is not a feather headdress, but rather a sealskin coat?

5

A collector in Europe wishes to donate some pieces of scrimshaw to your museum.

How do you proceed?

Glossary

Accession: (1) An object acquired by a museum as part of its permanent collection; (2) the act of recording/processing an addition to the permanent collection. [Naunert] (3) One or more objects acquired at one time from one source constituting a single transaction between the museum and a source, or the transaction itself. [Burcaw] (4) accessioning is the formal process used to accept and record an item as a collection object. [Malaro]

Accession Number: A control number, unique to an object, the purpose of which is identification, not description. [Naunert]

Accompanier: A courier who oversees transport of another museum's shipment while it is traveling with the courier's own shipment.

Accredited Scientist: Any individual associated with, employed by, or under contract to and accredited by an accredited scientific institution for the purpose of conducting biological or medical research, whose research activities are approved and sponsored by the scientific institution granting accreditation.

Accredited Scientific Institution: Any public museum, public zoological park, accredited institution of higher education, accredited member of the American Zoo and Aquarium Association, accredited member of the American Association of Systematic Collections, or any State or Federal government agency that conducts biological or medical research.

Acetone: Dimethyl ketone, a colorless, low boiling, volatile liquid soluble in water and many other organic liquids. Commonly used as a solvent for adhesives. Highly flammable. [Rose and de Torres]

Acid Migration: The transfer of an acid from a more acidic material to a less acidic material with which it is in contact. [Naunert]

Acid-free: A term loosely used for papers and other materials which are often pH neutral or alkaline buffered; could be any pH from 6 to 11. [Rose & de Torres]

Acidic: Acid-forming or containing an excess of acid-forming substances. Having a pH less than 7.0

Actual Notice: Written notice that is received in fact by the person to be notified.

Adverse Possession: A method of acquiring title to property by possession under certain conditions including that the possession must be adverse to the owner, actual, continuous, and exclusive.

Airbill: See Airwaybill

Airwaybill: The basic shipping document in airfreight; it is both the contract of carriage between the shipper and carrier and the receipt for the shipment. [Case]

Alkaline: Having a pH value greater than 7.

All-cargo Aircraft: An aircraft, able to accommodate large shipments, which does not carry passengers except couriers by arrangement.

All-risk: An insurance policy that covers damage by all perils except those specifically excluded in the policy. (Contrast with Named or Specific Perils Contract). [GANYS]

Anoxic: Condition of having insufficient oxygen to sustain life.

Aperture: Hole in the lens through which light travels to strike the film. In most photographic lenses, the aperture size is adjustable and measured in f-stops.

Archival Value: The value of documentary materials for continuing preservation in an archival institution. [Daniels and Walch]

Archives: (1) The non-current records of an organization or institution preserved because of their continuing value. (2) The agency responsible for selecting, preserving, and making available records determined to have permanent or continuing value. (3) The building in which an archival institution is located. [Daniels and Walch]

Arrangement: The archival process of organizing documentary materials in accordance with archival principles. [Daniels and Walch]

Backup, Full: Copying all computer files onto disk or, more usually, tape for safekeeping.

Backup, Incremental: Copying newly made computer files to disk or, more usually, tape for safekeeping.

Bailment: A legal relationship created between a lender and borrower of property whereby the borrower keeps the property until the lender reclaims it.

Bailor, Bailee: The bailor (lender) is the part who delivers the property to the bailee (borrower) in a bailment relationship.

Bar Code: Variable-width stripes on packaging or tags that identify the item and provide other data when read by an optical scanner. [Duckworth]

Batting: Non-woven natural or synthetic fiber wadded into a fibrous mass used for padding or stuffing. [Rose and de Torres]

Best: An independent rating firm that grades companies on their financial soundness.

Bill of Lading: The basic document in van, truck, or ocean shipping; it is both the contract of carriage between the shipper and carrier and the receipt for the shipment. See also Airway bill. [Naunert]

Black and White Negative: A negative, colorless photographic image on a clear film base. Sizes range from 35 mm color slides to 8 x10 in. (203 x 254 mm) sheet film transparencies.

Blanket Insurance Policy: An insurance contract that covers several classes of property at a single location or at multiple locations. [GANYS]

Boom: The extension arm of a crane that allows the equipment to "reach" the object to be moved.

Brace pack: This basic packing style for 3-D objects holds objects in place by simple wooden braces (typically 2 x 4s or T-braces) which are secured to the walls of the crate or inner crate.

Buffer: A substance containing both a weak acid and its conjugal weak base, used to restrain the acid migration of a material. Acid-free paper products are often buffered.

Cable Release: A flexible wire that screws onto a shutter release button, making it possible to depress the shutter release button at a distance from the camera. It is also used to decrease vibrations during film exposure.

Calipers: A measuring device consisting of a pair of movable, curved legs fastened at one end with a screw or rivet, used to measure the diameter or thickness of an object. [Naunert]

Cargo Close-out: The time by which shipments must be checked in to enable aircraft to be properly loaded and balanced.

Cargo Terminal: A cargo handling shed where shipments are loaded onto pallets or into containers, usually distant from the passenger terminal.

Case: Strong, closed, waterproof box constructed from a variety of hard materials. Used to protect museum objects during periods of movement or in storage. A crate.

Cause of Action: Facts which give a person the right to bring his or her claim to court.

Cavity Pack/Foam Cut-out: The object fits into a space cut or made to conform to the shape of the object. Cavities can be lined with tissue or soft inert fabric.

Center of Gravity: The point of an object at which it will balance when lifted. For a safe and stable lift, the load line must be directly above this point. The ability to discern the center of gravity is the responsibility of the rigger.

Certificate of Insurance: A document, signed by the insurance company or its agent, that provides written evidence of insurance in force at the time of issuance. Museums or lenders often require certificates of insurance from one another before releasing objects on loan. [Naunert]

Certified Cargo Screening Program (CCSP): TSA-implemented program to ensure security on all passenger flights leaving from US airports to domestic and international destinations, through screening of cargo prior to loading.

Chain of Custody: For TSA, control of cargo from the time of screening until its release to the carrier. This is implemented through control of physical access, certification of personnel, documentation, and physical control of the cargo and its conveyance.

Chain Fall: A reduction gear hoisting device that uses a continuous chain to raise or lower heavy objects. Used primarily with gantry or "A" frame; the capacity is rated by tons.

Claim: In insurance, a formal, written demand by the insured for payment for a loss coming under the terms of the insurance contract. [GANYS]

Climate Control: The ability to adjust and regulate the temperature and relative humidity of a particular environment. [Naunert]

Climate-controlled Van: One in which the temperature and relative humidity can be adjusted and regulated within certain limits. [Naunert]

Co-insurance Clause: A property provision which requires that the policy-holder carry insurance equal to a specified percentage of the property's value. [GANYS]

Color Negative: A negative color photographic image on a clear film base. Sizes range from 35 mm color slides to 8 x 10 in. (203 x 254 mm) sheet film transparencies.

Color Transparency: A positive color photographic image on a clear film base. Sizes range from 35 mm color slides to 8 x 10 in. (203 x 254 mm) sheet film transparencies. [1]

Combination Flight: An aircraft able to accommodate cargo containers and pallets as well as a reduced load of passengers.

Commercial Activity: Related to the offering for sale or resale, purchase, trade, barter, or the actual or intended transfer in the pursuit of gain or profit, of any item of wildlife and includes the use of any wildlife article for the purpose of facilitating such buying and selling, provided, however, that it does not include exhibition of such articles by museums or similar cultural or historical organizations.

Commercial Invoice: A document included in international shipping papers stating the object name, date, country of origin, materials, value, owner, and whether or not the object will be returned.

Common Law: Refers to legal principles which do not rest for their authority on any express statute, but rather upon statements of principles found in court decisions.

Compactor Storage: High density storage system with moveable units on rails, accessed by one aisle the location of which can be changed by moving units with manual or electric controls.

Condition: (1) The physical state of an object. (2) A contract provision or stipulation. [Naunert]

Condition Photograph: A photograph or series of photographs that clearly document the defects, damages, and physical condition of an object. [Naunert]

Conservation: Maximizing the endurance or minimizing the deterioration of an object through time, with as little change in the object as possible. [Lord and Lord]

Conservator: Trained professional who treats objects to repair damage, maximize endurance, and minimize deterioration.

Constructive Notice: Notice that is implied by law rather than notice that is actually mailed and received by the person being notified, such as legal notices published in a newspaper.

Container Number: Large identifying number on the outside of each container, usually 3 letters followed by 4 numbers, to aid in tracking of shipments.

Continuous Custody: (1) In contemporary U.S. usage, the archival principle that to guarantee archival integrity, archival material should either be retained by the creating organization or transferred directly to an archival institution. (2) In British usage, the principle that non-current records must be retained by the creating organization or its successor in function to be considered archival. [Daniels and Walch]

Contour Bracing/Yokes/Guillotines: Braces made the same size as the crate's interior. The yokes or guillotines are formed by cutting the shape of the object out of the brace and then cutting them in half. The front halves of the braces are held in slots and the back parts of the braces are glued or screwed into place to help stabilize the container.

Country of Exportation: The last country from which the animal or plant was exported before importation into the United States.

Country of Origin: The country where the animal or plant was taken from the wild, or the country of natal origin of the animal.

Courier: An individual, usually a representative of the owner of an object, who travels with the object to ensure its proper care and safe arrival.

Crane: A mobile unit equipped with boom, cable, and draw works, capable of 360-degree rotation around a center pin. Rated in ton capacity.

Crate Markings: Symbols, numbers, and letters stenciled on the outside of a crate indicating proper handling, size, and weight of packed crate; identifying initials.

Cross Docking: The transfer of a load one or more times from truck to truck or truck to warehouse

Escort: A security guard who protects the shipment from unexpected interference during transit.

Cross-link: A crosswise part that connects parallel chains in a complex chemical molecule. In a polymer, two or more small molecules may combine to form larger molecules. The resulting molecules may have different chemical properties from the original molecules, including solubility, etc.

Customs Broker: An individual or firm that arranges customs clearance of objects traveling between countries;

frequently employed also as a Freight-forwarding Agent for international shipments.

Customs Seal: A warning tag or label affixed to a shipping box by a customs official at the original Port-of-Entry. It is a guarantee to the customs official who makes the inspection at the ultimate destination that the contents have not been tampered with. [Naunert]

DAMS: Digital Asset Management System: A system used to control and access all digital assets of an institution.

Deaccession: (1) An object that has been removed permanently from the museum's collection. (2) Formal removal of accessioned objects from the museum's permanent collection. Objects removed from unaccessioned collections of the museum are not considered deaccessions but need to go through a formal removal process. See also Disposal.

Deed of Gift: A contract that transfers ownership of an object or objects from a donor to an institution. It should include all conditions of the gift.

Depth of Field: Zone from the points closest to the camera to the points farthest from the camera that are in acceptable focus.

Desiccation: Complete drying out, removal of all moisture.

Digital Image: An electronic photograph taken with a digital camera or scanned from an original document. It is composed of pixels, the smallest units displayed by computer monitors. Each pixel is assigned a tonal value (black, white, a shade of gray, or color) and is stored in binary code (zeros and ones).

Disposal: The act of physically removing an object or objects from a museum collection. See also Deaccession.

Dolly: A low, two- or four-wheeled flat cart or platform used to move objects.

Domestic shipment: The shipment of objects within one country. [Naunert]

Double-crating: One box or case inside another with cushioning between.

DNG: Digital negative, Adobe's archival RAW format. The preferred archival or lossless file format for conversion of RAW files after image capture.

Drawer or Rack Style Case: This sideways slot-style case, in which individual boxes slide into the case like drawers, provides a particularly effective method of packing traveling exhibitions containing many small 3-D objects.

Emulsion: (1) A suspension of small globules of one liquid in a second liquid with which the first will not mix. (2) A photosensitive coating, usually of silver halide grains in a thin gelatin layer, on photographic film, paper, or glass.

Endangered Species: Any species which is in danger of extinction throughout all or a significant portion of its range, other than a species of the Class Insecta determined by the Secretary of Interior, Commerce, or Agriculture to constitute a pest the protection of which under the provisions of an Act would present an overwhelming and over-riding risk to man. A species of wildlife and plants listed as "endangered" pursuant to specific act. (e.g., Endangered Species Act, CITES)

Endorsement: In insurance, a form attached to the basic insurance contract which alters certain provisions in the policy. [GANYS]

Ephemera: Plural of ephemeron. Usually refers to paper objects that are intended to last only a short time.

Expired Loans: Loans of limited duration for which the termination dates have passed.

Export: To depart from, to send from, to ship from, or to carry out of, or to attempt to depart from, to send from, to ship from, or to carry out of, or to consign to a carrier in any place subject to the jurisdiction of the United States with an intended destination of any place not subject to the jurisdiction of the United States.

Export License: Permission, usually granted by a governmental agency, to ship a native cultural object out of the country. [Naunert]

Export Shipment: The shipment of an object or a group of objects out of a country. [Naunert]

Extended Loan: An object loaned to a museum for long-term, sometimes indefinite, use. In terms of record keeping, extended loans are often treated as a part of the Permanent Collection.

Fish or Wildlife: Any member of the animal kingdom, alive or dead, including without limitation any mammal, fish, bird (including any migratory, non-migratory, or endangered bird for which protection is also afforded by treaty or other international agreement), amphibian, reptile, mollusk, crustacean, arthropod, coelenterate, or other invertebrate, whether or not bred, hatched, or born in captivity, and including any part, product, egg, or offspring thereof, or the dead body or parts thereof.

F-stop: Numerical indication of how large a lens opening (aperture) is. The larger the f-stop number, the smaller the opening; for example, f/16 represents a smaller aperture than f/2.

Flat-pack: Museum objects packed horizontally and separated by material (e.g., cardboard, Fome-Core). Generally has foam padding on sides, top, and bottom of case.

Foam Core: Layer of plastic foam laminated on the outside by paper-based material. [Rose and de Torres]

Foam-lined Box: The objects, often wrapped in poly or Bubblewrap, are placed into a box lined with foam which does not fit the contour of the object; the voids are filled with material such as tissue paper, newsprint, or scraps of foam.

Follow Car: A vehicle carrying an escort and sometimes a courier which follows the van(s) containing the objects. An escort should not be the driver.

Foxing: A discoloration of paper caused by the action of mold on iron salts, which are present in most paper. [Naunert]

Found-in-Collection (FIC): Undocumented objects that remain without status after all attempts to reconcile them to existing records of permanent collection and loan objects are completed. See Undocumented Objects.

Fractional Gift: A donation of an object or collection of objects to which the museum does not receive full title. A fractional interest gift is one in which the museum is given a present fractional interest and the donor retains the remaining fractional interest.

Freight Forwarding Agent: A person or company that organizes shipments for individuals or other companies. May also act as a carrier but typically acts only as an agent or logistics provider that dispatches shipments via asset-based carriers and that books or otherwise arranges space for these shipments. Freight forwarders typically arrange cargo movement to an international destination and have expertise that allows them to prepare and process documentation and perform related activities pertaining to international shipments.

Friable: Readily crumbled.

Gantry: Hoisting equipment consisting of vertical sides connected by a horizontal beam mounted high enough to provide a clear lift for an object below. Lift is usually provided by a chain hoist, and often a gantry can be constructed of two scaffolding towers connected by a beam.

General Facility Report: Current (2010) version of the Registrars Committee of the American Association of Museum's (RC-AAM) former Standard Facility report. See Standard Facility Report.

Glassine: A dense, slick-surfaced translucent paper resistant to the passage of air and dirt; used as a wrapping material or for separation sheets. [Naunert]

Gross Weight: For shipping purposes, the combined weight of the objects to be shipped, the packing materials, and the packing box. See also Net Weight, Tare Weight. [Naunert]

Guillotines: See Contour Bracing.

Hand-carry: A packed object which can be carried by one person and is transported on or under an aircraft passenger seat or in a passenger vehicle.

Hand Signals: Standardized and universal hand gestures developed by riggers to insure proper operation without verbal communication. Proper use is critical in rigging.

Harass: In the definition of "take" in the Endangered Species Act, an action which kills or injures wildlife. Such action may include significant habitat modification or degradation which kills or injures wildlife by significantly impairing essential behavioral patterns, including breeding, feeding, or sheltering.

Herbarium: A collection of dried plant specimens, usually mounted and systematically arranged for reference; a place that houses such a collection. [Rose and de Torres]

Hitch: A method of temporarily connecting by loop, hook, or noose, an object to be moved to a lifting device such as a crane or gantry. Examples are single hitch, bridle hitch, basket hitch, and choker hitches.

Hoist: (1) A common piece of equipment used for lifting objects. (2) The process of moving an object.

HVAC: The acronym used to refer to Heating, Ventilation, and Air Conditioning systems.

Hygroscopic Material: A material capable of absorbing moisture. [Naunert]

Hygrothermograph: An instrument that measures and records Temperature and Relative Humidity changes. [Naunert]

Import: To land on, bring into, or introduce into, or to attempt to land on, bring into, or introduce into any place subject to the jurisdiction of the United States, whether or not such landing, bringing, or introduction constitutes an importation within the meaning of the tariff laws of the United States.

Import Shipment: The shipment of an object or group of objects into the country. [Naunert]

Impounded Shipment: Objects in transit without proper permits or licenses which are seized by Customs upon arrival at an airport.

Incidental Taking: Any taking otherwise prohibited, if such taking is incidental to, and not the purpose of, the carrying out of an otherwise lawful activity.

Incoming Loan: An object borrowed by an institution. It is an incoming loan from the perspective of the borrowing institution; such a loan would be an Outgoing Loan to the lending institution. [Naunert]

Indefinite Loans: Loans that have no set duration.

Inert Materials: Materials that are devoid of active properties and unable or unlikely to form compounds.

Insurance Claim: A formal, written demand to an insurance company for reimbursement for loss of or damage to an insured object. [Naunert]

Integrated Pest Management: The selection, integration, and implementation of pest management methods based on predicted economic, ecological, and sociological consequences. A decision-making process which helps one decide if a treatment is necessary and appropriate, where the treatment should be administered, when treatment should be applied, and what strategies should be integrated for immediate and long-term results. [National Park Service]

J-Bar: Large shipper's tool in the shape of a "J" that allows leverage to be used when lifting a corner of a heavy package.

JPEG (or JPG) (Joint Photographic Experts Group) image format: The most widely used format for distribution but not for archival purposes. Each time an image is opened, saved, and closed, the image is compressed further. If it is opened and closed without saving, it is not altered. JPG works by analyzing images and discarding kinds of information that the eye is least likely to notice. [2] Images stored in this file format vary in size but are much smaller than TIFF formatted images and are ideal for use on the Internet. They require less storage space compared to a TIFF.

Laches: An unreasonable delay that makes it inequitable to give the relief sought by a party in court.

Lacquer: (1) Any varnish coating, particularly those found on metal. (2) A solution of cellulose nitrate that dries to form a film. (3) Urushi, or oriental lacquer

Load Line: The line that bears the weight of a lift.

Loan Agreement: A contract between a lender and a borrower of an object or objects, specifying the object(s) and outlining the conditions of loan and the respective responsibilities of each party.

Loss Limit: The maximum amount an insurance policy will pay for a single loss.

Lost in Inventory: An object that is claimed as lost (insurance) or noted as lost (inventory reconciliation) after a careful check of all areas where the object might reasonably be (storage, conservation, exhibition, loan) and after checking with all staff who might have had reason to interact with the object.

Lossless: A class of data compression algorithms that allows the exact original data to be reconstructed from the compressed data. See RAW and TIFF.

Lossy: A file compression technique that does not permit the decompression of data back to 100% of the original. Lossy methods provide high degrees of compression and result in very small compressed files, but there is a certain amount of loss when they are restored. See JPEG.

Marine Mammal: Any mammal which is a) morphologically adapted to the marine environment, including sea otters and members of the orders Sirenia, Pinnipedia, and Cetacea, or b) primarily inhabits the marine environment (such as the polar bear); and, for the purpose of this Act, includes any part of any such marine mammal, including its raw, dressed, or dyed fur or skin.

Material Safety Data Sheets (MSDS): Provided by manufacturers, these sheets include data on the volatility, flammability, toxicity, and other safety related information about a specific chemical or material.

Metadata: Data about data, for instance, the information attached to digital objects.

Microfoam: See Polyethylene/Polypropylene Foam.

Micro-environment: A climate-controlled and secure space for the display or storage of artifacts or specimens within a sealed case or frame, used in buildings where such control is not feasible in entire rooms. [Lord and Lord}

Net Weight: For shipping purposes, the weight of the object being shipped, exclusive of the weight of the box or packing materials. See also Gross Weight; Tare Weight. [Naunert]

Nitrile Rubber: A synthetic rubber which is highly oil resistant.

Nomenclature: A system of terms used in a particular science or discipline

Off-gassing: The process of releasing (usually slowly) volatile materials from woods, some paints, some polymers, etc. Many of these volatile materials contribute to the deterioration of objects. [Rose and de Torres]

Old Loans: Expired loans or loans of unlimited duration left unclaimed by lenders at the museum; the term includes unclaimed objects left at the museum under informal custody arrangements for study or examination by museum staff.

One-time/One-way Crate: A very simple crate used to send an object one-way only. It is usually destroyed after one use.

Original Order: The archival principle that records should be maintained in the order in which they were placed by the organization, individual, or family that created them. [Daniels and Walch]

Outgoing Loan: An object lent by a museum to another institution. It is an Outgoing Loan from the perspective of the lending institution; such a loan would be an Incoming Loan to the borrowing institution. [Naunert]

Pallet: A low, portable platform, usually of wood or metal, on which a heavy or bulky object is placed for storage, transport, or shipment. [Naunert]

Password: Secret code word used to restrict access. Used in computer and telephone systems, computer programs.

PCS Permit: Any document designated as a "permit," "license," "certificate," or any other document issued by the management authority or responsible agency or office to authorize, limit, or describe activity and signed by an authorized official.

pH: An expression indicating the hydrogen-ion concentration of a solution; the negative logarithm of the hydrogen-ion concentration. A measure of acidity.

Pick (Pick Point): The point above the center of gravity at which an object is lifted; the point at which the load line and the rigging meet.

Plant: Any member of the plant kingdom, including seeds, roots, and other parts thereof.

PNG: A lossless digital format that looks for patterns in the image that it can use to compress file size. The compression is exactly reversible, so the image is recovered exactly. [3] Images stored in this file format are larger than JPGs but smaller than TIFFs and may be used on the Internet when a lossless image is required. The PNG file format is good for archival storage and requires less storage space compared to a TIFF.

Polyethylene Foam: Foam made by the introduction of gas or by inclusion of a gas-evolving chemical in molten polyethylene; sheets of polyethylene foam are inert and stable.

Polyprophylene Foam: Foam made from polypropylene resin, similar in process to Polyethylene Foam. Sheets of polyprophylene are inert and stable.

Possession: The detention and control, or the manual or ideal custody of anything which may be the subject of property, for one's use and enjoyment, either as owner or as the proprietor of a qualified right in it, and either held personally or by another who exercises it in one's place and name. Possession includes the act or state of possessing and that condition of facts under which one can exercise his power over a corporeal thing at his pleasure to the exclusion of all other persons. Possession includes constructive possession, which means not actual but assumed to exist, where one claims to hold by virtue of some title, without having actual custody. (See Endangered Species article.)

Powder Coating: A coating made from spraying powdered thermosetting resins onto a metal substrate, which are then set by baking. [Rose and de Torres]

Print: A positive black and white or color image created from a negative or a printout from a digital print. Prints are usually made on paper and vary in size. A typical size for a print is 8 x 10 in.

Provenance: For works of art and historical objects, the background and history of ownership. The more common term for anthropological collections is "provenience," which defines an object in terms of the specific geographic location of origin. In scientific collections, the term "locality," meaning specific geographic point of origin, is more acceptable. [Naunert]

Psychrometer: An instrument for measuring the relative humidity by means of air flow across two thermometers, one of which (the wet-bulb) is covered by a moistened wick. Often used to help with calibration of hygrothermographs and as an independent check of relative humidity.

Rail and Trolley: A device that allows for the lateral movement of an object to be lifted. The trolley mounts to and rolls along the rail, the horizontal member of a gantry, usually an I-beam. Useful when an object is to be removed from a pedestal and then lowered to the floor or to a dolly.

RAW Image File: The preferred capture mode that produces a superior quality image. Contains unprocessed data from a digital camera and is sometimes considered as a digital negative (DNG). Camera make and model will determine the size of a RAW file.

Reciprocity Law: In photography, the theoretical relationship between the length of exposure (shutter speed) and the intensity of the light (aperture) which dictates that an increase in one will be balanced by a equal amount of decrease by the other. This means that if one meters a scene and decides the exposure will be f/5.6 at 1/60 second one could obtain the same exposure by doubling the f-stop and cutting exposure in half: f/4 at 1/125 second. Or the opposite, obtaining an exposure of f/8 at 1/30 second.

Reciprocity Failure: In photography, the failure of the reciprocity law to apply. This occurs at 1 second and longer when the normal ratio of aperture and shutter speed will underexpose the film and at 1/10,000 second and faster. When using black and white film with exposures of 1 second or longer exposures just need to be increased to avoid underexposure. When using color film in these conditions color shifts will occur because the three emulsions do not respond to the reciprocity effect in the same manner. To compensate, follow exposure and filtering instructions provided with the film along with a little trial and error.

Re-Export: Export of wildlife or plants that have been previously imported.

Registration: The process of developing and maintaining an immediate, brief, and permanent means of identifying an object for which the institution has permanently or temporarily assumed responsibility. [Naunert]

Relative Humidity (RH): The proportion of vapor pressure of air to its saturation vapor pressure at that temperature.

Rigging: (1) The art of combining and securing the proper slings and hitches to the proper pick point of an object to be lifted. The person responsible for this is the rigger. (2) The slings and equipment used in moving large objects.

Risk Assessment: Evaluation of a museum object for its suitability to travel.

Seal: A metal wire and numbered disc which are used to seal locks on vehicle or container doors to deter and monitor tampering with shipments in holding areas or in transit.

Seamless: A backdrop used in photography to create an even background for the main subject. Materials usually consist of large rolls of paper or large pieces of fabric.

Series: A body of file units or documents arranged in accordance with a unified filing system or maintained by the record creator as a unit because of some relationship arising out of their creation, receipt, or use. [Daniels and Walch]

Shellac: A preparation of lac, usually dissolved in alcohol, and used chiefly as a wood finish.

Shipping Agent: See Freight-forwarding Agent

Sight Line: The range of a guard's view of objects on display in which large objects do not obscure small objects.

Sight Measurement: An approximate measurement of an object, usually a painting or a work of art on paper, taken when the full extremities of the piece are inaccessible. [Naunert]

Silica Gel: A granular substance that has high moisture-absorbing and emitting properties and is used as a moisture stabilizer in packing, storing and exhibiting humidity sensitive objects.

Slat Case: A case with a minimal amount of wood and no solid sides; consists of slats instead of sheets.

Sliding Tray Case: A case with rigid trays that slide out of a side opening.

Sling Psychrometer: See Psychrometer.

Slings: The rope, cables, or woven straps used in rigging.

Slot Style Crating: A traditional style of packing for multiple, usually 2-D, objects, which allows each object to be unpacked as needed without handling the others in the crate. Individual, usually framed, objects fit into their own slots, and the ability to move directly from crate to wall and the same in reverse makes for efficient and safe installation, minimizing handling of the object.

Soft Packed: Packing an object without enclosing it in a hard shell box or case using a variety of soft materials

Solander Box: A ready-made box of acid-free board; frequently used for the storage of documents, unframed works on paper, etc. [Naunert]

Species: Any subspecies of fish, wildlife, or plants and any distinct population segment of any species of vertebrate fish or wildlife which interbreeds when mature.

Specimen: Any animal or plant, or any part, product, egg, seed, or root of any animal or plant.

Standard Facility Report: A form developed by the RC-AAM, completed by the borrower of objects to demonstrate suitability as a venue to lenders of objects.

Statutes of Limitations: Laws that require claims to be brought to court within a limited time period or otherwise the right to claim is lost.

Stowage Requirements: The structure of an object dictates which way up it can be placed, how far off center it can be tipped when handled, and which plane of travel is preferable.

Straight Truck: A truck, from 12 to 24 feet long, designed with body and cab connected.

Subgroup: A body of related records within a record group, usually consisting of the records of a primary subordinate administrative unit or of records series related chronologically, functionally, or by subject. [Daniels and Walch]

Substrate: In conservation, the immediate surface to which a coating or adhesive material is applied, e.g., the lacquer on a lacquered metal, not the metal seen beneath the lacquer.

Systematics: The science of classifying all organisms, both living and extinct, and of investigating the relationships between them; the field of science concerned with taxonomy and phylogeny. [Duckworth]

Tag Line: One or more control lines that are attached to an object before a lift takes place; used to control the sway, stability, and placement of the object.

Take: To harass, harm, pursue, hunt, shoot, wound, kill, trap, capture, or collect a living specimen, or to attempt to engage in any such conduct.

Tare Weight: For shipping purposes, the weight of the packing box, including packing materials, without the object it was built to contain. The term can also be used to indicate the weight of an empty vehicle. See also Gross Weight, Net Weight.

Taxidermy: The process of preparing animal skins and stuffing them in a lifelike form.

Taxonomy: The science or technique of classification; the discipline devoted to the identification, naming and classification of organisms. [Duckworth]

Temperature: A degree of hotness or coldness. May be expressed in Centigrade or Fahrenheit scales.

Threatened Species: Any species which is likely to become an endangered species within the foreseeable future throughout all or a significant portion of its range. A species of wildlife or plants listed as "threatened" pursuant to specific act. (e.g., Endangered Species Act, CITES)

TIFF (Tagged Image File Format): The most widely used archival format to save processed images. Flexible and universally supported across operating system platforms. Maintains all original color information and supports embedded color profiles needed for printing, as well as metadata in the file.

Touring Crate: A container that is built to stand up to a multi-venue tour, usually with reusable fastening hardware on the lid. It is built to withstand abuse from handling and is weather and usually water resistant.

Tractor Trailer: A two-part truck. The tractor is the cab where the driver sits and the trailer, hooked to the tractor, hauls the freight.

Transportation: To ship, convey, carry, or transport by any means whatever and deliver or receive for such shipment, conveyance, carriage, or transportation.

Travel Frame: (1) New or replacement frame used for travel instead of the original frame. (2) Wood collar to which an object is attached for travel to allow wrapping. Used on paintings with ornate frames, paintings without frames or with minimal frames, flat sculptural works, and unusual works where the surface may not be touched by packing material.

Traveling: Any horizontal movement.

Traveling Case: Case built to withstand a multi-stop tour, usually with reusable fastening hardware on the lid. Usually water-resistant.

Tray Pack: Objects placed into a tray or drawer using a foam cut-out to cushion the object. Trays or drawers can be stacked into a foam-lined case, the weight is absorbed by the sides of the tray or drawer, avoiding pressure on the object.

TSA: Transportation Safety Administration. Federal agency responsible for the security of the United States' transportation systems for public and commercial use.

Two-way Crate: A case built to send an object there and back, but not to withstand extensive travel.

Undocumented Objects: Similar to collections and found in collections areas but with no numbers, no information in their housing, nor any characteristics that might connect them to documentation.

Ultraviolet Filter: A filter that can be placed over windows, skylights, and fluorescent light tubes, between the light source and museum object, to remove or reduce harmful ultraviolet rays in the light. [Naunert]

Ultraviolet Radiation: Radiation of wavelengths shorter than 400mm, found in light from the sun, sky, and most artificial light sources; it is invisible and has a strongly damaging effect on collections.

Vapor Barrier: A treated paper or combination of papers used in lining a shipping box to protect the contents from the effects of water.

Varnish: A resin dissolved in a solvent or solvent mixture;

used to coat a surface with a hard, glossy, transparent film.

Worksheet: An informal document used to record basic catalogue information pertaining to an object. From the worksheet, catalog cards and accession sheets can be prepared. [Naunert]

Yokes: See Contour Bracing.

[1] DocuSource on NC, LLC. "Education Materials for Digital Printing: Glossary." DocuSource, of NC, LLC. http://www.docusourceofnc.com/pages/techtips/glossary.php (accessed on November 24, 2008).

[2] Ibid.

[3] Ibid.

BIOGRAPHIES | AUTHORS AND CONTRIBUTORS

Co-Editors

Rebecca A. Buck and Jean Allman Gilmore have published, through the American Association of Museums, four books: *New Museum Registration Methods* (1998), *On the Road Again: Developing and Managing Traveling Exhibitions* (2003), *Collection Conundrums: Solving Collections Management Mysteries* (2007), and *Museum Registration Methods 5th Edition* (2010). Both have served as Chair of RC-MAAM. They were awarded the Dudley Wilkinson Award for Excellence by the Registrars Committee of AAM in 2001.

Rebecca A. Buck

Rebecca A. Buck is Deputy Director for Collection Services and Chief Registrar at the Newark Museum. She was formerly Curator of Collections, Eastern Washington State Historical Society, Registrar, Hood Museum of Art, Dartmouth College, and Registrar, University of Pennsylvania Museum of Archaeology and Anthropology, Philadelphia. She served as an Adjunct Professor in Seton Hall University's Museum Professions Programs (1996–2007) and as Chair of the Registrars Committee of AAM (1999–2001). She holds degrees from Oberlin College and Boston University. She was awarded the John Cotton Dana Award by the New Jersey Association of Museums in 2004, and in 2006 was recognized on AAM's Centennial Honor Roll as one of the museum world's "one hundred champions" of the past 100 years.

Jean Allman Gilmore

Jean Allman Gilmore has been registrar of the Brandywine River Museum, Chadds Ford, Pennsylvania, since 1982. She earned a B.A. degree from Wittenberg University and a M.A. degree from the University of Wyoming, and completed the Museum Studies Program at the University of Delaware. She has served as Chairman of the Mid-Atlantic Association of Museums Registrars Committee, Secretary of the MAAM Board of Governors, and co-editor, with Rebecca Buck, of the journal *Registrar*, published by the AAM Registrars Committee.

Authors

Allen, Bill

Bill Allen, with the late Patricia Hayes, founded Henderson Phillips Insurance.

Arnone, Olivia

Olivia Arnone received her B.A. in Photography from Rutgers University in 2002 and went on to work as a freelance photographer and as an assistant at a contemporary American art gallery. She received her Masters degree from Ryerson University, Toronto, in conjunction with the George Eastman House, Rochester, in Photographic Preservation and Collections Management. Her educational and professional experience includes inventorying, archiving, and re-housing documentary and fine art photography collections. She is an associate registrar at The Newark Museum.

Bakke, Julia

Julie Bakke has been Chief Registrar at the Museum of Fine Arts, Houston since 2001. She was formerly registrar at The Menil Collection (1985–2001) and assistant registrar at the Philadelphia Museum of Art (1979–1985). She holds a B.A. degree from Mount Holyoke College.

Benas, Jeanne

Jeanne Benas has been the Registrar at the Smithsonian's National Museum of American History since 1994. Her collections management career began at the Smithsonian in 1977. She was Assistant Registrar at the National Air and Space Museum from 1982 to 1985, then returned to American History as manager of the acquisition and deaccession program. She has served as Co-Chair of the Mid-Atlantic Association of Museums Registrars Committee's Old Loan Task Force, chair of the MAAM Registrars Committee, Secretary of the Registrars Committee of AAM and has completed two terms as Chair of the RC-AAM.

Bennett, K. Sharon

K. Sharon Bennett is project archivist at the College of Charleston, where she is establishing a new Women's History Collection. She was formerly the archivist for The Charleston Museum and project consultant for the South Carolina Education Project. She is a frequent lecturer on preservation topics and a specialist in disaster planning and recovery.

Berkow, Racine

Racine Berkow is President and founder of Racine Berkow Associates, Inc., licensed customs brokers and freight forwarders specializing in handling fine arts, antiques and museum exhibitions. She has served as Registrar of The Jewish Museum in New York and was a founding member of the Registrar's Committee of the American Association of Museums. Ms. Berkow holds a B.F.A. from Ohio State University and professional certificates from The School of Visual Arts and the World Trade Institute. She is a member of ArtTable, Inc. and presently serves on the Board of Directors of The Tel Aviv Museum of Art.

Bitz, Gwen

Gwen Bitz is Registrar at Walker Art Center, Minneapolis, where she began museum work in 1972. In 1983 she left the Walker to serve as Registrar for The Museum Fund, Minneapolis and New York, and for the Minneapolis Institute of Arts. She returned to Walker as Registrar in 1990.

Breisch, Nancy L.

Nancy Breisch is a specialist in urban entomology and integrated pest management at the University of Maryland, College Park. Her research interests include the ecology and behavior of structural pests. Active in technical outreach efforts, Dr. Breisch coordinates one of the principal annual training and recertification conferences for the structural pest management industry.

Carnell, Clarisse

Clarisse Carnell is Registrar for the Collections at the Philadelphia Museum of Art. She began work in the library of the museum in 1975 and has been in the Registrar's Office since 1980. Ms. Carnell is also a classically trained pinhole photographer with works in the permanent collection of the Victoria and Albert Museum, the International Center for Photography, and the George Eastman House.

Cato, Paisley S.

Paisley S. Cato is Assistant Director and Curator for the Western Center for Archaeology & Paleontology, California, where she has implemented numerous museum policies and procedures for collections care and management, and exhibition and interpretive programming. In her 30-year career, she has worked at the San Diego Natural History Museum, Virginia Museum of Natural History, TCWC of Texas A&M University, The Museum at Texas Tech University, and the Denver Museum of Natural History.

Cline, Judith

Judith Cline has been the Associate Registrar for Outgoing Loans at the National Gallery of Art since 1992. She has held many Assistant Registrar positions at the National Gallery of Art between 1992 and 1984 and also worked for the Publications Department at the National Gallery of Art, 1980–1984. She has also served on two AAM panels, speaking on the subjects of courier requirements and training.

Daly, Karen D.

Karen D. Daly has been a museum registrar at the Virginia Museum of Fine Arts since 1996. In 2003, she became VMFA's Administrator of Provenance Research, serving as the museum's contact person for information related to World War II-era provenance, and as its coordinator of provenance research. She holds a Masters of Arts degree in art historical studies from Virginia Commonwealth University and a B.A in Philosophy and Religious Studies from Louisiana State University. She is a frequent lecturer and is a contributor to *Vitalizing Memory: International Perspectives in Provenance Research* (AAM, 2005).

DeAngelis, Ildiko Pogany

Ildiko Pogany DeAngelis is an attorney and former Director of the Museum Studies Program at The George Washington University, where she taught graduate courses in legal and ethical issues arising from the management of museum collections. She has published articles and served as faculty and steering committee member for the annual ALI/ABA Legal Problems of Museum Administration seminars. After graduating from the Washington College of Law in 1980, she joined the firm of Steptoes & Johnson and spent many years as a member of the Smithsonian's legal staff, concentrating on collections-related issues. She currently lives in Beijin and teaches graduate courses via distance education.

Difanis, Anita

Anita Difanis joined the Association of Art Museum Directors in 1992 as its first Director of Government Affairs. Prior to that, she taught French at the University of Wisconsin-Oshkosh, followed by 10 years at the Vie de France Corporation, where she was Vice President of Business Development. She has traveled and lived abroad extensively and currently makes her home in the D.C. area.

Demeroukas, Marie

Marie Demeroukas has been the photo archivist and research librarian at the Shiloh Museum of Ozark History in Springdale, Arkansas, since 2005. She was the collections manager at the Rogers Historical Museum for 18 years. She is active in the Southeastern Museums Conference and the Southeastern Registrars Association (SERA), and has had a hand in producing *Nomenclature 3.0,* as well as two SERA publications, *Steal This Handbook: A Template for Creating a Museum's Emergency Preparedness Plan and Basic Condition Reporting: A Handbook* (3rd edition).

Douglas, Anne Fuhrman

Anne Fuhrman Douglas worked in the field of collections management for more than 15 years. She was Registrar at the Ackland Art Museum, University of North Carolina at Chapel Hill, and has also worked at the Metropolitan Museum of Art and the Philadelphia Museum of Art. She received her M.A. from the College of William and Mary and her B.A. from Drew University.

Dowd, Mary

Mary Dowd is Manager of Administrative Services at the Newark Museum. She formerly served as paralegal for the Law Office of Margaret E. Padovano, Esq., and as Supervisor, Reconsideration and Continuing Disability Units for the State of New Jersey, Division of Disability Determinations.

Edwards, Alison

Alison Edwards is Director of Special Projects and Exhibition Planning at the Newark Museum. She was the Project Director of the Religion and the Arts Initiative at the Center for the Study of World Religions, Harvard University, and is co-editor of the volume *Stewards of the Sacred* (AAM 2004), which documents new policy and best practices for the care, research, and interpretation of culturally sensitive collections. Edwards received her Masters degree and is completing her doctorate at Harvard's Graduate School of Education.

Engel, Bethany

Bethany Engel is the Associate Registrar and Rights & Reproductions Coordinator at the Brandywine River Museum. She previously worked at the University of Pennsylvania Museum of Archaeology and Anthropology in the Traveling Exhibitions Department. She earned a B.A. in Anthropology from Rutgers University.

Fisher, Genevieve

Genevieve Fisher is Registrar at the Peabody Museum of Archaeology and Ethnology, Cambridge, Mass. She serves as a peer reviewer for AAM's Museum Assessment Program and has lectured in museum studies at both Tufts and Harvard Universities. She holds degrees in anthropology and European archaeology from the University of Pennsylvania and the University of Oxford.

Frantz, Sara

Sara L. Frantz has worked for Nevada Museum of Art for nine years, initially as Capital Campaign Coordinator, and as Registrar shortly thereafter. She completed her Master's degree in Museum Studies at John F. Kennedy University, Berkeley, California, in 2007, and received the *2007 Outstanding Student, School of Education and Liberal Arts Award.* She also received the *Gail Anderson Award for Outstanding Scholarship in Museums and Social Responsibility.* She is Chairperson for Nevada Museum of Art's Sustainable Practices Team.

Freitag, Sally

Sally Freitag has been Chief Registrar at the National Gallery of Art since 1992. She was previously Registrar at the Worcester Art Museum, Worcester, Mass. She also served as Associate Registrar at National Gallery of Art from 1973 to 1983 and has served on the Art and Artifacts Indemnity Panel.

Greene, Albert

Al Greene originated the U. S. General Services Administration's IPM program in 1988 and serves as the agency's nationwide point of contact for pest management issues. He has assisted in the implementation of IPM programs for a wide range of building types, including museums, archives, and records storage facilities, for virtually every major federal agency, as well as dozens of states, municipalities, and school systems.

Grossman, Janet

Janet Burnett Grossman earned her Ph.D. in Art History from the Institute of Fine Arts, New York University. In 2008, she retired after 17 years as a curator of ancient art at the J. Paul Getty Museum in Los Angeles. She now lives in Spokane, Washington, and is completing a manuscript on ancient gravestones excavated from the Agora in Athens, Greece, and is working on a catalogue of Greek sculptures in the J. Paul Getty Museum.

Hankins, Scott

Scott Hankins is the Assistant Registrar at the Ackland Art Museum, University of North Carolina at Chapel Hill. He previously served as the Associate Registrar at the Newark Museum. He holds a M.A. in Museum Studies from Seton Hall University. He is also a contributor to the R.A.R.I.N Wiki.

Holahan, Mary

Mary F. Holahan is Curator of Collections and Exhibitions at the Delaware Art Museum. She received her Ph.D. in Art History from the University of Delaware in 1978. She has taught and lectured widely on art history and fine arts collections management and has been active in various professional committees.

Holl, Jennifer

Jennifer M. Holl is the Collections Registrar at the Delaware Art Museum. She was previously the Collections Manager at the Delaware Historical Society. She earned a B.A. from Denison University and a M.A. degree in history from the University of Delaware, with her certificate in museum studies.

Hummel, Charles

Charles Hummel is Curator Emeritus and Adjunct Professor of Advanced Studies at Winterthur Museum. He retired from Winterthur in 1991 as Deputy Director for the Museum and Library Department. Mr. Hummel has served as Secretary of the American Association of Museums and was the recipient of the Katherine Coffee Award from the Mid-Atlantic Association of Museums in 1989.

Hurst, Kara J.

Kara J. Hurst has been Registrar at the Utah Museum of Natural History at the University of Utah since 2004 and teaches museum collections management at the University. She previously worked as Curator of Exhibitions & Education at the Price Tower Arts Center. Hurst has a B.A. in Anthropology from Pacific Lutheran University and an M.A. in Museum Science from Texas Tech University. She regularly lectures on museum collections and repository issues and is actively involved in state, regional and national organizations.

Jacobson, Claudia

Claudia Jacobson, Milwaukee Public Museum Registrar, has over 25 years of experience working with both cultural and natural history collections. She has headed committees to develop Ethics, Collections, Emergency Preparedness policies, and has prepared AAM Accreditation submissions. She teaches the collections management course for the Museum Studies Program of the University of Wisconsin-Milwaukee Graduate School and is active in state, regional and national museum associations.

Janzen, Mark

Mark Janzen has been the Registrar/Collection

Manager at the Ulrich Museum of Art in Wichita, Kansas, since 2001. He received his Masters degree from Texas Tech University's Museum Science program in 1994, and is currently working toward a Ph.D. in American History from Texas A&M University. He is the Chair of the Mountain Plains Museum Association Registrars Committee and a member of several standing committees, including the Scholarship and Membership committees. He regularly mentors new professionals in the MPMA region as at AAM.

Johnston, Tamara

Tamara Johnston has worked in collections care for 15 years. She is currently Preservation Coordinator at the Kohler Foundation; Preservation Consultant for the American Geographical Society Library at UW-Milwaukee; adjunct instructor at the Milwaukee Institute of Art and Design; volunteer Collections Manager for the National Speedskating Museum and Hall of Fame; and Chair of Education for the AAM's Registrars Committee. She is a graduate of the University of Wisconsin, Madison in Art History and the Museum Studies Program at The George Washington University.

Klein, Janice

Janice Klein has over 25 years of museum experience, including as Registrar of the Department of Anthropology at The Field Museum, Chicago, and as Executive Director of the Mitchell Museum of the American Indian, Evanston, Illinois. She currently runs her own company, EightSixSix Consulting, which specializes in collection management and small museum administration. She has served as Chair of AAM's Registrars Committee and Small Museum Administrators Committee, as well as on the American Association for State and Local History's Small Museums Committee, Task Force on Graduated Standards and Professional Development (Nominating) Committee.

Longstreth-Brown, Kittu

Kittu Longstreth-Brown retired as a Division Director at the Colorado Historical Society, Collection Services and Access, in 2001. She previously served as Registrar at the University of New Mexico Art Museum, Albuquerque, Head Registrar at the Portland (Oregon) Art Museum and as Chief Registrar at the Fine Arts Museums of San Francisco. Ms. Longstreth-Brown has a B.A. from Oberlin College and a M.Ed. from Harvard University.

Lord, Allyn

Allyn Lord is Director at Shiloh Museum of Ozark History in Fayetteville, Arkansas. She formerly served as assistant director at the Rogers Historical Museum in Rogers, Arkansas, and as registrar at The University Museum, University of Arkansas. Lord has been involved in numerous museum organizations and currently serves as AAM's Board liaison for the Standing Professional Committee council. She has written and co-edited *Basic Condition Reporting: A Handbook* and *Steal This Handbook! A Template for Creating a Museum's Emergency Preparedness Plan*. She received the Southeastern Museums Conference Leadership Award in 1996.

Malaro, Marie C.

Marie C. Malaro is a lawyer, author and retired university professor. For many years she was legal counsel for the Smithsonian Institution, and later was Director of the Graduate Program in Museum Studies at The George Washington University, where she is Professor Emerita, periodically teaching online. She is widely known for her books and many articles, as well as her 20 years of participation in the American Law Institute/American Bar Association's annual seminar, "Legal Problems of Museum Administration."

McGrew, T. Ashley

T. Ashley McGrew is a Lead Preparator for Exhibition Installation at the J. Paul Getty Museum, Los Angeles. Previously he worked as the Assistant Move Coordinator for Collections and Packing at the Smithsonian Institution's National Museum of the American Indian in the Bronx. He has worked commercially as a crate designer and packing supervisor in fine arts services and was Chief Preparator at the University of Oklahoma Museum of Art. He is currently Chair of Publications for PACIN (Packing, Art handling and Crating Information Network), a Professional Interest Committee of AAM.

McCormick, Maureen

Maureen McCormick is Chief Registrar at the Princeton University Art Museum, where she has worked since 1984. She began her museum career in the Registrar's Office at the Columbus Museum of Art, Ohio, and subsequently administered a traveling exhibition program at the Ohio Foundation for the Arts. She holds an M.F.A. in printmaking from the Tyler School of Art, Temple University, and paints icons in the Russian Byzantine style in her spare time.

McKeown, C. Timothy

C. Timothy McKeown is an anthropologist with the Department of the Interior. He served in various roles implementing the Native American Graves Protection and Repatriation Act (NAGPRA) from 1991–2009, promulgating regulations and representing the Secretary to the review committee. He lectures widely and writes on the subject of repatriation.

Meador-Woodruff, Robin

Robin Meador-Woodruff began her museum career in 1986 as the Assistant Registrar at the University of Michigan Museum of Art. She became the Coordinator of Museum Collections at the Kelsey Museum of Archaeology, University of Michigan, and later Curator of Slides and Photographs there. Most recently she served as Guest Curator for "Pompeii: Tales from an Eruption" at the Birmingham Museum of Art, where she is now a consultant.

Molini, John

John Molini is the Manager of Packing and Crating at The Art Institute of Chicago where he has worked since 1985, and where he created the packing and crating department. He was the leader in the innovation of hybrid crate designs and developed the first exclusive designs related to the highly sensitive transport of pastel works on paper. A former Chair of PACIN, he has taught at the Campbell Center for Historic Preservation in Mount Carroll, Illinois, since 1994.

Montgomery, Renee

Renee Montgomery, Assistant Director, Collections at the Los Angles County Museum of Art, was formerly Registrar at that museum. She holds an M.A. in Art History from the University of California, Riverside, and has served the RC-AAM as Development Officer, Vice Chair and, from 1988–1990, Chair.

Morris, Martha

Martha Morris is Associate Professor and Assistant Director of Museum Studies at The George Washington University. She was formerly the Deputy Director of the National Museum of American History and Registrar of the Corcoran Gallery of Art. She holds degrees from GWU and the University of Maryland. Her research and teaching are in the areas of museum management and leadership. She is co-author of *Planning Successful Museum Building Projects,* 2009.

Moser, Antonia

Antonia Moser holds a Masters degree in Museum Professions from Seton Hall University, as well as degrees in English literature from Boston College and Vanderbilt University. She currently serves as Associate Registrar at the Newark Museum.

Murphy, Amanda

Amanda Murphy is the Assistant Registrar at the Smithsonian National Zoo, Washington, D.C. Previously she worked with the National Park Service in developing the NAGPRA grant program and providing technical assistance and training.

Neilson, Dixie

Dixie Neilson teaches in the graduate Museum Studies program at the University of Florida, and is the Director of Art Care, a collections care consulting agency. She has more than 20 years experience in the museum field. She is past chair of the Southeastern Registrars Association (SERA) and presently serves as RC-AAM's Liaison for Museum Studies Programs, and is on the advisory board of PACIN. She is a contributor to *Basic Condition Reporting: A Handbook and Encyclopedia of Library and Information Sciences.*

Peak, Deborah

Deborah Peak, Senior Vice President, Aon/Huntington T. Block Insurance Agency, Inc., has more than 30 years of experience in all aspects of fine arts insurance. Widely respected as an authority in this highly specialized field, she is the manager of the fine art commercial team at Aon.

Powell, Brent

Brent Powell is the current Chair of PACIN (Packing Arthandling Crating Information Network) Professional Interest Committee of the American Association of Museums. He has worked and managed Art Handling staff since 1985 at The Nelson-Atkins Museum of Art in Kansas City, National Gallery of Victoria in Melbourne Australia and is presently the Head of Preparation at the Asian Art Museum in San Francisco. Commercial Fine Art employment has been with Fortress FAE in Baltimore and International Art Services in Sydney Australia. He has conducted numerous workshops, sessions and complied publications on packing, crating, storage and art handling through out the Untied States, Australia and Malaysia.

Quigley, Suzanne

Suzanne Quigley is President of art & artifact services, LLC, a consulting and art management company. She served as Head Registrar, Collections and Exhibitions, at the Solomon R. Guggenheim Museum, and was also Head Registrar at the Detroit Institute of Arts and Audio-Visual Librarian at Olin Library, Kenyon College. She has been a board member of the Museum Computer Network and editor of its quarterly magazine, *Spectra*. She holds an MLS degree from the University of Wisconsin, Madison.

Ryan, David

David Ryan is the Registrar at the Colorado Springs Pioneers Museum. He served previously as Assistant Curator of Collections and Registrar at the Albuquerque Museum. He holds a Masters of Liberal Studies with a museum emphasis from the University of Oklahoma and has served as Chair of the Mountain-Plains Museum Association Registrars Committee.

Schansberg, Jennifer

Jennifer Schansberg assisted C. Timothy McKeown in the office of the Departmental Consulting Archaeologist, National Park Service, Washington, DC, in the implementation of the Native American Graves Protection and Repatriation Act (NAGPRA). She later founded Artsy-Cartsy, an independent consulting firm.

Schlemmer, Mark B.

Mark B. Schlemmer is on the registrarial staff of the Solomon R. Guggenheim Museum where he focuses on collection exhibitions for the New York museum and for the Guggenheim Foundation's affiliates in Bilbao, Berlin, Venice and Abu Dhabi. Mark has an M.A. in Museum Professions-Museum Registration from Seton Hall University. He worked for a decade in Barcelona after spending a year in Lyon, France as a Fulbright Student Fellow. As a graduate student, he began his research into the registrarial challenges of Installation and New Media Art, and he continues to develop these passions at the Guggenheim.

Segal, Terry

Terry Segal has served as an Associate Registrar at the Detroit Institute of Arts since 1984. Previously she held positions at Henry Ford Museum & Greenfield Village, the Columbia Historical Society, Washington, DC, and the Smithsonian Institution Traveling Exhibition Service (SITES). She has a B.A. in Art History from the University of Michigan and an M.A. in Museum Studies and American Studies from The George Washington University. She is past Chair of the Midwest Registrars Committee.

Simmons, John E.

John E. Simmons is president of *Museologica*, a consulting company, and Adjunct Curator of Collections at the Earth and Mineral Sciences Museum & Art Gallery at Penn State University. He previously worked at the Fort Worth Zoological Park, the California Academy of Sciences, and the University of Kansas, where he was a collections manager in the Natural History Museum and director of the Museum Studies Program. He has a B.S. in systematics and ecology and an M.A. in historical administration and museum studies.

Slaney, Deborah C.

Deborah C. Slaney has been Curator of History for The Albuquerque Museum of Art and History since 2001. She was formerly Registrar of The Heard Museum and the Anniston Museum of Natural History. She holds a B.A. in Anthropology from the University of Arizona and an MLS/Museum Emphasis from the University of Oklahoma.

Speckart , Kathryn G.

Kathryn Speckart is the Collections Manager at the U.S. Diplomacy Center, U.S. Department of State. Previously she was on the collections management staff at the Smithsonian's National Museum of American History, the National Archives, and the Los Angeles County Museum of Art. Kathryn received a Masters in Museum Studies from The George Washington University in 1999, receiving the Marie Malaro Excellence in Research and Writing Award upon graduation.

Steiner, Christine

Christine Steiner is an attorney whose practice emphasizes visual arts, art law, intellectual property, publishing, and business transactions. Before she entered private practice she served as Secretary and General Counsel, J. Paul Getty Trust; Assistant General Counsel, Smithsonian Institution; and Assistant Attorney General of Maryland for state colleges and universities. She is an adjunct professor of law at Loyola Law School, and has been a visiting professor of international art law in Florence, Italy, and Cambridge, England. She is editor of *A Museum Guide to Copyright and Trademark,* (AAM, 2000). She is an honors graduate of Johns Hopkins University (B.A.) and the University of Maryland (J.D.), and is admitted to the bars of California and Maryland, as well as the Supreme Court of the United States.

Sully, Perian

Perian Sully is Collection Information Manager and Web Programs Strategist at The Magnes, Berkeley, California. An acknowledged authority on the intersection of technology, culture, and the arts, she frequently teaches technology workshops, and serves on the board of AAM's Media and Technology Standing Professional Committee. She is a regular contributor to the Musematic blog and is responsible for the development of Wikimuse, an online portal for technology use in museums. She earned her Bachelor of Arts in Studio Art (sculpture) at the University of California, Davis.

Summers, Cherie

Cherie Summers has been Chief Registrar at the Santa Barbara Museum of Art since 1988. She was formerly Chief Registrar at the Solomon R. Guggenheim Museum and Associate Registrar at the Museum of Modern Art, New York. She is a frequent participant on panels and workshops and has written on various registration topics. A MAP surveyor, she also serves on the Professional Advisory Council for the Museum of Art, Brigham Young University, and Advisory Council for the Mesilla Valley Historical Museum, New Mexico.

Swain, Lynn

Lynn Swain, formerly registrar at the Winterthur Museum and Gardens, is Membership Manager of the Isabella Stewart Gardner Museum. She has worked at Historic Deerfield, in Deerfield, Mass., the Fogg Art Museum, Harvard University, the Denver Art Museum, Colorado Historical Society, Denver Museum of Natural History, and Rocky Mountain National Park. She was also Curator of Collections, then Director of the Estes Park Area Historical Museum, in Estes Park, Colo.

Tanner-Kaplesh, Dr. Sonja

Dr. Sonja Tanner-Kaplash has taught in the Cultural Resource Management Program, University of Victoria, B.C., since 1983. She has edited *Museum Quarterly,* has been Registrar at the Royal Ontario Museum and has spoken and published widely on the museum profession. She received her Ph.D. in Museum Studies from the University of Leicester, U.K.

Tarpey, Sean

Sean B. Tarpey was registrar at the Mount Holyoke College Art Museum, South Hadley, Mass. He now operates Northern Artery, a small art shipping company in New England.

Taurins, Irene

Irene Taurins is Senior Registrar at the Philadephia Museum of Art where she has been since 1978. From 1972 to 1978 she was Registrar/Administrator for Sotheby's, New York. She is a member of AAM, ICOM, and MAAM. As Senior Registrar at the Philadelphia Museum of Art she has safely shipped countless museum objects.

Tompkins, William G.

William G. Tompkins is national collections coordinator of the Smithsonian Institution, Washington, D.C. He serves as principal advisor to senior Smithsonian management, museum directors, and staff on matters relating to collections management policies, procedures, and standards. He was formally assistant director of the Smithsonian's Office of the Registrar and collections manager in the National Numismatic Collections at the National Museum of American History.

Warden, Lea Foster

Lea T. F. Warden has been working in the museum field since 2000. Her research on environmental sustainability and traveling exhibitions was supported by a 2007 Smithsonian Fellowship in Museum Practice. She is a graduate of The George Washington University's Museum Studies Program.

Young, Holly

For the past 26 years, Holly Young has worked in archaeological repositories in Arizona. Currently the Curator of Collections at the Pueblo Grande Museum, she developed that institution's repository and collections policies and procedures. Her areas of expertise include the curation and management of archaeological collections and archives and the preservation of museum collections through preventive conservation. She currently serves on the boards of the Registrars Committee of AAM and the Museum Association of Arizona.

SELECTED BIBLIOGRAPHY

Alderson, William T., ed. *Mermaids, Mummies, and Mastodons: The Emergence of the American Museum.* Washington, DC: American Association of Museums, 1992.

Alexander, Edward P. *Museum Masters: Their Museums and Their Influence.* Nashville, TN: American Association for State and Local History, 1983.

_____, and Mary Alexander. *Museums in Motion: An Introduction to the History and Functions of Museums.* Lanham, MD: AASLH / AltaMira Press, 2007.

ALI-ABA (American Law Institute | American Bar Association). *Course of Studies Materials: Legal Problems of Museum Administration.* Philadelphia, PA: ALI-ABA, published annually since 1973.

American Association of Museums. *A Higher Standard: Museum Accreditation Program Standards.* Washington, DC: American Association of Museums, 2005.

American Institute for Conservation. *AIC Directory,* Washington, DC: American Institute for Conservation of Historic and Artistic Works, annual.

Bachmann, Konstanze, ed. *Conservation Concerns: A Guide for Collectors and Curators.* Washington, DC: Smithsonian Institution Press, 1992.

Bennett, G. W., J. M. Owens, and R. M. Corrigan. *Truman's Scientific Guide to Pest Management Operations,* 6th ed. Cleveland, OH: Advanstar Communications, 2003.

Booth, E. T., under the direction of John Cotton Dana. *Apprenticeship: Newark Museum.* 1928.

Bourcier, Paul, Ruby Rogers, and The AASLH *Nomenclature Committee. Nomenclature 3.0 for Museum Cataloging.* Nashville, TN: AltaMira Press, 2009.

Bowser, Eileen, and John Kuiper. *A Handbook for Film Archives.* New York: Garland Publishing, Inc., 1991.

Bradley, Susan. *A Guide to the Storage, Exhibition and Handling of Antiquities, Ethnographia and Pictorial Art.* London: British Museum, 1993.

Bressor, Julie P. *Caring for Historical Records.* Storrs, CT: University of Connecticut, 1990.

Brokerhof, Agnes W. "Applying the Outcome of Climate Research in Collection Risk Management." In Padfield, T., and K. Borchersen, eds. *Museum Microclimates.* Copenhagen: National Museum of Denmark, 2007. Available on-line at http://www.padfield.org/tim/cfys/mm/brokerhof/brokerhof.pdf.

Brown, Kim. *How to Photograph Your Artwork.* Ransom Canyon, TX: Canyonwinds, 1995.

Buck, Rebecca A., and Jean Allman Gilmore. *Collection Conundrums.* Washington, DC: American Association of Museums, 2007.

_____, eds. *New Museum Registration Methods.* Washington, DC: American Association of Museums, 1998.

_____. *On the Road Again: Developing and Managing Traveling Exhibitions.* Washington, DC: American Association of Museums, 2003.

Burke, R. B., and S. Adeloye. *A Manual of Basic Museum Security.* Washington, DC: International Committee on Museum Security and Leicestershire Museums, 1986.

Butcher-Younghams, Sherry. *Historic House Museums.* New York: Oxford University Press, 1993.

Campbell, N. J. *Writing Effective Policies and Procedures: A Step-by-Step Resource for Clear Communication.* New York: American Management Association, 1998.

Case, Mary, ed. *Registrars on Record: Essays on Museum Collections Management.* Washington, DC: American Association of Museums, 1988.

Darling, Pamela W. *Preservation Planning Program: An Assisted Self-Study Manual for Libraries.* Washington, DC: Association of Research Libraries, 1993.

Depocas, Alain, Jon Ippolito, and Caitlin Jones, eds. *The Variable Media Approach.* New York: Guggenheim Museum Publications, 2003.

Din, Herminia, and Phyllis Hecht, eds. Introduction by Selma Thomas. *The Digital Museum, A Think Guide.* Washington, DC: American Association of Museums, 2007.

Dorge, Valerie, and Sharon L. Jones, compilers. *Building an Emergency Plan: A Guide for Museums and Other Cultural Institutions.* Los Angeles, CA: The Getty Conservation Institute, 1999. Available on-line at http://www.getty.edu/conservation/publications/pdf_publications/emergency_plan.pdf

Druzik, James, and Bent Eshøj. "Museum Lighting: Its Past and Future Development." In Padfield, T., and K. Borchersen, eds. *Museum Microclimates.* Copenhagen: National Museum of Denmark, 2007. Available on-line at http://www.padfield.org/tim/cfys/mm/druzik/druzik.pdf.

Duncan, C., and R. Unterberger. *The Rough Guide to Shopping with a Conscience.* London: Rough Guides Ltd., 2007.

Ellis, Margaret Holben. *The Care of Prints and Drawings.* Lanham, MD: AltaMira Press, 1995.

Frey, Franziska, Dawn Heller, Dan Kushel, Timothy Vitale, Jeffrey Warda, ed., and Gawain Weaver. *The AIC Guide to Digital Photograph and Conservation Documentation.* Washington, DC.: AIC, 2008.

Gardner, James, and Elizabeth Merrit. *AAM Guide to Collections Planning.* Washington, DC: American Association of Museums, 2004.

Gillies, Teresa, and Neal Putt. *The ABCs of Collections Care,* rev. ed. Winnipeg: Manitoba Heritage Conservation Service, 1991.

Gorman, G. E., and Sydney J. Shep, eds. *Preservation Management of Libraries, Archives and Museums.* London: Facet Publishing, 2006.

Ham, F. Gerald. *Selecting and Appraising Archives and Manuscripts.* Chicago: The Society of American Archivists, 1993.

Heritage Preservation, *The National Institute for Conservation. Emergency Response and Salvage Wheel.* Washington, DC: Heritage Preservation, Inc., 2005.

Hoagland, K. Elaine, ed. *Guidelines for Institutional Policies and Planning in Natural History Collections.* Washington, DC: Association of Systematics Collections, 1994.

Holliday, C. O., S. Schmidheiny, and P. Watts. *Walking the Talk: The Business Case for Sustainable Development.* San Francisco: Berrett-KoehlerPublishers, 2002.

Jessup, W. C. "Pest Management." In Rose, C. L., C. A. Hawks, and H. H. Genoways, eds. *Storage of Natural History Collections: A Preventive Conservation Approach.* Iowa City, IA: Society for the Preservation of Natural History Collections, 1995.

Jones, B. G. *Protecting Historic Architecture and Museum Collections from Natural Disaster.* London: Butterworths, 1986.

LeCompte, Elise. *Handling Information for Natural History Objects.* 2008.

Long, Jane S., and Richard W. Long. *Caring for Your Family Treasures.* New York: Harry N. Abrams, Inc., Publishers, 2000.

Lord, Allyn, Carolyn Reno, and Marie Demeroukas. *Steal This Handbook! A Template for Creating a Museum's Emergency Preparedness Plan.* Columbia, SC: Southeastern Registrars Association, 1994.

Lord, G. D., and B. Lord, eds. *The Manual of Museum Planning.* London: HMSO, 1991.

Malaro, Marie C. *Museum Governance.* Washington, DC: Smithsonian Institution Press, 1994.

_____. *A Legal Primer on Managing Museum Collections.* Washington, DC: Smithsonian Institution Press, 1998.

Mallis, A. *Handbook of Pest Control,* 9th ed. Richfield, OH: GIE Media, 2004.

Mecklenburg, Marion F., et al. *Art in Transit: Handbook for Packing and Transporting Paintings.* Washington, DC: National Gallery of Art, 1991.

Merritt, E. E., ed. *Covering Your Assets: Facilities and Risk Management in Museums.* Washington, DC: American Association of Museums, 2005.

_____. *National Standards and Best Practices for U. S. Museums.* Washington, DC: American Association of Museums, 2008.

Miller, Frederic M. *Arranging and Describing Archives and Manuscripts.* Chicago: The Society of American Archivists, 1990.

Moses, Nancy. *Lost in the Museum: Buried Treasures and the Stories They Tell.* Nashville, TN: AltaMira Press, 2008.

Museums & Galleries Commission. *Standards in the Museum Care of Archeological Collections.* London: Museums & Galleries Commission, 1992.

The National Committee to Save America's Cultural Collections, Arthur W. Schultz, Chairman. *Caring for Your Collections.* New York: Harry N. Abrams, Inc., Publishers, 1992.

National Fire Protection Association. *NFPA 40: Standard for Storage and Handling of Cellulose Nitrate Film.* Quincy, MA: National Fire Protection Association, 2007.

National Parks Service. *Museum Handbook, Part I, Museum Collections.* Washington, DC: National Park Service, 2007.

National Trust. *The National Trust Manual of Housekeeping: The Care of Collections in Historic Houses Open to the Public.* Oxford and Burlington, MA: Butterworth-Heinemann, 2006.

Odegaard, Nancy. *A Guide to Handling Anthropological Museum Collections.* Los Angeles, CA: Western Association for Art Conservation, 1992.

_____, and Alyce Sadongei. *Old Poisons, New Problems: A Museum Resource for Managing Contaminated Cultural Materials.* Lanham, MD: AltaMira Press, 2005.

Ogden, Sherelyn, ed. *Caring for American Indian Objects: A Practical and Cultural Guide.* St. Paul: Minnesota Historical Society Press, 2004.

_____. *Preservation of Library and Archival Materials: A Manual,* 3rd ed. Andover, MA: Northeast Document Conservation Center, 1999.

Pearce, S. M. *Museums, Objects and Collections: A Cultural Study.* Washington, DC: Smithsonian Institution Press, 1993.

Perry, K. D., ed. *The Museum Forms Book,* rev. ed. Austin, TX: Texas Association of Museums, 1999.

Pinniger, David. *Pest Management in Museums, Archives, and Historic Houses.* London: Archetype Publications, 2001.

Porter, Elsa, chair. *The Archives of the Future: Archival Strategies for the Treatment of Electronic Databases. A Report for the National Archives and Records Administration.* Springfield,

VA: U. S. Department of Commerce, 1991.

Randolph, Pamela Young. *Museum Housekeeping: Developing a Collections Management Program.* Richmond: Virginia Association of Museums, 1987.

Rose, Carolyn L., Catharine A. Hawks, and Hugh H. Genoways, eds. *Storage of Natural History Collections: A Preventive Conservation Approach.* Iowa City, IA: Society of the Preservation of Natural History Collections, 1995.

Rose, Cordelia. *Courierspeak.* Washington, DC: Smithsonian Institution Press, 1993.

Selwitz, C., and S. Maekawa. Inert Gases in the Control of Museum Insect Pests. Los Angeles, CA: Getty Conservation Institute, 1998. Available on-line at http://www.getty.edu/conservation/publications/pdf_publications/inertgases.pdf

Shapiro, Michael, and Brett I. Miller, Morgan, Lewis & Bockius, LLP. Christine Steiner, ed. *A Museum Guide to Copyright and Trademark.* Washington, DC: American Association of Museums, 1999.

Simmons, John E. Things Great and Small: Collection Management Policies. Washington, DC: American Association of Museums, 2005

Sixsmith, Mike, ed. *Touring Exhibitions: The Touring Exhibition Group's Manual of Good Practice.* Oxford, England: Butterworth-Heineman Ltd., 1995.

Sullivan, Lawrence E., and Alison Edwards. *Stewards of the Sacred.* Washington, DC: American Association of Museums, 2004.

Various. *Code of Ethics for Museums.* Washington, DC: American Association of Museums, 2000.

Visual Resource Association. Cataloging Cultural Objects: A Guide to Describing Cultural Works and Their Images. Atlanta, GA: ALA Editions, 2006.

Weil, Stephen E. *A Deaccession Reader.* Washington, DC: American Association of Museums, 1997.

_____. *Making Museums Matter.* Washington, DC: Smithsonian Institution Press, 2002.

_____. *Rethinking the Museum and Other Meditations.* Washington, DC: Smithsonian Institution Press, 1990.

Wythe, Debora, ed. *Museum Archives: An Introduction.* Chicago: Society of American Archivists, 2004.

Yeide, Nancy, Akinsha Konstantin, and Amy Walsh. *The AAM Guide to Provenance Research.* Washington, DC: American Association of Museums, 2001.

Zorich, D. M. *Developing Intellectual Property Policies: A How-to Guide for Museums.* Ottawa: Canadian Heritage Information Network, 2003. Available on-line at http://www.chin.gc.ca/English/Publications/developing_policies.html

APPENDIX | REGISTRATION FORMS

MRM5 MUSEUM
123 Any Street, Any Town, Any State
Telephone: 000-000-0001
Fax: 000-000-0002

INCOMING LOAN AGREEMENT

AGREEMENT   The undersigned ("Lender") hereby lends to MRM5 Museum the object(s) described herein for the purposes, and subject to the terms and conditions set forth.

EXHIBITION   Exhibition:
Dates:
Venues:
Sampler Museum Registrar:

LENDER   Lender:
Address:
Telephone: (business)   (home)
FAX:
Contact Person:
Credit: Lent by
(Exact wording of lender's name for catalog, labels and publicity)

OBJECT   Artist/Maker:
Object/Title:
Medium:
Date of Work:

DIMENSIONS   Painting/Print   height   in.   width   in. (unframed)
                              height   in.   width   in. (framed)
                Object   height   in.   width   in.   depth   in.
approximate weight   lbs
May we reframe, remat or remount if necessary for the safety of the work? _____ Yes _____No
May we substitute
Plexiglass for glass? _____Yes _____No May we fix secure hanging devices onto frame? _____Yes _____No

INSURANCE   Total value (estimated fair market value in US $):
Please see reverse   MRM5 Museum will insure unless otherwise advised.
for conditions   Do you prefer to maintain your own insurance? _____Yes _____No If yes, estimated cost of premium:
Do you require a certificate of insurance? ____Yes ____ No

PHOTOGRAPHY   If black & white photographs and/or color transparencies suitable for reproduction are available, please
Please see reverse   state type and where they may obtained.
for conditions

SHIPPING/   Date required for receipt of loan:
HANDLING   Pick-up and/or return address if different from address above. _____Pick-up _____Return
Address:
Telephone: (business)   (home)
Name of contact if other than Lender:
Please list any special instructions for handling, packing, shipping or installation:

SIGNATURE   The Lender acknowledges that he/she has full authority and power to make this loan, that he/she has read the conditions above and on the back of this form and that he/she agrees to be bound by them.

Signature:_____   Date:_____
           Lender or authorized agent

Signature:_____   Date:_____
           For MRM5 Museum

Please complete, sign and return both copies to MRM5 Museum Registrar. A countersigned copy will be sent to you.

CONDITIONS GOVERNING INCOMING LOANS
(Version 12/3/02)

Care and Handling

1. MRM5 Museum (the "Museum") will exercise the same care with respect to the work of art on loan (the "work") as it does with comparable property of its own.
2. The Museum will not alter, clean or repair the work without prior express written permission of the Lender or except when the safety of the work makes such action imperative.

Packing and Transportation

1. The Lender certifies that the work is in good condition and will withstand ordinary strains of packing and transportation. Evidence of damage to the work at the time of receipt or while in the Museum's custody will be reported immediately to the Lender. The work will be returned packed in the same or similar materials unless otherwise authorized by the Lender. Costs of transportation and packing will be borne by the Museum unless the loan is at the Lender's request. Customs regulations will be adhered to in international shipments.

Insurance

1. Unless the Lender expressly elects to maintain his/her own insurance coverage, the Museum will insure the work wall-to-wall under its fine arts policy against risks of physical loss or damage from external cause while in transit and on location during the period of the loan. The insurance coverage contains the usual exclusions of loss or damage due to such causes as wear and tear, gradual deterioration, moths, vermin, inherent vice, war, invasion, hostilities, insurrections, nuclear reaction or radiation, confiscation by order of any government or public authority, risk of contraband or illegal transportation and/or trade and any repairing, restoration or retouching authorized by the Lender.
2. Insurance will be placed in the amount specified by the Lender which must reflect fair market value. In case of damage or loss, the insurance company may ask the Lender to substantiate the insurance value. If the Lender fails to indicate an amount, the Museum will set a value for purposes of insurance only for the period of the loan. The United States Government Arts and Artifacts Indemnity Act may be applicable to this loan. If so, the Lender agrees to said coverage at U.S. dollar valuation as specified in this loan agreement. If a work which has been industrially fabricated is damaged or lost and can be repaired or replaced to the artist's specifications, the Museum's liability shall be limited to the cost of such replacement. The Lender agrees that in the event of loss or damage, recovery shall be limited to such amount, if any, as may be paid by the insurer hereby releasing the Museum and the Trustees, officers, agents and employees of the Museum from liability for any and all claims arising out of such loss or damage.
3. If the Lender chooses to maintain his or her own insurance, the Museum must be supplied with a certificate of insurance naming the Museum as an additional insured or waiving subrogation against the Museum. If the Lender fails to supply the Museum with such a certificate, this loan agreement shall constitute a release of the Museum from any liability in connection with the work. The Museum cannot accept responsibility for any error in the information furnished to the Lender's insurer or for any lapses in coverage.

Reproduction and Credit

1. The Museum assumes the right, unless specifically denied by the Lender, to photograph, videotape, and reproduce the work for documentation, publicity, publication and educational purposes connected with this exhibition and to produce slides of the work to be distributed for educational use.
2. The general public will not be allowed to photograph works on loan to MRM5 Museum.

3. Unless otherwise instructed in writing, the Museum will give credit to the Lender in any labels and publications as specified on the face of the agreement.

Ownership and Change in Ownership

1. The Lender hereby warrants that he/she has full legal title to the work or that he/she is the duly authorized agent of the owner or owners of the work. The Lender will indemnify, defend and hold the Museum harmless from any losses, damages and expenses, including attorney's fees, arising out of claims by individuals, institutions or other persons claiming full or partial title to the work..
2. The Lender will notify the Museum promptly in writing of any change of ownership of the work whether by reason of death, sale, insolvency, gift or otherwise. If ownership shall change during the period of this loan, the Museum reserves the right to require the new owner, prior to the return of the work, to establish his or her right to possession by proof satisfactory to the Museum. The new owner shall succeed to Lender's rights and obligations under this agreement, including, but not limited to, the loan period and any insurance obligations.

Loan Period, Extension, Return

1. The work shall remain in the possession of the Museum for the time specified on the reverse, but may be withdrawn from exhibition at any time by the Museum. The Lender agrees that he/she cannot withdraw the work during the period of this agreement without prior written consent of the Museum Director.
2. The terms of this agreement shall apply to any extension of the loan period.
3. Unless the Lender requests otherwise in writing, the Museum will return the work only to the Lender and only at the address specified in this agreement. The Lender shall promptly notify the Museum in writing of any change of address. The Museum assumes no responsibility to search for a Lender who cannot be reached at the address specified in this agreement. The Lender will pay additional costs, if any, if the Lender request the return of the work to another address.
4. The Museum's right to return the loan shall accrue absolutely at the termination of the loan. If, after pursuing all possible means of contact, and in accordance with any legal requirements, the Lender cannot be found or the Lender refuses to accept the return of the work, it shall be deemed abandoned and become the property of the Museum. [This clause must comply with state law.]

Interpretation

1. This agreement constitutes the entire agreement between the Lender and the Museum and may be amended or modified only in writing signed by both parties. Any changes herein of printed text or written additions must bear the initial of both parties. This agreement shall be governed and interpreted according to the laws of the State of Any State.
2. If the terms of this agreement conflict with the forms, agreements or correspondence of the Lender, the terms of this agreement will be controlling.

MRM5 Museum
TRAVELING EXHIBITION CONTRACT

Please note: This contract is a sample only. Consult with legal counsel before adapting or using this form.

General Information

Exhibition Title:

Organizing exhibitor:
Address:
Contact:
Telephone:
Fax:
E-mail:
Loan period dates:
Exhibition public opening date:
Exhibition first event:
Exhibition closing date:
Participation Fee:
Fee includes:

Shipping:
Shipping Fee:
Contents of exhibition:

Other requirements:
Insurance:
Insurance value:
Credit:

1 AGREEMENT TO BORROW

This Agreement is made this ___date___ between ___**Legal name and location of organizer**___ (___**Short name for Organizer** ___ or "___**Organizer**___"), and ___**Legal name and location of exhibitor**____ ("Exhibitor").

___ **Organizer** ___has prepared an exhibition for circulation entitled ___**Title of Exhibition**___ ("the Exhibition"). The Exhibitor desires to display the Exhibition according to the terms and conditions set forth herein. Exhibitor hereby agrees to borrow and ___**Organizer**___ agrees to loan the Exhibition for the purpose of the exhibition ("loan purpose") on the Exhibitor's premises (the "approved location") during the period ____ dates___ (the "exhibition period"); ___ time ___ will be allowed before and after the exhibition period for transportation, unpacking/packing, and installation/deinstallation.. The Exhibitor agrees to pay in consideration of the loan the amount of $_____

The Exhibition consists of the objects as set forth in Appendix A (which is attached and made part of this agreement), object mounts and/or installation hardware, text and other panels and labels (collectively the "exhibition materials").

Exhibitor will comply with all special instructions of ___**Organizer**___ as outlined herein and in all written registration notes accompanying the Exhibition with respect to condition, care, handling, installation, presentation, security, and packing of the Exhibition. Care and handling instructions can be found in Appendix B, attached.

2 FEES/PAYMENT SCHEDULE

Exhibitor agrees to pay the loan fee to ___ **Organizer** ___ in two installments as follows: (1) $_____ to be sent with the executed original of the Agreement and (2) $_____ to be paid by the first day of the exhibition period, or not later than ___**date**___. ___**Organizer**___ will provide an invoice to exhibitor for all payments. The fee for the exhibition includes use of a fully researched and assembled exhibition with labels, educational materials, publicity packet, and insurance. It also includes catalogs and/or brochures, as noted below. Packing and crating are included. All costs for ___**Organizer** ___ courier, who will help with installation and deinstallation, are included. If lenders require couriers for specific works, the cost of those couriers (transport and per diem), will be borne by the Exhibitor. Shipping costs are not included in the exhibition fee.

Each exhibitor is responsible for all local costs incurred in presenting the exhibition, including but not limited to its unpacking/repacking, crate storage, installation, publicity, programming, receptions, etc. The Exhibitor is also responsible for any additional costs that may be specifically outlined in correspondence between ___**Organizer**___ and Exhibitor.

3 INSURANCE

___**Organizer**___, as part of the exhibition loan fee, shall continuously insure the exhibition materials on a wall-to-wall basis against all risks of physical loss or damage from any external cause except wear and tear, gradual deterioration, terrorism, and other exclusions standard to fine arts policies. Exhibitor shall report to the Registrar, ___**Organizer**___ any damage to the exhibition materials while in transit to or on the Exhibitors' premises, regardless of who may be responsible. Report to:

Registrar ___ **Phone** ___

Exhibitor must preserve all parts, packing materials, and other evidence or result of damage and provide photographs documenting damage and action taken in response.

Exhibitor shall be held responsible for any damage to the exhibition materials that results from its negligence or failure to comply with this agreement, including but not limited to its failure to comply with ___**Organizer**___ registration notes and instructions regarding security, unpacking/repacking, handling, installation/deinstallation and shipment, as well as any and all damages to the exhibition materials during the loan period which ___**Organizer**___ does not recover from an insurance carrier.

4 EXHIBITION DISPLAY/RESTRICTIONS

Exhibitor shall exhibit all exhibition materials as listed in Appendix A unless express written permission to the contrary has been obtained in advance from ___**Organizer** ___. Exhibitor will not show the Exhibition at more than one location without prior written permission from ___**Organizer** ___. Further, Exhibitor agrees to provide a secure and environmentally suitable storage area for any exhibition materials withdrawn from the Exhibition (as outlined in the care and handling regulations, Appendix B) for any reason and/or to pay any additional transportation or courier costs which may be incurred as a result of withdrawals of exhibition materials from the Exhibition.

___ **Organizer** ___ shall provide Exhibitor with a detailed set of guidelines for the handling and display of the exhibition materials ___ amount of time ___ before the opening of thee exhibition.. Exhibitor shall make such guidelines accessible to its installation and design staff, and other applicable staff, and shall be responsible for ensuring strict adherence to such guidelines.

5 CREDIT LINES/SPONSORSHIPS

The following credit shall be included on invitations and official press releases and posted at the entrance to the exhibition.

___Title ___was organized by ___**Organizer**___. The exhibition has received funding from the ___ **Funders names** ___. Additional support has been received from ___**foundations, corporations, and individuals**___. Other promotional and related programmatic materials will carry the first sentence of the above credit.

6 SHIPPING

The Exhibitor is responsible for the cost of shipping, which will be pro-rated [or actual, or a combination of the two] among all exhibitors. The estimated cost of shipping is $_____ and is payable upon receipt of the exhibition materials. Adjustments to shipping payments will be made at the end of the tour of the Exhibition. For foreign venues, and for Alaska and Hawaii, the Exhibitor must pay incoming shipping costs from the port-of-exit in the contiguous 48 states of the United States in addition to the pro-rated shipping costs. The foreign exhibitor is also required to pay all charges for customs clearance the Exhibition leaving or re-entering the United States.

___ **Organizer** ___or the previous Exhibitor shall pack the exhibition materials for shipment to the Exhibitor and arrange for their delivery to Exhibitor not later than the first day of the loan period, by a carrier selected and scheduled in advance by ___ **Organizer** ___. Exhibitor agrees to meet all transportation schedules required for the safety of objects and the timely shipment to other exhibitors. Exhibitor agrees that if it is unable to receive and ship the Exhibition in compliance with the necessary transportation schedule, it will absorb the cost of an acceptable interim storage facility and other expenses resulting from its inability to comply with such schedule.

7 PACKING/HANDLING/CARE/CONDITION REPORTING

Exhibitor shall ensure that all packing and unpacking instructions given by ___ **Organizer** ___ are followed explicitly by competent packers who are trained in museum object handling and that the exhibition materials are handled with special care at all times to protect against damage or deterioration. All unloading, unpacking, handling, repacking and reloading shall occur under the surveillance of the Exhibitor's registrar in consultation with the Exhibitor's conservators and security staff, or applicable staff. Exhibition material shall be handled with at least the same care as Exhibitor uses in handling its own property of a similar nature.

In preparing exhibition materials for their outgoing shipment, Exhibitor shall ensure that the exhibition materials are packed in the same manner in which they were delivered to Exhibitor and are thus prepared for outgoing shipment no later than the last day of the loan period. Exhibitor shall notify immediately, by telephone or fax, the Registrar, The MRM5 Musuem, of any loss or damage to the packing materials or packing crates which in any way might impair their ability to protect the exhibition materials. Exhibitor, at its own expense, shall, in consultation with the Registrar, ___ **Organizer** ___, replace packing materials or crates lost or damaged while in its care with comparable materials.

Exhibitor must examine the exhibition materials after a 24-hour acclimation but within seven days of their receipt and report on their condition. If any damage to the objects is discovered then or at any time, then or during the loan period, reports must be made immediately in writing, with photographic documentation and sent to the Registrar, ___ **Organizer** ___. Exhibitor agrees that it may not alter or repair any of the exhibition materials without first obtaining the express written permission of ___ **Organizer** ___.

ADD LANGUAGE ABOUT CONDITION REPORTS, ETC.

8 FACILITIES

Exhibitor shall, at its own expense, provide adequate security and environmental conditions for the exhibition materials, and shall comply with any and all special instructions put forth by ___ **Organizer** ___ for the care of the exhibition materials. Exhibitor shall provide ___ **Organizer** ___ with a copy of its Standard Facility Report as developed by the Registrars Committee of the American Association of Museums; ___ **Organizer** ___ will review the SFR as part of the contractual process.

All objects must be displayed according to guidelines provided by the **Organizer**.

Exhibitor shall assign security guard(s) as noted to the exhibition space during open hours. The Exhibitor must, as a security minimum during closed hours, have electronic surveillance systems that report to a central station manned 24 hours per day. Permission to use plants in the galleries must be obtained from the Registrar, ___ **Organizer** ___; food and drink will NOT be allowed in the exhibition galleries, storage areas, or anywhere the exhibition materials are kept.

The Exhibitor shall maintain 50% ±5% relative humidity and 68-72 degrees Fahrenheit. Light levels shall be maintained according to the guidelines provided.

The public shall be admitted to the exhibition without discrimination or segregation, and regardless of race, color, creed, sex, age or national origin. Additionally, the Exhibitor represents that there is full access to the exhibition for the physically disabled, as stipulated in Section 504 of Federal Public Law 93-112, as amended. The Exhibitor shall be in compliance with the Americans with Disabilities Act (Public Law 101-336, enacted July 26, 1990).

9 PUBLICITY

___ **Organizer** ___ will supply Exhibitor with a press release and a selection of photographs which may be used in preparing publicity and related materials for the Exhibition. The Exhibitor agrees to clear its own press release with the Public Relations department of ___ **Organizer** ___ before use.

Exhibitor shall forward promptly to ___ **Organizer** ___ contact person, all publicity releases, reviews, and other similar matter relating to the exhibition. At the end of the loan period, Exhibitor will forward attendance figures to ___ **Organizer** ___.

___ **Organizer** ___ reserves to itself the right to copy, photograph or reproduce the exhibition materials. Exhibitor shall not permit any of the exhibition materials to be copied, photographed or reproduced, and in the event of their public exhibition, shall contain in their photography guidelines a statement advising persons attending the Exhibition that the exhibition materials may not be copied, photographed or reproduced. Notwithstanding the foregoing sentence, Exhibitor may cause the exhibition materials to be photographed for curatorial and registrarial purposes provided that such photographs are made without removal of frames or mounts and are not released without ___ **Organizer** ___'s prior written consent and provided further that ___ **Organizer** ___ will be supplied with a duplicate set of prints.

___ **Organizer** ___ will provide the Exhibitor with ___number ___ copies of the catalog ___ Title ___. Additional copies of the catalog can be purchased at cost from ___ **Organizer** ___ Shop

10 DAMAGES, BREACH OF AGREEMENT

The Exhibitor must notify ___ **Organizer** ___ in writing to cancel the signed Agreement. The parties understand that it will be difficult, if not impossible, to calculate or estimate the serious and substantial damage to ___ **Organizer** ___ which would be caused by breach of this Agreement by Exhibitor, and therefore the parties agree that in the event Exhibitor cancels this Agreement prior to the beginning of the loan period, for any reason whatsoever (other than the inability of ___ **Organizer** ___ to perform hereunder), Exhibitor shall pay to ___ **Organizer** ___, as liquidated damages and not as a penalty, the total loan fee, which balance shall be due and payable immediately upon such cancellation.   However, in the event that ___ **Organizer** ___ arranges for an alternate venue for the Exhibition acceptable to ___ **Organizer** ___ during the loan period, the fees received from that venue, less the cost of procuring such alternate venue, shall be applied to reduce the amount payable to ___ **Organizer** ___under this paragraph. ___ **Organizer** ___, however, shall have no obligation to procure such alternate sponsor and the Exhibitor is entitled to no reduction of the loan fee for ___ **Organizer** ___'s failure to procure such alternate venue.

In the event Exhibitor fails to pay any amount when due under this Agreement, including but not limited to costs payable under paragraphs 1 and 3 above, such failure continuing for a period of 10 business days, the amount at the rate of 15% per annum from the date the unpaid amount originally was due will accrue until the late payment is received by ___ **Organizer** ___. Nothing in this Agreement shall be construed as an express or implied agreement by ___ **Organizer** ___ to forbear in the collection of any delinquent payment. Further, this Agreement shall not be construed as in any way giving Exhibitor the right, express or implied, to fail to make timely payments hereunder, whether upon payment of such interest rate or otherwise. Should the Exhibitor not receive the first payment before the scheduled shipment date, ___ **Organizer** ___ reserves the right to cancel the contract at its own discretion.

The parties further understand that, while ___ **Organizer** ___ shall endeavor to make all reasonable effort to assure delivery of the Exhibition to Exhibitor prior to the scheduled opening as stated above:

a) In the event that ___ **Organizer** ___ is unable to perform hereunder, ___ **Organizer** ___ shall promptly refund to Exhibitor the fee already paid by Exhibitor in full and complete satisfaction of its obligation to Exhibitor. Upon prior written notice, ___ **Organizer** ___ may terminate this Agreement prior to the beginning of the loan period for events beyond its control. Exhibitor shall release, indemnify and hold ___ **Organizer** ___ harmless from and against any and all loss arising from Exhibitor's inability to display the Exhibition because of loss or damage to the exhibition materials while in transit; and

b) In the event ___ **Organizer** ___ for any reason withdraws any work of art from the Exhibition while it is in circulation, Exhibitor shall promptly comply with all packing and shipping instructions given by ___ **Organizer** ___ in the course of such withdrawal. ___ **Organizer** ___ shall concurrently reimburse Exhibitor for its costs and expenses of packing and shipping incurred by such withdrawal.

11 NOTICES
Except as otherwise required specifically herein, all notices and other communication provided for or permitted hereunder shall be made by hand-delivery, pre-paid, first-class mail, fax, or e-mail. All notices are considered delivered when delivered by hand, four days after deposit of first class mail, and when receipt is acknowledged for fax and e-mail. In the case of extreme emergencies, immediate verbal consent should be sought by the exhibitor and followed as soon as possible in writing.

If to ___ **Organizer** ___
Name and title
Address
Phone
Fax
e-mail

If to the Exhibitor

Name and title
Address
Phone
Fax
e-mail

12 SUCCESSORS AND ASSIGNS

The Agreement shall inure to the benefit of and be binding upon the successors of each of the parties. This Agreement may not be assigned by either party without the prior written consent of the other.

13 WAIVERS, REMEDIES

No delay on the part of any party hereto in exercising any right, power or privilege hereunder shall operate as a waiver thereof, nor shall any waiver on the part of any party hereto of any right, power or privilege hereunder operate as a waiver of any right, power, or privilege hereunder.

14 ENTIRE AGREEMENT

This Agreement, together with all written special instructions accompanying the Exhibition, is intended by the parties as a final expression of their agreement and is a complete and exclusive statement of the agreement and understanding of the parties. This Agreement supersedes all prior agreements and understandings between the parties with respect to the subject matter contained herein.

15 ATTORNEYS' FEES

In any action or proceeding brought to enforce any provision of this Agreement, or where any provision hereof is validly asserted as a defense, the successful party shall be entitled to recover reasonable attorneys' fees in addition to any other available remedy.

16 SEVERABILITY

In the event that any one or more of the provisions contained herein, or the application thereof in any circumstances, is held invalid, illegal or unenforceable in any respect for any reason, the validity, legality and enforceability of any such provision in every other respect and of the remaining provisions hereof shall not in any way be impaired or affected, it being intended that all of the rights and privileges contained herein shall be enforceable to the fullest extent permitted by law.

17 GOVERNING LAW

This Agreement shall be governed by and construed in accordance with the State of Any State.

18 SIGNATURES

19 APPENDICES/ATTACHMENTS/SCHEDULES

This contract was developed initially by the Office of General Counsel, University of Pennsylvania, for the University of Pennsylvania Museum of Archaeology and Anthropology. It was modified at The Newark Museum, expanded with S.I.T.E.S. statements, and edited by two lawyers.

**MRM5 Museum
EXHIBITION FEE WORK SHEET**

Exhibition/Marketing:
Catalogues $_____
Photography $_____
Replacement of panels/graphics $_____
Exhibition design/installation manual $_____
Education/Marketing packets $_____

Registrarial:
Loan Fees $_____
Crating $_____
Insurance $_____
Conservation review for travel $_____
Condition Report Book $_____
Courier costs $_____
Object replacement/rotation costs $_____

Administrative:
Consultants: $_____
Postage, Telephone, FedEx $_____

Contingency:
Contingency: storage $_____
Contingency: damage $_____
Contingency: frame/crate replacement $_____

OVERHEAD (Operating budget) $_____

               Total: $_____

A   **Divided by number of venues (_____)** $_____
B   **+ Reasonable addition to approach current fees for exhibition** $_____
C   **Profit** $_____
               Fee (A + B + C) : $_____

MRM5 MUSEUM
MUSEUM INCIDENT REPORT

Brief description of incident:

Date/Time:

Location:

Collection:

Accession numbers and object descriptions, if applicable:

Reported by:

Witnesses and other persons involved:

Actions taken:

Notification to:

❑ Director   ❑ Director of Facilities:

❑ Registrar   ❑ Director of Security:

❑ Curator:

Other involved party:

[on back of form]
Please describe the incident as well as possible and the condition of any objects involved.

Index

AMERICAN ASSOCIATION OF MUSEUMS

Your Resource, Voice, Community

Be a part of the largest museum association—the national service organization that represents your professional interests. Membership brings you exceptional benefits:

- Expert help and confidential, customized guidance on any museum matter, from finance and ethics to facilities management and collection stewardship—*AAM's Information Center*

- Deep discounts on education and professional development opportunities—*AAM's Annual Meeting and MuseumExpo™*, *Seminars* and *Webinars*

- Access to the most complete, accurate and timely information for and about museums —*Museum* magazine, *Aviso Online* and *AAM Action Alerts & Legislative Updates*

- Significant discounts on professional literature covering every museum subject from audience research to technology —the *AAM Bookstore*

- Opportunities to network with colleagues who work in the same field or have similar interests —*AAM's Standing Professional Committees* and *Professional Interest Committees*

- A voice in Washington to make the case for museums with Congress, policymakers and the media —*AAM's Government Relations Department* and *Museum Advocacy Day*

- Collective buying power of more than 20,000 members to save you time and money on insurance, shipping and other services—*AAM's Affinity Partner Program*

- Opportunities to apply for funding assistance for AAM professional development—*AAM Fellowships*

- Ability to receive instant alerts about new job opportunities and post your resume so that hundreds of museums can find you—*AAM's JobHQ*

"The wheels are in motion to use the webinar series as a professional development opportunity for many of our staff. We thank you for modeling this way of learning and for making great information and people available to us at such reasonable prices. **It is yet another way my AAM membership gives me value!**" —*Connie Bodner, Ohio Historical Society, Columbus OH*

Join AAM Today

For more information on becoming a member and all the member benefits and discounts visit
www.aam-us.org/joinus or call **866.226.2150.**